THE ROYAL
HIGHLAND REGIMENT

The Black Watch

MEDAL ROLL

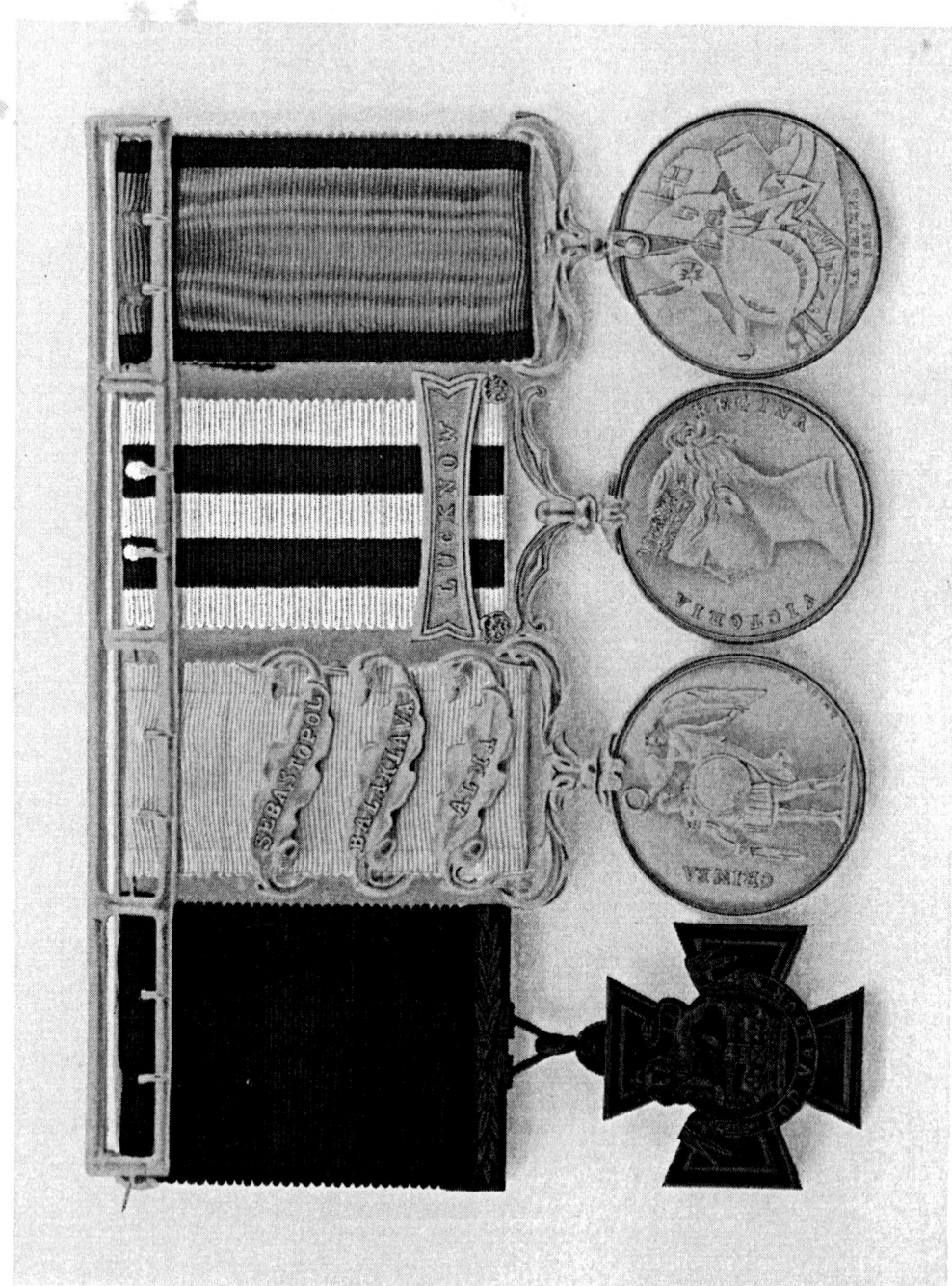

MEDALS AWARDED TO QUARTER-MASTER-SERJEANT JOHN SIMPSON, 42ND FOOT

THE ROYAL HIGHLAND REGIMENT

The Black Watch

FORMERLY

42nd and 73rd Foot

MEDAL ROLL

1801-1911

EDINBURGH

PRINTED BY T. AND A. CONSTABLE

PRINTERS TO HIS MAJESTY

1913

FOREWORD

In this Roll every endeavour has been made to ensure accuracy regarding Names, Regimental Numbers, and the Clasps to which individuals are entitled. It can be readily understood that in the compilation of the *original* Medal Rolls inaccuracies may have, in fact must have occurred, and therefore, if one or two are found in this volume, the compiler hopes that the cause thereof will be understood. Any such inaccuracies brought to notice will be rectified in any subsequent edition of the Roll. When differences occur in two or more Rolls of one campaign, they are mentioned either in a footnote, or, say in the case of a difference in number, thus 262$\frac{7}{8}$, which denotes that in one Roll the man's number is 2627 and in another 2628, either of which may be correct. The Rolls have been exceedingly carefully copied from the originals, and the compiler takes this opportunity to express his deep gratitude to Miss M. Gillett for her invaluable assistance in copying the originals, and also to all at the War Office who have been approached and have rendered very material assistance.

It is hoped that this work, dry in itself, and uninteresting to most, may be of value in time to come when the ink has faded, as it is fast doing, from many of the original Rolls, and no decipherable record remains of those who not only gained honourable distinction in, but helped to add laurels to the Colours of first, the 42nd, later 42nd and 73rd, and now The Royal Highland Regiment, The Black Watch.

J. S.

EDINBURGH,
22nd November 1912.

CONTENTS

ILLUSTRATIONS

42ND

ADJUTANT'S ROLL

OF THE

FIELD, STAFF, AND REGTL. OFFICERS, N.C. OFFICERS
AND MEN OF THE 42ND REGIMENT OF FOOT

WHO WERE PRESENT AT THE

BATTLE OF WATERLOO

AND THE ACTION WHICH PRECEDED IT

On the 15th and 18th June 1815

A

ADJUTANT'S ROLL of the Field and Staff-Officers, 42nd Regiment of Foot, who were present at the Battle of Waterloo, and the Action which preceded it, on the 15th and 18th June 1815.

Lieut.-Colonel Robert Henry Dick.
Major Archibald Menzies.
Adjutant James Young.
Quarter-Master Donald M'Intosh.
Surgeon Swinton M'Leod.
Assistant Surgeon in the Regulars, } Donald M'Pherson.
or Surgeon's Mate in the Militia } John Stewart.
Captain Duncan Stewart.

CAPTAIN AND LIEUT.-COLONEL JOHN CAMPBELL'S COMPANY.

Captain John Campbell, Lt.-Col.
Lieut. John Malcolm.
   ,,   Andrew L. Fraser.
Serjeant-Major Finlay King.
Quarter-Master Alexander Grant.
Pay-Master Serjt. or } William Watson.
   Pay-Master's Clerk }
Armourer as Sjt. Edward Patoun.
Drum-Major as Sjt. Hugh Martin.

SERJEANTS.	CORPORALS.
John Forbes.	William Chisholm.
Andrew Johnston.	Mitchel Henderson.
George Morris.	Duncan Mathieson.
Donald Ross.	Donald M'Pherson.

PRIVATE MEN.

Duncan Campbell.	Donald Holmes.	Donald M'Grigor, 2nd.	John Pringle.
Kenneth Campbell.	William Holmes.	James M'Intosh.	Charles Riddell.
William Clarke.	Alexander Melville, 1st.	Angus M'Kay.	Dawson Ross.
Michael Conolly.	Alexander Melville, 2nd.	George M'Kay.	Finlay Ross.
Archibald Cunningham.	John Moodie.	Kenneth M'Kay.	Hugh Ross.
Andrew Cruickshanks.	James M'Cann.	Robert M'Kay.	James Robertson.
Donald Davidson.	Alexander M'Donald.	Alexander M'Lea.	Donald Roy.
James Ferguson.	Donald M'Donald.	John M'Lean.	Robert Roycross.
Donald Fraser.	John M'Donald.	Murdoch M'Linnan.	John Smith.
Hugh Fraser.	Roderick M'Donald.	Neil M'Phie.	James Stevenson.
Peter Gray.	John M'Glashan.	John Nicolson.	William Sweeny.
Peter Grant.	Alexander M'Grigor.	Robert Patoun.	Joseph Wilson.
James Gavins.	Donald M'Grigor, 1st.	Lewis Polson.	

CAPTAIN AND BREVET-MAJOR MURDOCH M'LAINE'S COMPANY.

Lieut. Donald Mackenzie.
Ensign Alexander Cumming.

SERJEANTS.	DRUMMERS OR FIFERS.	CORPORALS.
James Anton.	Barney Mooney.	William Bowman.
Robert May.	Donald M'Donald.	Donald Murray.
John M'Cole.		Duncan M'Grigor.
Donald M'Grigor.		Lauchlan M'Lachlan.
		Alexander Scott.

PRIVATE MEN.

John Adge.	Alexander Fraser.	John Metcalf.	Peter M'Ewan.
John Anderson.	Robert Gourdie.	John Munro.	William M'Grigor.
Duncan Beattie.	James Grant.	James M'Donald.	John M'Intosh.
John Bennett.	William Hocknell.	John M'Donald.	John M'Kay.
William Bennett.	William Hilliard.	Ronald M'Donald.	William M'Kenzie.
Duncan Cameron.	John Innes.	William M'Donald.	David Smart.
Robert Carry.	James Irvine.	Alexander M'Tavish.	Robert Stark.
Alexander Chisholm.	Patt Kelly.	Alexander Noble.	Archibald Tanch.
John Clachar.	Alexander Kilgour.	James O'Kane.	George Tough.
John Davidson.	Donald Leith.	William Pool.	John Watson.
George Edoms.	James Loag.	James Reid.	Charles Whitelaw.
Alexander Edgar.	Alexander Lumsden.	Donald Ross.	John Wilson.

CAPTAIN MUNGO M'PHERSON'S COMPANY.

Captain Mungo M'Pherson.
Lieut. Hugh A. Fraser.
  ,,   Alexander Dunbar.
  ,,   Alexander Innes.

SERJEANTS.	DRUMMERS OR FIFERS.	CORPORALS.
William Duff.	John M'Kenzie.	John Hutchieson.
John M'Gregor.	Sinclair Sutherland.	David Kay.
James M'Conachie.		John M'Donald.
Alexander M'Leod.		Angus M'Pherson.
Donald Robertson.		John Reid.

PRIVATE MEN.

James Affleck.	William Mathieson.	Walter M'Kenzie.	James Smolett.
Donald Anderson.	William Miller.	Dougal M'Pherson.	Kenneth Simson.
John Beattie.	Walter Mitchell.	John M'Pherson.	Charles Stewart.
Peter Bennett.	Alexander Muckle.	Edward M'Manus.	Bartholomew Stobbs.
George Buist.	Dennis Milliea.	Alexander M'Kinnon.	Peter Sweeny.
William Calder.	John Morton.	John M'Lean.	George Taylor.
James Dallas.	Alexander Morrison.	George Orr.	James Turner.
William Davidson.	Donald Morrison.	James Pride.	John Warnock.
Thomas Foster.	Colin M'Donald.	James Rutledge.	James Waugh.
James Guillan.	Richard M'Donald.	George Ross.	Robert Webster.
George Jessiman.	James M'Intosh.	James Russell.	
Alexander Martin.	Donald M'Kay.		

CAPTAIN AND LIEUT.-COL. THOMAS F. WADE'S COMPANY.

Lieut. Kenneth M'Dougall.

SERJEANTS.	DRUMMERS OR FIFERS.	CORPORALS.
Robert Ferrie.	John Duff.	Duncan Grant.
James M'Iver.	Malcolm M'Innes.	James Martin.
Hugh Polson.		

PRIVATE MEN.

John Baggray.	Neil Gaw.	John M'Intosh.	Robert Ross.
John Banks.	James Halliday.	Donald M'Kay.	John Smith.
William Barclay.	Alexander Harvey.	Archibald M'Killop.	Robert Stewart.
James Barker.	James Hughes.	John M'Linnan.	James Stevenson.
Andrew Begbie.	William Jack.	Hugh M'Manus.	Arthur Sutherland.
William Blainey.	Joseph Kane.	Henry M'Tavish.	James Sutherland.
Roderick Cameron.	James Loudon.	Richard Pearce.	William Sutherland.
Archibald Campbell.	Roderick Mathieson.	George Randall.	Charles Taylor.
James Conolly.	John Morris.	George Reid.	John Warwick.
John Dent.	Alexander M'Allister.	David Robertson.	William Walton.
Henry Duff.	Donald M'Donald.	Andrew Ross.	Gilbert Wilson.
Andrew Gilmaur.	John M'Grigor.	Matthew Ross.	

CAPTAIN DONALD M'DONALD'S COMPANY.

Captain Donald M'Donald.
Lieut. James Brander.
„   Roger Stewart.
„   John Grant.

SERJEANTS.	DRUMMERS OR FIFERS.	CORPORALS.
John Christie.	Thomas Aitcheson.	Alexander Bethune.
William Graham.	William Murphy.	Alexander Campbell.
George M'Donald.	William Mackenzie.	Edward M'Kay.
William Ross.		

PRIVATE MEN.

Charles Anderson.	William Henderson.	Alexander M'Lean.	George Sharpe.
James Anderson.	David Morrison.	Duncan M'Linnan.	William Stedman.
George Baillie.	Colin M'Arthur.	Murdoch M'Linnan.	Daniel Sterratt.
John Bain.	Hugh M'Connell.	Owen M'Pherson.	William Sutherland.
Donald Cameron.	Donald M'Donald.	James Paterson.	Donald Swanson.
William Campbell.	Ronald M'Donald.	John Ritchie.	John Sweeny.
David Carroll.	Thomas M'Donald.	James Robertson.	John Tour.
William Coghill.	John M'Dougall.	James Rourke.	William Towns.
John Delaney.	Donald M'Kay.	Alexander Ross, 1st.	John Turnbull.
Hugh Douglas.	William M'Kinlay.	Alexander Ross, 2nd.	James Waters.
John Fraser.	Archibald M'Kessack.	John Ross.	William White.
James Haliburton.	Donald M'Leod.	Neil Shaw.	Andrew Weeley.

CAPTAIN DANIEL M'INTOSH'S COMPANY.

Captain Daniel M'Intosh.
Lieut. James Robertson.

SERJEANTS.

William Bankier.
Thomas Evans.
John Young.

CORPORALS.

Alexander Munro.
Colin Mackenzie.
John Smith.

PRIVATE MEN.

William Adams.	John Green.	Alexander M'Grigor.	David Robertson.
Angus Anderson.	Arthur Holmes.	John M'Intosh.	Alexander Ross.
James Barrie.	Donald Jackson.	John M'Kay, 1st.	Donald Ross.
Christopher Brannon.	William Johnston.	John M'Kay, 2nd.	William Ross.
John Campbell.	Charles Kelly.	William M'Kay.	Donald Smith.
Lewis Cattnach.	James Kennedy.	Hugh M'Donald.	James Symons.
Gibson Condy.	David Levach.	Donald Mackenzie.	John Watson.
David Duncan.	John Milne.	James M'Laren.	James Whittle.
Donald Ferguson.	Duncan Munro.	John M'Leod.	William Wilson.
Alexander Fraser.	Hugh Munro.	William M'Leod.	
Kenneth Fraser.	Donald M'Culloch.	William Nicol.	
John Grant.	Angus M'Donald.	James Panton.	

CAPTAIN ROBERT BOYLE'S COMPANY.

Captain Robert Boyle.

SERJEANTS.

Donald Sutherland.
Donald White.

DRUMMERS OR FIFERS.

James Watt.

CORPORALS.

John Mackenzie.

PRIVATE MEN.

George Aitken.	James Hamilton.	Donald M'Kay.	Archibald Russell.
James Campbell.	Thomas Hetherington.	George M'Kay.	James Ryrie.
William Campbell.	Colin Lindsay.	James M'Kay.	William Smith.
John Crunchie.	Walter Little.	John M'Kechnie.	Alexander Stewart.
Alexander Craib.	Martin Martin.	Hugh M'Kechnie.	John Stewart.
Thomas Curtain.	John Merson.	David M'Kenzie.	John Sutherland.
James Downie.	Donald Munro.	Donald M'Kenzie.	William Sutherland.
John Downie.	John Munro.	Murdoch Nicolson.	William Thomson.
John Fenner.	Peter M'Arthur.	Daniel Parsons.	Gilbert Tulloch.
John Fowler.	Donald M'Callum.	Peter Robertson.	Mathew Wallace.
Alexander Graham.	George M'Ellray.	Alexander Ross.	Samuel Yardley.
Hugh Hamilton.	Angus M'Kay.	John Ross.	

CAPTAIN JAMES STIRLING'S COMPANY.

Lieut. George Gun Munro.
„ Alexander Brown.

SERJEANTS.	DRUMMERS OR FIFERS.	CORPORALS.
William Dunn.	Angus M'Leod.	Hugh M'Intosh.
Thomas Gourlay.		Alexander M'Ewan.

PRIVATE MEN.

Ewan Cameron.	William Mason.	John M'Lean.	James Sheriffs.
Walter Caldwell.	William Mitchell.	Donald M'Laren.	James Smith.
Duff Chambers.	John M'Callum.	Colin M'Linnan.	Donald Smith.
Roderick Chisholm.	Alexander M'Donald.	John Randall.	John Smith.
George Dare.	Angus M'Donald.	Robert Riddell.	Peter Smith.
William Donald.	Ronald M'Donald.	William Ritchie.	Robert Smith.
William Duncan.	James M'Cawan.	James Robertson.	James Smith.
Timothy Driscoll.	Charles M'Hardy.	Donald Ross.	John Sutherland.
Donald Fraser, 1st.	Donald M'Intosh.	John Ross.	Benjamin Vint.
Donald Fraser, 2nd.	James M'Intosh.	William Ross.	James Wylie, 1st.
James Gunn.	Donald M'Lean.	Duncan Scott.	James Wylie, 2nd.

CAPTAIN ALEXANDER FRASER'S COMPANY.

Lieut. John Orr.
„ William Fraser.

SERJEANTS.	DRUMMERS OR FIFERS.	CORPORALS.
Donald Shaw.	Lauchlan M'Kenzie.	William Bain.
John Shaw.	John Still.	Roderick Henderson.
Ninian Thomson.		John Smith.
James Watson.		

PRIVATE MEN.

Alexander Bain.	Alexander Gillies.	David Munro.	Daniel O'Neal.
Charles Barker.	James Gosnell.	William Munro.	Donald Ross.
John Barclay.	Duncan Grant.	Joseph M'Callie.	William Shuan.
William Barber.	James Gunn.	Donald M'Donald.	William Sinclair.
Donald Brown.	George Graham.	Robert M'Donald.	John Sutherland.
John Bremner.	Andrew Henderson.	William M'Kay.	James Taitt.
James Caie.	Patt Hanilan.	Alexander Mackenzie.	Joseph Thomson.
Alexander Cameron.	Peter Henderson.	William M'Kinlay.	Steven Veitch.
John Cameron.	William Johnston.	James M'Lachlan.	Thomas Wallace.
John Dogherty.	John Longstaff.	David M'Lean.	William Wilson.
James Fife.	William Miller.	Donald M'Leod.	
Francis William Geddes.	John Moir.	Donald Roy.	

CAPTAIN DONALD CHISHOLM'S COMPANY.

Captain Donald Chisholm.
Lieut. Donald Mackay.

SERJEANTS.	DRUMMERS OR FIFERS.	CORPORALS.
Michael Barlow.	William Paterson.	John Arnott.
William Bissett.		Frederick Forrester.
William Paterson.		Robert Leslie.

PRIVATE MEN.

Doctor Batchelor.	James Johnston.	Alexander M'Craw.	Hugh Ross.
John Cairns.	Alexander Kirkwood.	Hector M'Donald.	Walter Ross.
William Campbell.	Robert Kyle.	John M'Donald.	Archibald Sinclair.
James Duncan.	James Lamont.	Thomas M'Gibbon.	James Sneiddon.
John Emmerson.	John Lawson.	Alexander M'Intosh.	George Sutherland.
Smith Fife.	William Lawson.	Hugh M'Donald.	David Stewart.
Daniel Fisher.	John Lawsell.	Donald M'Kay, 1st.	James Stewart.
Thomas Fleming.	Murray Miller.	Donald M'Kay, 2nd.	James Taylor.
William Gunn.	William Miller.	John M'Leod.	George Watt.
Andrew Harper.	Francis Mullen.	Lauchlan M'Pherson.	John Watt.
John Hutchieson.	John Munro.	Duncan Robertson.	Andrew Wiseman.

The Muster for the Period of this Roll was taken at Cheby Camp on the 8th Day of Septr. 1815, by John Home, Pay Master.

The foregoing Roll, after due examination, is certified by

R. H. DICK, *Lt.-Col., Commanding Officer.*
JAS. YOUNG, *Lt. and Adjutant.*

TOTALS.

	Officers.	W. Ors.	Serjts.	Corpls.	Musi- cians.	Private Men.	TOTAL.
STAFF	8	—	—	—	—	—	8[1]
Capt. and Lt.-Col. John Campbell's Company, . .	3	2	7	4	—	51	67
Capt. and Bt.-Major Murdoch M'Laine's Company,	2	—	4	5	2	48	61
Capt. Mungo M'Pherson's Company, ...	4	—	5	5	2	45	61
Capt. and Lt.-Col. Thomas F. Wade's Company, .	1	—	3	2	2	47	55
Capt. Donald M'Donald's Company, ...	4	—	4	3	3	48	62
Capt. Daniel M'Intosh's Company, . .	2	—	3	3	—	45	53
Capt. Robert Boyle's Company, ...	1	—	2	1	1	47	52
Capt. James Stirling's Company, ...	2	—	2	1	2	44	51
Capt. Alexander Fraser's Company, ...	2	—	4	3	2	46	57
Capt. Donald Chisholm's Company, ...	2	—	3	3	1	44	53
TOTAL, .	31	2	37	30	15	465	580

[1] C.O., 2nd in Commd., Adjt., Qr.-Mr., 3 Surgeons, 1 Capt. unattd.

73RD

ADJUTANT'S ROLL

OF THE

OFFICERS, N.C. OFFICERS AND MEN
OF THE SECOND BATTN. 73RD REGIMENT OF FOOT

ENTITLED WATERLOO MEN

7TH SEPTEMBER 1815

With a List of Medals returned to the C.-in-Chief's Office

ADJUTANT'S ROLL OF THE MEN OF THE SECOND BATTN. 73RD REGIMENT OF FOOT entitled WATERLOO MEN, 7th September 1815.

Lieut.-Colonel Honble. W. G. Harris (Col.).
Major Dawson Kelly (Lt.-Col.) on Staff Employ.
Adjutant Patrick Hay.
Surgeon Dr. M'Dearmid.
Assistant Surgeon in the Regulars, } Jno. Reach.
    or Surgeon's Mate in the Militia } F. B. White.
Pay-Master Jno. Williams.
Captn. Henry Coane.
Lieut. Richd. Leyne.
    ,,   Jno. M'Connell.
Ensign R. G. Heselridge.
    ,,   Wm. M'Bean.
    ,,   Thos. Deacon.
Supernumerary Officers, { C. B. Eastwood.
    or Officers Ex Second { G. D. Bridge.
                     { Geo. Hughes.

CAPTAIN RICHARD DREWE'S COMPANY.

Lieut. Thomas Reynolds.
    ,,   J. Y. Lloyd.
Armourer as Serjt. John Taylor.

SERJEANTS.		DRUMMERS OR FIFERS.	CORPORALS.	
James Fenning.		James Johnson.	Thomas Bonser.	*No. 24.
Thomas Scarrett.	*No. 22.	David M'Naught.	Garrett Eagen.	
Luke M'Laughlin.			Joseph Jones.	
			John Ward.	

PRIVATE MEN.

	REMARKS.		REMARKS.
William Barnes.		Patk. Lindon.	*No. 47.
Phenicis Bell.	*No. 31.	James Lowe.	
James Badger.		Miles Lynn.	
Samuel Brumwell.		Jonn. M'Night.	*No. 50.
Thomas Brown.		George M'Laren.	
Lewis Colgan.	*No. 35.	Peter M'Naught.	
John Conway.	*No. 36. Not entitled, Medal returned.	William Morris.	
		Daniel Murphy.	
James Curran.		James Naughton.	
Richard Eaton.		John Patterson.	Place of Birth, Parish of Ballyclear. Bleacher.
Mathw. Feagan.			
John Feeley.		John Ryan.	
Michael Gonnon.		William Scarrett.	
David Gowens.		Thomas Taylor.	
Joseph Grey.		James Walker.	*No. 60.
Henry Holton.	*No. 44.	Michl. Whynn.	
Morice Horan.		Joseph Yates.	
Henry Izzard.			

SECOND BATTALION 73RD REGIMENT

CAPTAIN JNO. PIKE, LATE PERCH'S COMPANY.

Lieut. Joseph Dowling.
„ Robert Stewart.

SERJEANTS.	DRUMMERS OR FIFERS.	CORPORALS.
Michl. Horan. *No. 66.	John Barber.	John Horan.
John Meade.	Thomas Freeman.	John Strealton. Place of Birth,
John Quinlan.		Ballyridy. A Labourer.

PRIVATE MEN.

	REMARKS.		REMARKS.
William Bray.	*No. 73.	John Hott.	
Samuel Barron.		Henry Jones.	
James Brian.		John Kelly.	
Thomas Bryant.		John Lauder.	
Joseph Bromley.		Christopher Lynham.	
John Broom.		Thomas Mandus.	
James Carr.		Alexr. M'Arthur.	
Daniel Carter.		Thomas M'Grane.	
Michl. Conner.	*No. 81.	Edward M'Gregor.	
James Conghlan.		Alexr. M'Laren.	*No. 102.
Thomas Curtis.		John Murray.	*No. 103.
Robert Dickson.	Place of Birth, Parish of Douglas. A Shoemaker.	John Nichols.	
		John Parrott.	
Patrick Fitzgerald.		William Pearce.	
George Flanigan.		Robert Salmon.	
Lawrance Flanigan.	*No. 87.	Richard Smith.	
Michael Flanigan.		Thomas Seward.	
William Galvin.		John Simmonds.	
Abraham Harris.		Andw. Sullivan.	
William Henderson.	*No. 91.	John Tracey.	
John Hobley.			

CAPTAIN MORGAN CARROL'S COMPANY.

SERJEANTS.	DRUMMERS OR FIFERS.	CORPORALS.
David Inglis.	Charles Ball.	William Dunlop. *No. 117.
John Murphy.	James Varley.	John Eagen.
John Smith. Place of Birth, Parish of Alfrid. A Musician.		James Eaton.

PRIVATE MEN.

	REMARKS.		REMARKS.
George Allen.		Edward Horan.	
Thomas Atkins.	Place of Birth, Effingham. A Labourer.	William Jackson.	
		Joseph Johnson.	
John Barnett.		Miles Kenning.	
Jeremh. Bates.		Patrick Kerrigan.	
Benjn. Bumstead.		John Lacey.	*No. 147.
John Clarke.		William Marriott.	
Patrick Connus.	Place of Birth, F. Mary, Droheda. *No. 128.	John Maskerry.	
		John Masey.	
Henry Counsell.		Thomas Masey.	
William Counsell.		Henry Nichols.	
Thomas Cross.		James Ostler.	
Martin Durrant.		John Parker.	
William Evans.	*No. 133.	John Plunket.	
John Fluke.		Josh. Porter.	
James Ford.		John Rice.	
Edward Gardiner.		Anty. Sellers.	
Edward Hawes.		George Sheppard.	
Joseph Heaton.		John Simpson.	
James Hifford.		Stephen Smallfield.	*No. 161.
Patrick Hogan.	*No. 140.	John Woods.	
William Hopgood.			

CAPTAIN WILLIAM WHARTON'S COMPANY.

Captain William Wharton.

SERJEANTS.	DRUMMERS OR FIFERS.	CORPORALS.
Patrick Cassins.	William Gorman.	William Marshall.
William Kirk.	John Wilson. Place of Birth,	
Robert M'Nish.	Parish of Oldchurch, Kent.	

PRIVATE MEN.

	REMARKS.		REMARKS.
Edward Argent.		Thomas Murray.	
John Arnold.		George Poole.	
John Benfield.	*No. 172.	George Porter.	*No. 193.
Solomon Bullock.		Joseph Reynor	
William Clewes.		William Rogers.	
James Conway.		John Salt.	
Michl. Cowan.		Roger Sellers.	
Andw. Davidson.		John Smith.	Place of Birth, Parish of St. George's. A Clerk.
William Dent.			
James Ely.		Thomas Taylor.	Place of Birth, Parish of Killmain. Labr.
Fredk. Fitter.			
Jerh. Fitzgerald.		William Terry.	
Richd. Gardiner.		Moses Thorogood.	
Robt. Harrison.		Benjn. Wakefield.	*No. 202.
George Johns.		George Weston.	
Richard Lucitt.		Thomas Wilkinson.	Place of Birth, Parish of Stoke. A Potter.
Thomas Mansell.	*No. 186.		
Joseph Mantle.		John Wilson.	Place of Birth, Parish of Olman. Labr.
Henry M'Gilson.	*No. 198.		
James M'Mahon.	*No. 189.	John Winterbourne.	
Thomas M'Naught.		John White.	

CAPTAIN JOHN GARLAND'S COMPANY.

Captain John Garland.
Ensign A. Blennerhassit.

SERJEANT.	DRUMMERS OR FIFERS.	CORPORALS.
William Eaves.	Thomas Faux.	Daniel M'Crohan.
	John Lewis.	John Reids.

PRIVATE MEN.

	REMARKS.		REMARKS.
Downie Alles.		Mathw. Kelly.	
George Batts.		William Lancaster.	
James Bacon.	*No. 217. Not entitled, Medal returned.	Mathw. M'Grath.	
		Daniel Neighbour.	
William Motherton.		Jno. Parkins.	*No. 238.
James Brown.		Charles Payne.	*No. 239.
George Cheadle.		Joseph Pridney.	
Joseph Cheadle.		Joseph Quitter.	
John Chipman.		Joseph Reid.	
James Caulaghan.		James Roach.	
John Courtes.		William Rose.	
Robert Dickson.	Place of Birth, Castle-Douglas. A Labr.	James Rudden.	*No. 245. Spelt Rudding.
		William Sheath.	
Nichls. Dobson.		Edward Sheppard.	
John Flattery.		Robert Smalley.	*No. 248.
John Godolphin.		John Smith.	Place of Birth, Ashford, Kent. Labr.
George Graham.	*No. 229.		
William Hammond.		Joseph Vicars.	
Josh. Harvey.		James Vincent.	*No. 251.
Francis James.		John Wade.	
John Johnson.			

CAPTAIN ROBERT CRAWFORD'S (Bt.-Lt.-Col.) COMPANY.

SERJEANTS.
John Cobbett.
Edward M'Elroy.
Patrick O'Leary.   *No. 256.

CORPORALS.
Thomas Cummings.   *No. 257.
William Smith.
John Sutherland.

PRIVATE MEN.

	REMARKS.		REMARKS.
Richard Ashford.		James M'Elroy.	
Thomas Aitkins.		Walter Murray.	
Robert Beagent.		William Napier.	
Anty. Bell.	*No. 263.	Charles O'Leary.	
Thomas Bell.		Samuel Pierce.	
William Bird.		Paul Robertshaw.	
George Bradwell.		Isaac Rodbett.	
Richard Clarke.		William Rollison.	
James Cochrane.		John Serwin.	*No. 292. Spelt M'Scriven.
William Coachman.		Thomas Simpson.	
Henry Edwards.		John Smith, 1st.	Place of Birth, Parish of Cutton. A Labourer.
Archd. Elliott.			
John Friswell.		John Smith, 2nd.	Place of Birth, Parish of St. Nichols. A Tailor.
William Goadlett.			
Joseph Graham.	*No. 274.	William Smith.	*No. 296. Place of Birth, Parish of Glencairn. A Labr.
James Hull.	*No. 275.		
Alfred Isaac.		Charles Shears.	
Benjn. Jevens.		Thomas Stewart.	
Robert Lenham.	*No. 278.	Benjn. Stocks.	*No. 299.
Peter Leonard.		Jno. Tinsley.	
Andw. Linton.		Richd. Upton.	*No. 301.
George Metcalf.		Richd. Uzzle.	
Patrick M'Kenny.		John Woodall.	
Alexander M'Killigan.		William York.	

CAPTAIN WILLIAM CHESLEYN, Late MORICE'S COMPANY.

SERJEANTS.
John Van Hulton.
William Weston.

DRUMMERS OR FIFERS.
John Wilson (or Urtson—J. S., 24/3/10).
Place of Birth, Edinburgh. Tinsmith.

PRIVATE MEN.

	REMARKS.		REMARKS.
William Allen.		Patrick Hanify.	*No. 329.
Thomas Aitkins.	Place of Birth, Parish of Dycott. Labourer.	Peter Hanify.	
		James Lambert.	
John Barclay.		Simon Lynch.	*No. 332.
John Bartle.		William M'Coane.	
William Beasley.		John Martin.	
Patrick Birmingham.	*No. 314.	Archd. M'Donald.	
James Boggins.		Robert Moore.	*No. 336.
Henry Bowles.		Benjn. Palmer.	
William Buggins.		James Remmington.	
John Burroughs.		James Reynolds.	
James Chaplin.		Benjn. Scarf.	*No. 340.
William Cox.	Place of Birth, St. Ann's, Blackfriars. Butcher.	David Smith.	
		Samuel Taylor.	
James Dawson.		George Tyrrell.	*No. 343.
Thomas Draper.		William Waples.	
William Durbin.		Patrick Warrington.	
Thomas Elles.		Thomas Wilkinson.	
John Frost.		Samuel White.	
John Gormon.		Noah Wood.	
John Griffen.		William Warmonth.	*No. 349.
Judd Harding.	*No. 328.	Richd. Young.	*No. 350.

CAPTAIN HENRY B. LYNCH, LATE PIKE'S COMPANY.

SERJEANTS.	DRUMMERS OR FIFERS.	CORPORALS.
Adam Denby.	George Argue.	John Ellam.
James Groombridge.	Samuel Hudson.	Thomas Watts.
Samuel Lowe.		
John M'Lean.		
Richd. Pickett.		

PRIVATE MEN.

	REMARKS.		REMARKS.
John Alwright.		Jesse Hurley.	
William Ashenden.		William Jowers.	
Richard Barton.	*No. 363.	John Kinnair.	*No. 384.
John Beville.		John Kennock.	*No. 385.
James Binder.		John Lowe.	
Francis Bishop.		John Lower.	
George Brooks.		George Malkin.	
William Burridge.		Luke Miller.	
Charles Creeke.		John Milwood.	
John Cutton.		James Moore.	
Joseph Deeks.		Hugh Morris.	
William Duff.		Edward Murphy.	
Isaac Eabourne.		John Phillips.	
George East.		George Rose.	*No. 395.
Mathw. Evans.	*No. 375.	Michl. Ryan.	*No. 396.
Charles Eyles.		Peter Sundell.	
Stowell Fleming.		James Taylor.	*No. 398.
James Handforth.	*No. 378.	Benjn. Tyler.	
James Hindes.		Henry Webster.	
John Hobley.	Place of Birth, Nuneaton. Labourer.	James Westwood.	
		Daniel Wilmott.	
William Howe.			

CAPTAIN DUNCAN DEWER, LATE ROBERTSON'S COMPANY.

SERJEANTS.		DRUMMERS OR FIFERS.	CORPORALS.
William Dunn.	*No. 404.	James Stretton.	Henry Atkinson.
John Burton.			Michl. Lone.
Peter M'Cormick.	*No. 406.		

PRIVATE MEN.

	REMARKS.		REMARKS.
John Arnold.	Place of Birth, Parish of Leeds. Carpetweaver.	John Mannerly.	
		William Mathews.	
Thomas Banford.	*No. 411.	James M'Cabe.	
John Burley.		John Melsor.	
George Carey.	*No. 413.	Thomas Morice.	
Jno. Cole.		William Morrison.	
Jno. Conner.		John Mott.	
Thomas Daniels.		Edward Palmer.	
John Davey.		William Pardoe.	*No. 435.
Patk. Downey.		John Patterson.	Place of Birth, Paisley. Weaver.
Thomas Elwell.			
John Gee.		James Quinn.	*No. 437.
Bernd. Greenham.		Joseph Rice.	
Francis Harmon.		William Robertson.	*No. 439.
Elias Hill.		William Saxby.	
Jno. Hunter, 1st.	Place of Birth, Dumfries. Taylor.	James Siviter.	
		Thomas Stanton.	
Jno. Hunter, 2nd.	Place of Birth, Edinburgh. Shoemaker.	Ralph Surtis.	*No. 443.
		Richd. Stanley.	
Samuel Kirton.		John Tolly.	

VACANT, LATE CAPTAIN KENNEDY'S COMPANY.

SERJEANTS.	DRUMMERS OR FIFERS.	CORPORALS.
George Austin.	George Holland.	Thomas Edwards.
Henry Bell.	George Holt.	James Fleet.
John Farrow.		John Rennie.

PRIVATE MEN.

	REMARKS.		REMARKS.
Denis Abbis.		Charles Hockady.	
Edward Aldridge.	*No. 455.	Joseph Jones.	Place of Birth, Nottingham.
James Allen.			S. Weaver.
Michl. Armstrong.	*No. 457.	Richard Mathews.	
William Ashby.		Mathew M'Grath.	
Benjn. Baker.	*No. 459.	Alexr. M'Millan.	*No. 480.
Richd. Ball.		Michl. Murray.	*No. 481.
William Barrett.		James O'Neil.	
J. L. Bayley.		Thomas Oxley.	*No. 484.
Willm. Bayley.	*No. 463. Spelt Bailey.	Joseph Parrott.	
Benjn. Broxton.		James Quinlan.	
Thomas Chandler.		Alexr. Reid.	
Patrick Conner.	*No. 466.	Phillip Reily.	
Edward Cooke.		Alexr. Scott.	
William Cox.		William Shea.	
Thomas Crowson.		Robt. Smith.	
William Daily.		Benjn. Thompson.	
Patrick Donahue.	*No. 471. Spelt Donaghue.	George Turton.	
John Dove.		Thomas Walker.	*No. 494.
John Foley.		James Waterfield.	
John Gormon.	*No. 474.	Michl. Whitaker.	
Richard Hammond.		William Wilkinson.	
William Hawkes.		Delmer Wright.	

The foregoing Roll, after due examination, is certified by

L. OWEN, *Captn., Commanding Officer.*
JOHN YUDEN LLOYD, *Lt., Adjutant.*

NOTE.—On the next page will be found a list, which is attached to the original Roll now in the War Office, giving the names of men whose medals were returned to the C.-in-C.'s Office, with reasons for doing so. From the numbers given therein I have discovered that the whole of the survivors of Waterloo were numbered from the Colonel down to "Delmer Wright," of the "Vacant," late Capt. Kennedy's Company. I have given those men in the above Roll, who are mentioned on the next page, their numbers taken therefrom.—J. S.

TOTALS AS GIVEN BY THE ABOVE ROLL.

NOTE.—In this summary the undermentioned officers have not been included, as in no list do their names appear as having taken part in the Battle with the Regt. Capts. Dewer, Lynch, Cheslyn, Crawford, Carrol, Pike, and Drewe.—J. S.
25/3/1910.

Companies.	Officers.	W. O's.	Serjts.	Corpls.	Musicians.	Private Men.	TOTAL.
STAFF	16	—	—	—	—	—	16
Capt. Richd. Drewe's, . . .	2	—	4	4	2	33	45
Capt. J. Pike, late Perch's, .	2	—	3	2	2	40	49
Capt. Morgan Carrol's, . . .	—	—	3	3	2	41	49
Capt. William Wharton's, . .	1	—	3	1	2	38	45
Capt. John Garland's, . . .	2	—	1	2	2	38	45
Capt. (Bt.-Lt.-Col.) Crawford's,	—	—	3	3	—	45	51
Capt. W. Cheslyn, late Morice's,	—	—	2	—	1	42	45
Capt. H. B. Lynch, late Pike's,	—	—	5	2	2	42	51
Capt. D. Dewer, late Robertson's,	—	—	3	2	1	36	42
Vacant, late Kennedy's, . .	—	—	3	3	2	45	53
TOTALS, .	23	—	30	22	16	400	491

LIST OF MEDALS RETURNED TO THE COMMANDER-IN-CHIEF'S OFFICE BY THE SECOND BN. 73RD REGT., the men to whom they belong being Dead, Discharged, Transferred, etc.

NOTTINGHAM, 5th May 1816.

RANK AND NAMES.	NUMBER.	REMARKS.
Private Lawrance Flanagan	87	
,, James Walker	60	
,, John Murray	103	
,, Benjn. Wakefield	202	
,, Jos. Graham	274	
,, Bn. Stocks	299	
,, Robert Lenham	278	
,, Richard Barton	363	*Deceased.*
,, Michael Armstrong	457	
,, James Quinn	437	
,, Benjn. Scarfe	340	
,, Morrice M'Grath	480	
,, Bn. Baker	459	
,, Judd Harding	328	
,, Thomas Walker	494	
Corporal Thomas Cummings . . .	257	
Private Phineas Bell	31	Sent Augt. 20.
,, Johnathn. M'Knight . . .	50	Sent to address 17th July.
,, Patk. Connors	128	Recd.
,, William Evans	133	Sent 21 June '16.
,, Stephen Smallfield	161	Sent 20 Aug.
,, Jno. Benfield	172	Sent to the O. Cmg. Regt., Nottgh., 27 J.
,, Geo. Porter	193	Recd.
,, James Rudding	245	28th Jan. '17.
,, Patk. Birmingham	314	Sent 27 July.
,, Simion Lynch	332	Sent 2 Aug. '16.
,, Jos. Hanoforth	378	Sent 5 Sept.
,, W. Bailey	463	Sent to Birmingham.
,, Patk. Donaghue	471	Sent 24 Sept. 1816.
,, John Gorman	474	Sent 7 Sept.
Serjt. P. O'Leary	256	Recd. Sent to Lord Aylmer.
,, P. M'Cormick	406	Sent 15 July.
Private M'Scriven	292	Exchanged to 12th Foot. Sent 28 Aug.
Serjt. William Dunn	404	16 Novr.
Private Anthy. Bell	263	Sent to Nottingham Offr. Comdg.
,, Richard Upton	301	
,, Wm. Warmouth	349	
Serjt. Michl. Horan	66	Sent to his address.
Private Patk. Lindon	47	12th Dec.
,, Patk. Hogan	140	Recd.
,, Michl. Ryan	396	Sent.
,, P. Conners	466	Sent to Tralee 7 June '16.

Remarks spanning "Geo. Porter" through "P. M'Cormick": *Discharged to Chelsea Pension. Places of Residence unknown.*

Remarks spanning "Anthy. Bell" through "Wm. Warmouth": *Sick, absent in France; not expected to join the Battn.*

Remarks spanning "Patk. Lindon" through "P. Conners": *Sick, absent Strand Bridge Bks., London; not expected to join the Battn.*

RANK AND NAMES.	NUMBER.	REMARKS.
Serjt. Thos. Scarrett	22	Sent Col. Nooper 27 May 1816.
Corpl. Thos. Bonsor	24	
„ Wm. Dunlop	117	Recd.
Private Lewis Colgan	35	Sent 22 July.
„ Henry Holton	44	Sent 16 Nov. '16.
„ Michl. Connor	81	Recd.
„ W. Henderson	91	
„ Henry M'Gilsen	198	*Sick, absent at Colchester ; wounded men not expected to join the Battn.*
„ Jas. M'Mahon	189	
„ Wm. Smith	296	
„ Robt. Moore	336	
„ Richd. Young	350	
„ George Rose	395	
„ George Carey	413	
„ Wm. Robertson	439	Recd.
„ Alexr. M'Millan	481	
„ Edwd. Aldridge	455	
Private John Lacey, ...	147	17th Feb.
„ Thos. Mansell	186	3 Garr.Bn. Sent 10 July.
„ Jas. Vincent	251	Recd. 12 June '16.
„ Wm. Bray	73	3 Garr.Bn. Sent 10 July.
„ George Tyrrell	343	Sent 22 July.
„ Charles Payne	239	Recd.
„ Wm. Pardoe	435	Sent.
„ John Kennach	385	Sent 20 Aug.
„ Matthew Evans	375	Recd. 12 June.
„ John Parkins	238	28 Jany.
„ Robt. Smalley	248	Recd.
„ James Hull	275	Sent 14 Aug.
„ Patk. Henaffy	329	3 Gn. Bn. Sent 10 July.
„ Ralph Surtes	443	*Sick, absent Chelsea or Chatham ; not expected to join the Battn.*
„ John Conway	36	} *Returned in the Waterloo list by mistake, not being entitled.*
„ James Beacon	217	
„ Thomas Bamford	411	*Deserted* 21st March ; not yet heard of.
„ Jno. Kennair	384	*Deserted* 1st March ; sent to the Isle of Wight.
„ Geo. Graham	229	*Deserted* 12th March ; not yet heard of.
„ Alexr. M'Laren	102	*Deserted* 12th Novr. '15 ; sent back to the Regt.
„ Thos. Oxley	484	{ Recd. Sent to Lord Aylmer. { Discharged to Chelsea Pension.
„ James Taylor	398	{ Recd. 12th June 1816. { Sick, absent Colchester ; not expected to join Bn.

L. OWEN, *Captn.*,

Comm. 2nd Bn. 73rd Foot.

42ND

ROLL OF OFFICERS, N.C. OFFICERS AND MEN OF THE
42ND REGIMENT OF FOOT

WHO WERE ALIVE IN 1847

AND RECEIVED THE GENERAL SERVICE MEDAL

PENINSULA AND EGYPT

ROLL of Officers, N.C. Officers and Men, 42nd Foot, who were alive in 1847, and received the General Service Medal (Peninsula and Egypt).

NAME.	Corunna.	Busaco.	F. d'Onor.	C. Rodrigo.	Salamanca.	Pyrenees.	Nivelle.	Nive.	Orthes.	Toulouse.	Talavera.	Egypt.	REMARKS.
OFFICERS.													
Brander, J., Lieut.-Col. . .			1	1		1	1	1	1				
Campbell, P. Colin (Vol.), late Capt.										1			
Fraser, Hugh A., Subst. Maj. Unattd.	1	1	1	1	1					1			
Gordon, Geo., Ensn. Lt. H.P. 85th							1	1	1	1			
Geddes, Jas., Ensn. Lt. H.P. 42nd										1			
Hane, John, Ensn., late Pay-Master	1				1	1	1	1	1	1			
M'Innes, Dond., Capt., late Capt.	1				1								
M'Donald, Dond., Lt., Barrack-Master	1	1	1	1									
Mackay, Dond., Qr.-Mr. . .		1	1										
Mackay, Lachlan, Ensn. Lt. H.P. 42nd						1	1	1	1	1			
M'Niven, Thos. Wm., Lt., Lt.-Col. Unattd. . . .									1	1			
Menzies, Archd., Capt., late Major					1								
Nicholson, H., Lt., Capt. H.P. Gd. Guards							1	1	1	1			42nd Regimental Collection.
Stewart, Duncan, Lt., Capt. Unattd.					1	1	1	1	1				
Fraser, A. Simon, Vol. Ensn. Lt. H.P. Unattd. . . .						1	1	1					
Innes, Alexr., Ensn. Lt. H.P. Unattd.										1			
Orr, John, Ensn. and Lt., Lt. Retd. Full Pay (Capt. Edinr. Militia)					1	1							
RANK AND FILE.													
Holms, William		1	1	1	1	1	1	1	1	1			
Hutchison, John		1	1	1									
Hutchison, John		1	1	1	1	1	1	1	1	1			
Hegginbottom, Chas. . .					1	1			1	1			Capt. Stewart's Collection.
Hawarth, John					1	1							
Harper, John, ...		1	1	1	1	1	1		1	1			
Hawson, Darbey	1												
Henderson, William . . .	1				1								
Holmes, Arthur			1	1	1	1	1	1	1	1			

Name.	Corunna.	Busaco.	F. d'Onor.	C. Rodrigo.	Salamanca.	Pyrenees.	Nivelle.	Nive.	Orthes.	Toulouse.	Talavera.	Egypt.	Remarks.
Rank and File.													
Jackson, Donald	1				1	1	1		1	1			
Jack, William, ...		1	1	1	1	1	1	1	1	1	1		
Jefferay, Thos.	1												
Johnston, David	1				1	1	1	1	1	1			
Johnstone, William . . .	1				1	1	1	1	1	1		1	Egypt.
Kyle, Robert						1	1	1	1	1			
Keir, William, *Serjt.* . . .		1	1	1									
Kerr, Alexr.		1			1								Capt. Stewart's Collection.
Kerry, Michael, *Serjt.* . .		1	1										
Kay, David,[1]	1		1		1	1	1	1	1	1			
Kennedy, James			1		1					1			
Kelly, Daniel					1					1			
Lunndane, Alex.					1	1			1	1			
Lemon, John		1	1	1	1								
Lamont, James	1				1	1			1	1			
Hamilton, Thos.	1											1	Egypt. Capt. Stewart's Collection.
Campbell, William . . .							1		1	1			
Cox, John					1				1				
Campbell, Wm., *Serjt.* . .		1	1	1	1	1	1	1	1	1			
Clark, Wm.					1							1	Egypt.
Connolly, Jas., *Serjt.* . . .						1	1	1	1	1			
Catnock, Alexr.											1		
Cavines, John			1				1	1	1	1			
Cameron, Alexr.										1	1		
Clark, Donald	1												
Cruikshanks, Alexr., *Serjt.* .	1				1	1		1	1	1			
Croll, Francis	1				1				1	1			
Campbell, William . . .	1				1	1	1	1	1	1			
							Pris	oner	of	War.			
Dent, John	1			1	1	1	1	1	1	1			Capt. Stewart's Collection. Also his Waterloo and Regtl. medals.
Donaldson, William . . .										1			
Durham, John, *Serjt.* . .	1											1	Egypt.
Dow, Alexr.		1	1				1	1	1	1			
Duncan, James	1				1	1	1	1	1	1			
Dougherty, John, *Corpl.* .			1	1	1	1	1	1	1	1			
Dallas, James, *Corpl.* . .		1	1	1	1	1	1	1	1	1			
Davidson, John		1	1	1	1					1			
Downie, James					1	1	1	1	1	1			
Donoghue, Michael . . .	1				1				1	1			
Cameron, John		1	1	1	1	1	1	1	1	1			
M'Bain, Robert							1	1	1	1			
M'Donald, Alexr. (1) . . .						1	1	1	1	1			
M'Donald, Donald . . .	1											1	Egypt.
M'Donald, Robt.					1	1							
M'Gregor, Donald . . .	1	1	1	1	1	1			1	1	1		
M'Gregor, James (3) . . .	1				1								

[1] See additional List, page 30.

NAME.	Coruña.	Busaco.	F. d'Onor.	C. Rodrigo.	Salamanca.	Pyrenees.	Nivelle.	Nive.	Orthes.	Toulouse.	Talavera.	Egypt.	REMARKS.
RANK AND FILE.													
M'Intosh, Hugh, *Corpl.*	1	1	1	1	1	1	1	1	1	1			
M'Intosh, James	1				1	1	1		1	1			
M'Intosh, James	1				1	1	1	1	1				
M'Intosh, John	1				1								
M'Kennion, Peter					1	1	1	1	1	1			
M'Kenzie, John, *Corpl.*	1		1		1	1	1	1	1	1		1	Egypt. In Col. Eaton's Collection, U.S. Institute.
M'Kenzie, William		1	1	1	1				1	1			
M'Lean, John (1)	1				1	1			1	1			In Col. Eaton's Collection, U.S. Institute. This was one of the men who carried Sir J. Moore to the grave.
M'Lennan, John					1								
M'Leod, John (2)	1			1	1	1	1	1	1	1		1	Egypt.
M'Naughton, Alexr.										1			
M'Pherson, Dond., *Serjt.*					1	1	1	1	1	1			
Mathieson, Finlay	1				1	1			1	1			
Munro, John					1								
Munro, John,	1			1	1	1	1	1	1				
Munro, Neil	1				1	1						1	Egypt. Capt. Stewart's Collection.
M'Kenzie, Colin, *Corpl.*	1				1	1	1	1	1	1			
M'Kennon, Hector, *Corpl.*	1		1		1	1	1	1	1	1	1		
Monteith, John	1		1		1								
Martin, James, *Serjt.*		1	1	1	1	1	1	1	1				
M'Donald, John					1								
M'Dougall, Alexr.	1				1	1							
M'Dougall, John, *Serjt.*	1												
M'Glasban, John					1	1	1	1	1				
M'Kinlay, Wm.	1				1	1	1	1	1				Capt. Stewart's Collection. Also this man's Waterloo and Regtl. medals.
Metcalf, John					1	1			1	1			
Munro, John	1				1	1							
M'Connell, Hugh, *Serjt.*	1		1		1	1	1		1	1			
Mitchell, Wm.		1	1	1	1				1	1			
M'Kay, Wm.	1				1	1			1				
Oliver, Thomas		1	1	1									
		Cor pora l.											
Patterson, Hugh, *Corpl.*	1				1	1			1				
Pride, James					1								
Patterson, Willm., *Corpl.*			1	1	1	1	1	1	1	1			
Paton, Robert	1				1	1	1	1		1			
Petrie, James	1				1	1			1	1		1	Egypt.
Peddie, William	1					1	1	1	1	1			
Perry, George	1				1					1			
Patterson, Wm., *Dr.*	1		1		1	1	1	1	1	1			
Playfair, James		1	1	1	Sick								
Ritchie, John	1				1								
Ross, John		1	1	1		1				1			

NAME.	Corunna.	Busaco.	F. d'Onor.	C. Rodrigo.	Salamanca.	Pyrenees.	Nivelle.	Nive.	Orthes.	Toulouse.	Talavera.	Egypt.	REMARKS.
RANK AND FILE.													
Ross, Hugh, *Serjt.*							1	1	1	1			
Redburn, John, *Corpl.*	1				1	1	1		1	1	Not present.		
Ross, Alexander									1	1			
Robertson, James	1				1					1			
Riddle, Archibald	1				1							1	Egypt.
Robertson, James		1					1	1	1	1			
Robertson, Duncan					1	1						1	Egypt.
Reid, John, *Serjt.*		1	1			1	1	1	1				
Skinner, Donald	1												
Sutherland, Robt., *Buglr.*					1								
Sutherland, George		1	1		1	1			1	1			
Sinclair, James	1				1	Disallowed.							
Sweeney, John		1		1	1				1	1			
Sutherland, Walter		1			1								
Sutherland, William										1			
Thomson, Willm.					1								
Thomson, Robt.					1		1	1	1	1			
Taylor, George		1			1	1 Sick	1 Absent	1	1	1			
Turner, James		1	1	1	1	Not	present.	1	1	1			
Towers, John	1				1	1	1	1	1	1			
Urquhart, John	1				1					1			Capt. Stewart's Collection.
Urquhart, Robt.		1	1	1	1								
Wiseman, Andrew							1	1	1	1			
Whitlar, David	1												
Wilson, Gilbert	1				1	1	1		1	1			
Warren, George, *Dr.*		1	1	1	1							1	Egypt.
Wilson, Joseph	1				1	1	1	1	1	1			
Wylie, James, *Dr.*		1	1										
Wylie, Andrew		1	1										
Wilson, James										1			
White, William	1				1	1	1	1	1	1	1		
Watt, James	1					1			1	1	1		
Watters, James		1	1	1	1	1	1	1	1	1	1		
Waugh, James					1	1			1	1			
Young, Alexr.									1				
Young, Private	1			1	1	1			1	1			
Adam, David		1	1	1	1	1	1	1	1	Recruiting Edinburgh.			
Boag, John		1			1	1	1	1	1	1			
Barker, James					1								
Burke, Thomas		1	1	1	1	1			1	1			
Bismell, John					1	1				1			
Cameron, Donald		1	1	1	1	1	1	1	1	1	1		This is the man who wrote the account of the Red Hackle for Drysdale. He died at Inverness, 1854.

Name.	Corunna.	Busaco.	F. d'Onor.	C. Rodrigo.	Salamanca.	Pyrenees.	Nivelle.	Nive.	Orthes.	Toulouse.	Talavera.	Egypt.	Remarks.
RANK AND FILE.													
Campbell, Duncan . . .					1								
Duff, John		1	1	1	1	1			1	1	Sick		
Downie, John					1	1		1	1	1			
Fowler, John		1	1		1	1	1	1	1	1			
Frazer, William . . .	1												
Ferguson, James . . .							1	1	1	1			Capt. Stewart's Collection.
Fife, Smith									1	1			
Findlay, Robt. . . .					1	1	1	1					
Fraser, Donald, *Serjt.* . .							1	1	1	1			
Gilchrist, David . . .		1	1		1	1			1	1			
Gordon, Alexr. . . .		1	1	1									
Graham, James . . .		1	1	1									
Henderson, Alexr. . .		1	1			1	1	1	1	1			
Horn, John		1	1	1	1	1							
Gunn, James										1			
Jones, John					1	1	1	1	1	1			
Jenkins, John, *Corpl.* . .	1	1	1	1	1	1	1	1	1	1			
King, John	1												
Kerth, William		1	1	1		1			1				
Leslie, Robert, *Corpl.* . .					1	1	1	1	1	1			
Duncan, William . . .					1								
Gow, John										1			
Johnson, William . . . Prince Edward Island	1				1	1	1	1		1			
Logan, Richard		1			Sick 1	1				1			
Lennon, George									1	1			
M'Donald, John . . .		1	1		1	1		1	1	1			
M'Kenzie, Rodk. . . .		1	1	1	1	1	1	1	1	1			Capt. Stewart's Collection.
M'Kenzie, Hugh . . .		1	1	1	1	1			1	1			
M'Kimmie, Jno.	1												
Solson, Lewis					1	1		1	1	1			
Sutherland, Alexr. . .		1				1				1			
Shepherd, Andw. . . .		1	1	1	1	1	1	1	1	1			
Sutherland, Sinclair . .										1			
Tait, James	1				1	1		1	1	1			
Vint, Benjamin					1	Sick 1	1	1	1	1			
Murray, James	1												
Mason, William . . .					1	1	1	1	1	1			
M'Lardy, James . . .		1	1	1	1	1			1	1			
M'Leod, James	1				1	1			1	1			
M'Pheil, Charles . . .		1	1	1	1	1	1	1	1	1	Not present		

NAME.	Coruna.	Busaco.	F. d'Onor.	C. Rodrigo.	Salamanca.	Pyrenees.	Nivelle.	Nive.	Orthes.	Toulouse.	Talavera.	Egypt.	REMARKS.
RANK AND FILE.													
Munro, Duncan, *Dr.*		1	1	1									
M'Intosh, John	1												
Murray, William						*1* (Not present.)	1	1	*1* (Sick.)	*1*			
M'Kenzie, K.		1	*1* (Sick.)	*1*			1		1	1			
M'Gregor, John		1	1	1	1					1			
M'Intosh, Donald									1	1			
Peattie, Paul		1	1	1	1	1	1	1	1	1			In W. E. Gray's Collection (2 Rutland Park, Sheffield).
Panton, James		1	1	1	1	1	1	1	1	1			
Pyne, Sutherland		1	1	1	1				1	1			
Roy, George					*1* (Sick)	1			1	1	*1* (Not present.)		
Ross, William		1	1	1	1	1			1	1			
Ross, Thomas		1	1	1		1			1	1			
Ross, John			1	1	1								
Ross, Donald	1												
Speedie, Thos., *Corpl.*		1	1	1									
Suttie, William		1			1	1				1			Capt. Stewart's Collection.
Sewell, Robert						1	1	1	1	1			
Smith, John	1												
Scott, John		1	*1*	1	1	1	1		1	1			
Rigg, Benjamin		1	1	1									
Ross, Robt.						1			1	1			
Swanson, Magnus		1					1		1	1			
Mackay, William		1	1	1	1	1	1	1	1	1			
Weir, William		*1*	1	1									
M'Pherson, John		1					1	1	1	1			
M'Farish, Henry								1	1	1			
M'Intosh, John						1			1	1			
Ross, John		1	1	1	1	1	1	1	1	1			In Col. Murray's (Polmaise) Collection.
Baillie, Geo.		1	1	1	1	1	1	1	1				
Duff, John		1	1	1	1	1	1	1	1	1			
Case, James			1	1	1	1	1		1	1			
Fraser, John	1								1				
Cochran, Angus	1			*1*	1	*1* (Not entitled.)							
Mackinnin, Norman						1		1					
M'Donald, Colin		1	1	1	1	1	1	1	1	1			
M'Intosh, John	1			*1*	1	1			1	1	*1* (Not entitled.)		
M'Donald, Hugh	1			1	1	1			1	1			
Munro, John	1				1								
Mackenzie, John	1				1	1	1	1	1				
Nicholson, Murdock	1	*1* (Not present.)	*1*	*1*	1	1	1	1	1	1			
Nicol, Donald		*1*	1	*1*	1	1	1	1	1	*1*			
M'Phie, Neil					1								
Mackay, John		1			1		1	1	1				

NAME.	Corunna.	Busaco.	F. d'Onor.	C. Rodrigo.	Salamanca.	Pyrenees.	Nivelle.	Nive.	Orthes.	Toulouse.	Talavera.	Egypt.	REMARKS.
RANK AND FILE.													
M'Leod, Donald,	1				1	1				1			
Ross, William, *Serjt.*		1	1	1									Capt. Stewart's Collection.
Ross, John	1												
Ross, Donald					1	1	1	1	1	*1*	Sick		
Ross, George, *Serjt.*					1	1			1	1			
Robb, Wm.	1				1	*1*	On	com	md.	*1*		1	Egypt. Capt. Stewart's Collection.
Urquhart, Duncan	1				1	1				1			Capt. Stewart's Collection.
Bottie, Duncan			1	1	1	1	1	1		1			
Cottenach, Lewis					1	1	1	1	1	1			
Randell, George	1					1	1	1	1	1			
Riddell, Robt., *Serjt.*					1	1	1	1	1	1			
Rutledge, James	1				1	1			1	1			
Ross, Donald		1	1	1	1	1	1	1	1	1			
Robertson, Peter [1]					1	1	1	1	1	1			
Ritchie, John (2)					1	1	1	1	1				
Russell, James	1				1	1	1	1	1	1			
Sutherland, John (1)	1				1					1			
Sutherland, James					1	1	1	1	1	1			
Still, John	1											1	Egypt.
Smith, John, *Corpl.*	1				1	1	1	1	1	1			In Col. Murray's (Polmaise) Collection.
Symons, Charles	1		*1*		1	1	1	1	1	1			
Sutherland, John (2)	1												
Steadman, Wm.		1	1										
Smith, John	1												
Shields, Andrew				*1*	1	1			1	1			
Stewart, Donald								1	1	1			
Scott, John	1				1	1		1	1	1			
Stewart, Robert		1	1	1	1	1			1	1			Capt. Stewart's Collection.
Stevenson, James	*1*		*1*		1	1	1		1	1	1		
Sutherland, John			1	1	1	1							
Sutherland, John (2)			1	1	*1*	1	1	1	1	1			
Sutherland, Wm.	1				1								
Smith, William	*1*	*1*	1	1	1	1	1	1	1	1			
Symons, James	1				1	1	1	1	1	1			
Sutherland, Wm., *Serjt.*						1	1	1	1	1			
									No claim.				
Stewart, John	1				*1*				*1*	*1*			
Swanson, Malcolm	1				1	1	1	1	1	1			
Swanson, Dond., *Serjt.*		1	1	1									
Slidders, David	1	Dru	mm	er.									
Stormson, John	1				1	1	1		1				
Smith, John	1				1	1	1	1	1	1			
M'Gregor, Wm., *Serjt.*	1												
M'Lean, John											1	1	Egypt.
M'Leod, John			1	1		1			1	1			
Morrison, David, *Dr.*	1				1	*1*	1	1	1	1			
M'Dermaid, Jno.	1				1								
Muller, Murray								1	1	1	1		
M'Donald, Wm., *Corpl.*			1				1	1	1	1	1		

[1] Also clasps for 'Roleia,' 'Vimiera,' and 'Corunna' in 71st Foot.

NAME.	Corunna.	Busaco.	F. d'Onor.	C. Rodrigo.	Salamanca.	Pyrenees.	Nivelle.	Nive.	Orthes.	Toulouse.	Talavera.	Egypt.	REMARKS.
RANK AND FILE.													
Mackey, Donald		1			1	1	1	1	1	1			
Mackay, Robert						1	1	1	1	1			
Macleod, John, *Serjt.*	1				1	1	1	1	1				
Macleod, Murdock	1				1								
Mackay, Donald (1)	1				1				1				
Mackay, Donald (2)	1		1			1	1	1	1	1			
M'Kay, Kenneth		1	1	1	1	1	1	1	1	1			
M'Kenzie, Hugh, *Serjt.*	1				1	1	1	1	1	1			
M'Kenzie, Wm., *Corpl.*					1	1	1	1	1	1			Capt. Stewart's Collection.
M'Leod, Angus		1	1	1	1	1	1	1	1	1			
M'Pherson, Lachlan						1	1	1					
M'Gregor, Alexr.						1	1						
M'Kay, Robert	1				1	1	1	1	1	1			
M'Donald, Donald						1	1	1	1	1			
M'Kay, Wm.		1	1	1	1	1	1	1	1	1			Capt. Stewart's Collection.
M'Lennan, Colin					1	1	1	1	1	1			
Mason, William	1				1								Capt. Stewart's Collection.
Melville, Alexr.	1				1	1			1				
M'Lintock, Peter		1	1		1					1			
M'Pherson, Wm.	1				1	1				1			
M'Arthur, Colin	1				1				1	1			
M'Donald, Angus	1			1	1	1	1		1	1		1	
Adams, George	1	1	1	1	1	1		1					
Anderson, Charles						1	1		1	1			
Anton, James, *Qr.-M. Serjt.*							1	1	1	1			
Aitken, Alex., *Serjt.*	1											1	Egypt. This N.C.O. was a drummer in Egypt.
Armott, John, *Serjt.*	1				1	1	1	1	1	1			
Allan, James	1					1			1	1			
Abernethy, Thos., *Corpl.*	1				1				1	1			
Anderson, John	1				1	1	1	1	1	1			Capt. Stewart's Collection.
Bowman, Wm., *Serjt.*							1	1	1	1			
Berkley, Peter	1												
Bankier, Wm., *Serjt.*	1		1		1	1	1		1	1			
Brown, Thos.		1	1	1	1	1			1	1			
Buchanan, Wm.,		1	1	1	1	1		1	1	1			
Bigbie, Andw.	1				1	1		1	1	1			
Bain, John						1	1	1	1	1			
Bennett, Wm.		1	1	1	1	1		1	1	1			
Bissett, Wm., *Serjt.*			1										
Batchelor, Docter	1				1	1	1	1	1	1			
Beath, Adam						1	1		1	1			
Balmain, John			1	1	1	1		1	1	1			
Bain, Donald				1	1					1			
Bremner, Alexr.		1											
Chambers, Duff		1	1		1	1							
Crab, Alexr.					1	1				1			
Chisholm, Roderick		1	1	1	1	1	1	1	1	1			
Campbell, Alexr.	1				1	1			1	1			
Campbell, Duncan	1				1	1			1	1			

NAME.	Corunna.	Busaco.	F. d'Onor.	C. Rodrigo.	Salamanca.	Pyrenees.	Nivelle.	Nive.	Orthes.	Toulouse.	Talavera.	Egypt.	REMARKS.
RANK AND FILE.													
Campbell, John					1	1			1	1			
Fyfe, James (or John) . .						*1*	1	1	1	1			In Col. Murray's (Polmaise) Collection.
Fleming, Thos.										1			
Fraser, Wm.	1												In Col. Murray's (Polmaise) Collection.
Fraser, Donald (1) . . .		1	1		1	1	1	1	1	1			
Fraser, Evan	1				1				1	1			
Fraser, Hugh	1				1				1	1			In Regtl. Collection. Also a silver Maltese ✠ to same man.
Fraser, Donald (2) . . .						1	1	1	1	1			Capt. Stewart's Collection.
Fraser, Alexr. (4)	1												
Fraser, John, *Serjt.* . . .		1	1	1	1	1	1	1	1	1			
Wounded in left eye; not present.													
Fraser, Kenneth	*1*				1					1			
Glen, Thomas	1					1			1	1			
Gillies, Alexr.	1			*1*	1	1	1	1	1	1			
Gunn, James	1				1	1	1	1	1	1			
Gearns, James					1	1	1		1	1			In Col. Murray's (Polmaise) Collection.
Gilmour, Andw.	1		*1*		1	1	1	1		1			
Grant, Hugh		1	1	1	1								
Grey, Peter, *Corpl.* . . .					1	1	1		1	1			
Gunn, William									1	1			
Gosnell, James						1	1	1	1	1			
Grant, James			1	1	1				1	1			
Galloway, Wm., *Dr.* . . .										1			
Gourlay, Thos., *Serjt.* . .		1	1										
Gowrie, James		1	*1*		1	1			1	1			
Gray, Peter	1				1	1			1				
Graham, Findlay . . .		1		1	1								
Grant, Duncan, *Serjt.* . .					1	1	1	1	1	1			
Gray, William	1				1							1	Egypt.
Graham, Wm., *Serjt.* . .		1	1	1									
M'Intyre, Dugald . . .		1	1	1	1	1				1			Capt. Stewart's Collection.
Finniston, Fras.												1	Egypt.
M'Dougall, Wm.												1	Egypt.
M'Cord, Samuel		1		1	1	1	1		1	1			
Murray, Robert					1				1	1			
M'Connell, Alexr. . . .					1	1							
M'Kay, Edward					1	1	1	1	1				
M'Nally, Edwd.			1										Capt. Stewart's Collection.
M'Craw, Alexr.					1	1				1			
M'Ewan, Alexr., *Serjt.* . .	1												
Murphy, Wm., *Serjt.* . .					1	1	1	1	1				In Col. Eaton's Collection, U.S. Institute.
M'Lennan, Murdock . . .	1			*1*	1	1				1	*1*		
M'Namara, John	1					1	1	1	1				
M'Kenzie, James		1	1	*1*	1	1							Capt. Stewart's Collection.
M'Kenzie, Alexr.		1		1					1	1			
M'Ivor, James, *Serjt.* . .	1		*1*			1	1	1	1	1			Capt. Stewart's Collection. Also his Waterloo medal.

Name.	Corunna.	Busaco.	F. d'Onor.	C. Rodrigo.	Salamanca.	Pyrenees.	Nivelle.	Nive.	Orthes.	Toulouse.	Talavera.	Egypt.	Remarks.
RANK AND FILE.													
M'Leod, Alexr.		1											
Nicholson, John	1				1	*1*			*1*	*1*			
Nichol, Wm.	1				1	1							
Miller, Wm.					1	1	1	1					
Muller, Francis . . .					1								
M'Laren, Donald . . .		1			*1*	1	1	1	1	1			
Mathieson, Wm.						1	1	1	*1*	*1*		1	Egypt.
Murray, James	1												
M'Gregor, Alexr. . . .		1	1	1	1	1	1	1	1	1			
M'Pherson, Dougal . . .		1	1	1									
M'Pherson, Angus, *Serjt.* .		1	1	1									
Merson, John		1	1		1	1				1			
Munro, Donald (1) . . .					1	1		1	1	1			}1 { One of these men got the 'Egypt' bar.
Munro, Donald		1	1	*1*									
Murray, Andrew	1												
M'Laren, James		1			1								
Muro (?), David					1	1	1		1	1			
Matheson, Hugh	1				1	1	1	1	1	1			
Morrison, Alex.	1			*1*		1	1	1	1	1			
M'Alpin, Thos.					1				*1*	1			
M'Bain, John	1				1	1				1			
M'Connachie, Jas., *Serjt.* .	1				1	1	1	1	1	1			
M'Donald, Chas.	1				1	1	1	1	1	1			Capt. Stewart's Collection.
M'Kay, Donald, *Serjt.* . .		1	1										
M'Kay, George		1	1	1		1	1	1	1	1			In Capt. John Stansfield's Collection.

Since going to Press the following additional names have been discovered in various Supplementary Rolls at the War Office :—

Sgt. Alexr. Ross.[1]   Fuentes d'Onor, Ciudad Rodrigo, Salamanca, Pyrenees, Nive, Nivelle, Orthes, Toulouse.

Pte. Alexr. Ross.[2]   Corunna, Busaco, Fuentes d'Onor, Ciudad Rodrigo, Salamanca, Pyrenees, Nive, Nivelle, Orthes, Toulouse.

Pte. Wm. Smith.   Fuentes d'Onor, Ciudad Rodrigo, Salamanca, Pyrenees, Nive, Nivelle, Orthes, Toulouse.

Pte. John Horn.   Busaco, Fuentes d'Onor, Ciudad Rodrigo, Salamanca, Pyrenees.

Pte. David Kay.   See page 22, and add Clasp for Maida (from Second Supplementary List, d/20/2/1850).

Pte. Peter Robertson.[3]   Salamanca, Orthes, Toulouse.

Corpl. John Jenkins.[4]   Talavera, Busaco, Fuentes d'Onor, Ciudad Rodrigo, Salamanca, Pyrenees, Toulouse.

[1] Sent to Gibraltar.   [2] Sent to Eldon, Canada.   [3] From List No. 15.   [4] From List No. 16.

RECIPIENTS OF THE MEDAL AND CLASP FOR EGYPT, 1801.

The men who received the Bar for Egypt only, had already received the Medal for other engagements.—J. S.

Alexander, Jno.		M'Donald, Donald	Bar	Allan, George.		Ross, Donald.	
Allardice, Jas.		M'Lean, John.	Bar	Aitken, Alexr., *Dmr.*	Bar	Still, John.	Bar
Andrews, George.		Robb, Wm. Capt.		Clarke, Wm.	Bar	Smith, John.	
Baird, Robert. Capt.		Stewart's Collec-		Campbell, David.		Ross, John.	
Stewart's Collection		tion.		Finnistone, Fras.	Bar	Thomson, Jas.	
Blair, John.		Robertson, Duncan.	Bar	Fraser, Hector.		Gray, Wm.	Bar
Cameron, Alex., *Cpl.*		Ramsay, Alex., *Cpl.*		Fjuley, Alex.		Harlan, Wm.	
Campbell, Hugh.		Rogers, Andw. Capt.		M'Donald, John.		Johnston, Wm.	Bar
Crookshanks, Geo.		Stewart's Collec-		M'Dougall, Wm.	Bar	Mathison, Wm.	Bar
Denham, John.	Bar	tion.		M'Leod, Thomas.		M'Intosh, Donald.	
Dallas, Jas., *Corpl.*		Scott, John.		Munro, Murdock.		M'Kenzie, John.	Bar
Hamilton, Thos.	Bar	Stewart, Jas.		M'Hardy, John,		Munro, Donald.	Bar
Home, Geo.		Simpson, John.		*Corpl.*		M'Leod, John.	Bar
Kennedy, Lachlan.		Tait, John.		Murray, Hugh.		M'Cullock, Michael.	
M'Bean, John (or		Walker, Robert.		Petrie, Jas.	Bar	Nicoll, Jas.	
M'Bain).	Bar	Warren George,		M'Kay, Donald.	Bar	Young, Geo.	
M'Lean, Kenneth.		*Drummer.*	Bar	Munro, Neil.	Bar	M'Kenzie, John,	
M'Leod, John.		Wilkins, William.		Riddle, Archd.	Bar	*Corpl.*	Bar

For Description of these Medals see List of Illustrations.

73RD

FIRST REPORT OF THE COMMITTEE OF GENERAL OFFICERS ON THE CLAIMS OF OFFICERS, N.C.O.'S AND MEN

NOW OR LATELY SERVING IN THE ARMY

TO THE MEDAL FOR SERVICE IN THE

WARS WITH THE KAFFIRS

1834-5, 1846-7, 1850 TO 1853

Shewing the period at which they were severally present
in the Field against the Enemy

Also a List of OFFICERS, N.C.O.'S AND MEN whose claims to the

CAPE OF GOOD HOPE MEDAL

For Service in the Wars against the Kaffirs, have been
investigated and found valid.

A.-G.'S OFFICE,
HORSE GUARDS, Dec. 1858.

E

FIRST REPORT OF THE COMMITTEE OF THE CONSOLIDATED BOARD OF GENERAL OFFICERS on the Claims of Officers now, or lately, serving in the Army, to the Medal for Service in the Wars with the Kaffirs, shewing the periods at which they were severally present in the Field against the Enemy.

NAME OR PRESENT RANK.	Rank and Situation at the time.	Period when Engaged.			REMARKS.
		1834-5.	1846-7.	1850-53.	
OFFICERS.					
Amiel, Francis J. T., late Lt. 73rd Foot. Capt. R. Lancs. Mila.	Lieut. 73rd Foot	..	..	1	Ashton-under-Lyne, 22/11.
Bewes, Wyndham E., Bt. Major 73rd Foot.	Bt.-Major ,,	..	1	1	Cover, Walmer, 20/11.
Bicknell, Philip B., Captain 73rd Foot.	Capt. ,,	..	1	..	Phi. Bicknell, Capt. 73rd Foot.
Burne, Godfrey, Captain 73rd Foot.	Capt. ,,	..	..	1	Cape of Good Hope, 3/1.
Barnes, James W., Captain 73rd Foot.	Lieut. ,,	..	1	1	J. W. Barnes, Capt. 73rd Foot.
Booth, Edward, Surgeon 73rd Foot.	Surgn. ,,	..	..	1	Cape of Good Hope, 3/1.
Campbell, Robt. Parker, Major 90th Foot.	Capt. ,,	..	..	1	R. Campbell, Lt.-Col. 90th L.I.
Combe, C. W., late Capt. 73rd Foot.	Capt. ,,	..	1	..	Jersey, 24/11.
Carson, John, Qr.-Master 73rd Foot.	Qr.-Mr. ,,	..	1	1	Cape of Good Hope, 3/1.
Cochrane, John T., late Pay-master 73rd Foot.	P. Mr. ,,	..	..	1	Sent Backham, nr. Woking-ham, Berks. No. of medal 106.
Davies, George, Lieut. 73rd Foot.	Lieut. ,,	..	..	1	Cape of Good Hope, 3/1.
Evans, Edward, Lieut. 73rd Foot.	Lieut. ,,	..	..	1	Medal sent him 13/9/56.
Gawler, John Cox, Capt. 73rd Foot.	Lieut. ,,	..	..	1	Cape of Good Hope, 3/1.
Hoghton, Chas., Capt. 4 Lancs. Militia.	Lieut. ,,	..	1	..	Col. Blackhame, 4 W. Y. Mila., Berwick-on-Tweed, 26/10.
Hodgson, Wm. P., Asst. Surgn. 73rd Foot.	Ast. Sn. ,,	..	1	..	
Knox, Alfred C., Captain 73rd Foot.	Capt. ,,	..	1	1	Depot, Jersey, 5/1.
Littlehales, Chas., Capt. Dorset Militia.	Capt. ,,	..	1	..	Dorset Mila.
Lucas Gould, A., Lieut., 73rd Foot.	Lieut. ,,	..	..	1	Cape of Good Hope, 3/1.
M'Kenzie, Hugh, Lieut. 73rd Foot.	Lieut. ,,	..	..	1	Depot, Jersey, 24/11.

NAME OR PRESENT RANK.	Rank and Situation at the time.	Period when Engaged.			REMARKS.
		1834-5.	1846-7.	1850-53.	
OFFICERS.					
O'Connell, M. C., late Capt. 73rd Foot. Capt. Kerry Mila.	Capt. 73rd Foot.	..	1	..	Castle Barracks, Limerick.
Owen, Hugh C., late Lieut. 73rd Foot.	Lieut. ,,	..	1	..	Llanstenan House, Haverford West, 7/1.
Pinckney, Fredk. G. A., Lt.-Col. 73rd Foot.	Major ,,	..	1	1	⎫ Cape of Good Hope, 3/1.
Peto, William L., Captain 73rd Foot.	Lieut. ,,	..	1	..	⎭
Poole, Wellington W., Staff Surgeon, 2nd Class.	Ast. Sn. ,,	..	..	1	Wellington W. W. Poole, Staff Surgeon, 2nd Class.
Reeve, Fredk., Captain 73rd Foot.	Lieut. ,,	..	..	1	Cape of Good Hope, 3/1.
Renny, George, Captain 73rd Foot.	Capt. ,,	..	..	1	⎫ Depot, Jersey, 24/11.
Rennie, William, Ensign 73rd Foot.	Sgt.-Major ,,	..	1	1	⎭
Smith, George, Bt. Lt.-Col. 73rd Foot.	Major ,,	..	1	..	Cape of Good Hope, 3/1.
Vandermenlen, C. J., late Lt.-Col. 73rd Foot.	Lt.-Col. ,,	..	1	..	Recd. C. J. Vandermenlen, 5 Priory St., Cheltenham. No. of medal 499. Delivered 1/11/56.
Williams, John J. L., Lieut. 73rd Foot.	Lieut. ,,	..	..	1	Capt. Stewart's Collection.
Hall, S. W., Barrack Master, Shorncliffe.	Lieut. ,,	..	1	..	Delivered to him 15/9/56.
Eyre, William, Brigadier-General.	Lt.-Col. ,,	..	..	1	
Hickson, B. M., Capt. Glamorgan Mila.	Ensn. ,,	..	1	..	Medal recd., J. G. Hickson, 15/4/57.
Reeve, Frederick, Capt. 73rd Foot.	Capt. ,,	..	..	1	Sent to C. of Good Hope, 29/7/57.
RANK AND FILE.					
Atkinson, Swayne, Serjt., now serving ...		..	..	1	
Arnold, James, Corpl., ,, ...		..	..	1	
Ashfield, Wm., ,, ,, ...		..	..	1	
Adby, Geo., Private, ,, ...		..	..	1	
Ahern, Timy., ,, ,, ...		..	..	1	
Allen, James, ,, ,, ...		..	..	1	
Allibone, Anthy., ,, ,, ...		..	..	1	
Ambrose, Chas., ,, ,, ...		..	..	1	
Anderson, Chas., ,, ,, ...		..	..	1	
Archer, Thos., ,, ,, ...		..	..	1	Returned. Deserted.
Arnold, Wm., ,, ,, ...		..	..	1	
Anderson, John, ,, discharged ...		..	1	..	
Anderton, John, ,, now serving .		..	1	1	Medal sent to S.O. Prs., Birmingham, 20/12/56.
Bayley, Willm., Actg. Sjt.-Major, ,, .		..	1	..	Now an Ensn. The Regtl. Depot, Jersey.
Burgos, Henry, O.R.C. Sjt., ,, ..		..	..	1	Capt. Stewart's Collection.

NAMES.	Period when Engaged.			REMARKS.
	1834-5.	1846-7.	1850-53.	

RANK AND FILE.				
Brown, John, Hospl. Serjt., now serving	..	..	1	
Barson, J., Colr.-Serjt., ,,	..	..	1	
Bird, Reuben, Serjt., ,,	..	..	1	
Bishop, Thos., ,, ,,	..	..	1	
Bromwich, David, ,, ,,	..	..	1	
Bromwich, Saml., ,, ,,	..	..	1	
Buchanan, Wm. H., ,, ,,	..	..	1	
Bennett, John, Drummer, ,,	..	..	1	
Best, John, ,, ,,	..	..	1	
Burke, Wm., ,, ,,	..	..	1	
Bailey, Richd., Private, ,,	..	..	1	
Balham, Robt., ,, ,,	..	..	1	Returned. Deserted.
Ball, James ,, ,,	..	..	1	
Ballance, John, ,, ,,	..	..	1	
Banks, James, ,, ,,	..	..	1	
Barry, Thos., ,, ,,	..	..	1	
Barnett, John, ,, ,,	..	..	1	
Bateman, Thos., ,, ,,	..	..	1	
Bateman, Wm., ,, ,,	..	..	1	
Beesley, Robt., ,, ,,	..	..	1	
Bettington, John, ,, ,,	..	..	1	
Bingham, Willm., ,, ,,	..	..	1	
Bird, Geo., ,, ,,	..	..	1	
Bird, Michl., ,, ,,	..	..	1	
Blackist, John, ,, ,,	..	..	1	
Bligh, Andw., ,, ,,	..	..	1	
Bond, Willm., ,, ,,	..	..	1	
Booth, John, ,, ,,	..	..	1	
Bottoms, Samuel, ,, ,,	..	..	1	Returned. Dead.
Bouchier, Thos., ,, ,,	..	..	1	
Bowden, Willm., ,, ,,	..	..	1	
Boyde, John, ,, ,,	..	..	1	
Brazier, Willm., ,, ,,	..	..	1	Medal sent to W.O., 580017/2; 15/1/57.
Button, Willm., ,, ,,	..	..	1	
Brocklehurst, Geo., ,, ,,	..	..	1	
Brooker, Jas., ,, ,,	..	..	1	
Browett, John, ,, ,,	..	..	1	
Brown, Willm., 1st., ,, ,,	..	..	1	
Brown, Willm., 2nd. ,, ,,	..	..	1	
Buckley, John, ,, ,,	..	..	1	
Burke, James, ,, ,,	..	..	1	Sent to the O.C. Cape Mounted Rifles, 21/12/57.
Burke, John, ,, ,,	..	..	1	
Burke, Willm., ,, ,,	..	..	1	
Burrows, Heny., ,, ,,	..	..	1	
Burns, Martin, ,, ,,	..	..	1	Returned. Dead.
Burton, Thos., ,, ,,	..	..	1	
Butcher, John, ,, ,,	..	..	1	
Byrne, John, ,, ,,	..	..	1	
Byrne, Thos., ,, ,,	..	..	1	

NAMES.			Period when Engaged.			REMARKS.
			1834-5.	1846-7.	1850-53.	
RANK AND FILE.						
Byrnes, John,	Private,	now serving	..	..	1	
Bew, Abraham,	,,	,,	..	1	1	Medal sent S.O. of Prs., Jersey, 18/9/56.
Brias, Thos.,	,,	,,	..	1	1	Medal sent O.C. Depot, 4/6/56.
Bennett, John,	,,	discharged	..	1	..	
Boole, Willm.,	,,	,,	..	1	1	Sent to Genl. Officer at Cape Town, 13/11/58.
Burnett, Geo.,	,,	,,	..	1	1	S.O. of Pensrs., Newcastle-under-Lyme, 28/12.
Byrne, Patk.,	,,	now serving	..	..	1	
Baker, Willm.,	,,	,,	..	1	..	
Conway, Willm.,	Drum-Major,	,,	..	..	1	Medal sent O.C. Depot, 4/6/56.
Cosslet, Thos.,	Colr.-Serjt.,	,,	..	..	1	
Carr, John,	Corpl.,	,,	..	..	1	
Collins, Richd.,	,,	,,	..	..	1	Returned. Deserted.
Connor, John,	,,	,,	..	..	1	
Cuddihy, Patk.,	,,	,,	..	..	1	
Coney, Willm.,	Drummer,	,,	..	..	1	
Croft, Geo.,	,,	,,	..	..	1	Medal sent O.C. Depot, 4/6/56.
Cooper, Timy.,	,,	,,	..	..	1	Medal sent O.C. Depot, 4/6/56.
Callaghan, Mathw.,	,,	,,	..	..	1	
Campbell, Joseph,	,,	,,	..	..	1	Capt. Stewart's Collection.
Cargill, Thos.,	,,	,,	..	..	1	
Carroll, Patk.,	,,	,,	..	..	1	
Campbell, Michl.,	Private,	,,	..	..	1	
Casey, John,	,,	,,	..	..	1	
Cash, Thos.,	,,	,,	..	..	1	
Cassidy, Patk.,	,,	,,	..	..	1	
Clarke, Chrisr.,	,,	,,	..	..	1	
Clune, Michl.,	,,	,,	..	..	1	
Coates, Willm.,	,,	,,	..	..	1	
Cody, James,	,,	,,	..	..	1	
Collins, John,	,,	,,	..	..	1	
Collins, Patk.,	,,	,,	..	..	1	
Coney, Robt.,	,,	,,	..	..	1	
Conlan, Patk.,	,,	,,	..	..	1	
Connolly, Nichs.,	,,	,,	..	..	1	
Connors, James,	,,	,,	..	..	1	
Conway, Jeremiah,	,,	,,	..	..	1	
Coonan, Willm.,	,,	,,	..	..	1	
Carey, John,	,,	,,	..	..	1	
Corcorane, John,	,,	,,	..	..	1	Medal sent O.C. Depot, 4/6/56.
Carrigan, Willm.,	,,	,,	..	..	1	
Cox, John,	,,	,,	..	..	1	
Corder, Ezekiel,	,,	,,	..	..	1	
Coyne, John,	,,	,,	..	..	1	

NAMES.	Period when Engaged.			REMARKS.
	1834-5.	1846-7.	1850-53.	
RANK AND FILE.				
Crawforth, John, Private, now serving	..	..	1	
Creedon, Richd., ,, ,,	..	..	1	
Croft, Joseph, ,, ,,	..	..	1	
Culliman, Lot, ,, ,,	..	..	1	
Cusack, Patk., ,, ,,	..	..	1	
Campbell, Willm., ,, Pensioner	..	1	1	
Carson, Saml., ,, discharged	..	1	1	Sent to S.O. of Penrs., Freemantle, W. Australia, 22/1/59.
Cloves, Willm., ,, ,,	..	1	1	Sent care of S.O. Prs., Wolverhampton, 23/11/58.
Corrigan, John, ,, now serving	..	..	1	
Cock, Willm., ,, discharged	..	..	1	
Darling, William, Qr.-Mr.-Serjt., now serving	..	..	1	
Darvill, James, Serjeant, ,,	..	..	1	
Duff, Hope, Staff-Serjt., Cumberland Ma., Serjeant, now serving.	..	1	1	Delivered to Honble. Col. Lowther, 10/5/56.
Daly, John, Corporal, now serving	..	..	1	
Dumbreck, John, ,, ,,	..	..	1	
Dally, Peter, Private, now serving	..	..	1	
Dafter, Richard, ,, ,,	..	..	1	
Daniells, Henry, ,, ,,	..	..	1	
Darsey, Nicholas, ,, ,,	..	..	1	
Dash, Thomas,[1] ,, ,,	..	..	1	Capt. Stewart's Collection.
Dashwood, Robt. Henry, ,, ,,	..	..	1	
Davies, Morris, ,, ,,	..	..	1	
Day, Manns, ,, ,,	..	..	1	
Dennis, Wm. Coyde, ,, ,,	..	..	1	
Devane, Thomas, ,, ,,	..	..	1	Sent care of S.O. Prs., Clifden, 6/3/67.
Devitt, John, ,, ,,	..	..	1	
Dixon, Richard, ,, ,,	..	..	1	
Dinan, John, ,, ,,	..	..	1	
Dobson, James, ,, ,,	..	..	1	
Donaldson, James, ,, ,,	..	..	1	
Donoghue, John, ,, ,,	..	..	1	
Doran, James, ,, ,,	..	..	1	
Doyle, James, ,, ,,	..	..	1	
Doyle, Michael, ,, ,,	..	..	1	
Drinkwater, Thos., ,, ,,	..	..	1	
Duffy, Patrick, ,, ,,	..	..	1	
Dynan, William, ,, ,,	..	..	1	
Donoghoe, Thos., ,, ,,	..	..	1	
Edwards, David, ,, ,,	..	..	1	
Edwards, Geo., ,, ,,	..	..	1	
Elliot, John, ,, ,,	..	..	1	
Elwart, Thos., ,, ,,	..	..	1	
Enwright, John, ,, ,,	..	..	1	
Evens, Chas., ,, ,,	..	..	1	
Evans, John, ,, ,,	..	..	1	Returned. Deserted.
Exell, Thos., ,, ,,	..	..	1	

[1] 'William,' not 'Thomas,' engraved on medal.—J. S.

NAMES.	Period when Engaged.			REMARKS.
	1834-5.	1846-7.	1850-53.	
RANK AND FILE.				
Early, John, Private, now serving . . .	..	1	..	Medal sent O.C. Depot, 4/6/56.
Fitzgerald, Jas., Colr.-Serjt., ,, . . .	..	..	1	Medal sent O.C. Depot, 4/6/56. L.S. and G.C. medal in Capt. Stewart's Collection.
Flannagan, John, Serjt., ,, . . .	..	..	1	
Freebairn, John, Corpl., ,, . . .	..	..	1	
Flinn, Willm., Drummer, ,, . . .	..	..	1	
Fearnley, Chris., Private, now serving . .	..	1	1	Medal sent O.C. Depot, 4/6/56.
Fell, Joshua, ,, ,, . . .	..	..	1	
Fenaughty, Patk., ,, ,, . . .	..	..	1	
Finch, John, ,, ,, . . .	..	..	1	
Fisher, John, ,, ,, . . .	..	..	1	
Fitzgerald, Thos., ,, ,, . . .	..	..	1	
Fitzpatrick, James, ,, ,, . . .	..	..	1	
Flanagan, Michl., ,, ,, . . .	..	..	1	
Flemming, Cornelius, ,, ,, . . .	..	..	1	
Fletcher, Richd., ,, ,, . . .	..	..	1	
Friend, James, ,, ,, . . .	..	..	1	
Funnell, Henry, ,, discharged . .	..	1	1	
Flanagan, Joseph, ,, ,, . .	..	1	1	
Foley, Thos., ,, ,, . .	..	..	1	
Green, Terence, Corporal, now serving . .	..	1	1	Medal sent O.C. Depot, 4/6/56.
Garlick, Willm., ,, ,, . . .	..	..	1	
Gage, James, ,, ,, . . .	..	..	1	
Graham, John, ,, ,, . . .	..	..	1	
Garrett, Chas., Private, ,, . . .	..	..	1	
Gilbert, John P., ,, ,, . . .	..	..	1	Medal sent O.C. Depot, 4/6/56.
Gill, Thos., , ,, . . .	..	..	1	
Gobell, Richd., ,, ,, . . .	..	..	1	
Gracey, Willm., ,, ,, . . .	..	..	1	
Green, Patk., ,, ,, . . .	..	..	1	
Greenwood, Robt., ,, ,, . . .	..	..	1	
Gilmore, Hugh, ,, discharged . . .	..	..	1	Sent to 138 Long St., Cape Town, 27/4/58.
Holihan, James, Colr.-Serjt., now serving . .	..	..	1	Medal sent O.C. Depot, 4/6/56.
Hickey, James, Serjt., ,, . . .	..	..	1	
Harris, Willm., ,, ,, . . .	..	..	1	
Hare, Eyre, Armr. Serjt., discharged . . .	..	..	1	
Hallicy, Andw., Corpl., now serving . .	..	..	1	
Hatch, Geo., ,, ,, . . .	..	..	1	
Halehy, James, Drummer, ,, . . .	..	..	1	
Hawkes, John, Corpl., ,, . . .	..	..	1	Returned from the Cape, and sent to Depot 73rd, 13/3/57.
Hall, John, Private, ,, . . .	..	..	1	

NAMES.		Period when Engaged.			REMARKS.
		1834-5.	1846-7.	1850-53.	

RANK AND FILE.

NAMES.		1834-5.	1846-7.	1850-53.	REMARKS.
Hall, Richd.,	Private, now serving	..	..	1	
Halloran, Patk.,	,, ,,	..	..	1	
Hannin, Michl.,	,, ,,	..	..	1	
Hare, Dennis,	,, ,,	..	..	1	
Hare, John,	,, ,,	..	..	1	
Hardy, Daniel,	,, ,,	..	..	1	
Harteope, Thos.,	,, ,,	..	..	1	
Haughey, James,	,, ,,	..	..	1	
Hawkins, Wm.,	,, ,,	..	..	1	
Hayes, Patk.,	,, ,,	..	..	1	
Haslehurst, Edwd.,	,, ,,	..	..	1	
Heavey, Danl.,	,, ,,	..	..	1	
Henry, Joseph,	,, ,,	..	..	1	
Herrick, Patk.,	,, ,,	..	..	1	
Hazlehurst, Willm.,	,, ,,	..	..	1	
Higgins, Willm.,	,, ,,	..	..	1	
Hill, Thos.,	,, ,,	..	..	1	
Hilliard, Willm.,	,, ,,	..	..	1	
Hoddoway, Joseph,	,, ,,	..	..	1	
Hogan, Edwd., 1st,	,, ,,	..	..	1	
Hogan, Edwd., 2nd,	,, ,,	..	..	1	
Hogan, Patk.,	,, ,,	..	..	1	
Holihan, John,	,, ,,	..	..	1	
Hoolihan, James,	,, ,,	..	..	1	
Holton, Geo.,	,, ,,	..	..	1	
Hopkins, John,	,, ,,	..	..	1	
Hooker, Willm.,	,, ,,	..	..	1	Medal sent O.C. Depot at Portsmouth, 13/10/56.
Hopper, James,	,, ,,	..	..	1	
Horan, James,	,, ,,	..	..	1	
Howley, Michl.,	,, ,,	..	..	1	
Hill, Chas.,	,, discharged	..	1	1	Sent to the Custom House, Cape Town, 8/9/57.
Hutchinson, Thos.,	Serjt., now serving	..	1	1	Medal sent O.C. Depot, 4/6/56.
Holihan, Edwd.,	Private, ,,	..	..	1	
Hawkins, Fredk.,	,, ,,	..	1	1	} Medals sent O.C. Depot, 4/6/56.
Hayman, Chas.,	,, ,,	..	1	1	
Hoskin, John,	,, ,,	..	1	1	
Herlihey, Michl.,	,, ,,	..	..	1	
Henley, Willm. J.,	,, ,,	..	1	1	Medal sent him at Roeland Street, Cape Town, 15/5/57.
Halfpenny, Willm.,	,, ,,	..	..	1	Medal sent O. C. Depot, 4/6/56.
Irwin, Alex.,	,, ,,	..	..	1	
Irwin, Thos.,	Serjt., ,,	..	..	1	
Ilsley, James,	Private, ,,	..	..	1	
Irwin, James,	,, ,,	..	..	1	
Ingram, Joseph,	,, ,,	..	..	1	

NAMES.			Period when Engaged.			REMARKS.
			1834-5.	1846-7.	1850-53.	
RANK AND FILE.						
Ibbett, John,	Private,	now serving · ·	..	..	1	
Jones, Elias,	Serjeant,	,, · · ·	..	..	1	
Jones, Daniel,	Corporal,	,, · · ·	..	..	1	
Jordon, John,	,,	,, · · ·	..	..	1	
Joice, Amos Henry,	Drummer,	,, · · ·	..	..	1	Medal sent O.C. Depot, 4/6/56.
Jackman, James,	Private,	,, · · ·	..	..	1	
Jones, William,	,,	,, · · ·	..	..	1	
Jordon, John,	,,	,, · · ·	..	..	1	
Jordon, Patrick,	,,	,, · · ·	..	..	1	
James, William,	,,	,, · · ·	..	1	1	Medal sent O.C. Depot, 4/6/56.
Kilkeary, Bernard,	Serjt.,	,, · · ·	..	..	1	
Kedwell, James,	Private,	,, · · ·	..	..	1	Sent O.C. 73rd Foot, 20th Jany./59.
Keliher, Daniel,	,,	,, · · ·	..	..	1	
Kelly, John,	,,	,, · · ·	..	..	1	
Kent, John,	,,	,, · · ·	..	..	1	
Kerr, Michael,	,,	,, · · ·	..	..	1	
Kildea, John,	,,	,, · · ·	..	..	1	Sent to O.C., 20 Jany./59.
King, Michael,	,,	,, · · ·	..	..	1	
Knott, George,	,,	,, · · ·	..	..	1	
Lucas, Geo.,	Corpl.,	,, · · ·	..	..	1	
Lever, Geo.,	Drummer,	,, · · ·	..	..	1	
Lacey, Stephen,	Private, now serving · ·		..	..	1	
Ladds, Fredk.,	,,	,, · · ·	..	..	1	
Lane, George,	,,	,, · · ·	..	..	1	Returned. Dead.
Lawes, Fredk.,	,,	,, · · ·	..	..	1	
Leary, Michael,	,,	,, · · ·	..	..	1	
Lewin, John,	,,	,, · · ·	..	..	1	
Lewin, Patrick,	,,	,, · · ·	..	..	1	
Joice, Corns. John,	,,	,, · · ·	..	..	1	This name should follow Jordon, Patk.
Lewis, Richard,	,,	,, · · ·	..	..	1	
Lindsay, John,	,,	,, · · ·	..	..	1	
Lines, John,	,,	,, · · ·	..	..	1	
Loal, Henry,	,,	,, · · ·	..	..	1	
Lock, Peter,	,,	,, · · ·	..	..	1	
Lockwood, Abraham,	,,	,, · · ·	..	..	1	
Lingstaff, William,	,,	,, · · ·	..	..	1	
Lord, Samuel,	,,	,, · · ·	..	..	1	
Lough, John,	,,	,, · · ·	..	..	1	
Loughrin, Bryan,	,,	,, · · ·	..	..	1	Medal sent to Lt.-Col. Pinckney at the Cape, 30/3/57.
Lunnon, Wm.,	,,	,, · · ·	..	..	1	
Lye, George,	,,	,, · · ·	..	..	1	Medal sent O.C. Depot, 4/6/56.
Lynch, Patrick,	,,	,, · · ·	..	..	1	
Legate, James,	,,	,, · · ·	..	..	1	Medal sent O.C. Depot, 4/6/56.

NAMES.	Period when Engaged.			REMARKS.
	1834-5.	1846-7.	1850-53.	
RANK AND FILE.				
Lester, Edward, Private, Pensioner	..	..	1	Medal sent him at 5 Alfred St., Leicester, 12/5/57.
M'Glashen, James, Colr.-Serjt., now serving	..	..	1	
M'Querrie, Alexr., Serjt., „	..	..	1	
Morrison, Geo., Colr.-Serjt., „	..	1	1	Medal sent to Major Bunbury, 27/11/56.
Murtough, John, Serjt., „	..	..	1	Capt. Stewart's Collection.
Martin, Peter, „ „	..	..	1	
M'Kinley, James, Private, discharged	..	1	..	Medal sent him, 7/10/56.
M'Masters, James, Corpl., now serving	..	..	1	
M'Menomie, Patk., „ „	..	1	1	Medal sent O.C. Medical Staff Corps, Chatham, 24/1/57.
M'Nally, Bernard, Private, „	..	..	1	Medal sent O.C. Depot, 4/6/56.
Martin, Michael, „ „	..	..	1	Medal sent O.C. Depot, 4/6/56.
Miller, John, „ „	..	1	1	Medal sent O.C. Depot, 4/6/56. Returned from the Cape, and sent to Depot 73rd.
M'Carthy, Danl., 1st, „ „	..	..	1	
M'Carthy, Danl., 2nd, „ „	..	..	1	
M'Combe, Thos., „ „	..	..	1	
M'Donald, Alexr., „ „	..	..	1	
M'Grath, John, „ „	..	..	1	
M'Grath, Michl., „ „	..	..	1	
M'Grigor, John, „ „	..	..	1	
M'Kearney, Patk., „ „	..	..	1	
M'Kinlay, Robt., „ „	..	..	1	
M'Lean, Willm., „ „	..	..	1	
M'Mahon, James, 1st, „ „	..	..	1	
M'Mahon, James, 2nd, „ „	..	..	1	
M'Nally, John, „ „	..	..	1	
M'Signe, Martin, „ „	..	..	1	
Maddagan, John, „ „	..	..	1	
Mahoney, Danl., „ „	..	..	1	
Maloney, Danl., „ „	..	..	1	
Maloney, James, „ „	..	..	1	Returned. Deserted.
Maloney, Patk., „ „	..	..	1	
M'Namara, Denis, „ „	..	..	1	
M'Nutty, James, „ „	..	..	1	Returned. Deserted.
Manley, Willm., „ „	..	..	1	Returned. Dead.
Maddigan, Patk., „ „	..	..	1	
Martin, James, „ „	..	..	1	
Matheson, Alexr., „ „	..	..	1	
May, Patk., „ „	..	..	1	
Mayes, John, „ „	..	..	1	
Mills, Willm., „ „	..	..	1	
Milne, Alexr., „ „	..	..	1	
Mitchell, Geo., „ „	..	..	1	

NAMES.		Period when Engaged.			REMARKS.
		1834-5.	1846-7.	1850-53.	
RANK AND FILE.					
Moffatt, Saml.,	Private, now serving . .	..	..	1	
Molloy, Michl.,	,, ,, . . .	..	..	1	
Mongavon, John,	,, ,, . . .	..	..	1	
Moore, James,	,, ,, . . .	..	..	1	
Moore, Peter,	,, ,, . . .	..	..	1	Returned from the Cape and sent to Depot, 18/3/57.
Moran, John,	,, ,, . . .	..	..	1	
Moran, Patk., 1st,	,, ,, . . .	..	..	1	
Moran, Patk., 2nd,	,, ,, . . .	..	..	1	
Moran, Patk., 3rd,	,, ,, . . .	..	..	1	
Morgan, Saml.,	,, ,, . . .	..	..	1	
Morgan, Willm.,	,, ,, . . .	..	..	1	
Morwood, Wm. J.,	,, ,, . . .	..	..	1	
Muirhead, Malcome,	,, ,, . . .	..	..	1	
Munger, David,	,, ,, . . .	..	..	1	
Murnance, Danl.,	,, ,, . . .	..	..	1	
Murnance, John,	,, ,, . . .	..	..	1	Sent to W.O. E/71/2; 1/7/58. Returned. Dead.
Murphy, Patk.,	,, ,, . . .	..	..	1	
Murray, John,	,, ,, . . .	..	..	1	
Murray, Patk.,	,, ,, . . .	..	..	1	
Muspratt, Geo.,	,, ,, . . .	..	..	1	
Miles, Stephen,	,, ,, . . .	..	1	..	To Col. Sonench, 23/4.
Murphy, John,	Drummer ,, . . .	..	1	1	Medal sent O.C. Depot, 4/6/56.
Norrie, James,	Serjt., ,, . . .	..	..	1	
Neal, Robt.,	Private, ,, . . .	..	..	1	
Newton, James,	,, ,, . . .	..	..	1	
Nolon, Thos.,	,, ,, . . .	..	..	1	
Norman, Anthy.,	,, ,, . . .	..	..	1	
O'Brien, Edwd.,	,, ,, . . .	..	..	1	Medal sent to O.C. Depot, 4/6/56.
O'Brien, James,	,, ,, . . .	..	..	1	Medal sent to O.C. Depot, 4/6/56.
O'Brien, Thos.,	,, ,, . . .	..	..	1	
O'Bryan, Martin,	,, ,, . . .	..	..	1	
O'Connor, Mathew,	,, ,, . . .	..	..	1	
O'Donoghoe, Willm.,	,, ,, . . .	..	..	1	
O'Grady, John,	,, ,, . . .	..	..	1	
O'Reilly, Patk.,	,, ,, . . .	..	..	1	
Oriel, John,	Corporal, ,, . . .	..	..	1	
Pegler, Mathew,	Serjt., discharged . . .	..	..	1	Medal sent to Lt.-Col. Pinckney at the Cape, 30/3/57.
Pegler, Saml.,	,, ,, . . .	..	1	1	
Pouldon, Willm.,	Corpl., now serving . . .	..	..	1	
Powell, James,	,, ,, . . .	..	..	1	
Perry, Fredk.,	,, ,, . . .	..	..	1	
Popple, John,	Private, ,, . . .	..	1	..	Medal sent O.C. Depot, 4/6/56.

NAMES.	Period when Engaged.			REMARKS.
	1834-5.	1846-7.	1850-53.	
RANK AND FILE.				
Page, James, Private, now serving . . .	..	..	1	
Parfitt, Robt., ,, ,, . . .	..	..	1	
Parker, Patk., ,, ,, . . .	..	..	1	
Parkinson, John, ,, ,, . . .	..	..	1	
Payne, Robt., ,, ,, . . .	..	..	1	
Penrose, Geo., ,, ,, . . .	..	..	1	
Pettitt, Robt., ,, ,, . . .	..	..	1	
Powell, Thos., ,, ,, . . .	..	..	1	
Prendergust, Michl., ,, ,, . . .	..	..	1	
Proudley, Richd., ,, ,, . . .	..	..	1	
Prosser, Chas., ,, ,, . . .	..	..	1	
Payne, John, ,, discharged . . .	..	1	1	Medal sent W.O., 25/7/56.
Quill, John, ,, now serving . . .	..	..	1	
Quilter, William, ,, ,,	..	..	1	Sent to the O.C. Cape Mounted Rifles, 21/12/57.
Rennie, Francis, Serjeant-Major, discharged . .	..	1	..	Sent to the C. of Good Hope, 8/8/57.
Rennie, Alexander, Colour-Serjt., now serving .	..	..	1	
Rowland, Thomas, ,, ...	..	..	1	
Robins, Edward, Serjeant, ...	..	..	1	
Roberts, Charles, ,, ...	..	..	1	
Rowland, William, ,, discharged . . .	..	1	..	Medal delivered to Capt. Curtin, Governor of Gosport Prison, for him, 27/9/56.
Ryan, Matthew, Corporal	..	..	1	
Robinson, James ,, ...	..	..	1	
Ryan, Michael, ,, ...	..	..	1	
Rawley, Richard, Private	..	..	1	
Renny, William, ,, ...	..	..	1	
Reynolds, Michael, ,, ...	..	..	1	
Rice, John, ,, ...	..	..	1	
Rich, John, ,, ...	..	..	1	
Richards, Richard, ,, ...	..	..	1	
Roach, Rimney, ,, ...	..	..	1	
Roberts, Meredith, ,, ...	..	..	1	
Rorke, Edward, ,, ...	..	..	1	Medal sent O.C. Depot, 4/6/56.
Rooney, John, ,, ...	..	..	1	
Ryan, Patrick, ,, ...	..	..	1	
Rogers, James, Serjt., discharged	..	1	..	Medal sent to him 5/6/56, p. post.
Scott, J. Gortley, Serjeant-Major, ...	..	..	1	
Stupart, Alexander, Colour-Serjt., ...	..	..	1	
Shaughnessy, Dermot, Serjt., ...	..	..	1	
Shorter, George, ,, ...	..	..	1	
Smith, Robert, ,, ...	..	..	1	
Stafford, Henry, ,, ...	..	..	1	
Sanderson, Herbert, Corporal	..	..	1	
Shaw, Robert, ,, ...	..	..	1	
Smith, Alexander, ,, ...	..	..	1	

NAMES.		Period when Engaged.			REMARKS.
		1834-5.	1846-7.	1850-53.	
RANK AND FILE.					
Swayne, Robert,	Corporal	..	..	1	
Scivier, John,	Drummer	..	..	1	
Seaburn, Michael,	,,	..	..	1	Returned. Deserted.
Stretton, John,	,,	..	..	1	Medal sent to Lt.-Col. Pinckney at the Cape, 30/3/57. Medal returned from Col. Pinckney, and delivered to Stretton, 17/8/57.
Salsbury, William,	Private	..	..	1	
Smith, George,	,,	..	..	1	Medal sent O.C. Depot, 4/6/56.
Scannell, James,	,,	..	..	1	
Seymour, Jesse,	,,	..	..	1	
Shannon, Peter,	,,	..	..	1	
Sharkey, James,	,,	..	..	1	
Sheehan, Daniel,	,,	..	..	1	
Shuttle, George,	,,	..	..	1	
Sims, Charles,	,,	..	..	1	
Simms, George,	,,	..	..	1	
Sinclair, Thomas,	,,	..	..	1	
Sinnott, William,	,,	..	..	1	
Slattery, Michael,	,,	..	..	1	
Smith, Henry,	,,	..	..	1	
Smith, John,	,,	..	..	1	
Snell, William,	,,	..	..	1	
Sparkman, George,	,,	..	..	1	
Spier, Charles,	,,	..	..	1	
Soper, Charles,	,,	..	..	1	
Steel, John,	,,	..	..	1	
Stewart, Robert,	,,	..	..	1	
Stockdale, Phillip,	,,	..	..	1	
Sullivan, Daniel,	,,	..	..	1	
Sullivan, Murty,	,,	..	..	1	Sent to O.C. 81st Regt., 26/9/64; 156212/385.
Sullivan, Patrick,	,,	..	..	1	
Sullivan, Timothy,	,,	..	..	1	
Sworton, David,	,,	..	..	1	
Sweeney, Thomas,	,,	..	..	1	
Swonson, William,	,,	..	..	1	
*Stoneham, Noah,	,, discharged	..	1	1	Medal sent S.O. of Prs., Gloucester, 10/9/56.
Saunders, Robert,	,, ,,	..	1	1	
Shanahan, John,	,, ,,	..	..	1	Sent to the Custom House, Cape Town, 8/57.
Smith, John,	,,	..	..	1	
Salt, Henry,	,, discharged	..	..	1	Medal sent him, 7/10/56.
Sullivan, John,	,,	..	..	1	
*Stoneham, Noah,	,, discharged	..	1	1	
Trydell, John, Corporal		..	1	1	Medal sent O.C. Depot, 4/6/56.
Trydill, James,	Private	..	..	1	Returned. Dead.

NAMES.	Period when Engaged.			REMARKS.
	1834-5.	1846-7.	1850-53.	
RANK AND FILE.				
Taylor, Patrick, Private	..	..	1	
Thomas, William, ,,	..	..	1	
Thompson, Alexr., ,,	..	..	1	
Thompson, William, ,,	..	..	1	
Thorndyke, Jeremiah, ,,	..	..	1	
Tilley, John, ,,	..	..	1	
Trendall, John, ,,	..	..	1	
Turner, John, ,,	..	..	1	
Turnbull, Adam, ,,	..	..	1	
Turner, Edward, ,,	..	..	1	
Taylor, Benjamin, ,, discharged	..	1	..	Sent to care of S.O.P., Wolverhampton, 23/11/58.
Vicars, John Hy., Drummer, ,,	..	..	1	Sent to him at the Cape, 23/3/57.
Viney, David, Private	..	..	1	
Vincent, David, ,,	..	..	1	
Walker, William, Serjeant, discharged	..	1	..	Medal sent O.C. 2 Surrey Mila., 13/6/56.
Walsh, John, Private	..	..	1	Returned. Dead.
Walsh, Joseph, ,,	..	..	1	
Ward, William, ,,	..	..	1	
Waterman, John, ,,	..	..	1	
Waters, James Smith, ,,	..	..	1	
Watson, Aaron, ,,	..	..	1	
Watt, John, ,,	..	..	1	
Walton, George, ,,	..	..	1	
Weadock, Daniel, ,,	..	..	1	
White, James, ,,	..	..	1	
White, Patrick, ,,	..	..	1	
Wilgram, James, ,,	..	..	1	
Williams, Frederick, ,,	..	..	1	
Williams, John, ,,	..	..	1	
Williamson, Frederick, ,,	..	..	1	Returned. Dead.
Wilson, Frederick, ,,	..	..	1	
Wilson, John, ,,	..	..	1	
Wiltshire, Henry, ,,	..	..	1	
Wood, Joseph, ,,	..	..	1	
Woolcott, Samuel, ,,	..	..	1	
Wright, Isaac, ,,	..	..	1	
Wright, John, ,,	..	..	1	
Walker, Godfrey, ,,	..	1	..	
Wallace, John, ,,	..	..	1	
Walsh, Thomas, ,,	..	..	1	
West, William, ,,	..	1	1	Medals sent O.C. Depot, 4/6/56.
Whitby, Robert, Corporal	..	..	1	
Williams, Joseph, Private	..	..	1	
Witham, William, ,,	..	1	1	
Ward, John, Serjeant	..	..	1	
Watson, Thomas, ,,	..	..	1	
Warman, Francis, Corporal	..	..	1	
Young, John, Drum-Major, discharged	..	1	1	Medal sent to 18 Barrack St., Cape Town, 25/6/57.

LIST OF OFFICERS, NON-COMMISSIONED OFFICERS AND PRIVATES, whose Claims to the CAPE OF GOOD HOPE MEDAL, for Service in the Wars against the Kaffirs, have been investigated and found valid.

ADJUTANT-GENERAL'S OFFICE,
HORSE GUARDS, December 1858.

Regtl. No.	Rank and Name.	Year for which claimed.	Remarks.
1	Private Robert Laurence	1846-7	
1546	„ Patk. Collevan	1846-7 / 1850-3	Sent 11/2/59.
	Captain Christopher Harrison	1850-1	
756	Private Thos. Musgrave	1846-7	Sent to Major Pigott, 22/4/58.
1866	„ Israel Thorndike	1846-7	Sent 21/4/58.
704	„ William Steel	1846-7 / 1850-1-2	Sent to Capt. Bayly, 22/4/58.
943	„ Jno. M'Cann	1846-7	Sent 21/4/58.
2068	„ James Lynch	1846-7 / 1850-1-2	Sent 21/4/58.
702	Serjt. Wm. Kitchen	1846-7 / 1850-1-2	Sent 21/4/58.
979	Private Jno. Anderson	1846-7	Sent to O.C. at Limerick, 24/4/58.
1984	„ James Bailey	1846-7 / 1850-1-2	Sent 23/4/58.
1309	Cr.-Serjt. James Donnelly	1852-53	Sent 13/8/58.
1268	Private Josiah Trump	1846-7	Sent 27/8/58.
812	„ James Fitzpatrick	1847 / 1850-1-2	Returned 11/8/58. Sent 9/8/58. {This man's medal appears to have been mislaid, since it has been returned to this office. Cancelled medal sent to H. J. R. to engrave for this man 15/10/59. Given to him 19/10/59.
1085	„ Michael Bourke	1846-47	Sent 13/8/58.
760	„ George Merchant	1846-47	Sent 13/8/58.
831	„ Michl. Shruan	1846-7 / '50-1-2-3	Sent 13/8/58.
	„ James Stewart	1846-7	Sent 25/3/58.
	„ John Lourie	1846-7 / 1850-1	
	„ David Smith	1846-7 / 1850-1	
	„ James Kerry	1846-7 / 1850-1	

Regtl. No.	NAMES.	RANK.	1834-5.	1846-7.	1850-3.	REMARKS.
	James Hennessy .	Private	..	..	1	Pensioner.
2373	Michl. FitzGerald .	,,	..	..	..	Claim retained by War Office.
1684	Thos. Watkinson .	,,	..	..	..	,, ,, ,, Sent (3/6/59).
	Bolton, Alexander .	,,	..	1	..	Pensioner (sent care of S.O.P., Cardiff, 16/9/57).
	Candler, Samuel .	,,	..	1	..	Pensioner (sent to 14 Frederick Place, Commercial Rd., Rotherhithe, 10/1/57).
	Cannon, Charles .	,,	..	1	..	(Sent to 9 Abernethy Place, North End, Fulham, 22/12/57).
	Conway, John . .	,,	..	1	..	Serving (sent to the O.C., Cape of Good Hope, 1/6/58).
	Evens, Edmund .	,,	..	1	..	(Sent to Sir Jas. Jackson, K.C.B., 27/5/58).
	Finley, William .	,,	..	1	1	Pensioner (medal sent S.O.P., Perth, 28/7/57).
	Fitzgerald, Michael	,,	..	1	..	Serving.
	Gaten, George . .	,,	..	1	..	(Sent to Sir Jas. Jackson, K.C.B., 27/5/58).
	Gibbens, Thomas .	,,	..	..	1	Sent to 15 Whitehart Street, Drury Lane, 3/8/57.
	Gordon, Thomas .	,,	..	1	..	Dischd. Cape Town (sent to Sir Jas. Jackson, K.C.B., 27/5/58).
	Huntley, Henry .	,,	..	..	1	Pensioner (sent to S.O.P., Trowbridge, 12/9/57).
	Lockhart, John . .	,,	..	1	..	Pensioner (sent care of Mr. Jas. Brown, 273 George St., Glasgow, 3/10/57).
	M'Namara, Thomas	,,	..	1	..	Pensioner (sent to Major Pigott, S.O.P., Exeter, 24/4/58).
	M'Glashen, Peter .	,,	..	1	..	Pensioner (sent S.O.P., 1st Edinburgh District, 29/8/57).
	M'Kay, Hugh . .	Colr.-Serjt.	..	1	..	Pensioner (sent to 190 Borthwicks Close, High St., Edinburgh, 6/8/57).
	Malone, John . .	Private	..	1	..	Serving (sent to O.C. 73rd Regt., Cape of Good Hope, 7/7/58).
	Morgan, John . .	,,	..	1	..	(Sent to the Conevil Police Station, near Carmarthen, 11/12/57).
	Neal, James . .	,,	..	1	..	Pensioner (sent to the Paddington Infirmary, 6/8/57). Returned and sent to Mrs. Seymours, 12 Leonard St., Finsbury, 10/8/57).
	Peate, George . .	,,	..	1	..	(Sent to Sir Jas. Jackson, K.C.B., 27/5/58).
	Roberts, John B. .	Qr.-Mr.-Serjt.	..	1	..	Pensioner (medal delivered to him to-day, 27/8/57).
	Small, William . .	Serjt.	..	1	1	Pensioner (medal returned 20/1/58, he having left the district. Sent to Thomastown, Co. Kilkenny, 10/7/58).
	Trowell, John . .	Private	..	1	..	Serving (sent to the O.C. 73rd Regt., 10/8/58).
	Watkinson, Thomas	,,	..	1	..	Serving (sent to the O.C. 73rd Regt., 10/8/58).
	Williams, Samuel .	Corporal	..	1	..	

42ND

ROYAL HIGHLANDERS

NOMINAL LIST OF OFFICERS, WARRANT OFFICERS,
N.C.O.'S AND MEN

ENTITLED TO RECEIVE MEDALS

FOR SERVICE IN THE

CRIMEA

42ND ROYAL HIGHLANDERS

NOMINAL LIST of Officers, Non-Commissioned Officers and Soldiers entitled to receive Medals for Service in the Crimea.

RANK.	NAME.	Clasps.				REMARKS.
		Alma.	Inker-man.	Bala-klava.	Sebas-topol.	
Lt.-Colonel	Duncan A. Cameron, Col.	Yes.	..	Yes.[1]	Yes.[2]	Brigadier-General.[4]
Major	G. Burrell Cumberland .	Yes.	..	Yes.[3]	Yes.	Retired.[4]
,,	Thomas Tulloch (Lt.-Col.)	Yes.	..	Yes.[5]	Yes.	Exchanged to H. Pay.[4]
Captain	John C. Macpherson (M.)	Yes.	..	..	Yes.	Full Pay Retired.[4]
,,	Honble. Robert Rollo (Lt.-Col.)	Yes.	..	Yes.	Yes.	Unattached.[4]
,,	Alexander Cameron (M.)	Yes.	..	Yes.[6]	Yes.	On Leave.[4]
,,	Archibald C. Campbell .	Yes.	..	Yes.[6]	Yes.	Retired.[4]
,,	Fredk. G. Wilkinson .	Yes.	..	..	Yes.	
,,	Andrew Pitcairn . .	Yes.	..	Yes.	Yes.	
,,	Honble. G. H. E. Grant	Yes.	..	Yes.	Yes.	Retired.[4]
,,	Charles C. Graham . .	..	..	..	Yes.	Left at Varna 29 Aug. (1854). Joined from Varna 27 Decr., at Balaklava.
Lieutenant	Rowland A. Frazer .	Yes.	..	Yes.[7]	Yes.	Deceased.[4]
,,	John C. Macleod . .	Yes.	..	Yes.[7]	Yes.[8]	
,,	Robert C. Cunninghame	Yes.	..	Yes.[7]	Yes.[8]	Deceased.[4]
,,	Thomas H. Montgomery	Yes.	..	Yes.[7]	Yes.[8]	
,,	Willm. C. Ward . .	Yes.	..	Yes.	Yes.[8]	
,,	John G. Campbell . .	Yes.	..	Yes.	Yes.	On Leave.[4]
,,	Henry C. Jervoise . .	Yes.	..	Yes.	..	
,,	J. C. R. Grove . .	Yes.	..	Yes.	Yes.[8]	
,,	W. G. E. Webber . .	Yes.	..	Yes.	Yes.[8]	
,,	Francis C. Scott . .	Yes.	..	Yes.	Yes.	
,,	Sir P. A. Halkett, Bart.	Yes.	..	Yes.	Yes.[8]	
,,	Rothes L. Dunbar . .	..	..	..	Yes.	Joined at Balaklava from England, 2nd Decr. 1854.
,,	Robert Whigham . .	..	..	..	Yes.	Joined at Balaklava from England, 2 Decr. 1854.
Ensign	John Wilson . . .	..	..	Yes.[9]	Yes.	Left at Varna 29 Aug. Joined before Sebastopol Oct. 1854.
,,	M. D. Viscount Forth .	Yes.	..	..	Yes.	Resigned his Commission 17 Oct. 1854.
Adjutant	John Drysdale, Lieut. .	Yes.	..	Yes.[7]	Yes.[8]	
Surgeon	John G. Wood . . .	Yes.	..	Yes.	..	
Asst. Surgeon	W. A. M'Kinnon . .	Yes.	..	Yes.	Yes.	
Asst. Surgeon	Alexr. M'Lean . .	..	..	Yes.	Yes.	
Qr.-Master	William Wood . . .	Yes.	..	Yes.[10]	Yes.[11]	
Pay-Master	John Wheatley . . .	Yes.	..	..	Yes.	Depot Bn., Winchester. A., B., and S. Clasps 6/2/56.[4] To England on Sick Leave.
Surgeon	J. S. Furlong . . .	..	..	..	Yes.	
Pay-Master	J. A. Bazalgette . .	..	..	..	Yes.	

[1] Commanding the Highland Brigade at the time.   [2] Brigadier-General.   [3] Retired from the Service.
[4] These entries are from the Supplementary Sebastopol Clasp List.   [5] Sent to the Depot.
[6] In England.   [7] Major.   [8] Captain.   [9] Lieut.   [10] Ensn. and Adjt.   [11] Lt. and Adjt.

Regtl. No.	RANK.	NAME.	Clasps.				REMARKS.
			Alma.	Inkerman.	Balaklava.	Sebastopol.	
1061	Sjt.-Major	William Lawson . .	Yes.	..	Yes.[1]	Yes.[2]	
785	Qr.-Mr.-Sjt.	Alexr. M'Gregor .	Yes.	..	..	Yes.[3]	See D.C. Medal Roll.
1327	Py.-Mr.-Sjt.	James Brown . . .	Yes.	..	..	Yes.	
1196	Armr.-Sjt.	James Pattison . .	Yes.	..	..	Yes.	
821	Drum-Maj.	James Walker . . .	Yes.	..	Yes.	Yes.	Died at Balaklava 3rd Nov. 1854.
2136	,,	George Benzies . .	Yes.	..	Yes.	Yes.[4]	
2120	Hospl.-Sjt.	Thomas Steven . .	Yes.	..	..	Yes.	
1975	O.R. Clerk	Will. A. Connell .	Yes.	..	..	Yes.	
1964	Pipe-Major	George Irvine . .	Yes.	..	Yes.	Yes.	
1480	Cr.-Sgt.	Charles Christie . .	Yes.	..	Yes.	Yes.	
1718	,,	James Fraser . . .	Yes.	..	Yes.	Yes.[5]	
1093	,,	John Granger . . .	Yes.	..	Yes.	..	
924	,,	James Louden . . .	Yes.	..	..	..	Wounded at Alma. Died at sea 26 Sept. 1854, on passage to Scutari.
1406	,,	Alexr. Reid	Yes.	..	Yes.	Yes.	
2220	,,	John Simpson . . .	Yes.	..	Yes.	Yes.[6]	
2255	,,	John Steven . . .	Yes.	..	Yes.[7]	Yes.[8]	
2647	,,	Thomas Torrance . .	Yes.	..	Yes.	Yes.	
2230	,,	Peter White	Yes.	..	Yes.	Yes.[9]	See D.C. Medal Roll.
2070	Serjt.	David Barclay . . .	Yes.	..	..	Yes.	At Scutari.[10]
1153	,,	Wilson Brown . . .	Yes.	..	..	Yes.	
1068	,,	John Chisholm . . .	Yes.	..	Yes.	Yes.	Died at Balaklava 5 Jan. ? 1855.[10]
1223	,,	David Dalgleish . .	Yes.	..	..	Yes.[11]	
822	,,	George Donald . . .	Yes.	..	Yes.	Yes.	
1581	,,	William Ferguson . .	Yes.	..	..	Yes.	Deceased 20th Dec. '54.[10]
1539	,,	James Fraser . . .	Yes.	..	..	Yes.	Deceased 25th Jan. '55.[10]
1469	,,	William Gardiner . .	..	..	..	Yes.[11]	Left at Varna 26th Aug. Joined at Balaklava 27th Decr. (1854).
2160	,,	John Jamieson . . .	Yes.	..	..	Yes.	Died at Balaklava 8th Decr. (1854).
1999	,,	Andrew Johnstone . .	Yes.	..	Yes.	Yes.	
2188	,,	Hugh Lockhart . . .	Yes.	..	Yes.	..	Sent home 26 Decr. (1854).
1844	,,	Peter Menzies . . .	Yes.	..	Yes.	Yes.	At Hulali.[10]
1439	,,	James Murray . . .	Yes.	..	Yes.	Yes.	At Hulali.[10]
1046	,,	Archibald M'Callum .	Yes.	..	..	Yes.	
1749	,,	William M'Callum . .	Yes.	..	Yes.	Yes.	
1379	,,	Donald M'Lardy . .	Yes.	..	Yes.	Yes.[12]	
2094	,,	Robert M'Nair . . .	Yes.	..	Yes.	Yes.[12]	
2321	,,	Edward M'Sally . .	Yes.	..	Yes.	Yes.	
2027	,,	George Rankin . . .	..	..	..	Yes.	Left at Varna 29th Aug. Joined at Balaklava 2nd Nov. (1854).
2293	,,	William Rankin . .	Yes.	..	..	Yes.	Sent home 23 March.[10]
2589	,,	Thomas Ridley . . .	Yes.	..	Yes.	Yes.[11]	
1580	,,	Charles Robertson . .	Yes.	..	Yes.	Yes.	
2098	,,	William Ross . . .	Yes.	..	Yes.	Yes.	
1875	,,	George Scott . . .	Yes.	..	Yes.	Yes.	
1089	,,	John Scott	Yes.	..	..	..	Died of cholera at Belbeck, 25th Septr. '54.
1721	,,	William Spyron . .	Yes.	..	..	Yes.	
1857	,,	James Stewart . . .	Yes.	..	..	..	Wounded at Alma. Died at Scutari 4 Oct. (1854).

[1] Promoted Ensign.   [2] Lieut.   [3] Promoted Qr.-Master.   [4] Benzie.
[5] 'Frazier.'   [6] Qr.-Mr.-Serjt.
[7] Stephen.   [8] Sergeant in Sebastopol Clasp List; also name spelt Stephen.   [9] Sjt.-Major in Sebastopol List.
[10] These entries are from the Supplementary Sebastopol Clasp List.   [11] Cr.-Sergt.   [12] Private.

Regtl. No.	Rank.	Name.	Alma.	Inkerman.	Balaklava.	Sebastopol.	Remarks.
2156	Serjt.	William Strathearn .	Yes.	..	Yes.	Yes.	
2221	,,	William Taylor . . .	Yes.	..	..	Yes.[1]	
2500	,,	John Watt	Yes.	..	..	Yes.[2]	
1062	,,	Alexr. Watson . . .	Yes.	..	..	Yes.[1]	
1993	,,	John Fisher	Yes.	..	Yes.	Yes.	Died at Balaklava 30th Novr. (1854).
2711	,,	Alexr. Armstrong . .	Yes.	..	Yes.	Yes.	
1054	,,	John Nicholson . . .	Yes.	..	..	Yes.	
2121	,,	William Walker . .	Yes.	..	Yes.	Yes.	
2638	,,	James Hunter . . .	Yes.	..	Yes.	Yes.	
2154	,,	John Reid . . .	Yes.	..	Yes.	Yes.	
1407	,,	William Reid . . .	Yes.	..	..	..	Died at Balaklava 29th Septr. (1854).
2106	Corpl.	Thomas Adams . . .	Yes.	..	Yes.	Yes.[3]	
1966	,,	Alexr. Aden	Yes.	..	Yes.	Yes.[3]	
2789	,,	James Anderson . .	Yes.	..	Yes.	Yes.[4]	
2648	,,	George Boyle . . .	Yes.	..	..	Yes.	Died at Balaklava 12 Oct. (1854).
2258	,,	William Cameron . .	Yes.	..	Yes.	..	
2449	,,	Alexr. Campbell . .	Yes.	..	Yes.	Yes.	Deceased [5] 9 Feb. '55.[6]
1672	,,	James Christie . . .	Yes.	..	Yes.	Yes.[1]	
2079	,,	Mathew Craig . . .	..	..	Yes.	Yes.[1]	Left at Varna 29 Aug. Joined before Sebastopol 21 Oct. (1854).
1485	,,	Daniel Cameron . . .	Yes.	..	Yes.	Yes.	
2273	,,	Charles Evans . . .	Yes.	..	..	Yes.[7]	
1584	,,	William Ford . . .	Yes.	..	Yes.	Yes.	
3194	,,	Donald Fraser . . .	Yes.	..	Yes.	Yes.	Died at Balaklava 24 Decr. (1854).
1249	,,	George Fraser . . .	Yes.	..	Yes.	Yes.[8]	
1782	,,	Joseph Gemmell . .	Yes.	..	Yes.	Yes.[9]	
2573	,,	George Johnstone . .	Yes.	..	Yes.	Yes.	
2253	,,	William Kimmett . .	Yes.	..	..	Yes.	
2768	,,	John Malcolm . . .	Yes.	..	..	Yes.	Died at Balaklava 10 Oct. (1854).
3211	,,	Benjamin Mawson . .	Yes.	..	Yes.	Yes.[4]	
2050	,,	William Minnes . . .	Yes.	..	Yes.	Yes.[1]	
2084	,,	Alexr. Moir	Yes.	..	Yes.	Yes.	Sent home 22 March.[6]
1978	,,	David Murie . . .	Yes.	..	..	Yes.[3]	At Scutari.[6]
2406	,,	William Murdoch . .	Yes.	..	Yes.	Yes.	
1209	,,	James M'Clelland . .	Yes.	..	Yes.	Yes.[4]	See D.C. Medal Roll.
2621	,,	George M'Culloch . .	Yes.	..	Yes.	Yes.	
1150	,,	Donald M'Kenzie . .	Yes.	..	..	Yes.[1]	
3012	,,	Malcm. M'Phee . . .	Yes.	..	Yes.	Yes.[4]	
1618	,,	Donald M'Tavish . .	Yes.	..	Yes.	Yes.[4]	
3209	,,	Joseph Mumford . .	Yes.	..	Yes.	Yes.	See D.C. Medal Roll.
1391	,,	Alexr. Mackie . . .	Yes.	..	Yes.	Yes.	
1646	,,	John Mathie . . .	Yes.	..	Yes.	..	
1554	,,	Robert M'Kenzie . .	Yes.	..	Yes.	Yes.	Sent home 28th April.[6]
2233	,,	John M'Millan . . .	Yes.	..	Yes.	Yes.	
1619	,,	John Patterson . . .	Yes.	..	Yes.[10]	Yes.[10][4]	See D.C. Medal Roll.
1204	,,	Willm. Petrie . . .	Yes.	..	Yes.	Yes.	See D.C. Medal Roll.
2925	,,	Archd. Ritchie . . .	Yes.	..	Yes.	Yes.[1]	
2780	,,	Walter Robertson . .	Yes.	..	Yes.	Yes.	
1184	,,	William Simpson . .	Yes.	..	Yes.	Yes.[4]	
2089	,,	John Smith	Yes.	..	..	Yes.[4]	
1420	,,	James Stewart . . .	Yes.	..	..	Yes.	

[1] Private. [2] Cr.-Sergt. [3] Sergt. [4] Sergt. in Sebastopol Clasp List.
[5] This entry from *Balaklava* Clasp List. [6] These entries are from the Supplementary Sebastopol Clasp List.
[7] Drummer. [8] Spelt Frazier. [9] Private in Sebastopol Clasp List. [10] Spelt Paterson.

Regtl. No.	Rank.	Name.	Clasps.				Remarks.
			Alma.	Inker-man.	Bala-klava.	Sebas-topol.	
1952	Corpl.	James Sievwright . .	Yes.	..	Yes.	Yes.	Deceased 28th Jan.[1]
1823	,,	John Thompson . .	Yes.	..	Yes.	Yes.[2]	
1111	,,	Robert Wilson . .	Yes.	..	Yes.	Yes.[3]	
2210	,,	Peter Yule . . .	Yes.	..	Yes.	Yes.	
2987	Drumr.	John Allan . . .	Yes.	..	..	Yes.	
775	,,	James Carden . .	Yes.	..	Yes.	..	
2814	,,	David Clarke . .	Yes.	..	Yes.	Yes.	
2791	,,	Andrew Hepburn .	Yes.	..	Yes.	Yes.	
2244	,,	Edward Locke . .	Yes.	..	Yes.	Yes.	
2068	,,	Andrew Morrison .	Yes.	..	Yes.	Yes.	
2764	,,	James Morrison . .	..	..	..	Yes.	
2625	,,	John M'Donald . .	Yes.	..	Yes.	Yes.	
1388	,,	James M'Gregor .	Yes.	..	Yes.	Yes.	
2714	,,	Lewis M'Kenzie .	Yes.	..	Yes.	Yes.	
2762	,,	James M'Leod . .	Yes.	..	Yes.	Yes.	
2756	,,	Alexr. Reid . .	Yes.	..	Yes.	Yes.	Deceased 23 Feb.[1]
2754	,,	Chas. D. Wilson .	Yes.	..	Yes.	Yes.	
959	Piper	Donald Bain . .	Yes.	..	Yes.	Yes.[3]	On Certif. Depot 20/11/7.[4]
2284	,,	David Muir . . .	Yes.	..	Yes.	Yes.	
1254	,,	John M'Donald . .	Yes.	..	Yes.	Yes.[3]	
1957	,,	James M'Intosh .	Yes.	..	Yes.	Yes.	
1200	,,	Donald M'Pherson .	Yes.	..	Yes.	Yes.	Sent home 15th April.[1]
1677	Private	Robert Adam, 1st .	Yes.	..	Yes.	Yes.	
3033	,,	Robert Adam, 2nd .	Yes.	..	Yes.	Yes.	
2680	,,	George Adams . .	..	..	..	Yes.	On Certif. Depot 20/11/7.[1]
3193	,,	John Allan . . .	Yes.	..	Yes.	Yes.	
1103	,,	George Anderson .	Yes.	..	Yes.	Yes.	Sent home.[1]
2504	,,	James Anderson .	Yes.	..	Yes.	Yes.	
2190	,,	John Anderson . .	Yes.	..	Yes.	Yes.	
2015	,,	Robert Anderson, 1 .	Yes.	..	..	Yes.	Died at Balaklava (Scutari ?) 27 Novr. '54.
3306	,,	Robert Anderson, 2 .	Yes.	..	Yes.	Yes.	Deceased.[5]
1990	,,	William Anderson, 1 .	Yes.	..	Yes.	Yes.	Died at Balaklava 10 Novr. '54.
2373	,,	William Anderson, 2 .	Yes.	..	Yes.	..	Died at Balaklava 10 Novr. (1854).
3310	,,	Stephen Andrews .	Yes.	..	Yes.	Yes.	
3154	,,	John Angus . . .	Yes.	..	Yes.	Yes.	
2611	,,	George Arbuckle .	Yes.	..	Yes.	Yes.[6]	
2910	,,	Henry Archibald .	Yes.	..	Yes.	Yes.	
3032	,,	William Archibald .	Yes.	..	Yes.	Yes.	Sent home 18 May.[1]
2434	,,	Thomas Armour .	Yes.	..	Yes.	Yes.	
3000	,,	James Armstrong .	Yes.	..	Yes.	Yes.	
3111	,,	Frank Ashton . .	Yes.	..	Yes.	Yes.	
3049	,,	Mark Axe . . .	Yes.	..	..	Yes.	
3166	,,	John Bain . . .	Yes.	..	Yes.	Yes.	
1835	,,	William Bain . .	Yes.	..	Yes.	Yes.	
1426	,,	John Baird . . .	Yes.	..	Yes.	Yes.	Deceased 25 Feby. 1855.[4]
3291	,,	William Ballard .	Yes.	..	..	Yes.	
2411	,,	John Bannerman .	Yes.	..	Yes.	Yes.	Deceased 4 June 1855.[4]
2181	,,	William Barber . .	Yes.	..	..	Yes.	Died at Balaklava 10 October '54.
2854	,,	John Barclay . .	Yes.	..	..	Yes.[6]	
1812	,,	William Barclay, 1 .	Yes.	..	Yes.	Yes.	

[1] These entries are from the Supplementary Sebastopol Clasp List.   [2] Sergt. in Sebastopol Clasp List.
[3] Private.   [4] From the Sebastopol Clasp List.   [5] This entry from *Balaklava* Clasp List.
[6] Corporal in Sebastopol Clasp List.

Regtl. No.	Rank.	Name.	Clasps.				Remarks.
			Alma.	Inker-man.	Bala-klava.	Sebas-topol.	
2117	Private	William Barclay, 2 . .	Yes.	..	Yes.	Yes.	
3248	,,	James Barnes . . .	Yes.	..	Yes.	Yes.	
2569	,,	Allan Barr . . .	Yes.	..	Yes.	Yes.	
2300	,,	John Barr . . .	Yes.	..	Yes.	..	
2429	,,	Ronald Bathgate . .	Yes.	..	Yes.	Yes.	Sent home 13 June.[1]
2774	,,	Alexr. Baxter . . .	Yes.	..	..	Yes.	Deceased 16 July '55.[1]
3288	,,	John Baxter . . .	Yes.	..	Yes.	Yes.	
3249	,,	John Beattie . . .	Yes.	..	Yes.	Yes.	
2099	,,	James Bell . . .	Yes.	..	Yes.	Yes.	
2325	,,	William Bell . . .	Yes.	..	Yes.	Yes.	
3081	,,	John Bennett . . .	Yes.	..	Yes.[2]	Yes.	
1357	,,	William Bennett . .	Yes.	..	..	..	
3007	,,	Edward Billington . .	..	..	..	Yes.	
1266	,,	George Binnie . . .	..	..	Yes.[3]	Yes.	Deceased 2nd Septr. '55.[1]
2832	,,	John Black . . .	Yes.	..	Yes.	Yes.	
1115	,,	Ronald Black . . .	Yes.	..	Yes.	..	
1525	,,	Robert Blackie . . .	Yes.	..	Yes.	Yes.	
2965	,,	John Blackley . . .	Yes.	..	Yes.	Yes.	
3250	,,	David Blair	Yes.	..	Yes.	Yes.	
3014	,,	George Blanny . . .	Yes.	..	Yes.	Yes.	
1728	,,	John Bullock . . .	Yes.	..	Yes.	Yes.[4][5]	
3294	,,	Samuel Blott . . .	..	..	Yes.	Yes.	Sent home 16th Feby. '55.[1]
2040	,,	Francis Blyth . . .	Yes.	..	..	Yes.	Died before Sebastopol 3rd Octr.
3167	,,	Robert Boag . . .	Yes.	..	Yes.	Yes.	
1234	,,	Joseph Boggle . . .	Yes.	..	Yes.	Yes.	Sent home 24 Augt.[1]
2660	,,	Angus Borthwick . .	Yes.	..	Yes.	Yes.	
886	,,	Thomas Borthwick . .	Yes.	..	..	..	
3085	,,	George Bowers . . .	Yes.	..	Yes.	Yes.	
2217	,,	Angus Bowie . . .	Yes.	..	Yes.	Yes.	See D.C. Medal Roll.
3239	,,	James Boyle . . .	Yes.	..	Yes.	Yes.	
2182	,,	Richard Brackey . .	Yes.	..	Yes.	Yes.	
3231	,,	Peter Brennan . . .	Yes.	..	Yes.	Yes.[6]	
1424	,,	William Brims . . .	Yes.	..	Yes.	Yes.	Sent home 2 June '55.[1]
1478	,,	Adam Brodie . . .	Yes.	..	Yes.	Yes.	
2550	,,	James Brodie . . .	..	..	Yes.	Yes.	
2983	,,	James Brewster . . .	Yes.	..	..	Yes.	
3097	,,	Willm. Brooks . . .	Yes.	..	..	Yes.	
3251	,,	Charles Brothwell . .	Yes.	..	..	Yes.	
1146	,,	Alexr. Brown . . .	..	..	Yes.	Yes.	
2816	,,	Andrew Brown . . .	..	..	..	Yes.	
3089	,,	Charles Brown . . .	Yes.	..	Yes.	Yes.	
1411	,,	David Brown . . .	..	..	..	Yes.	Provisnl. Bn., Malta.[1]
2532	,,	George Brown . . .	Yes.	..	Yes.	Yes.	
1471	,,	James Brown, 1 . .	Yes.	..	Yes.	Yes.	
3215	,,	James Brown, 2 . ..	Yes.	..	Yes.	Yes.	
2889	,,	John Brown . . .	Yes.	..	Yes.	Yes.	
3327	,,	Michael Brown . . .	Yes.	..	Yes.	Yes.[7]	
2897	,,	Robert Brown . . .	Yes.	..	Yes.	Yes.	
1125	,,	Thomas Brown, 1 . .	Yes.	..	Yes.	Yes.	
2703	,,	Thomas Brown, 2 . .	Yes.	..	Yes.	Yes.	
2733	,,	Thomas Brown, 3 . .	..	..	Yes.	Yes.	

[1] These entries are from the Supplementary Sebastopol Clasp List.   [2] Spelt Bennet.   [3] Spelt Bennie.
[4] Corporal in Sebastopol Clasp List.   [5] Blellock.   [6] James Brennan.
[7] 3617 in Sebastopol Roll.

Regtl. No.	Rank.	Name.	Alma.	Inkerman.	Balaklava.	Sebastopol.	Remarks.
1981	Private	William Brown, 1 . .	Yes.	..	Yes.	Yes.	
2582	,,	William Brown, 2 . .	..	..	..	Yes.	
2724	,,	David Bruce, 1 . .	Yes.	..	Yes.	Yes.	Deceased 22 March.[1]
3158	,,	David Bruce, 2 . .	Yes.	..	..	Yes.	Sent home 28 March '55.[1]
2761	,,	Henry Bruce . .	Yes.	..	Yes.	Yes.	Sent home 9 June '55.[1]
3022	,,	Robert Bruce . .	Yes.	..	..	..	
2700	,,	John Bryson . .	Yes.	..	Yes.	Yes.	
3020	,,	Andw. Buchanan .	Yes.	..	Yes.	Yes.	
2520	,,	James Buchanan .	Yes.	..	Yes.	Yes.	
3055	,,	James Brookes .	Yes.	..	Yes.	Yes.[2]	Deceased 1 Feby. '55.[1]
1809	,,	John Buchanan .	Yes.	..	Yes.	Yes.	
3054	,,	Thomas Buller . .	Yes.	..	Yes.	..	
3252	,,	George Butler . .	Yes.	..	..	Yes.	Deceased 21 Feby. 1855.[3]
3206	,.	Michael Burke . .	Yes.	..	..	Yes.	
2580	,,	William Burns . .	Yes.	..	Yes.	Yes.[4]	
3052	,,	Emanl. Butt . .	Yes.	..	Yes.	Yes.	Sent home 15th May '55.[1]
2182	,,	Thomas Cadger . .	Yes.	..	..	Yes.	Died 22 Novr. at Balaklava.
2848	,,	John Cairns . . .	Yes.	..	..	Yes.	
2830	,,	William Cairns . .	Yes.	..	Yes.	Yes.	
2502	,,	Duncan Cameron .	Yes.	..	Yes.	Yes.	
3005	,,	Ewen Cameron . .	Yes.	..	Yes.	Yes.	
3031	,,	Hugh Cameron . .	Yes.	..	Yes.	Yes.	
3217	,,	James M. Cameron .	Yes.	..	Yes.	Yes.	Sent home 22 Aug. '55.[1]
2345	,,	John Cameron . .	Yes.	..	Yes.	Yes.	
1299	,,	Peter Cameron . .	Yes.	..	Yes.	Yes.	Deceased 3 March 1855.[3]
3035	,,	William Cameron .	Yes.	..	Yes.	Yes.	
2840	,,	Archd. Campbell .	Yes.	..	Yes.	Yes.	Deceased 8 Feby. '55.[1]
3039	,,	Arthur Campbell .	Yes.	..	Yes.	Yes.	
3285	,,	James Campbell .	Yes.	..	..	Yes.	
2557	,,	John Campbell . .	Yes.	..	Yes.	Yes.	
1713	,,	Malcm. Campbell .	Yes.	..	Yes.	Yes.	Deceased 9 March 1855.[3]
2806	,,	Neil Campbell . .	Yes.	..	..	..	Killed at Alma 20 Septr. 54.
1164	,,	Robert Campbell .	Yes.	..	Yes.	Yes.[5]	
3225	,,	Ralph Canny . .	Yes.	..	Yes.	Yes.	
3143	,,	Daniel Carmichael .	Yes.	..	Yes.	Yes.	
1170	,,	Neil Carmichael .	Yes.	..	Yes.	Yes.	
1237	,,	Robert Carphin . .	Yes.	..	Yes.	Yes.	
2737	,,	Hugh Carr . . .	Yes.	..	Yes.	Yes.	Deceased 18 June 1855.[3]
2924	,,	John Carrick . .	Yes.	..	..	Yes.	Sent home 20th Decr. '54.[1]
2649	,,	Nichol Cassills . .	..	..	..	Yes.[6]	
2912	,,	John Caw . . .	Yes.	..	Yes.	Yes.	At Scutari.[1]
3253	,,	James Charlton . .	Yes.	..	Yes.	Yes.	
1351	,,	Alexr. Chisholm .	Yes.	..	Yes.	Yes.	
1777	,,	Andw. Christie . .	Yes.	..	Yes.	Yes.	
2753	,,	George Christie . .	Yes.	..	Yes.	Yes.	
888	,,	Charles Christison .	Yes.	..	Yes.	Yes.	See D.C. Medal Roll.
2845[7]	,,	John S. Clarke . .	..	..	Yes.	Yes.	Sent home 15 April 1855.[3] [7]
3137	,,	John Clarke, 1 . .	Yes.	..	..	Yes.	Deceased 15 Augt. 1855.[3]
3197	,,	John Clarke, 2 . .	Yes.	..	Yes.	Yes.[8]	
1551	,,	Robert Clarke . .	Yes.	..	Yes.	Yes.[9]	Deceased [10] 22 Feby. '55.[1]
1945	,,	Thomas Clarke, 1 . .	Yes.	..	Yes.	Yes.[8]	

[1] These entries are from the Supplementary Sebastopol Clasp List.   [2] Brooks.   [3] From Sebastopol Clasp List.
[4] No. 2560 in Supplementary Sebastopol List.   [5] Corporal in Sebastopol Clasp List.   [6] Nicol Cassils.
[7] No. 2485.   [8] Clark.   [9] 1550.   [10] These entries are from Balaklava Clasp List.

Regtl. No.	RANK.	NAME.	Clasps.				REMARKS.
			Alma.	Inkerman.	Balaklava.	Sebastopol.	
3240	Private	Thomas Clarke, 2 . .	Yes.	..	..	Yes.[1]	
2567	,,	James Clunie . . .	Yes.	..	..	Yes.	
2865	,,	John Calvin	Yes.	..	Yes.[2]	Yes.	
2601	,,	John Connell . . .	Yes.	..	..	Yes.	
1116	,,	Quintin Connell . .	Yes.	..	..	Yes.	
981	,,	Thomas Campbell . .	Yes.	..	..	Yes.	Died 7 Octr., Balaklava, 1854.
2157	,,	James Conning . . .	Yes.	..	Yes.	Yes.	
820	,,	Edward Connolly . .	Yes.	..	Yes.	Yes.	
3307	,,	William Campbell . .	Yes.	..	Yes.	..	
3046	,,	Charles Cook . . .	Yes.	..	Yes.	Yes.	Died at Balaklava 25 Decr. 1854.
3229	,,	Samuel Cooper . . .	Yes.	..	Yes.	Yes.	
2866	,,	Thomas Cooper . . .	Yes.	..	..	Yes.	Died before Sebastopol, 5 Octr. 1854.
3304	,,	Francis Cootes . . .	Yes.	..	Yes.	Yes.	
2037	,,	George Copeland . .	Yes.	..	Yes.	Yes.	At Scutari.[3]
3141	,,	Alexr. Cormack . . .	Yes.	..	Yes.	Yes.	
3057	,,	Andrew Coull . . .	Yes.	..	..	Yes.	Sent home 27 Augt. '55.[3]
925	,,	Robert Coulter . . .	..	..	Yes.	Yes.	Deceased 13th Feby. 1855.[3]
3254	,,	William Cox . . .	Yes.	..	Yes.	Yes.	
1924	,,	James Craig	Yes.	..	Yes.	Yes.	
2195	,,	Duncan Cram . . .	Yes.	..	Yes.[4]	Yes.[4]	
2856	,,	John Crawford, 1 . .	..	..	..	Yes.[5]	Killed in the trenches on the 8th Septr.[3]
3010	,,	John Crawford, 2 . .	Yes.	..	..	Yes.[5]	
3189	,,	Walter Cerar . . .	..	..	..	Yes.	Died before Sebastopol, 21 Octr. 1854.
3228	,,	John Crockwell . . .	Yes.	..	Yes.	Yes.	
2817	,,	Andrew Crombie . .	Yes.	..	Yes.	Yes.	Sent home 7 Septr. '55.[3]
2610	,,	James Crone . . .	Yes.	..	Yes.	..	
2897	,,	William Cross . . .	..	..	..	Yes.	
3091	,,	Mathew Crowley . .	Yes.	..	Yes.	Yes.	
3315	,,	Wm. Cruikshank . .	Yes.	..	Yes.[6]	Yes.[6]	Sent home 22 Septr. '55.[3]
2290	,,	James Cumpsty . .	Yes.	..	..	Yes.	
1724	,,	Charles Cuninghame .	Yes.	..	Yes.[7]	Yes.	
2862	,,	John Currie . . .	Yes.	..	..	Yes.	
3132	,,	Patrick Daughney . .	Yes.	..	Yes.	Yes.	
3115	,,	James Davidson . .	Yes.	..	Yes.	Yes.	Deceased 9 Augt. 1855.[8]
1959	,,	John Davidson, 1 . .	Yes.	..	..	Yes.	Sent home 2 May '55.[3]
2640	,,	John Davidson, 2 . .	Yes.	..	Yes.	Yes.	
3029	,,	William Davidson . .	Yes.	..	Yes.	Yes.	
1394	,,	William Davie . . .	Yes.	..	..	Yes.	Transfd. 5 April '55.[3]
3159	,,	James Davis . . .	Yes.	..	Yes.	Yes.	
3255	,,	John Davis	Yes.	..	Yes.	Yes.	
3245	,,	Thomas Davis . . .	Yes.	..	..	Yes.	Died at Balaklava 7 Octr. 1854 (1855).[3]
3118	,,	Alfred Dawson . . .	Yes.	..	Yes.	Yes.	Sent home 31 Augt. '55.[3]
1300	,,	John Dempster . . .	Yes.	..	..	Yes.	Certif. Depot 20/11/7.[3]
2623	,,	James Devine . . .	Yes.	..	Yes.	Yes.	Deceased 24 Augt. '55.[3]
2081	,,	William Dewar . . .	Yes.	..	Yes.	..	
2113	,,	Alexr. Dick	Yes.	..	Yes.	Yes.	Deceased 9 Feby. '55.[3]
2236	,,	Thomas Dick . . .	Yes.	..	Yes.	Yes.	
2926	,,	John Dickson . . .	..	..	Yes.[9]	Yes.	
2838	,,	Robert Dickson . . .	Yes.	..	Yes.	Yes.	

[1] Clark. [2] Colvin. [3] These entries are from the Supplementary Sebastopol Clasp List.
[4] Cramb. [5] Corporal in Sebastopol List. [6] Cruickshanks. [7] Cunningham.
[8] From Sebastopol Clasp List. [9] Described as John Dickson 2nd in this List.

Regtl. No.	Rank.	Name.	Clasps.				Remarks.
			Alma.	Inker-man.	Bala-klava.	Sebas-topol.	
2954	Private	Peter Dickson . . .	Yes.	..	Yes.	Yes.	
2867	,,	Thomas Dickson . .	..	..	Yes.	Yes.	Died at Balaklava 2nd Novr. 1854.
2197	,,	William Dodds . . .	Yes.	..	Yes.	Yes.[1]	
734	,,	John Donald . . .	Yes.	..	Yes.	Yes.[2]	
1537	,,	Alexr. Donaldson . .	Yes.	..	..	Yes.	
1428	,,	James Donaldson . .	Yes.	..	..	Yes.	At Scutari.[3]
3317	,,	Robert Donnolly . .	Yes.	..	Yes.[4]	Yes.	
3078	,,	John Donovan . . .	Yes.	..	Yes.	Yes.	
3074	,,	Michael Dougherty .	Yes.	..	..	Yes.	
2347	,,	David Douglas . . .	Yes.	..	Yes.	Yes.	Sent home 12 Augt. '55.[3]
2483	,,	Robert Dow . . .	Yes.	..	..	Yes.	Deceased 9 Feby. '55.[5]
3034	,,	William Dow . . .	Yes.	..	..	Yes.	Deceased 1 Jany. '55.[3]
3070	,,	Henry Dowdall . . .	..	..	..	Yes.	Deceased 18th Feby. '55.[3]
2627	,,	Robert Downie . . .	Yes.	..	Yes.	Yes.	
3106	,,	Francis Doyle . . .	Yes.	..	Yes.	Yes.	
2918	,,	Angus Drummond . .	Yes.	..	Yes.	Yes.	
2252	,,	Ferdinand Drysdale .	Yes.	..	..	Yes.	Deceased 24 Novr. '55,[3] at Scutari.
1853	,,	Robert Drysdale . .	Yes.	..	Yes.	Yes.	Deceased 30 Novr. '54,[5] Balaklava.
1381	,,	Henry Drewitt . . .	Yes.	..	..	Yes.	Deceased 8th Oct. 1854, Sebastopol.
1570	,,	Peter Dudgeon . . .	Yes.	..	Yes.	Yes.	On Certif. R18/8/58.[5]
3200	,,	Lewis Dudley . . .	..	..	..	Yes.	Deceased 24 Octr. '54.[3]
1630	,,	John Dunbar . . .	Yes.	..	Yes.	Yes.	
1427	,,	Alexr. Duncan . . .	Yes.	..	..	Yes.	
1566	,,	James Duncan . . .	Yes.	..	..	Yes.	Deceased 1 Octr. 1854, Balaklava.
3158	,,	John Duncan . . .	Yes.	..	Yes.	Yes.[6]	
1804	,,	William Duncan . .	Yes.	..	Yes.	Yes.	
3172	,,	David Dunlop . . .	Yes.	..	..	Yes.	
2934	,,	James Duns . . .	Yes.	..	Yes.	Yes.	
2431	,,	Edward Durney . .	Yes.	..	Yes.	Yes.	
2977	,,	James Eaddie . . .	Yes.	..	Yes.[7]	Yes.[7]	
2726	,,	John Early	Yes.	..	Yes.	Yes.	
3075	,,	Joseph Eaton . . .	Yes.	..	Yes.	Yes.	
2519	,,	David Edgar . . .	..	..	..	Yes.	Sent home 24th Septr. '55.[3]
2417	,,	Thomas Elliott . . .	Yes.	..	..	..	Died of wounds recd. at Alma.
3123	,,	George Eno	Yes.	..	Yes.	Yes.	Sent home 9th Jany. '55.[3]
3184	,,	John Etchison . . .	Yes.	..	Yes.	Yes.[8]	
3235	,,	Richard Fadden . .	Yes.	..	..	..	Killed at Alma 20 Septr. '54.
3216	,,	Archd. Fairbairn . .	Yes.	..	Yes.	Yes.	
1631	,,	William Fairley . .	Yes.	..	Yes.	Yes.	
3113	,,	James Farmer . . .	..	..	Yes.	..	
3072	,,	Thomas Farraday . .	Yes.	..	Yes.	Yes.	
1863	,,	Alexr. Doig	..	..	..	Yes.	Sent to Scutari 14 Sept. '54.
3241	,,	John Fegan	..	..	Yes.	Yes.	
2836	,,	John Featherstone . .	Yes.	..	..	Yes.	
2469	,,	Donald Ferguson . .	Yes.	..	Yes.	Yes.	Deceased [9] 3 Jany. '55,[3] Balaklava.
1928	,,	John Ferguson, 1 . .	Yes.	..	Yes.	Yes.	
2717	,,	John Ferguson, 2 . .	Yes.	..	Yes.	Yes.	
1865	,,	William Ferguson . .	Yes.	..	Yes.	Yes.	Deceased [9] 6 Jany. '55,[5] Balaklava.
1332	,,	James Fife	Yes.	..	Yes.	Yes.	
2841	,,	Malcolm Finlayson .	Yes.	..	..	Yes.	Deceased 2 May 1855.[5]
3173	,,	Peter Finney . . .	Yes.	..	Yes.	Yes.	

[1] No. 2127 in this List. [2] Corporal in Sebastopol List. [3] These entries are from the Supplementary Sebastopol Clasp List.
[4] Donnelly. [5] From Sebastopol Clasp List. [6] No. 3138 in this List. [7] Eadie.
[8] Etchinson. [9] These entries are from Balaklava Clasp List.

Regtl. No.	Rank.	Name.	Alma.	Inker-man.	Bala-klava.	Sebas-topol.	Remarks.
			Clasps.				
2396	Private	James Fisher . . .	Yes.	..	Yes.	Yes.	Deceased [1] 23rd July '55.[2]
3103	,,	Philip Fitzgerald . .	Yes.	..	Yes.	Yes.	
3112	,,	Richard Fitzgerald . .	Yes.	..	Yes.	Yes.	
3040	,,	Patrick Flynn . . .	Yes.	..	..	Yes.	
1185	,,	Alexr. Forbes . . .	Yes.	..	..	..	Wounded at Alma 20 Septr. '54.
1897	,,	David Forbes . . .	Yes.	..	Yes.	Yes.	
2305	,,	James Forbes . . .	Yes.	..	Yes.	Yes.	Deceased [1] 24 Jany. '55.[2]
2825	,,	John Forbes . . .	Yes.	..	Yes.	Yes.[3]	
1449	,,	Willm. Forrester, 1 .	Yes.	..	..	..	Wounded at Alma, d.at Scutari 17 Oct.
3157	,,	Willm. Forrester, 2 .	Yes.	..	Yes.	Yes.	
2946	,,	George Fox . . .	Yes.	..	..	Yes.	Transfd. 4 April '55.[2]
3024	,,	Donald Fraser, 1 . .	Yes.	..	Yes.	Yes.	Clasp given as they both possess Balaklava Clasp.[4] [5]
3151	,,	Donald Fraser, 2 . .	Yes.	..	Yes.	Yes.[6]	
3150	,,	Peter Fraser . . .	Yes.	..	..	..	
2174	,,	Robert Fraser . . .	Yes.	..	Yes.	Yes.	Deceased 24 Jany. '55.[2]
3187	,,	William Fraser . . .	Yes.	..	..	Yes.	Deceased 12 Novr.[2]
2551	,,	William Frew . . .	Yes.	..	..	Yes.	
2242	,,	George Fleming . . .	Yes.	..	Yes.	Yes.	
1285	,,	James Gaff . . .	Yes.	..	..	Yes.	Deceased 27 March 1855.[4]
3036	,,	Robert Galbraith . .	Yes.	..	Yes.	Yes.	
3218	,,	James Garrow . . .	Yes.	..	Yes.	Yes.	
3256	,,	John Gaskell . . .	Yes.	..	..	Yes.	Deceased 14 April 1855.[4]
3016	,,	William Gibb . . .	Yes.	..	..	Yes.	
3006	,,	William Gibbons . .	Yes.	..	Yes.	Yes.	
1616	,,	James Gibson, 1 . .	Yes.	..	Yes.	Yes.	Deceased 8 May 1855.[4]
2145	,,	James Gibson, 2 . .	Yes.	..	Yes.	Yes.	
1076	,,	William Gibson, 1 . .	Yes.	..	Yes.	Yes.	
2041	,,	William Gibson, 2 . .	Yes.	..	Yes.	Yes.	
2407	,,	James Gilchrist, 1 . .	..	..	..	Yes.	
2566	,,	James Gilchrist, 2 . .	..	..	..	Yes.	
2972	,,	Peter Gilfillan . .	Yes.	..	Yes.	Yes.	
3063	,,	James Farrell . . .	..	..	..	..	Sent to Scutari 17 Sept.
3053	,,	George Gingell . . .	..	..	Yes.	Yes.	Died at Balaklava 20 Decr. 1854.
1622	,,	John Girvan . . .	Yes.	..	Yes.	Yes.	
2134	,,	George Glenn . . .	Yes.	..	..	Yes.[7]	
3195	,,	Thomas Goldie . . .	Yes.	..	Yes.	Yes.	Deceased 20 Jany. '55.[2]
3060	,,	Thomas Goodbury . .	Yes.	..	Yes.	Yes.	Died at Balaklava 29 Novr. 1854.
2940	,,	Alfred Goodwin . .	Yes.	..	Yes.	Yes.	Deceased 27th Feby. 1855.[4]
3134	,,	John Gready . . .	Yes.	..	Yes.	Yes.	
3079	,,	William Graham . .	Yes.	..	Yes.	Yes.	
1751	,,	John Grahams . . .	Yes.	..	Yes.	Yes.	
805	,,	George Grant . . .	Yes.	..	Yes.	Yes.	
2129	,,	James Grant . . .	Yes.	..	Yes.	Yes.	Deceased [1] 15th Feby. '55.[2] See D.C. Medal Roll.
1678	,,	Charles Gray . . .	Yes.	..	Yes.	..	
1877	,,	William Gray . . .	Yes.	..	Yes.	Yes.	Deceased 23 June 1855.[4]
3234	,,	Michael Grehan . .	Yes.	..	Yes.	Yes.	
3237	,,	John Green . . .	Yes.	..	Yes.	Yes.	
3061	,,	Robert Green . . .	Yes.	..	Yes.	Yes.	
3059	,,	David Grimwood . .	Yes.	..	Yes.	Yes.	

[1] These entries are from Balaklava Clasp List.   [2] These entries are from the Supplementary Sebastopol Clasp List.
[3] Corporal in Sebastopol Clasp List.   [4] From the Sebastopol Clasp List.
[5] This entry is not understood ; it is copied exactly from the Sebastopol List.   [6] Frazier.   [7] Glen.

Regtl. No.	Rank.	Name.	Alma.	Inker-man.	Bala-klava.	Sebas-topol.	Remarks.
					Clasps.		
3301	Private	James Groves, 1 . .	Yes.	..	Yes.	Yes.	
3319	,,	James Groves, 2 . .	..	..	..	Yes.	
1940	,,	John Guthrie . . .	Yes.	..	Yes.	Yes.	
1075	,,	David Haddow . . .	Yes.	..	..	Yes.	See D.C. Medal Roll.
3098	,,	Thomas Hadley . .	..	..	..	Yes.	
2901	,,	James Haggart . . .	..	..	..	Yes.	
2990	,,	Thomas Haig . . .	..	..	..	Yes.	Deceased 21 Jany. '55.[1]
3095	,,	Henry Hamilton . .	Yes.	..	..	..	
2959	,,	William Hamilton . .	Yes.	..	Yes.	Yes.	
3133	,,	Daniel Hammett . .	Yes.	..	Yes.[2]	Yes.	
2039	,,	Robert Hall . . .	Yes.	..	Yes.	Yes.	Deceased 12 Jany. 1855.[3]
3082	,,	Thomas Hanlon . .	Yes.	..	Yes.	Yes.	
3100	,,	Patrick Hanahan . .	Yes.	..	Yes.	Yes.	Deceased 19 Augt. 1854.[3]
1358	,,	Thomas Hardie . .	Yes.	..	..	Yes.	Sent home 15th April '55.[1]
1632	,,	Alexr. Harper . . .	Yes.	..	Yes.	..	
3129	,,	John Harris . . .	Yes.	..	Yes.	Yes.	
1899	,,	John Harrow . . .	Yes.	..	Yes.	Yes.	Sent home 15 April.[1]
1840	,,	David Hart . . .	Yes.	..	..	..	Killed at Alma 20th Septr.
3233	,,	Michael Hart . . .	Yes.	..	..	Yes.	Deceased 9 Feby. '55.[1]
3107	,,	William R. Hart . .	Yes.	..	Yes.	Yes.	
1986	,,	Joseph Hartley . . .	Yes.	..	Yes.	Yes.[4]	See D.C. Medal Roll.
3048	,,	Fredk. Harvey . . .	Yes.	..	..	Yes.	Deceased 14 Augt. '55.[1]
3202	,,	Willm. Haynes . . .	Yes.	..	Yes.	Yes.	
3258	,,	James Healey, 1 . .	Yes.	..	Yes.	Yes.	
3308	,,	James Healey, 2 . .	Yes.	..	Yes.	Yes.	
1456	,,	William Heeley . . .	Yes.	..	Yes.	Yes.[5]	
1900	,,	John Heggie . . .	Yes.	..	..	Yes.	
1187	,,	Alexr. Henderson . .	Yes.	..	Yes.	Yes.	
2944	,,	James Henderson . .	Yes.	..	Yes.	Yes.	
2855	,,	John Henderson . .	Yes.	..	Yes.	Yes.	
3208	,,	Dennis Hennessy . .	Yes.	..	..	Yes.	
2103	,,	Alexr. Herron . . .	Yes.	..	Yes.	Yes.	
3259	,,	Arthur Herron . . .	Yes.	..	Yes.	Yes.	
2801	,,	Robert Hewitt . . .	Yes.	..	Yes.	Yes.	
2552	,,	John Hiddle . . .	Yes.	..	Yes.	Yes.[4]	
3116	,,	William Hill . . .	Yes.	..	Yes.	Yes.	Died at Balaklava 16th Novr. 1854.
1336	,,	David Hislop . . .	Yes.	..	..	Yes.	See D.C. Medal Roll.
3026	,,	Hugh Hodge . . .	Yes.	..	Yes.	Yes.	
3314	,,	Arthur Hogan . . .	Yes.	..	Yes.	Yes.	
3119	,,	Timothy Holland . .	Yes.	..	..	Yes.	Died at Balaklava 4 Novr. 1854.
3260	,,	Joseph Holligan . .	Yes.	..	..	Yes.	Died before Sebastopol, 5 Octr. 1854.
1156	,,	Robert Holmes . . .	Yes.	..	Yes.	Yes.	See D.C. Medal Roll.
1963	,,	Alexr. Hood . . .	Yes.	..	Yes.	Yes.	
1004	,,	David Hope . . .	Yes.	..	Yes.	Yes.	
2850	,,	Alexr. Hossack . . .	Yes.	..	Yes.	Yes.	
2353	,,	Archd. Hossack . .	Yes.	..	Yes.	Yes.	
3101	,,	Thomas Houlder . .	Yes.	..	..	Yes.	
3093	,,	George Honnsom . .	Yes.	..	..	..	
3261	,,	Henry How	Yes.	..	Yes.	Yes.	
1615	,,	James Howden . . .	Yes.	..	Yes.	Yes.	
998	,,	George Howison . .	Yes.	..	Yes.	Yes.	

[1] These entries are from the Supplementary Sebastopol Clasp List.   [2] Hammitt.   [3] From the Sebastopol Clasp List.
[4] Corporal in Sebastopol Clasp List.   [5] Healey.

Regtl. No.	Rank.	Name.	Clasps.				Remarks.
			Alma.	Inker-man.	Bala-klava.	Sebas-topol.	
2980	Private	John Hugill	Yes.	..	..	Yes.	
1596	,,	Thomas Hume . . .	Yes.	..	..	Yes.	
2274	,,	William Hunter . .	Yes.	..	..	..	
3044	,,	Charles Hussey . . .	Yes.	..	Yes.	Yes.	
1348	,,	Robert Hutchison . .	Yes.	..	Yes.	Yes.	Sent home 11 Jany. '55.[1]
1157	,,	Robert Hutton . . .	Yes.	..	Yes.	Yes.[2]	
3278	,,	Peter Hynd	Yes.	..	Yes.	Yes.	
1732	,,	Peter Ingram . . .	Yes.	..	Yes.	Yes.	
1520	,,	Robert Ingram . . .	Yes.	..	Yes.	Yes.[2]	
3186	,,	James Irvine . . .	Yes.	..	..	Yes.	Deceased 7 March 1855.[3]
2225	,,	James Jack . . .	Yes.	..	Yes.	Yes.	
2585	,,	Robert Jack . . .	Yes.	..	Yes.	Yes.	
3170	,,	Thomas Jackson . .	Yes.	..	Yes.	Yes.	
3051	,,	Daniel Jacobs . . .	Yes.	..	..	Yes.	
3117	,,	Richard James, 1 . .	..	..	Yes.	Yes.	Deceased 26 Feby. '55.[1]
3136	,,	Richard James, 2 . .	Yes.	..	Yes.	Yes.	
3109	,,	John Jeffries . . .	Yes.	..	Yes.	Yes.	Sent home 26 Feby.[1]
1439	,,	William Hossack . .	..	..	..	..	Sent to Scutari 17 Septr.
1654	,,	George Johnstone . .	Yes.	..	..	..	
1552	,,	John Johnstone . .	..	..	Yes.	Yes.	Left on board ship 14 Sept. Joined 24 Octr. 1854.
3142	,,	Peter Johnstone . .	Yes.	..	Yes.	..	Deceased 11 Jany. '55.[1]
1982	,,	Robert Johnstone . .	Yes.	..	..	Yes.	
3045	,,	James Jones . . .	Yes.	..	Yes.	Yes.	
2163	,,	John Joss . . .	Yes.	..	Yes.	Yes.	
3105	,,	Thomas Kain . . .	Yes.	..	..	Yes.[4]	
1441	,,	James Keay, 1 . . .	Yes.	..	Yes.	Yes.[4]	
2961	,,	James Keay, 2 . . .	Yes.	..	Yes.	Yes.	
2534	,,	Hugh Kelly . . .	Yes.	..	Yes.	Yes.	
3124	,,	Thomas Kelly . . .	Yes.	..	Yes.	Yes.	
3244	,,	Michael Kennedy . .	Yes.	..	Yes.	Yes.	
1003	,,	William Kennedy . .	Yes.	..	Yes.	Yes.[5]	
2593	,,	John Kerr	..	..	..	Yes	Left at Varna 29 Augt. Joined at Balaklava 25 Decemr.
2879	,,	Thomas Kerr . . .	Yes.	..	Yes.	Yes.	
1025	,,	William Kerr . . .	Yes.	..	Yes.	Yes.	See D.C. Medal Roll.
1695	,,	William Kesson . .	Yes.	..	Yes.	Yes.	
1492	,,	John Kincaid . . .	Yes.	..	Yes.	Yes.	
2877	,,	William King . . .	Yes.	..	Yes.	Yes.	
3083	,,	James Kittle . . .	Yes.	..	Yes.	Yes.	
2588	,,	Adam Laidlaw, 1 . .	Yes.	..	Yes.	Yes.	Deceased[6] 20 March 1855.[3]
2936	,,	Adam Laidlaw, 2 . .	Yes.	..	Yes.	Yes.[7]	
1740	,,	James Laird . . .	Yes.	..	Yes.	Yes.	
2869	,,	James Lamb . . .	Yes.	..	..	Yes.	
1331	,,	Henry Lane	Yes.	..	Yes.	Yes.	Deceased 30 Jany. '55. This clasp was given to a living man in error.[1]
2771	,,	William Lang . . .	Yes.	..	..	Yes.	Died before Sebastopol, 3 Octr. 1854.
2978	,,	Andrew Law . . .	Yes.	..	Yes.	Yes.	Deceased 7 Feby. 1855.[3]
1094	,,	David Lawson . . .	Yes.	..	..	Yes.	Transferred 5 April.[1]
3230	,,	Conner Lavin . . .	Yes.	..	Yes.	Yes.	
3128	,,	Andrew Lee	Yes.	..	Yes.	Yes.	

[1] These entries are from the Supplementary Sebastopol Clasp List. [2] Corporal in Sebastopol Clasp List.
[3] From the Sebastopol Clasp List. [4] Kean. [5] No. 3003.
[6] These entries are from the Balaklava Clasp List. [7] *Andrew* Laidlaw.

Regtl. No.	Rank.	Name.	Clasps.				Remarks.
			Alma.	Inker-man.	Bala-klava.	Sebas-topol.	
2993	Private	John Leishman . . .	Yes.	..	Yes.	Yes.	
1138	,,	Thomas Leitch . . .	Yes.	..	..	..	
1263	,,	John Leonard . . .	Yes.	..	Yes.	Yes.	
2554	,,	John Leslie	Yes.	..	Yes.	Yes.	Sent home 24 April.[1]
3086	,,	Peter Lettimer . . .	Yes.	..	Yes.	Yes.	
1324	,,	Matthew Liddle . .	Yes.	..	Yes.	Yes.	Died at Balaklava 1 Novr. 1855.
2359	,,	James Lightbody . .	Yes.	..	Yes.	Yes.	
2446	,,	Alexr. Lindsay . . .	Yes.	..	Yes.	Yes.	
451	,,	Hugh Littlejohn . .	Yes.	..	..	..	Died at Balaklava 30 Septr.[2]
2669	,,	Andw. M. Livingston .	Yes.	..	Yes.[3]	Yes.	
3263	,,	James Lochrie . . .	Yes.	..	Yes.	Yes.	Deceased March '55.[1]
3219	,,	Samuel Loggie . . .	Yes.	..	Yes.	Yes.	
3220	,,	John Loggie . . .	Yes.	..	Yes.	Yes.	
1626	,,	James Lockhart . . .	Yes.	..	Yes.	Yes.	
918	,,	Daniel Logg	Yes.	..	Yes.	Yes.	See D.C. Medal Roll
3084	,,	William Lott . . .	Yes.	..	Yes.	Yes.	Deceased.[1]
3178	,,	John Loven	Yes.	..	Yes.	Yes.	
2087	,,	John Lowden . . .	Yes.	..	Yes.[4]	Yes.[4]	
1264	,,	Mathew Low . . .	Yes.	..	Yes.	Yes.	
1303	,,	Alexr. Lowrie . . .	Yes.	..	Yes.	Yes.	Deceased 18 June 1855.[5]
1260	,,	Thomas Lucas . . .	Yes.	..	Yes.	Yes.	
3325	,,	William Luckins . .	Yes.	..	Yes.	Yes.	
1112	,,	James Lunnan . . .	Yes.	..	Yes.[6]	Yes.[6]	
1923	,,	John Lyle	Yes.	..	Yes.	Yes.[7]	
3080	,,	Timothy Lynch . .	Yes.	..	..	Yes.	
1729	,,	Andw. Lyon . . .	Yes.	..	Yes.	Yes.	Wounded at Alma 20 Septr.
3204	,,	James Lyon	Yes.	..	Yes.	Yes.	At Scutari.[1]
3019	,,	William Lyon . . .	Yes.	..	Yes.	Yes.	At Scutari.[1]
1367	,,	Thomas Lyle . . .	Yes.	..	..	..	Wounded at Alma 20th Septr.[2]
3041	,,	Edward Meaguer . .	Yes.	..	Yes.[8]	Yes.[8]	
3205	,,	Michael Mahoney, 1 .	Yes.	..	Yes.[9]	Yes.	Deceased 31 July 1855.[5]
3305	,,	Michael Mahoney, 2 .	Yes.	..	Yes.[9]	Yes.	
2999	,,	John Malcolm . . .	Yes.	..	Yes.	Yes.	
1811	,,	James Manson . . .	Yes.	..	Yes.	Yes.	
3282	,,	Thomas Murray . .	Yes.	..	Yes.[10]	Yes.[11]	
3181	,,	Willm. Marshall . .	Yes.	..	..	..	Deceased 19 Jany. '55.[1]
2111	,,	James Martin . . .	Yes.	..	Yes.	Yes.	Sent to England 19 Octr. 1855.[5]
2819	,,	John Martin . . .	Yes.	..	Yes.	Yes.	
2536	,,	Thomas Martin . . .	Yes.	..	Yes.	Yes.	Sent home 12 Augt.[1]
1309	,,	Andw. Mason . . .	Yes.	..	Yes.	Yes.	
3147	,,	Alexr. Mathieson . .	Yes.	..	Yes.	Yes.	
2953	,,	John Mathews . . .	Yes.	..	Yes.	Yes.	
2896	,,	James May	Yes.	..	Yes.	Yes.	Deceased [2] 21 Novr. 1855.[5]
1575	,,	John Menteith . . .	Yes.	..	Yes.[12]	Yes.[12]	
2505	,,	James Menzies . . .	Yes.	..	Yes.	Yes.	
2481	,,	Robert Menzies . . .	..	..	..	..	Deceased 20th Feby. '55.[1]
2798	,,	Willm. Merriman . .	Yes.	..	Yes.[13]	Yes.[7]	
1446	,,	Robert Michie . . .	Yes.	..	..	Yes.	
1512	,,	Robert Middleton . .	..	..	..	Yes.	
1353	,,	David Mill	Yes.	..	Yes.	Yes.	
1701	,,	David Miller . . .	..	..	..	Yes.	Deceased 6 April 1855.[5]

[1] These entries are from the Supplementary Sebastopol Clasp List.　　[2] From Balaklava Clasp List.　　[3] Livingstone.
[4] Louden.　　[5] From Sebastopol Clasp List.　　[6] Lunnen.　　[7] Corporal in Sebastopol Clasp List.　　[8] Magner.
[9] Mahony.　　[10] Marry.　　[11] Murry.　　[12] Menteath.　　[13] Willm. H. Merriman.

Regtl. No.	Rank.	Name.	Alma.	Inker-man.	Bala-klava.	Sebas-topol.	Remarks.
1802	Private	Duncan Miller	Yes.	..	Yes.	Yes.	
2243	"	Henry Miller	Yes.	..	Yes.	Yes.	
1748	"	James Miller, 1	Yes.	..	Yes.	Yes.[1]	
3163	"	James Lipp	..	..	..	Yes.	
2405	"	James Miller, 2	Yes.	..	Yes.	Yes.	
2499	"	James Miller, 3	..	..	Yes.	Yes.	Sent to England 19 Octr. 1855.[2]
3161	"	James Miller, 4	Yes.	..	Yes.	Yes.	
1545	"	John Miller	Yes.	..	..	Yes.	
2004	"	Joseph Miller	..	..	..	Yes.	
1368	"	Robert Miller, 1	..	..	Yes.	Yes.[3]	
1768	"	Robert Miller, 2	Yes.	..	..	Yes.	
1319	"	William Miller	Yes.	..	Yes.	Yes.	At Scutari.[4]
3015	"	Alexr. Milne	Yes.	..	Yes.	Yes.	
3149	"	John Milne	Yes.	..	..	..	Deceased 11 July '55.[4]
2049	"	Robert Milne	..	..	..	Yes.	
2690	"	James Mitchell	Yes.	..	Yes.	Yes.	
2923	"	John Mitchell, 1	Yes.	..	..	Yes.	Died before Sebastopol 6 Octr. 1854.
3002	"	John Mitchell, 2	Yes.	..	Yes.	..	Deceased 1st Feby. '55.[4]
3008	"	Thomas Mitchell	Yes.	..	Yes.	Yes.	Deceased 17 Jany. '55.[2]
2821	"	Robert Moffatt	Yes.	..	..	..	Died at Balaklava 2 Octr. '54.
3037	"	John Monachan	Yes.	..	Yes.	Yes.[5]	
1333	"	George Monroe	Yes.	..	Yes.[6]	Yes.[6]	
1297	"	James Montgomery	Yes.	..	..	Yes.	
2820	"	David Moodie	..	..	..	Yes.	
2929	"	James Moodie	Yes.	..	..	Yes.	
3323	"	Edward Morris	..	..	Yes.	Yes.	
3121	"	George Mortimer	Yes.	..	Yes.	Yes.	
1717	"	Robert Morton	Yes.	..	..	Yes.	Died at Balaklava 5 Octr.
1755	"	Archd. Moss	Yes.	..	..	Yes.	
3236	"	John Mugen	Yes.	..	Yes.[7]	Yes.	
3162	"	John Muir	Yes.	..	Yes.	Yes.	Deceased 26 July '55.[4]
2207	"	William Muir, 1	Yes.	..	Yes.	Yes.	
2324	"	William Muir, 2	Yes.	..	Yes.	Yes.	
1568	"	John Mullins	Yes.	..	Yes.	Yes.[1]	
1400	"	Alexr. Munroe	Yes.	..	Yes.[6]	Yes.	
1165	"	George Munro	Yes.	..	Yes.	Yes.	Deceased 18 April '55.[2]
1335	"	Johnathan Munro	Yes.	..	Yes.[8]	Yes.	
3269	"	Levi Murden	Yes.	..	Yes.	Yes.	
3038	"	Francis Murphy	Yes.	..	..	Yes.	
1988	"	John Murray	..	..	Yes.	Yes.	Deceased 17 Feb. '55.[4]
1662	"	Robert Murray, 1	Yes.	..	Yes.	Yes.	At Scutari.[4]
1984	"	Robert Murray, 2	Yes.	..	..	Yes.	Died at Balaklava (before Sebastopol) 15 Octr. '54.
1730	"	John Mutrie	Yes.	..	Yes.	Yes.	
3183	"	Thomas M'Adams	Yes.	..	Yes.[9]	Yes.[9]	Sent home 22 Septr. '55.[4]
3108	"	Michael M'Aleer	Yes.	..	..	Yes.	Deceased 1 Jany. '55.[4]
1797	"	John M'Allister	Yes.	..	..	Yes.	Died before Sebastopol, 5 Octr. 1855.
3171	"	Mathew M'Allum	..	..	Yes.	Yes.	
2847	"	Archd. M'Alpin	Yes.	..	Yes.	Yes.[10]	
2000	"	John M'Alpin	..	..	..	Yes.[10]	
1792	"	John M'Arthur	Yes.	..	Yes.	Yes.	

[1] Corporal in Sebastopol Clasp List.　　[2] From Sebastopol Clasp List.　　[3] Millar.
[4] These entries are from the Supplementary Sebastopol Clasp List.　　[5] Monacham.　　[6] Munro.
[7] Murgan.　　[8] 'Jonathan' in Balaklava Roll.　　[9] M'Adam.　　[10] M'Alpine.

I

Regtl. No.	Rank.	Name.	Clasps.				Remarks.
			Alma.	Inker-man.	Bala-klava.	Sebas-topol.	
1747	Private	Patrick M'Auley	Yes.	..	Yes.[1]	Yes.[2]	
2581	,,	David M'Ausland	Yes.	..	Yes.	Yes.	
3264	,,	Patrick M'Bristy	Yes.	..	Yes.	Yes.[3]	
2144	,,	Archd. M'Callum	Yes.	..	Yes.	Yes.	
3265	,,	Patrick M'Cann	Yes.	..	..	Yes.	Deceased 2 March 1855.[4]
3281	,,	Thomas M'Cann	Yes.	..	Yes.[5]	Yes.	
3293	,,	Andrew M'Crabbie	Yes.	..	Yes.	Yes.	Sent home 30 March '55.[6]
2362	,,	Robert M'Cready	Yes.	..	..	Yes.[7]	
2960	,,	William M'Crory	Yes.	..	Yes.	Yes.	
1913	,,	Daniel M'Culloch	Yes.	..	Yes.	Yes.	Sent home 22 Septr. '55.[6]
2101	,,	John M'Culloch	..	..	..	Yes.	
2681	,,	Peter M'Culloch	Yes.	..	Yes.	Yes.	
3313	,,	William M'Dead	Yes.	..	Yes.	Yes.	
3025	,,	Alexr. M'Donald	Yes.	..	Yes.	Yes.	
861	,,	Angus M'Donald, 1	Yes.	..	Yes.	Yes.	
1991	,,	Angus M'Donald, 2	Yes.	..	Yes.	Yes.	
2247	,,	David M'Donald	Yes.	..	Yes.	Yes.	Sent home 6 Oct. '55.[6]
1935	,,	Donald M'Donald, 1	Yes.	..	Yes.	Yes.	
2800	,,	Donald M'Donald, 2	Yes.	..	..	..	
2984	,,	James M'Donald	Yes.	..	..	..	Died of wounds received at Alma, 21 Septr.
1034	,,	John M'Donald, 1	Yes.	..	..	Yes.	On Certif.
3139	,,	John M'Donald, 2	Yes.	..	Yes.	Yes.	Died at Balaklava 7 Decr. 1854.
2369	,,	Duncan M'Dougall, 1	Yes.	..	Yes.	Yes.	
2908	,,	Duncan M'Dougall, 2	Yes.	..	..	Yes.	Deceased 20 July 1855.[4]
3266	,,	John M'Dowall	Yes.	..	..	Yes.	Died at Balaklava 2 Octr. '54.
3023	,,	Duncan M'Fadyen	Yes.	..	Yes.	Yes.	
2974	,,	John M'Fadyen	Yes.	..	Yes.	Yes.	
1915	,,	Archd. M'Farlane	Yes.	..	..	Yes.	
2100	,,	Daniel M'Farlane	..	..	..	Yes.	Died at Balaklava 7 Novr. (6 Nov.) '54.[6]
1974	,,	Duncan M'Farlane	Yes.	..	Yes.	Yes.	
3242	,,	Willm. M'Gawley	Yes.	..	..	Yes.	Deceased.[6]
2620	,,	John M'George	Yes.	..	Yes.	Yes.	Sent home 11 June '55.[6]
3148	,,	John M'Glawn	..	..	Yes.	Yes.	Deceased 28 Jany. '55.[4]
2307	,,	Daniel M'Gregor	Yes.	..	..	Yes.	Died at Sebastopol 4 Octr. 1854.
3246	,,	John M'Gregor	Yes.	..	..	Yes.	
2093	,,	Malcm. M'Gregor	Yes.	..	..	Yes.	Died at Sebastopol 14 Octr. 1854.
1846	,,	Archd. M'Inness	Yes.	..	Yes.	Yes.	Deceased 26 March.[6]
2438	,,	Wm. M'Leod	Yes.	..	..	Yes.[8]	
1337	,,	John M'Inness	..	..	..	Yes.[9]	
2947	,,	Wm. M'Intosh	Yes.	..	Yes.	Yes.	
1450	,,	John M'Intyre	Yes.	..	Yes.	Yes.	
2389	,,	George M'Kay	Yes.	..	Yes.	Yes.	
1231	,,	John M'Kay, 1	Yes.	..	Yes.	Yes.	
2622	,,	John M'Kay, 2	Yes.	..	..	Yes.	Sent home 24 June '55.[6]
1401	,,	Robert M'Kay, 1	Yes.	..	Yes.	Yes.	
2722	,,	Robert M'Kay, 2	Yes.	..	Yes.	Yes.	
2542	,,	James M'Kechnie	Yes.	..	Yes.	Yes.	Deceased 31 Jany. 1855.[4]
2609	,,	Neil M'Kechnie	Yes.	..	Yes.	Yes.	
1911	,,	Wm. M'Kendrick	..	..	..	Yes.	Deceased 20 March.[6]
2313	,,	Alexr. M'Kenzie, 1	Yes.	..	Yes.	Yes.	

[1] M'Aulley. [2] M'Auley. [3] M'Briarty. [4] From Sebastopol Clasp List.
[5] No. 328. [6] These entries are from the Supplementary Sebastopol Clasp List.
[7] M'Creaddie. [8] M'Loud, and a *Piper*. [9] John M'Innes.

Regtl. No.	Rank.	Name.	Clasps.				Remarks.
			Alma.	Inkerman.	Balaklava.	Sebastopol.	
3169	Private	Alexr. M'Kenzie, 2	Yes.	..	Yes.	..	Absent without leave since 27 December. Deserted. Supposed dead.[1]
1389	,,	Fredk. M'Kenzie	Yes.	..	Yes.	Yes.	
2658	,,	John M'Kenzie, 1	Yes.	..	Yes.	Yes.	
2705	,,	John M'Kenzie, 2	Yes.	..	Yes.	Yes.	
3212	,,	Willm. M'Kenzie	Yes.	..	..	..	Killed at Alma 20 Sept.
2397	,,	John M'Killop	Yes.	..	Yes.	..	
995	,,	James M'Kinnon	Yes.	..	Yes.	Yes.	
1908	,,	John M'Kinnon	Yes.	..	Yes.	Yes.	
889	,,	Alexr. M'Lachlan	Yes.	..	Yes.[2]	Yes.	
2900	,,	James M'Laren	..	..	Yes.	Yes.	
3174	,,	Hugh M'Laughlin	..	..	Yes.[3]	Yes.	
1519	,,	David M'Lean, 1	Yes.	..	Yes.	Yes.	Deceased 28 Feby.[4]
3280	,,	David M'Lean, 2 [5]	..	..	..	..	
2607	,,	George M'Lean	Yes.	..	Yes.	Yes.	
1461	,,	James M'Lean	..	..	..	Yes.	Deceased 27 Feby. 1855.[6]
3247	,,	John M'Lean	Yes.	..	Yes.	Yes.	
1307	,,	Neil M'Lean	Yes.	..	..	..	
2689	,,	Roderick M'Lean	Yes.	..	Yes.	Yes.	Died at Balaklava 26 Decr. 1854.
1874	,,	Alexr. M'Leod	Yes.	..	Yes.	Yes.	Deceased 24 Jany.[4]
2976	,,	Angus M'Leod	Yes.	..	Yes.	Yes.	
1444	,,	Donald M'Leod	Yes.	..	Yes.	Yes.	
982	,,	John M'Leod, 1	Yes.	..	..	Yes.	Died at Sebastopol 8 Octr. 1854.[7]
1166	,,	John M'Leod, 2	Yes.	..	Yes.	Yes.	
2482	,,	John M'Leod, 3	Yes.	..	..	..	Killed at Alma 20 Septr.
3185	,,	Norman M'Leod	..	..	..	Yes.	
1550	,,	Thomas M'Leod	Yes.	..	Yes.	Yes.	Deceased[1] 16 Feby. '55.[4]
2014	,,	William M'Lusky	Yes.	..	Yes.	Yes.	
978	,,	William M'Math	Yes.	..	..	Yes.	Wounded at Alma.
1151	,,	Charles M'Millan	Yes.	..	Yes.	Yes.	
1031	,,	Edward M'Millan	Yes.	..	Yes.	Yes.	
1780	,,	Robert M'Morran	Yes.	..	Yes.	Yes.	
3267	,,	James M'Mutrie	Yes.	..	Yes.	Yes.	
1976	,,	Andrew M'Murray	Yes.	..	Yes.	Yes.	
846	,,	David M'Nab	..	..	Yes.	Yes.	
1762	,,	James M'Nair	Yes.	..	Yes.	Yes.	
1236	,,	Duncan M'Naughton	Yes.	..	Yes.	Yes.	Sent to England 19th Octr. 1855.[6]
1235	,,	John M'Naughton	Yes.	..	..	Yes.	Deceased 25 May 1855.[6]
1635	,,	Robert M'Neil	Yes.	..	..	Yes.	
2846	,,	John M'Nichol	Yes.	..	Yes.[8]	Yes.	
1860	,,	John M'Nish	Yes.	..	Yes.	Yes.	
2885	,,	Archd. M'Phail	Yes.	..	Yes.	Yes.	
3177	,,	John M'Phail	Yes.	..	..	Yes.	
1056	,,	Alexr. M'Pherson, 1	Yes.	..	..	Yes.	Died at Balaklava 1 Octr. 1854.
2478	,,	Alexr. M'Pherson, 2	..	..	..	Yes.	
2281	,,	James M'Pherson, 1	Yes.	..	..	Yes.	
3140	,,	James M'Pherson, 2	Yes.	..	Yes.	Yes.	
1773	,,	John M'Pherson	Yes.	..	Yes.	Yes.	
3155	,,	Roderick M'Rae	Yes.	..	..	Yes.	
2430	,,	John M'Tear	Yes.	..	Yes.	Yes.	Deceased[1] 24 Feby. 1855.[6]
2860	,,	John M'Vicar	Yes.	..	Yes.	Yes.	

[1] These entries are from the Balaklava Clasp List. [2] M'Lauchlan.
[3] M'Lauchlin. [4] These entries are from the Supplementary Sebastopol Clasp List.
[5] David M'Lean, 2, appears on the Alma Roll 'not entitled to Clasp,' and does not appear on either Balaklava or Sebastopol Rolls.
[6] From Sebastopol Clasp List. [7] 3rd Oct. in Sebastopol Roll. [8] M'Nicol.

Regtl. No.	Rank.	Name.	Alma.	Inker-man.	Bala-klava.	Sebas-topol.	Remarks.
2935	Private	Willm. M'Callum	..	..	..	Yes.	
1763	,,	John Neven	Yes.	..	..	Yes.	
1425	,,	John Newlands	Yes.	..	Yes.	..	
2970	,,	Alexr. Nicholson	Yes.	..	..	Yes.	Deceased 13 March 1855.[1]
1128	,,	John Nicholson	Yes.	..	..	Yes.	
2214	,,	William Nicol	Yes.	..	..	Yes.	Transfd. 4 April '55.[2]
3071	,,	John Nixon	Yes.	..	..	Yes.	Deceased. No date known.[2]
3094	,,	John Noonan	Yes.	..	Yes.	Yes.	
3203	,,	Benjn. Norfolk	Yes.	..	..	..	Wounded at Alma. Died at Scutari 23 Oct.
3114	,,	Henry Nott	Yes.	..	Yes.	Yes.	
3131	,,	Charles Nowell	Yes.	..	Yes.	Yes.	Died at Balaklava 26 Decr. 1854.
3042	,,	Francis Oakley	Yes.	..	Yes.	Yes.	
3066	,,	Patrick O'Brine	Yes.	..	Yes.	Yes.[3]	
2451	,,	Francis O'Neill	Yes.	..	Yes.	Yes.[4]	
1664	,,	William O'Neill	Yes.	..	Yes.	Yes.	Deceased 25 May 1855.[1]
1796	,,	John Orr	Yes.	..	Yes.	Yes.	
2971	,,	John Park	Yes.	..	..	Yes.	At Scutari.[2]
3102	,,	George Parker	Yes.	..	..	Yes.	Died at Balaklava 21 Decr. 1855.[1]
3207	,,	Samuel Parsons	Yes.	..	Yes.	Yes.	
3028	,,	Edward Patterson	Yes.	..	Yes.[5]	Yes.[5]	
1604	,,	John Paterson, 1	..	..	..	Yes.	
2694	,,	John Paterson, 2	..	..	Yes.	Yes.	
3013	,,	George Paul	Yes.	..	Yes.	Yes.	
3160	,,	Thomas Paul	Yes.	..	Yes.	Yes.	
3168	,,	Gavin Peacock	Yes.	..	Yes.	Yes.	
3165	,,	Alexr. Pearson	Yes.	..	Yes.	Yes.	
3271	,,	Edwin Pearson	..	..	Yes.	Yes.	Died at Balaklava 25 Decr. 1854.
3201	,,	Willm. Perkins	Yes.	..	Yes.	..	
1711	,,	William Petrie, 1	Yes.	..	Yes.	Yes.	
2769	,,	William Petrie, 2	Yes.	..	Yes.	Yes.	
2462	,,	Robert Pettinew	Yes.	..	Yes.[6]	Yes.[6]	
3062	,,	John Phillipps	Yes.	..	..	..	
2998	,,	Andrew Philp	Yes.	..	..	..	Deceased 12 Jany. '55.[2]
3227	,,	Charles S. Prercy	Yes.	..	Yes.[7]	Yes.[8]	
1692	,,	William Prain	Yes.	..	..	..	Deceased 4 June '55.[2]
3130	,,	John Pring	Yes.	..	Yes.	Yes.	Died at Balaklava 26 Octr. '54.
3004	,,	George Price	..	..	..	Yes.	
1232	,,	George Pringle	Yes.	..	Yes.	Yes.	
3056	,,	William Quin	Yes.	..	..	Yes.	
1838	,,	William Rae	Yes.	..	Yes.	Yes.	Died at Balaklava 12 Decr. 1854.
3156	,,	Robert Ramsay	Yes.	..	Yes.	Yes.	
2808	,,	Robert Rattray	Yes.	..	Yes.	Yes.	Deceased 18th Decr. '54.[2]
909	,,	Alexr. Reid	..	..	Yes.	Yes.	Left at Varna 3 Septr. Joined 21 Octr. Died at Balaklava 10 Decemr. 1854.
1862	,,	Robert Reid	Yes.	..	Yes.	Yes.	Sent home 11 June '55.[2]
2997	,,	William Rennie	Yes.	..	Yes.	Yes.	
1735	,,	Alexr. Richardson	Yes.	..	Yes.	Yes.	
1912	,,	Thomas Richardson	Yes.	..	Yes.	Yes.	Died at Balaklava 16 Novr. 1854.
951	,,	Francis Richmond	Yes.	..	Yes.	Yes.	Deceased 6 March 1855.[1]

[1] From Sebastopol Clasp List.
[2] These entries are from the Supplementary Sebastopol Clasp List.
[3] O'Brien.   [4] O'Neil.   [5] Paterson.   [6] Petticrew.
[7] Piercy.   [8] Corporal Piercey in Sebastopol Clasp List.

Regtl. No.	Rank.	Name.	Clasps.				Remarks.
			Alma.	Inker-man.	Bala-klava.	Sebas-topol.	
3311	Private	James Richmond . .	Yes.	..	Yes.	Yes.	
2423	,,	Mathew Richmond .	Yes.	..	Yes.	Yes.	
1413	,,	George Ritchie . . .	Yes.	..	Yes.	Yes.	
2545	,,	John Ritchie . .	Yes.	..	..	Yes.	Died at Balaklava 26 Octr. 1854.
1694	,,	William Ritchie, 1 . .	Yes.	..	..	Yes.	
3145	,,	William Ritchie, 2 . .	Yes.	..	Yes.	Yes.	
3001	,,	Alexr. Robb . . .	Yes.	..	..	Yes.	
2330	,,	George Robb . . .	Yes.	..	Yes.	Yes.	
1167	,,	James Robb, 1 . . .	Yes.	..	Yes.	Yes.	
2880	,,	James Robb, 2 . . .	Yes.	..	..	Yes.	Died at Balaklava 1 Novr. '54.
1936	,,	William Robb . .	Yes.	..	Yes.	Yes.	
2058	,,	Alexr. Robbin . .	Yes.	..	Yes.	Yes.	
2472	,,	James Roberton . .	Yes.	..	Yes.	Yes.	
2968	,,	William Roberton .	Yes.	..	Yes.	Yes.	
1361	,,	Alexr. Robertson, 1 .	Yes.	..	..	..	Wounded at Alma 20 Septr.
1398	,,	Alexr. Robertson, 2 .	Yes.	..	Yes.	Yes.	Died at Balaklava 14 Novr. 1854.
3214	,,	David Robertson .	Yes.	..	Yes.	Yes.	
2069	,,	James Robertson, 1 .	Yes.	..	Yes.	Yes.[1]	Died at Balaklava 5 Octr. 1854.
3190	,,	James Robertson, 2 .	Yes.	..	..	Yes.	
1364	,,	John Robertson, 1 . .	Yes.	..	Yes.	Yes.	
2930	,,	John Robertson, 2 . .	Yes.	..	Yes.	Yes.	Sent to England 1 Octr. 1855.[2]
2995	,,	John Robertson, 3 . .	Yes.	..	Yes.	Yes.	
1325	,,	William Robertson, 1 .	Yes.	..	Yes.	Yes.	
1745	,,	William Robertson, 2 .	Yes.	..	Yes.	Yes.	Deceased 25 Feby. '55.[3]
3199	,,	Noah Robinson . .	Yes.	..	Yes.	Yes.	
3210	,,	James Roddis . .	Yes.	..	Yes.	Yes.	
3009	,,	John Rolie	Yes.	..	Yes.	Yes.	
1706	,,	Alexr. Ross	..	..	..	Yes.[4]	
2790	,,	David Ross	Yes.	..	Yes.	Yes.	
3175	,,	William Ross . . .	Yes.	..	Yes.	Yes.	
2992	,,	David Reid	Yes.	..	..	Yes.	
3069	,,	Thomas Rouse . .	Yes.	..	..	Yes.	Died at Balaklava 1 Octr. '54.
3099	,,	Patrick Salmon . .	Yes.	..	Yes.	Yes.	Sent home 24 April '55.[3]
1712	,,	Charles Sanderson . .	Yes.	..	Yes.	Yes.[5]	
3086	,,	William Saxton . .	Yes.	..	..	Yes.	Died at Balaklava 26 Octr. 1854.
2945	,,	John Scott . . .	Yes.	..	..	Yes.[4]	
3030	,,	Robert Scott . .	Yes.	..	Yes.	Yes.	
2905	,,	William Scott . . .	Yes.	..	Yes.	Yes.	
2034	,,	Charles Shanks . .	Yes.	..	Yes.	Yes.	Deceased 21 Feby. '55.[3]
3226	,,	James Sharkey . .	..	..	..	Yes.	
1648	,,	Thomas Shaw . .	Yes.	..	Yes.	Yes.	
3144	,,	Robert Shaw . . .	Yes.	..	Yes.	Yes.	
1415	,,	John Shearer . . .	Yes.	..	Yes.	Yes.	Deceased 23 Feby. '55.[3]
1045	,,	Andrew Sheddan . .	Yes.	..	Yes.[6]	Yes.[6]	Sent home 11 June '55.[3]
2881	,,	Joseph Shillinglaw . .	Yes.	..	Yes.	Yes.	
1772	,,	Robert Sibbalds . .	Yes.	..	Yes.	Yes.	
2061	,,	William Sideserf . .	Yes.	..	Yes.	Yes.	
2467	,,	Peter Sim	..	..	..	Yes.[4]	
3018	,,	Isaac Simpkins . . .	Yes.	..	Yes.	Yes.	
1352	,,	William Simpson . .	Yes.	..	Yes.	Yes.	
3188	,,	James Sinclair . . .	Yes.	..	..	..	Died at Sebastopol (Balaklava) 8 Octr.

[1] Date of death 5th Decr. '54 in Sebastopol Roll.
[2] From Sebastopol Clasp List.
[3] These entries are from the Supplementary Sebastopol Clasp List.
[4] Corporal in Sebastopol List.
[5] No. 1717.
[6] Shedden.

Regtl. No.	Rank.	Name.	Alma.	Inker-man.	Bala-klava.	Sebas-topol.	Remarks.
				Clasps.			
2985	Private	James Skene	Yes.	..	..	..	Died at Scutari 20 Novr.
3068	,,	Joseph Slack	Yes.	..	..	Yes.	Transferred 5 April '55.
2802	,,	Robert Sloane	Yes.	..	Yes.	Yes.	
3279	,,	Samuel Small	Yes.	..	Yes.	Yes.	
3125	,,	Albert Smith	Yes.	..	Yes.	Yes.	
2957	,,	Alexr. Smith	Yes.	..	Yes.	Yes.	
2116	,,	George Smith	Yes.	..	Yes.	..	
2391	,,	James Smith	..	..	Yes.	Yes.	
2132	,,	John Smith, 1	Yes.	..	Yes.	Yes.	
2902	,,	John Smith, 2	Yes.	..	..	Yes.	
3283	,,	Peter Smith	Yes.	..	Yes.	Yes.	
2803	,,	Robert Smith, 1	Yes.	..	..	Yes.	At Scutari.[1]
2826	,,	Robert Smith, 2	Yes.	..	Yes.	Yes.	
2590	,,	Thomas Smith, 1	Yes.	..	Yes.	Yes.	
3309	,,	Thomas Smith, 2	Yes.	..	Yes.	Yes.	
2982	,,	William Smith	Yes.	..	Yes.	Yes.	Deceased. No date known.[1]
2340	,,	Bernard Smyth	Yes.	..	Yes.	Yes.[2]	
2939	,,	Andrew Souter	Yes.	..	Yes.	Yes.	Sent home 22 March.[1] On Certif. Regt. 18/8/58.[3]
2948	,,	Robert Spalding	Yes.	..	Yes.	Yes.	Deceased 25 Decr. '54.[1]
1567	,,	Daniel Spence	Yes.	..	Yes.	Yes.	
1377	,,	John Spence	Yes.	..	Yes.	Yes.	
1380	,,	John Spittal	Yes.	..	Yes.	Yes.	
2019	,,	Thomas Steele	Yes.	..	Yes.	Yes.	
1412	,,	Alexr. Stephen	Yes.	..	Yes.[4]	Yes.	
1769	,,	James Steven	Yes.	..	Yes.	Yes.	Died at Balaklava 30 Oct. (Nov.) 1854
2414	,,	William Stevens	Yes.	..	..	Yes.	Died at Sebastopol (Scutari) 26 Octr. 1854.
3272	,,	Andw. Stevenson	Yes.	..	Yes.	Yes.	
1029	,,	James Stevenson	Yes.	..	Yes.	Yes.	
1876	,,	John Stewart, 1	Yes.	..	Yes.	Yes.	Deceased 24 Augt. 1855.[3]
2937	,,	John Stewart, 2	Yes.	..	Yes.	Yes.	
2185	,,	George Storrie	Yes.	..	Yes.	Yes.	Deceased 14 Feby. 1855.[3]
1386	,,	John Strachan	Yes.	..	..	Yes.	
1655	,,	Robert Strachan	Yes.	..	Yes.	Yes.	
2447	,,	Thomas Surrill	Yes.	..	..	Yes.	Died at Balaklava 22 Novr.
2942	,,	George Sutherland	Yes.	..	Yes.	..	
3462	,,	Daniel Sutherland	Yes.	..	..	Yes.	Deceased 16 July 1855.[3]
1422	,,	George Swan	Yes.	..	Yes.	Yes.	
1894	,,	Mathew Tanner	..	..	..	Yes.[5]	
2599	,,	Peter Tannch	Yes.	..	Yes.[6]	Yes.[6]	
3302	,,	Henry Taylor	Yes.	..	Yes.	Yes.	
2191	,,	John Taylor	..	..	Yes.	Yes.	Died at Balaklava 5 Novr. 1854.
3273	,,	Joseph Taylor	..	..	Yes.	Yes.	Died at Balaklava 18 Decr. '54.
2933	,,	Peter Taylor	Yes.	..	Yes.	Yes.	
2517	,,	William Taylor, 1	Yes.	..	Yes.		
3064	,,	William Taylor, 2	..	..	..	Yes?[7]	Deceased 12 Jany. '55.[1] [7]
3090	,,	William Taylor, 3	..	..	..		
2043	,,	John Telfer	Yes.	..	Yes.	Yes.	Deceased 18 June 1855.[3]
1731	,,	David Tennant	Yes.	..	..	Yes.	
3213	,,	William Thom	Yes.	..	Yes.	Yes.	Sent home 13th Sept. '55.[1]

[1] These entries are from the Supplementary Sebastopol Clasp List.
[3] From Sebastopol Clasp List.   [4] Stephens.   [5] No. 1874.   [2] Smythe.
[7] One of these only, but the number is not given in the Sebastopol Clasp List.   [6] Taunch.

Regtl. No.	Rank.	Name.	Clasps.				Remarks.
			Alma.	Inker-man.	Bala-klava.	Sebas-topol.	
1559	Private	Alexr. Thompson . .	Yes.	..	Yes.	Yes.[1]	
2454	,,	John Thompson, 1 . .	Yes.	..	Yes.	Yes.	
2843	,,	John Thompson, 2 . .	Yes.	..	Yes.	Yes.[1]	
2966	,,	Robert Thompson . .	Yes.	..	Yes.	Yes.	
2336	,,	Thomas Thompson . .	Yes.	..	Yes.	Yes.	
2828	,,	William Thompson, 1 .	Yes.	..	..	Yes.	
3274	,,	William Thompson, 2 .	Yes.	..	Yes.	Yes.	
1292	,,	David Todd . . .	Yes.	..	Yes.	Yes.	
2916	,,	Richard Torrance . .	Yes.	..	Yes.	Yes.	
3067	,,	George Tronson . .	Yes.	..	Yes.	Yes.	
2941	,,	John Tulloch . . .	Yes.	..	..	Yes.	Died at Sebastopol (Balaklava) 3 Oct. 1854.
2950	,,	John Turnbull . . .	..	..	..	Yes.	Deceased 15 Jany. '55.[2]
3153	,,	William Turnbull . .	Yes.	..	Yes.	Yes.	
3232	,,	Philip Tooley . .	Yes.	..	Yes.	Yes.	
3275	,,	George Veal . . .	Yes.	..	Yes.	Yes.	
2201	,,	William Valentine . .	Yes.	..	Yes.	Yes.[3]	
3300	,,	Charles Wagstaff . .	Yes.	..	Yes.	Yes.	
3065	,,	Samuel Wainwright .	Yes.	..	Yes.	Yes.	Deceased 9th Feb. '55.[2]
3076	,,	James Walklett . .	..	..	..	Yes.	Died at Scutari 15 Novr. '55.
3135	,,	Michael Wallace . .	Yes.	..	Yes.	Yes.	
3092	,,	John Warner . . .	Yes.	..	Yes.	Yes.	
1703	,,	John Walters . . .	Yes.	..	Yes.	Yes.	
3110	,,	George Watson . . .	Yes.	..	..	Yes.	
2920	,,	James Watson . . .	..	..	Yes.	..	
3287	,,	William Watson . .	Yes.	..	..	Yes.	
2535	,,	John Watt . . .	Yes.	..	Yes.	Yes.	
3017	,,	William Watt . . .	Yes.	..	Yes.	Yes.	Died at Balaklava 1 Decr. 1854.
2887	,,	Johnston Weir . . .	Yes.	..	Yes.	Yes.[4]	
3120	,,	Wm. Whichello . . .	Yes.	..	..	..	Died at Balaklava 27 Sept.
2130	,,	Duncan White . . .	Yes.	..	Yes.	Yes.	
1770	,,	John White . . .	Yes.	..	..	Yes.	Deceased 18 April '55.[2]
3104	,,	Thomas White . . .	Yes.	..	Yes.	Yes.	Deceased 24 Feby. '55.[2]
1347	,,	Walter White . . .	Yes.	..	..	Yes.	
3073	,,	James Whitehead . .	..	..	Yes.	Yes.	Deceased 15 Feby. '55.[2]
1583	,,	James Whitelaw . .	Yes.	..	Yes.	Yes.	
3192	,,	David Whittel . . .	Yes.	..	..	Yes.	Died at Balaklava 11 Novr. 1854.
3299	,,	George Wiggins . . .	Yes.	..	..	Yes.	
2878	,,	John Wilkie . . .	Yes.	..	Yes.	Yes.	
1553	,,	Walter Wilkie . . .	Yes.	..	Yes.	Yes.	
1127	,,	Mathew Willack . .	Yes.	..	..	Yes.	Sent home 27 Aug. '55. A. and S. Clasp sent.[2]
1197	,,	John Williamson, 1 .	Yes.	..	Yes.	Yes.	
3312	,,	John Williamson, 2 .	Yes.	..	Yes.	Yes.	
3122	,,	John Wright . . .	Yes.	..	Yes.[5]	Yes.	
2527	,,	Edward Wilson . .	Yes.	..	..	..	
2602	,,	James Wilson, 1 . .	Yes.	..	..	..	Died at Belbeck 24 Septr.
2815	,,	James Wilson, 2 . .	Yes.	..	Yes.	Yes.	
1901	,,	John Wilson, 1 . . .	Yes.	..	..	Yes.	
3276	,,	John Wilson, 2 . . .	Yes.	..	Yes.	Yes.	
1979	,,	Robert Wilson . . .	Yes.	..	Yes.	Yes.	

[1] Corporal in Sebastopol List.
[2] These entries are from the Supplementary Sebastopol Clasp List.
[3] Vallentine.
[4] Johnstone Weir.
[5] Wight.

Regtl. No.	Rank.	Name.	Clasps.				Remarks.
			Alma.	Inker-man.	Bala-klava.	Sebas-topol.	
2652	Private	Patrick Wyness	Yes.	..	Yes.	Yes.	
2223	,,	Alexr. Yorkston	Yes.	..	Yes.[1]	Yes.[2]	At Scutari.[3]
2943	,,	George Yorkston	Yes.	..	Yes.[1]	Yes.[2]	
1909	,,	John Yorston	Yes.	..	Yes.	Yes.[4]	
2118	,,	George Young	Yes.	..	Yes.	Yes.	
2996	Boy	Robert Robertson	..	..	Yes.	Yes.[5]	

JOINED FROM ENGLAND 2ND DECEMBER 1854.

Regtl. No.	Rank.	Name.	Clasps.				Remarks.
			Alma.	Inker-man.	Bala-klava.	Sebas-topol.	
2218	Corpl.	James M'Kay	..	..	..	Yes.[5]	
3338	Private	Patrick Aigen	..	..	..	Yes.	
3324	,,	George Ansell	..	..	..	Yes.	Sent home 26 March.[3]
3404	,,	Thomas Asberry	..	..	..	Yes.	Deceased 27 Jany. 1855.[6]
3415	,,	Joseph Bailey	..	..	..	..	
3322	,,	Owen Bawn	..	..	..	Yes.[7]	
3333	,,	Edmond Birmingham	..	..	..	Yes.	
3377	,,	James Bolger	..	..	..	Yes.	
2492	,,	Henry Boyle	..	..	..	Yes.	
3096	,,	John Brien	..	..	..	Yes.	
2327	,,	Patrick Burke	..	..	..	Yes.[8]	
3408	,,	Robert Burns	..	..	..	Yes.	
3351	,,	John Cameron	..	..	..	Yes.	
3342	,,	Henry Chalmers	..	..	..	Yes.	Sent home 31 March.[3]
3352	,,	Walter Chalmers	..	..	..	Yes.	
3368	,,	Hugh Connell	..	..	..	Yes.	At Scutari.[3]
3328	,,	Joseph Cooper	..	..	..	Yes.	
3353	,,	Thomas Dingwall	..	..	..	Yes.	
3390	,,	David Downie	..	..	..	Yes.	
3360	,,	John Duncan	..	..	..	Yes.	
3406	,,	John Dunwoodie	..	..	..	Yes.	
3369	,,	Robt. Fulerton	..	..	..	Yes.	Deceased. No date known.[3]
2882	,,	Daniel Fulton	..	..	..	Yes.	
3355	,,	William Gibb	..	..	..	Yes.[9]	
3358	,,	James Gracey	..	..	..	Yes.[2]	
3389	,,	William Gray	..	..	..	..	
3350	,,	Peter Hanagan	..	..	..	Yes.[10]	Deceased 16 May.[3]
3388	,,	George Irvine	..	..	..	Yes.	
3326	,,	Stephen Keen	..	..	..	Yes.	
3341	,,	John Ledwidge	..	..	..	Yes.	
3348	,,	William Malley	..	..	..	Yes.[11]	
3379	,,	Robert Martin	..	..	..	Yes.	Deceased 22 Feby. '55.[3]
3318	,,	John Mays	..	..	..	Yes.	Deceased 21 Novr. 1855.
3416	,,	George Mead	..	..	..	Yes.	
880	,,	Peter Milroy	..	..	..	Yes.	
3343	,,	Edmund Murphy	..	..	..	Yes.	
3364	,,	Peter M'Auley	..	..	..	Yes.	
3356	,,	Donald M'Donald	..	..	..	Yes.	

[1] Yorkstone. [2] Corporal in Sebastopol Clasp List. [3] These entries are from the Supplementary Sebastopol Clasp List.
[4] No. 1907. [5] Private. [6] From Sebastopol Clasp List. [7] Bawan.
[8] No. 3337. [9] John Gibb. [10] Flanagan. [11] Marley.

Regtl. No.	Rank.	Name.	Clasps.				Remarks.
			Alma.	Inkerman.	Balaklava.	Sebastopol.	
3373	Private	Hugh M'Kechnie . .	..	..	..	Yes.	
3340	,,	John M'Kennarney .	..	..	..	Yes.[1]	
3359	,,	Alexr. M'Kimmie . .	..	..	..	Yes.	Deceased 14 March 1855.[2]
3400	,,	Alexr. M'Leod . . .	..	..	..	Yes.	Deceased 4 July 1855.[2]
3286	,,	William M'Millan . .	..	..	..	Yes.	
3370	,,	William Newall . . .	..	..	..	Yes.	
3384	,,	James O'Neill . .	..	..	..	Yes.	
3298	,,	James Penman . .	..	..	..	Yes.[3]	
3380	,,	Thomas Sweeny . .	..	..	..	Yes.	
3378	,,	George Walker . . .	..	..	..	Yes.	
3320	,,	John Wall	..	..	..	Yes.	
3299	,,	Alexr. Wallace . . .	..	..	..	Yes.	Deceased 12 Feby. '55.[4]
3335	,,	John Waterson . . .	..	..	..	Yes.	

[1] Corporal in Sebastopol Clasp List.   [2] From Sebastopol Clasp List.   [3] John.
[4] These entries are from the Supplementary Sebastopol Clasp List.

REMARKS.

The Regiment being part of the Force stationed on the Height of Balaklava for the protection of the base of operations, was necessarily not engaged at Inkerman, but remained under Arms during the Battle, a strong force of Cavalry, Artillery, and Infantry threatening its front throughout the day.

K

42ND ROYAL HIGHLANDERS

SUPPLEMENTARY LIST OF OFFICERS, NON-COMMISSIONED OFFICERS AND SOLDIERS entitled to receive MEDALS for Service in the CRIMEA.

RANK.	NAME.	Clasps.				REMARKS.
		Alma.	Inker-man.	Bala-klava.	Sebas-topol.	
Major	Charles Murray . . .	..	..	..	Yes.	Joined from England 15 June 1855.
Lieut.	Wilsone Black . . .	..	..	..	Yes.	Joined from England 14 July 1855.
,,	W. A. Crompton . .	..	..	..	Yes.[1]	do. do.
,,	Adam Ferguson . .	..	..	..	Yes.	do. do.
,,	William Baird . . .	..	..	..	Yes.	do. do.
,,	William Green . . .	..	..	..	Yes.	do. do.
,,	F. E. A. Farquharson .	..	..	..	Yes.[2]	do. do.
,,	Honble. R. Stewart .	..	..	..	Yes.	do. do.
Ensign	W. P. Hesketh . . .	..	..	..	Yes.	do. do.
,,	H. J. Bramley . . .	..	..	..	Yes.[3]	do. do.
Regtl. No.						
2140 Private	John Arneil . . .	..	..	..	Yes.	Joined from Scutari 11 June 1855.
3176 ,,	George Watson . .	..	..	..	..	do. do.
3519 Serjt.	Alexr. Fraser . .	..	..	..	Yes.[4]	Joined from England 3 June 1855.
3367 Private	Andw. Allan . . .	..	..	..	Yes.	do. do.
3493 ,,	Francis Anderson . .	..	..	..	Yes.	do. do.
3354 ,,	Andrew Bain . . .	..	..	..	Yes.	do. do.
3431 ,,	James Brown . . .	..	..	..	Yes.	do. do.
3336 ,,	Hugh Byrnes . . .	..	..	..	Yes.[5]	do. do.
3547 ,,	Duncan Cameron . .	..	..	..	Yes.	do. do.
3536 ,,	William Clarke . .	..	..	..	Yes.	do. do.
3513 ,,	Henry Cook . . .	..	..	..	Yes.	do. do.
3620 ,,	William Dick . . .	..	..	..	..	do. do.
3533 ,,	Thomas Dickson . .	..	..	..	Yes.	do. do.
3435 ,,	Alfred Dixon . . .	..	..	..	Yes.	do. do.
3375 ,,	Guildford Dudley . .	..	..	..	Yes.	do. do.
3616 ,,	Peter Elliott . .	..	..	..	Yes.	do. do.
3495 ,,	David Ferguson . .	..	..	..	Yes.	do. do.
3512 ,,	John Few . . .	..	..	..	Yes.	do. do.
3517 ,,	John Formby . . .	..	..	..	Yes.	Transferred 4 April '55.[6] Joined from England 3 June 1855.
3634 ,,	John Fraser . . .	..	..	..	Yes.	do. do.
3511 ,,	Alexr. Gibbs . . .	..	..	..	Yes.	do. do.
3567 ,,	William Hadden . .	..	..	..	Yes.	15 June 1855.[7] Deceased. Joined from England 3 June 1855.
3549 ,,	Archd. Graham . .	..	..	..	Yes.	do. do.
3502 ,,	Festus Heanne . .	..	..	..	..	do. do.
3592 ,,	John Land . . .	..	..	..	Yes.	do. do.
3595 ,,	James Lavell . . .	..	..	..	Yes.	Sent home 7 Septr. 1855.[6] Joined from England 3 June 1855.
3508 ,,	Wm. Matheson . . .	..	..	..	Yes.	do. do.
3478 ,,	James Miller . . .	..	..	..	..	do. do.

[1] W. H. Crompton.   [2] F. E. H. Farquharson.   [3] A. J. Bramley.   [4] Serjt.   [5] Hugh Burns.
[6] These entries are from the Supplementary Sebastopol Clasp List.   [7] From Sebastopol Clasp List.

Regtl. No.	Rank.	Name.	Alma.	Inker-man.	Bala-klava.	Sebas-topol.	Remarks.
				Clasps.			
3521	Private	George Miller	..	..	..	Yes.	Joined from England 3 June 1855.
3569	,,	Alexr. Mill	..	..	..	Yes.[1]	do. do.
3499	,,	Wm. Milner	..	..	..	Yes.	do. do.
3449	,,	Hugh Mitchell	..	..	..	Yes.	do. do.
3563	,,	William Morrison	..	..	..	Yes.	do. do.
							Deceased 25 June 1855.[2]
3487	,,	William Morrison	..	..	..	Yes.[3]	Joined from England 3 June 1855.
3548	,,	William M'Donald	..	..	..	Yes.	do. do.
3610	,,	Dugald M'Phee	..	..	..	Yes.	do. do.
3554	,,	John M'Gurk	..	..	..	Yes.	do. do.
3488	,,	Donald M'Innes	..	..	..	Yes.[4]	do. do.
3590	,,	George M'Laughlin	..	..	..	Yes.	do. do.
3461	,,	Samuel M'Nie	..	..	..	Yes.[5]	do. do.
3568	,,	Stewart Nicol	..	..	..	Yes.	do. do.
3442	,,	Andw. M'Donald	..	..	..	Yes.	do. do.
3490	,,	William Nelson	..	..	..	Yes.[6]	do. do.
3623	,,	John Oliver	..	..	..	Yes.	do. do.
3498	,,	Wm. Pentland	..	..	..	Yes.	do. do.
3660	,,	Robert Redman	..	..	..	Yes.	do. do.
3429	,,	Henry Scobie	..	..	..	Yes.	do. do.
3552	,,	Thomas Turnbull	..	..	..	Yes.	do. do.
3372	,,	Samuel Wade	..	..	..	Yes.	do. do.
3413	,,	William Webster	..	..	..	Yes.	do. do.
3467	,,	George Yeats	..	..	..	Yes.	do. do.
3624	,,	William Young	..	..	..	Yes.	do. do.
3588	Corpl.	Andw. M'Murray	..	..	..	Yes.	Joined from England 15 June 1855.
3596	Private	Peter Anderson	..	..	..	Yes.	do. do.
3509	,,	William Bevis	..	..	..	Yes.	do. do.
3433	,,	Robert Blair	..	..	..	Yes.	do. do.
3537	,,	William Brown	..	..	..	Yes.	do. do.
3542	,,	William Campbell	..	..	..	Yes.	do. do.
							Deceased 29 June 1855.[2]
3524	,,	Michael Convery	..	..	..	Yes.	Joined from England 15 June 1855.
3875	,,	John Cameron	..	..	..	Yes.[7]	do. do.
							Deceased 1 June '55.[8]
3541	,,	Alexr. Cruickshanks	..	..	..	Yes.	Joined from England 15 June 1855.
3119	,,	Francis Curr	..	..	..	Yes.[9]	do. do.
3576	,,	Robert Dawson	..	..	..	Yes.	do. do.
3539	,,	Robert Dow	..	..	..	Yes.	do. do.
3558	,,	James Downie	..	..	..	Yes.	do. do.
3585	,,	David Ford	..	..	..	Yes.	do. do.
3629	,,	Charles Fraser	..	..	..	Yes.[10]	do. do.
3538	,,	Lewis Fraser	..	..	..	Yes.	do. do.
							Sent to England 19 Octr. 1855.[2]
3594	,,	John Grubb	..	..	..	Yes.	Joined from England 15 June 1855.
3424	,,	Edward Hill	..	..	..	Yes.	do. do.
3386	,,	James Hamilton	..	..	..	Yes.	do. do.
3618	,,	James Hope	..	..	..	Yes.	do. do.
3583	,,	Andrew Hurst	..	..	..	Yes.	do. do.
3540	,,	Robert Jamieson	..	..	..	Yes.	do. do.
3537	,,	William Jamieson	..	..	..	Yes.	do. do.

[1] Milne.   [2] From the Sebastopol Clasp List.   [3] No. 3489.   [4] Duncan M'Innes.
[5] M'Nil.   [6] Neilson.   [7] 2875.
[8] These entries are from the Supplementary Sebastopol Clasp List.   [9] Carr, 3619.   [10] Frazier.

Regtl. No.	Rank.	Name.	Clasps.				Remarks.
			Alma.	Inkerman.	Balaklava.	Sebastopol.	
3582	Private	John Johnstone	..	..	..	Yes.	Joined from England 15 June 1855.
3593	,,	James Logan	..	..	..	Yes.	do. do.
3575	,,	Willm. Murray	..	..	..	Yes.	do. do.
3597	,,	Charles Muirhead	..	..	..	Yes.	do. do.
3422	,,	Donald M'Donald	..	..	..	Yes.	do. do.
3485	,,	James M'Donald	..	..	..	Yes.	do. do.
3470	,,	Daniel M'Ewan	..	..	..	Yes.	do. do.
							Sent to England 19 Octr. 1855.[1]
3571	,,	John M'Ilwaine	..	..	..	Yes.	Joined from England 15 June 1855.
3602	,,	Duncan M'Keen	..	..	..	Yes.	do. do.
3523	,,	Thomas M'Learn	..	..	..	Yes.[2]	do. do.
3643	,,	Fredk. M'Lean	..	..	..	Yes.	do. do.
3469	,,	John M'Gregor	..	..	..	Yes.	do. do.
3659	,,	James Nichollass	..	..	..	Yes.[3]	do. do.
3270	,,	James Neill	..	..	..	Yes.	do. do.
3572	,,	John Nowland	..	..	..	Yes.[4]	do. do.
3598	,,	Angus Scott	..	..	..	Yes.	do. do.
3578	,,	George Smith	..	..	..	Yes.	do. do.
3539	,,	William Steven	..	..	..	Yes.	do. do.
3448	,,	William Stewart	..	..	..	Yes.	do. do.
——	,,	William Stewart	..	..	..	..	do. do.
3662	,,	William Tomlinson	..	..	..	Yes.	do. do.
—	,,	David Walker	..	..	..	..	do. do.
3441	Serjt.	John Malins	..	..	..	Yes.	Joined from England 11 July 1855.
3025	Private	Robert Armstrong	..	..	..	Yes.	do. do.
							At Scutari.[5]
3617	,,	Michael Brown	..	..	..	Yes.	Joined from England 11 July 1855.
3615	,,	George Campbell	..	..	..	Yes.	do. do.
5555	,,	John Harrison	..	..	..	Yes.	do. do.
3575	,,	Martin Hyland	..	..	..	Yes.[6]	do. do.
3564	,,	Thomas Lithead	..	..	..	Yes.	do. do.
							Deceased 17 Aug. 1855.[5]
3630	,,	David Lyell	..	..	..	Yes.	Joined from England 11 July 1855.
3639	,,	Archd. Morrison	..	..	..	Yes.	do. do.
3532	,,	James M'Donald	..	..	..	Yes.	do. do.
							Sent to England 19 Octr. 1855.[1]
3565	,,	James Queen	..	..	..	Yes.	Joined from England 11 July 1855.
3661	,,	James Sharpless	..	..	..	Yes.	do. do.
3641	,,	John Templeton	..	..	..	Yes.	do. do.
							At Kulali.
3640	,,	James Watt	..	..	..	Yes.	Joined from England 11 July 1855.
3654	Corpl.	Robert Adams	..	..	..	Yes.	Joined from England 14th July 1855.
3682	,,	Arthur Robb	..	..	..	Yes.	do. do.
2280	Drumr.	James Cameron	..	..	..	Yes.	do. do.
3763	Private	David Bell	..	..	..	Yes.	do. do.
2525	,,	Edward Bonner	..	..	..	Yes.[7]	do. do.
3459	,,	Mathew Bourbank	..	..	..	Yes.	do. do.
							Deceased 6 Aug. 1855.[1]
3520	,,	John Brown	..	..	..	Yes.	Joined from England 14th July 1855.
3678	,,	William Brown	..	..	..	Yes.	do. do.
3697	,,	Alexr. Burgess	..	..	..	Yes.	do. do.

[1] From the Sebastopol Clasp List.　　　[2] M'Laren.　　　[3] Nicholas.　　　[4] John Nolan.
[5] These entries are from the Supplementary Sebastopol Clasp List.　　　[6] No. 3573.　　　[7] No. 2523.

Regtl. No.	Rank.	Name.	Clasps.				Remarks.
			Alma.	Inker-man.	Bala-klava.	Sebas-topol.	
3635	Private	Thomas Burns . . .	..	..	..	Yes.	Joined from England 14th July 1855.
3734	,,	James Campbell . .	..	..	..	Yes.	do. do.
3681	,,	James Davidson . .	..	..	..	..	do. do. Deceased.
3680	,,	David Deas . . .	..	..	..	Yes.[1]	do. do.
3152	,,	Quintin Devine . . .	..	..	..	Yes.	do. do.
3724	,,	James Drummond . .	..	..	..	Yes.	do. do.
3671	,,	William Fairlie . .	..	..	..	Yes.	do. do.
3747	,,	John Fleming . .	..	..	..	Yes.	do. do.
3730	,,	John Gillespie . .	..	..	..	Yes.[2]	do. do.
3332	,,	Edwd. Gilligan . .	..	..	..	Yes.	do. do.
3698	,,	Alexr. Hutton . .	..	..	..	Yes.	do. do.
3464	,,	Michael Leonard . .	..	..	..	Yes.[3]	do. do.
3759	,,	Wm. Matthew . .	..	..	..	Yes.	do. do.
3666	,,	James Moffatt . .	..	..	..	Yes.	do. do.
3673	,,	Henry Morrison . .	..	..	..	Yes.	do. do.
3708	,,	James Moubray . .	..	..	..	Yes.	do. do.
3476	,,	Richd. M'Donald . .	..	..	..	Yes.	Deceased 12 Aug. 1855.[4]
3712	,,	James M'Dougal . .	..	..	..	Yes.	Joined from England 14th July 1855.
3649	,,	Peter M'Intosh . .	..	..	..	Yes.	do. do.
3713	,,	Hugh M'Intyre . .	..	..	..	Yes.	do. do.
3704	,,	Alexr. M'Laughlin .	..	..	..	Yes.	do. do.
3700	,,	Neil M'Neil . . .	..	..	..	Yes.	Deceased 13 Augt. 1855.[5]
3497	,,	Alexr. Napier . .	..	..	..	Yes.	Joined from England 14th July 1855.
3688	,,	John Neilson . .	..	..	..	Yes.	do. do.
3677	,,	James Nichol . .	..	..	..	Yes.	do. do.
3684	,,	William Nimmo . .	..	..	..	Yes.[6]	do. do.
2777	,,	Alexr. Ogilvie . .	..	..	..	Yes.	do. do.
3223	,,	John O'Reilly . .	..	..	..	Yes.	Sent to England 19 Octr. 1855.[5]
3699	,,	David Plain . . .	..	..	..	Yes.	Joined from England 14th July 1855.
3653	,,	William Ramage . .	..	..	..	Yes.	do. do.
3723	,,	Thomas Ritchie . .	..	..	..	Yes.	do. do.
3696	,,	James Rodgers . .	..	..	..	Yes.	do. do.
3760	,,	Robert Ross . .	..	..	..	Yes.	do. do.
3773	,,	William Ross . .	..	..	..	..	do. do.
3676	,,	Thomas Shepherd . .	..	..	..	Yes.	do. do.
3748	,,	Thomas Small . .	..	..	..	Yes.	do. do.
3462	,,	Daniel Sutherland . .	..	..	..	..	do. do. Deceased.
3790	,,	Andw. Thompson . .	..	..	..	Yes.	do. do.
3652	,,	John Thompson . .	..	..	..	Yes.	do. do.
3664	,,	Philip Ward . .	..	..	..	..	do. do.
3721	,,	Alexr. Watson . .	..	..	..	Yes.	do. do.
3727	,,	John Williamson . .	..	..	..	Yes.	do. do.
1727	,,	David Wilson . .	..	..	..	Yes.	do. do.
3344	,,	John Hayslip . .	..	..	..	Yes.	do. do.

The above names all appear in the Roll first made out for the Crimea Medal and Alma-Inkerman Clasps. The draft joining on 2nd Decr. 1854, and the Supplementary List, are at the end of the original.

[1] 3682 Sebastopol Roll. [2] No. 2730. [3] Mathew Leonard.
[4] These entries are from the Supplementary Sebastopol Clasp List. [5] From Sebastopol Clasp List.
[6] William Kimms.

In addition to the above, the following names are in the Sebastopol Clasp Roll, but not in either the Alma-Inkerman or Balaklava Clasp Rolls. Judging from the high Regimental Numbers of the majority of these men, it seems likely that they formed part of the last draft sent to the Regiment, but there appears to be no reason why they should not receive the Medal if entitled to the Sebastopol Clasp.—J. S.

Regtl. No.	Rank.	Name.	Regtl. No.	Rank.	Name.	Regtl. No.	Rank.	Name.
2289	Corpl.	John Dickson.	3164	Piper	Dond. M'Pherson.	3791	Pte.	Wm. M'Gavin.
1673	Pte.	George Campbell.[1]	3599	Pte.	Andw. Brown.	3767	,,	Wm. M'Kenzie.
3224	,,	Patk. Donohoe.[2]	3638	,,	John Cameron.	3817	,,	Jas. M'Kinnon.
2991	,,	James Finlayson.[3]	3768	,,	John Hicks.	3321	,,	Henry Naxton.
3238	,,	George Gill.[4]	2612	,,	John Kenniburgh.	2898	,,	Wm. Small.
2771	,,	Wm. Gordon.[5]	3243	,,	Bernd. Malady.	2428	,,	James Trainer.
—	,,	Wm. Mathes.[6]	—	,,	Alexr. Miller.	—	,,	Charles Walker.
—	,,	Wm. Muirhead.[7]	3191	,,	Thos. M'Ennis.	—	,,	Thos. Ward.

The following are the entries against the names in the 'Remarks' Column:—

[1] Deceased 27 May.   [2] At Kulali.   [3] Deceased 23 July '55.   [4] Sent home 14 Oct. '54.
[5] Sent home 9 June '54.   [6] At Scutari.   [7] Deceased 13 Jany. '55.

42ND

ROLL OF OFFICERS, N.C.O.'S AND MEN

OF

HER MAJESTY'S 42ND ROYAL HIGHLAND REGIMENT

WHO HAVE BEEN EMPLOYED IN THE SUPPRESSION OF

THE MUTINY IN INDIA

ROLL OF OFFICERS AND MEN OF H.M. 42ND ROYAL HIGHLAND REGIMENT who have been employed in the Suppression of the MUTINY IN INDIA.

CAMP PHILLEEBEET, 25th October 1858.

Services for which entitled to Medal } Engaged in the late Campaign in the open Field in the N.W. Provinces.

RANK AND NAMES.	If engaged in the Operations against Lucknow from 2nd to 16th March /58.	REMARKS.
Lt.-Col. A. Cameron	Yes.	Died of fever, 9th Augst. /58.
„ G. E. Thorold	No.	Proceeded down country 1st Jany. /58. Retired on Full Pay 16th March 1858.
„ F. G. Wilkinson	Yes.	Coming home on leave.
„ E. R. Priestly	„	
Major J. C. M'Leod	„	
„ Jno. Drysdale	„	
Capt. Geo. Fraser	„	
„ W. C. Ward	„	
„ Duncan M'Pherson . . .	„	
„ J. C. R. Grove	„	
„ F. C. Scott	„	
„ R. H. Gordon	No.	
„ H. H. Moseley	Yes.	
„ W. Baird	„	
„ Jno. Wilson	„	
„ Will Lawson	„	Died of wounds, 19 August 1859.
Lieut. Chas. Douglas	„	Died of wounds 17th April /58.
„ Will Green	„	
„ F. E. H. Farquharson . . .	„	Coming home.
„ M. M'Leod	„	
„ G. W. Cockburn	„	
„ Hon. R. H. Stewart . . .	„	
„ F. J. Bramley	„	Killed in action, 15th Apr. 1858.
„ R. K. Bayly	„	Coming home.
„ P. M. Bosworth	„	Died of dysentery 19th June 1858.
„ G. A. Furse	„	
„ W. James	„	
Ensgn. A. J. Ceely	„	
„ J. E. Christie	„	
„ W. H. Spooner	„	
„ S. G. M'Dakin	„	
„ F. G. Coleridge	„	Promoted to a Lieutenancy in the 25th Foot, 2nd Battn.
„ W. S. Walter	„	
„ H. W. Fielden	„	
Adjt. W. Wood (Lieut.)	„	Coming home.
Surgeon J. S. Furlong . . .	„	
Asst. Surgn. A. M'Lean . . .	„	
„ T. A. Thornhill . . .	„	Exchanged to the 7th Hussars.
„ A. Hooper	„	
Qr.-Mr. A. M'Gregor	„	Transferred to 22nd Depot Battalion, Stirling Castle.
Pay-Mr. J. A. Bazalgette	„	Coming home.

L

	RANK AND NAMES.	If engaged in the Operations against Lucknow from 2nd to 16th March /58.	REMARKS.
	Serjt.-Major Peter White (2230) . .	Yes.	
	Qr.-Mr.-Sjt. John Simpson (2220) . .	,,	
	P.-Mr.-Serjt. James Brown (1327) .	,,	
	Insr. of Musky. James Anderson (104).	,,	
	As. Serjt. Henry Bancroft (3) . . .	,,	
	Drum-Major George Benzie (2136) .	,,	
Regtl. No.			
2120	Hospl. Serjt. Steven, Thomas .		
2995	O.R. Clerk Robertson, John .	,,	
1964	Pipe-Major Irvine, George .	,,	
1153	Cr.-Serjt. Brown, Wilson . .	,,	
2825	,, Forbes, John . .	,,	
1469	,, Gardner, William .	,,	
1999	,, Johnstone, Andrew .	,,	
2986	,, Landles, Andrew .	,,	Killed in action, Jany. 1859.
2589	,, Ridley, Thomas . .	,,	Died of wounds, 3 May 1858.
2156	,, Strathearn, William .	,,	
2647	,, Torrance, Thomas .	,,	
2500	,, Watt, John . . .	,,	
1223	,, Dalgleish, David .	,,	Died 1st May 1858.
1869	,, Peebles, David .	,,	
2253	,, Stephen, John . .	,,	
2106	Serjt. Adams, Thomas . .	,,	Died 1st July 1858.
1966	,, Aden, Alexander. . .	,,	
4076	,, Aymers, George . . .	,,	Medal returned. Deserted Put with Duplicate Medals.
2845	,, Barclay, John . . .	,,	
3609	,, Barr, John	,,	
2832	,, Black, John	,,	
3454	,, Butters, James . . .	,,	
1249	,, Fraser, George . . .	,,	Died 6th October /58.
1718	,, Fraser, James . . .	,,	Killed 15th April /58.
1986	,, Hartley, Joseph . .	,,	
2552	,, Hiddle, John	,,	Died 31st May /58.
2638	,, Hunter, James . . .	,,	Drowned on his way to England, 1859.
2573	,, Johnstone, George . .	,,	Discharged 19th Jany. 1860.
1277	,, Leitch, Alexr. . . .	,,	Died 20th May /58.
1748	,, Miller, James, 1 . . .	,,	
3161	,, Miller, James, 2 . . .	,,	
1138	,, Leitch, Thomas . .	,,	
2289	,, Dickson, John . . .	,,	
2496	,, · Fox, George . . .	,,	
64	,, French, Wm. H. . .	,,	
2084	,, Moir, Alexr.	,,	
2820	,, Moodie, David . . .	,,	
1568	,, Mullins, John . . .	,,	
1429	,, Murray, James . . .	,,	
3209	,, Mumford, Joseph . .	,,	
3438	,, M'Arthur, George . .	,,	
2581	,, M'Ausland, David . .	,,	Discharged 19th Jany. 1860.
2621	,, M'Culloch, George . .	,,	Died 9th Apr. /58.
1563	,, M'Kay, Alexr. . . .	,,	
4206	,, M'Kay, Dick	,,	
2233	,, M'Millan, John . . .	,,	Died 22nd May /58.

Regtl. No.	Rank and Names.	If engaged in the Operations against Lucknow from 2nd to 16th March /58.	Remarks.
2199	Serjt. M'Pherson, Duncan . .	Yes.	Died 11th Augt. /58.
2321	,, M'Sally, Edward . .	,,	
1618	,, M'Tavish, Donald . .	,,	
2027	,, Rankin, George . . .	,,	
2154	,, Reid, John	,,	Died 19th Apr. /58.
1580	,, Robertson, Charles . .	,,	
1875	,, Scott, George . . .	,,	Died 19th July /58.
2221	,, Taylor, William . . .	,,	
1823	,, Thompson, John, 1 . .	,,	
2843	,, Thompson, John, 2 . .	,,	
2754	,, Wilson, Charles . . .	,,	
3632	,, Wilson, James . . .	,,	
2188	,, Lockhart, Hugh . . .	,,	
1930	Corpl. Allan, John	,,	
2611	,, Arbuckle, George . .	,,	Discharged 19th Aug. 1860.
1835	,, Bain, William . . .	,,	
1525	,, Blacklie, Robert . . .	,,	Died 14th June /58.
1728	,, Blellock, John . . .	,,	
2816	,, Brown, Andrew . . .	,,	
1125	,, Brown, Thomas . . .	,,	
4127	,, Cameron, Hugh . . .	,,	
1428	,, Donaldson, James . .	,,	
3078	,, Farrady, Thomas . . .	,,	
2242	,, Fleming, George . . .	,,	
3358	,, Gracie, James . . .	,,	
805	,, Grant, George . . .	,,	Died 8th May /58.
2791	,, Hepburn, Andrew . .	,,	
3363	,, Hynd, John	,,	
1520	,, Ingram, Robert . . .	,,	
3830	,, Lillie, John	,,	
65	,, Livestone, William . .	No.	Died 15th Decr. /57.
1319	,, Miller, William . . .	Yes.	
2050	,, Minnes, William . . .	,,	
66	,, M'Crory, John . . .	,,	Transferred to 24th Foot, 1st Battalion, May 1858.
1974	,, M'Farlane, Duncan . .	,,	
1388	,, M'Gregor, James . . .	,,	
1957	,, M'Intosh, James . . .	,,	
1150	,, M'Kenzie, Donald . .	,,	
1379	,, M'Lardy, Donald . .	,,	Died 24th May '58.
3995	,, M'Laren, Thomas . .	,,	
1166	,, M'Leod, John . . .	,,	
4256	,, M'Lellan, Hugh . . .	,,	
2094	,, M'Nair, Robert . . .	,,	
2846	,, M'Nichol, John . . .	,,	
3042	,, Oakley, Francis . . .	,,	
2925	,, Ritchie, Archd. . . .	,,	
2780	,, Robertson, Walter . .	,,	
2098	,, Ross, William, 1 . .	,,	
3417	,, Ross, William, 2 . .	,,	Died 12 Sept. '58.
2881	,, Shillinglan, Joseph . .	,,	
3018	,, Simpkins, Isaac . . .	,,	
2803	,, Smith, Robert . . .	,,	
1377	,, Spence, John	,,	
2916	,, Torrance, Richard . .	,,	

Regtl. No.	Rank and Names.	If engaged in the Operations against Lucknow from 2nd to 16th March /58.	Remarks.
1559	Corpl. Thompson, Alexr. . .	Yes.	
2966	,, Thompson, Robert . .	,,	Died 21 Sept. '58.
2336	,, Thompson, Thomas . .	,,	
68	,, Warner, William . .	,,	
3176	,, Watson, George . .	,,	
69	,, Whitelaw, John . .	,,	
1979	,, Wilson, Robert . . .	,,	
67	,, Wilson, George . . .	,,	
1909	,, Yovestone, John . .	,,	
2118	,, Young, George . . .	,,	
2210	,, Yule, Peter	,,	
4048	Drummer Bonnar, Andrew .	,,	
3394	,, Brodie, Robert . .	,,	
3411	,, Cribbes, Robert . .	,,	
3456	,, Duncan, Henry . .	,,	
2273	,, Evans, Charles . .	,,	
3802	,, Fraser, Alexder. .	,,	
3393	,, Lawson, John . .	,,	Died 26 June '58.
4331	,, Jamieson, William .	,,	
4025	,, Milne, Archd. .	,,	
4065	,, Moore, William . .	,,	
2068	,, Morrison, Andrew .	,,	
3636	,, Mullins, Hugh . .	,,	
3791	,, M'Gavin, William .	,,	
2714	,, M'Kenzie, Lewis .	,,	Died 18 June '58.
2762	,, M'Leod, James . .	,,	
3401	,, M'Leod, William .	,,	
3398	,, Ross, James . . .	,,	
3810	,, Russell, David . .	,,	
3809	,, Wilson, James . .	,,	
4024	,, Gibson, Angus . .	,,	
2284	,, Muir, David . . .	,,	
4054	,, M'Kay, Thomas .	,,	
2976	,, M'Leod, Angus . .	,,	
2438	,, M'Leod, William .	,,	
3164	,, M'Pherson, Donald .	,,	
1677	Private Adam, Robert . . .	,,	
3316	,, Adams, John . . .	,,	
3033	,, Adams, Robert, 1 . .	,,	
3654	,, Adams, Robert, 2 . .	,,	
3857	,, Aitken, William . .	,,	
38	,, Aitken, George . .	,,	
3193	,, Allan, John . . .	,,	
3844	,, Allan, William . . .	,,	
4163	,, Anderson, Henry . .	,,	Died 14 May '58.
2504	,, Anderson, James, 1 .	,,	Discharged 19 Jany. 1860.
2676	,, Anderson, James, 2 .	,,	
3750	,, Anderson, James, 3 .	,,	
11	,, Anderson, James, 4 .	,,	
2190	,, Anderson, John, 1 .	,,	
4143	,, Anderson, John, 2 .	,,	
3596	,, Anderson, Peter . .	,,	
3306	,, Anderson, Robert . .	,,	Died 10 Septr. '58.
3840	,, Anderson, Smith . .	,,	
3154	,, Angus, John . . .	,,	

Regtl. No.	RANK AND NAMES.	If engaged in the Operations against Lucknow from 2nd to 16th March /58.	REMARKS.
3324	Private Ansell, George . . .	Yes.	
2910	,, Archibald, Henry . .	,,	
3926	,, Armer, John . . .	,,	Deserted 5 March '58.
2140	,, Arniel, John . . .	,,	
4328	,, Auld, Robert . . .	,,	
3049	,, Axe, Mark	,,	
3166	,, Bain, John	,,	
3560	,, Baird, William . .	,,	
4159	,, Bates, Joseph . . .	,,	Died of wounds 12 May '58.
4240	,, Ballard, John . . .	,,	
70	,, Barber, Thomas . .	,,	
1812	,, Barclay, William, 1 .	,,	To England 4 Augst. '58.
2117	,, Barclay, William, 2 .	,,	
3248	,, Barnes, James . . .	,,	Died 2 May '58.
2569	,, Barr, Allan . . .	,,	Discharged 28th Feby. 1860.
2429	,, Bathgate, Ronald . .	,,	
16	,, Bateman, Charles . .	,,	
3288	,, Baxter, John . . .	,,	
2099	,, Bell, James . . .	,,	
4068	,, Bell, Thomas . . .	,,	Died 18 April '58.
3445	,, Bell, William . . .	,,	
3081	,, Bennett, John . . .	,,	
71	,, Blaber, William . .	,,	
3250	,, Blair, David . . .	,,	
3433	,, Blair, Robert . . .	,,	
1115	,, Black, Ronald . . .	,,	Died 3 July '58.
3167	,, Boag, Robert . . .	,,	
1234	,, Bogle, Joseph . . .	,,	
3377	,, Bolger, James . . .	,,	
72	,, Bland, William . .	,,	
4283	,, Bonnar, John . . .	,,	Died 9 Augst. '58.
2660	,, Borthwick, Angus . .	,,	
2217	,, Bowie, Angus . . .	,,	
3823	,, Boyle, William . .	,,	
2182	,, Brackie, Richard . .	,,	To England 23 Sept. '58. Discharged 24 March 1859.
73	,, Braeslane, Daniel . .	,,	
4074	,, Brennan, James . .	,,	
3231	,, Brennan, Peter . .	,,	
4023	,, Brenton, John . . .	,,	
1478	,, Brodie, Adam . . .	,,	Killed 15 Apr. '58.
3097	,, Brooks, William . .	,,	
3251	,, Brothwell, Charles .	,,	
3599	,, Brown, Andrew . .	,,	
3089	,, Brown, Charles . .	,,	Died 18 June '58.
1411	,, Brown, David . . .	,,	Discharged 28 Feby. 1860.
2532	,, Brown, George . .	,,	
3215	,, Brown, James, 1 . .	,,	
3431	,, Brown, James, 2 . .	,,	
2889	,, Brown, John, 1 . .	,,	
3957	,, Brown, John, 2 . .	,,	
74	,, Brown, John, 3 . .	,,	To England 14 July '58. Discharged.
3617	,, Brown, Michael . .	,,	
75	,, Brown, Richard . .	,,	
2897	,, Brown, Robert . .	,,	

Regtl. No.	Rank and Names.	If engaged in the Operations against Lucknow from 2nd to 16th March /58.	Remarks.
2703	Private Brown, Thomas, 1 .	Yes.	
2733	,, Brown, Thomas, 2	,,	
1981	,, Brown, William, 1 .	,,	
2582	,, Brown, William, 2 .	,,	
3678	,, Brown, William, 3 .	,,	
2761	,, Bruce, Henry . . .	,,	
4184	,, Bryson, Andrew . .	,,	
2700	,, Bryson, John . . .	,,	
3020	,, Buchanan, Andrew .	,,	Killed 5 May '58.
2520	,, Buchanan, James . .	,,	Died 4 June '58.
1809	,, Buchanan, John . .	,,	
4282	,, Bunch, James . . .	,,	
3697	,, Burgess, Alexder. . .	,,	Died 12 June '58.
3206	,, Burke, Michael . .	,,	
3337	,, Burke, Patrick . .	,,	
—	,, Burns, Robert . . .	,,	
2508	,, Burns, William . .	,,	Died 5 July 1858.
76	,, Burrows, William . .	,,	
2830	,, Cairns, William . .	,,	Died 7 June '58.
4111	,, Calderwood, John . .	,,	
2502	,, Cameron, Duncan . .	,,	Discharged.
3963	,, Cameron, John . .	,,	
3035	,, Cameron, William . .	,,	
4318	,, Campbell, Angus . .	,,	
2020	,, Campbell, Duncan .	,,	
3285	,, Campbell, James, 1 .	,,	
3734	,, Campbell, James, 2 .	,,	Died 8 Apr. '58.
4092	., Campbell, James, 3 .	,,	
2557	,, Campbell, John, 1 .	,,	
3843	,, Campbell, John, 2 .	,,	
3225	,, Canny, Ralph . . .	,,	
4252	,, Carrabine, John . .	,,	
1237	,, Carplin, Robert . .	,,	Died 9 Sept. '58.
2649	,, Casills, Nichol . . .	,,	Discharged 19 Jany. 1860.
2912	,, Caw, John	,,	
3352	,, Chalmers, Walter . .	,,	
28	,, Chalmers, William .	,,	
1351	,, Chisholm, Alexder. .	,,	
2753	,, Christie, George .	,,	
1672	,, Christie, James .	,,	
2814	., Clark, David . . .	,,	
2485	,, Clark, John, 1 . . .	,,	
3197	,, Clark, John, 2 . . .	,,	
3240	,, Clark, Thomas . . .	,,	
3536	,, Clark, William, 1 . .	,,	
4179	,, Clark, William, 2 . .	,,	
35	,, Clark, William, 3 . .	,,	
2567	,, Clunie, James . . .	,,	Discharged 19th Jany. 1860.
4121	,, Colvin, David . . .	,,	
2865	,, Colvin, John . . .	,,	
3780	,, Connor, Archd. . .	,,	
3886	,, Cook, Alexander . .	,,	
4033	,, Cook, William . .	,,	
62	,, Cook, Walter . . .	,,	
4086	,, Cooper, Quibell . .	,,	

Regtl. No.	RANK AND NAMES.	If engaged in the Operations against Lucknow from 2nd to 16th March /58.	REMARKS.
3405	Private Cooper, Robert, 1 . .	Yes.	
77	,, Cooper, Robert, 2 . .	,,	
3229	,, Cooper, Samuel . .	,,	
4071	,, Corbet, Samuel . .	,,	
3141	,, Cormack, Alexder. .	,,	Died 20 June '58.
78	,, Corry, John . . .	,,	
79	,, Coulter, Robert . .	,,	
80	,, Cox, James . . .	,,	
3254	,, Cox, William . . .	,,	
1924	,, Craig, James . . .	,,	
2079	,, Craig, Mathew . . .	,,	
81	,, Cronan, John . . .	,,	Died 6 Oct. '58.
126	,, Cronan, David . . .	,,	
2893	,, Cross, William . . .	,,	
4102	,, Crosson, Robert . .	,,	
82	,, Cronghan, James . .	,,	
2290	,, Cumsty, James . .	,,	
3619	,, Curr, Francis . . .	No.	Died 7 July '58.
4154	,, Currie, George . . .	Yes.	
2195	,, Cramb, Duncan . .	,,	Died 15 June '58.
3010	,, Crawford, John . .	,,	
3091	,, Crawley, Mathew . .	,,	
83	,, Daly, Richard . . .	,,	
3133	,, Daughney, Patrick .	,,	
3115	,, Davidson, James . .	,,	
2640	,, Davidson, John . .	,,	Discharged 19th Jany. 1860.
3159	,, Davies, James . . .	,,	
3118	,, Dawson, Alfred . .	,,	
3576	,, Dawson, Robert . .	,,	
84	,, Deere, James . . .	,,	
85	,, Delaney, Thomas . .	,,	
2081	,, Dewar, William . .	,,	
2236	,, Dick, Thomas . . .	,,	
3938	,, Dick, Walter . . .	No.	Died 22 May 1858.
2926	,, Dickson, John . . .	Yes.	
2954	,, Dickson, Peter . .	,,	
2838	,, Dickson, Robert . .	,,	
3553	,, Dickson, Thomas . .	,,	
4268	,, Digby, George . . .	,,	
3353	,, Dingwall, Thomas .	,,	
3435	,, Dixon, Alfred . . .	,,	
4211	,, Docherty, Patrick . .	,,	
4259	,, Dodd, Michael . . .	,,	Died 4 July '58.
2127	,, Dodds, William . .	,,	
1863	,, Doig, Alexder. . . .	,,	
3679	,, Donaldson, Wemyss .	,,	
3224	,, Donohoe, Patrick . .	,,	
86	,, Dorthwaite, John . .	,,	
3074	,, Dougherty, Michael .	,,	
17	,, Douglas, Robert . .	,,	
3558	,, Downie, James . .	,,	
2627	,, Downie, Robert . .	,,	Discharged 19th Jany. 1860.
3851	,, Downie, William . .	,,	
3106	,, Doyle, Francis . . .	,,	Died of wounds, 11 March '58.
87	,, Doyle, Joseph . . .	,,	

Regtl. No.	Rank and Names.	If engaged in the Operations against Lucknow from 2nd to 16th March /58.	Remarks.
53	Private Draper, Henry . .	Yes.	
3724	„ Drummond, James .	„	
1570	„ Dudgeon, Peter . .	„	
3375	„ Dudley, Guildford . .	„	
3138	„ Duncan, John, 1 . .	„	
3360	„ Duncan, John, 2 . .	„	
3942	„ Duncan, Thomas . .	„	
1804	„ Duncan, William . .	„	Died of wounds, 16th April 1858.
3172	„ Dunlop, David . .	„	
2934	„ Dunns, James . . .	„	Died of wounds 28 April '58.
3406	„ Dunwoodie, John . .	„	
2977	„ Eadie, James . . .	„	Killed 15 April '58.
2726	„ Early, John . . .	„	
3076	„ Eaton, Joseph . . .	„	
88	„ Eldridge, Ambrose .	„	
3616	„ Elliott, Peter . . .	„	Died 4 Augst. '58.
3184	„ Etchison, John . .	No.	Died 17 May '58.
3510	„ England, George . .	Yes.	
3671	„ Fairley, William . .	„	Died 17 April '58.
4108	„ Farmer, Henry . .	„	
34	„ Faulkner, Henry . .	„	
3892	„ Fenwick, John . .	„	
3921	„ Fergie, David . . .	„	
3495	„ Ferguson, David . .	„	
1928	„ Ferguson, John, 1 . .	„	
2717	„ Ferguson, John, 2 . .	„	
3829	„ Ferguson, John, 3 . .	„	
63	„ Ferguson, William .	„	
3512	„ Few, John	„	
3103	„ Fitzgerald, Philip . .	„	
89	„ Flannagan, David . .	„	
3040	„ Flynn, Patrick . .	„	
3157	„ Forrester, William .	„	
4232	„ Forsyth, Jacob . .	„	
4180	„ Foy, William . . .	„	
3629	„ Fraser, Charles . .	„	Killed 15 April '58.
3151	„ Fraser, Donald . .	„	
4142	„ Fraser, Simon . . .	„	
2551	„ Frew, William . . .	„	Discharged 19th Jany. 1860.
56	„ Fuse, Henry . . .	„	
4197	„ Fullarton, James . .	„	
2882	„ Fulton, Daniel . . .	„	
3036	„ Galbraith, Robert . .	„	
90	„ Gatcliffe, John . .	„	Died 11 May 1858.
3434	„ Gardner, William . .	„	
4287	„ Gardner, John . . .	„	Killed 9 March '58.
3669	„ Gavin, James . . .	„	
3355	„ Gibb, John	„	
3835	„ Gibson, John . . .	„	
2407	„ Gilchrist, James . .	„	
3871	„ Gilderthorpe, Charles .	„	
57	„ Gill, William . . .	„	
3836	„ Gilles, Joseph . . .	„	
3658	„ Gillespie, George . .	„	
3332	„ Gilligan, Edward . .	„	

Regtl. No.	Rank and Names.	If engaged in the Operations against Lucknow from 2nd to 16th March /58.	Remarks.
2134	Private Glen, George . . .	Yes.	
55	„ Goodman, Samuel .	„	
3932	„ Gordon, Thomas . .	„	
4085	„ Gordon, David . .	„	
3701	„ Gorrin, Fredk. . . .	„	
3466	„ Gourlay, Robert . .	„	
4004	„ Gourlay, Thomas . .	„	
91	„ Gowers, William . .	„	
3549	„ Graham, Archd. . .	„	
1751	„ Graham, John, 1 . .	„	
4029	„ Graham, John, 2 . .	„	
92	„ Graham, Robert . .	„	Died 31 July '58.
3079	„ Graham, William . .	„	
4050	„ Grant, James . . .	„	
58	„ Grant, Mark . . .	No.	Killed 5 Decr. '57.
52	„ Grant, Thomas . .	Yes.	Drowned 29 Augt. '58.
1678	„ Gray, Charles . . .	„	
3858	„ Gray, Martin . . .	„	
3785	„ Gray, Thomas . . .	„	
1877	„ Gray, William . . .	„	
4110	„ Greig, Robert . . .	„	
14	„ Greive, Hugh . . .	„	
3059	„ Grimwood, David . .	„	
3301	„ Groves, James . . .	„	
3594	„ Grubb, John . . .	„	
3985	„ Gunnes, John . . .	„	
1940	„ Guthrie, John . . .	„	
3567	„ Hadden, William . .	„	
93	„ Hales, William . .	„	
3095	„ Hamilton, Henry . .	„	
3386	„ Hamilton, James . .	„	
4018	„ Hamilton, William .	„	Killed 15 April '58.
3133	„ Hammitt, Daniel . .	„	
3082	„ Hanlon, Thomas . .	„	
3555	„ Harrison, John . .	„	
3392	„ Harper, Alexder. . .	No.	(Died 3 Decr. '57.) This man's No. is 1632.
1899	„ Harrow, John . . .	Yes.	
3107	„ Hart, William . . .	„	
3202	„ Haynes, William . .	„	Died 3 Sept. '58.
3344	„ Hayslip, John . . .	„	
3358	„ Heally, James, 1 . .	„	
3308	„ Heally, James, 2 . .	„	
1456	„ Heally, William . .	„	
30	„ Henderson, James, 1 .	„	
3870	„ Henderson, John . .	„	
3208	„ Hennessy, Dennis . .	„	Died 30 April '58.
3502	„ Henne, Festus . . .	„	
4196	„ Hepburn, John . .	„	Killed 15 April '58:
2103	„ Herron, Alexder. . .	„	
3259	„ Herron, Arthur . .	„	
2801	„ Hewitt, Robert . .	„	
3768	„ Hicks, John . . .	No.	
4324	„ Hill, George . . .	Yes.	
1156	„ Holmes, Robert, 1 .	„	Killed 11 March '58.

M

Regtl. No.	Rank and Names.	If engaged in the Operations against Lucknow from 2nd to 16th March /58.	Remarks.
4039	Private Holmes, Robert, 2 .	Yes.	
95	,, Holland, Joshua . .	,,	
3960	,, Honeyford, John . .	,,	
4309	,, Honeyman, James .	,,	
96	,, Howard, George . .	,,	
3261	,. Howe, Henry . . .	,,	
998	,, Howison, George . .	,,	
3421	,, Hutcheson, John . .	,,	
1348	,, Hutcheson, Robert .	,,	
3933	,, Hutton, Peter . .	,,	
3573	,, Hyland, Martin . .	,,	Died 7 June '58.
3278	,, Hynd, Peter . . .	,,	
4078	,, Inglis, Thomas . .	,,	Died 20 Aug. '58.
97	,, Irvine, John . . .	,,	
4219	,, Irvine, Robert . . .	,,	
3170	,, Jackson, Thomas . .	,,	
3051	,, Jacobs, Daniel . .	.,	
3136	,, James, Richard . .	,,	
3546	,, Jamieson, Robert . .	,,	
2364	,, Jeffrey, John . . .	,,	
3752	,, Jenkins, Robert . .	,,	
25	,, Johnstone, David . .	,,	
1552	,, Johnstone, John, 1 .	,,	
3582	,, Johnstone, John, 2 .	,,	
1982	,, Johnstone, Robert .	,,	
2961	,, Kay, James . . .	,,	
3929	,, Kean, John . . .	,,	
3326	,, Keen, Stephen . . .	,,	
2534	,, Kelly, Hugh . . .	,,	
3124	,, Kelly, Thomas . .	,,	
2593	,, Kerr, John	,,	Discharged 19 Jany. 1860.
3451	,, Kidd, Charles . . .	,,	
2253	,, Kimmitt, William . .	,,	
90	,, Kirkwood, Alexder. .	,,	
1695	,, Kesson, William . .	,,	
3939	,, King, William . . .	,,	
51	,, Knight, Richard . .	,,	
3928	,, Knowles, George . .	,,	
4113	,, Knox, William . .	.,	
18	,, Lafferty, James . .	,,	
2936	,, Laidlaw, Adam . .	,,	
1740	,, Laird, James . . .	,,	Died 18th May '58.
4217	,, Lammond, John . .	,,	
99	,, Latey, Thomas . .	,,	
3595	,, Lavell, James . . .	,,	
3230	,, Lavin, Connor . . .	,,	
1094	,, Lawson, David . .	,,	Died 25 Augst. '58.
100	,, Lawler, James . . .	,,	
4235	,, Leckie, James, A. . .	,,	
4295	,, Leishman, Robert . .	,,	
101	,, Leathem, Joseph . .	,,	
3464	,, Leonard, Michael . .	,,	
3655	,, Lennie, Alexder. . .	,,	
2554	,, Leslie, John . . .	,,	Discharged 19 Jany. 1860.
2359	,, Lightbody, James . .	,,	

Regtl. No.	RANK AND NAMES.	If engaged in the Operations against Lucknow from 2nd to 16th March /58.	REMARKS.
2446	Private Lindsay, Alexander .	Yes.	
3788	,, Lindsay, William . .	,,	
2669	,, Livestone, Andrew .	,,	Discharged 28th Feby. 1860.
59	,, Little, Thomas . .	,,	
3593	,, Logan, James . . .	,,	
3220	,, Loggie, John . . .	,,	
3219	,, Loggie, Samuel . .	,,	Died 11 June '58.
1626	,, Lockhart, James . .	,,	
4253	,, Long, George . . .	,,	
3178	,, Loven, James . . .	,,	
2087	,, Lowden, John . . .	,,	
1260	,, Lucas, Thomas . .	,,	
1112	,, Lunnen, James . .	,,	
4038	,, Lyall, William . . .	,,	
3633	,, Lyness, James . . .	,,	
3080	,, Lynch, Timothy . .	,,	
3204	,, Lyon, James . . .	,,	
3019	,, Lyon, William . . .	,,	Died of wounds 24 Apr. '58.
1391	,, Mackie, Alexder. . .	,,	Died 12 June '58.
3041	,, Magnor, Edward . .	,,	
3305	,, Mahoney, Michael . .	,,	
2999	,, Malcolm, John . .	,,	
3775	,, March, John . . .	,,	Died 2 Septr. 1858.
3711	,, Marshall, Thomas . .	,,	
13	,, Martin, George . .	,,	
2819	,, Martin, John . . .	,,	
1309	,, Mason, Andrew . .	,,	Killed 9 March '58.
4124	,, Mason, John . . .	,,	
3409	,, Mathieson, William .	,,	
2953	,, Mathews, John . .	,,	
2896	,, May, James . . .	,,	
3437	,, Meiklim, Peter . .	,,	
1575	,, Menteath, John . .	,,	Died of wounds 31 March '58.
2505	,, Menzies, James . .	,,	
3577	,, Merrilees, William .	,,	
2798	,, Merriman, William .	,,	
1353	,, Mill, David . . .	,,	
1802	,, Miller, Duncan . .	,,	
3521	,, Miller, George . . .	,,	
2243	,, Miller, Henry . . .	,,	
2405	,, Miller, James, 1 . .	,,	
2499	,, Miller, James, 2 . .	,,	
3478	,, Miller, James, 3 . .	,,	
2322	,, Miller, John . . .	,,	Died 22 June '58.
2004	,, Miller, Joseph . . .	,,	
3407	,, Milne, Alexder., 1 .	,,	Died 12 Sept. '58.
3569	,, Milne, Alexder., 2 .	,,	
3896	,, Mills, Thomas . . .	,,	
2662	,, Mitchell, Andrew . .	,,	
3449	,, Mitchell, Hugh . .	,,	
2690	,, Mitchell, James . .	,,	
3666	,, Moffatt, James . .	,,	Died 25 Augst. '58.
61	,, Molloy, James . . .	,,	
19	,, Morton, James . . .	,,	
3037	,, Monachan, John . .	,,	Died 20th Augst. '58.

Regtl. No.	Rank and Names.	If engaged in the Operations against Lucknow from 2nd to 16th March /58.	Remarks.
1297	Private Montgomery, James .	Yes.	
3898	,, Montague, Henry . .	,,	
4308	,, Moodie, Alexder. . .	,,	
2929	,, Moodie, James . .	,,	Killed 10th March '58.
3323	,, Morris, Edward . .	,,	
3762	,, Morris, James . . .	,,	
1158	,, Morrison, Douglas .	,,	
3673	,, Morrison, Henry . .	,,	
2764	,, Morrison, James . .	,,	Transferred to 93 Hrs., 1 July '58.
3489	,, Morrison, William . .	,,	
3121	,, Mortimer, George . .	,,	
3708	,, Mowbray, James . .	,,	
3399	,, Mowat, Thomas . .	,,	
109	,, Muir, John	,,	
3597	,, Muirhead, Charles . .	,,	
3781	,, Mullins, Patrick . .	,,	
1335	,, Munro, Jonathan . .	,,	
3343	,, Murphy, Edward . .	,,	
4210	,, Murray, Alexder. . .	,,	
4258	,, Murray, John, 1 . .	,,	
110	,, Murray, John, 2 . .	,,	
3575	,, Murray, William . .	,,	
102	,, M'Aloese, Patrick . .	,,	
3866	,, M'Allister, Peter . .	,,	
2847	,, M'Alpine, Archd. . .	,,	
2000	,, M'Alpin, John . . .	,,	
1792	,, M'Arthur, John . .	,,	
3264	,, M'Brierty, Patrick .	,,	
2144	,, M'Callum, Archd. . .	,,	
1749	,, M'Callum, William, 1 .	,,	Died 3 Octr. '58.
2935	,, M'Callum, William, 2 .	,,	
3281	,, M'Cann, Thomas . .	,,	
2362	,, M'Cready, Robert . .	,,	Died 26 May '58.
1991	,, M'Donald, Angus . .	,,	Died 23 March '58.
2	,, M'Donald, Charles .	,,	
4207	,, M'Donald, Daniel . .	,,	
3422	,, M'Donald, Donald .	,,	
3532	,, M'Donald, James . .	,,	
2625	,, M'Donald, John . .	,,	
3706	,, M'Ewan, Andrew . .	,,	
3470	,, M'Ewan, Daniel . .	,,	
3023	,, M'Fadyen, Duncan . .	,,	
2975	,, M'Fadyen, John . .	,,	
1915	,, M'Farlane, Archd. . .	,,	
26	,, M'Farlane, David . .	,,	
4083	,, M'Farlane, John . .	,,	
103	,, M'Geery, John . .	,,	
104	,, M'Grath, James . .	,,	
3246	,, M'Gregor, John, 1 . .	,,	
3469	,, M'Gregor, John, 2 . .	,,	
105	,, M'Guire, Hugh . .	,,	
3554	,, M'Gurk, John . . .	,,	
3488	,, M'Innes, Duncan . .	,,	Died 27 April '58.
4195	,, M'Innes, James . .	,,	
3649	,, M'Intosh, Peter . .	,,	

Regtl. No.	RANK AND NAMES.	If engaged in the Operations against Lucknow from 2nd to 16th March /58.	REMARKS.
2947	Private M'Intosh, William .	Yes.	
4009	,, M'Intyre, Duncan . .	,,	Died 23 April '58.
3713	,, M'Intyre, Hugh . .	,,	
3976	,, M'Intyre, John, 1 . .	,,	
4036	,, M'Intyre, John, 2 . .	,,	Killed 15 April '58.
3814	,, M'Kay, Andrew . .	,,	
3296	,, M'Kay, Donald . .	,,	
984	,, M'Kay, Daniel . .	,,	
2389	,, M'Kay, George . .	,,	
4303	,, M'Kay, John . . .	,,	
1401	,, M'Kay, Robert, 1 . .	,,	Died 6 Septr. '58.
2722	,, M'Kay, Robert, 2 . .	,,	Died 14 June '58.
3373	,, M'Kechnie, Hugh . .	,,	
2609	,, M'Kechnie, Neil . .	,,	
2313	,, M'Kenzie, Alexder., 1 .	,,	
3169	,, M'Kenzie, Alexder., 2 .	,,	
1389	,, M'Kenzie, Fredk. . .	,,	Discharged 19 Jany. 1860.
2658	,, M'Kenzie, John, 1 .	,,	
2705	,, M'Kenzie, John, 2 .	,,	Died of wounds 18 March '58.
1554	,, M'Kenzie, Robert . .	,,	Died 12 April '58.
4319	,, M'Kenzie, Hugh . .	,,	
4008	,, M'Karnie, James . .	,,	
107	,, M'Kervy, Patrick . .	,,	
3443	,, M'Innarney, Terance .	,,	
1908	,, M'Kinnon, John, 1 .	,,	
4279	,, M'Kinnon, John, 2 .	,,	
4007	,, M'Laren, Alexder. .	,,	
3900	,, M'Laren, James . .	,,	
3544	,, M'Laren, William . .	,,	
108	,, M'Laughlan, James .	,,	
3643	,, M'Lean, Frederick .	,,	
2607	,, M'Lean, George . .	,,	
3733	,, M'Lean, Robert . .	,,	
1444	,, M'Leod, Donald . .	,,	Discharged.
4043	,, M'Lorns, John . . .	,,	
4216	,, M'Lure, Hugh . . .	,,	Died 5 June '58.
2014	,, M'Lusky, William . .	,,	
4086	,, M'Mahon, Peter . .	,,	
3919	,, M'Manns, Charles . .	,,	
1151	,, M'Millan, Charles . .	,,	
3975	,, M'Millan, James . .	,,	
3286	,, M'Millan, William . .	,,	
3726	,, M'Muinemy, Hugh .	,,	
1780	,, M'Moran, Robert . .	,,	
1976	,, M'Murray, Andrew .	,,	
3267	,, M'Murtrie, James . .	,,	
3645	,, M'Nab, James . . .	,,	
4302	,, M'Neil, John . . .	,,	
2436	,, M'Nutty, William . .	,,	
3610	,, M'Fie, Dugald . . .	,,	
3012	,, M'Phee, Malcolm . .	,,	
2478	,, M'Pherson, Alexder. .	,,	
2281	,, M'Pherson, James, 1 .	,,	
3140	,, M'Pherson, James, 2 .	,,	
3607	,, M'Pherson, John, 2 .	,,	

Regtl. No.	Rank and Names.	If engaged in the Operations against Lucknow from 2nd to 16th March /58.	Remarks.
7	Private M'Queen, Donald . .	Yes.	
3155	,, M'Rae, Roderick . .	,,	Died 4 May '58.
2860	,, M'Vicar, John . .	,,	
3497	,, Napier, Alexder. . .	,,	
4275	,, Napier, James . .	,,	
3321	,, Naxton, Henry . .	,,	
37	,, Neave, David . . .	,,	
3270	,, Neill, James . . .	,,	
4047	,, Neill, Peter . .	,,	
3688	,, Neilson, John . .	,,	
3490	,, Neilson, William . .	,,	
3370	,, Newal, William . .	,,	
111	,, Niblock, William . .	,,	
3677	,, Nichol, James . . .	,,	
2214	,, Nicoll, William . .	,,	
3659	,, Nicholas, James . .	,,	
1054	,, Nicholson, John, 1 .	,,	
1128	,, Nicholson, John, 2 .	,,	
3094	,, Noonan, John . . .	,,	
3114	,, Nott, Henry . . .	,,	
4231	,, Nowlin, Michael . .	,,	
3066	,, O'Brien, Patrick . .	,,	
3623	,, Oliver, John . .	,,	
2451	,, O'Neill, Francis . .	,,	
112	,, O'Neill, Hugh . . .	,,	Died 26 Sept. '58.
1252	,, O'Neill, James . .	,,	
1796	,, Orr, John	,,	
3953	,, Osborne, William . .	,,	
2663	,, Pallister, Thomas . .	,,	Died 25 June '58.
4314	,, Panton, Thomas . .	,,	
3207	,, Parsons, George . .	,,	Discharged 18 Jany. 1860.
3959	,, Paterson, Daniel . .	,,	Died 21 April '58.
3685	,, Paterson, James . .	,,	
2694	,, Paterson, John . .	,,	
3930	,, Paterson, William . .	,,	
3013	,, Paull, George . . .	,,	
3160	,, Paul, Thomas . . .	,,	
3165	,, Pearson, Alexder. . .	,,	
3227	,, Piercy, Charles . .	,,	
3699	,, Plain, David . . .	,,	
2678	,, Pollock, Alexder. . .	,,	
3004	,, Price, George . . .	,,	
1232	,, Pringle, George . .	,,	
3966	,, Proven, James . .	,,	
113	,, Quigley, Thomas . .	,,	
3057	,, Quinn, William . .	,,	Died 5 Septr. '58.
3653	,, Ramage, William . .	,,	Died 18 May /58.
3156	,, Ramsay, Robert . .	,,	
49	,, Rainer, William . .	,,	
3660	,, Redman, Robert . .	,,	
3935	,, Reid, James . . .	,,	
4103	,, Reid, John . . .	,,	
2005	,, Reid, Robert . . .	,,	Died 8 April '58.
3777	,, Rennie, James . .	,,	
4116	,, Rennie, John . . .	,,	

Regtl. No.	RANK AND NAMES.	If engaged in the Operations against Lucknow from 2nd to 16th March /58.	REMARKS.
114	Private Richardson, Charles .	Yes.	
4177	,, Richardson, James .	,,	
3311	,, Richmond, James . .	,,	
2423	,, Richmond, Mathew .	,,	
4273	,, Riddle, Robert . .	,,	
1413	,, Ritchie, George, 1 . .	,,	
4316	,, Ritchie, George, 2 . .	,,	
3723	,, Ritchie, Thomas . .	,,	
1694	,, Ritchie, William . .	,,	
3001	,, Robb, Alexder. . .	,,	
3682	,, Robb, Arthur . . .	,,	
2058	,, Robbin, Alexder. . .	,,	
3909	,, Robert, John . . .	,,	
2968	,, Roberton, William .	,,	
3214	,, Robertson, David, 1 .	,,	
4322	,, Robertson, David, 2 .	,,	
3873	,, Robertson, Hugh . .	,,	
1364	,, Robertson, John, 1 .	,,	
2930	,, Robertson, John, 2 .	,,	
1325	,, Robertson, William, 1	,,	
3853	,, Robertson, William, 2	,,	
3199	,, Robinson, Noah . .	,,	Discharged 19 Jany. 1860.
3901	,, Rodgers, Robert . .	,,	
3009	,, Rollie, John . . .	,,	
115	,, Rolestone, Joseph . .	,,	
3043	,, Rose, Thomas . . .	,,	
3692	,, Ross, Archd. . . .	,,	Died 25 April '58.
2790	,, Ross, David . . .	,,	
4317	,, Ross, Roderick . .	,,	
3175	,, Ross, William . . .	,,	
3477	,, Ross, Samuel . . .	,,	
50	,, Rowland, Charles . .	,,	
3993	,, Russell, Alexder. . .	,,	
4000	,, Russell, James . .	,,	
3746	,, Russell, John . . .	,,	
116	,, Ryan, Thomas . .	,,	
3099	,, Salmon, Patrick . .	,,	
8	,, Samuel, George . .	,,	
1712	,, Sanderson, Charles .	,,	
3880	,, Schooler, William . .	,,	
3429	,, Scobie, Henry . . .	,,	
3598	,, Scott, Angus . . .	,,	
47	,, Scott, John . . .	,,	
3783	,, Scott, James . . .	,,	
4175	,, Scott, Robert . . .	,,	
2905	,, Scott, William . . .	,,	
3226	,, Sharkey, James . .	,,	
3826	,, Sharpe, James . . .	,,	
117	,, Sharpe, William . .	,,	
3661	,, Sharples, James . .	,,	
29	,, Sharry, John . . .	,,	
3144	,, Shaw, Robert . . .	,,	Died 23rd May 1858.
3936	,, Shearer, Robert . .	,,	
4013	,, Shields, Bernard . .	,,	
118	,, Short, Samuel . . .	,,	

Regtl. No.	Rank and Names.	If engaged in the Operations against Lucknow from 2nd to 16th March /58.	Remarks.
1772	Private Sibbalds, Robert . .	Yes.	
2061	,, Sideserf, William . .	,,	
1184	,, Simpson, William, 1 .	,,	
1352	,, Simpson, William, 2 .	,,	
4222	,, Simington, Charles .	,,	
3946	,, Sinclair, Hugh . .	,,	
2802	,, Sloane, Robert . .	,,	
3279	,, Small, Samuel . . .	,,	
2957	,, Smith, Alexder. . .	,,	
119	,, Smith, James . . .	,,	
2089	,, Smith, John, 1 . .	,,	
2132	., Smith, John, 2 . .	,,	
2902	,, Smith, John, 3 . .	,,	
4	,, Smith, John, 4 . .	,,	
2826	,, Smith, Robert . . .	,,	
2590	,, Smith, Thomas, 1 . .	,,	Died 22 May '58.
120	,, Smith, Thomas, 2 . .	,,	
3872	,, Smith, William . .	,,	
2939	,, Soutar, Andrew . .	,,	
121	,, Spence, Edward . .	,,	Died of wounds 18 April /58.
48	,, Spilling, John . . .	,,	Died 24 June '58.
1412	,, Stephen, Alexder. . .	,,	
3539	,, Stephen, William . .	,,	Died 7 May '58.
1420	,, Stewart, James . .	,,	
2937	,, Stewart, John . . .	,,	
4298	,, Stirling, Robert . .	,,	
4296	,, Stirling, William . .	,,	
33	,, Swanson, Walter . .	,,	Died 29 Augst. '58.
2942	,, Sutherland, George .	,,	
3863	,, Symington, Alexder. .	,,	
122	,, Tarry, Richard . .		
2599	,, Taunch, Peter . . .	,,	
3302	,, Taylor, Henry . . .	,,	
2933	,, Taylor, Peter . . .	,,	
32	,, Temple, John . . .	,,	
1731	,, Tennant, David . .	No.	Died 28 April '58.
3790	,, Thompson, Andrew .	Yes.	
3884	,, Thompson, James, 1 .	,,	
4294	,, Thompson, James, 2 .	,,	
2454	., Thompson, John, 1 .	,,	Died 17 April '58.
3652	,, Thompson, John, 2 .	,,	
2828	,, Thompson, William, 1	,,	
3274	,, Thompson, William, 2	,,	
4293	,, Todd, John . . .	,,	Died 7 July '58.
3662	,, Tomlinson, William .	,,	
3067	,, Tronson, George . .	,,	
4093	,, Tully, Bernard . .	,,	
3552	,, Turnbull, Thomas . .	,,	
3153	,, Turnbull, William . .	,,	
4227	,, Turner, Duncan . .	,,	
4141	,, Turner, William . .	,,	
2281	,, Valentine, William .	,,	
3372	,, Wade, Samuel . . .	,,	
3300	,, Wagstaff, Charles . .	,,	
3378	,, Walker, George . .	,,	

Regtl. No.	RANK AND NAMES.	If engaged in the Operations against Lucknow from 2nd to 16th March /58.	REMARKS.
4012	Private Walker, Robert . .	Yes.	
3320	,, Wall, John . . .	,,	
6	,, Wall, Richard . . .	,,	
3133	,, Wallace, Michael .	,,	
23	,, Walsh, John . . .	,,	
3664	,, Ward, Philip . . .	,,	
3224	,, Ward, Thomas . .	,,	Died 1 July '58.
3335	,, Waterson, John . .	,,	To England 14 July '58.
1862	,, Watson, Alexder. .	,,	Discharged 19 Jany. 1860.
2535	,, Watt, John . . .	,,	
15	,, Watt, Thomas . . .	,,	
3413	,, Webster, William . .	,,	Discharged 19th Jany. 1860.
4166	,, Weir, John	,,	
3955	,, Wells, John . .	,,	
2130	,, White, Duncan . .	,,	
3904	,, White, John, 1 . .	,,	
123	,, White, John, 2 . .	,,	
1347	,, White, Walter . . .	,,	
122	,, Wright, John . . .	,,	
2878	,, Wilkie, John . .	,,	
1553	,, Wilkie, Walter . .	,,	
3312	,, Williamson, John . .	,,	
4299	,, Willis, John . . .	,,	
3376	,, Wilson, Hugh . . .	,,	Died 25th April '58.
124	,, Wilson, Alexder. . .	,,	
125	,, Wilson, David . . .	,,	
4112	,, Wilson, Isaac . . .	,,	
1901	,, Wilson, John, 1 . .	,,	
4323	,, Wilson, John, 2 . .	,,	
1546	,, Wilson, Joseph . .	,,	
1111	,, Wilson, Robert, 1 . .	,,	Died 19 June '58.
3958	,, Wilson, Robert, 2 . .	,,	
3801	,, Wilson, Thomas, 1 .	,,	
3950	,, Wilson, Thomas 2 .	,,	
4305	,, Wilson, William . .	,,	
4118	,, Woods, James . . .	,,	Died 22 April '58.
4267	,, Wright, James . .	,,	Died 5 May '58.
3881	,, Wright, Robert . .	,,	
4028	,, Wright, William . .	,,	
4181	,, Wyness, John . . .	,,	
2652	,, Wyness, Patrick . .	,,	
3467	,, Yates, George . . .	,,	
45	,, Bartie, John . . .	No.	
131	,, Boyd, Fullarton . .	No.	
143	,, Brown, William . .	No.	
149	,, Cameron, James . .	No.	
134	,, Campbell, James . .	No.	
153	,, Crosson, Peter . .	No.	
4204	,, Docharty, John . .	No.	
160	,, Edgar, Thomas . .	No.	
158	,, Galbraith, George . .	No.	
136	,, Galford, Andrew . .	No.	
43	,, Gillanders, Robert .	No.	
127	,, Glen, John	No.	
4271	,, Gordon, George . .	No.	

Regtl. No.	Rank and Names.	If engaged in the Operations against Lucknow from 2nd to 16th March /58.	Remarks.
138	Private Grey, John	No.	
139	„ Hume, Thomas . .	No.	
129	„ Johnstone, Robert .	No.	
2869	„ Lamb, James . . .	No.	
2986	„ Lettimer, Peter . .	No.	Died 11 Aug. '58.
156	„ Lodge, Lewis . . .	No.	
145	„ Lundie, Joseph . .	No.	
151	„ Lyle, Robert . . .	No.	
155	„ Marshall, Andrew . .	No.	
166	„ Murdoch, John . .	No.	
157	„ Mutch, Alexder. .	No.	Died 7 Sept. '58.
3183	„ M'Adam, Thomas . .	No.	
132	„ M'Cormack, Thomas .	No.	
42	„ M'Farlane, John . .	No.	
141	„ M'Gan, Samuel . .	No.	
130	„ M'Gregor, Charles . .	No.	
3832	„ M'Lean, Alexder. . .	No.	
149	„ M'Turk, William . .	No.	
142	„ Nicoll, George . . .	No.	
154	„ Paterson, John . .	No.	
3920	„ Ramage, James . .	No.	
135	„ Rankin, William . .	No.	
176	„ Robertson, Alexder. .	No.	
152	„ Shaw, Francis . . .	No.	
3309	„ Smith, Thomas . .	No.	Died 8 May '58.
148	„ Smith, William . .	No.	
173	„ Stewart, James . .	No.	
168	„ Stewart, Robert . .	No.	
1422	„ Swan, George . . .	No.	
128	„ Tevendale, George .	No.	
133	„ Thompson, James . .	No.	
147	„ Young, Fredk. . . .	No.	

893 With Clasps for the Operations against Lucknow.

54 Without Clasps.

Total, 947

NOT ENTITLED. 42ND ROYAL HIGHLANDERS.

SUPPLEMENTARY ROLL of the above CORPS, who claim the INDIAN MUTINY MEDAL under the provisions of General Order by the Commander-in-Chief, 4th September 1858, and whose Names have not been included in any previous Return.

BAREILLY, 24th January 1861.

	Regtl. No.	RANK AND NAMES.	REMARKS.
In actual Conflict with the Enemy at Kirkhut Ghur under Captain Gordon, 42nd Royal Highlanders, *vide* Despatch of Brigadier-General Douglas, G.O.C., No. 135 of 1859.	1400	Corporal Alex. Munro.	Sent home 16th Novr. 1860.
	1209	,, James M'Lellan.	Sent home 13th Feby. 1860.
	4321	Drummer James M'Lean.	
	4281	,, Warren M'Leod.	Died 13th Novr. 1858.
	279	Private William Archer.	
	357	,, Robert Auld.	
	245	,, John Beattie.	
	235	,, Norman Blair.	
	4157	,, Alex. Brown.	
	319	,, Andrew Buchan.	
	284	,, John Cameron.	
	359	,, Daniel Campbell.	
	322	,, Charles Chancellor.	
	199	,, John Chancellor.	
	344	,, George Combe.	
	174	,, James Cooper.	
	259	,, John Cowan.	
	328	,, James Crane.	
	294	,, Alex. Crombie.	
	300	,, Michael Crombie.	Died 18th April 1859. M. Crombie's medal recd.
	318	,, David Cunningham.	
	162	,, Robert Cunningham.	
	324	,, Archibald Davidson.	
	244	,, George Deans.	
	267	,, James Denham.	
	280	,, Alex. Donaldson.	
	261	,, Thomas Fairbairn.	
	306	,, Robert Farrell.	
	268	,, John Farrow.	
	333	,, William Farquharson.	
	305	,, Alex. Finlayson.	Transferred to 8th Hussars 31st Augt. 1859.
	327	,, Alex. Forrest.	
	331	,, John Galbraith.	
	182	,, Charles Gibson.	
	4159	,, John Gillespie.	
	186	,, Robert Grant.	Died 15th April 1860.
	351	,, James Guild.	
	249	,, George Gunn.	
	246	,, Robert Haddow.	
	331	,, Joseph Hannah.	
	293	,, David Hutchison.	
	326	,, James Hutchison.	

Regtl. No.	Rank and Names.	Remarks.
321	Private Robert Howie.	
196	,, George Inglish.	
228	,, James Johnstone.	
287	,, John Jordine.	
221	,, James King.	
179	,, William Laird.	
349	,, Hugh Lammond.	
212	,, Cain Lancaster.	Died 12th May 1859.
323	,, Thomas Lochead.	
317	,, David Locke.	
346	,, Robert Menzies.	
341	,, Robert Methren.	
3787	,, John Miller.	
210	,, Henry Mitchell.	
206	,, John Mitchell.	
281	,, James Morrison.	
312	,, Finlay M'Culloch.	
355	,, Archibald M'Intosh.	
320	,, Charles M'Queen.	
203	,, John M'Tavish.	
339	,, Finlay Nicholson.	
302	,, Samuel Nicholson.	
3600	,, Robert Oliver.	Died 10th August 1860.
233	,, James Philp.	
181	,, John Pollock.	
193	,, David Robertson.	
194	,, John Robertson.	
335	,, Thomas Robertson.	
311	,, Michael Rowley.	Died — January 1859.
278	,, James Russell.	Transferred to 79th Highlanders 1st Augt. 1859.
340	,, Thomas Sage.	
330	,, James Savage.	
190	,, Robert Scarlett.	
283	,, Peter Smith.	
241	,, Robert Stark.	
145	,, John Stewart.	
254	,, John Stewart.	
260	,, John Stewart.	
269	,, William Street.	Transferred to 23rd Coy. Royal Engrs. 30th Augt. 1859.
342	,, Peter Taylor.	
310	,, James Tennant.	
307	,, John Thompson.	
373	,, Simpson Wallis.	
200	,, James Walker.	
299	,, William White.	
266	,, William Wilkie.	
234	,, Alexander Wilson.	
198	,, Samuel Wilson.	

In actual Conflict with the Enemy at Kirkhut Ghur under Captain Gordon, 42nd Royal Highlanders, vide Despatch of Brigadier-General Douglas, G.O.C., No. 135 of 1859.

Note.—Although in the original roll the 'Supplementary Roll' is headed 'Not Entitled,' it would appear (from the fact that No. 300, Pte. M. Crombie, received his medal) that at least some of the men on this list did actually receive the medal.—J. S.

73RD

ROLL OF OFFICERS, N.C.O.'S AND MEN

OF

HER MAJESTY'S 73<small>RD</small> REGIMENT OF FOOT

WHO HAVE BEEN EMPLOYED IN THE SUPPRESSION OF

THE MUTINY IN INDIA

ROLL OF OFFICERS AND MEN OF HER MAJESTY'S SEVENTY-THIRD REGIMENT OF FOOT who have been employed in the Suppression of the MUTINY IN INDIA.

HEAD QUARTERS CAMP,
DHUKUREE, 12th March 1859.

RANK AND NAME.	Services for which entitled to Medal.			REMARKS.
Colonel F. G. A. Pinckney, C.B. .	Commanded Field Force Soraon, and Brigade in Oude.			Died.
„ G. H. Smith	Commanded H.M.'s 73rd Regt. with Brigr. Rowcroft's Force.			
Bt.-Lt.-Col. Thos. Ross . . .	Served with H.M.'s 73rd Regt. with Brigr. Rowcroft's Force.			
Major W. L. Peto	„	„	„	
Captain J. W. Barnes	„	„	„	Medal given to him, 7/8/61.
„ W. H. Barry	„	„	„	Depot.
„ A. H. Godfrey . . .	„	„	„	
„ R. H. Hereford . . .	„	„	„	
„ W. C. O'Brien . . .	„	„	„	
„ F. Reeve	„	„	„	Medal to Depot, 8/7/61.
Lieut. M. S. Blyth	„	„	„	Retired.
„ F. T. Greatrex	„	„	„	
„ P. Gibant	„	„	„	Given to him, 12/7/61.
„ T. W. S. Miles	„	„	„	Medal given to him, 28/6/61.
„ W. J. L. Milligan . . .	„	„	„	
„ H. Fraser	„	„	„	
„ W. H. S. Pigott . . .	„	„	„	
„ A. H. Sharp	„	„	„	
„ P. F. Shieldham . . .	„	„	„	Retired.
Ensign J. Kirk	„	„	„	„
Surgeon E. Booth	„	„	„	Dead.
Asst. Surgn. J. Anderson . . .	„	„	„	
„ R. T. Scott . . .	„	„	„	
„ J. M'Kinnell . .	„	„	„	
Pay-Mastr. L. Cassidy . . .	„	„	„	
Qr.-Mr. J. G. Scott	„	„	„	
Regtl. No. 2766 Serjt. - Major Joseph T. Murray	„	„	„	
1631 Qr. - Mr. - Serjt. William Darling	„	„	„	
2740 Paymr. - Serjt. Bernard Kilkeary	„	„	„	Discharged.
Asst.-Serjt. George W. Hawkins .	„	„	„	Died.

Arrived in India March 1858.

Regtl. No.	RANK AND NAMES.	REMARKS.
1903	Dr.-Major John Conway.	
3207	Or. Clerk Willm. Stanley Sampson.	
1794	Cr.-Serjt. James S. Barson.	
2729	„ Edwd. Doyle.	Discharged.
2322	„ John Flinn.	
2273	„ Edwd. Robins.	
2800	„ James Rowland.	
1561	„ Thomas Rowland.	
2602	„ Dermot Shaughnessy.	
2178	„ George Shuter.	
1547	„ Alexr. Stupart.	
2133	„ John Jordon.	
3516	Serjt. Reuben Arbon.	
1890	„ Swain Atkinson.	
1725	„ Richard Bailey.	
3612	„ Mark Berry.	
2934	„ Thomas Berry.	
2747	„ David Bromage.	Discharged.
1655	„ Samuel Bromwich.	Died 11 Septr. '58.
2095	„ Henry Buckanan.	
2271	„ Henry Burgess.	Discharged. Now in England.
3234	„ George Coaten.	
2570	„ Stephen Collins.	
3265	„ George Coleman.	
1450	„ John Daly.	Transferred to Indian Army.
2888	„ Roger Dougherty.	
3510	„ George Fuller.	
1575	„ John Graham.	
2609	„ William Harris.	Transferred to Indian Army.
2469	„ Daniel Hickey.	
2218	„ George Holton.	
1342	„ Richard Hornsby.	Discharged.
3167	„ Joseph Lawson.	
2647	„ John Lewen.	
2044	„ George Lucas.	
2873	„ Stuart Lafferty.	
2183	„ William Longstaff.	Woolwich Division Royal Marines.
1573	„ William M'Lean.	
1651	„ James M'Masters.	
1339	„ Alexr. M'Quarrie.	
2999	„ George Pomphrey.	Died.
2073	„ William Poulden.	
6	„ Eli Sumners.	
1793	„ Edward Turner.	Discharged.
3212	„ James Walsh.	
3006	„ Jonathan Watkinson.	
1881	„ Thomas Watson.	Discharged.
3061	„ John Wilcox.	Medal to Depot, 8/7/61.
3542	Lc.-Serjt. J. M. Jones.	War Office. Issued 1/3/04. Off 68/42/837.
2028	Corpl. John Bettington.	
2002	„ Reuben Bird.	
3441	„ Samuel Bland.	
3032	„ Fredk. Brooks.	
2926	„ Fredk. Burnop.	Died 24 Sep. '58.
1407	„ John Carr.	
2731	„ Patrick Cuddihy.	

Regtl. No.	Rank and Names.	Remarks.
3468	Corpl. John Dell.	
3564	,, Joseph Dell.	
1825	,, Thomas Drinkwater.	
2992	,, William Fogarty.	
2088	,, William Garlick.	
3080	,, Henry Hermon.	
2018	,, Daniel Jones.	Discharged.
1093	,, Michael King.	Discharged.
2055	,, Richard Lewis.	
2117	,, Alexr. M'Donald.	
3231	,, William Mayden.	
3365	,, John Mewitt.	Transferred to Bengal Horse Artillery.
3725	,, Michael Mulcahy.	
1549	,, George Penrose.	
1755	,, George Shuttle.	
3572	,, John Smith.	
2340	,, Alexr. Smith.	Discharged.
1795	,, Herbert Sanderson.	
2338	,, John Rice.	
2221	,, Charles Roberts.	
2258	,, Charles Soper.	
2927	,, George Tims.	
2061	,, John Williams.	
3152	,, William Woods.	
2067	,, Nicholas Connolly.	
3170	,, Edward Thipps.	Died.
3269	,, James Hooper.	Transferred to Bengal Foot Artillery.
2047	,. John Coyne.	Died 3 Jany. 1859.
2533	,, George Watton.	Died Sept. 9, 1858.
1020	Drummer John Best.	
3348	,, Thomas Bunting.	
2719	,, William Burke.	
2236	,, William Coney.	
3529	,, Edward Downey.	Transferred to 23rd Foot.
1926	,, William Flinn.	
3084	,, John Fox.	
3350	,, James Gilligan.	
2764	,, James Herlihey.	
2193	,, James Horan.	
2052	,, Frederick Jones.	
2862	,, Michael Kiney.	
2254	,, George Lever.	Discharged.
3413	,, Henry Morrisey.	
2757	,, James Reynolds.	
1757	,, John Scivier.	
3073	,, John Scott.	
2323	,, Benjamin Shemels.	
3495	,, Michael Stephenson.	
3075	,, James Thompson.	
2021	Pte. George Adby.	Died.
2653	,, Timothy Ahern.	
1698	,, Antony Allibone.	
3076	,, William Alsford.	
1406	,, Charles Ambrose.	
1626	,, Charles Anderson.	
3388	,, Thomas Archer.	

Regtl. No.	RANK AND NAMES.	REMARKS.
2874	Pte. George Armstrong.	
2038	,, James Arnold.	
2017	,, William Arnold.	
3040	,, Thomas Ashcroft.	
3331	,, John Axtell.	
3336	,, John Bailey.	
2833	,, Henry Baker.	
52	,, George Baker.	
3338	,, Emanuel Baldwin.	Not.
3012	,, Henry Bale.	Died.
2560	,, John Ballance.	
2082	,, James Banks.	
4	,, William Barker.	
2137	,, John Barnett.	Died.
2596	,, Thomas Barry.	
2227	,, William Bateman.	
3483	,, William Battin.	
2903	,, John Bean.	
3178	,, Daniel Beattie.	
3420 or 3426	,, John Beckley. ? See Depot List.	Medal to Depot, 8/7/61.
3342	,, Robert Beesley.	Died.
3248	,, Thomas Beetles.	
3355	,, George Bennett.	Died.
3239	,, Henry Bennett.	
1786	,, John Bennett.	
3746	,, William Bennett.	
2030	,, William Bingham.	
2967	,, William Birchfield.	Died.
3404	,, Edwin Bird.	
2743	,, Michael Bird.	
1756	,, Thomas Bishop.	
1136	,, John Blackist.	
3344	,, Robert Blakely.	Died.
2956	,, Aaron Blizzard.	
3116	,, William Blunsome.	
1554	,, William Bond.	
2	,, William Bonnyman.	Discharged.
1613	,, John Booth.	Died.
3157	,, George Bott.	
2306	,, Thomas Boucher.	
2253	,, William Bowden.	
2861	,, James Boyce.	
3117	,, William Brandon.	Died.
3464	,, William Bray.	Transferred to Bengal Foot Artillery.
3096	,, Henry Breen.	
3029	,, Edward Brett.	
1429	,, William Britton.	
2163	,, George Brocklehurst.	Discharged.
3174	,, John Brooks.	
3646	,, Stephen Brooks.	
3447	,, William Brooks.	
2245	,, James Brooker.	
3320	,, James Brown.	
3357	,, Joseph Brown.	

Regtl. No.	Rank and Names.	Remarks.
3579	Pte. Thomas Brown.	
2870	,, Joseph Brownlow.	
45	,, John Bryant.	
3130	,, William Bryant.	
3109	,, Samuel Bucke.	
2444	,, John Buckley.	
26	,, David Buckingham.	
3786	,, William Bunting.	
3008	,, Martin Burke.	
3145	,, Michael Burke.	
3088	,, Patrick Burke.	
3201	,, Thomas Burke.	
2828	,, William Burke.	
3712	,, Thomas Burnes.	
1835	,, Henry Burrows.	
78	,, Tom Burton.	
3362	,, Charles Butler.	
3353	,, Joseph Butler.	
2198	,, John Byrne.	Died.
2982	,, Michael Byrne.	
2214	,, John Burke.	
3541	,, Charles Burgham.	
1347	,, Joseph Campbell.	
2411	,, John Carey.	
1601	,, Thomas Cargill.	
13	,, Owen Carmen.	91st Depot.
2892	,, George Carroll.	
33	,, Josiah Carter.	
1211	,, John Casey.	Discharged.
2754	,, Thomas Cash.	Medal to Depot, 8/7/61.
1349	,, Patrick Cassidy.	
3406	,, James Clarke.	
3695	,, James Clarke.	
50	,, James Clarke.	
3249	,, Joseph Clarke.	
3303	,, Thomas Clarke.	
3369	,, Samuel Clewes.	
1380	,, Michael Clune.	
3149	,, George Cobb.	Medal to Depot, 8/7/61.
2658	,, James Cody.	
2974	,, Denis Coleman.	
2856	,, James Coleman.	
3363	,, Samuel Coleman.	
3351	,, David Collins.	
2424	,, John Collins.	
2558	,, Patrick Collins.	
76	,, John Combes.	
1826	,, Robert Cooney.	Died.
1865	,, Patrick Conlon.	
3728	,, John Connell.	
2166	,, James Connors.	
3715	,, Patrick Considine.	
37	,, Abraham Cooke.	
34	,, Thomas Cooke.	
3803	,, George Cooper.	
3190	,, Edwin Cooper.	Died 20 Augt. '58.

Regtl. No.	RANK AND NAMES.	REMARKS.
2940	Pte. Patrick Corcoran.	
1440	,, Eziekiel Corder.	Died.
1612	,, John Corrigan.	Medal to Depot, 8/7/61.
3505	,, John Cotter.	
3079	,, George Cox.	
2126	,, John Cox.	
3557	,, John Cox.	
47	,, William Crack.	
3266	,, John Crockford.	
2550	,, Daniel Croneen.	
27	,, William Croos.	Died.
3439	,, John Crossbie.	
1392	,, Lot Culliman.	
3729	,, James Cummins.	
3500	,, Thomas Cummins.	Died.
2944	,, John Curtis.	
3115	,, John Curtis.	
3611	,, Samuel Curry.	Transferred to Bengal Foot Artillery.
2923	,, John Cusick.	Died 18 Sept. '58.
2784	,, William Coonan.	Discharged.
3297	,, David Daniels.	
1934	,, Henry Daniels.	
2857	,, Daniel Darsey.	
1372	,, Nicholas Darsey.	
3308	,, Francis Davidson.	Died.
1737	,, Morris Davies.	
3311	,, Joseph Davies.	
3123	,, John Dawson.	
2167	,, Manns Day.	
3606	,, William Day.	Transferred to Bengal Horse Artillery.
3411	,, David Deacon.	
1410	,, John Devitt.	
3623	,, James Diaper.	
2889	,, Josiah Dick.	
2511	,, John Donoghue.	
2650	,, Thomas Donoghue.	
2157	,, James Doran.	
3416	,, John Dorman.	
3372	,, Alexr. Downie.	Transferred to Bengal Foot Artillery.
22	,, James Downey.	
2851	,, John Doyle.	
2759	,, Michael Doyle.	Discharged.
201	,, Martin Duffy.	
2744	,, Patrick Duffy.	Discharged.
5	,, George Duncan.	
3403	,, Alfred Duncombe.	Transferred to Bengal Horse Artillery.
3372	,, Jacob Durham.	
3709	,, Thomas Dykes.	
1444	,, William Dynan.	Died.
40	,, Robert Drake.	
3666	,, Alfred Edwards.	
3478	,, Richard Edwards.	
3396	,, William Elliment.	
3329	,, Henry Elsden.	
3299	,, William Enwright.	
1360	,, John Enwright.	

Regtl. No.	Rank and Names.	Remarks.
3461	Pte. George Erney.	
938	„ Charles Evans.	Died.
3339	„ William Ewer.	
1722	„ George Edwards.	Died 20 Decr. '58.
3722	„ James Farrell.	
3347	„ John Farrell.	
1711	„ Joshua Fell.	
3790	„ Robert Fell.	
2504	„ Patrick Finaughty.	
3	„ Alexander Ferguson.	
3256	„ Thomas Field.	
3524	„ Thos. Branch Field.	Transferred to Bengal Horse Artillery.
1402	„ John Finch.	Died.
1966	„ John Fisher.	
3001	„ John Fisher.	
3077	„ Wm. Henry Fisher.	
2373	„ Michael Fitzgerald.	
2487	„ Thomas Fitzgerald.	
2839	„ James Fitzpatrick.	
2359	„ Michael Flanagan.	
1895	„ Richard Fletcher.	
3135	„ William Flint.	
2917	„ Morgan Foley.	Discharged.
3706	„ Charles Ford.	
3083	„ George Ford.	
31	„ Joseph Forsbury.	
3490	„ Josiah Foster.	
3143	„ William Frame.	
3283	„ Joseph Freeman. .	Transferred to Bengal Horse Artillery.
2614	„ James Friend.	Died.
3169	„ Samuel Fryer.	
3498	„ William Fuller.	
3656	„ William Gandy.	
3738	„ John Gannon.	
2108	„ Charles Garrett.	
3327	„ Isaac Gazeley.	
2991	„ George Geffries.	
2896	„ John Glann.	
2928	„ Frederick Goodfellow.	
19	„ John Gorey.	
2852	„ John Gorman.	
3370	„ George Gosling.	Died.
3000	„ William Gough.	
2771	„ John Grady.	Died.
3698	„ James Grant.	
3218	„ Joshua Gravestock.	
3251	„ Thomas Gravestock.	
2404	„ Patrick Green.	
1697	„ Robert Greenwood.	Died.
2619	„ Michael Griffin.	
2691	„ George Grimwood.	Transferred to Bengal Horse Artillery.
3356	„ Geo. Henry Groves.	
3323	„ James Groves.	
3743	„ George Gunn.	Transferred to Bengal Horse Artillery.
1621	„ Richard Gobell.	
3401	„ James Gardener.	Died.

Regtl. No.	Rank and Names.	Remarks.
3068	Pte. John Hail.	
3064	,, Walter Hale.	Died.
3271	,, William Hale.	
2354	,, John Hall.	Discharged.
3367	,, John Hall.	Transferred to Bengal Foot Artillery.
3368	,, Josiah Hall.	
1857	,, Richard Hall.	
1393	,, Patrick Halloran.	
3379	,, Frederic Harcourt.	
1460	,, Daniel Hardy.	
1141	,, Denis Hare.	
2866	,, Michael Harper.	
3108	,, Charles Harris.	Medal to Depot, 8/7/61.
3712	,, Standish Harris.	
3460	,, Thomas Harris.	
3453	,, Arthur Harrison.	Transferred to Bengal Foot Artillery.
3268	,, Charles Harrison.	Died 13th Novr. '58.
1769	,, Thomas Hartrope.	
2938	,, Charles Harvey.	
1388	,, James Haughey.	Medal to Depot, 8/7/61.
3275	,, John Hewen.	
2484	,, Patrick Hayes.	
3513	,, Thomas Hayter.	
1609	,, William Hazlehurst.	Died 10 Octr. '58.
3031	,, Alfred Hearn.	
3057	,, Richard Hearn.	
2910	,, Patrick Hearnes.	
3285	,, James Heages.	
3332	,, John Henderson.	Transferred to Bengal Artillery.
1852	,, James Henry.	
2739	,, Patrick Herrick.	
3098	,, Andrew Hickey.	
1090	,, Patrick Hickey.	Discharged.
3755	,, Michael Heffernan.	
2528	,, William Higgins.	
3318	,, James Hill.	
3317	,, Matthew Hill.	Transferred to Bengal Foot Artillery.
1978	,, Thomas Hill.	
3121	,, Henry Hiscock.	
3635	,, Israel Hobbs.	
2536	,, Patrick Hogan.	
3097	,, William Hogan.	
2199	,, John Holihan.	
21	,, Patrick Holihan.	Discharged.
3670	,, Thomas Holmes.	
2627	,, John Hopkins.	
1336	,, James Hopper.	
2994	,, Cornelius Horgan.	Died.
24	,, Joseph Horne.	
3658	,, Henry Horner.	
3028	,, Thomas Horsey.	
3494	,, Denis Howigan.	
3449	,, William Howard.	
3196	,, John Howell.	
3319	,, Thomas Howell.	
2637	,, Michael Howley.	

Regtl. No.	Rank and Names.	Remarks.
3385	Pte. James Humphrey.	Died.
3295	,, Job Hunt.	
3492	,, Thomas Hunt.	
2932	,, Robert Hunter.	
1295	,, Charles Hurlstone.	Discharged.
3302	,, John Hutchinson.	
2384	,, John Ibbett.	
2022	,, James Ilsley.	
3665	,, Henry Iron.	
1446	,, James Irwin.	
1263	,, James Jackman.	
3629	,, William Jackson.	
32	,, Frederick James.	
3051	,, William James.	
3387	,, Henry Jandrell.	
3970	,, James Jarmeny.	Died.
3574	,, Joseph Jewett.	
3583	,, William Johnson.	Died.
39	,, John Jerrett.	
3386	,, William Johnson.	
3531	,, Joseph Johnstone.	
2334	,, Cornelius John Joice.	
2884	,, Michael Jones.	
3005	,, Richard Jones.	
2056	,, William Jones.	
2475	,, Patrick Jordon.	
3056	,, Richard Jordon.	
2210	,, John Jordon.	
1814	,, James Kedwell.	
2880	,, Denis Kelly.	
3342	,, Edward Kent.	Died.
2148	,, Michael Kerr.	
38	,, John Kightly.	
2678	,, John Kildea.	
3469	,, James Kilkenny.	
3750	,, Charles Kinnirey.	
3763	,, Patrick Kishane.	
3713	,, William Knight.	
3085	,, James Knowles.	
3307	,, Jeremiah Knowles.	
3291	,, William Knowles.	Died.
2220	,, Charles Lang.	
3389	,, Thomas Lavison.	
1248	,, Michael Leary.	Medal to Depot, 8/7/61.
7	,, John Lennon.	
2962	,, Thomas Lewis.	
1396	,, John Lindsay.	Discharged.
1987	,, Peter Lock.	
3429	,, James Logan.	
2996	,, Timothy Long.	
1200	,, Samuel Lord.	Died 12 Augt. 1858.
1997	,, John Lough.	
3482	,, George Ludby	
41	,, Richard Lumbey.	
2087	,, William Lunnon.	
3412	,, Christopher Lye.	

Regtl. No.	Rank and Names.	Remarks.
3036	Pte. Thomas Lygo.	
2564	„ Patrick Lynch.	
3601	„ Neil M'Allister.	
3164	„ Laurence M'Ardle.	
3377	„ Hugh M'Cartney.	
1672	„ Thomas M'Combe.	
3687	„ John M'Cormick.	
3470	„ Charles M'Cullough.	
3179	„ Philip M'Enany.	
2883	„ Edward M'Garvey.	
2466	„ John M'Grath.	
3471	„ Joseph Mack.	
3445	„ John M'Kewen.	
2864	„ Henry M'Laughlin.	
3090	„ Denis M'Mahon.	
2480	„ James M'Mahon.	Died.
3754	„ John M'Mahon.	
3507	„ Patrick M'Mahon.	
3757	„ Thomas M'Mahon.	
3225	„ James M'Manns.	
2154	„ Bernard M'Nally.	
1538	„ John M'Nally.	
3263	„ William M'Nally.	
3499	„ James M'Namara.	
3407	„ William M'Naughton.	Died 27th Novr. 1858.
2582	„ Thomas M'Namara.	
3481	„ Michael M'Nulty.	
3335	„ Richard M'Queen.	
2557	„ John Maddigan.	
2443	„ Daniel Mahony.	
2481	„ Thomas Mahony.	
2698	„ Daniel Maloney.	Died.
1384	„ Patrick Maloney.	
2993	„ Patrick Manoke.	
2149	„ James Martin.	
1797	„ Peter Martin.	
1614	„ Alexander Matheson.	
238	„ Roderick Matheson.	
2846	„ John May.	
2845	„ Patrick May.	
3013	„ William Mayzey.	Died.
3334	„ James Menzies.	Died 5th Octr. '58.
3037	„ George Miles.	
3596	„ William Miller.	
1557	„ William Mills.	Died.
1552	„ George Mitchell.	
2937	„ James Mitchell.	
2909	„ William Mitchell.	
1310	„ Samuel Moffatt.	
2742	„ Michael Molloy.	
3684	„ Daniel Monk.	
3657	„ Thomas Molyneux.	
3394	„ Alexander Moore.	Died 2nd Jany. '59.
2205	„ James Moore.	
3538	„ William Moore.	
2512	„ Patrick Moran.	

Regtl. No.	Rank and Names.	Remarks.
2639	Pte. Patrick Moran.	
2683	,, Patrick Moran.	
3313	,, Michael Moran.	Died.
1276	,, Peter Moore.	Died 6 Septr. 1858.
1583	,, Samuel Morgan.	Died.
2467	,, John Mungavan.	Died.
2035	,, William Morgan.	
2200	,, David Munger.	Discharged.
3418	,, William Munt.	
2414	,, Daniel Murnane.	
2206	,, John Murphy.	
1408	,, Patrick Murphy.	
2853	,, Patrick Murphy.	
2381	,, Patrick Murray.	
3477	,, Henry Musslewhite	
2345	,, John Myers.	Died 8 Oct. '58.
3463	,, John Murphy.	
2793	,, Michael M'Grath.	
3044	,, William Maddock.	Transferred to S. Musketry, Hythe.
2790	,, Robert Neal.	Discharged.
9	,, William Newman.	Discharged.
1212	,, James Newton.	
3187	,, George Heny. Noble.	
2651	,, Thomas Nolan.	
1913	,, James Norrie.	Died.
2607	,, Antony Noonan.	Died 9 Septr. '58.
2886	,, Michael O'Brien.	Died 18 Novr. '58.
2471	,, Thomas O'Brien.	
3113	,, William O'Brien.	
2965	,, Jeremiah O'Creavy.	Died.
2347	,, John O'Grady.	
3631	,, Richard O'Kelly.	
3767	,, Patrick O'Loughlin.	Transferred to Bengal Horse Artillery.
662	,, John Oriel.	Discharged.
3604	,, William Orris.	
1891	,, James Page.	Discharged.
23	,, William Pannell.	Died.
1692	,, Robert Parfett.	
3288	,, John Parkins.	
3521	,, Joseph Parkins.	
3555	,, Thomas Parrott.	
3203	,, Richard Partridge.	
1195	,, Robert Payne.	
3705	,, George Peacock.	
3603	,, Joseph Peake.	
3295	,, Thomas Penny.	
3128	,, Joseph Perry.	Transferred to 4th Batt. Royal Artillery.
3111	,, Stephen Perry.	
1844	,, Robert Pettitt.	Transferred to the Royal Marines.
3605	,, Walter Philips.	
3245	,, Benjamin Phipps.	
30	,, John Pyke.	
2988	,, William Playle.	Medal to Depot, 8/7/61.
3043	,, James Popple.	
2049	,, Thomas Powell.	Discharged.
3298	,, James Pratt.	Transferred to Bengal Horse Artillery.

Regtl. No.	Rank and Names.	Remarks.
3627	Pte. Samuel Prior.	
2309	,, Charles Prosser.	Died.
1898	,, Richard Proudley.	
3616	,, Alfred Parrott.	
3417	,, Charles Putman.	Died.
3686	,, James Putman.	Transferred to Bengal Horse Artillery.
3514	,, William Quenault.	
3289	,, George Quick.	
3334	,, William Quick.	
2843	,, Peter Quinn.	
2566	,, Michael Quinlivan.	
3273	,, Thomas Radwell.	
3578	,, Henry Rawson.	
43	,, Walter Rayner.	
3467	,, William Reed.	Dead.
3455	,, Richard Rennie.	Died.
3458	,, Isiah Rowbottom.	
3677	,, Williams Reynolds.	
3042	,, John Rich.	
2026	,, Richard Richards.	
11	,, David Rielly.	
3692	,, William Rielly.	
2911	,, James Richie.	
2470	,, Remmy Roach.	
1161	,, Meredith Roberts.	Discharged.
15	,, John Robinson.	
3039	,, William Robinson.	
3252	,, Hugh Rogen.	Died.
3352	,, George Rogers.	
2603	,, John Rooney.	
3210	,, Alexander Ross.	
3448	,, Thomas Ross.	
3129	,, William Rowe.	
3024	,, John Ruddy.	Medal to Depot, 8/7/61.
3230	,, Matthew Ryan.	Died.
3432	,, Timothy Ryan.	
3543	,, William Robertson.	Died 9 Septr. '58.
3154	,, Edward Scally.	
3112	,, Philip Sage.	
3619	,, Charles Samuels.	
3444	,, Joseph Sandy.	
3133	,, Thomas Sanger.	
3215	,, William Saunders.	
3476	,, Philip Sayer.	Discharged.
3437	,, John Schursley.	
2763	,, John Seaburn.	
3358	,, James Seagrave.	
25	,, George Sexton.	
3257	,, William Shadbolt.	
1416	,, James Sharkey.	
2158	,, Robert Shaw.	Discharged.
2677	,, Daniel Sheehan.	
2219	,, Charles Sims.	Discharged.
1568	,, George Sims.	
1414	,, Thomas Sinclair.	Died.
2875	,, William Sloan.	

Regtl. No.	Rank and Names.	Remarks.
3345	Pte. Peter Storach.	Died 17 Octr. '58.
1401	,, John Smith.	Discharged.
2799	,, John Smith.	
3671	,, John Smith.	
3232	,, William Smith.	
3473	,, William Smith.	
3788	,, William Smith.	
2298	,, William Snell.	Died.
3609	,, Charles Songer.	
1780	,, George Sparkman.	
2125	,, Charles Spier.	
2286	,, Henry Stafford.	
2144	,, John Steel.	
3700	,, Robert Stewart.	
2953	,, Edward Still.	
3588	,, William Stimpson.	
1629	,, Robert Stockdale.	
3702	,, Joseph Storey.	
3279	,, William Stratton.	
3651	,, William Stringer.	
3693	,, Charles Stewart.	
2337	,, Daniel Sullivan.	Died.
2831	,, John Sullivan.	
2380	,, Murtey Sullivan.	
2654	,, Patrick Sullivan.	
3753	,, Patrick Sullivan.	
2659	,, Timothy Sullivan.	
3390	,, William Summerville.	Transferred to Bengal Horse Artillery.
46	,, William Sutton.	
2004	,, William Swanson.	Discharged.
2812	,, Patrick Tayler.	
3280	,, Joseph Tearle.	
3433	,, John Teft.	
2349	,, Alexander Thompson.	
3326	,, Mark Thompson.	
3110	,, Henry Tibbles.	
3058	,, John Ticktom.	
1974	,, John Tilley.	
3364	,, James Tims.	Transferred to Bengal Foot Artillery.
3496	,, William Tomsett.	
3427	,, John Toner.	
3527	,, Thomas Treacher.	
2124	,, John Trendell.	
2436	,, John Trowell.	
3074	,, Michael Troy.	
3770	,, William Truscott.	
3426	,, Henry Trydell.	
3675	,, Robert Trydell.	
2918	,, Nicholas Tucker.	
2348	,, Adam Turnbull.	Discharged.
2633	,, John Turner.	
3682	,, John Turner.	
3267	,, Thomas Turner.	
2931	,, William Tyler.	
1925	,, William Thompson.	Died 6 Septr. '58.
3440	,, Richard Vine.	

Regtl. No.	Rank and Names.	Remarks.
3391	Pte. Thomas Vokes.	
2863	„ James Wallace.	Died 16th Septr. '58.
3021	„ John Wallace.	
10	„ John Walsh.	
1594	„ John Ward.	
2144	„ James Waters.	Discharged.
1684	„ Thomas Watkinson.	
2878	„ Hamilton Watson.	Died.
1229	„ John Watt.	
2175	„ Daniel Weadock.	
3026	„ Frederick Webster.	
3415	„ David West.	
3636	„ George Watkinson.	
35	„ George White.	
1192	„ James White.	Discharged.
2445	„ Patrick White.	
3049	„ Reuben White.	Died.
3614	„ Thomas Whitehead.	
1439	„ James Wilgram.	
8	„ William Wilkins.	
3454	„ Abel Wilcock.	Discharged.
175	„ David Williams.	
3219	„ George Williams.	
3162	„ Charles Willis.	
3337	„ James Willis.	
3573	„ James Wilson.	
3475	„ John Wilson.	
3341	„ Thomas Wilson.	Transferred to Bengal Foot Artillery.
2356	„ Frederick Wilson.	Died 10 Aug. '58.
3373	„ John Wilson.	Died 24 Decr. '58.
2039	„ Henry Wiltshire.	
3618	„ James Wing.	
3378	„ George Windsor.	
14	„ Frederick Winterbottom.	Discharged.
3533	„ George Wood.	
3214	„ Charles Woodward.	
3393	„ Charles Woodward.	
2264	„ Isaac Wright.	Discharged.
3186	„ William Wylie.	
2738	„ Henry Wallace.	
3150	„ Thomas Wiltshire.	
1892	„ John Waterman.	Died 20th Decr. '58.
1599	„ John White.	
2983	„ Timothy Sullivan.	

42ND

ROYAL HIGHLAND REGIMENT 'THE BLACK WATCH'

NOMINAL LIST OF OFFICERS, N.C.O.'S AND MEN

ENTITLED TO THE SILVER MEDAL

FOR SERVICES ON

THE GOLD COAST

Under G.O. 43 of 1874

42ND ROYAL HIGHD. REGIMENT 'THE BLACK WATCH.'
NOMINAL LIST OF OFFICERS AND MEN entitled to the SILVER
MEDAL for Services on the GOLD COAST under G.O. 43 of 1874.

PORTSMOUTH, 1874.

RANK AND NAMES.	Whether entitled to the Clasp.		REMARKS.
Colonel Sir John C. M'Leod, K.C.B.	Yes.	..	Malta.
Major Duncan Macpherson, C.B.	,,	..	Malta.
,, F. C. Scott, C.B.	,,	..	Retired.
Captain William Baird (Major)	,,	..	Deceased.
,, William Green (Major)	..	No.	Malta.
,, F. E. H. Farquharson, V.C.	Yes.	..	Malta.
,, R. K. Bayly	,,	..	Perth, 57 Bde. Depot.
,, G. A. Furse	,,	..	Staff (India).
,, Edmond Whitehead	,,	..	40th Regt. O.C.
,, T. G. C. Moore	,,	..	Malta.
,, A. F. Kidston	,,	..	Perth.
,, A. M. Creagh	,,	..	Malta.
Lieut. E. P. Hicks	..	No.	do.
,, Walker Aitken	Yes.	..	do.
,, R. C. Coveny	,,	..	do.
,, G. B. M. Cumberland	,,	..	do.
,, R. H. L. Brickenden	..	No.	do.
,, R. C. Annesley	Yes.	..	79th Regt., Aldershot.
,, C. J. Eden	,,	..	Malta.
,, A. G. Wauchope	,,	..	Perth.
,, J. D. K. M'Callum	,,	..	79th Regt.
,, N. W. P. Brophy	,,	..	Malta.
,, W. K. Suther	..	No.	do.
,, J. E. A. Harvey	Yes.	..	do.
,, M. J. Scobie	,,	..	do.
,, W. A. Berwick	,,	..	Retired.
,, E. G. Grogan	,,	..	Malta.
,, W. H. H. C. Moubray	,,	..	Perth.
Sub.-Lieut. G. M. Munro	,,	..	Malta.
Adjt. A. S. Stevenson (Lt.)	,,	..	do.
Py.-Master Frank Samwell (Major)	..	No.	do.
Qr.-Master John Forbes	Yes.	..	do.
Regtl. No.			
2854 Serjt.-Major John Barclay	Yes.	..	Appld. for List 1. Discharged (Isle of W.). See D.C. Medal Roll.
386 Qr.-Mr.-Serjt. Andrew Graham	Yes.	..	Malta.
269 Serjt. I. of M. William Street	Yes.	..	do. See D.C. Medal Roll.
1551 Pay-Mr.-Serjt. Charles Bateman	Yes.	..	do.
3685 Color-Serjt. James Paterson	Yes.	..	do.
526 Pioneer-Serjt. Peter Gairns	Yes.	..	Perth.
841 Drum-Major Adam Bunch	..	No.	Malta.
1373 Pipe-Major John M'Donald	Yes.	..	do.
— Ar.-Serjt. Thomas Pinkney	..	No.	do.

Regtl. No.	Rank and Names.	Whether entitled to the Clasp.		Remarks.
2173	Hospl. Serjt. John Hynd . . .	Yes.	..	A.H. Corps, D.G.A.M.W.
4086	Color-Serjt. Quibel Cooper . .	Yes.	..	1st Berks. R. Vols.
1419	,, Alexander Dunbar .	Yes.	..	Perth.
333	,, William Farquharson	Yes.	..	Malta.
1370	,, Ronald Fraser . .	Yes.	A.-G.List 140.	Deserted.
1386	,, William Mitchell .	Yes.	..	Malta.
4321	,, James M'Lean . .	Yes.	..	Perth.
172	,, John Todhunter . .	Yes.	..	Malta.
921	Serjeant Henry Barton . . .	Yes.	..	do. See D.C. Medal Roll.
1927	,, Peter Bateman . .	Yes.	..	do.
3454	,, James Butters . . .	Yes.	..	do.
1690	,, John Campbell . . .	Yes.	..	do.
888	,, James Chapman . .	Yes.	..	do.
653	,, James Cornfoot . .	Yes.	..	do.
1375	,, John George . . .	..	No.	do.
941	,, George Gordon . .	Yes.	..	do.
1320	,, Simpson Henderson .	..	No.	do.
797	,, Daniel Kelly . . .	Yes.	..	Perth.
1452	,, Joseph Knight . . .	Yes.	..	do.
232	,, John M'Leish . . .	Yes.	..	Malta.
3995	,, Thomas M'Laren . .	Yes.	..	Dalkeith Militia.
1701	,, Thomas Quirk . . .	Yes.	..	Malta.
1523	,, Thomas Reid . . .	Yes.	..	do.
1602	,, Alexander Short . .	..	No.	Perth.
624	,, John Simpson . . .	Yes.	..	Malta.
1613	,, James Thompson . .	Yes.	..	Deserted.
889	,, Joseph Tyson . . .	..	No.	Malta.
1379	,, Thomas Watt . . .	Yes.	..	do.
1756	,, Isaac Young . . .	Yes.	..	do.
1254	Corporal Thomas Allan . . .	Yes.	..	do.
1490	,, John C. Ayton . . .	Yes.	..	Deceased.
1765	,, John Banks	Yes.	..	Deserted.
1900	,, Donald Cameron . .	..	No.	Discharged.
1893	,, Alexander Clark . .	..	No.	Deserted.
1000	,, John Cochrane . . .	Yes.	..	Malta.
506	,, William Cockburn . .	Yes.	..	do.
1744	,, Robert Geddes . .	Yes.	..	do.
1355	,, Graham Gillies . .	Yes.	..	do.
548	,, James Gunn . . .	Yes.	..	do.
231	,, Andrew Howie . . .	Yes.	..	do.
1944	,, David Marshall . . .	Yes.	..	do.
476	,, Thomas Milne . . .	Yes.	..	do.
1101	,, William Murray . .	Yes.	..	do.
1988	,, Alexander M'Donald .	Yes.	..	do.
1685	,, James M'Donald . .	Yes.	..	do.
141	,, Samuel M'Gaw . . .	Yes.	..	do.
178	,, Charles M'Intosh . .	Yes.	..	Deceased.
264	,, Hugh M'Kernie . .	Yes.	..	Malta.
1585	,, James M'Laren . . .	Yes.	..	Discharged.
1294	,, John M'Neil . . .	Yes.	..	Malta.
896	,, John M'Vean . . .	Yes.	..	do.
151	,, John Ritchie . . .	Yes.	..	79th Regt. (Aldershot).
488	,, Alexander Robertson .	Yes.	..	Malta.
1929	,, James Ruffle . . .	..	No.	do.

Regtl. No.	RANK AND NAMES.	Whether entitled to the Clasp.		REMARKS.
1857	Corporal William Sherlaw . .	Yes.	..	Malta.
101	,, James Sweeney . . .	Yes.	..	79th Regt. (Aldershot).
117	,, William Wallace . .	Yes.	..	do. do.
1413	,, Ebenezer Walton . .	..	No.	Malta.
1810	,, Robert Welsh . . .	Yes.	..	Discharged.
855	,, William Whitson . .	..	No.	Malta.
234	,, Alexander Wilson . .	Yes.	..	do.
198	,, Samuel Wilson . . .	Yes.	..	do.
1243	,, William Wilson . . .	..	No.	do.
2065	Drummer Francis Bunch . .	..	No.	Deceased.
1539	,, William Coupland . .	..	No.	Malta.
1661	,, William Campbell . .	Yes.	..	do.
1492	,, Joseph Clark . . .	Yes.	..	do.
1621	,, John Gordon . . .	Yes.	..	Perth.
1644	,, James Lennie . . .	Yes.	..	Malta.
1666	,, James N. M'Kay . .	Yes.	..	do.
1451	,, Donald M'Kenzie . .	Yes.	..	do.
4306	,, Thomas Neill . . .	Yes.	..	do.
1313	,, James Smith . . .	Yes.	..	Discharged.
1758	,, John Spence . . .	..	No.	Perth.
3036	Piper Robert Galbraith . . .	Yes.	..	do.
4024	,, Angus Gibson . . .	Yes.	..	Malta.
1562	,, James Honeyman . .	Yes.	..	do.
7	,, Donald M'Queen . . .	Yes.	..	do.
1187	,, James Weatherspoon . .	Yes.	..	Deceased. See D.C. Medal Roll.
272	Private Samuel Adams . . .	..	No.	Perth.
1800	,, Thomas Adams . . .	Yes.	..	Malta. See D.C. Medal Roll.
1980	,, David Adamson . . .	Yes.	..	do.
77	,, James Adamson . . .	..	No.	do.
2151	,, David Alexander . .	..	No.	do.
39	,, James Alexander . .	..	No.	do.
43	,, James Alexander . .	Yes.	..	do.
2069	,, Robert Alexander . .	Yes.	..	do.
1861	,, George Allan . . .	Yes.	..	Deserted.
2182	,, James Allan . . .	Yes.	..	Deserted.
3193	,, John Allan (1) . . .	..	No.	Perth.
2035	,, John Allan (2) . . .	Yes.	..	Malta.
2127	,, John Allan . . .	..	No.	do.
1445	,, Alexander Anderson .	Yes.	..	do.
184	,, Cornelius Anderson .	Yes.	..	do.
1735	,, George Anderson . .	Yes.	..	do.
1671	,, Hugh Anderson . .	Yes.	..	do.
1402	,, John Anderson (1) . .	Yes.	..	Perth.
2157	,, John Anderson (2) . .	Yes.	..	Malta.
1782	,, Thomas Anderson . .	Yes.	..	do.
122	,, William Anderson (1) .	Yes.	..	79th Regt.
139	,, William Anderson (2) .	Yes.	..	Malta.
3154	,, John Angus . . .	Yes.	..	Discharged.
2011	,, Christopher Armstrong .	Yes.	..	Malta.
203	,, William Armstrong . .	Yes.	..	do.
2154	,, John Arnot . . .	Yes.	..	do.
1808	,, John Arthur . . .	Yes.	..	do.
1478	,, Alexander Bain . . .	Yes.	..	do.
162	,, James Bain	Yes.	..	79th Foot (Appld. for).
1950	,, Joseph Bain	Yes.	..	Malta.

Regtl. No.	Rank and Names.	Whether entitled to the Clasp.		Remarks.
271	Private Peter Baird	Yes.	..	79th Regt., Aldershot.
1781	,,　John Bain	Yes.	..	Malta.
164	,,　Edward Balfour . . .	Yes.	..	do.
559	,,　James Balfour . . .	Yes.	..	Discharged.
1832	,,　John Banks	Yes.	..	Deserted.
166	,,　Michael Barrie . . .	Yes.	..	79th Regt., Aldershot.
45	,,　John Bartie	Yes.	..	Malta.
2017	,,　Joseph Bather . . .	Yes.	..	do.
2016	,,　Samuel Bather . . .	Yes.	..	do.
1707	,,　David Beattie . . .	Yes.	..	do.
186	,,　James Beck	..	No.	79th Regt., Aldershot.
154	,,　William Bell . . .	Yes.	..	Discharged.　See D.C. Medal Roll.
1390	,,　Samuel Bell	Yes.	..	Perth.
400	,,　Michael Bennett . . .	Yes.	..	Discharged.
192	,,　Matthew Bennie . . .	Yes.	..	79th Regt., Aldershot.
193	,,　John Berrie	..	No.	do.
1863	,,　Henry Binny	..	No.	Malta.
53	,,　Edward Black . . .	..	No.	Perth.
198	,,　James Black	Yes.	..	79th Regt., Aldershot.
1844	,,　John Blyth	Yes.	..	Deserted.
2159	,,　William Blyth . . .	Yes.	..	Discharged.
217	,,　William Bowie . . .	..	No.	79th Regt., Aldershot.
131	,.　Fullarton Boyd . . .	Yes.	..	Malta.
1496	,,　John Brands	Yes.	..	Perth.
155	,,　John Broadley . . .	..	No.	79th Regt.
1896	,,　Alexander Brown . . .	Yes.	..	Malta.
1928	,,　Charles Brown . . .	Yes.	..	do.
1870	,,　David Brown . . .	Yes.	..	do.
2020	,,　George Brown . . .	Yes.	..	do.
2226	,,　George Brown . . .	Yes.	..	Deceased.
772	,,　James Brown . . .	Yes.	..	Malta.
1567	,,　James Brown . . .	Yes.	..	Perth.
2075	,,　James Brown . . .	Yes.	..	Malta.
1958	,,　Alexander Bruce . . .	Yes.	..	Discharged.
1610	,,　Charles Buchan . . .	Yes.	..	Malta.
2217	,,　George Buchan . . .	..	No.	do.
2218	,,　Thomas Buchan . . .	Yes.	..	do.
1146	,,　James Buchanan . . .	Yes.	..	do.
303	,,　John Buckley . . .	Yes.	..	do.
1709	,,　David Burnett . . .	Yes.	..	Deserted.
1982	,,　Robert Burnett . . .	..	No.	Malta.
1983	,,　William Burnett . . .	..	No.	Deserted.
2206	,,　John Burns	..	No.	Malta ?
2089	,,　James Burt	..	No.	do.
128	,,　John Butler	Yes.	..	79th Regt., Aldershot.
1485	,,　James Cairnie . . .	Yes.	..	Malta.
2124	,,　David Cairns	Yes.	..	do.
1912	,,　Alexander Cameron . .	..	No.	Perth.
2048	,,　Alexander Cameron . .	..	No.	Malta.
952	,,　Angus Cameron . . .	Yes.	..	do.
1974	,,　John Cameron . . .	..	No.	do.
2023	,,　John Cameron . . .	..	No.	do.
1340	,,　William Cameron . . .	Yes.	..	61st Bde. Depot.
180	,,　Donald Cameron . . .	Yes.	..	79th Regt., Aldershot.
209	,,　George Cameron . . .	Yes.	..	do.　　　do.　　See D.C. Medal Roll.

Regtl. No.	RANK AND NAMES.	Whether entitled to the Clasp.		REMARKS.
168	Private Peter Cameron . . .	Yes.	..	79th Regt.
4111	,, John Calderwood . .	Yes.	..	Malta.
2077	,, James Caldwell . . .	Yes.	..	do.
2025	,, William Callander . .	Yes.	..	Discharged.
419	,, James Campbell . . .	Yes.	..	Discharged.
275	,, Joseph Campbell . .	Yes.	..	Deceased.
2042	,, Daniel Campbell . .	Yes.	..	Malta.
1626	,, Henry Campbell . . .	Yes.	..	do.
2139	,, James Campbell . . .	Yes.	..	do.
65	,, James Campbell . . .	Yes.	..	Perth.
156	,, Charles Campbell . .	Yes.	..	79th Regiment.
1839	,, John Carmichael . .	Yes.	..	Malta.
188	,, James Carnaghan . .	Yes.	..	79th Regiment.
2183	,, Michael Carrigan . .	Yes.	..	Malta.
2099	,, David Carse	Yes.	..	do.
2158	,, George Chalmers . .	Yes.	..	do.
199	,, John Chancellor . . .	Yes.	..	do.
1776	,, Robert Chandler . . .	..	No.	do.
1972	,, Samuel Chisholm . .	Yes.	..	Malta.
2131	,, William Chisholm . .	Yes.	..	Deserted.
4311	,, Methven Clark . . .	Yes.	..	Malta.
1821	,, Robert Clark	Yes.	..	do.
2013	,, Thomas Clark . . .	..	No.	do.
1724	,, William Clark . . .	Yes.	..	do.
2119	,, Arthur Clelland . . .	..	No.	do.
169	,, John Clelland . . .	Yes.	..	79th Regiment.
130	,, William Clelland . . .	Yes.	..	do. do.
1997	,, John Cochrane . . .	Yes.	..	Malta.
119	,, William Cockburn . .	..	No.	79th Regt.
1969	,, John Collins	Yes.	..	Deserted.
2138	,, Joseph Collins . . .	Yes.	..	Malta.
2173	,, William Coulin . . .	Yes.	..	do.
2223	,, James Connan . . .	..	No.	do.
1633	,, John Connell	Yes.	..	Deserted.
1899	,, Walter Cook	..	No.	Malta.
174	,, James Cooper . . .	..	No.	Perth.
1111	,, Fergus Cowan . . .	Yes.	..	Malta.
2072	,, Dugald Cowan . . .	Yes.	..	do.
132	,, Nicholas Cowan . . .	Yes.	..	79th Regiment.
1949	,, James Coupar . . .	Yes.	..	Perth.
189	,, William Cormack . .	Yes.	..	79th Regiment, Aldershot.
1925	,, James Craig	..	No.	Malta.
1627	,, Peter Craig	Yes.	..	Deceased.
1745	,, Thomas Craig . . .	Yes.	..	Malta.
1895	,, Thomas Craig . . .	Yes.	..	do.
2137	,, Peter Crane	Yes.	..	Discharged.
1996	,, James Crighton . . .	Yes.	..	Malta.
2197	,, Hugh Cross	..	No.	do.
1976	,, John Crow	Yes.	..	do.
1913	,, William Curran . . .	..	No.	do.
1888	,, Robert Currie . . .	Yes.	..	do.
1731	,, John Cuthbertson . .	Yes.	..	do.
2144	,, Michael Davie . . .	Yes.	..	do.
2015	,, John Davis	Yes.	..	do.
2193	,, John Devany . . .	Yes.	..	do.

Regtl. No.	Rank and Names.	Whether entitled to the Clasp.		Remarks.
591	Private James Dewar . . .	Yes.	..	Malta.
1890	,, John Dickson . . .	Yes.	..	do.
1606	,, Alexander Dobbie . .	..	No.	do.
211	,, James Dobbin . . .	Yes.	..	79th Regt., Aldershot.
195	,, Charles Donald . . .	Yes.	..	79th Regt.
1791	,, William Donald . . .	..	No.	Malta.
1653	,, James Donaldson . .	Yes.	..	do.
1837	,, James Donaldson . .	Yes.	..	do.
2156	,, David Dougal . . .	Yes.	..	Discharged.
2196	,, William Dougal . . .	..	No.	Deserted.
1623	,, James Douglas . . .	Yes.	..	Malta.
2233	,, John Douglas . . .	Yes.	..	do.
1789	,, James Downie . . .	..	No.	do.
123	,, Thomas Downie . . .	Yes.	..	79th Regiment.
206	,, Alexander Drummond .	Yes.	..	do. do.
124	,, Charles Drummond . .	Yes.	..	do. do.
2201	,, John Drummond . .	Yes.	..	Malta.
702	,, George Dudley . . .	Yes.	..	Malta.
3375	,, Guildford Dudley . .	Yes.	..	Died of wounds.
2171	,, James Duff	..	No.	Malta.
2186	,, William Duncan . . .	Yes.	..	do.
1783	,, Thomas Duncanson . .	..	No.	do.
422	,, Martin Dunn	Yes.	..	Perth.
1420	,, John Edwards . . .	Yes.	..	Malta.
187	,, Michael Ellard . . .	Yes.	..	79th Regiment.
804	,, John Ellison . . .	Yes.	..	Malta.
2100	,, Alexander Falconer . .	Yes.	..	do.
1804	,, John J. Farquharson .	Yes.	..	do.
194	,, Robert Farquharson .	Yes.	..	79th Regiment.
2204	,, Robert Ferguson . .	Yes.	..	Malta.
63	,, William Ferguson . .	Yes.	..	do.
102	,, Robert Findlay . . .	..	No.	79th Regiment.
305	,, Alexander Finlayson .	Yes.	..	Malta.
1960	,, Robert Finlayson . .	Yes.	..	Discharged.
2130	,, James Forbes . . .	..	No.	Malta.
55	,, John Fortune . . .	..	No.	Perth.
1394	,, Alexander Fraser . .	Yes.	..	do.
1703	,, David Fraser	..	No.	Malta.
1457	,, Duncan Fraser . . .	..	No.	Discharged.
1833	,, George Fraser . . .	..	No.	Malta.
1185	,, James Fraser . . .	Yes.	..	do.
2046	,, William Fraser . . .	Yes.	..	do.
56	,, Henry Fuee	Yes.	..	Perth.
158	,, George Galbraith . .	Yes.	..	Malta.
1937	,, George Galbraith . .	Yes.	..	do.
1560	,, John Gardiner . . .	Yes.	..	Discharged.
1658	,, John Gardiner . . .	..	No.	Malta.
2076	,, Burnet Gibb	Yes.	..	do.
3355	,, John Gibb	Yes.	..	Perth.
1930	,, James Gillespie . . .	Yes.	..	Malta.
1860	,, Ellar Gillies	Yes.	..	do.
273	,, William Glasgow . .	Yes.	..	79th Regt. (Aldershot).
1489	,, Alexander Goodfellow .	Yes.	..	Malta.
1698	,, John Gordon	Yes.	..	do.
54	,, Alexander Graham . .	Yes.	..	Deserted.

Regtl. No.	RANK AND NAMES.	Whether entitled to the Clasp.		REMARKS.
1965	Private James Graham . . .	Yes.	..	Malta.
1901	,, John Graham . . .	Yes.	..	Deserted.
2005	,, William Graham . . .	Yes.	..	Malta.
104	,, John Grainger . . .	..	No.	Deceased.
63	,, Henry Grant	Yes.	..	Discharged.
274	,, James Grant . . .	Yes.	..	79th Regiment.
1249	,, John Grant . . .	Yes.	..	Malta.
186	,, Robert Grant . . .	Yes.	..	do.
182	,, Daniel Grantan . . .	Yes.	..	79th Regiment.
1851	,, David Gray	Yes.	..	D.G.A.M.D.—A.H. Corps.
2120	,, Peter Gray	Yes.	..	Malta.
213	,, William Gray . . .	..	No.	79th Regiment.
2008	,, John Greenlees . . .	Yes.	..	Malta.
1918	,, David Grieve . . .	Yes.	..	do.
1945	,, Andrew Griffith . . .	..	No.	Deserted.
202	,, Robert Hall	Yes.	..	79th Regiment.
1455	,, George Halliday . . .	..	No.	Malta.
1670	,, Henry Hargrave . . .	Yes.	..	Discharged.
163	,, Robert Harley . . .	Yes.	..	Perth.
2236	,, William Hart . . .	Yes.	..	Malta.
2114	,, John Hay	..	No.	do.
576	,, William Haynes . . .	Yes.	..	do.
1635	,, James Henderson . .	..	No.	do.
1797	,, James Henderson . .	..	No.	do.
1733	,, Robert Henderson . .	Yes.	..	do.
475	,, Thomas Henderson . .	Yes.	..	Deceased.
579	,, Thomas Hindon . . .	Yes.	..	Malta.
196	,, James Hill	Yes.	..	79th Regiment.
2175	,, Alexander Hodge . .	Yes.	..	Discharged.
170	,, Alexander Hogg . . .	Yes.	..	79th Regiment
1715	,, David Hogg	Yes.	..	Malta.
1942	,, William Holland . . .	..	No.	do.
2083	,, George Houston . . .	Yes.	..	do.
2134	,, Richard Howie . . .	..	No.	do.
2207	,, Andrew Hume . . .	Yes.	..	do.
126	,, Peter Hume	Yes.	..	do.
212	,, James Hunter . . .	Yes.	..	79th Regt., Aldershot.
2215	,, Andrew Hunter . . .	..	No.	Malta.
326	,, James Hutchison . .	Yes.	..	do.
105	,, John Hutchison . . .	Yes.	..	Deceased.
1904	,, John Inglis	..	No.	Malta.
2148	,, William Inglis . . .	..	No.	do.
167	,, Alexander Imray . .	Yes.	..	79th Regiment.
177	,, Alexander Imray . .	..	No.	79th Regiment.
1975	,, William Jackson . . .	..	No.	Malta.
106	,, George Jamieson . .	Yes.	..	79th Regiment.
218	,, George Jamieson . .	..	No.	79th Regiment.
2078	,, James Jeffrey . . .	Yes.	..	Malta.
1770	,, Peter Jeffrey	Yes.	..	Perth.
120	,, Henry Jones	Yes.	..	79th Regiment. See D.C. Medal Roll.
2136	,, Robert Jones . . .	..	No.	Malta.
1407	,, Alexander Johnston . .	..	No.	Deceased.
208	,, Charles Johnston . .	Yes.	..	79th Regiment.
118	,, George Johnston . .	Yes.	..	79th Regiment.
362	,, William Johnston . .	Yes.	..	Malta.

Regtl. No.	Rank and Names.	Whether entitled to the Clasp.		Remarks.
2140	Private David Jolly	..	No.	Malta.
3929	,, John Kean	..	No.	Perth.
1858	,, William Kennan	Yes.	..	Malta.
1531	,, David Kirk	..	No.	do.
107	,, Oliver Kirkwood	Yes.	..	Deserted.
18	,, James Lafferty	..	No.	Malta.
646	,, Peter Lafferty	Yes.	..	do.
147	,, Charles Lamond	Yes.	..	79th Regiment.
212	,, Cain Lancaster	Yes.	..	Malta.
113	,, Gilbert Lawrie	Yes.	..	79th Regt., Aldershot.
2132	,, John Lawrie	Yes.	..	Malta.
1921	,, Peter Lawrie	..	No.	Discharged.
1780	,, Andrew Lawrie	Yes.	..	Malta.
1823	,, David Laing	Yes.	..	do.
1919	,, David Lamb	Yes.	..	do.
2001	,, James Lamb	Yes.	..	do.
2002	,, John Lawns	Yes.	..	do.
1241	,, Alexander Lawrence	Yes.	..	do.
2079	,, William Lawrence	Yes.	..	do.
1655	,, David Lawson	Yes.	..	Deserted.
1281	,, Robert Lawson	Yes.	..	Perth.
1326	,, James Leckie	..	No.	Deserted.
1922	,, Thomas Lee	Yes.	..	Malta.
2006	,, Thomas Leitch	..	No.	do.
210	,, James Liddle	Yes.	..	79th Regt., Aldershot.
1836	,, David Lindsay	Yes.	..	Deserted.
1087	,, George Little	Yes.	..	Malta.
2036	,, John Livingstone	..	No.	do.
2212	,, John Lockie	Yes.	..	Discharged.
165	,, James Logan	Yes.	..	79th Regiment.
2237	,, William Lorimer	Yes.	..	Deceased.
1657	,, John Love	Yes.	..	do.
1825	,, Thomas Lowe	Yes.	..	Malta.
157	,, William Lumsden	Yes.	..	79th Regiment.
201	,, Matthew Lynch	Yes.	..	79th Regiment.
2051	,, Peter Lyons	..	No.	Perth.
2112	,, Matthew W. Mair	Yes.	..	Malta.
2034	,, Jasper Malcolm	Yes.	..	do.
2122	,, Robert Manners	..	No.	do.
2110	,, Samuel Marchbank	..	No.	do.
155	,, Andrew Marshall	Yes.	..	do.
199	,, David Marshall	Yes.	..	79th Regiment.
2057	,, Daniel Martin	..	No.	Malta.
13	,, George Martin	Yes.	..	do.
571	,, James Matthew	Yes.	..	do.
2170	,, John Matthew	..	No.	do.
1885	,, Duncan Matheson	Yes.	..	do.
1886	,, James May	Yes.	..	do.
2033	,, Charles F. Menteath	Yes.	..	Discharged.
1434	,, Alexander Michie	..	No.	Malta.
197	,, Peter Millan	Yes.	..	79th Regiment.
1955	,, Charles Millar	..	No.	Malta.
1716	,, Alexander Millar	Yes.	..	do.
1794	,, James Millar	Yes.	..	do.
1934	,, James Millar	..	No.	do.

Regtl. No.	RANK AND NAMES.	Whether entitled to the Clasp.		REMARKS.
1856	Private John Millar	Yes.	..	Malta.
1705	,, William Millar . . .	..	No.	Deserted.
404	,, Robert Millar . . .	..	No.	Malta.
904	,, Robert Millar . . .	Yes.	..	do.
1683	,, Henry Milne	Yes.	..	do.
270	,, John Milne	Yes.	..	do.
210	,, Henry Mitchell . . .	Yes.	..	Deceased.
2690	,, James Mitchell . . .	Yes.	..	Deceased.
2155	,, Thomas Mitchell . . .	Yes.	..	Malta.
1577	,, David Morrison . . .	..	No.	do.
2152	,, Robert Morton . . .	Yes.	..	Perth.
56	,, Thomas Muir . . .	Yes.	..	Malta.
1729	,, Alexander Munro . .	..	No.	Discharged.
1630	,, William Munro . .	Yes.	..	Malta.
2047	,, George Munro . . .	Yes.	..	do.
51	,, James Murray . . .	Yes.	..	do.
173	,, John Murphy . . .	Yes.	..	Deceased.
1767	,, John M'Avoy . . .	Yes.	..	Deceased.
2185	,, John M'Allister . .	..	No.	Malta.
1820	,, William M'Allister . .	Yes.	..	do.
1898	,, John M'Arthur . .	Yes.	..	do.
1153	,, James M'Cabe . . .	Yes.	..	Deceased.
727	,, William M'Cudden . .	Yes.	..	Malta.
1841	,, Henry M'Culloch . .	Yes.	..	do.
4207	,, Daniel M'Donald . .	..	No.	do.
2181	,, Edward M'Donald . .	..	No.	Perth.
2052	,, George M'Donald . .	Yes.	..	Malta.
2133	,, Robert M'Donald . .	Yes.	..	Perth.
108	,, Robert M'Donald . .	Yes.	..	79th Regt., Aldershot.
1811	,, Stephen M'Donald . .	Yes.	..	Malta.
172	,, Francis M'Donald . .	Yes.	..	79th Regiment.
72	,, John M'Donald . . .	..	No.	Malta.
2070	,, James M'Dougal . .	Yes.	..	do.
620	,, Andrew M'Farlane . .	Yes.	..	do.
2166	,, James M'Farlane . .	Yes.	..	Discharged.
2189	,, William M'Farlane . .	..	No.	Malta.
140	,, William M'Feat . .	Yes.	..	79th Regiment.
179	,, Michael M'Gowan . .	Yes.	..	79th Regiment.
1993	,, James M'Gregor . .	Yes.	..	Malta.
1792	,, John M'Gregor . .	Yes.	..	Discharged.
22	,, John M'Gregor . .	Yes.	..	Malta.
191	,, Malcolm M'Gregor .	Yes.	..	79th Regiment.
2187	,, James M'Guigan . .	..	No.	Malta.
1971	,, John M'Innes . .	Yes.	..	do.
214	,, Alexander M'Intosh .	Yes.	..	79th Regiment.
2229	,, Donald M'Intosh . .	Yes.	..	Deserted.
175	,, William M'Intosh . .	Yes.	..	Malta.
153	,, Silvester M'Ivor . .	Yes.	..	79th Regiment.
127	,, Michael M'Ivor . .	..	No.	79th Regiment.
1984	,, William M'Iver . .	..	No.	Malta.
185	,, David M'Kay . . .	Yes.	..	Perth.
2037	,, Ewan M'Kay . . .	Yes.	..	Deceased.
434	,, James M'Kay . . .	Yes.	..	Malta.
1482	,, James M'Kay . . .	Yes.	..	Discharged.
109	,, Hugh M'Kay . . .	Yes.	..	79th Regt. (Aldershot).

Regtl. No.	Rank and Names.	Whether entitled to the Clasp.		Remarks.
2058	Private William M'Kendrie . .	Yes.	..	Perth.
2118	,, Alexander M'Kenzie .	Yes.	..	Malta.
2090	,, Hugh M'Kenzie . . .	Yes.	..	do.
1764	,, Charles M'Kenzie . .	Yes.	..	do.
159	,, Robert M'Kenzie . .	Yes.	..	79th Regiment.
1619	,, Robert M'Kenzie . .	..	No.	Perth.
158	,, Thomas M'Kenzie . .	Yes.	..	79th Regiment.
1372	,, William M'Kenzie . .	Yes.	..	Malta.
2177	,, Alexander M'Kinnon .	..	No.	do.
753	,, Archibald M'Laughlan .	Yes.	..	do.
2161	,, William M'Lachlan . .	Yes.	..	do.
1694	,, John M'Laren . . .	Yes.	..	do.
1883	,, Robert M'Laren . . .	..	No.	do.
1761	,, Archibald M'Lean . .	Yes.	..	do.
2045	,, Dugald M'Lean . . .	Yes.	..	Perth.
114	,, John M'Lean	Yes.	..	79th Regiment.
1967	,, John M'Leish . . .	Yes.	..	Malta.
2021	,, Patrick M'Leish . . .	..	No.	Deserted.
2172	,, Donald M'Leod . . .	..	No.	Malta.
142	,, Duncan M'Leod . . .	Yes.	..	79th Regiment.
1910	,, Alexander M'Lennan .	Yes.	..	Malta.
2101	,, Donald M'Lennan . .	Yes.	..	Discharged.
2222	,, Robert M'Lennan . .	Yes.	..	Malta.
1381	,, Allan M'Lucas . . .	Yes.	..	do.
1872	,, Alexander M'Mahon .	Yes.	..	do.
1719	,, Duncan M'Martin . .	..	No.	do.
2085	,, Hugh M'Millan . . .	..	No.	do.
1617	,, John M'Millan . . .	Yes.	..	Discharged.
149	,, John M'Millan . . .	Yes.	..	Malta.
1563	,, William M'Nulty . .	..	No.	Perth.
190	,, David M'Lure . . .	..	No.	Discharged.
545	,, William M'Nie . . .	Yes.	..	Malta.
1795	,, Alexander M'Phail . .	Yes.	..	Discharged.
1542	,, Johnstone M'Pherson .	Yes.	..	Malta.
2117	,, James M'Queen . . .	Yes.	..	Deserted.
133	,, Alexander M'Rae . .	Yes.	..	79th Regiment.
152	,, Archibald M'Rae . .	Yes.	..	79th Regiment.
1818	,, Alexander M'Swain . .	Yes.	..	Malta.
1759	,, John M'Tavish . . .	Yes.	..	do.
2228	,, James Neilson . . .	..	No.	do.
1882	,, William Nicoll . . .	Yes.	..	do. See D.C. Medal Roll (Sgt.).
2115	,, John C. Niven . . .	Yes.	..	do.
174	,, Henry Ogden . . .	Yes.	..	do.
2235	,, Robert Ogilvie . . .	Yes.	..	do.
110	,, Hugh O'Neil	Yes.	..	79th Regiment.
165	,, James O'Neil	Yes.	..	Malta.
149	,, John O'Neil	..	No.	79th Regiment.
1897	,, Alexander Pairman . .	Yes.	..	Discharged.
4314	,, Thomas Panton . . .	..	No.	Malta.
1875	,, John Paterson . . .	..	No.	do.
2004	,, William Paterson . .	..	No.	do.
205	,, Richard Park . . .	Yes.	..	do.
2050	,, George Paul	Yes.	..	do.
137	,, Peter Paxton . . .	Yes.	..	79th Regt., Aldershot.
2082	,, James Pearson . . .	Yes.	..	Malta.

Regtl. No.	Rank and Names.	Whether entitled to the Clasp.		Remarks.
134	Private Thomas Pickard . . .	Yes.	..	79th Regt., Aldershot.
1801	„ George Pilmer . . .	Yes.	..	Discharged.
725	„ David Purvis . . .	Yes.	..	Malta.
1951	„ Hugh Rankin . . .	Yes.	..	do.
2220	„ David Reid	Yes.	..	Discharged.
204	„ James Reid	Yes.	..	79th Regiment.
332	„ Peter Reid	Yes.	..	Killed in action 31/1/74.
1641	„ William Rennie . . .	..	No.	Malta.
2010	„ James Renton . . .	..	No.	Deserted.
1909	„ Alfred Raich	Yes.	..	Malta.
705	„ William Rhodes . . .	Yes.	..	do.
1392	„ William Richardson . .	..	No.	do.
1561	„ George Ritchie . . .	Yes.	..	do. See D.C. Medal Roll.
1398	„ Alexander Robertson .	Yes.	..	Deserted.
2093	„ David Robertson . .	Yes.	..	Malta.
144	„ James Robertson . .	Yes.	..	Discharged
176	„ James Robertson . .	Yes.	..	79th Regiment.
2214	„ James Robertson . .	Yes.	..	Discharged.
112	„ Thomas Robertson . .	Yes.	..	79th Regiment.
376	„ John Robertson . . .	..	No.	Perth.
2232	„ John Robertson . .	Yes.	..	Malta.
1675	„ Thomas Robertson . .	Yes.	..	do.
2103	„ William Robertson . .	Yes.	..	do.
136	„ William Robertson . .	Yes.	..	79th Regt.
416	„ Michael Rodgers . . .	Yes.	..	Malta.
1466	„ Donald Ross	Yes.	..	Discharged.
111	„ George Ross . . .	Yes.	..	79th Regt.
1135	„ Robert Ross	Yes.	..	Malta.
1962	„ James Roy	Yes.	..	Perth.
1884	„ James Russell . . .	Yes.	..	Malta.
1502	„ John Salmond . . .	Yes.	..	do.
8	„ George Samuel . . .	Yes.	..	Died of wounds.
781	„ John Scott	Yes.	..	Malta.
1418	„ Alexander Sandison . .	Yes.	..	Perth.
1961	„ James Satterthwaite .	Yes.	..	Malta.
1537	„ William Scott . . .	Yes.	..	do.
143	„ James Scott	Yes.	..	79th Regiment.
135	„ Robert Scott	Yes.	...	Discharged.
1940	„ Thomas Scrymgeour .	Yes.	..	Died of wounds.
1966	„ James Seaton . . .	Yes.	..	Deserted.
1935	„ Andrew Shedden . .	Yes.	..	Malta.
892	„ Joseph Sharpless . .	Yes.	..	do.
2039	„ William Sheil . . .	Yes.	..	do.
1779	„ Donald Sim	Yes.	..	Perth.
2125	„ John Sim	Yes.	..	Malta.
639	„ John Sime	Yes.	..	do.
1843	„ Stephen Sime . . .	Yes.	..	do.
1963	„ Andrew Stewart . . .	Yes.	..	do.
121	„ James W. Stewart . .	..	No.	79th Regt., Aldershot.
2098	„ James Stewart . . .	Yes.	..	Discharged.
161	„ James Stewart . . .	Yes.	..	79th Regiment.
138	„ Duncan Stewart . . .	..	No.	79th Regiment.
3018	„ Isaac Simpkins . . .	Yes.	..	Discharged.
1448	„ Alexander Simpson . .	Yes.	..	Malta.
1399	„ Hugh Simpson . . .	Yes.	..	Perth.

Regtl. No.	RANK AND NAMES.	Whether entitled to the Clasp.		REMARKS.
444	Private George F. Simpson . .	Yes.	..	Malta.
200	,, Henry Simpson . . .	Yes.	..	79 Regiment.
2143	,, Robert Skeine . . .	Yes.	..	Malta.
948	,, Joseph Skillings . . .	Yes.	..	do.
2147	,, Andrew Skinner . . .	..	No.	Perth.
786	,, John Slattie	..	No.	Malta.
2225	,, Alexander Smith . .	..	No.	do.
1503	,, Charles Smith . . .	Yes.	..	do.
1437	,, David Smith	Yes.	..	do.
1855	,, George Smith . . .	Yes.	..	Discharged.
703	,, Henry Smith	Yes.	..	Malta.
2014	,, James Smith	Yes.	..	Deserted.
33	,, James Smith	Yes.	..	Deceased.
1741	,, John Smith	Yes.	..	Malta.
20	,, John Smith	..	No.	do.
129	,, Patrick Smith . . .	Yes.	..	79th Regiment.
160	,, William Smith . . .	Yes.	..	79th Regiment.
2104	,, William Smith . . .	Yes.	..	Deceased.
2184	,, William Smith . . .	..	No.	Malta.
146	,, William Smith . . .	..	No.	Deceased.
1624	,, James Sorbie	Yes.	..	Malta.
2126	,, James Spence . . .	..	No.	do.
1968	,, Robert Spence . . .	..	No.	do.
2199	,, Thomas Sproul . . .	Yes.	..	do.
537	,, Archibald Stevenson .	Yes.	..	Deceased.
1708	,, James Stevens . . .	Yes.	..	Malta.
148	,, John Stalker	Yes.	..	79th Regiment.
374	,, Alexander Stewart . .	Yes.	..	Malta.
2102	,, Alexander Stewart . .	..	No.	do.
7	,, George Stewart . . .	..	No.	79th Regiment.
1747	,, Kenneth Stewart . . .	Yes.	..	Malta.
207	,, John Stewart . . .	Yes.	..	79th Regiment.
1696	,, Peter Stewart . . .	Yes.	..	Malta.
1766	,, Robert Stewart . . .	Yes.	..	do.
1695	,, Thomas Stewart . . .	Yes.	..	Perth.
1702	,, John Stobie	..	No.	Malta.
2007	,, William Strachan . .	..	No.	do.
2092	,, William Strachan . .	Yes.	..	do.
183	,, Andrew Strachan . .	Yes.	..	79th Regiment.
2028	,, William Strath . . .	Yes.	..	Perth.
2071	,, Duncan Strong . . .	Yes.	..	Malta.
2205	,, Henry Stuart . . .	..	No.	Discharged.
116	,, William Stuttart . .	Yes.	..	79th Regiment.
1939	,, Alexander Sutherland .	Yes.	..	Malta.
2942	,, George Sutherland . .	Yes.	..	Discharged.
85	,, George Sutherland . .	Yes.	..	Discharged.
1946	,, Hugh Sim	..	No.	Malta.
150	,, Thomas Tackney . .	Yes.	..	79th Regiment.
2024	,, Andrew Tait . . .	Yes.	..	Malta.
2210	,, David Taylor . . .	Yes.	..	Discharged.
1894	,, John Taylor . . .	Yes.	..	Malta.
1917	,, David Telford . . .	Yes.	..	do.
215	,, Archibald Telford . .	Yes.	..	79th Regt., Aldershot.
1616	,, James Tevendale . .	Yes.	..	Malta.
1566	,, Charles Thompson . .	Yes.	..	do.

Regtl. No.	Rank and Names.	Whether entitled to the Clasp.		Remarks.
115	Private Henry Thompson . .	Yes.	..	79th Regt., Aldershot.
145	,, James Thompson . .	Yes.	..	79th Regiment.
617	,, John Thompson . . .	..	No.	Malta.
1866	,, John Thompson . . .	Yes.	..	do.
1926	,, John Thompson . . .	Yes.	..	do.
2208	,, Robert Thompson . .	..	No.	do.
2019	,, Thomas Thompson . .	Yes.	..	Killed 31/1/74.
42	,, William Thompson . .	Yes.	..	Malta.
2200	,, John Todd	..	No.	do.
692	,, Luke Todd	Yes.	..	do.
684	,, Frank Turner . . .	..	No.	do.
2146	,, William Turnbull . .	Yes.	..	Discharged.
2054	,, Alexander Urquhart .	..	No.	Malta.
1907	,, John Waddle . . .	Yes.	..	do.
200	,, James Walker . . .	Yes.	..	do.
425	,, James Walker . . .	Yes.	..	do.
103	,, James Walker . . .	Yes.	..	79th Regiment.
1806	,, Peter Walker . . .	Yes.	..	Malta.
1985	,, William Walker . . .	Yes.	..	Malta.
125	,, James Wallace . . .	Yes.	..	79 Regt., Aldershot.
1827	,, Peter Walls	Yes.	..	Discharged.
1905	,, Charles Warren . . .	Yes.	..	Malta.
638	,, James Watson . . .	..	No.	do.
1920	,, John Watson . . .	..	No.	do.
171	,, Robert Watson . . .	Yes.	..	do.
1991	,, Adam Watt . . .	Yes.	..	do.
2128	,, Peter Watt	Yes.	..	Discharged.
1663	,, James Weatherspoon .	..	No.	Malta.
2026	,, William Weir . . .	Yes.	..	do.
2238	,, Hector White . . .	..	No.	do.
1534	,, John White	Yes.	..	Discharged. See D.C. Medal Roll.
2073	,, Peter Whittaker . . .	..	No.	Malta.
1615	,, John Williamson . .	..	No.	do.
2000	,, George Willis . . .	Yes.	..	do.
181	,, James Wilson . . .	Yes.	..	79 Regiment.
1710	,, John Wilson	Yes.	..	Malta.
2062	,, Robert Wilson . . .	Yes.	..	do.
2221	,, Thomas Wilson . . .	Yes.	..	Deserted.
216	,, Thomas Wilson . . .	Yes.	..	79th Regiment.
1674	,, Robert Woods . . .	Yes.	..	Perth.
52	,, Alexander Young . .	Yes.	..	Malta.
131	,, William Younger . .	Yes.	..	79th Regt., Aldershot.
1954	,, Peter Yule	..	No.	Malta.

For Description of these Medals see List of Illustrations.

42ND

1st BATTN. THE BLACK WATCH (ROYAL HIGHLANDERS)

LIST OF OFFICERS, WARRANT OFFICERS, N.C.O.'S AND
MEN ENTITLED TO WAR MEDAL

FOR THE

EGYPTIAN CAMPAIGN
1882

1st BATTN. THE BLACK WATCH (ROYAL HIGHLANDERS).
LIST OF OFFICERS, WARRANT OFFICERS, N.C. OFFICERS AND MEN entitled to WAR MEDAL for the EGYPTIAN CAMPAIGN.

CAIRO, 14th Novr. 1882.

RANK AND NAME.	Regtl. No. and Rank at the time the Medal was earned.	Whether entitled to Clasp for Tel-el-Kebir.	Whether serving with Regt., Depot, dead, discharged, deserted, etc.	REMARKS.	Bronze Star 1882.
Colonel D. Macpherson, C.B.	Colonel.	Yes.	With Bn.		Got.
Lt.-Colonel W. Green . .	Lieut.-Colonel.	,,	,,		Got.
Major R. K. Bayly . . .	Major.	,,	,,		Got.
,, A. F. Kidston . . .	,,	,,	,,		Got.
,, J. S. Walker . . .	,,	,,	,,		Got.
,, W. Aitken	,,	,,	,,	Medal presented by Her Majesty 20/11/82.	Got.
Captain R. C. Coveny . .	Captain.	,,	,,	Medal issued 8/2/83.	Got.
,, G. M. Fox . . .	,,	,,	,,		Got.
,, C. J. Eden . . .	,,	,,	,,		Got.
,, A. G. Wauchope, C.M.G.	,,	,,	,,		Got.
,, N. W. Brophy . .	,,	,,	,,		Got.
Lieut. H. F. Elliot . . .	Lieutenant.	,,	,,		Got.
,, Lord A. Kennedy .	,,	,,	,,		Got.
,, E. P. Campbell . .	,,	,,	,,		Got.
,, A. G. Duff . . .	,,	,,	,,		Got.
,, N. MacLeod . . .	,,	No.	,,		Got.
,, J. F. A. Kennedy .	,,	Yes.	,,		Got.
,, F. L. Speid . . .	,,	,,	,,		
,, J. A. Park . . .	,,	,,	Dead. Adjt.Genl.	Died of wounds.	
,, G. S. A. Harvey . .	,,	,,	With Bn.		Got.
,, J. G. Maxwell . .	,,	,,	,,		Got.
,, T. J. Graham Stirling	,,	,,	Dead. Adjt.Genl.	Issd. 20/1/83 ; 77878/12. Killed in action.	
,, J. Home	,,	,,	With Bn.		Got.
,, C. P. Livingstone .	,,	,,	,,		Got.
,, K. M. M. Cox . . .	,,	No.	,,		Got.
,, J. G. M'Neill . . .	,,	Yes.	Dead. Adjt.Genl.	Issd. 26/2/83 ; 79886/11. Killed in action.	
,, J. N. E. F. Livingstone	,,	,,	With Bn.		Got.
,, E. Lee, Adjutant . .	,,	,,	,,		Got.
Surg.-Major C. F. Pollock .	Surgeon-Major.	,,	,,		Got.
Pay-Mr. W. R. Thornhill .	Captain.	No.	,,		Got.
Qr.-Mr. J. Forbes . . .	Quarter-Master.	Yes.	,,		Got.
Warrt. Officer John M'Neill .	1294 Serjt.-Major.	,,	Dead.	A.G. List 130. Killed in action.	
Private James Abbott . .	RH/1527 Private.	,,	With Bn.		
Serjeant Thomas Adams .	1800 Serjeant.	,,	,,		Got.
Private James Adamson .	RH/154 Private.	,,	,,		Got.
,, James Aitken . .	RH/1522 ,,	,,	Depot.		

RANK AND NAME.	Regtl. No. and Rank at the time the Medal was earned.	Whether entitled to Clasp for Tel-el-Kebir.	Whether serving with Regt., Depot, dead, discharged, etc.	REMARKS.	Bronze Star 1882.
Piper Thomas Aitken . .	57B/2314 Piper.	Yes.	With Bn.		Got. Depot.
Private Donald Alexander .	RH/1413 Private.	,,	Depot.		
,, Samuel Alexander .	RH/1364 ,,	,,	,,		
,, David Allan . . .	57B/2898 or 2398 Private.	,,	With Bn.		Got. Depot.
,, James Allison . .	RH/63 Private.	,,	,,		Got.
,, Charles Amy . .	57B/2637 ,,	,,	,,	Spelt Amey in 'Star' Roll.	Got.
,, Andrew Anderson .	57B/2605 ,,	,,	,,		Got.
,, David Anderson .	RH/192 ,,	,,	,,		Got.
,, James Anderson .	RH/706 ,,	,,	,,		Got.
,, James Anderson .	RH/1136 ,,	,,	,,	E/93095/20.	
,, John Anderson . .	57B/2694 ,,	,,	,,		Got.
Lce.-Serjt. Samuel Anderson	57B/997 Lce.-Serjt.	,,	,,		Got.
Corpl. William Anderson .	57B/2415 Corpl.	,,	,,		Got.
Private John Arnott . . .	RH/170 Private.	,,	,,		Got.
,, James Armstrong .	RH/292 ,,	,,	,,		Got.
,, John Arthur . .	1808 ,,	,,	Depot.	Medal presented by Her Majesty 21/11/82.	Got.
,, Walter Atken . .	RH/1046 ,,	,,	With Bn.	Spelt Aitken in 'Star' Roll.	Got.
,, John Auld . . .	RH/1438 ,,	,,	Depot.		
,, David Baird . . .	57B/2360 ,,	,,	With Bn.		Got.
,, John Bain . . .	1781 ,,	,,	,,		Got.
,, Robert Bain . . .	RH/1582 ,,	,,	Depot.		
Piper William Bain . . .	57B/2370 Piper.	,,	With Bn.		Got.
Private Martin Baker . .	57B/2504 Private.	,,	,,		Got.
,, Frederick Baldwin .	RH/1051 ,,	,,	,,		Got.
,, James Balfour . .	RH/1310 ,,	,,	,,		
Lce.-Corpl. James Bannigan	1629 Lce.-Corpl.	,,	Dead.	A.G. List 170. Killed in action.	
Private Thomas Barber . .	RH/1358 Private.	,,	With Bn.		
,, John Barrie . . .	57B/449 ,,	,,	,,		Got.
,, William Barrowman .	RH/209 ,,	,,	,,		Got.
,, Spencer Barwood .	57B/595 ,,	,,	,,		Got.
Corpl. William Bateman .	57B/1154 Corporal.	,,	Dead.	A.G. List 118. Dead.	
Drummer William Bateman .	57B/2381 Drummer.	,,	With Bn.		Got.
Private Thomas Battison .	57B/2333 Private.	,,	,,		Got.
Corpl. John Baxter . . .	57B/2650 Corporal.	,,	,,		Got.
Private Joseph Baxter . .	57B/2651 Private.	,,	,,		Got.
,, Frederick Beaching .	RH/1532 ,,	,,	,,		
,, George Bedson . .	RH/1247 ,,	,,	Depot.		Got.
,, Peter Bell . . .	57B/2668 ,,	,,	,,		
,, William Bell . . .	57B/2431 ,,	,,	,,		Got. Depot.
,, James Bellamy . .	RH/815 ,,	,,	With Bn.		Got.
,, David Berry . .	RH/1681 ,,	,,	Depot.		
,, Stewart Berry . .	57B/2434 ,,	,,	With Bn.		Got.
,, William Beveridge .	RH/1526 ,,	,,	,,		
,, Owen Biggan . .	No number recd. ,,	,,	,,		
,, Thomas Biggan . .	RH/112 ,,	,,	,,		Got.
,, David Bishop . .	RH/36 ,,	,,	,,		Got.
,, Samuel W. Bissett .	RH/15 ,,	,,	,,		Got.
,, John Blackhall . .	57B/2429 ,,	,,	,,		Got.

Rank and Name.	Regtl. No. and Rank at the time the Medal was earned.	Whether entitled to Clasp for Tel-el-Kebir.	Whether serving with Regt., Depot, dead, discharged, deserted, etc.	Remarks.	Bronze Star 1882.
Private Adam Blackley	RH/7 Private.	Yes.	With Bn.		Got.
,, David Blackwood	RH/203 ,,	,,	,,		Got.
,, Albert Blunden	RH/1059 ,,	,,	,,		Got.
,, John Boardman	RH/263 ,,	,,	Depot.	Medal presented by Her Majesty 29/11/82.	Got. Depot.
,, John Boas	RH/169 ,,	,,	With Bn.	In prison. Has not got star.	
Drummer Joseph Bogle	57B/2280 Drummer.	,,	,,		Got.
Lce.-Corpl. Frank Booth	57B/2563 Lce.-Corp.	,,	,,		Got.
Private William Borland	57B/2683 Private.	,,	,,		Got.
,, John Bowers	RH/1558 ,,	,,	Depot.		
,, Thomas Bowser	57B/2356 ,,	,,	With Bn.		Got.
,, Kennedy Boyd	57B/2399 ,,	,,	,,	See 68742/495.	Got.
,, George Breach	57B/2298 ,,	,,	,,		Got.
,, David Bremner	RH/156 ,,	,,	,,	Bremner in 'Star' Roll.	Got.
Lce.-Corpl. Walter Brimble	RH/1103 ,,	,,	,,		Got.
Private John Brophy	RH/213 ,,	,,	,,		Got.
,, Thomas Brough	RH/1525 ,,	,,	,,		
,, James Bruce	57B/2403 ,,	,,	,,		Got.
,, Alexander Brown	RH/691 ,,	,,	,,		Got.
Piper Alexander Brown	57B/1155 Piper.	,,	Depot.	Capt. Stewart's Collection.	Got. Depot.
Private John Brown	RH/1674 Private.	,,	With Bn.		
,, Robert Brown	RH/1564 ,,	,,	Dead.	A.G. List 140.	
,, William Brown	RH/1438 ,,	,,	With Bn.		
,, Alexander Brown	RH/207 ,,	,,	,,		Got.
Lce.-Corpl. George Buchan	57B/2288 Lce.-Corp.	,,	,,		Got.
Private Henry Bullock	RH/1047 Private.	,,	,,		Got.
Serjeant Robert Burnett	1982 Serjeant.	,,	Depot.		Got.
Private William Burns	RH/1371 Private.	No.	Depot.		
,, David Byres	57B/2470 ,,	Yes.	With Bn.		Got.
,, John Byrne	RH/1371 ,,	,,	,,		
,, Peter Cairns	RH/114 ,,	,,	Depot.		Got. Depot.
,, George Caldwell	RH/57 ,,	,,	With Bn.		Got.
Lce.-Corpl. James Callander	RH/653 Lce.-Corpl.	,,	,,		Got.
Private Alexander Cameron	1912 Private.	,,	,,		Got.
Corpl. Alexander Cameron	57B/2286 Corpl.	,,	,,		Cot.
Private Alexr. Cameron	57B/2469 Private.	,,	,,		Got.
Corpl. Donald Cameron	57B/2378 Corporal.	,,	,,		Got.
Private Donald Cameron	RH/172 Private.	,,	,,		Got. Depot.
,, Hector Cameron	RH/1436 ,,	,,	,,		
,, Robert Cameron	57B/2564 ,,	,,	,,		Got.
,, William Cameron	RH/1461 ,,	,,	Depot.		
,, Alexander Campbell	RH/814 ,,	,,	With Bn.		Got.
,, Daniel Campbell	57B/2511 ,,	,,	,,		Got.
,, Henry Campbell	1629 ,,	,,	,,		
,, James Campbell	RH/1245 ,,	,,	,,	Forfeited on confession of desertion, 68/42/133. Restored, 68/42/580.	
,, John Campbell	RH/67 ,,	,,	,,		Got.
,, John Campbell	RH/1633 ,,	,,	,,		
,, Joseph Campbell	RH/1667 ,,	,,	,,		
Serjeant William Campbell	1661 Serjeant.	,,	Depot.	E/91077/12.	Got.

Rank and Name.	Regtl. No. and Rank at the time the Medal was earned.	Whether entitled to Clasp for Tel-el-Kebir.	Whether serving with Regt., Depot, dead, discharged, deserted, etc.	Remarks.	Bronze Star 1882.
Serjeant John Campion	57B/249 Serjeant.	Yes.	With Bn.	E/90631/15.	Got.
„ John Carmichael	1839 „	„	„		Got.
Lce.-Corpl. James Carstairs	RH/197 Lce.-Corpl.	„	„		Got.
Drumr. David Carter	57B/1068 Drummer.	„	„		Got.
Private William Carter	RH/230 Private.	„	„		Got.
Serjeant Ernest V. Chadwick	RH/1676 Serjeant.	„	„		
Lce.-Corpl. William Chalmers	RH/32 Lce.-Corpl.	„	„		Got.
Corpl. Robert Chapman	57B/2685 Corporal.	„	„		Got.
Private James Chisholm	RH/115 Private.	„	„		Got.
Lce.-Corpl. William Christie	RH/146 Lce.-Corpl.	„	„		Got.
„ Ernest Christoph	RH/1042 „	„	„		Got.
Corpl. James Clancey	RH/1072 Corporal.	„	„		Got.
Private Peter Clark	57B/1134 Private.	„	„		Got.
„ Thomas M. Clark	RH/792 „	„	Dead.	E/92120/18. A.G.List 122. Killed in action.	
Serjt.-Dmr. William Clark	1724 Sjt.-Drummer.	„	With Bn.		Got.
Private Ebenezer Claydon	RH/1065 Private.	„	„		Got.
„ Oliver Coates	RH/785 „	„	„		Got.
„ Charles Cochrane	RH/1436 „	„	Depot.		
„ Robert Cochrane	57B/2391 „	„	With Bn.		Got.
„ Thomas Cocking	RH/760 „	No.	Depot.		Got.
„ Peter Coles	RH/1675 „	Yes.	With Bn.		
Corporal Edwin H. Collier	57B/2574 Corporal.	No.	Depot.	No. 2514 'Star' Roll.	Got. Depot.
Private William Collins	1195 Private.	„	With Bn.		Got.
Lce.-Corpl. James Constable	57B/2699 Lce.-Corp.	Yes.	Depot.		
Pio.-Serjt. James Connan	2223 Pioneer-Serjt.	„	With Bn.		Got.
Private Andrew Connell	RH/1626 Private.	„	Depot.		
„ James Connolly	57B/2673 „	„	With Bn.		Got.
Drummer Edward Cook	1753 Drummer.	„	„		Got.
Private Albert C. Corrall	RH/1031 Private.	„	„		Got.
„ John Courtney	RH/240 „	„	„		Got.
„ Charles Coutts	RH/1559 „	„	„		
„ Andrew Coyle	RH/1382 „	„	„	Issued 68/72 ? 002/487 ?	
„ David Cowan	RH/241 „	„	„		Got.
„ James Cowper	57B/2362 „	„	„		Got.
„ George Cox	1552 „	„	„		Got.
„ Alexr. Craig	57B/555 „	„	Depot.		
„ William Crawford	57B/2567 „	„	With Bn.		Got.
„ Peter Crichton	57B/2506 „	„	„		Got.
„ Henry Crowe	57B/2495 „	„	„		Got.
„ Adam Cruickshank	57B/2388 „	„	„		Got.
„ John Cruickshank	RH/1344 „	„	„		
Corporal John Cruickshank	57B/2412 „	„	„	'Forfeited' 68/42/133 on conviction of theft.	
Private David Cunningham	RH/1477 „	„	„		
„ James Cunningham	RH/1192 „	„	Depot	Medal presented by Her Majesty 29/11/82.	Got. Depot.
„ Abrahim Curtis	RH/1492 „	„	„		
„ Robert Cuthill	57/2473 „	„	With Bn.		Got.
„ William Dalgleish	57B/928 Lce.-Serjt.	No.	„		Got.
„ George Davidson	57B/2363 Private.	Yes.	„		Got.
„ Henry Davidson	RH/1422 „	„	„		

Rank and Name.	Regtl. No. and Rank at the time the Medal was earned.	Whether entitled to Clasp for Tel-el-Kebir.	Whether serving with Regt., Depot, dead, discharged, etc.	Remarks.	Bronze Star 1882.
Private James Davidson	RH/1636 Private.	Yes.	With Bn.	William in 'Star' Roll.	
Lce.-Corpl. William Davidson	RH/21 ,,	,,	,,		Got.
Private George Deans	RH/35 ,,	,,	,,		Got.
,, Michael Delaney	RH/1692 ,,	,,	,,		
,, Martin Dempsey	RH/68 ,,	,,	Depot.	Medal presented by Her Majesty 29/11/82.	Got.
,, Charles Dick	RH/1388 ,,	,,	With Bn.		
,, James Dickson	RH/248 ,,	,,	,,		Got.
,, Alexander Dobbie	1606 ,,	,,	,,	E/88952/24.	Got.
,, James Dods	57B/1112 ,,	,,	,,		Got.
,, William Donald	1620 ,,	,,	Depot.	Medal presented by Her Majesty 21/11/82.	Got.
Serjt.-Cook James Donaldson	1653 Serjt.-Cook.	,,	With Bn.		Got.
Private Peter Donaldson	57B/2507 Private.	,,	,,		Got.
,, George Douglas	57B/2552 ,,	No.	Depot.		Got.
,, Hugh Dow	RH/194 ,,	Yes.	Depot.	Deserter 68/42/123. Restored 29/8/87. A.G. List 235.	
,, John Dowie	57B/1081 ,,	,,	With Bn.		Got.
,, James Downie	1789 ,,	,,	,,		Got.
,, John Downie	57B/2410 ,,	- ,,	,,		Got.
,, Robert Downie	RH/693 ,,	,,	,,		Got.
,, David Driver	RH/116 ,,	,,	,,		Got.
Corpl. Cecil E. P. Drouêt	57B/2593 Corporal.	,,	,,		Got.
Private David Drummond	RH/1383 Private.	,,	,,		
,, George Drummond	RH/110 ,,	,,	,,		Got.
Corpl. Henry Drummond	57B/2652 Corporal.	,,	Depot.		Got.
Private James Drummond	RH/1631 Private.	,,	With Bn.		
,, John Drummond	57B/1158 ,,	,,	,,		Got.
,, William Dryborough	57B/1029 ,,	,,	,,		Got.
,, Alexander Duff	RH/188 ,,	,,	,,		Got.
,, Hope Duff	RH/1196 ,,	,,	Dead.	Died of wounds. A.G. List 130.	
,, John Duff	57B/2383 ,,	,,	With Bn.		Got.
Cr.-Serjt. Louis Dunbar	57B/487 Cr.-Serjt.	,,	,,		Got. Depot.
Lce.-Corpl. James Duncan	RH/69 Lce.-Corpl.	,,	,,		Got.
Private James Duncan	RH/295 Private.	,,	,,		Got.
,, Charles Durrant	RH/1027 ,,	,,	,,		Got.
,, John Durward	RH/251 ,,	,,	,,		Got.
,, John Edmonds	RH/1116 ,,	,,	,,		Got.
,, Thomas Edwards	RH/235 ,,	,,	,,		Got.
,, William Edwards	RH/967 ,,	,,	,,		Got.
,, Henry Ellis	RH/140 ,,	,,	,,		
,, William Ellis	RH/1463 ,,	,,	,,		Got.
,, John Elliot	57B/2538 ,,	,,	,,		Got.
,, William Elvin	RH/247 ,,	,,	,,		
,, Henry Elwood	RH/1365 ,,	,,	Depot.		
Lce.-Corpl. John Ewen	RH/175 Lce.-Corpl.	,,	With Bn.	Spelt Ewan in 'Star' Roll.	Got.
Corpl. John Falconer	57B/2628 Corporal.	,,	Depot.		Got. Depot.
Private George Farmer	RH/1214 Private.	,,	With Bn.		Got.
,, David Farrell	RH/1599 ,,	,,	,,		
,, Robert Ferguson	57B/1074 ,,	,,	,,		Got.

Rank and Name.	Regtl. No. and Rank at the time the Medal was earned.	Whether entitled to Clasp for Tel-el-Kebir.	Whether serving with Regt., Depot, dead, discharged, etc.	Remarks.	Bronze Star 1882.
Private William Fenn	RH/1119 Private.	Yes.	With Bn.		Got.
„ William Fiddler	RH/1492 „	„	„		
Lce.-Corpl. Frederick Field	57B/608 Lce.-Corpl.	„	„		Got.
Private George L. Finlay	RH/941 Private.	„	„	Findlay in 'Star' Roll.	Got.
„ James Flynn	RH/698 „	„	„		Got.
Lce.-Corpl. Butler W. Ford	RH/286 Lce.-Corpl.	„	„		Got.
Private David Ford	RH/782 Private.	„	„		Got.
„ George Ford	RH/1571 „	„	Depot.		
„ Andrew Frame	RH/72 „	„	With Bn.		Got.
„ George Franklin	RH/1572 „	„	„		
„ Alexander Fraser	RH/682 „	„	„		Got.
„ Hugh Fraser	57B/2493 „	„	„		Got.
Corpl. John Frazer	RH/73 Corporal.	„	„		Got.
Private John Fraser	57B/2609 Private.	„	„		Got.
Serjeant Ronald Fraser	1370 Serjeant.	„	„		Got.
Private Charles Fryer	RH/1100 Private.	„	„	Medal presented by Her Majesty 29/11/82.	
„ George Galbraith	1937 „	„	„		Got.
„ Neil Galbraith	RH/846 „	„	„		Got.
Corpl. William Garlick	57B/2631 Corporal.	„	Dead.	A.G. List 130.	
Private Joseph Garner	57B/1251 Private.	„	With Bn.		Got. Depot.
„ James Gascoigne	RH/900 „	„	„		Got.
„ James George	57B/2599 „	„	„		Got.
„ William Gettins	RH/1534 „	„	„		
„ William Gibbons	RH/1533 „	„	Depot.		
„ Andrew Gilbert	RH/1260 „	„	With Bn.		Got.
„ Thomas Gilbert	RH/75 Lce.-Corpl.	„	„		Got.
Lce.-Corpl. James Gill	RH/76	„	„		Got.
Serjeant James Gillespie	1930 Serjeant.	Yes.	„	Forfeited on desertion ?	
Private George Glass	RH/1465 Private	„	„		
Corpl. Thomas Glen	1625 Corporal.	„	„		Got.
Private William Glen	57B/2407 Private.	„	„		Got.
„ William Gloag	RH/176 „	„	„		Got.
„ John Goodfellow	57B/2546 „	„	„		Got.
„ William Godwin	RH/1524 „	„	„		
„ David Gordon	RH/879 „	„	„		Got.
„ John Gordon	RH/2549 „	„	„		Got.
Lce.-Corpl. James Govan	57B/2424 Lce.-Corp.	„	„		Got.
Private George Graham	RH/252 Private.	„	„		Got.
„ James Graham	RH/10 „	„	„		Got.
„ Peter Graham	RH/1529 „	„	„		
„ Thomas Graham	57B/2348 „	„	„		Got.
„ John Grakin	RH/1158 „	„	„	? Forfd. on desertion.	
„ Alexr. Grant	RH/78 „	No.	„		Got.
„ James Grant	RH/177 „	Yes.	„		Got.
„ James Gray	RH/257 „	„	Depot.	Forfeited 68/42/246.	
„ James Gray	RH/1319 „	„	Dead.	E/92216/22. A.G.List 122.	
„ James Gray	RH/1381 „	„	With Bn.		
„ James Gray	RH/12 „	„	„		Got.
Lce.-Corpl. Peter Gray	57B/896 Lce.-Corpl.	„	„	E/93094/13.	Got.
Private William Gray	57/2524 Private.	„	„		Got.
„ James Greenaway	RH/1409 „	„	Depot.		

Rank and Name.	Regtl. No. and Rank at the time the Medal was earned.	Whether entitled to Clasp for Tel-el-Kebir.	Whether serving with Regt., Depot, dead, discharged, deserted, etc.	Remarks.	Bronze Star 1882.
Private John Greenlaw . .	57B/2408 Private.	Yes.	With Bn.		Got.
,, Archd. Gregor . .	RH/933 ,,	,,	,,	Spelt Grigor in 'Star' Roll.	Got. Depot.
,, Thomas Haig . .	RH/780 ,,	,,	,,		Got.
,, Alexr. Hailstones .	RH/816 ,,	,,	,,		
,, Stephen Hall . .	RH/1070 ,,	,,	,,		Got.
,, William Hamilton .	57B/1093 ,,	,,	,,		Got.
,, John Hamill . .	RH/1519 ,,	,,	Depot.		
,, Thomas Handy . .	57B/2542 ,,	,,	With Bn.		Got.
,, Peter Hanlon . .	RH/1672 ,,	,,	Depot.		
,, George Hardie . .	RH/178 ,,	,,	With Bn.		
,, Robert Hare . .	RH/1120 ,,	,,	,,		Got.
,, Robert Hargraves .	RH/1662 ,,	,,	,,		
,, John Hargraves	No number received. ,,	,,	Dead.	A.G. List 170.	
,, John Harris . . .	RH/1638 ,,	,,	Depot.		
,, James Harley . .	57B/2667 ,,	,,	With Bn.		Got.
,, John Harper . .	57B/1067 ,,	,,	,,		Got.
,, Charles Harrow . .	57B/837 ,,	,,	,,		Got. Depot.
,, Robert Harrow . .	57B/892 ,,	,,	,,		Got.
,, George Harvey . .	RH/1401 ,,	,,	,,	Harvie in 'Star' Roll.	
,, John Hastie . . .	RH/117 ,,	,,	,,		Got.
,, John Hastie . . .	57B/2686 ,,	,,	,,		Got.
,, George Hastings .	RH/133 ,,	,,	Dead.	A.G. List 140.	
,, George Hay . . .	1529 ,,	,,	With Bn.		Got.
,, John Hay . . .	57B/2373 ,,	,,	,,		Got.
,, James Henderson .	1797 ,,	,,	,,		Got.
,, David Herd . . .	RH/2334 ,,	,,	Dead.	A.G. List 126.	
,, John Hillis . . .	RH/79 ,,	,,	With Bn.		Got.
,, David Hind . . .	RH/1393 ,,	,,	Depot.		
Lce.-Corpl. George Hodges .	RH/1351 Lce.-Corp.	,,	,,		Got.
Private William Hogg . .	RH/158 Private.	,,	With Bn.		Got. Depot.
,, Ephraim Holdsworth	RH/238 ,,	,,	,,		Got.
,, William Holland .	1942 ,,	,,	,,		Got.
,, Robert Hood . .	57B/2422 ,,	,,	,,		
,, William Holahan .	RH/1467 ,,	,,	Depot.	Medal presented by Her Majesty 29/11/82.	
,, John Hooligan . .	57B/2466 ,,	,,	,,		Got. Depot.
,, George Howieson .	57B/2369 ,,	,,	With Bn.		Got.
,, James Houston . .	57B/1039 ,,	,,	,,		Got.
,, James Howden . .	RH/193 ,,	,,	,,	Forfeited /629.	Got.
,, Thomas Hughes .	RH/1661 ,,	,,	,,		
,, John Hunter . .	RH/1523 ,,	,,	,,		
,, James Hutchison .	RH/22 ,,	,,	,,		Got.
,, George Illingsworth .	RH/231 ,,	,,	,,		Got.
,, Henry Inch . . .	RH/1053 ,,	,,	,,		
,, Samuel Ingerson .	RH/1565 ,,	,,	,,		Got.
Drummer David Inglis . .	57B/610 Drummer.	,,	,,		Got.
Private William Inkson .	RH/675 Private.	,,	Depot.		Got.
Lce.-Corpl. James Innes .	1536 Lce.-Corpl.	,,	With Bn.		
Private John Irvine . . .	RH/1398 Private.	No.	Depot.		
,, Richard Irvine . .	57B/1164 ,,	Yes.	With Bn.		Got.
,, William Irving . .	RH/1468 ,,	,,	Depot.		

Rank and Name.	Regtl. No. and Rank at the time the Medal was earned.	Whether entitled to Clasp for Tel-el-Kebir.	Whether serving with Regt., Depot, dead, discharged, etc.	Remarks.	Bronze Star 1882.
Private John Jamieson . .	57B/724 Private.	Yes.	With Bn.		Got.
„ John Jarvie . . .	RH/1378 „	„	„		
„ Peter Jeffrey . .	1770 „	„	„		Got.
„ Charles O. Jeffs . .	RH/700 „	„	„		Got.
„ Andrew Johnstone .	RH/1399 „	No.	Depot.		
„ David Johnstone .	57B/2696 „	Yes.	With Bn.		
„ Felix Johnstone .	RH/1604 „	„	„		Got.
Lce.-Corpl. James Johnstone	RH/38 Lce.-Corpl.	„	„		Got.
Private John Johnston . .	RH/1396 Private.	„	Depot.		
„ John Johnston . .	RH/1531 „	„	„		
Lce.-Corpl. John Johnstone .	RH/198 Lce.-Corpl.	„	„		Got.
Private John Johnstone . .	RH/138 Private.	„	With Bn.	E/90632/17.	Got.
„ Lawrence Johnston .	RH/1435 „	„	Depot.		
Serjt. Michael Johnston . .	57B/465 Serjeant.	„	With Bn.		Got.
Private Robert Johnstone .	RH/1445 Private.	„	„		
„ Stephen Johnstone .	RH/739 „	„	„		Got.
„ Thomas Johnstone .	RH/1073 „	„	„		Got.
„ William Johnson .	RH/1360 „	„	Depot.	Medal issued 2/1/83 ; /2.	
„ James Judson . .	RH/1493 „	„	With Bn.		
Corpl. David Kay . . .	RH/80 Corporal.	„	„		Got.
Private Charles Kelly . .	RH/1215 Private.	„	„		Got.
„ Thomas Kelly . .	RH/1560 „	„	Depot.		
„ James Kemp . .	57B/25 „	„	With Bn.		Got.
„ Thomas Kemp .	57B/2377 „	„	„		Got.
„ Archd. Kennedy .	RH/1135 „	„	„		Got.
„ John Kenny . .	RH/1494 „	„	Depot.		
Lc.-Corpl. John H. Kerr .	RH/243 Lc.-Corpl.	„	„		Got. Depot.
„ Alexr. Kessack .	RH/284 „	„	With Bn.		Got.
Private William Kidd .	RH/81 Private	„	„		Got.
„ William Kincaird .	57B/2614 „	„	„		Got.
„ David King . . .	57B/2687 „	„	„		Got.
„ John King . .	RH/705 „	„	„		Got.
Corpl. John King . . .	57B/2477 Corporal.	„	Depot.		Got. Depot.
Private Paul Kirkby . . .	RH/716 Private.	„	With Bn.		Got.
„ George Laing . .	RH/1642 „	„	„		
„ James Laird . . .	RH/1109 „	„	„		Got.
„ William Lang . .	RH/1495 „	„	Depot.		
„ William Langlands .	RH/2613 „	„	With Bn.		Got.
„ William Law . .	RH/294 „	No.	Depot.		
„ Alexr. Lawrence .	1241 „	Yes.	With Bn.		
„ Andrew Lawrie . .	1780 „	„	„		Got.
„ John Lawrie . .	RH/82 „	„	„		Got.
„ Edward Ledran . .	57B/2478 „	„	„		Got.
„ James Lee . . .	RH/1350 „	„	„		Got.
„ John Lee . . .	57B/2279 „	„	„		
„ Richard Lee . . .	57B/1003 „	„	„		Got.
„ Thomas Lee . . .	1922 „	No.	„		Got.
„ James Leith . .	RH/155 „	Yes.	Depot.	E/90684/13. Medal to W'wich 20/678368/42/129/284.	Got.
Lc.-Corpl. Robert Leslie .	2213 Lce.-Corpl.	„	With Bn.		
Private William Leslie .	57B/2347 Private.	„	„		Got.
„ Charles Lever . .	RH/1630 „	„	„		Got.

Rank and Name.	Regtl. No. and Rank at the time the Medal was earned.	Whether entitled to Clasp for Tel-el-Kebir.	Whether serving with Regt., Depot, dead, discharged, etc.	Remarks.	Bronze Star 1882.
Private Charles Lewin . .	RH/1561 Private.	Yes.	Depot.		
,, James Lewis . .	RH/1107 ,,	,,	With Bn.		Got.
,, George Lies . . .	RH/1050 ,,	,,	,,		Got.
,, Robert Lindsay . .	RH/144 ,,	,,	,,		Got.
,, Peter Linn . . .	RH/1414 ,,	,,	,,		
Serjt. John Linning . . .	RH/2342 Serjeant.	,,	,,		Got.
Private William Lithgow .	RH/1668 Private.	,,	Depot.		
Cr.-Serjt. John Lockhart .	1887 Cr.-Serjeant.	,,	With Bn.		Got.
Lce.-Corpl. Alexr. Logan . .	RH/83 Lce.-Corpl.	,,	,,		Got.
Cr.-Serjt. Robert Logan . .	57B/343 Cr.-Serjt.	,,	,,		Got.
Private James Louth . .	RH/788 Private.	,,	,,		Got.
,, William Love . .	RH/1353 ,,	,,	,,		
,, George Low . . .	57B/2660 ,,	,,	,,		Got.
,, William Low . .	RH/1664 ,,	,,	,,		
Lce.-Serjt. George Luscombe .	57B/1444 Lce.-Serjt.	No.	,,		Got.
Private Robert Lyle . . .	57B/2710 Private.	Yes.	Dead.		Got.
,, John Lynch . . .	RH/1062 ,,	,,	With Bn.		
Lce.-Corpl. James Lynn . .	RH/1231 Lce.-Corpl.	,,	,,		Got.
Private John Maccorist . .	57B/2513 Private.	,,	,,		Got.
Lce.-Corpl. George Mackie .	RH/1238 Lce.-Corp.	,,	,,	E/90679/15.	Got.
Private Henry Madden . .	RH/962 Private.	,,	Dead.	A.G. List 170.	
,, John Mann . . .	RH/1335 ,,	,,	Depot.		Got.
,, Andrew Manson .	RH/1332 ,,	,,	With Bn.		
,, George Marsh . .	RH/1446 ,,	,,	,,		
,, Thomas Marsh . .	RH/1696 ,,	,,	,,		
,, Alexr. Marshall . .	RH/1384 ,,	,,	,,		
Lce.-Corpl. James Marshall .	RH/160 Lce.-Corpl.	,,	,,		Got.
Private Bernard Martin . .	RH/1634 Private.	,,	Dead.	A.G. List 132.	
,, William Martin .	57B/2468 ,,	,,	With Bn.		Got.
,, John Mason . . .	RH/107 ,,	,,	,,		Got.
,, Edward Mather . .	RH/216 ,,	,,	,,		Got.
,, George Matthews .	57B/2659 ,,	,,	,,		Got.
,, George Maxwell .	RH/55 ,,	,,	,,		Got.
,, Robert Maxwell .	57B/2427 ,,	,,	,,		Got.
,, Henry Maxwell . .	RH/1038 ,,	,,	,,		Got.
,, James Meek . . .	RH/111 ,,	,,	Depot.		Got. Depot.
,, Robert Meldrum .	RH/1394 ,,	,,	With Bn.		
,, Robert Mercer . .	57B/2588 ,,	,,	,,		Got.
,, Joseph Metcalf . .	RH/1033 ,,	,,	,,		Got.
,, Alexr. Michie . .	1434 ,,	,,	Dead.	A.G. List 130. Killed in action.	
,, James Middleton .	RH/164 ,,	,,	With Bn.		Got.
,, David Miller . .	57B/1135 ,,	,,	Depot.		
Lce.-Corpl. John Miller . .	RH/290 Lce.-Corpl.	,,	With Bn.		Got.
Private James Miller . .	1794 Private.	,,	,,		Got.
,, John Miller . . .	57B/2480 ,,	,,	,,		Got.
,, Peter Miller . .	RH/971 ,,	,,	,, .		Got.
,, Robert Miller . .	57B/609 ,,	,,	,,		Got.
,, Anthony Milne . .	RH/1612 ,,	,,	,,		
,, Alex. Mitchell . .	57B/2566 ,,	,,	,,		Got.
,, Francis Mitchell .	RH/1625 ,,	,,	Depot.		
,, James Mitchell . .	57B/1117 ,,	,,	,,		

Rank and Name.	Regtl. No. and Rank at the time the Medal was earned.	Whether entitled to Clasp for Tel-el-Kebir.	Whether serving with Regt., Depot, dead, discharged, etc.	Remarks.	Bronze Star 1882.
Private John Mitchell	RH/1077 Private.	Yes.	With Bn.		Got.
„ David Moodie	RH/278 „	„	„		Got.
„ Robert More	57B/2402 „	„	„		Got.
„ Frank Morgan	57B/2587 „	„	„		Got.
„ John Morrison	57B/2380 „	„	„		Got.
„ William Morrison	57B/14 Serjeant.	„	„		Got.
„ William Morrison	RH/1379 Private.	„	„		
„ Henry Morton	57B/2654 „	„	„		Got.
„ John Morton	RH/1385 „	„	„		
„ Thomas Motion	RH/88 „	„	„		Got.
„ Samuel Moubray	57B/685 „	„	„	865 in 'Star' Roll.	Got. Depot.
Corpl. David Murrie	57B/2406 Corporal.	„	„	Spelt Muirrie in 'Star' Roll.	Got.
Drummer Henry E. Mumford	57B/2565 Drummer.	„	„		Got.
Piper Donald Munro	57B/1040 Piper.	„	„		Got.
Private James Munro	57B/982 Corporal.	„	„		Got.
„ George Murphy	RH/1448 Private.	„	Depot.		
„ James Murphy	RH/1521 „	„	„		
„ Michael Murphy	RH/768 „	„	Dead.	A.G. List 126.	
„ John Murray	57B/2420 „	„	With Bn.		Got.
„ John Murray	RH/1498 „	„	„		
„ James M'Arthur	57B/1102 „	„	„		Got.
„ Donald M'Bain	RH/1416 „	„	„		
„ Peter M'Cafferty	RH/1489 „	„	„		Got.
„ Patrick M'Cann	RH/120 „	„	„		Got.
„ Arch. M'Cartney	57B/1129 „	„	„		Got.
Corporal Robert M'Clay	57B/2595 Corporal.	„	„		Got.
Private Mathew M'Clune	RH/1447 Private.	„	Depot.		
„ Henry M'Culloch	1841 „	„	With Bn.	1847 in 'Star' Roll.	Got.
„ Malcolm M'Callum	RH/1467 „	„	Depot.	1469 in 'Star' Roll.	
Drummer John W. M'Dine	57B/2331 Drummer.	No.	With Bn.		Got.
Lce.-Corpl. Alex. M'Donald	1988 Lce.-Corpl.	Yes.	„		Got.
Private Donald M'Donald	57B/1075 Private.	„	„		Got.
Cr.-Serjt. James M'Donald	1685 Cr.-Serjeant.	„	Depot.	Medal presented by Her Majesty 29/11/82.	Got. Depot.
Private James M'Donald	RH/1576 Private.	„	„		
Serjt.-Piper John M'Donald	1373 Serjt.-Piper.	„	With Bn.		Got.
Piper John M'Donald	57Bde./72 Piper.	„	„		Got.
Private John M'Donald	RH/845 Private.	„	„		Got.
„ William M'Donald	RH/1336 „	„	„		
„ William M'Donald	57B/2475 „	„	„		Got.
„ James M'Dougall	RH/1343 „	„	„		Got.
„ Francis M'Ewan	RH/1528 „	„	Depot.	A.G. List 333.	
„ James M'Farlane	R/H1496 „	„	„		
„ John M'Farlane	RH/1644 „	„	With Bn.		
„ Donald M'Geoch	57B/2716 „	„	Depot.		Got.
„ Andrew M'George	RH/701 „	„	With Bn.		Got.
„ James M'Gregor	57B/2358 „	No.	„		Got.
„ Robert M'Gregor	RH/1099 „	„	„		Got.
„ William M'Gregor	RH/33 „	Yes.	„		Got.
„ James M'Quicken	RH/1338 „	„	Depot.		
Lce.-Corpl. James M'Intosh	57B/2416 Lc.-Corpl.	„	„		Got.

Rank and Name.	Regtl. No. and Rank at the time the Medal was earned.	Whether entitled to Clasp for Tel-el-Kebir.	Whether serving with Regt., Depot, dead, discharged, deserted, etc.	Remarks.	Bronze Star 1882.
Piper William M'Intosh . .	RH/1390 Piper.	Yes.	With Bn.		
Private Alexr. M'Intyre . .	RH/26 Private.	,,	,,		Got.
,, Murdoch M'Iver .	57/2578 ,,	,,	,,		Got.
,, Donald M'Kay . .	RH/148 ,,	,,	,,	E/90685/12.	Got.
Drummer James N. M'Kay .	1666 Drummer.	,,	,,	E/91108/13.	Got.
Cr.-Serjt. John M'Kay . .	57B/1156 Cr.-Serjt.	,,	,,		Got.
Private John M'Kay . .	57/2623 Private.	,,	,,		Got.
,, Robert M'Kay . .	RH/1617 ,,	,,	,,		
,, Andrew M'Kechnie .	57B/1037 ,,	,,	,,		Got.
Serjeant George M'Kechnie .	57B/1012 Serjeant.	No.	,,		Got. Depot.
Private John M'Kee . .	57B/2496 Private.	Yes.	,,	Spelt M'Kie in 'Star' Roll.	
,, David M'Kendrick .	RH/1130 ,,	,,	,,		Got.
,, Andrew M'Kenzie .	57B/2393 ,,	,,	,,		Got.
Serjeant Donald M'Kenzie .	1451 Serjeant.	,,	,,	E/92920/10.	Got.
Private Evan M'Kenzie .	RH/128 Private.	,,	,,		Got.
,, Fergus M'Kenzie .	57B/2572 ,,	,,	,,		Got.
,, George M'Kenzie .	RH/1415 ,,	,,	Depot.		
,, George M'Kenzie .	57Bde/938 ,,	,,	With Bn.		Got.
,, George M'Kenzie .	RH/84 ,,	,,	,,		Got.
Corpl. James M'Kenzie .	2180 Corporal.	,,	,,		Got.
Serjt. Murdoch M'Kenzie .	RH/1548 Serjeant.	,,	,,		
Private Ronald M'Kenzie .	RH/205 Private.	,,	,,		Got.
,, Alexander M'Kenzie .	RH/1437 ,,	,,	Depot.		
,, William M'Kenzie .	1372 ,,	,,	With Bn.		Got. Depot.
Serjt. Duncan M'Lachlan .	57B/757 Sergeant.	,,	,,		Got.
Private Lachlan M'Lauchlan.	57B/2436 Private.	,,	,,		Got.
Qr.-Mr.-Serjeant William M'Lachlan.	2161 Cr.-Serjeant.	,,	,,		Got.
Private James M'Laren . .	57B/2346 Private.	,,	,,		Got.
,, David M'Latchie .	RH/34 ,,	,,	,,		Got.
,, John M'Lean . .	RH/934 ,,	,,	,,	Forfeited 68/42/538.	Got.
,, Lachlan M'Lean .	RH/963 ,,	,,	,,		Got.
,, Thomas M'Lean .	57B/2615 ,,	,,	,,		Got.
Lce.-Corpl. Angus M'Leod .	RH/1556 Lce.-Corp.	,,	,,		
Private Angus M'Leod . .	RH/279 Private.	,,	,,		Got.
,, James M'Leod . .	RH/1470 ,,	,,	Depot.		
,, Murdoch M'Leod .	RH/859 ,,	,,	With Bn.		Got.
,, Allan M'Lucas . .	1381 ,,	,,	,,		Got.
,, Archd. M'Lucas . .	57B/697 ,,	,,	Depot.		Got.
,, James M'Mahon .	RH/1618 ,,	,,	,,		
,, John M'Master . .	57B/929 ,,	,,	With Bn.		Got.
Serjt. Archd. M'Millan . .	57B/2330 Serjeant.	,,	Depot.		Got. Depot.
Private Henry M'Millan . .	RH/1034 Private.	,,	With Bn.		Got.
,, William M'Millan .	RH/1041 ,,	,,	,,		Got.
Lc.-Serjt. Livingstone M'Nair	57B/2349 Cr.-Serjt.	,,	,,		Got.
Private George M'Night .	RH/1395 Private.	,,	Depot.		
,, Finlay M'Pherson .	57B/2714 ,,	,,	With Bn.		Got.
,, James M'Pherson .	RH/1039 ,,	Yes.	,,		Got.
,, William M'Pherson .	RH/1363 ,,	,,	Depot.		
,, Thomas M'Phin . .	57B/327 ,,	,,	With Bn.		Got.
Serjeant Alexr. M'Swain .	1818 Serjeant.	,,	,,		Got.
Private Francis Nelson . .	57B/2674 Private.	,,	,,		Got.

Rank and Name.	Regtl. No. and Rank at the time the Medal was earned.	Whether entitled to Clasp for Tel-el-Kebir.	Whether serving with Regt., Depot, dead, discharged, deserted, etc.	Remarks.	Bronze Star 1882.
Private James Nelson	57B/1163 Private.	Yes.	With Bn.		Got.
,, William Nelson	57B/2583 ,,	,,	,,		Got.
,, Richard Nesbit	RH/1563 ,,	,,	,,		
,, John New	RH/1057 ,,	,,	,,		Got.
,, George Newton	57B/2306 ,,	,,	,,		Got.
,, William Nicol	RH/1562 ,,	,,	Depot.		
,, Alexr. Nicholson	57B/2627 ,,	,,	With Bn.		
,, Alexr. Niven	57B/2711 ,,	,,	,,		
,, Joseph Nixon	RH/1487 ,,	,,	,,		
,, John Norton	RH/1471 ,,	,,	,,		
,, James O'Brien	RH/1432 ,,	,,	,,		
,, David Ogilvie	57B/2430 ,,	,,	,,		Got.
,, George Ogilvie	RH/777 ,,	,,	,,		Got.
,, William Paden	57B/1159 ,,	,,	,,		Got.
,, Alfred Page	RH/735 ,,	No.	Depot.	Deserted /515. Restored /564. L/Cpl.in'Star' Roll	Got. Depot.
,, Henry Palmer	RH/1104 ,,	Yes.	With Bn.		Got.
,, Joseph Parker	RH/59 ,,	,,	,,		Got.
,, Silas Parker	57B/2535 ,,	,,	,,	E/90630/19.	Got.
,, James Patton	57B/2423 ,,	,,	,,	Spelt Paton in 'Star' Roll.	Got.
,, Francis Patterson	RH/1673 ,,	,,	,,		
,, George Paterson	57B/2705 ,,	,,	,,	Spelt Patterson in 'Star' Roll.	Got.
,, William Paterson	RH/975 ,,	,,	,,	Spelt Patterson in 'Star' Roll.	Got.
,, Alfred Payne	57B/2641 ,,	,,	Depot.		Got. Depot.
,, John Payne	RH/795 ,,	,,	With Bn.		Got.
,, Richard Peacock	RH/1620 ,,	,,	Depot.		
,, William Pearson	RH/964 ,,	,,	With Bn.		Got.
Ar.-Serjt. Thomas Pinkney	371 Armourer-Serjt.	,,	,,		Got.
Serjt. David Pirie	57B/2310 Serjeant.	,,	,,		Got.
Private Robert Pollock	RH/1663 Private.	,,	,,		
,, Charles Porter	57B/2530 ,,	,,	,,		Got.
Corpl. Alfred Poskitt	RH/1346 Corporal.	,,	Dead.	E/88414/10. A.G. List 122.	
Lce.-Corpl. Alexr. Pratt	RH/91 Lc.-Corporal.	,,	With Bn.		Got.
Private Frank Prime	RH/214 Private.	,,	,,	E/91096/7.	Got.
,, George Pringle	RH/1225 ,,	,,	,,		Got.
Serjt. James Pringle	57B/100 Serjeant	,,	,,		Got.
Corpl. Thomas Proudfoot	57B/529 Corporal.	,,	Depot.		
Private Thomas Pugh	RH/1337 Private.	,,	,,		Got. Depot.
Corpl. Andrew Pullar	RH/1425 Corporal.	,,	With Bn.		
Private John Quinn	RH/1500 Private.	,,	Depot.		
,, Thomas Rassall	RH/1501 ,,	,,	With Bn.		
,, William Rattray	RH/1472 ,,	,,	Depot.		
,, George H. Redfearn	57B/2600 ,,	No.	,,		Got. Depot.
Serjt. David Reid	57B/2365 Serjeant.	Yes.	With Bn.		Got.
Private James Reid	RH/1102 Private.	,,	,,		Got.
,, James Reid	57B/2392 ,,	,,	,,		Got.
Corpl. John E. Reid	57B/80 Corporal.	,,	,,	E/91082/7.	Got.
Private Joseph O'Reade	RH/1106 Private.	,,	,,		Got.

Rank and Name.	Regtl. No. and Rank at the time the Medal was earned.	Whether entitled to Clasp for Tel-el-Kebir.	Whether serving with Regt., Depot, dead, discharged, deserted, etc.	Remarks.	Bronze Star 1882.
Serjeant Thomas Reid . .	57B/1092 Serjeant.	Yes.	With Bn.		Got.
Private Robert Reilly . .	RH/1424 Private.	,,	Depot.		
Drummer William Reilly .	RH/1153 Drummer	,,	With Bn.		Got.
Corpl. John Rennie . . .	RH/8 Corporal.	,,	,,		Got.
Serjt. Josiah Rhodes . .	57/1252 Serjeant.	,,	,,		Got.
Private Alexander Robertson	RH/28　Private.	,,	,,		Got. Depot.
,,　David Robertson .	RH/694　　,,	,,	,,		Got. Depot.
,,　Ebenezer Robertson	RH/265　　,,	,,	,,	237 in 'Star' Roll.	
,,　George Robertson .	57/2485　　,,	,,	Dead.	A.G. List 118.　Killed in action.	
Lce.-Serjt. John Robertson .	57B/2325 Lce.-Serjt.	No.	With Bn.	'Forfeited'　68/42/133. Forfeited on desertion.	
Private John Robertson .	RH/1255 Private.	Yes.	,,		Got.
Lc.-Corpl. Robert Robertson	57B/2604 Lc.-Corpl.	,,	,,		Got.
Private William Robertson .	57/2515 Private.	,,	,,		Got.
Corporal William Robertson	57B/1019 Corporal.	,,	,,		Got.
Private William Robertson .	RH/1640 Private.	,,	,,		
Corpl. Andrew S. Ross . .	1737 Corporal.	,,	,,		Got.
Private Charles Ross . .	RH/260 Private.	,,	,,		Got.
Drummer George Ross . .	RH/681 Drummer.	,,	,,		Got.
Corpl. James Ross . . .	57B/2451 Corporal.	,,	,,		Got.
Private William Ross . .	RH/1341 Private.	,,	Depot.		
Serjeant John Roy . . .	57/989　Serjeant.	,,	With Bn.		Got.
Private Alexr. Russell . .	RH/1578　　,,	,,	,,		
,,　Allan Russell . .	57B/2397　　,,	,,	,,		Got.
,,　David Russell . .	RH/1367　　,,	,,	,,		Got.
,,　John Russell . .	57B/1143　　,,	,,	,,		Got.
,,　John Russell . .	RH/761　　,,	,,	,,		
,,　Mathew Russell .	RH/16　　,,	,,	Depot.	Dead.	
,,　Charles Ryan . .	No Regtl. No. received.　　,,	,,	,,		
,,　John Ryan . . .	RH/219　　,,	,,	With Bn.	'Forfeited'　68/42/133. Restored 14/9/88; /620. Forfeited on conviction of desertion.	
Lce.-Corpl. Benjamin Saddler	RH/800 Lce.-Corpl.	,,	,,		Got.
Private. Michael Sands . .	RH/1387 Private.	,,	,,		Got.
,,　William Schofield .	RH/1105　　,,	,,	,,		Got.
,,　William Scobbie .	RH/1428　　,,	,,	,,		
,,　Edward Scott . .	RH/1374　　,,	,,	Depot.		
,,　James Scott . . .	RH/1502　　,,	,,	With Bn.		
,,　John Scott . . .	RH/20　　,,	,,	,,		Got.
,,　Thomas Scott . .	691　　,,	,,	,,		Got.
,,　James Seaton . .	1966　　,,	,,	,,		Got.
,,　George Seth . . .	57B/2644　　,,	,,	,,		Got. Depot.
,,　John Sharp . . .	57B/2386　　,,	,,	,,		Got.
,,　John Sharp . . .	RH/870　　,,	,,	,,		Got.
,,　Frederick Shaw . .	RH/1110　　,,	,,	,,		Got.
,,　Robert Shaw . .	57B/2555　　,,	,,	,,		Got.
,,　Robert Shaw . .	RH/1622　　,,	,,	Depot.		
,,　Samuel Shaw . .	RH/289　　,,	,,	With Bn.		Got.
,,　Charles Shearer . .	57B/2620　　,,	,,	,,		Got.

Rank and Name.	Regtl. No. and Rank at the time the Medal was earned.	Whether entitled to Clasp for Tel-el-Kebir.	Whether serving with Regt., Depot, dead, discharged, deserted, etc.	Remarks.	Bronze Star 1882.
Private Henry Shepston .	RH/232 Private.	Yes.			Got.
„　William Shelton .	RH/1334 „	„			
„　Henry Shires . .	RH/223 „	„		'Forfeited' 42/312. Forfeited on conviction of theft.	
„　James Shirra . .	RH/17 „	„			Got.
„　Edward Shoesmyth .	57B/2658 „	„	Depot.	E/88815/9.	Got.
Corpl. Robert Sime . . .	RH/182 Corporal.	„	With Bn.		Got.
Drummer Thomas E. Simpson	57B/86 Drummer.	„	„		Got.
Private William Simpson .	RH/1503 Private.	„	„		
„　William J. Simpson .	RH/224 „	„	„		
Qr.-Mr.-Sjt. Charles Sinclair .	1618 Qr.-Mr.-Sjt.	„	„		Got.
Serjeant Daniel Sinclair .	57B/966 Serjeant.	„	„		Got.
Private David Sinclair . .	RH/1423 Private.	„	„	Medal presented by Her Majesty 29/11/82.	
„　Thomas Slack . .	RH/1688 „	„	„		Got. Depot.
„　David Slater . .	RH/93 „	„	„		Got.
Drummer John Slattie .	57B/2467 Drummer	„	„		Got.
Lce.-Corpl. Alexr. Smith .	RH/1449 Lc.-Corpl.	„	Depot.	Medal presented by Her Majesty 29/11/82.	
Private Alexr. Smith . .	RH/1454 Private.	„	Dead.	E/90053/14. A.G. List 122.	
„　Alexr. Smith . .	57B/2387 „	„	With Bn.		Got.
„　Andrew Smith . .	RH/40 „	„	„		Got.
„　Charles Smith . .	RH/237 „	„	„		Got.
„　Charles Smith . .	RH/94 „	„	„		Got.
„　Charles Smith . .	RH/1419 „	„	„		
„　James Smith . .	RH/1408 „	„	„		
„　James Smith . .	RH/53 „	„	„		Got.
Corporal James Smith . .	57B/2664 Corporal.	„	„		Got.
Private John Smith . . .	57B/634 Private.	„	„		Got.
„　Ralph Smith . .	RH/1535 „	„	„		Got. Depot.
„　Robert Smith . .	57B/2390 „	„	„		Got.
„　Thomas Smith . .	RH/1040 „	„	„		Got.
„　James Smyth . .	RH/225 „	„	„	E/93031/19.	Got.
„　John Smyth . . .	RH/1580 „	„	„		
„　Archd. Speid . .	RH/285 „	„	„		Got.
„　George Spence . .	RH/18 „	„	„		Got.
Lce.-Corpl. William Statham	57/596 Lce.-Corpl.	„	„		Got.
Private David Steedman .	2191 Private.	„	„		Got.
„　Alex. Steel . .	RH/1627 „	No.	Depot.		
„　Francis Steel . .	RH/1642 „	Yes.	„		
„　Peter Steel . . .	RH/165 „	„	„	68/Egypt/602.	
Serjt. John Stephen . . .	57/2261 Serjeant.	„	With Bn.		Got.
Private Robert Stevenson .	RH/300 Private.	„	Dead.	A.G. List 118.　Killed in action.	
„　Alex. Stewart . .	RH/1359 „	„	With Bn.		
„　Alex. Stewart . .	RH/13 „	„	„		Got.
„　David Stewart . .	RH/1376 „	„	„		
„　Donald Stewart . .	RH/908 „	„	„		Got.
„　Donald Stewart . .	RH/947 „	„	„		Got.
Corpl. George Stewart . .	RH/125 Corporal.	„	„		Got.

Rank and Name.	Regtl. No. and Rank at the time the Med l was earned.	Whether entitled to Clasp for Tel-el-Kebir.	Whether serving with Regtl. Depot, dead, discharged, deserted, etc.	Remarks.	Bronze Star 1882.
Private George Stewart . .	57B/2471 Private.	Yes.	With Bn.		Got.
„ Henry Stewart . .	R.H/1421 „	„	„		
Lce.-Corpl. John Stewart .	R.H/1386 Lce.-Corp.	„	„		
Private John Stewart .	R.H/95 Private.	„	„		Got.
„ Peter Stewart . .	57/686 „	„	„		Got.
„ Peter Stewart . .	R.H/1154 „	„	„		Got.
„ William Stewart .	R.H/906 „	„	„		Got.
„ Charles Stobbie . .	57B/2646 „	„	„		Got.
„ David Stoddart . .	R.H/1016 „	„	„		Got.
Lce.-Serjt. Alex. Storm .	R.H/1555 Lce.-Serjt.	„	„		
Private Andrew Strachan .	57B/2371 Private.	„	„		Got. Depot.
„ David Strachan .	R.H/1637 „	„	„		
„ George Strachan .	57B/2676 „	„	„		Got.
Piper John Struthers .	R.H/1377 Piper.	„	„		
Private William Struthers .	R.H/1380 Private.	„	„		
Drummer Alex. H. Stuart .	57B/2492 Drummer	„	„		Got.
Corporal Norman Stewart .	R.H/96 Corporal.	„	„		Got.
Private Henry Stubbings .	R.H/1504 Private.	„	„		
Lc.-Corpl. Harry Studley .	R.H/47 Lce.-Corpl.	„	„		Got.
Private Alex. Sutherland .	R.H/97 Private.	„	„		Got.
„ James Sutherland .	57B/282 „	„	„		Got.
Lce.-Corpl. John Sutherland	57/2374 „	„	„		Got.
Private William Swan . .	R.H/293 „	„	„	No. 273. Swann in 'Star' Roll.	
„ James Sweeney . .	R.H/1410 „	„	„		
„ John Taplin . . .	R.H/1417 „	„	„		
„ George Taylor . .	R.H/1391 „	„	„		Got.
„ George Taylor . .	No number received.	„	Depot.		Got.
„ Alexr. Thompson .	57/955 „	„	With Bn.		Got.
„ David B. Thompson .	R.H/98 „	„	„		Got.
„ George Thompson .	R.H/99 „	„	„		Got.
„ James Thompson .	57B/2709 „	„	„		Got.
„ James Thompson .	R.H/139 „	„	„		Got.
„ John Thompson .	1866 „	„	„		Got.
„ John Thompson .	57B/790 „	„	„		Got.
„ William Thompson .	R.H/105 „	„	„		Got.
Drummer James Thorburn .	57B/758 Drummer.	„	„	Forfeited 68/42/133. Restored /570. Forfeited on conviction of theft.	
Private Owen Tiernay . .	R.H/1680 Private.	„	Depot.		
„ William Todd . .	57B/520 „	„	With Bn.		Got.
„ James Tonner . .	R.H/1628 „	„	„		
„ David Tosh . . .	57B/2474 „	„	„		Got.
„ Thomas Totten . .	R.H/1032 „	„	„		Got.
„ John Towers . .	R.H/30 „	„	Dead.	A.G. List 170.	
„ Peter Toy . . .	57B/2548 „	„	With Bn.		Got.
„ Robert Trench . .	R.H/254 „	„	„		
„ George Tucker . .	57B/597 „	„	„		Got.
„ George Turnbull .	57B/1103 „	„	Depot.		
„ John Turnbull . .	R.H/24 „	„	With Bn.		Got. Depot.
„ Alex. Turner . .	R.H/268 „	„	„		Got.

RANK AND NAME.	Regtl. No. and Rank at the time the Medal was earned.	Whether entitled to Clasp for Tel-el-Kebir.	Whether serving with Regt., Depot, dead, discharged, etc.	REMARKS.	Bronze Star 1882.
Drummer James M. Turner .	57B/2321 Drummer.	No.	Depot.		Got.
Private William Turner . .	RH/1687 Private.	Yes.	With Bn.		
Cr.-Serjt. James Tweedie .	57B/2294 Serjt.	,,	,,		Got.
Private William Urquhart .	RH/1018 Private.	,,	,,		Got.
,, John Vair . . .	57B/2509 ,,	,,	,,		Got.
,, Robert Vair . . .	RH/49 ,,	,,	,,		Got.
,, William Vallance .	RH/258 ,,	,,	,,		Got.
,, John Waddle . .	1907 ,,	,,	,,		
,, John Waddle . .	RH/1431 ,,	,,	Depot.		Got.
,, Mark Wadmore . .	RH/737 ,,	,,	With Bn.		Got.
,, Alfred Walker . .	57B/2543 ,,	,,	,,		Got.
,, Christopher Walker .	57B/2437 ,,	,,	,,		Got.
,, Daniel Walker . .	RH/1342 ,,	No.	,,		
,, James Walker . .	57B/1016 ,,	Yes.	,,	E/95556/11.	Got.
Serjt. Peter Walker . . .	1806 Serjeant.	,,	Depot.	Died of wounds.	
Private Robert Walker . .	RH/912	,,	With Bn.		Got. Depot.
Corporal Robert Walker .	RH/1660 Corporal.	,,	,,		
Private Robert Walker . .	RH/1418 Private.	,,	,,		
,, William Walker . .	RH/688 ,,	,,	Depot.		
,, Davidson Wallace .	RH/1629 ,,	,,	With Bn.		
,, Robert Wallbanks .	57B/2545 ,,	No.	Depot.		Got. Depot.
,, Henry Ward . .	57B/2562 ,,	Yes.	With Bn.	Medal presented by Her Majesty 29/11/82.	Got.
,, John Wassall . .	RH/1115 ,,	,,	,,		
Cr.-Serjt. Alex. B. Watson .	57/538 Cr.-Serjt.	No.	,,		Got.
Serjeant Adam Watt . .	1991 Serjeant.	No.	,,		Got.
Private George Watt . .	RH/183 Private.	Yes.	,,		Got.
,, John Watt . . .	57B/2666 ,,	,,	,,		Got.
C.-Serjt. Thomas Watt . .	1379 Cr.-Serjt.	,,	,,		Got.
Private James Weatherspoon	1663 Private.	,,	,,		Got.
,, David Webster . .	RH/123 ,,	,,	,,		Got.
,, John Welsh . . .	57B/495 ,,	,,	,,		Got.
,, George West . .	RH/152 ,,	,,	,,		Got.
,, Andrew White . .	57B/2617 ,,	,,	,,	E/92718/14.	Got.
Lce.-Corpl. George White .	RH/748 Lce.-Corpl.	,,	,,	Forfeited on account of confession of fraudulent enlistment. A.G. List 126. Specially granted, see 68/42/97.	Got.
Cr.-Serjt. Hector White . .	2238 Cr.-Serjt.	,,	,,		Got.
Private Hugh White . . .	RH/915 Private.	,,	,,		Got.
,, Joseph White . .	RH/221 ,,	,,	,,		Got.
,, Thomas White . .	57B/2625 ,,	,,	,,		Got.
,, Thomas White . .	RH/786 ,,	,,	,,		Got.
Lc.-Corpl. Francis L. Wilkin	57B/2669 Lc.-Corpl.	,,	,,		Got.
,, William Wilkie .	57B/2527 ,,	,,	,,		Got.
Private Henry Wilkinson .	RH/1689 Private.	,,	,,		
,, George Wilks . .	RH/742 ,,	,,	,,		Got.
,, John Williamson .	57B/2379 ,,	,,	,,		Got.
,, William Willox . .	57B/2671 ,,	,,	,,		Got.
,, William Willox . .	RH/199 ,,	,,	,,		Got.
,, Charles Wilson . .	RH/48 ,,	,,	,,		Got.

RANK AND NAME.	Regtl. No. and Rank at the time the Medal was earned.	Whether entitled to Clasp for Tel-el-Kebir.	Whether serving with Regt., Depot, dead, discharged, deserted, etc.	REMARKS.	Bronze Star 1882.
Private Charles Wilson . .	57B/2589 Private.	Yes.	With Bn.		Got. Depot.
„ Hugh Wilson . .	R.H/1669 „	„	Depot.		
„ James Wilson . .	R.H/1474 „	„	With Bn.		
„ James Wilson . .	R.H/1244 „	„	Depot.	'Deserted' 68/42/123.	
„ James Wilson . .	57B/29 „	„	With Bn.		Got.
„ John Wilson . .	R.H/100 „	„	„		Got.
„ John Wilson . .	R.H/1690 „	„	„		
„ John Wilson . .	R.H/184 „	„	„		Got.
„ Robert Wilson .	57B/1121 „	„	„		
„ Thomas Wilson . .	R.H/1412 „	„	Depot.		Got.
„ Thomas Wilson . .	57B/1028 „	„	With Bn.		
„ William Wilson . .	R.H/1506 „	„	Depot.		Got.
„ William Wilson . .	R.H/101 „	„	With Bn.		Got.
„ James Winter . .	R.H/54 „	„	„		Got.
Sergt. John Wishart . . .	R.H/1392 Serjeant.	„	„		
Private Henry Wood . .	R.H/1049 Private.	„	„		Got.
Lce.-Corpl. John T. Wood .	R.H/770 Lce.-Corpl.	„	„		Got.
Serjt. Robert Wood . . .	1674 Serjeant.	„	„		Got.
Private Thomas Woods . .	R.H/1475 Private.	„	„		
Serjeant William Woodage .	1852 Serjeant.	„	„		Got.
Private David Wooley . .	R.H/215 Private.	„	„		Got.
„ Alex. Young . .	R.H/23 „	„	„		Got.
„ Andrew Young . .	R.H/102 „	„	„	E/95557/13.	Got.
„ Henry Young . .	57B/1089 „	„	Dead.	A.G. List 132. Died of wounds.	
Cr.-Serjt. Isaac Young . .	1756 Cr.-Serjt.	„	With Bn.		Got.
Private John Young . . .	R.H/1635 Private.	„	„		
„ William Young . .	R.H/14 „	„	„		Got.
„ Robert Younger .	R.H/103 „	„	„		Got.
Captain G. B. M. Cumberland. (George Bentinck Macleod).	Captain. Asst. Provost Marshal.	Yes.	Staff.	Bronze Star issued 27/3/83 ; 68/42/53.	
Lce.-Corpl. Geo. White .	} 748	Yes. {	{ With Regiment.	{ Earned the Medal whilst in a state of desertion from 3/Grenr. Guards. Forfeited 68/42/97.	
Jno. Marriott					

NOTE.—At the end of the Bronze 'Star' Roll is written the following :—

Bronze Stars received,	.	.	560
„ „ issued,	.	.	514
Returned to H. Gds.,	.	.	14

42ND

1st BATTN. THE BLACK WATCH (ROYAL HIGHLANDERS)

ROLL OF OFFICERS, WARRANT OFFICERS, N.C.O.'S AND MEN

ENTITLED TO THE

WAR MEDAL OR CLASP

FOR OPERATIONS IN THE VICINITY OF

SUAKIN

1884

1st BATTN. THE BLACK WATCH (ROYAL HIGHLANDERS). ROLL of Officers, Warrant Officers, Non-Commissioned Officers and Men entitled to the War Medal or Clasp for Operations in the vicinity of Suakin, 1884.

Medals Issued 23/10/84. Cairo, 20th July 1884.

*=Bronze Star.

Rank and Name at the time the Medal was earned.	Whether in possession of Egypt Medal, 1882.	Whether entitled to Clasp, Suakin.	Whether at action of El-Teb.	Whether at action of Tamaai.	Whether serving with Regiment or Depot, dead, discharged, deserted, etc.
Lt.-Col. W. Green	Yes.	Yes.	Yes.	Yes.	With Regiment.
,, R. H. Bayly	,,	,,	,,	No.	do.
Major A. F. Kidston	,,	,,	,,	,,	do.
,, W. Aitken	,,	,,	,,	Yes.	Killed at Tamaai. A.G. List 149.
Bt.-Lt.-Col. R. C. Coveny . . .	,,	,,	,,	,,	With Regiment.
Major C. J. Eden	,,	,,	,,	,,	do.
Capt. N. W. P. Brophy . . .	,,	,,	,,	,,	do.
* ,, A. Scott Stevenson . .	No.	No.	No.	,,	do.
,, H. F. Elliot	Yes.	Yes.	Yes.	No.	do.
Lieut. Lord A. Kennedy . . .	,,	,,	,,	Yes.	do.
,, N. MacLeod	,,	,,	,,	,,	Depot.
,, J. F. A. Kennedy . . .	,,	,,	,,	,,	With Regiment.
,, F. L. Speid	,,	,,	,,	,,	do.
,, J. Home	,,	,,	,,	No.	do.
,, C. P. Livingstone . . .	,,	,,	,,	Yes.	do.
* ,, A. C. Bald	No.	No.	,,	,,	do.
* ,, N. W. Cuthbertson . . .	,,	,,	No.	No.	do.
* ,, D. A. M'Leod	,,	,,	Yes.	Yes.	do.
* ,, A. G. Ferrier-Kerr . . .	,,	,,	,,	,,	do.
* ,, W. G. Wolrige-Gordon . .	,,	,,	,,	No.	do.
* ,, J. Macrae	,,	,,	No.	Yes.	do.
Lt. and Adjt. A. G. Duff . . .	Yes.	Yes.	Yes.	,,	do.
Qr.-Master C. Sinclair . . .	,,	,,	,,	,,	do.
WARRANT OFFICER.					
Serjt.-Major Isaac Young . . .	Yes.	Yes.	Yes.	Yes.	With Regiment.
Regtl. No.					
*2085 Pte. Andrew Adams . .	No.	No.	Yes.	Yes.	With Regiment.
*2045 ,, James Adams . . .	,,	,,	,,	,,	do.
*2570 ,, John Adams . . .	,,	,,	,,	,,	do.
154 ,, James Adamson . .	Yes.	Yes.	,,	,,	do.
2314 Piper Thomas Aitken . .	,,	,,	,,	,,	do.
2398 Pte. David Allan . . .	,,	,,	,,	,,	do.
*1176 ,, James Allan . . .	No.	No.	,,	,,	do. Forfeited 68/42/443. Restored 25/8/87. See 68/12/129.
2637 ,, Charles Amey . . .	Yes.	Yes.	,,	,,	With Regiment.
2605 ,, Andrew Anderson . .	,,	,,	,,	No.	Discharged. A.G. List 163.
192 ,, David Anderson . .	,,	,,	,,	Yes.	With Regiment.
1136 ,, James Anderson . .	,,	,,	,,	,,	Killed at Tamaai. A.G. List 149.
*2077 ,, John Anderson . .	No.	No.	,,	,,	With Regiment.

Regtl. No.	Rank and Name at the time the Medal was earned.	Whether in possession of Egypt Medal, 1882.	Whether entitled to Clasp, Suakin.	Whether at action of El-Teb.	Whether at action of Tamaai.	Whether serving with Regiment or Depot, dead, discharged, deserted, etc.
2694	Lc.-Corpl. John Anderson .	Yes.	Yes.	Yes.	Yes.	With Regiment.
2415	Lc.-Sjt. William Anderson .	,,	,,	,,	,,	Killed at Tamaai. A.G. List 149.
*2689	Pte. James Angus . . .	No.	No.	,,	No.	With Regiment.
*1152	,, Henry Anson . . .	,,	,,	No.	Yes.	do.
*1060	,, Shem Arbon . . .	,,	,,	Yes.	,,	do.
292	,, James Armstrong . .	Yes.	Yes.	No.	No.	do.
170	,, John Arnott . . .	,,	,,	Yes.	Yes.	do.
*2695	,, Alexr. Arthur . . .	No.	No.	,,	,,	Killed at Tamaai. A.G. List 149.
1808	,, John Arthur . . .	Yes.	Yes.	,,	,,	With Regiment.
1046	,, Walter Atkin . . .	,,	,,	,,	,,	do.
2370	Piper William Bain . .	,,	,,	,,	,,	do.
2360	Pte. David Baird . . .	,,	,,	,,	No.	do.
2504	,, Martin Baker . . .	,,	,,	,,	Yes.	do.
* 212	Lc.-Corpl. Wm. Ballantine .	No.	No.	,,	,,	do.
* 932	Pte. Andrew Barclay . .	,,	,,	,,	,,	Killed at Tamaai. A.G. List 149.
209	,, William Barrowman .	Yes.	Yes.	Yes.	Yes.	Killed at Tamaai. A.G. List 149.
595	,, Spencer Barwood . .	,,	,,	,,	,,	With Regiment.
2381	Drummer William Bateman	,,	,,	No.	,,	do.
* 954	Private John Bates . .	No.	No.	Yes.	No.	Depot.
2333	,, Thomas Battison .	Yes.	Yes.	,,	Yes.	With Regiment.
2651	,, Joseph Baxter . .	,,	,,	,,	,,	do.
*1005	,, James Beaton . .	No.	No.	,,	,,	Depot.
1247	Lce.-Corpl. George Bedson .	Yes.	Yes.	,,	No.	With Regiment.
* 744	Private Charles Belcher .	No.	No.	,,	Yes.	do.
815	,, James Bellamy .	Yes.	Yes.	,,	,,	do.
* 249	,, Gilbert Berry . .	No.	No.	,,	,,	do.
2434	,, Stewart Berry . .	Yes.	Yes.	,,	No.	do.
*1995	,, John J. Best . .	No.	No.	,,	Yes.	do.
*2559	,, Andrew Beveridge .	,,	,,	,,	No.	do.
112	,, Thomas Biggan .	Yes.	Yes.	,,	Yes.	do.
*2016	,, Alexander Birse .	No.	No.	,,	No.	do.
36	,, David Bishop . .	Yes.	Yes.	,,	Yes.	Killed at Tamaai. A.G. List 149.
15	,, Samuel Bissett .	,,	,,	,,	,,	With Regiment.
*2717	,, Donald Black . .	No.	No.	,,	No.	do.
* 65	,, James Black . .	,,	,,	Yes.	Yes.	Killed at Tamaai. A.G. List 149.
2429	,, John Blackhall .	Yes.	Yes.	,,	,,	do. do.
203	Corporal David Blackwood	,,	,,	,,	No.	With Regiment.
*1265	Private William Blair .	No.	No.	,,	Yes.	do.
1059	,, Albert Blunden .	Yes.	Yes.	,,	,,	do.
*2606	,, George Blyth . .	No.	No.	,,	,,	Killed at Tamaai.
*1274	,, James Blyth . .	,,	,,	,,	,,	With Regiment.
2280	Drummer Joseph Bogle .	Yes.	Yes.	,,	,,	do.
*1064	Private Samuel Boon . .	No. 68/42/374	No. 68/42/374	,,	,,	do.
2563	Corporal Frank Booth . .	Yes.	Yes.	,,	,,	do.
2683	Lce.-Corpl. William Boreland	,,	,,	,,	,,	do.
* 923	Private William Boycott .	No.	No.	,,	No.	Killed at El-Teb. A.G. List 149.
* 805	,, James Boyd . .	,,	,,	,,	Yes.	With Regiment.
*1961	,, William Boynes .	,,	,,	,,	,,	do.
2356	,, Thomas Bowser .	Yes.	Yes.	,,	No.	do.
*2462	,, George Brailsford .	No.	No.	,,	Yes.	do.
2298	,, George Breach . .	Yes.	Yes.	Yes.	No.	Discharged. A.G. List 184.
156	,, David Bremner .	,,	,,	,,	,,	With Regiment.

Regtl. No.	RANK AND NAME at the time the Medal was earned.	Whether in possession of Egypt Medal, 1882.	Whether entitled to Clasp, Suakin.	Whether at action of El-Teb.	Whether at action of Tamaai.	Whether serving with Regiment or Depot, dead, discharged, deserted, etc.
1103	Private Walter Brimble	Yes.	Yes.	Yes.	Yes.	With Regiment.
*2597	„ William Britton	No.	No.	,,	,,	do.
*2078	„ David Brodie	,,	,,	,,	,,	do.
* 113	„ Hugh Broggan	,,	,,	,,	No.	do.
213	Corporal John Brophy	Yes.	Yes.	,,	,,	do.
691	Lce.-Corpl. Alexr. Brown	,,	,,	,,	,,	do.
207	Private Alexr. Brown	,,	,,	,,	Yes.	do.
*1968	„ John Brown	No.	No.	,,	No.	do.
* 756	„ Harry Browning	,,	,,	,,	Yes.	do.
*1200	„ Alexr. Bruce	,,	,,	,,	,,	do.
*1216	„ William Bruce	,,	,,	No.	No.	do.
2403	„ James Bruce	Yes.	Yes.	Yes.	Yes.	do.
2288	Lce.-Corpl. George Buchan	,,	,,	No.	No.	do.
1047	Private Henry Bullock	,,	,,	Yes.	Yes.	do.
1982	Serjeant Robert Burnett	,,	,,	,,	,,	do.
*2715	Private Charles Burns	No.	No.	,,	No.	do.
*1183	„ Morris Burton	,,	,,	,,	,,	do.
*1716	„ David Butters	,,	,,	,,	,,	Depot.
*1985	„ William Button	,,	,,	,,	,,	With Regiment.
2470	„ David Byres	Yes.	Yes.	Yes.	,,	do.
* 825	„ John Cains	No.	No.	,,	Yes.	Killed at Tamaai. A.G. List 149.
2317	„ John Cairns	,,	,,	,,	,,	With Regiment.
* 66	„ Duncan Calder	,,	,,	,,	,,	do.
57	„ George Caldwell	Yes.	Yes.	,,	,,	do.
*1052	„ Edward Calver	No.	No.	,,	No.	do.
* 976	„ John Callaghan	,,	,,	,,	Yes.	do.
653	Lce.-Serjt. James Callander	Yes.	Yes.	,,	,,	Depot.
2199	Serjeant Alexr. Cameron	,,	,,	,,	No.	With Regiment.
2469	Private Alexr. Cameron	,,	,,	,,	Yes.	do.
*2484	„ David Cameron	No.	No.	,,	,,	do.
*2502	„ James Cameron	,,	,,	,,	,,	do.
2564	Lce.-Corpl. Robert Cameron	Yes.	Yes.	,,	,,	do.
814	Private Alexr. Campbell	,,	,,	,,	,,	do.
*1934	„ Archd. Campbell	No.	No.	,,	,,	do.
2511	Piper Daniel Campbell	Yes.	Yes.	,,	,,	do.
*1981	Private Daniel Campbell	No.	No.	,,	,,	do.
*1245	„ James Campbell	,,	,,	,,	No.	do.
67	„ John Campbell	Yes.	Yes.	No.	,,	do.
* 959	„ Thomas G. Campbell	No.	No.	Yes.	Yes.	do.
1661	Serjeant William Campbell	Yes.	Yes.	,,	,,	Killed at Tamaai. A.G. List 149.
* 245	Private William Campbell	No.	No.	,,	,,	With Regiment.
*2661	Corpl. William Carcary	,,	,,	,,	,,	do.
*2057	Private Alexr. Cargill	,,	,,	,,	,,	do.
*2015	„ Robert Carmichael	,,	,,	,,	No.	do.
* 882	„ John Carnie	,,	,,	,,	Yes.	do.
*2519	„ Michael Carr	,,	,,	,,	,,	do. See 68/42/495 (Forfeited).
* 965	„ Robert Carr	,,	,,	,,	,,	With Regiment.
1031	„ Albert C. Carrol	Yes.	Yes.	,,	,,	do.
197	Corporal James Carstairs	,,	,,	,,	,,	do.
*1007	Private Adam Cavers	No.	No.	,,	,,	do.
*1312	Lce.-Corpl. Edward Chalmers	,,	,,	,,	,,	do.
32	Private William Chalmers	Yes.	Yes.	,,	,,	do.

Regtl. No.	RANK AND NAME at the time the Medal was earned.	Whether in possession of Egypt Medal, 1882.	Whether entitled to Clasp, Suakin.	Whether at action of El-Teb.	Whether at action of Tamaai.	Whether serving with Regiment or Depot, dead, discharged, deserted, etc.
*1264	Private George Charlton	No.	No.	Yes.	Yes.	With Regiment.
* 891	,, Robert Cheeny	,,	,,	,,	,,	do.
115	,, James Chisholm	Yes.	Yes.	,,	,,	do.
*2052	,, James Christie	No.	No.	,,	,,	Killed at Tamaai. A.G. List 149.
146	,, William Christie	Yes.	Yes.	Yes.	Yes.	With Regiment.
1724	Serjt.-Dr. William Clark	,,	,,	,,	,,	do.
1065	Private Ebenezer Claydon	,,	,,	,,	,,	do.
785	,, Oliver Coates	,,	,,	,,	,,	do.
2391	,, Robert Cochrane	,,	,,	No.	,,	do.
760	,, Thomas Cocking	,,	,,	Yes.	No.	do.
* 191	,, Walter Coe	No.	No.	,,	Yes.	do.
*1324	,, John Collins	,,	,,	,,	,,	do.
* 826	,, Robert Collins	,,	,,	,,	,,	do.
1195	,, William Collins	Yes.	Yes.	,,	,,	do.
2223	Cr.-Serjt. James Connon	,,	,,	,,	,,	do.
2673	Corporal James Connolly	,,	,,	,,	,,	do.
1753	Drummer Edward Cook	,,	,,	,,	,,	do.
2362	Private James Cooper	,,	,,	,,	,,	do.
*2635	,, Peter Coote	No.	No.	,,	,,	do.
*1035	,, James Costello	,,	,,	,,	,,	do.
* 743	,, Frank Coulthard	,,	,,	,,	,,	Killed at Tamaai. A.G. List 149.
240	,, John Courtney	Yes.	Yes.	,,	,,	With Regiment.
*2017	,, Andrew Coutts	No.	No.	,,	,,	do.
241	,, David Cowan	Yes.	Yes.	,,	No.	do.
*1126	,, John Cowan	No.	No.	,,	,,	do.
* 173	,, George Cowie	,,	,,	,,	Yes.	do.
1552	,, George Cox	Yes.	Yes.	,,	,,	do.
* 885	,, James Cox	No.	No.	,,	,,	do.
*2090	,, Charles Craig	,	,,	,,	,,	do.
*2113	,, Thomas Crawford	,,	,,	,,	,,	do.
2567	,, William Crawford	Yes.	Yes.	,,	,,	do.
2506	,, Peter Crichton	,,	,,	,,	,,	do.
2495	,, Henry Crowe	,,	,,	,,	No.	do.
2388	Lc.-Corpl. Adam Cruickshank	,,	,,	,,	,,	do.
*2412	Private John Cruickshank	No.	No.	,,	Yes.	Discharged.
*1099	,, William Crump	,,	,,	,,	,,	Killed at Tamaai. A.G. List 149.
*2053	,, David Currie	,,	,,	,,	,,	With Regiment.
*1081	Lce.-Corpl. William Curtis	,,	,,	,,	,,	do.
*2307	Private James Cuthbert	,,	,,	,,	,,	do.
*2656	,, James Cuthbertson	,,	,,	,,	No.	do.
2473	,, Robert Cuthill	Yes.	Yes.	,,	,,	do.
*1302	Corporal Joseph Daily	No.	No.	,,	Yes.	do.
928	Private William Dalgleish	Yes.	Yes.	,,	No.	do.
* 887	,, Alexr. Darrah	No.	No.	,,	Yes.	Killed at Tamaai. A.G. List 149.
*2479	,, David Davidson	,,	,,	,,	No.	With Regiment.
2363	,, George Davidson	Yes.	Yes.	,,	Yes.	do.
21	Lce.-Serjt. William Davidson	,,	,,	,,	,,	do.
*1719	Private William Davidson	No.	No.	,,	No.	do.
35	,, George Deans	Yes.	Yes.	,,	Yes.	do.
68	,, Martin Dempsey	,,	,,	,,	,,	do.
* 50	,, Robert Dick	No.	No.	,,	No.	do.
248	,, James Dickson	Yes.	Yes.	No.	,,	do.
* 784	,, Arthur Dixon	No.	No.	Yes.	Yes.	do.

Regtl. No.	RANK AND NAME at the time the Medal was earned.	Whether in possession of Egypt Medal, 1882.	Whether entitled to Clasp, Suakin.	Whether at action of El-Teb.	Whether at action of Tamaai.	Whether serving with Regiment or Depot, dead, discharged, deserted, etc.
*2190	Private Thomas Docherty	No.	No.	Yes.	No.	With Regiment.
* 283	„ Thomas Dodds	„	„	„	Yes.	do.
*2033	„ Alexr. Doig	„	„	„	„	do.
*2097	„ David Donald	„	„	„	No.	do.
*1330	„ Joseph Donald	„	„	„	„	do.
*1984	„ David Donaldson	„	„	„	Yes.	do.
* 946	„ George Donaldson	„	„	„	„	do.
1653	Serjt.-Cook James Donaldson	Yes.	Yes.	„	„	do.
2507	Lc.-Corpl. Peter Donaldson	„	„	„	„	do.
*1067	Private Henry Double	No.	No.	„	„	do.
2552	„ George Douglas	Yes.	Yes.	„	„	do.
*1210	„ Robert Douglas	No.	No.	No.	No.	With 2nd R.H., Aldershot.
*1194	„ William Douglas	„	„	Yes.	Yes.	Depot.
1789	„ James Downie	Yes.	Yes.	„	„	Killed at Tamaai. A.G. List 149.
2410	„ John Downie	„	„	„	„	With Regiment.
693	„ Robert Donnie	„	„	„	„	do.
116	„ David Drever	„	„	„	No.	do.
110	„ George Drummond	„	„	No.	Yes.	do.
2652	„ Henry Drummond	„	„	Yes.	„	do.
*1066	„ William Dudgeon	No.	No.	„	No.	Depot.
2383	„ John Duff	Yes.	Yes.	„	Yes.	With Regiment.
*1321	„ Alexr. Duncan	No.	No.	„	„	do.
69	Serjeant James Duncan	Yes.	Yes.	„	„	Killed at Tamaai. A.G. List 211.
295	Private James Duncan	„	„	„	„	With Regiment.
487	Cr.-Serjt. Louis S. Dunbar	„	„	„	„	do.
1027	Private Charles Durrant	„	„	„	„	Killed at Tamaai. A.G. List 149.
251	„ John Durward	„	„	„	No.	With Regiment.
*1164	„ David Eadie	No.	No.	No.	„	do.
* 822	Serjt. Philip Eames	„	„	Yes.	„	do.
* 143	Private David Edgar	„	„	„	Yes.	do.
*1725	„ John Edmondstone	„	„	„	„	do. Forfeited /622.
235	„ Thomas Edwards	Yes.	Yes.	„	68/Egypt/708	do.
967	„ William Edwards	„	„	„	„	do.
*1178	„ Bernard Egan	No.	No.	„	„	do.
*2616	„ William Elder	„	„	„	„	do.
* 731	„ Alfred Elcombe	„	„	„	No.	do.
2538	„ John Elliott	Yes.	Yes.	Yes.	No.	do.
247	„ William Elvin	„	„	„	Yes.	do.
*1141	„ Alfred Embrough	No.	No.	„	„	do.
*2584	„ Nathaniel Ennis	„	„	„	„	do.
* 762	„ Michael Enright	„	„	„	„	do.
*2011	„ Henry J. Evans	„	„	„	No.	do.
175	Lce.-Serjt. John Ewan	Yes.	Yes.	„	„	Depot.
*1728	Private Thomas Farley	No.	No.	„	Yes.	With Regiment.
1214	„ George Farmer	Yes.	Yes.	„	No.	do.
1119	„ William Fenn	„	„	„	Yes.	do.
*2503	„ Charles Ferguson	No. 68/42/479	No.	„	„	do.
*1229	„ Robert Ferguson	„	„	„	„	Depot.
*1074	Lce.-Corpl. William Ferguson	„	„	„	No.	With Regiment.
608	„ Frederick Field	Yes.	Yes.	Yes.	Yes.	do.
941	Private George Findlay	„	„	„	No.	do.

Regtl. No.	Rank and Name at the time the Medal was earned.	Whether in possession of Egypt Medal, 1882.	Whether entitled to Clasp, Suakin.	Whether at action of El-Teb.	Whether at action of Tamaai.	Whether serving with Regiment or Depot, dead, discharged, deserted, etc.
*2062	Lce.-Corpl. Percy Finlay	No.	No.	Yes.	Yes.	Killed at Tamaai. A.G. List 149.
* 239	Private Israel Firth	,,	,,	,,	,,	With Regiment.
* 733	,, George Fisher	,,	,,	,,	No.	do.
* 70	,, Robert Flood	,,	,,	,,	,,	do.
698	,, James Flynn	Yes.	Yes.	,,	Yes.	do.
* 998	,, John Flynn	No.	No.	,,	,,	do.
* 894	,, William Folwell	,,	,,	,,	,,	do.
*2442	,, Thomas Forbes	,,	,,	,,	No.	do.
*2577	,, William Forbes	,,	,,	,,	Yes.	do.
286	Serjeant Butler W. Ford	Yes.	Yes.	,,	,,	do.
752	Private David Ford	,,	,,	,,	,,	do.
* 71	,, Donald Foreman	No.	No.	,,	,,	do.
*1137	,, John Forrest	,,	,,	,,	No.	do.
* 229	,, Jesse Fowler	,,	,,	,,	Yes.	do.
* 960	,, George E. Foxwell	,,	,,	,,	,,	do.
682	,, Alexr. Fraser	Yes.	Yes.	,,	,,	do.
2609	,, John Fraser	,,	,,	,,	No.	do.
1370	Serjeant Ronald Fraser	,,	,,	,,	Yes.	Killed at Tamaai. A.G. List 149.
*2095	Private William Fraser	No.	No.	,,	,,	do. do.
*1186	Drummer George Fulton	,,	,,	,,	,,	With Regiment.
*1592	Private William Fulton	,,	,,	,,	,,	Killed at Tamaai. A.G. List 149.
*1179	,, John Furness	,,	,,	,,	,,	With Regiment. Forfeited 68/42/495.
*2579	,, Andrew Gaffney	No.	No.	Yes.	No.	With Regiment.
*2663	,, James Gagan	,,	,,	,,	,,	do.
846	,, Neil Galbraith	Yes.	Yes.	Yes.	Yes.	do.
* 984	,, Edward Gamwell	No.	No.	,,	No.	do.
*1704	,, John W. Gardiner	,,	,,	,,	,,	do.
900	,, James Gascoigne	Yes.	Yes.	,,	,,	do.
2599	,, James George	,,	,,	,,	Yes.	do.
* 783	,, Patrick Gerrity	No.	No.	,,	No.	do.
*2066	,, David Gibb	,,	,,	,,	Yes.	Depot.
*1319	,, George Gilbert	,,	,,	,,	,,	With Regiment.
75	Corporal Thomas Gilbert	Yes.	Yes.	,,	,,	do.
76	Private James Gill	,,	,,	,,	,,	do.
*2678	,, James Gillies	No.	No.	No.	No.	do.
*1947	,, Hugh Gillies	,,	,,	Yes.	Yes.	Killed at Tamaai. A.G. List 149.
*1930	,, James Gillespie	/370. No.	/370. No.	,,	,,	Discharged. A.G. List 158.
*1999	,, Samuel C. Glass	No.	No.	,,	,,	With Regiment.
1625	Lce.-Serjt. Thomas Glen	Yes.	Yes.	,,	,,	do.
2407	Private William Glen	,,	,,	,,	,,	do.
176	,, William Gloag	,,	,,	,,	No.	do.
* 714	,, John Golland	No.	No.	,,	,,	do.
* 751	James Goodall ,,	,,	,,	,,	Yes.	do.
879	Lc.-Corpl. David Gordon	Yes.	Yes.	,,	,,	do.
2549	,, John Gordon	,,	,,	,,	,,	do.
2424	Private James Goran	,,	,,	,,	,,	do.
*1243	,, Robert Gow	No.	No.	,,	,,	do.
*2083	,, James Gowans	,,	,,	,,	,,	do. Forfeited /569.
252	,, George Graham	Yes.	Yes.	,,	,,	do.
10	,, James Graham	,,	,,	,,	,,	do.
2348	,, Thomas Graham	,,	,,	,,	No.	Discharged. A.G. List 166.
78	Corporal Alexr. Grant	,,	,,	,,	Yes.	With Regiment.

Regtl. No.	RANK AND NAME at the time the Medal was earned.	Whether in possession of Egypt Medal, 1882.	Whether entitled to Clasp, Suakin.	Whether at action of El-Teb.	Whether at action of Tamaai.	Whether serving with Regiment or Depot, dead, discharged, deserted, etc.
177	Private James Grant . .	Yes.	Yes.	Yes.	Yes.	With Regiment.
* 918	,, John Grant . .	No.	No.	,,	,,	do.
*1992	,, Thomas Graveson .	,,	,,	,,	,,	Killed at Tamaai. A.G. List 149.
12	,, James Gray . .	Yes.	Yes.	,,	No.	With Regiment.
* 997	,, James Gray . .	No.	No.	,,	Yes.	do.
896	Serjeant Peter Gray . .	Yes.	Yes.	,,	,,	Killed at Tamaai. A.G. List 149.
2708	Private John Greenlaw .	,,	,,	,,	,,	With Regiment.
*2092	,, Matthew J. Greer .	No.	No.	,,	,,	do.
*2499	,, Henry Griffiths .	,,	,,	,,	,,	do.
*1145	,, Charles Haig . .	,,	,,	,,	,,	do.
780	,, Thomas Haig . .	Yes.	Yes.	Yes.	Yes.	do.
* 828	,, James Haines . .	No.	No.	,,	,,	do. Capt. Stewart's Collection.
1070	,, Stephen Hall . .	Yes.	Yes.	,,	,,	With Regiment.
*2601	,, Robert Hamilton .	No.	No.	,,	,,	do.
*1991	,, William Hamilton .	,,	,,	,,	,,	do.
2542	,, Thomas Handy .	Yes.	Yes.	,,	,,	do.
* 781	,, Richard Harding .	No.	No.	,,	No.	do.
*2021	,, Robert Harkness .	,,	,,	,,	,,	do.
* 994	Corporal Hugh Harley . .	,,	,,	,,	Yes.	do.
2667	Private James Harley . .	Yes.	Yes.	,,	,,	do.
117	,, John Hastie . .	,,	,,	,,	,,	do.
2686	,, John Hastie . .	,,	,,	,,	,,	do.
* 42	Corporal Edwin Hawkins .	No.	No.	,,	,,	do.
1529	Private George Hay . .	Yes.	Yes.	,,	,,	Discharged. A.G. List 153.
2373	Lce.-Corpl. John Hay . .	,,	,,	,,	,,	With Regiment.
* 935	Private William Hencher-wood	No.	No.	,,	No.	do.
*1654	Serjeant Alexr. Henderson	,,	,,	,,	Yes.	do.
1797	Private James Henderson .	Yes.	Yes.	,,	,,	do.
*2000	,, John Henderson .	No.	No.	,,	No.	Killed at El-Teb. A.G. List 149.
*2523	,, George Hendry .	,,	,,	,,	,,	With Regiment.
*2079	,, Thomas Higginson	,,	,,	,,	Yes.	do.
79	,, John Hillis . . .	Yes.	Yes.	,,	,,	do.
*1055	Lce.-Corpl. Joseph Hines .	No.	No.	,,	No.	do.
*1304	Private William Hislop .	,,	,,	,,	Yes.	do.
*1193	Lce.-Corpl. James Hogg .	,,	,,	,,	,,	do.
158	Private William Hogg . .	Yes.	Yes.	,,	No.	do.
*2035	,, George Holmes .	No.	No.	,,	,,	do.
2422	,, Robert Hood . .	Yes.	Yes.	,,	Yes.	do.
* 955	,, James Hope . .	No.	No.	,,	,,	do.
* 270	,, Robert Horn . .	,,	,,	,,	,,	do.
*2088	,, James Houston .	,,	,,	,,	,,	do.
*1976	,, William Howard .	,,	,,	,,	,,	do.
* 830	,, Edward Howarth .	,,	,,	,,	,,	do.
193	,, James Howden .	Yes.	Yes.	,,	,,	do. Forfeited /629.
2369	,, George Howieson .	,,	,,	,,	,,	do.
* 810	,, Richard Humphries .	No.	No.	,,	No.	Died of wounds. A.G. List 149.
*1314	Lce.-Corpl. George Hunt .	,,	,,	No.	Yes.	With Regiment.
*1955	Private John Hunter . .	,,	,,	Yes.	,,	do.
*2582	,, John Hunter . .	,,	,,	No.	No.	do.
*1157	,, George Huntingdon	,,	,,	Yes.	Yes.	do.
22	Corporal James Hutchison .	Yes.	Yes.	,,	No.	do.

Regtl. No.	Rank and Name at the time the Medal was earned.	Whether in possession of Egypt Medal, 1882.	Whether entitled to Clasp, Suakin.	Whether at action of El-Teb.	Whether at action of Tamaai.	Whether serving with Regiment or Depot, dead, discharged, deserted, etc.
*1966	Private Andrew Hutton	No.	No.	Yes.	Yes.	With Regiment.
610	Drummer David Inglis	Yes.	Yes.	,,	,,	Discharged. A.G. List 181.
675	Lce.-Corpl. William Inkston	,,	,,	,,	,,	Killed at Tamaai. A.G. List 149.
1536	Private James Innis	,,	,,	,,	,,	With Regiment.
*2700	,, John Irvine	No.	No.	,,	,,	do.
* 937	Lce.-Corpl. William Jack	,,	,,	,,	,,	do.
740	Private Charles O. Jeffs	Yes.	Yes.	,,	,,	do.
2696	,, David Johnston	,,	,,	,,	,,	Killed at Tamaai. A.G. List 149.
38	Corporal James Johnston	,,	,,	,,	,,	With Regiment.
198	Private John Johnston	,,	,,	,,	,,	do.
* 957	,, John Johnston	No.	No.	,,	,,	do. Forfeited 68/42/443.
465	Cr.-Serjt. Michael Johnston	Yes.	Yes.	,,	,,	Killed at Tamaai. A.G. List 149.
739	Private Stephen Johnston	,,	,,	,,	,,	With Regiment.
1071	,, Thomas Johnston	,,	,,	,,	,,	do.
*1275	,, William Johnston	No.	No.	,,	No.	do.
*1092	,, George Jones	,,	,,	,,	,,	do.
* 897	,, Thomas Jones	,,	,,	,,	Yes.	do.
* 907	,, Alexr. Joss	,,	,,	,,	No.	Depot. Capt. Stewart's Collection
80	Serjeant David Kay	Yes.	Yes.	Yes.	No.	With Regiment.
915	Private Hugh Kean	,,	,,	,,	,,	do.
* 6	,, David Keir	No.	No.	,,	Yes.	do.
*1975	,, Gilbert Kellar	,,	,,	,,	,,	do.
1215	,, Charles Kelly	Yes.	Yes.	No.	,,	Killed at Tamaai. A.G. List 151.
25	Drummer James Kemp	,,	,,	Yes.	,,	With Regiment.
2377	Private Thomas Kemp	,,	,,	,,	,,	do.
1135	Lce.-Corpl. Archd. Kennedy	,,	,,	,,	,,	do.
81	Private William Kidd	,,	,,	,,	No.	do.
*2565	,, William Kidd	No.	No.	,,	Yes.	do. Forfeited by desertion. Restored 1/693. A.G. List 342.
2687	,, David King	Yes.	Yes.	Yes.	Yes.	With Regiment.
703	,, John King	,,	,,	,,	,,	Killed at Tamaai. A.G. List 149.
2614	Lce.-Corpl. William Kincaid	,,	,,	Yes. 69/Egypt/708	,,	With Regiment.
* 255	Private Andrew Laidlaw	No.	No.	Yes.	Yes.	do.
*2003	,, William Laing	,,	,,	,,	,,	do.
*2551	,, Thomas Lang	,,	,,	,,	,,	do.
2613	,, William Langlands	Yes.	Yes.	Yes.	No.	do.
1241	,, Alexr. Laurence	,,	,,	No.	No.	do.
82	,, John Laurie	,,	,,	Yes.	Yes.	do.
* 938	,, Robert Laurie	No.	No.	,,	,,	do.
*1301	,, William Laurie	,,	,,	,,	,,	do.
*2056	,, David Law	,,	,,	,,	,,	do.
* 921	,, Charles Lee	,,	,,	,,	,,	Discharged. Bouverie Arms, Garden Lane, Chester.
* 218	,, Edward Lee	,,	,,	,,	,,	With Regiment.
2478	,, Edward Ledran	Yes.	Yes.	,,	,,	do.
*1644	Drummer James Lennie	No.	No.	,,	,,	do.
*1206	Private James Leslie	,,	,,	,,	,,	do.
2213	,, Robert Leslie	Yes.	Yes.	,,	,,	Discharged. A.G. List 183. Capt. Stewart's Collection.
*2394	,, William Leslie	No.	No.	,,	,,	With Regiment.
*1048	,, George Lewis	,,	,,	,,	,,	Depot.

Regtl. No.	Rank and Name at the time the Medal was earned.	Whether in possession of Egypt Medal, 1882.	Whether entitled to Clasp, Suakin.	Whether at action of El-Teb.	Whether at action of Tamaai.	Whether serving with Regiment or Depot, dead, discharged, deserted, etc.
1107	Private James Lewis	Yes.	Yes.	Yes.	Yes.	With Regiment.
1050	„ George Lies	„	„	„	„	do.
144	„ Robert Lindsay	„	„	„	„	do.
*717	„ Robert Lindsay	No.	No.	Yes. 68/Egypt/708	No.	do.
*1087	Lce.-Corpl. William Lindsay	„	„	Yes.	Yes.	do.
*1320	Private William Lindsay	„	„	„	„	do.
2342	Cr.-Serjt. John Linning	Yes.	Yes.	Yes.	No.	do.
83	Private Alexander Logan	„	„	„	„	do.
343	Cr.-Serjt. Robert Logan	„	„	„	Yes.	do.
*1269	Private David Louden	No.	No.	„	„	do.
788	„ James Louth	Yes.	Yes.	„	„	do.
2660	„ George Low	„	„	„	„	do.
2710	„ Robert Lyle	„	„	„	No.	do.
1231	Lce.-Serjt. James Lynn	„	„	„	Yes.	do.
2513	Private John Maccorist	„	„	„	No.	do.
*1001	„ William Major	No.	No.	„	Yes.	do.
*2441	„ Alexander Mann	„	„	„	„	do.
160	„ James Marshal	Yes.	Yes.	„	„	Killed at Tamaai. A.G. List 149.
*1068	„ Jonas Martin	No.	No.	„	„	With Regiment.
*2624	„ Thomas Martin	„	„	„	„	do.
2468	„ William Martin	Yes.	Yes.	„	No.	do.
107	„ John Mason	„	„	„	„	do.
*1284	Lce.-Corpl. William Mason	No.	No.	„	Yes.	do.
216	Private Edward Mather	Yes.	Yes.	„	No.	Depot.
*1960	„ John Mathieson	No.	No.	„	Yes.	With Regiment.
2659	„ George Matthews	Yes.	Yes.	Yes.	Yes.	do.
55	„ George Maxwell	„	„	„	„	do.
1038	„ Henry Maxwell	„	„	„	„	do.
2588	„ Robert Mercer	„	„	„	„	do.
164	„ James Middleton	„	„	„	No.	do.
*866	„ Alexr. Millar	No.	No.	„	Yes.	do.
1794	„ James Miller	Yes.	Yes.	„	„	do.
290	Corporal John Miller	„	„	„	„	do.
2480	Private John Miller	„	„	„	„	Killed in action. A.G. List 149.
971	„ Peter Miller	„	„	„	„	With Regiment.
609	Lce.-Corpl. Robert Miller	„	„	„	„	do.
*86	Serjt. James Milne	No.	No.	„	„	do.
2566	Private Alexr. Mitchell	Yes.	Yes.	Yes.	No.	do.
*1002	„ Benjamin Mitchell	No.	No.	„	Yes.	do.
*944	„ William Mitchell	„	„	„	„	do.
*2678	„ Robert Moffatt	„	„	„	„	do.
278	„ Daniel Moodie	Yes.	Yes.	„	„	do.
*2443	„ David Moodie	No.	No.	„	„	do.
2402	„ Robert More	Yes.	Yes.	„	„	do.
*2025	„ Alexr. Morgan	No.	No.	„	„	Killed in action. A.G. List 149.
2587	„ Frank Morgan	Yes.	Yes.	„	No.	With Regiment.
*832	„ Samuel Morgan	No.	No.	„	Yes.	Depot.
*1017	Serjt. David Morrison	„	„	„	„	With Regiment.
*1195	Private James Morrison	„	„	„	„	do.
2380	„ John Morrison	Yes.	Yes.	„	„	do.
*2438	„ John Morrison	No.	No.	„	„	do.
14	Corporal William Morrison	Yes.	Yes.	„	No.	do.

Regtl. No.	Rank and Name at the time the Medal was earned.	Whether in possession of Egypt Medal, 1882.	Whether entitled to Clasp, Suakin.	Whether at action of El-Teb.	Whether at action of Tamaai.	Whether serving with Regiment or Depot, dead, discharged, deserted, etc.
*1956	Private William Morrison	No.	No.	Yes.	No.	With Regiment.
2654	,, Henry Morton	Yes.	Yes.	,,	Yes.	do.
*1329	,, Hugh Morton	No.	No.	,,	,,	Killed at Tamaai. A.G. List 149.
*2622	,, Albert Moss	,,	,,	,,	,,	With Regiment.
88	,, Thomas Motion	Yes.	Yes.	,,	No.	do.
*986	,, James Mounted	No.	No.	,,	,,	do.
2655	Drummer Henry E. Mumford	Yes.	Yes.	Yes.	Yes.	do.
*977	Private William Murdoch	No.	No.	No.	,,	do.
*1036	,, John Murray	,,	,,	Yes.	,,	do.
2420	,, John Murray	Yes.	Yes.	,,	,,	do.
*1190	,, William Murray	No.	No.	,,	No.	do.
*1983	,, William Murrell	,,	,,	,,	,,	Depot.
2406	Serjeant David Murrie	Yes.	Yes.	Yes.	Yes.	With Regiment.
*2004	Private Robert M'Alpine	No.	No.	No.	No.	do.
*1248	,, John M'Call	,,	,,	Yes.	Yes.	do.
120	,, Patrick M'Cann	Yes.	Yes.	No.	,,	do.
*1722	,, James M'Cash	No.	No.	Yes.	,,	do.
2595	Serjeant Robert M'Clay	Yes.	Yes.	,,	,,	Killed at Tamaai. A.G. List 149.
1841	Private Henry M'Culloch	,,	,,	,,	No.	Discharged. A.G. List 219.
*2568	Lce.-Corpl. Angus M'Dermid	No.	No.	,,	Yes.	With Regiment.
*1989	Private Donald M'Dermid	,,	,,	,,	No.	do. Forfeited 68/42/453.
2331	Drummer John W. M'Dine	Yes.	Yes.	,,	,,	With Regiment.
1988	Private Alexr. M'Donald	,,	,,	,,	Yes.	Killed at Tamaai. A.G. List 149.
*1013	,, Archd. M'Donald	No.	No.	,,	,,	With Regiment.
*2018	,, Charles M'Donald	,,	,,	,,	,,	do.
*162	,, Donald M'Donald	,,	,,	,,	,,	do.
*683	,, Daniel M'Donald	,,	,,	No.	,,	do.
1373	Sjt.-Piper John M'Donald	Yes.	Yes.	Yes.	Yes.	do.
72	Piper John M'Donald	,,	,,	,,	No.	Discharged. c/o John Souter, 17 Albert St., Leith Walk, Edinburgh.
*1948	Private John M'Donald	No.	No.	Yes.		With Regiment.
*2517	,, John M'Donald	,,	,,	,,	Yes.	do.
*2010	,, William M'Donald	,,	,,	,,	,,	do.
2475	,, William M'Donald	Yes.	Yes.	,,	,,	do.
*1088	,, Charles M'Dougall	No.	No.	,,	,,	do.
1343	,, James M'Dougall	Yes.	Yes.	No.	,,	do.
*1300	,, Donald M'Farlane	No.	No.	Yes.	No.	Killed at Tamaai. A.G. List 149.
*1980	,, James M'Gann	,,	,,	,,	Yes.	With Regiment.
2716	,, Donald M'Geoch	Yes.	Yes.	,,	,,	do.
701	,, Andrew M'George	,,	,,	,,	,,	do.
*2001	,, Peter M'Glashan	No.	No.	,,	,,	do.
2358	,, James M'Gregor	Yes.	Yes.	Yes.	No.	do.
1199	,, Robert M'Gregor	,,	,,	,,	Yes.	do.
33	,, William M'Gregor	,,	,,	,,	,,	do.
*1118	,, Francis M'Guire	No.	No.	,,	,,	do.
*1711	,, William M'Innis	,,	,,	,,	,,	do.
2416	Corporal James M'Intosh	Yes.	Yes.	Yes.	,,	Depot.
*1982	Private William M'Intosh	No.	No.	,,	No.	Killed at Tamaai. A.G. List 149.
*1273	,, Daniel M'Intyre	,,	,,	,,	Yes.	With Regiment.
2578	,, Murdoch M'Iver	Yes.	Yes.	Yes.	,,	do.
1666	Drummer James M'Kay	,,	,,	,,	Yes.	Killed at Tamaai. A.G. List 149.
2623	Private John M'Kay	,,	,,	,,	,,	With Regiment.

Regtl. No.	RANK AND NAME at the time the Medal was earned.	Whether in possession of Egypt Medal, 1882.	Whether entitled to Clasp, Suakin.	Whether at action of El-Teb.	Whether at action of Tamaai.	Whether serving with Regiment or Depot, dead, discharged, deserted, etc.
*2302	Private John M'Kechnie .	No.	No.	Yes.	No.	With Regiment.
* 806	Corporal Andrew M'Kee .	,,	,,	,,	Yes.	do.
*2527	Private Thomas M'Kelvie .	,,	,,	,,	No.	do.
1130	,, David M'Kendrick	Yes.	Yes.	,,	,,	do.
2393	,, Andrew M'Kenzie .	,,	,,	,,	Yes.	do.
* 163	,, Duncan M'Kenzie .	No.	No.	,,	No.	do.
128	Lce.-Serjt. Evan M'Kenzie	Yes.	Yes.	,,	Yes.	do.
2572	Private Fergus M'Kenzie .	,,	,,	,,	,,	do.
2180	Serjeant James M'Kenzie .	,,	,,	,,	No.	do.
*1974	Private James M'Kenzie .	No.	No.	,,	Yes.	do.
205	Piper Ronald M'Kenzie .	Yes.	Yes.	,,	,,	do.
*1037	Private William M'Kenzie .	No.	No.	,,	,,	do.
757	Cr.-Serjt. Duncan M'Lachlan	Yes.	Yes.	Yes.	Yes.	do.
*1323	Private James M'Lachlan .	No.	No.	,,	,,	do.
2161	Qr. - Mr. - Serjeant William M'Lachlan	Yes.	Yes.	Yes. 68/Egypt/708	Yes.	do.
*1237	Private Alexr. M'Laren .	No.	No.	Yes.	Yes.	do.
2346	,, James M'Laren .	Yes.	Yes.	Yes.	No.	do.
*1263	,, John M'Laren . .	No.	No.	No.	Yes.	do.
*1250	,, Thomas M'Laren .	,,	,,	Yes.	No.	do. Restored /624.
*2580	Lce.-Corpl. William M'Laren	,,	,,	,,	Yes.	do. ,, 68/42/638.
34	Private David M'Latchie .	Yes.	Yes.	,,	,,	do.
2436	,, Lachlan M'Lauchlan	,,	,,	,,	No.	do.
* 692	,, Archd. M'Lean .	No.	No.	,,	,,	do.
*1161	,, Donald M'Lean .	,,	,,	,,	Yes.	do.
934	,, John M'Lean .	Yes.	Yes.	Yes.	Yes.	do. Forfeited 68/42/538.
963	,, Lachlan M'Lean .	,,	,,	,,	No.	Depot.
2615	,, Thomas M'Lean .	,,	,,	,,	Yes.	With Regiment.
279	,, Angus M'Leod . .	,,	,,	,,	,,	do.
*2433	,, John M'Leod . .	No.	No.	,, .	,,	Forfeited England. Discharged with ignominy.
859	,, Murdoch M'Leod .	Yes.	Yes.	Yes.	Yes.	With Regiment.
697	,, Archd. M'Lucas .	,,	,,	,,	No.	Depot.
929	,, John M'Master .	,,	,,	,,	Yes.	With Regiment.
1041	,, Henry M'Millan .	,,	,,	,,	,,	do.
1034	,, William M'Millan .	,,	,,	,,	,,	do.
2349	Serjeant Livingstone M'Nair	,,	,,	,,	No. *	do. Clasps issued 6/11/02. (A.G. 2/Medals/5543).
* 147	Private James M'Nally .	No.	No.	Yes.	Yes.	Killed at Tamaai. A.G. List 149.
* 766	,, Martin M'Namara .	,,	,,	,,	No.	With Regiment. Forfeited 68/42/443.
* 85	,, Chambers M'Naughton	No.	No.	Yes.	Yes.	With Regiment.
*1128	,, David M'Neil . .	,,	,,	,,	,,	do.
*2111	,, Alexr. M'Phee . .	,,	,,	,,	,,	do.
*1167	,, Alexr. M'Pherson .	,,	,,	,,	,,	do.
2714	,, Finlay M'Pherson .	Yes.	Yes.	Yes.	Yes.	Killed at Tamaai. A.G. List 149.
1039	,, James M'Pherson .	,,	,,	,,	,,	With Regiment.
*2014	,, Peter M'Que . .	No.	No.	,,	,,	do.
1818	Serjeant Alexr. M'Swain .	Yes.	Yes.	,,	No.	Depot.
*2626	,, Edwin Nadin . .	No.	No.	,,	,,	With Regiment.
*2684	Private Andrew Neil . .	,,	,,	,,	,,	do.
*2556	,, John Neish . . .	,,	,,	,,	Yes.	do.
2674	,, Francis Nelson . .	Yes.	Yes.	,,	Yes.	do.

Regtl. No.	Rank and Name at the time the Medal was earned.	Whether in possession of Egypt Medal, 1882.	Whether entitled to Clasp, Suakin.	Whether at action of El-Teb.	Whether at action of Tamaai.	Whether serving with Regiment or Depot, dead, discharged, deserted, etc.
1057	Private John New	Yes.	Yes.	Yes.	No.	With Regiment.
2306	,, George Newton	,,	,,	,,	,,	do.
*919	,, Jesse Newsome	No.	No.	,,	,,	do.
*1290	,, George Nicol	,,	,,	,,	,,	do.
*2117	,, Charles Nicoll	,,	,,	,,	Yes.	do.
*1140	,, Thomas Nicolson	,,	,,	,,	,,	do.
*2543	Corporal Donald Nicholson	,,	,,	,,	,,	do.
2430	Private David Ogilvie	Yes.	Yes.	,,	,,	Discharged. A.G. List 183.
777	,, George Ogilvie	,,	,,	,,	,,	With Regiment.
*2281	,, James O'Brien	No.	No.	,,	,,	do.
*747	,, George Paine	,,	,,	,,	No.	do.
1104	,, Henry Palmer	Yes.	Yes.	,,	Yes.	do.
*808	,, David Park	No.	No.	Yes. 68/Egypt/708	,,	do.
59	,, Joseph Parker	Yes.	Yes.	Yes.	No.	do.
*1283	Lce.-Corpl. Arthur Paterson	No.	No.	,,	Yes.	do.
*1024	Private Donald Paterson	,,	,,	,,	,,	Killed at Tamaai. A.G. List 149.
2705	,, George Paterson	Yes.	Yes.	,,	,,	With Regiment.
*2540	,, John Paton	No.	No.	,,	,,	do.
*1441	,, Joseph Patterson	,,	,,	,,	,,	do.
*1079	,, Thomas Paxton	,,	,,	,,	,,	do.
795	Lce.-Corpl. John Payne	Yes.	Yes.	,,	,,	do.
*2096	Private Owen Payne	No.	No.	,,	,,	do.
*1072	,, Thomas Peacock	,,	,,	,,	,,	Killed at Tamaai. A.G. List 149.
*1029	,, William Pearce	,,	,,	,,	No.	Dead. A.G. List 149.
*2638	Lce.-Corpl. James Pearson	No.	No.	No.	No.	With Regiment.
964	Private William Pearson	Yes.	Yes.	Yes.	,,	do.
*1061	,, John Peck	No.	No.	,,	Yes.	do.
*1205	,, Angus Peden	,,	,,	,,	,,	Depot.
*1063	,, Abraham Perkins	,,	,,	,,	,,	Discharged. A.G. List 162.
2310	,, David Pirie	Yes.	Yes.	,,	Yes.	With Regiment.
*1259	,, Henry Pike	No.	No.	,,	,,	do.
371	1st Class Armr.-Sjt. Thomas Pinkney	Yes.	Yes.	No.	No.	do.
*1220	Private John Pither	No.	No.	Yes.	Yes.	do.
*1098	,, William Pitts	,,	,,	,,	,,	do.
2530	,, Charles Porter	Yes.	Yes.	,,	,,	do.
*893	,, James Potterton	No.	No.	Yes.	,,	do.
91	Corporal Alexr. Pratt	Yes.	Yes.	,,	No.	do.
*2476	Private Robert Pratt	No.	No.	No.	No.	do.
214	,, Frank Prime	Yes.	Yes.	Yes.	Yes.	Killed at Tamaai. A.G. List 149.
1225	,, George Pringle	,,	,,	,,	,,	With Regiment.
*2064	,, John Pyper	No.	No.	,,	,,	do.
*2458	,, George Radley	,,	,,	,,	,,	do.
1102	,, James Read	Yes.	Yes.	,,	,,	do.
1106	,, Joseph O. Reade	,,	,,	,,	,,	do.
2392	Corporal James Reid	,,	,,	,,	,,	do.
80	Serjeant John E. Reid	,,	,,	,,	,,	Killed at Tamaai. A.G. List 149.
*1155	Private Robert Reid	No.	No.	,,	,,	With Regiment.
*2039	,, William Reid	,,	,,	,,	No.	do.
520	,, William Reid	Yes.	Yes.	,,	Yes.	do.
1153	Drummer William Reilly	,,	,,	,,	No.	do.
8	Pioneer-Sjt. John Rennie	,,	,,	,,	Yes.	do.

Regtl. No.	RANK AND NAME at the time the Medal was earned.	Whether in possession of Egypt Medal, 1882.	Whether entitled to Clasp, Suakin.	Whether at action of El-Teb.	Whether at action of Tamaai.	Whether serving with Regiment or Depot, dead, discharged, deserted, etc.
*2364	Private Simpson Rennie .	No.	No.	Yes.	Yes.	With Regiment.
1252	Cr.-Serjt. Josiah Rhodes .	Yes.	Yes.	,,	,,	do.
*2428	Private James Richards .	No.	No.	,,	No.	Depot.
*1080	,, James Richardson	,,	,,	,,	Yes.	With Regiment.
*2681	,, James Ritchie . .	,,	,,	,,	,,	do.
*1440	,, Hugh Roberts . .	,,	,,	No.	No.	do.
28	,, Alexr. Robertson .	Yes.	Yes.	Yes.	Yes.	do.
*2071	,, David Robertson .	No.	No.	,,	,,	do.
1255	,, John Robertson .	Yes.	Yes.	,,	No.	do.
*2074	,, John Robertson .	No.	No.	,,	Yes.	do.
*2418	,, John Robertson .	,,	,,	,,	,,	do. Forfeited 68/42/443.
2604	,, Robert Robertson .	Yes.	Yes.	,,	,,	With Regiment.
2515	,, William Robertson	,,	,,	,,	,,	do.
* 118	,, George Robson .	No.	No.	,,	,,	do.
* 928	,, Stephen Rose . .	,,	,,	,,	,,	do.
1737	Corporal Andrew S. Ross .	Yes.	Yes.	Yes.	Yes.	do.
260	,, Charles Ross . .	,,	,,	,,	,,	do.
681	Drummer George Ross . .	,,	,,	,,	,,	do.
2451	Corporal James Ross .	,,	,,	,,	,,	do.
*1361	Private James Ross . .	No.	No.	,,	,,	do.
*1112	,, William Roulston .	,,	,,	,,	No.	do.
*2497	,, James Rourke . .	,,	,,	Yes.	Yes.	do.
*1266	,, David Rowan . .	,,	,,	,,	,,	do.
*1056	,, Harry Rowe . .	,,	,,	,,	No.	Killed at El-Teb. A.G. List 149.
* 145	,, Robert Rowe . .	,,	,,	,,	,,	With Regiment.
* 220	,, Frederick Rowley .	,,	,,	,,	Yes.	do. See 68/42/495.
*1279	,, John Roy . . .	,,	,,	,,	,,	Killed at Tamaai. A.G. List 149.
2397	,, Allan Russell . .	Yes.	Yes.	Yes.	No.	With Regiment.
761	,, John Russell . .	,,	,,	,,	Yes.	do.
* 219	,, John Ryan . . .	No.	No.	,,	,,	do. See /620.
800	Corporal Benjamin Sadler .	Yes.	Yes.	,,	,,	do.
*2647	Drummer William Sadler .	No.	No.	,,	No.	do.
1387	Private Michael Sands .	Yes.	Yes.	Yes.	Yes.	Killed at Tamaai. A.G. List 149.
1105	,, William Schofield .	,,	,,	,,	,,	With Regiment.
* 773	,, Joseph Scothern .	No.	No.	,,	No.	do.
*1280	,, Alexr. Scott . .	,,	,,	,,	,,	do.
20	,, John Scott . . .	Yes.	Yes.	Yes.	No.	do.
691	,, Thomas Scott . .	,,	,,	,,	,,	do.
*2701	,, Thomas Scott . .	No.	No.	Yes.	Yes.	Killed at Tamaai. A.G. List 149.
*1707	,, William Scrimgeour	,,	,,	,,	,,	With Regiment.
870	,, John Sharp . .	Yes.	Yes.	Yes.	Yes.	do.
2386	,, John Sharp . .	,,	,,	,,	,,	Discharged. A.G. List 159.
1110	,, Frederick Shaw .	,,	,,	,,	,,	With Regiment.
2555	,, Robert Shaw . .	,,	,,	,,	,,	do.
289	,, Samuel Shaw . .	,,	,,	,,	,,	do.
2620	,, Charles Shearer .	,,	,,	,,	No.	do.
*2336	Lce.-Corpl. John Shepherd	No.	No.	Yes.	Yes.	do.
232	Private Henry Shepstone .	Yes.	Yes.	,,	,,	Killed at Tamaai. A.G. List 272.
*1949	,, Peter Sheridan .	No.	No.	,,	,,	With Regiment.
223	,, Henry Shires . .	Yes.	Yes.	Yes.	Yes.	do. Forfeited on conviction of theft.
182	Serjeant Robert Sime . .	,,	,,	,,	,,	Discharged. A.G. List 153.
*1443	Lce.-Corpl. Alexr. Simpson	No.	No.	,,	,,	With Regiment.

Regtl. No.	RANK AND NAME at the time the Medal was earned.	Whether in possession of Egypt Medal, 1882.	Whether entitled to Clasp, Suakin.	Whether at action of El-Teb.	Whether at action of Tamaai.	Whether serving with Regiment or Depot, dead, discharged, deserted, etc.
*1292	Private George Simpson	No.	No.	Yes.	Yes.	With Regiment.
86	Drummer Thomas Simpson	Yes.	Yes.	Yes.	Yes.	do.
*2115	Private William Simpson	No.	No.	,,	,,	do.
706	,, Donald Sinclair	Yes.	Yes.	,,	,,	do.
*2101	,, Alexr. Singer	No.	No.	,,	,,	do.
*1222	,, William Skeet	,,	,,	,,	No.	do.
* 847	Lc.-Corpl. George W. Skillings	,,	,,	,,	,,	do.
93	Private David Slattie	Yes.	Yes.	Yes.	Yes.	do.
2467	Drummer John Slattie	,,	,,	,,	No.	do.
*2382	,, Alexr. Small	No.	No.	,,	,,	do.
94	,, Charles Smith	Yes.	Yes.	Yes.	No.	do.
*1144	,, Frederick Smith	No.	No.	Yes.	Yes.	do.
2664	Serjeant James Smith	Yes.	Yes.	Yes.	No.	do.
53	Private James Smith	,,	,,	,,	,,	do.
*1997	,, James Smith	No.	No.	Yes.	Yes.	do.
*2603	,, James P. Smith	,,	,,	,,	No.	do.
634	,, John Smith	Yes.	Yes.	Yes.	Yes.	do.
2390	,, Robert Smith	,,	,,	,,	,,	do.
*1160	,, Thomas Smith	No.	No.	,,	,,	do.
* 836	,, William Smith	,,	,,	,,	,,	do.
*1187	,, William H. Smith	,,	,,	,,	,,	do.
*2516	,, William Smith	,,	,,	,,	,,	do.
*2061	Lce.-Corpl. William S. Smyth	,,	,,	Yes.	No.	Discharged /388. A.G. List 163.
* 840	Corpl. Joseph Snelling	,,	,,	,,	Yes.	do. A.G. List 153.
*2662	Private William Souter	,,	,,	,,	No.	With Regiment.
*1122	,, Robert Southgate	,,	,,	,,	,,	do.
* 837	,, Joseph Speckman	,,	,,	,,	Yes.	do.
* 775	,, Edward Speaks	,,	,,	,,	,,	do.
285	,, Archd. Speid	Yes.	Yes.	Yes.	Yes.	do.
*2435	,, Andrew Spence	No.	No.	,,	No.	do.
18	,, George Spencer	Yes.	Yes.	Yes.	Yes.	do.
*1010	,, Thomas Sprunt	No.	No.	,,	No.	do.
* 801	,, Francis Stanley	,,	,,	,,	Yes.	do.
596	Corporal William Statham	Yes.	Yes.	Yes.	No.	do.
2191	Private David Steadman	,,	,,	,,	,,	do. A.G. List 370.
* 765	,, James Stenson	No.	No.	Yes.	Yes.	do.
2261	Serjeant John Stephen	Yes.	Yes.	Yes.	Yes.	do.
*1174	Private John Stephenson	No.	No.	,,	No.	do.
2492	Drummer Alex. H. Stewart	Yes.	Yes.	Yes.	Yes.	do.
13	Private Alexr. Stewart	,,	,,	,,	,,	do.
*2073	,, Alexr. Stewart	No.	No.	,,	,,	Killed at Tamaai. A.G. List 149.
*2649	,, Alexr. Stewart	,,	,,	,,	,,	With Regiment.
908	,, Donald Stewart	Yes.	Yes.	Yes.	Yes.	do.
947	,, Donald Stewart	Yes.	Yes.	Yes. 68/Egypt/708	Yes.	do.
125	Serjeant George Stewart	Yes.	Yes.	Yes.	Yes.	Depot.
2471	Private George Stewart	,,	,,	,,	,,	With Regiment.
*1299	,, James Stewart	No.	No.	,,	No.	do.
95	,, John Stewart	Yes.	Yes.	Yes.	Yes.	do. 68/42/425.
96	,, Norman Stewart	,,	,,	,,	,,	do.
*1935	Serjeant Peter Stewart	No.	No.	,,	,,	do.
686	Private Peter Stewart	Yes.	Yes.	,,	No.	Depot.
906	,, William Stewart	,,	,,	,,	Yes.	With Regiment.

Regtl. No.	RANK AND NAME at the time the Medal was earned.	Whether in possession of Egypt Medal, 1882.	Whether entitled to Clasp, Suakin.	Whether at action of El-Teb.	Whether at action of Tamaai.	Whether serving with Regiment or Depot, dead, discharged, deserted, etc.
*1125	Private William Stewart	No.	No.	Yes.	Yes.	With Regiment.
*1226	„ William Stewart	„	„	„	No.	do.
2646	„ Charles Stobbie	Yes.	Yes.	Yes.	Yes.	do.
1016	„ David Stoddart	„	„	„	„	do.
* 726	„ George Stokes	No.	No.	„	„	do.
* 951	„ William Stokes	„	„	„	„	do.
2676	„ George Strachan	Yes.	Yes.	Yes.	Yes.	do.
*1271	„ John Stubbs	No.	No.	„	„	do.
47	Serjeant Harry Studley	Yes.	Yes.	Yes.	Yes.	do.
97	Private Alexr. Sutherland	„	„	„	„	do.
2374	Serjeant John Sutherland	„	„	„	„	do.
273	Private William Swan	„	„	„	„	Killed at Tamaai. A.G. List 149.
*1298	„ John Swanson	No.	No.	„	„	With Regiment.
*2558	„ David Taylor	„	„	„	„	do.
1391	„ George Taylor	Yes.	Yes.	Yes.	Yes.	do.
*1727	„ John Taylor	No.	No.	„	„	Killed at Tamaai. A.G. List 149.
*1252	„ William Taylor	„	„	„	„	With Regiment.
*2118	„ Alexr. Terras	„	„	„	„	do.
*2070	„ William Thom	„	„	„	„	do.
*1566	„ Charles Thompson	„	„	„	„	do.
98	„ David B. Thompson	Yes.	Yes.	Yes.	Yes.	Killed at Tamaai. A.G. List 149.
99	„ George Thompson	„	„	„	„	With Regiment.
2709	„ James Thompson	„	„	„	„	do.
139	„ James Thompson	„	„	„	„	do.
1866	„ John Thompson	„	„	„	„	do.
790	Lce.-Corpl. John Thompson	„	„	„	„	do.
*1019	Private William Thompson	No.	No.	„	No.	do.
105	„ William Thompson	Yes.	Yes.	Yes.	Yes.	do.
* 728	„ Charles Timberlake	No.	No.	„	„	do.
* 839	„ Alfred C. Tombs	„	„	„	No.	do.
2474	„ David Tosh	Yes.	Yes.	Yes.	No.	do.
1032	„ Thomas Totten	„	„	„	Yes.	do. Capt. Stewart's Collection.
*1705	„ William Tough	No.	No.	Yes.	„	With Regiment.
* 745	„ Henry Town	„	„	„	„	do.
2548	„ Peter Toy	Yes.	Yes.	Yes.	No.	do.
*2498	„ Thomas Toy	No.	No.	„	Yes.	do.
*1026	„ Michael Trainer	„	„	„	„	do.
* 226	„ Edwin Tuffitt	„	„	„	„	Killed at Tamaai. A.G. List 149.
268	„ Alexr. Turner	Yes.	Yes.	Yes.	Yes.	With Regiment.
2321	Drummer James M. Turner	„	„	„	„	do.
*2665	Private John Turner	No.	No.	„	„	do.
*1180	„ Charles Tuson	„	„	„	„	do.
2198	Cr.-Serjt. James Tweedie	Yes.	Yes.	Yes.	Yes.	do.
1018	Private William Urquhart	„	„	„	„	do.
258	„ William Vallance	„	„	„	No.	do.
2509	Lce.-Corpl. John Vair	„	„	„	Yes.	do.
49	„ Robert Vair	„	„	„	„	do.
* 746	Private James Vickers	No.	No.	„	„	do.
* 980	„ Frank Wade	„	„	No.	No.	do.
737	„ Mark Wadmore	Yes.	Yes.	Yes.	No.	do.
*1121	„ Simon Wagstaff	No.	No.	No.	No.	do.
2437	Lc.-Cpl. Christopher Walker	Yes.	Yes.	Yes.	Yes.	do.

Regtl. No.	RANK AND NAME at the time the Medal was earned.	Whether in possession of Egypt Medal, 1882.	Whether entitled to Clasp, Suakin.	Whether at action of El-Teb.	Whether at action of Tamaai.	Whether serving with Regiment or Depot, dead, discharged, deserted, etc.
1016	Private James Walker	Yes.	Yes.	Yes.	Yes.	Killed at Tamaai. A.G. List 149.
688	,, William Walker	,,	,,	,,	,,	With Regiment.
*1700	,, Robert Wallace	No.	No.	,,	,,	do.
*1950	,, William Wallace	,,	,,	,,	,,	do.
2562	,, Henry Ward	Yes.	Yes.	Yes.	No.	do.
*2093	,, Robert Watson	No.	No.	,,	Yes.	do.
*2318	,, Robert Watson	,,	,,	,,	No.	do.
*1012	,, Thomas Watson	,,	,,	,,	Yes.	do.
2247	Serjeant Adam Watt	Yes.	Yes.	Yes.	Yes.	do.
*2058	Private David Watt	No.	No.	,,	,,	do.
183	,, George G. Watt	Yes.	Yes.	,,	,,	do.
2666	,, John Watt	,,	,,	,,	No.	do.
1379	Serjeant Thomas Watt	,,	,,	,,	,,	do.
1663	Private James Weatherspoon	,,	,,	,,	Yes.	Discharged. A.G. List 153.
123	,, David Webster	,,	,,	,,	,,	With Regiment.
*2461	,, Herbert Webster	No.	No.	,,	,,	do.
*2320	,, Michael Welsh	,,	,,	,,	,,	do.
*2099	,, Fergus West	,,	,,	,,	,,	do.
152	,, George West	Yes.	Yes.	Yes.	Yes.	do.
*904	,, Alfred Wharton	No.	No.	,,	,,	do.
2238	Cr.-Serjt. Hector White	Yes.	Yes.	,,	No.	Depot.
221	Private Joseph White	,,	,,	,,	Yes.	do.
786	,, Thomas White	,,	,,	,,	,,	With Regiment.
2625	,, Thomas White	,,	,,	,,	,,	Killed at Tamaai. A.G. List 149.
*2491	,, James Whitelaw	No.	No.	,,	,,	With Regiment.
748	Corporal George Whyte	Yes.	Yes.	,,	No.	Discharged. A.G. List 177.
*1967	Private Daniel Whyte	No.	No.	,,	Yes.	With Regiment.
2379	,, John Williamson	Yes.	Yes.	,,	No.	do.
2669	Serjeant Francis L. Wilkin	,,	,,	,,	Yes.	do.
2537	Lce.-Serjt. William Wilkie	,,	,,	,,	,,	do.
2671	Private William Will	,,	,,	,,	,,	do.
48	,, Charles Wilson	,,	,,	,,	,,	do.
29	,, James Wilson	,,	,,	,,	,,	Depot.
*1959	,, James Wilson	No.	No.	,,	,,	With Regiment.
*185	Corporal John Wilson	,,	,,	,,	,,	do.
100	Private John Wilson	Yes.	Yes.	,,	,,	Discharged. A.G. List 184.
1028	,, Thomas Wilson	,,	,,	Yes.	No.	With Regiment.
*2640	,, Thomas Wilson	No.	No.	,,	Yes.	do.
101	,, William Wilson	Yes.	Yes.	,,	No.	do.
54	,, James Winter	,,	,,	,,	Yes.	do.
*1713	,, Alexr. Wishart	No.	No.	,,	,,	do.
*1069	,, Alfred Wright	,,	,,	,,	,,	do.
770	Corporal John T. Wood	Yes.	Yes.	Yes.	No.	Discharged. 167 King Street, Singley, Yorkshire.
1049	Private Henry Wood	,,	,,	,,	Yes.	With Regiment.
*1182	Lce.-Corpl. Sidney H. Wood	No.	No.	,,	,,	do.
1852	Band Sjt. William Woodage	Yes.	Yes.	,,	,,	do.
102	Private Andrew Young	,,	,,	,,	,,	Killed at Tamaai. A.G. List 149.
14	,, William Young	,,	,,	,,	,,	With Regiment.
103	,, Robert Younger	,,	,,	,,	,,	do.
*804	,, James P. Yule	No.	No.	,,	,,	do.

	Officers.	R. & F.			Officers.	R. & F.
Shown as Killed at El-Teb	—	3	Shown as Killed in action	.	—	2
,, Killed at Tamaai	1	55	,, Died of wounds	.	—	1

1st BATTALION THE BLACK WATCH.

NOMINAL ROLL of OFFICERS, NON-COMMISSIONED OFFICERS AND MEN OF ABOVE BATTALION, entitled to the EGYPTIAN STAR, 1884-85, who have become Non-Effective by DEATH, DISCHARGE, or TRANSFER.

Regtl. No.	RANK AND NAME at the time the Decoration was earned.	REMARKS.
	Lieut. T. M. M. Berkeley	2nd Bn. The Black Watch.
	,, St. G. E. W. Burton.	
	,, G. Silver	1st Bn. East Surrey Regt., Allahabad, Bengal.
969	Private Andrew Alexander	2nd Bn. The Black Watch.
823	,, William Asher	do. do.
1006	,, John Beattie	do. do.
1945	,, William Campbell	do. do.
2331	,, Alexr. Chapman	do. do.
451	,, John Clark	Army Reserve.
234	,, James Clines	do.
2133	,, William Cowper	Deceased.
2200	,, Hugh Dickson	do. E/104624/9.
174	,, James Dunnlevy	Deserted.
2114	,, Robert Edwards	Deceased.
2518	,, David Foley	Army Reserve.
978	,, David Gillard	Discharged.
1000	Serjeant Charles Halkett	do.
2044	Private John Halliday	1st Bn. Royal Fusiliers
719	,, Albert Harris	2nd Bn. The Black Watch.
2137	,, Frank Harrison	Deceased.
493	,, John Harroway	2nd Bn. The Black Watch.
2270	Lce.-Corpl. John E. Houghton	do. do.
2269	,, Robert F. Houghton	Deceased.
2163	Private Andrew Irvine	2nd Bn. The Black Watch.
739	,, Stephen Johnson	Forfeited (under Sec. 18 A.A. 1881).
2257	,, William Jowett	2nd Bn. The Black Watch.
2565	,, William Kidd	Forfeited (Desertion).
831	,, Herbert King	2nd Bn. The Black Watch.
1712	,, William Laird	do. do.
2009	,, John Lawrie	Deceased.
551	,, John Melvin	Army Reserve.
2094	,, John Mitchell	2nd Bn. The Black Watch.
210	,, William Muir	Deceased.
1134	,, Alexr. M'Intosh	2nd Bn. The Black Watch.
2034	,, Alexr. M'Phee	Discharged (Penal Servitude).
2643	,, John M'Pherson	Army Reserve.
1191	,, Robert M'Pherson	Discharged.
778	,, John Noon	Discharged with ignominy.
999	Serjeant Colin Orton	Deceased.
2289	Private George Reid	Deceased.
2418	,, John Robertson	Forfeited (under Sec. 18 A.A. 1881).
966	,, Thomas Sharp	2nd Bn. The Black Watch.
223	,, Henry Shires	Army Reserve.
2265	Lce.-Corpl. Francis Sausmarez Shortt	2nd Bn. The Black Watch.
2002	Private Robert Sloggie	do. do.
2160	,, Charles Thompson	Deserted.
1272	,, Matthew Tully	Discharged with ignominy.
2112	,, Thomas Turner	do. as incorrigible and worthless.

42ND..

1st BATTALION BLACK WATCH
(ROYAL HIGHLANDERS)

SUDAN MEDAL

SUDAN MEDAL

ROYAL HIGHLANDERS

Regtl. No.	Rank and Name at the time the Decoration was earned.	Whether in possession of Medal and Clasp for							Whether at Suakin between 26th March 1884 and 28th Feby. 1885.	Whether entitled to Clasps inscribed				Whether serving with Regt. or Depot, dead, discharged, deserted, etc.
		Egypt, 1882.	Tel-el-Kebir.	Medal Suakin, 1884.	Clasp Suakin, 1884.	El-Teb.	Tamaai.	El-Teb—Tamaai.		Nile, 1884-85.	Abu Klea.	Kirbekan.	Suakin, 1885.	
	Lieut. A. C. Bald	No	No	Yes	No	No	No	Yes	No	Yes	No	No	No	Regiment.
	Lieut.-Col. R. K. Bayly, C.B.	Yes	Yes	No	Yes	Yes	No	No	,,	Yes	No	Yes	No	,,
	Lieut. T. M. M. Berkeley	No	No	No	No	No	No	No	,,	Yes	No	No	No	2nd Bn. Aldershot /588.
	Bt.-Major N. W. P. Brophy	Yes	Yes	No	Yes	No	No	Yes	,,	Yes	No	No	No	Deceased. A.G. List 185.
	Lieut. St. G. E. W. Burton	No	No	No	No	No	No	No	,,	Yes	No	Yes	No	2nd Bn. Aldershot /588.
	Bt.-Lt.-Col. R. C. Coveny	Yes	Yes	No	Yes	No	No	Yes	,,	Yes	No	Yes	No	Deceased. A.G. List 185.
	Lt. and Adjt. A. G. Duff	Yes	Yes	No	Yes	No	No	Yes	,,	Yes	No	Yes	No	Regiment.
	Bt.-Lt.-Col. C. J. Eden	Yes	Yes	No	Yes	No	No	Yes	,,	Yes	No	Yes	No	,,
	Captain H. F. Elliot	Yes	Yes	No	Yes	Yes	No	No	,,	Yes	No	Yes	No	42nd Regtl. Dist., Perth, N.B.
	Lieut. G. H. L. Galbraith	No	No	No	No	No	No	No	,,	Yes	No	Yes	No	Regiment.
	,, W. G. Wolrige-Gordon	No	No	Yes	No	Yes	No	No	,,	Yes	No	Yes	No	,,
	Colonel W. Green, C.B.	Yes	Yes	No	Yes	No	No	Yes	,,	Yes	No	Yes	No	G.O.C. Assouan. Regiment.
	Lieut. J. Home	Yes	Yes	No	Yes	Yes	No	No	,,	Yes	No	Yes	No	Regiment.
	Captain Lord A. Kennedy	Yes	Yes	No	Yes	No	No	Yes	,,	Yes	No	Yes	No	,,
	Lieut. T. F. A. Kennedy	Yes	Yes	No	Yes	No	No	Yes	,,	Yes	No	Yes	No	,,
	Bt.-Lt.-Col. A. L. Kidston	Yes	Yes	No	Yes	Yes	No	No	,,	Yes	No	Yes	No	,,
	Lieut. A. G. Ferrier-Kerr	No	No	Yes	No	No	No	Yes	,,	Yes	No	Yes	No	,,
	,, C. P. Livingston	Yes	Yes	No	Yes	No	No	Yes	,,	Yes	Yes	No	No	,,
	,, P. J. C. Livingston	No	No	No	No	No	No	No	,,	Yes	No	Yes	No	,,
	,, D. A. M'Leod	No	No	Yes	No	No	No	Yes	,,	Yes	No	Yes	No	,,
	,, J. Macrae	No	No	Yes	No	No	Yes	No	,,	Yes	No	Yes	No	,,
	Captain W. H. H. C. Moubray	No	No	No	No	No	No	No	,,	Yes	No	Yes	No	,,
	Lieut. H. Rose	No	No	No	No	No	No	No	,,	Yes	No	Yes	No	,,
	Qr.-Mr. C. Sinclair	Yes	Yes	No	Yes	No	No	Yes	,,	Yes	No	Yes	No	,,
	Lieut. G. Silver	No	No	No	No	No	No	No	,,	Yes	No	Yes	No	2nd Bn. Aldershot.
	,, T. Souter	Yes	Yes	No	No	No	No	No	,,	Yes	No	Yes	No	Regiment.
	Captain A. S. Stevenson	No	No	Yes	No	No	Yes	No	,,	Yes	No	Yes	No	,,
	Major (Pay-Mr.) W. R. Thornhill	Yes	Yes	No	No	No	No	No	,,	Yes	No	No	No	Dist. Paymaster, Cyprus.
	Surgeon F. H. Treherne	No	No	Yes	No	No	No	Yes	,,	Yes	No	Yes	No	Egypt.
	Bt.-Lt.-Col. A. G. Wauchope, C.M.G.	Yes	Yes	No	Yes	Yes	No	No	,,	Yes	No	Yes	No	Regiment.
	Lieut. D. L. Wilson	No	No	No	No	No	No	No	,,	Yes	No	Yes	No	,,
710	Private David Adams	No	No	No	No	No	No	No	No	Yes	No	Yes	No	Regiment.
2570	,, John Adams	No	No	Yes	No	No	No	Yes	,,	Yes	No	Yes	No	,,
154	,, James Adamson	Yes	Yes	No	Yes	No	No	Yes	,,	Yes	No	Yes	No	,,
2398	,, David Allan	Yes	Yes	No	Yes	No	No	Yes	,,	Yes	No	Yes	No	,,

Regtl. No.	Rank and Name at the time the Decoration was earned.	Whether in possession of Medal and Clasp for							Whether at Suakin between 26th March 1884 and 28th Feby. 1885.	Whether entitled to Clasps inscribed				Whether serving with Regt. or Depot, dead, discharged, deserted, etc.
		Egypt, 1882.	Tel-el-Kebir.	Medal Suakin, 1884.	Clasp Suakin, 1884.	El-Teb.	Tamaai.	El-Teb—Tamaai.		Nile, 1884-85.	Abu Klea.	Kirbekan.	Suakin, 1885.	
1176	Private James H. Allan	No	No	Yes	No	No	No	Yes	No	Yes	No	Yes	No	Regiment.
854	,, William Allan	No	No	No	No	No	No	No	,,	Yes	No	Yes	No	,,
969	,, Andrew Alexander	No	No	No	No	No	No	No	,,	Yes	No	Yes	No	,,
63	,, James Allison	Yes	Yes	No	No	No	No	No	,,	Yes	Yes	No	No	A. Reserve.
2314	Piper Thomas Aitken	Yes	Yes	No	Yes	No	No	Yes	,,	Yes	No	Yes	No	Regiment.
1139	Private Arthur Aitkenson	No	No	No	No	No	No	No	,,	Yes	No	Yes	No	,,
192	,, David Anderson	Yes	Yes	No	No	No	No	Yes	,,	Yes	No	Yes	No	,,
2077	,, John Anderson	No	No	Yes	No	No	No	Yes	,,	Yes	No	Yes	No	,,
2694	Corporal John Anderson	Yes	Yes	No	Yes	No	No	Yes	,,	Yes	No	Yes	No	,,
2055	Private Samuel Anderson	No	No	No	No	No	No	No	,,	Yes	No	Yes	No	,,
2689	,, James Angus	No	No	Yes	No	Yes	No	No	,,	Yes	No	Yes	No	,,
1152	,, Henry Anson	No	No	Yes	No	No	Yes	No	,,	Yes	No	Yes	No	,,
1060	,, Shem Arbon	No	No	Yes	No	No	No	Yes	,,	Yes	No	No	No	Depot.
2342	,, Robert Archer	No	No	No	No	No	No	No	,,	Yes	No	Yes	No	Regiment.[1]
292	,, James Armstrong	Yes	Yes	No	Yes	No	No	No	,,	Yes	No	Yes	No	,,
170	,, John Arnott	Yes	Yes	No	Yes	No	No	Yes	,,	Yes	No	Yes	No	A. Reserve. A.G. List 216.
823	,, William Asher	No	No	No	No	No	No	No	,,	Yes	No	No	No	2nd Battalion.
1046	,, Walter Atken	Yes	Yes	No	Yes	No	No	Yes	,,	Yes	No	Yes	No	Regiment.
1085	,, George Alyward	No	No	No	No	No	No	No	,,	Yes	No	Yes	No	,,
2370	Piper William Bain	Yes	Yes	No	Yes	No	No	Yes	,,	Yes	No	Yes	No	,,
2360	Private David Baird	Yes	Yes	No	Yes	Yes	No	No	,,	Yes	No	Yes	No	,,
2504	,, Martin Baker	Yes	Yes	No	Yes	No	No	Yes	,,	Yes	No	No	No	,,
212	Corporal William Ballantine	No	No	Yes	No	No	No	Yes	,,	Yes	No	Yes	No	,,
2189	Private Fredk. Baldwin	No	No	No	No	No	No	No	,,	Yes	No	Yes	No	,, See D.C.M. Roll.
1217	,, John Barclay	No	No	No	No	No	No	No	,,	Yes	No	Yes	No	Regiment.
734	,, Edward Barnes	No	No	No	No	No	No	No	,,	Yes	No	No	No	,,
1305	Serjt. Arthur V. Barwood	No	No	No	No	No	No	No	,,	Yes	No	No	No	,,
595	Private Spencer Barwood	Yes	Yes	No	Yes	No	No	Yes	,,	Yes	No	Yes	No	,,
2069	,, Charles Batchelor	No	No	No	No	No	No	No	,,	Yes	No	Yes	No	,, Captain Stewart's Collection
2333	,, Thomas Battison	Yes	Yes	No	Yes	No	No	Yes	,,	Yes	No	Yes	No	Regiment.
2651	Lce.-Corpl. Joseph Baxter	Yes	Yes	No	Yes	No	No	Yes	,,	Yes	No	Yes	No	,,
2650	Serjt. Matthew Baxter	Yes	Yes	No	No	No	No	No	,,	Yes	No	Yes	No	,,
1006	Private John Beattie	No	No	No	No	No	No	No	,,	Yes	No	No	No	Depot.
1247	Corpl. George Bedson	Yes	Yes	No	Yes	Yes	No	No	,,	Yes	No	Yes	No	Regiment.
2324	Private Joshua Bedlington	No	No	No	No	No	No	No	,,	Yes	No	No	No	,,
815	,, James Bellamy	Yes	Yes	No	Yes	No	No	Yes	,,	Yes	No	No	No	Depot.
744	,, Charles Belcher	No	No	Yes	No	No	No	Yes	,,	Yes	No	No	No	,,
2124	,, James Belford	No	No	No	No	No	No	No	,,	Yes	No	Yes	No	Regiment.
2434	Corpl. Stewart Berry	Yes	Yes	No	Yes	Yes	No	No	,,	Yes	No	Yes	No	,,
1995	Private John J. Best	No	No	Yes	No	No	No	Yes	,,	Yes	No	Yes	No	,,
2559	,, Andrew Beveridge	No	No	Yes	No	Yes	No	No	,,	Yes	No	Yes	No	,,
112	,, Thomas Biggan	Yes	Yes	No	Yes	No	No	Yes	,,	Yes	No	Yes	No	,,
15	,, Samuel W. Bissett	Yes	Yes	No	Yes	No	No	Yes	,,	Yes	No	Yes	No	,,
2016	,, Alexr. Birse	No	No	Yes	No	No	No	No	,,	Yes	No	No	No	,,
1265	,, William Blair	No	No	Yes	No	No	No	Yes	,,	Yes	No	Yes	No	,,
2155	,, David Blackley	No	No	No	No	No	No	No	,,	Yes	No	No	No	,,
1059	,, Albert Blunden	Yes	Yes	No	Yes	No	No	Yes	,,	Yes	No	Yes	No	,,

[1] Star sent 30/5/88.

Regtl. No.	RANK AND NAME at the time the Decoration was earned.	Egypt, 1882.	Tel-el-Kebir.	Medal Suakin, 1884.	Clasp Suakin, 1884.	El-Teb.	Tamaai.	El-Teb—Tamaai.	Whether at Suakin between 26th March 1884 and 28th Feby. 1885.	Nile, 1884-85.	Abu Klea.	Kirbekan.	Suakin, 1885.	Whether serving with Regt. or Depot, dead, discharged, deserted, etc.
		Whether in possession of Medal and Clasp for								Whether entitled to Clasps inscribed				
1274	Private James Blyth	No	No	Yes	No	No	No	Yes	No	Yes	No	Yes	No	Regiment.
2280	Drummer Joseph Bogle	Yes	Yes	No	Yes	No	No	Yes	,,	Yes	No	Yes	No	,,
2563	Serjt. Frank Booth	Yes	Yes	No	Yes	No	No	Yes	,,	Yes	No	No	No	,,
2683	Corporal William Borland	Yes	Yes	No	Yes	No	No	Yes	,,	Yes	No	Yes	No	,,
2356	Private Thomas Bowser	Yes	Yes	No	Yes	Yes	No	No	,,	Yes	No	Yes	No	,,
2399	,, Kennedy Boyd	Yes	Yes	No	No	No	No	No	,,	Yes	No	No	No	,, See 68/42/495.
1306	,, William Boyd	No	No	No	No	No	No	No	,,	Yes	No	Yes	No	Regiment.
1961	,, William Boynes	No	No	Yes	No	No	No	Yes	,,	Yes	No	Yes	No	,,
2442	,, George Brailsford	No	No	Yes	No	No	No	Yes	,,	Yes	Yes	No	No	,,
156	,, David Bremner	Yes	Yes	No	Yes	Yes	No	No	,,	Yes	Yes	No	No	,,
2078	,, David Brodie	No	No	Yes	No	No	No	Yes	,,	Yes	No	No	No	Depot.
113	,, Hugh Broggan	No	No	Yes	No	Yes	No	No	,,	Yes	No	Yes	No	Regiment.
207	,, Alexr. Brown	Yes	Yes	No	Yes	No	No	Yes	,,	Yes	No	Yes	No	,,
1968	,, John Brown	No	No	Yes	No	Yes	No	No	/503 ,,	Yes	No	Yes	No	,,
2173	,, Andrew Browning	No	No	No	No	No	No	No	,,	Yes	No	Yes	No	,,
756	,, Henry Browning	No	No	Yes	No	No	No	Yes	,,	Yes	No	No	No	Discharged. A.G. List 196.
213	Corporal John Brophy	Yes	Yes	No	Yes	Yes	No	No	,,	Yes	No	Yes	No	Regiment.
1103	Private Walter Brimble	Yes	Yes	No	Yes	No	No	Yes	,,	Yes	No	Yes	No	A. Reserve. A.G. List 194.
2597	,, William Britton	No	No	Yes	No	No	No	Yes	,,	Yes	No	No	No	Regiment.
2154	Drummer Alexr. H. Bruce	No	No	No	No	No	No	No	,,	Yes	No	No	No	,,
1200	Private Alexr. Bruce	No	No	Yes	No	No	No	Yes	,,	Yes	No	Yes	No	,,
2403	,, James Bruce	Yes	Yes	No	Yes	No	No	Yes	,,	Yes	No	No	No	Deceased. A.G. List 209.
1216	,, William Bruce	No	No	Yes	No	No	No	No	,,	Yes	No	Yes	No	Regiment.
1047	,, Henry Bullock	Yes	Yes	No	Yes	No	No	Yes	,,	Yes	No	No	No	,,
721	,, Freeman Bullimore	No	No	No	No	No	No	No	,,	Yes	No	Yes	No	,,
1982	Cr.-Serjt. Robert Burnett	Yes	Yes	No	Yes	No	No	Yes	,,	Yes	No	Yes	No	,,
2327	Private Joshua F. Burley	No	No	No	No	No	No	No	,,	Yes	No	Yes	No	,,
1183	,, Morris Burton	No	No	Yes	No	Yes	No	No	,,	Yes	No	No	No	,,
2470	,, David Byres	Yes	Yes	No	Yes	Yes	No	No	,,	Yes	No	Yes	No	,,
2171	,, John Cairns	No	No	No	No	No	No	No	,,	Yes	No	Yes	No	,,
2317	Drummer John Cairns	No	No	Yes	No	No	No	Yes	,,	Yes	No	No	No	Depot.
66	Private Duncan Calder	No	No	Yes	No	No	No	Yes	,,	Yes	No	Yes	No	Regiment.
57	,, George Caldwell	Yes	Yes	No	Yes	No	No	Yes	,,	Yes	No	Yes	No	,,
976	,, John Callaghan	No	No	Yes	No	No	No	Yes	,,	Yes	No	No	No	,,
1052	,, Edward Calver	No	No	Yes	No	Yes	No	No	,,	Yes	No	Yes	No	Depot.
2199	Cr.-Serjt. Alexr. Cameron	Yes	Yes	No	Yes	Yes	No	No	,,	Yes	No	No	No	Deceased. A.G. List 187.
2649	Private Alexr. Cameron	Yes	Yes	No	Yes	No	No	Yes	,,	Yes	No	No	No	Regiment.
2484	,, David Cameron	No	No	Yes	No	No	No	Yes	,,	Yes	No	Yes	No	,,
2378	Serjeant Donald Cameron	Yes	Yes	No	No	No	No	No	,,	Yes	No	Yes	No	,,
2502	Private James Cameron	No	No	Yes	No	No	No	Yes	,,	Yes	No	Yes	No	,,
2564	Corporal Robert Cameron	Yes	Yes	No	Yes	No	No	Yes	,,	Yes	No	Yes	No	,,
814	Private Alexr. Campbell	Yes	Yes	No	Yes	No	No	Yes	,,	Yes	No	Yes	No	,,
2511	Lce.-Corpl. Daniel Campbell	Yes	Yes	No	Yes	No	No	Yes	No	Yes	No	Yes	No	,,
2255	Private Hugh Campbell	No	No	No	No	No	No	No	,,	Yes	No	No	No	,, Forfeited /688.

Regtl. No.	Rank and Name at the time the Decoration was earned.	Egypt, 1882.	Tel-el-Kebir.	Medal Suakin, 1884.	Clasp Suakin, 1884.	El-Teb.	Tamaai.	El-Teb—Tamaai.	Whether at Suakin between 26th March 1884 and 28th Feby. 1885.	Nile, 1884-85.	Abu Klea.	Kirbekan.	Suakin, 1885.	Whether serving with Regt. or Depot, dead, discharged, deserted, etc.
67	Private John Campbell	Yes	Yes	No	Yes	No	No	No	No	Yes	No	Yes	No	Regiment.
2158	Lce.-Corpl. Malcolm Campbell	No	No	No	No	No	No	No	,,	Yes	No	Yes	No	,,
704	Private Robert Campbell	No	No	No	No	No	No	No	,,	Yes	No	Yes	No	,,
1245	Corporal James Campbell	No	No	Yes	No	Yes	No	No	,,	Yes	No	Yes	No	,,
1945	Private William Campbell	No	No	No	No	No	No	No	,,	Yes	No	Yes	No	Depot.
245	,, William Campbell	No	No	Yes	No	No	No	Yes	,,	Yes	No	Yes	No	Regiment.
2661	Serjeant William Carcary	No	No	Yes	No	No	No	Yes	,,	Yes	No	Yes	No	,,
2057	Private Alexr. Cargill	No	No	Yes	No	No	No	Yes	,,	Yes	No	Yes	No	,,
2015	,, Robt. Carmichael	No	No	Yes	No	Yes	No	No	,,	Yes	No	Yes	No	,,
882	,, John Carnie	No	No	Yes	No	No	No	Yes	,,	Yes	No	Yes	No	,,
965	,, Robert Carr	No	No	Yes	No	No	No	Yes	,,	Yes	No	Yes	No	,,
2519	,, Michael Carr	No	No	Yes	No	No	No	Yes	,,	Yes	No	Yes	No	,, A.G. List 547; 20/4/63. Restored 35/42/147.
197	Corporal James L. Carstairs	Yes	Yes	No	Yes	No	No	Yes	,,	Yes	No	No	No	Regiment.
1007	Private Adam Cavers	No	No	Yes	No	No	No	Yes	,,	Yes	No	Yes	No	,,
1312	Lce.-Corpl. Edward Chalmers	No	No	Yes	No	No	No	Yes	,,	Yes	No	No	No	Depot.
32	Private William Chalmers	Yes	Yes	No	Yes	No	No	Yes	,,	Yes	No	Yes	No	Regiment.
2331	,, Alexr. Chapman	No	No	No	No	No	No	No	,,	Yes	No	Yes	No	Discharged. A.G. List 220; /588.
1264	Lce.-Corpl. George Charlton	No	No	Yes	No	No	No	Yes	,,	Yes	No	Yes	No	Regiment.
891	Private Robert Cheeney	No	No	Yes	No	No	No	Yes	,,	Yes	No	Yes	No	,,
115	,, James Chisholm	Yes	Yes	No	Yes	No	No	Yes	,,	Yes	No	Yes	No	Depot.
1072	,, James Clancy	Yes	Yes	No	No	No	No	No	,,	Yes	Yes	No	No	Regiment.
1724	Serjt.-Dr. William Clark	Yes	Yes	No	Yes	No	No	Yes	,,	Yes	No	Yes	No	,,
451	Private John Clark	No	No	No	No	No	No	No	,,	Yes	No	Yes	No	,,
1065	,, Ebenezr. Claydon	Yes	Yes	No	Yes	No	No	Yes	,,	Yes	No	Yes	No	,,
234	,, James Clines	No	No	No	No	No	No	No	,,	Yes	No	Yes	No	,,
785	,, Oliver Coates	Yes	Yes	No	Yes	No	No	Yes	,,	Yes	No	Yes	No	,,
2391	,, Robert Cochrane	Yes	Yes	No	Yes	No	Yes	No	,,	Yes	No	Yes	No	,,
760	,, Thomas Cocking	Yes	No	No	Yes	Yes	No	No	,,	Yes	No	Yes	No	,,
791	,, Walter Coe	No	No	Yes	No	No	No	Yes	,,	Yes	No	Yes	No	Depot.
1324	,, John Collins	No	No	Yes	No	No	No	Yes	,,	Yes	No	Yes	No	Regiment.
826	,, Robert E. Collins	No	No	Yes	No	No	No	Yes	,,	Yes	No	Yes	No	,,
2223	Cr.-Serjt. James Connon	Yes	Yes	No	Yes	No	No	Yes	,,	Yes	No	Yes	No	,, See D.C.M. Roll.
2673	Corporal James Connolly	Yes	Yes	No	Yes	No	No	Yes	,,	Yes	No	Yes	No	Regiment.
2635	Private Peter Coote	No	No	Yes	No	No	No	Yes	,,	Yes	No	Yes	No	,,
1031	,, Albert Corrall	Yes	Yes	No	Yes	No	No	Yes	,,	Yes	No	Yes	No	,,
1035	,, James Costello	No	No	Yes	No	No	No	Yes	,,	Yes	No	Yes	No	,,
240	,, John Courtney	Yes	Yes	No	Yes	No	No	No	,,	Yes	No	Yes	No	,,
2017	,, Andrew Coutts	No	No	Yes	No	No	No	Yes	,,	Yes	No	Yes	No	,,
1126	,, John Cowan	No	No	Yes	No	Yes	No	No	,,	Yes	No	Yes	No	,,
173	,, George Cowie	No	No	Yes	No	No	No	Yes	,,	Yes	No	Yes	No	,,
2362	,, James Cowper	Yes	Yes	No	Yes	No	No	Yes	,,	Yes	No	Yes	No	,,
2133	,, William Cowper	No	No	No	No	No	No	No	,,	Yes	No	No	No	Deceased. A.G. List 309.
1552	,, George Cox	No	No	Yes	No	No	No	Yes	,,	Yes	No	Yes	No	Regiment.
885	,, James Cox	No	No	Yes	No	No	No	Yes	,,	Yes	No	Yes	No	,,
2141	,, Robert Craig	No	No	No	No	No	No	No	,,	Yes	No	Yes	No	,,

Regtl. No.	RANK AND NAME at the time the Decoration was earned.	Whether in possession of Medal and Clasp for							Whether at Suakin between 26th March 1884 and 28th Feby. 1885.	Whether entitled to Clasps inscribed				Whether serving with Regt. or Depot, dead, discharged, deserted, etc.
		Egypt, 1882.	Tel-el-Kebir.	Medal Suakin, 1884.	Clasp Suakin, 1884.	El-Teb.	Tamaai.	El-Teb—Tamaai.		Nile, 1884-85.	Abu Klea.	Kirbekan.	Suakin, 1885.	
2090	Private Charles Craig	No	No	Yes	No	No	No	Yes	No	Yes	No	Yes	No	Regiment.
2567	,, William Crawford	Yes	Yes	No	Yes	No	No	Yes	,,	Yes	No	Yes	No	,,
2134	,, William Crawford	No	No	No	No	No	No	No	,,	Yes	No	Yes	No	,,
2113	,, Thomas Crawford	No	No	Yes	No	No	No	Yes	,,	Yes	No	No	No	,,
2506	,, Peter Crichton	Yes	Yes	No	Yes	No	No	Yes	,,	Yes	No	No	No	,,
2495	,, Henry Crowe	Yes	Yes	No	Yes	Yes	No	No	,,	Yes	No	Yes	No	Depot.
1159	,, Francis Curran	No	No	No	No	No	No	No	,,	Yes	No	Yes	No	Regiment.
2052	,, David Currie	No	No	Yes	No	No	No	Yes	,,	Yes	No	Yes	No	,,
1081	Corporal William Curtis	No	No	Yes	No	No	No	Yes	,,	Yes	No	Yes	No	,,
2307	Private James Cuthbert	No	No	Yes	No	No	No	Yes	,,	Yes	No	Yes	No	,,
2473	,, Robert Cuthill	Yes	Yes	No	Yes	Yes	No	No	,,	Yes	No	Yes	No	,,
928	,, William Dalgleish	Yes	No	No	Yes	Yes	No	No	,,	Yes	No	Yes	No	Depot.
1302	Serjeant Joseph Daily	No	No	Yes	No	No	No	Yes	,,	Yes	No	Yes	No	Regiment.
827	Private Thomas Davis	No	No	No	No	No	No	No	,,	Yes	No	No	No	,, Forfeited /691.
2479	,, David Davidson	No	No	Yes	No	Yes	No	No	,,	Yes	No	No	No	Regiment.
2363	,, George Davidson	Yes	Yes	No	Yes	No	No	Yes	,,	Yes	No	Yes	No	,,
21	Serjeant William D. F. Davidson	Yes	Yes	No	Yes	No	No	Yes	,,	Yes	No	Yes	No	,,
1719	Private William Davidson	No	No	Yes	No	Yes	No	No	/503 ,,	Yes	No	No	Yes	,,
35	,, George Deans	Yes	Yes	No	Yes	No	No	Yes	,,	Yes	No	Yes	No	Depot.
68	,, Martin Dempsey	Yes	Yes	No	Yes	No	No	Yes	,,	Yes	No	No	No	Regiment.
50	,, Robert Dick	No	No	Yes	No	Yes	No	No	,,	Yes	Yes	No	No	,,
2200	,, Hugh Dickson	No	No	No	No	No	No	No	,,	Yes	No	Yes	No	,, E/104624/9.
784	,, Arthur Dickson	No	No	Yes	No	No	No	Yes	,,	Yes	No	Yes	No	,,
283	Lce.-Corpl. Thomas Dodds	No	No	Yes	No	No	No	Yes	,,	Yes	No	Yes	No	,,
2190	Private Thomas Docherty	No	No	Yes	No	Yes	No	No	,,	Yes	No	Yes	No	Discharged. A.G. List 203.
2033	,, Alexr. Doig	No	No	Yes	No	No	No	Yes	,,	Yes	No	Yes	No	Regiment.
2097	,, David Donald	No	No	Yes	No	Yes	No	No	,,	Yes	No	No	No	,,
1330	,, Joseph Donald	No	No	Yes	No	Yes	No	No	,,	Yes	No	No	No	Depot.
1620	,, William Donald	Yes	Yes	No	No	No	No	No	,,	Yes	No	Yes	No	Discharged. A.G. List 432.
1984	,, David Donaldson	No	No	Yes	No	No	No	Yes	,,	Yes	No	Yes	No	Regiment.
946	,, George Donaldson	No	No	Yes	No	No	No	Yes	,,	Yes	No	Yes	No	,,
1653	Serjeant James Donaldson	Yes	Yes	No	Yes	No	No	Yes	,,	Yes	No	Yes	No	,,
2507	Corporal Peter Donaldson	Yes	Yes	No	Yes	No	No	Yes	,,	Yes	No	Yes	No	,,
2046	Private William Donaldson	No	No	No	No	No	No	No	,,	Yes	No	Yes	No	,,
759	,, George M. Dore	No	No	No	No	No	No	No	,,	Yes	No	Yes	No	,,
2119	,, Peter Dorward	No	No	No	No	No	No	No	,,	Yes	No	Yes	No	,,
1067	,, Henry Double	No	No	Yes	No	No	No	Yes	,,	Yes	No	Yes	No	,,
2552	,, George Douglas	Yes	No	No	Yes	No	No	Yes	,,	Yes	No	Yes	No	,,
2410	,, John Downie	Yes	Yes	No	Yes	No	No	Yes	,,	Yes	No	Yes	No	,,
693	Lce.-Corpl. Robert Downie	Yes	Yes	No	Yes	No	No	Yes	,,	Yes	No	Yes	No	Deceased. A.G. List 188.
116	Private David Drever	Yes	Yes	No	Yes	Yes	No	No	,,	Yes	No	No	No	Regiment.
2652	Lce.-Corpl. Henry Drummond	Yes	Yes	No	Yes	No	No	Yes	,,	Yes	No	No	No	,,
2383	Private John Duff	Yes	Yes	No	Yes	No	No	Yes	,,	Yes	No	Yes	No	,,
487	Qr.-Mr.-Serjt. Lewis Dunbar	Yes	Yes	No	Yes	No	No	Yes	,,	Yes	No	Yes	No	,,
1321	Private Alexr. Duncan	No	No	Yes	No	No	No	Yes	,,	Yes	No	Yes	No	,,
295	Corporal James Duncan	Yes	Yes	No	Yes	No	No	Yes	,,	Yes	No	Yes	No	,,

Regtl. No.	Rank and Name at the time the Decoration was earned.	Whether in possession of Medal and Clasp for							Whether at Suakin between 26th March 1884 and 28th Feby. 1885.	Whether entitled to Clasps inscribed				Whether serving with Regt. or Depot, dead, discharged, deserted, etc.
		Egypt, 1882.	Tel-el-Kebir.	Medal Suakin, 1884.	Clasp Suakin, 1884.	El-Teb.	Tamaai.	El-Teb—Tamaai.		Nile, 1884-85.	Abu Klea.	Kirbekan.	Suakin, 1885.	
174	Private James Dunlevey . .	No	No	No	No	No	No	No	No	Yes	No	No	No	Regiment. Forfeited 68/42/482.
251	,, John Durward . .	Yes	Yes	No	Yes	Yes	No	No	,,	Yes	No	Yes	No	Regiment.
2038	,, Thomas Dysart . .	No	No	No	No	No	No	No	,,	Yes	No	Yes	No	,,
1164	,, David Eadie . .	No	No	Yes	No	No	No	No	,,	Yes	No	No	No	,,
822	Drummer Philip Eames . .	No	No	Yes	No	Yes	No	No	,,	Yes	No	Yes	No	,,
464	Private James Easton . .	No	No	No	No	No	No	No	,,	Yes	No	Yes	No	,,
143	,, David Edgar . .	No	No	Yes	No	No	No	Yes	,,	Yes	No	Yes	No	,,
1725	,, John Edmonstone .	No	No	Yes	No	No	No	Yes	,,	Yes	No	No	No	,, Forfeited /622.
2114	,, Robert Edwards . .	No	No	No	No	No	No	No	,,	Yes	No	Yes	No	Deceased. A.G. List 209.
235	,, Thomas Edwards, V.C.	Yes	Yes	No	Yes	No	No	Yes	,,	Yes	No	Yes	No	Regiment.
967	,, William Edwards . .	Yes	Yes	No	Yes	No	No	Yes	,,	Yes	No	No	No	,,
1178	,, Bernard Egan . .	No	No	Yes	No	No	No	Yes	,,	Yes	No	Yes	No	,,
2616	,, William Elder . .	No	No	Yes	No	No	No	Yes	,,	Yes	No	No	No	,, Captain Stewart's Collection
2538	,, John Elliot . .	Yes	Yes	No	Yes	Yes	No	No	/503 ,,	Yes	No	No	No	Regiment.
247	,, William Elvin . .	Yes	Yes	No	Yes	No	No	Yes	,,	Yes	No	Yes	No	,,
1141	Lce.-Corpl. Alfred Embrough .	No	No	Yes	No	No	No	No	,,	Yes	No	No	No	,,
2584	Private Nathaniel Ennis .	No	No	Yes	No	No	No	Yes	,,	Yes	No	No	No	,,
762	,, Michael Enright . .	No	No	Yes	No	No	No	Yes	,,	Yes	No	Yes	No	,,
2011	,, Henry Evans . .	No	No	Yes	No	Yes	No	No	,,	Yes	No	No	No	,,
1728	,, Thomas Farley .	No	No	Yes	No	No	No	Yes	,,	Yes	No	Yes	No	,,
1214	,, George Farmer .	Yes	Yes	No	Yes	Yes	No	No	,,	Yes	No	Yes	No	,,
2448	,, Thomas Fay . .	No	No	No	No	No	No	No	,,	Yes	No	Yes	No	,, Star sent 30/5/88.
2503	,, Charles Ferguson .	No	No	Yes	No	No	No	Yes	,,	Yes	No	No	No	Regiment.
1074	Corporal William Ferguson .	No	No	Yes	No	Yes	No	No	,,	Yes	No	Yes	No	Depot.
941	,, George L. Finlay .	Yes	Yes	No	Yes	Yes	No	No	,,	Yes	No	Yes	No	Regiment.
239	Private Isreal Firth . .	No	No	Yes	No	No	No	Yes	,,	Yes	No	Yes	No	,,
733	,, George Fisher . .	No	No	Yes	No	Yes	No	No	,,	Yes	No	No	No	Depot.
70	,, Robert Flood . .	No	No	Yes	No	Yes	No	No	,,	Yes	No	Yes	No	Regiment. Captain Stewart's Collection
698	Lce.-Corpl. James Flynn .	Yes	Yes	No	Yes	No	No	Yes	,,	Yes	No	Yes	No	Depot.
998	Private John Flynn . .	No	No	Yes	No	No	No	Yes	,,	Yes	Yes	No	No	Regiment.
2518	,, David Foley . .	No	No	No	No	No	No	No	,,	Yes	No	Yes	No	,,
894	Lce.-Corpl. William Folwell .	No	No	Yes	No	No	No	Yes	,,	Yes	No	Yes	No	,,
2442	Private Thomas Forbes .	No	No	Yes	No	Yes	No	No	,,	Yes	No	Yes	No	Depot.
2577	,, William Forbes .	No	No	Yes	No	No	No	Yes	,,	Yes	No	Yes	No	Regiment.
71	,, Donald Foreman .	No	No	Yes	No	No	No	Yes	,,	Yes	No	Yes	No	Deceased. A.G. List 209.
1137	,, John Forrest . .	No	No	Yes	No	Yes	No	No	,,	Yes	No	No	No	Regiment.
229	,, Jesse Fowler . .	No	No	Yes	No	No	No	Yes	,,	Yes	No	Yes	No	,,
960	Lce.-Corpl. George E. Foxwell	No	No	Yes	No	No	No	Yes	,,	Yes	No	Yes	No	,,
682	Private Alexr. Fraser . .	Yes	Yes	No	Yes	No	No	Yes	,,	Yes	No	Yes	No	,,
1296	,, Hector Fraser . .	No	No	No	No	No	No	No	,,	Yes	No	Yes	No	,,
2050	,, John Fraser . .	No	No	No	No	No	No	No	,,	Yes	No	Yes	No	,,
2609	,, John Fraser . .	Yes	Yes	No	Yes	Yes	No	No	,,	Yes	No	No	No	,,
1186	Drummer George Fulton . .	No	No	Yes	No	No	No	Yes	,,	Yes	No	No	No	Depot.

Regtl. No.	Rank and Name at the time the Decoration was earned.	Egypt, 1882.	Tel-el-Kebir.	Medal Suakin, 1884.	Clasp Suakin, 1884.	El-Teb.	Tamaai.	El-Teb—Tamaai.	Whether at Suakin between 26th March 1884 and 28th Feby. 1885.	Nile, 1884-85.	Abu Klea.	Kirbekan.	Suakin, 1885.	Whether serving with Regt. or Depot, dead, discharged, deserted, etc.
1179	Private John Furness	No	No	Yes	No	No	No	Yes	No	Yes	No	Yes	No	Regiment. Forfeited 68/42/495.
2579	„ Andrew Gaffney	No	No	Yes	No	Yes	No	No	„	Yes	No	No	No	Regiment.
2663	„ James Gagan	No	No	Yes	No	Yes	No	No	„	Yes	No	Yes	No	„
846	„ Neil Galbraith	Yes	Yes	No	Yes	No	No	Yes	„	Yes	No	Yes	No	„
1704	„ John M. Gardner	No	No	Yes	No	Yes	No	No	„	Yes	No	No	No	„
2599	„ James George	Yes	Yes	No	Yes	No	No	Yes	„	Yes	Yes	No	No	„
783	„ Patrick Gerrity	No	No	Yes	No	No	No	No	„	Yes	No	Yes	No	„
1710	Lce.-Corpl. James Gibb	No	No	No	No	No	No	No	„	Yes	No	Yes	No	„
75	Corporal Thomas Gilbert	Yes	Yes	No	Yes	No	No	Yes	„	Yes	No	No	No	„
793	Private John Gilbert	No	No	No	No	No	No	No	„	Yes	No	Yes	No	„
1319	„ George Gilbert	No	No	Yes	No	No	No	Yes	„	Yes	No	No	No	„
76	„ James Gill	Yes	Yes	No	Yes	No	No	Yes	„	Yes	Yes	No	No	„ Captain Stewart's Collection
978	„ David Gillard	No	No	No	No	No	No	No	„	Yes	No	No	No	Discharged. A.G. List 274; /663.
1322	Lce.-Corpl. William Gillespie	No	No	No	No	No	No	No	„	Yes	No	Yes	No	Regiment.
2679	Private James Gillies	No	No	Yes	No	No	No	No	„	Yes	No	Yes	No	„
2088	„ Neil Gilmour	No	No	No	No	No	No	No	„	Yes	No	Yes	No	„
1625	Lce.-Serjt. Thomas Glen	Yes	Yes	No	Yes	No	No	Yes	„	Yes	No	Yes	No	„
176	Private William Gloag	Yes	Yes	No	Yes	Yes	No	No	„	Yes	No	Yes	No	„
714	„ John Golland	No	No	Yes	No	Yes	No	No	„	Yes	No	Yes	No	„
751	„ James Goodall	No	No	Yes	No	No	No	Yes	„	Yes	No	Yes	No	„
2546	Lce.-Corpl. John Goodfellow	Yes	Yes	No	No	No	No	No	„	Yes	No	Yes	No	„
879	Private David Gordon	Yes	Yes	No	Yes	No	No	Yes	„	Yes	Yes	No	No	„ Captain Stewart's Collection
2291	„ George Gordon	No	No	No	No	No	No	No	„	Yes	No	Yes	No	Regiment.
2549	Corporal John Gordon	Yes	Yes	No	Yes	No	No	Yes	„	Yes	No	Yes	No	„
2029	Boy William Goulden	No	No	No	No	No	No	No	„	Yes	No	Yes	No	„
2424	Private James Govan	Yes	Yes	No	Yes	No	No	Yes	„	Yes	No	Yes	No	„
2164	„ John Govan	No	No	No	No	No	No	No	„	Yes	No	Yes	No	„
1243	„ Robert Gow	No	No	Yes	No	No	No	Yes	„	Yes	No	No	No	„
2082	„ James Gowans	No	No	Yes	No	No	No	Yes	„	Yes	No	No	No	„ Forfeited /569.
251	„ George Graham	Yes	Yes	No	Yes	No	No	Yes	„	Yes	No	Yes	No	Regiment.
10	„ James Graham	Yes	Yes	No	Yes	No	No	Yes	„	Yes	No	Yes	No	„
2172	„ Henry Graham	No	No	No	No	No	No	No	„	Yes	No	No	No	„
78	„ Alexr. Grant	Yes	Yes	No	Yes	No	No	Yes	„	Yes	No	Yes	No	Discharged.
2123	„ James Grant	No	No	No	No	No	No	No	„	Yes	No	Yes	No	Regiment.
177	„ James Grant	Yes	Yes	No	Yes	No	No	Yes	„	Yes	No	Yes	No	A. Reserve.
918	„ John Grant	No	No	Yes	No	No	No	Yes	„	Yes	No	Yes	No	Regiment.
2524	„ William Gray	Yes	Yes	No	No	No	No	No	„	Yes	No	No	No	„
997	„ James Gray	No	No	Yes	No	No	No	Yes	„	Yes	No	No	No	„
12	Lce.-Corpl. James Gray	Yes	Yes	No	Yes	Yes	No	No	„	Yes	No	Yes	No	„
2708	Private John Greenlaw	Yes	Yes	No	Yes	No	No	Yes	„	Yes	No	No	No	„
2092	Lce.-Corpl. Matthew J. Greer	No	No	Yes	No	No	No	Yes	„	Yes	No	Yes	No	„
2499	Private Henry J. Griffiths	No	No	Yes	No	No	No	Yes	„	Yes	No	Yes	No	„
2205	„ James Haggarty	No	No	No	No	No	No	No	„	Yes	No	Yes	No	„
816	„ Alexr. Hailstones	Yes	Yes	No	No	No	No	No	„	Yes	No	Yes	No	„
1145	„ Charles Haig	No	No	Yes	No	No	No	Yes	„	Yes	No	Yes	No	„

Regtl. No.	RANK AND NAME at the time the Decoration was earned.	Whether in possession of Medal and Clasp for							Whether at Suakin between 26th March 1884 and 28th Feby. 1885.	Whether entitled to Clasps inscribed				Whether serving with Regt. or Depot, dead, discharged, deserted, etc.
		Egypt, 1882.	Tel-el-Kebir.	Medal Suakin, 1884.	Clasp Suakin, 1884.	El-Teb.	Tamaai.	El-Teb—Tamaai.		Nile, 1884-85.	Abu Klea.	Kirbekan.	Suakin, 1885.	
780	Private Thomas Haig . . .	Yes	Yes	No	Yes	No	No	Yes	No	Yes	No	Yes	No	Regiment.
1000	Serjeant Charles Halkett .	No	No	No	No	No	No	No	,,	Yes	No	Yes	No	,, /706.
1070	Private Stephen Hall . . .	Yes	Yes	No	Yes	No	No	Yes	,,	Yes	No	Yes	No	,,
2044	,, John Halliday . .	No	No	No	No	No	No	No	,,	Yes	No	Yes	No	,,
1991	,, William Hamilton .	No	No	Yes	No	No	No	Yes	,,	Yes	No	Yes	No	,,
2601	,, Robert Hamilton .	No	No	Yes	No	No	No	No	,,	Yes	No	Yes	No	,,
2542	,, Thomas Handy .	Yes	Yes	No	Yes	No	No	Yes	,,	Yes	No	Yes	No	Deceased. A.G. List 209.
781	,, Richard Harding .	No	No	Yes	No	Yes	No	No	,,	Yes	No	No	No	Regiment.
2021	,, Robert Harkness .	No	No	Yes	No	Yes	No	No	,,	Yes	No	No	No	,,
2667	Lce.-Corpl. James Harley .	Yes	Yes	No	Yes	No	No	Yes	,,	Yes	No	Yes	No	,,
994	Serjeant Hugh Harley . .	No	No	Yes	No	No	No	Yes	,,	Yes	No	Yes	No	,,
719	Private Albert Harris . .	No	No	No	No	No	No	No	,,	Yes	No	Yes	No	Depot /558.
2137	,, Frank Harrison .	No	No	No	No	No	No	No	,,	Yes	No	Yes	No	Deceased. A.G. List 209.
493	,, John Harroway .	No	No	No	No	No	No	No	,,	Yes	No	No	No	Depot. Medal sent to Mint /683.
2173	,, Thomas Hart .	No	No	No	No	No	No	No	,,	Yes	No	No	No	Regiment. Forfeited /579.
2686	,, John Hastie . .	Yes	Yes	No	Yes	No	No	Yes	,,	Yes	No	No	No	Regiment.
117	,, John Hastie . .	Yes	Yes	No	Yes	No	No	Yes	,,	Yes	No	Yes	No	,,
42	Serjeant Edwin Hawkins .	No	No	Yes	No	No	No	Yes	,,	Yes	No	Yes	No	,,
935	Private Wm. Hencherwood	No	No	Yes	No	Yes	No	No	,,	Yes	No	Yes	No	,,
1797	,, James Henderson .	Yes	Yes	No	Yes	No	No	Yes	,,	Yes	No	Yes	No	,,
1654	Serjeant Alexr. Henderson	No	No	Yes	No	No	No	Yes	,,	Yes	No	Yes	No	,, See D.C.M. Roll.
2523	Private George Hendry .	No	No	Yes	No	Yes	No	No	,,	Yes	No	Yes	No	Regiment.
2079	,, Thomas Higginson .	No	No	Yes	No	No	No	Yes	,,	Yes	No	Yes	No	,,
79	,, John Hillis . .	Yes	Yes	No	Yes	No	No	Yes	,,	Yes	No	No	No	A. Reserve. A.G. List 248.
1055	Corporal Joseph Hines .	No	No	Yes	No	Yes	No	No	,,	Yes	No	Yes	No	Regiment.
1304	Private William Hislop .	No	No	Yes	No	No	No	Yes	,,	Yes	No	Yes	No	,,
1193	Corporal James Hogg . .	No	No	Yes	No	No	No	Yes	,,	Yes	No	Yes	No	,,
158	Private William Hogg .	Yes	Yes	No	Yes	Yes	No	No	,,	Yes	No	Yes	No	,,
2035	,, George Holmes .	No	No	Yes	No	Yes	No	No	,,	Yes	No	Yes	No	,,
1218	,, Andrew Hood . .	No	No	No	No	No	No	No	,,	Yes	No	No	No	,,
2135	,, James Hood . .	No	No	No	No	No	No	No	,,	Yes	No	Yes	No	,,
2422	,, Robert Hood . .	Yes	Yes	No	Yes	No	No	Yes	,,	Yes	Yes	No	No	,,
955	,, James Hope . .	No	No	Yes	No	No	No	Yes	,,	Yes	No	No	No	,,
2314	,, Thomas Hopkins .	No	No	Yes	No	No	No	No	,,	Yes	No	Yes	No	,,
270	,, Robert Horn . .	No	No	Yes	No	No	No	No	,,	Yes	No	Yes	No	,,
2138	,, Wm. H. Horsfall .	No	No	No	No	No	No	No	,,	Yes	No	Yes	No	,, /684.
2270	Lce.-Corpl. John E. Houghton	No	No	No	No	No	No	No	,,	Yes	No	Yes	No	Depot.
2269	,, Robert F. Houghton	No	No	No	No	No	No	No	,,	Yes	No	Yes	No	Deceased. A.G. List 209.
2088	Private James Houston .	No	No	Yes	No	No	No	Yes	,,	Yes	No	No	No	Regiment.
1976	,, William Howard .	No	No	Yes	No	No	No	Yes	,,	Yes	No	Yes	No	,,
830	,, Edward Howarth .	No	No	Yes	No	Yes	No	No	,,	Yes	No	Yes	No	,,
2369	,, George Howieson .	Yes	Yes	No	Yes	No	No	Yes	,,	Yes	No	No	No	,,
1314	,, George Hunt . .	No	No	Yes	No	No	Yes	No	,,	Yes	No	Yes	No	,,

Regtl. No.	Rank and Name at the time the Decoration was earned.	Whether in possession of Medal and Clasp for							Whether at Suakin between 26th March 1884 and 28th Feby. 1885.	Whether entitled to Clasps inscribed				Whether serving with Regt. or Depot, dead, discharged, deserted, etc.
		Egypt, 1882.	Tel-el-Kebir.	Medal Suakin, 1884.	Clasp Suakin, 1884.	El-Teb.	Tamaai.	El-Teb—Tamaai.		Nile, 1884-85.	Abu Klea.	Kirbekan.	Suakin, 1885.	
1129	Private Alexr. Hunter	No	No	No	No	No	No	No	No	Yes	No	Yes	No	Regiment.
2582	,, John Hunter	No	No	Yes	No	No	No	No	,,	Yes	No	No	No	,,
1955	,, John Hunter	No	No	Yes	No	No	No	Yes	,,	Yes	No	Yes	No	,,
1157	,, George Huntingdon	No	No	Yes	No	No	No	Yes	,,	Yes	No	No	No	,,
22	Lce.-Serjt. James Hutchison	Yes	Yes	No	Yes	Yes	No	No	,,	Yes	No	Yes	No	,,
1966	Private Andrew Hutton	No	No	Yes	No	No	No	Yes	,,	Yes	No	Yes	No	,,
1053	,, Henry Inch	Yes	Yes	No	No	No	No	No	,,	Yes	No	Yes	No	,,
1536	,, James Innes	Yes	Yes	No	Yes	No	No	Yes	,,	Yes	No	No	No	Discharged.
2163	,, Andrew Irvine	No	No	No	No	No	No	No	,,	Yes	No	Yes	No	Depot.
2700	,, John Irvine	No	No	Yes	No	No	No	Yes	,,	Yes	No	No	No	Regiment.
937	,, William Jack	No	No	Yes	No	No	No	Yes	,,	Yes	No	No	No	,,
900	,, Andrew Jamieson	Yes	Yes	No	Yes	Yes	No	No	,,	Yes	No	No	No	,,
910	,, David Jamieson	No	No	No	No	No	No	No	,,	Yes	No	Yes	No	,,
1770	,, Peter Jeffrey	Yes	Yes	No	No	No	No	No	,,	Yes	No	No	No	,,
740	,, Charles O. Jeffs	Yes	Yes	No	Yes	No	No	No	,,	Yes	No	Yes	No	,,
739	Lce.-Corpl. Stephen Johnson	No	No	No	No	No	No	No	,,	Yes	No	Yes	No	,, Forfeited.
2291	Private Charles Johnston	No	No	No	No	No	No	No	,,	Yes	No	Yes	No	Regiment.
198	Lce.-Corpl. John Johnston	Yes	Yes	No	Yes	No	No	Yes	,,	Yes	No	Yes	No	,,
957	Private John Johnston	No	No	Yes	No	Yes	No	No	,,	Yes	No	No	No	,, Forfeited.
1071	,, Thomas Johnston	Yes	Yes	No	Yes	No	No	Yes	,,	Yes	No	Yes	No	Regiment.
2575	,, Alfred C. Jones	No	No	No	No	No	No	No	,,	Yes	No	Yes	No	,,
1092	,, George Jones	No	No	Yes	No	Yes	No	No	,,	Yes	No	Yes	No	,,
1262	,, James Jones	No	No	No	No	No	No	No	,,	Yes	No	Yes	No	,,
897	,, Thomas Jones	No	No	Yes	No	No	No	Yes	,,	Yes	No	No	No	,,
2257	,, William Jowett	No	No	No	No	No	No	No	,,	Yes	No	No	No	Depot /588.
80	,, David Kay	Yes	Yes	No	Yes	Yes	No	No	,,	Yes	No	Yes	No	Regiment.
915	,, Hugh Kean	Yes	Yes	No	Yes	Yes	No	No	,,	Yes	No	Yes	No	,,
1975	,, Gilbert Keillor	No	No	Yes	No	No	No	Yes	,,	Yes	No	Yes	No	,,
1135	,, Archd. Kennedy	Yes	Yes	No	Yes	No	No	Yes	,,	Yes	No	Yes	No	,,
2195	,, George Kennedy	No	No	No	No	No	No	No	,,	Yes	No	Yes	No	,,
6	,, David Keir	No	No	Yes	No	No	No	Yes	,,	Yes	No	Yes	No	,,
25	,, James Kemp	Yes	Yes	No	Yes	No	No	Yes	,,	Yes	No	Yes	No	,,
2377	,, Thomas Kemp	Yes	Yes	No	Yes	No	No	Yes	,,	Yes	No	Yes	No	,,
2565	,, William Kidd	No	No	No	No	No	No	No	,,	Yes	No	No	No	,, Restored /693.
81	,, William Kidd	Yes	Yes	No	Yes	Yes	No	No	,,	Yes	No	Yes	No	Regiment.
789	,, Arthur Kightly	No	No	No	No	No	No	No	,,	Yes	No	No	No	,,
2687	,, David King	Yes	Yes	No	Yes	No	No	Yes	,,	Yes	No	Yes	No	,,
831	,, Herbert King	No	No	No	No	No	No	No	,,	Yes	No	No	No	Depot.
2614	Corporal William Kincaid	Yes	Yes	No	Yes	No	No	Yes	,,	Yes	No	Yes	No	Regiment.
716	Private Paul Kirkby	Yes	Yes	No	No	No	No	No	,,	Yes	No	Yes	No	,,
255	,, Andrew Laidlaw	No	No	Yes	No	No	No	Yes	,,	Yes	No	No	No	,,
2003	,, William Laing	No	No	Yes	No	No	No	Yes	,,	Yes	No	Yes	No	,,
1712	,, William Laird	No	No	No	No	No	No	No	,,	Yes	No	Yes	No	,, /604.
2022	,, Robert Lamb	No	No	No	No	No	No	No	,,	Yes	No	No	No	Regiment.
2551	,, Thomas Lang	No	No	Yes	No	No	No	Yes	,,	Yes	No	Yes	No	,,
2613	,, William Langlands	Yes	Yes	No	Yes	Yes	No	No	,,	Yes	No	Yes	No	,,
1951	,, James Laurie	No	No	No	No	No	No	No	,,	Yes	No	Yes	No	,,
82	,, John Laurie	Yes	Yes	No	Yes	No	No	Yes	,,	Yes	No	Yes	No	,,
938	,, Robert Laurie	No	No	Yes	No	No	No	Yes	,,	Yes	No	Yes	No	,,

Regtl. No.	RANK AND NAME at the time the Decoration was earned.	Whether in possession of Medal and Clasp for							Whether at Suakin between 26th March 1884 and 28th Feby. 1885.	Whether entitled to Clasps inscribed				Whether serving with Regt. or Depot, dead, discharged, deserted, etc.
		Egypt, 1882.	Tel-el-Kebir.	Medal Suakin, 1884.	Clasp Suakin, 1884.	El-Teb.	Tamaai.	El-Teb—Tamaai.		Nile, 1884-85.	Abu Klea.	Kirbekan.	Suakin, 1885.	
2056	Private David Law	No	No	Yes	No	No	No	Yes	No	Yes	No	Yes	No	Regiment.
294	,, William Law	Yes	No	No	No	No	No	No	,,	Yes	No	Yes	No	,,
2009	,, John Lawrie	No	No	No	No	No	No	No	,,	Yes	No	No	No	Deceased. A.G. List 209.
2283	,, John Laurie	No	No	No	No	No	No	No	,,	Yes	No	Yes	No	Regiment. Captain Stewart's Collection
1301	,, William Lawrie	No	No	Yes	No	No	No	Yes	,,	Yes	No	Yes	No	Regiment.
2478	,, Edward Ledran	Yes	Yes	No	Yes	No	No	Yes	,,	Yes	No	Yes	No	,,
218	,, Edward Lee	No	No	Yes	No	No	No	Yes	,,	Yes	No	Yes	No	,,
1644	Drummer James Lennie	No	No	Yes	No	No	No	Yes	,,	Yes	No	Yes	No	Depot.
1206	Private James Leslie	No	No	Yes	No	No	No	Yes	,,	Yes	No	Yes	No	Regiment.
2394	,, William Leslie	No	No	Yes	No	No	No	Yes	,,	Yes	No	Yes	No	,,
1107	,, James Lewis	Yes	Yes	No	Yes	No	No	Yes	,,	Yes	No	No	No	,,
1050	,, George Lies	Yes	Yes	No	Yes	No	No	Yes	,,	Yes	No	Yes	No	,,
717	,, Robert Lindsay	No	No	Yes	No	Yes	No	No	,,	Yes	No	No	No	,,
1320	,, William Lindsay	No	No	Yes	No	No	No	Yes	,,	Yes	No	No	No	,,
1087	Corporal William Lindsay	No	No	Yes	No	No	No	Yes	,,	Yes	No	Yes	No	,,
2342	Cr.-Serjt. John Linning	Yes	Yes	No	Yes	Yes	No	No	,,	Yes	No	Yes	No	,,
83	Private Alexr. Logan	Yes	Yes	No	Yes	Yes	No	No	,,	Yes	No	Yes	No	,,
343	Cr.-Serjt. Robert Logan	Yes	Yes	No	Yes	No	No	Yes	,,	Yes	No	Yes	No	Depot.
1269	Private David Louden	No	No	Yes	No	No	No	Yes	,,	Yes	No	No	No	Regiment.
788	,, James Louth	Yes	Yes	No	Yes	No	No	Yes	,,	Yes	No	Yes	No	Depot.
2660	,, George Low	Yes	Yes	No	Yes	No	No	Yes	,,	Yes	No	Yes	No	Regiment.
1444	Serjeant George Luscombe	Yes	No	No	No	No	No	No	,,	Yes	No	Yes	No	,,
2710	Private Robert Lyle	Yes	Yes	No	Yes	Yes	No	No	,,	Yes	Yes	No	No	,,
1231	Serjeant James Lynn	Yes	Yes	No	Yes	No	No	Yes	,,	Yes	No	Yes	No	,,
2513	Private John Maccorist	Yes	Yes	No	Yes	No	No	Yes	,,	Yes	No	Yes	No	Depot. Captain Stewart's Collection
939	,, John Magee	No	No	No	No	No	No	No	,,	Yes	No	Yes	No	Regiment.
1001	,, William Major	No	No	Yes	No	No	No	Yes	,,	Yes	Yes	No	No	,,
2441	,, Alexr. Mann	No	No	Yes	No	No	No	Yes	,,	Yes	No	Yes	No	,,
2080	,, William Marshal	No	No	No	No	No	No	No	,,	Yes	No	Yes	No	,,
1068	,, Jonas Martin	No	No	Yes	No	No	No	Yes	,,	Yes	No	No	No	,,
2624	,, Thomas Martin	No	No	Yes	No	No	No	No	,,	Yes	No	Yes	No	Depot.
107	,, John Mason	Yes	Yes	No	Yes	Yes	No	No	,,	Yes	No	No	No	Regiment.
1284	,, William Mason	No	No	Yes	No	No	No	Yes	,,	Yes	No	Yes	No	,,
2659	,, George Matthews	Yes	Yes	No	Yes	No	No	Yes	,,	Yes	No	Yes	No	,,
1960	,, John Matthieson	No	No	Yes	No	No	No	Yes	,,	Yes	No	No	No	,,
55	,, George Maxwell	Yes	Yes	No	Yes	No	No	Yes	,,	Yes	No	No	No	,,
1038	,, Henry Maxwell	Yes	Yes	No	Yes	No	No	Yes	,,	Yes	No	Yes	No	,,
2299	,, George Melville	No	No	No	No	No	No	No	,,	Yes	No	No	No	,,
551	,, John Melvin	No	No	No	No	No	No	No	,,	Yes	No	No	No	,, 68/42/482.
2234	,, Thomas Menary	No	No	No	No	No	No	No	,,	Yes	No	Yes	No	,,
1025	,, John Menzies	No	No	No	No	No	No	No	,,	Yes	No	No	No	,,
2588	,, Robert Mercer	Yes	Yes	No	Yes	No	No	Yes	,,	Yes	No	Yes	No	,,
164	,, James Middleton	Yes	Yes	No	Yes	Yes	No	No	,,	Yes	No	Yes	No	,,
866	,, Alexr. Miller	No	No	Yes	No	No	No	Yes	,,	Yes	No	Yes	No	,,
290	Corporal John Miller	Yes	Yes	No	Yes	No	No	Yes	,,	Yes	Yes	No	No	,,
971	Private Peter Miller	Yes	Yes	No	Yes	No	No	Yes	,,	Yes	No	No	No	,,
609	Lce.-Corpl. Robert Miller	Yes	Yes	No	Yes	No	No	Yes	,,	Yes	No	Yes	No	,,

Regtl. No.	RANK AND NAME at the time the Decoration was earned.	Whether in possession of Medal and Clasp for							Whether at Suakin between 26th March 1884 and 28th Feby. 1885.	Whether entitled to Clasps inscribed				Whether serving with Regt. or Depot, dead, discharged, deserted, etc.
		Egypt, 1882.	Tel-el-Kebir.	Medal Suakin, 1884.	Clasp Suakin, 1884.	El-Teb.	Tamaai.	El-Teb—Tamaai.		Nile, 1884-85.	Abu Klea.	Kirbekan.	Suakin, 1885.	
86	Serjeant James Milne . . .	No	No	Yes	No	No	No	Yes	No	Yes	No	Yes	No	Regiment.
1044	Private Fredk. Minns . . .	No	No	No	No	No	No	No	,,	Yes	No	No	No	,,
2566	,, Alexr. Miller . . .	Yes	Yes	No	Yes	Yes	No	No	,,	Yes	No	Yes	No	,,
1002	,, Benj. Mitchell . . .	No	No	Yes	No	No	No	Yes	,,	Yes	No	No	No	,,
2176	,, David Mitchell . .	No	No	No	No	No	No	No	,,	Yes	No	Yes	No	,,
2143	,, James Mitchell . .	No	No	No	No	No	No	No	,,	Yes	No	Yes	No	,,
2094	,, John Mitchell . . .	No	No	No	No	No	No	No	,,	Yes	No	Yes	No	Depot.
1077	,, John Mitchell . . .	Yes	Yes	No	No	No	No	No	,,	Yes	No	Yes	No	Regiment.
944	,, William Mitchell .	No	No	Yes	No	No	No	Yes	,,	Yes	No	Yes	No	Depot.
2678	,, Robert Moffat . . .	No	No	Yes	No	No	No	Yes	,,	Yes	No	No	No	Regiment.
278	,, Daniel Moodie . . .	Yes	Yes	No	Yes	No	No	Yes	,,	Yes	No	No	No	Depot.
2443	,, David Moodie . . .	No	No	Yes	No	No	No	Yes	,,	Yes	No	Yes	No	Regiment.
2587	,, Frank Morgan . . .	Yes	Yes	No	Yes	Yes	No	No	,,	Yes	No	Yes	No	,,
1017	Cr.-Serjt. David Morrison . .	No	No	Yes	No	No	No	Yes	,,	Yes	No	Yes	No	,, See D.C. Medal Roll.
1195	Private James Morrison . .	No	No	Yes	No	No	No	Yes	,,	Yes	No	Yes	No	Regiment.
2438	,, John Morrison . .	No	No	Yes	No	No	No	Yes	,,	Yes	No	No	No	Depot.
2380	,, John Morrison . .	Yes	Yes	No	No	No	No	Yes	,,	Yes	No	Yes	No	Regiment.
14	Serjeant William Morrison .	Yes	Yes	No	Yes	Yes	No	No	,,	Yes	No	Yes	No	,,
1956	Private William Morrison .	No	No	Yes	No	Yes	No	No	,,	Yes	No	Yes	No	,,
2654	,, Henry Morton . .	Yes	Yes	No	Yes	No	No	Yes	,,	Yes	No	Yes	No	,,
1228	,, Thomas Morton . .	No	No	No	No	No	No	No	,,	Yes	No	Yes	No	,,
2622	Lce.-Corpl. Albert Moss . .	No	No	Yes	No	No	No	Yes	,,	Yes	No	Yes	No	,,
210	Private William Muir . . .	No	No	No	No	No	No	No	,,	Yes	No	Yes	No	Deceased. A.G. List 209.
2655	Lce.-Corpl. Henry E. Mumford	Yes	Yes	No	Yes	No	No	Yes	,,	Yes	No	Yes	No	Regiment. See D.C.M. Roll.
190	Private Robert Murdoch . .	No	No	No	No	No	No	No	,,	Yes	No	No	No	Regiment.
997	,, William Murdoch .	No	No	Yes	No	No	Yes	No	,,	Yes	No	Yes	No	Depot.
280	,, David Murray . .	No	No	No	No	No	No	No	,,	Yes	No	Yes	No	Regiment.
1036	,, John Murray . .	No	No	Yes	No	No	No	Yes	,,	Yes	No	Yes	No	,,
2420	,, John Murray . .	Yes	Yes	No	Yes	No	No	Yes	,,	Yes	No	No	No	Depot.
1190	,, William Murray .	No	No	Yes	No	Yes	No	No	,,	Yes	No	Yes	No	Regiment.
2406	Serjeant David Murrie .	Yes	Yes	No	Yes	No	No	Yes	,,	Yes	No	Yes	No	,,
2004	Private Robert M'Alpine .	No	No	Yes	No	No	No	No	,,	Yes	No	Yes	No	,,
1284	Lce.-Corpl. John M'Call .	No	No	Yes	No	No	No	Yes	,,	Yes	No	Yes	No	,,
120	Private Patrick M'Cann .	Yes	Yes	No	Yes	No	Yes	No	,,	Yes	No	No	No	,,
1722	,, James M'Cash . .	No	No	Yes	No	No	No	Yes	,,	Yes	No	Yes	No	Depot.
2193	,, Matthew M'Culloch .	No	No	No	No	No	No	No	,,	Yes	No	No	No	Regiment.
2568	Lce.-Corpl. Angus M'Dermid .	No	No	Yes	No	No	No	No	,,	Yes	No	No	No	Depot.
2331	Drummer John M'Dine .	Yes	Yes	No	Yes	Yes	No	No	,,	Yes	No	Yes	No	Regiment.
1013	Private Archd. M'Donald .	No	No	Yes	No	No	No	Yes	,,	Yes	No	No	No	,,
2018	,, Charles M'Donald .	No	No	Yes	No	No	No	Yes	/503 ,,	Yes	No	No	No	,,
683	,, Daniel M'Donald .	No	No	Yes	No	No	Yes	No	,,	Yes	No	Yes	No	,,
162	,, Donald M'Donald .	No	No	Yes	No	No	No	Yes	,,	Yes	No	No	No	,,
1948	,, John M'Donald .	No	No	Yes	No	No	No	Yes	,,	Yes	No	Yes	No	,,
2517	,, John M'Donald .	No	No	Yes	No	No	No	Yes	,,	Yes	No	No	No	Deceased. A.G. List 190.
845	,, John M'Donald .	Yes	Yes	No	No	No	No	No	,,	Yes	No	Yes	No	Regiment.
2475	,, William M'Donald .	Yes	Yes	No	Yes	No	No	Yes	,,	Yes	No	Yes	No	,,

Regtl. No.	RANK AND NAME at the time the Decoration was earned.	Whether in possession of Medal and Clasp for							Whether at Suakin between 26th March 1884 and 28th Feby. 1885.	Whether entitled to Clasps inscribed				Whether serving with Regt. or Depot, dead, discharged, deserted, etc.
		Egypt, 1882.	Tel-el-Kebir.	Medal Suakin, 1884.	Clasp Suakin, 1884.	El-Teb.	Tamaai.	El-Teb—Tamaai.		Nile, 1884-85.	Abu Klea.	Kirbekan.	Suakin, 1885.	
2180	Private William M'Donald .	No	No	No	No	No	No	No	No	Yes	No	No	No	Regiment.
2010	,, William M'Donald	No	No	Yes	No	No	No	Yes	,,	Yes	No	Yes	No	,,
1088	,, Charles M'Dougall	No	No	Yes	No	No	No	Yes	,,	Yes	No	Yes	No	,,
1343	,, James M'Dougall .	Yes	Yes	No	Yes	No	No	No	,,	Yes	No	Yes	No	,,
2716	,, Donald M'Geoch .	Yes	Yes	No	Yes	No	No	Yes	,,	Yes	No	Yes	No	,,
701	,, Andrew M'George	Yes	Yes	No	Yes	No	No	Yes	,,	Yes	No	Yes	No	,,
2001	,, Peter M'Glashan .	No	No	Yes	No	Yes	No	No	,,	Yes	No	Yes	No	,,
2266	,, James M'Gregor .	No	No	No	No	No	No	No	,,	Yes	No	Yes	No	,, Captain Stewart's Collection
2358	Lee.-Corpl. James M'Gregor .	Yes	No	No	Yes	No	No	Yes	,,	Yes	No	Yes	No	Regiment.
1199	Private Robert M'Gregor .	Yes	No	No	Yes	No	No	Yes	,,	Yes	No	Yes	No	,,
33	,, William M'Gregor .	Yes	Yes	No	Yes	No	No	Yes	,,	Yes	No	Yes	No	,,
1118	,, Francis M'Guire .	No	No	Yes	No	No	No	Yes	,,	Yes	No	Yes	No	,,
1711	,, William M'Innes .	No	No	Yes	No	No	No	Yes	,,	Yes	No	Yes	No	Deceased. A.G. List 209.
1134	,, Alexr. M'Intosh .	No	No	No	No	No	No	No	,,	Yes	No	Yes	No	Depot.
1273	,, Daniel M'Intyre .	No	No	Yes	No	No	No	Yes	,,	Yes	No	No	No	Regiment.
2578	,, Murdoch M'Iver .	Yes	Yes	No	Yes	No	No	Yes	,,	Yes	No	Yes	No	,,
2623	,, John M'Kay . .	Yes	Yes	No	Yes	No	No	Yes	,,	Yes	No	Yes	No	,,
2125	,, John M'Kechnie .	No	No	No	No	No	No	No	,,	Yes	No	Yes	No	,,
806	Serjeant Andrew M'Kee .	No	No	Yes	No	No	No	Yes	,,	Yes	No	Yes	No	,,
2527	Private Thomas M'Kelvie .	No	No	Yes	No	Yes	No	No	/503 ,,	Yes	No	Yes	No	,,
1130	,, David M'Kendrick .	Yes	Yes	No	Yes	Yes	No	No	,,	Yes	No	Yes	No	,,
2082	,, Andrew M'Kenzie .	No	No	No	No	No	No	No	,,	Yes	No	Yes	No	,,
2393	,, Andrew M'Kenzie .	Yes	Yes	No	Yes	No	No	Yes	,,	Yes	Yes	No	No	,,
128	Serjeant Evan M'Kenzie .	Yes	Yes	No	Yes	No	No	Yes	,,	Yes	No	No	No	,,
2572	Private Fergus M'Kenzie .	Yes	Yes	No	Yes	No	No	Yes	,,	Yes	No	Yes	No	,,
205	Piper Ronald M'Kenzie .	Yes	Yes	No	Yes	No	No	Yes	,,	Yes	No	Yes	No	,,
1037	Private William M'Kenzie .	No	No	Yes	No	No	No	Yes	,,	Yes	No	No	No	Depot.
1974	,, James M'Kenzie .	No	No	Yes	No	No	No	Yes	,,	Yes	No	Yes	No	Regiment.
757	Cr.-Serjt. Duncan M'Lachlan .	Yes	Yes	No	Yes	No	No	Yes	,,	Yes	No	Yes	No	,,
1323	Corporal James M'Lachlan .	No	No	No	No	No	No	Yes	,,	Yes	No	No	No	,,
2414	Qr.-Mr.-Sjt. William M'Lachlan	Yes	Yes	No	Yes	No	No	Yes	/503 ,,	Yes	No	Yes	No	,,
1237	Private Alexr. M'Laren .	No	No	No	No	No	No	Yes	,,	Yes	No	Yes	No	,, Captain Stewart's Collection
2346	,, James M'Laren .	Yes	Yes	No	Yes	Yes	No	No	,,	Yes	No	No	No	Regiment.
1263	,, John M'Laren . .	No	No	Yes	No	No	Yes	No	,,	Yes	No	Yes	No	,,
1250	,, Thomas M'Laren .	No	No	Yes	No	Yes	No	No	,,	Yes	No	No	No	,, See /624.
2580	,, William M'Laren .	No	No	Yes	No	No	No	Yes	,,	Yes	No	Yes	No	,, See /638.
34	,, David M'Latchie .	Yes	Yes	No	Yes	No	No	Yes	,,	Yes	No	Yes	No	,,
2436	,, Lachlan M'Lauchlan .	Yes	Yes	No	Yes	Yes	No	No	,,	Yes	No	No	No	,,
692	,, Archd. M'Lean .	No	No	Yes	No	Yes	No	No	,,	Yes	No	No	No	,,
1161	,, Donald M'Lean .	No	No	Yes	No	No	No	Yes	,,	Yes	No	No	No	,,
934	,, John M'Lean . .	Yes	Yes	No	Yes	No	No	Yes	,,	Yes	Yes	No	No	,, Forfeited 68/42/538.
2615	,, Thomas M'Lean .	Yes	Yes	No	Yes	No	No	Yes	,,	Yes	No	Yes	No	Regiment.
279	,, Angus M'Leod .	Yes	Yes	No	Yes	No	No	Yes	,,	Yes	No	Yes	No	,,
802	,, Kenneth M'Leod .	No	No	No	No	No	No	No	,,	Yes	No	Yes	No	,,
859	,, Murdoch M'Leod .	Yes	Yes	No	Yes	No	No	Yes	,,	Yes	No	Yes	No	,,
929	,, John M'Master .	Yes	Yes	No	Yes	No	No	Yes	,,	Yes	Yes	No	No	Deceased. A.G. List 194.

Regtl. No.	Rank and Name at the time the Decoration was earned.	Whether in possession of Medal and Clasp for							Whether at Suakin between 26th March 1884 and 28th Feby. 1885.	Whether entitled to Clasps inscribed				Whether serving with Regt. or Depot, dead, discharged, deserted, etc.
		Egypt, 1882.	Tel-el-Kebir.	Medal Suakin, 1884.	Clasp Suakin, 1884.	El-Teb.	Tannaai.	El-Teb—Tannaai.		Nile, 1884-85.	Abu Klea.	Kirbekan.	Suakin, 1885.	
1041	Private Henry M'Millan	Yes	Yes	No	Yes	No	No	Yes	No	Yes	No	Yes	No	Regiment.
1034	„ William M'Millan	Yes	Yes	No	Yes	No	No	Yes	„	Yes	No	Yes	No	„
2149	„ William M'Nal	No	No	No	No	No	No	No	„	Yes	No	Yes	No	„
766	„ Martin M'Namara	No	No	Yes	No	No	No	Yes	„	Yes	No	No	No	Discharged. Forfeited.
1128	„ David M'Neil	No	No	Yes	No	No	No	Yes	„	Yes	No	Yes	No	Regiment.
2111	„ Alexr. M'Phee	No	No	Yes	No	No	No	Yes	„	Yes	No	Yes	No	Depot.
2034	„ Alexr. M'Phee	No	No	No	No	No	No	No	„	Yes	No	No	No	Regiment. Forfeited 68/42/495.
1167	„ Alexr. M'Pherson	No	No	Yes	No	No	No	Yes	„	Yes	No	Yes	No	Regiment.
1039	„ James M'Pherson	Yes	Yes	No	Yes	No	No	Yes	„	Yes	No	Yes	No	„
2643	„ John M'Pherson	No	No	No	No	No	No	No	„	Yes	No	Yes	No	„
1191	„ Robert M'Pherson	No	No	No	No	No	No	No	„	Yes	No	No	No	„ 68/42/482. A.G. List 431. Star issued 28/7/96 /716.
2014	„ Peter M'One	No	No	Yes	No	No	No	Yes	„	Yes	No	No	No	Depot.
2250	„ Robert M'Stravick	No	No	No	No	No	No	No	„	Yes	No	No	No	Regiment.
1093	„ Albert Neal	No	No	No	No	No	No	No	„	Yes	No	Yes	No	„
187	„ William Neave	No	No	No	No	No	No	No	„	Yes	No	Yes	No	„
2684	„ Andrew Neil	No	No	No	No	Yes	No	No	„	Yes	No	No	No	„
1972	„ Henry Neil	No	No	No	No	No	No	No	„	Yes	No	No	No	„
700	„ James Neish	No	No	No	No	No	No	No	„	Yes	No	Yes	No	„
2556	„ John Neish	No	No	Yes	No	No	No	Yes	„	Yes	No	No	No	„
1057	„ John New	Yes	Yes	No	Yes	Yes	No	No	„	Yes	No	Yes	No	„
919	„ Jesse Newsome	No	No	Yes	No	Yes	No	No	„	Yes	No	No	No	„
2306	„ George Newton	Yes	Yes	No	Yes	Yes	No	No	„	Yes	No	Yes	No	A. Reserve. A.G. List 196.
1290	„ George Nicol	No	No	Yes	No	Yes	No	No	„	Yes	No	No	No	Deceased. A.G. List 199.
2117	„ Charles Nicoll	No	No	Yes	No	No	No	Yes	„	Yes	No	Yes	No	Regiment.
2617	„ Alexr. Nicolson	Yes	Yes	No	No	No	No	No	„	Yes	No	Yes	No	„
2453	Serjeant Donald Nicolson	No	No	Yes	No	No	No	Yes	„	Yes	No	Yes	No	„
1014	Private John Niven	No	No	No	No	No	No	No	„	Yes	No	No	No	„
778	„ John Noon	No	No	No	No	No	No	No	„	Yes	No	Yes	No	„
999	Serjeant Colin Orton	No	No	No	No	No	No	No	„	Yes	No	Yes	No	„ E/91731/13 E/91731/14.
2281	Private James O'Brien	No	No	Yes	No	No	No	Yes	„	Yes	No	No	No	Discharged.
747	„ George Paine	No	No	Yes	No	Yes	No	No	„	Yes	No	No	No	Regiment.
1104	„ Henry Palmer	Yes	Yes	No	Yes	No	No	Yes	„	Yes	No	Yes	No	„
808	„ David Park	No	No	Yes	No	No	No	Yes	/503 „	Yes	No	Yes	No	„
59	„ Joseph Parker	Yes	Yes	No	Yes	Yes	No	No	„	Yes	No	No	No	„
1142	„ John Parkes	No	No	No	No	No	No	No	„	Yes	No	Yes	No	„
1441	„ Joseph Patterson	No	No	Yes	No	No	No	Yes	„	Yes	No	Yes	No	„
1283	Corporal Arthur Patterson	No	No	Yes	No	No	No	Yes	„	Yes	No	Yes	No	Deceased. A.G. List 209.
2373	Private Robert Patterson	No	No	No	No	No	No	No	„	Yes	No	Yes	No	Regiment.
975	„ William Patterson	Yes	Yes	No	No	No	No	No	„	Yes	No	No	No	„
2423	„ James Patton	Yes	Yes	No	No	No	No	No	„	Yes	No	Yes	No	„
2540	„ John Patton	No	No	Yes	No	No	No	Yes	„	Yes	No	No	No	„
2147	„ Henry Paul	No	No	No	No	No	No	No	„	Yes	No	Yes	No	„

Regtl. No.	Rank and Name at the time the Decoration was earned.	Whether in possession of Medal and Clasp for							Whether at Suakin between 26th March 1884 and 28th Feby. 1885.	Whether entitled to Clasps inscribed				Whether serving with Regt. or Depot, dead, discharged, deserted, etc.
		Egypt, 1882.	Tel-el-Kebir.	Medal Suakin, 1884.	Clasp Suakin, 1884.	El-Teb.	Tamaai.	El-Teb—Tamaai.		Nile, 1884-85.	Abu Klea.	Kirbekan.	Suakin, 1885.	
1079	Private Thomas Paxton	No	No	Yes	No	No	No	Yes	No	Yes	No	Yes	No	Regiment.
795	Corporal John Payne	Yes	Yes	No	Yes	No	No	Yes	,,	Yes	No	Yes	No	Depot.
2096	Private Owen Payne	No	No	Yes	No	No	No	Yes	,,	Yes	No	Yes	No	Regiment.
964	,, William Pearson	Yes	Yes	No	Yes	Yes	No	No	,,	Yes	No	Yes	No	,,
2638	Lce.-Corpl. James Peerson	No	No	Yes	No	No	No	No	,,	Yes	No	No	No	,,
1061	Private John Peck	No	No	Yes	No	No	No	No	,,	Yes	No	Yes	No	,,
2310	,, David Perie	Yes	Yes	No	Yes	No	No	Yes	,,	Yes	No	Yes	No	A. Reserve. A.G. List 215.
1114	,, James Perks	No	No	No	No	No	No	No	,,	Yes	No	No	No	Regiment /658.
834	,, Edward Perring	No	No	No	No	No	No	No	,,	Yes	No	Yes	No	Regiment.
1259	,, Henry Pike	No	No	Yes	No	No	No	Yes	,,	Yes	No	Yes	No	,,
1098	,, William Pitts	No	No	Yes	No	No	No	Yes	,,	Yes	No	Yes	No	,,
371	Armr.-Sgt. Thomas Pinkney	Yes	Yes	No	Yes	No	No	No	,,	Yes	No	Yes	No	,,
2530	Private Charles Porter	Yes	Yes	No	Yes	No	No	Yes	,,	Yes	No	Yes	No	,,
1326	,, James Porter	No	No	No	No	No	No	No	,,	Yes	No	No	No	,,
893	,, James Potterton	No	No	No	No	No	No	Yes	,,	Yes	No	No	No	,,
776	,, John Powell	No	No	No	No	No	No	No	,,	Yes	No	No	No	,,
91	Serjeant Alexr. Pratt	Yes	Yes	No	Yes	Yes	No	No	,,	Yes	No	Yes	No	,,
774	Private Stephen Preston	No	No	No	No	No	No	No	,,	Yes	No	No	No	,,
1225	,, George Pringle	Yes	Yes	No	Yes	No	No	Yes	,,	Yes	No	Yes	No	,,
851	,, James Pullar	No	No	No	No	No	No	No	,,	Yes	No	Yes	No	,,
2064	,, John Pyper	No	No	Yes	No	No	No	Yes	,,	Yes	No	Yes	No	,,
901	,, Andrew Queen	No	No	No	No	No	No	No	,,	Yes	No	Yes	No	,,
1223	,, James Ralston	No	No	No	No	No	No	No	,,	Yes	Yes	No	No	,,
2298	,, Jacob Railton	No	No	No	No	No	No	No	,,	Yes	No	Yes	No	,, 68/42/613.
520	,, William H. Reade	Yes	Yes	No	Yes	No	No	Yes	,,	Yes	No	Yes	No	Regiment.
1102	,, James Reed	Yes	Yes	No	Yes	No	No	Yes	,,	Yes	No	Yes	No	,,
1106	,, Joseph O. Reade	Yes	Yes	No	Yes	No	No	Yes	,,	Yes	No	No	No	,,
2289	,, George Reid	No	No	No	No	No	No	No	,,	Yes	No	No	No	Deceased. A.G. List 212.
2392	Lce.-Serjt. James Reid	Yes	Yes	No	Yes	No	No	Yes	,,	Yes	No	Yes	No	Discharged. A.G. List 194.
1155	Private Robert Reid	No	No	Yes	No	No	No	Yes	,,	Yes	No	No	No	Depot.
2039	,, William Reid	No	No	Yes	No	Yes	No	No	,,	Yes	No	Yes	No	Regiment.
8	Pioneer-Sjt. John Rennie	Yes	Yes	No	Yes	No	No	Yes	,,	Yes	No	No	No	,,
2564	Lce.-Corpl. Simpson Rennie	No	No	Yes	No	No	No	Yes	,,	Yes	No	Yes	No	,,
1252	Cr.-Serjt. Josiah Rhodes	Yes	Yes	No	Yes	No	No	Yes	,,	Yes	No	Yes	No	,,
1080	Private James Richardson	No	No	No	No	No	No	Yes	,,	Yes	No	Yes	No	,,
1153	Drummer William Riley	Yes	Yes	No	Yes	Yes	No	No	,,	Yes	No	Yes	No	,,
2681	Private James Ritchie	No	No	Yes	No	No	No	Yes	,,	Yes	No	Yes	No	,,
1440	,, Hugh Roberts	No	No	Yes	No	No	No	No	,,	Yes	No	Yes	No	,,
28	,, Alexr. Robertson	Yes	Yes	No	Yes	No	No	Yes	,,	Yes	No	Yes	No	,,
917	,, Alexr. Robertson	No	No	No	No	No	No	No	,,	Yes	No	Yes	No	,,
2071	,, David Robertson	No	No	Yes	No	No	No	Yes	,,	Yes	No	Yes	No	Depot.
694	,, David Robertson	Yes	Yes	No	No	No	No	No	,,	Yes	No	No	No	Regiment.
2418	,, John Robertson	No	No	No	No	No	No	No	,,	Yes	No	Yes	No	,, Forfeited.
2074	,, John Robertson	No	No	Yes	No	No	No	Yes	,,	Yes	No	Yes	No	Regiment.
1255	,, John Robertson	Yes	Yes	No	Yes	Yes	No	No	,,	Yes	No	Yes	No	,,
2252	,, Robert Robertson	No	No	No	No	No	No	No	,,	Yes	No	Yes	No	,,
2280	,, Thomas Robertson	No	No	No	No	No	No	No	,,	Yes	No	Yes	No	,,

Regtl. No.	Rank and Name at the time the Decoration was earned.	Egypt, 1882.	Tel-el-Kebir.	Medal Suakin, 1884.	Clasp Suakin, 1884.	El-Teb.	Tamaai.	El-Teb—Tamaai.	Whether at Suakin between 26th March 1884 and 28th Feby. 1885.	Nile, 1884-85.	Abu Klea.	Kirbekan.	Suakin, 1885.	Whether serving with Regt. or Depot, dead, discharged, deserted, etc.
118	Lce.-Corpl. George Robson	No	No	Yes	No	No	No	Yes	No	Yes	No	No	No	Regiment.
928	Private Stephen Rose	No	No	Yes	No	No	No	Yes	,,	Yes	No	Yes	No	Depot.
1973	,, Arthur Ross	No	No	No	No	No	No	No	,,	Yes	No	Yes	No	Regiment.
260	Corporal Charles Ross	Yes	Yes	No	Yes	No	No	Yes	,,	Yes	No	Yes	No	,,
681	Private George Ross	Yes	Yes	No	Yes	No	No	Yes	,,	Yes	No	Yes	No	,,
1246	,, Henry Ross	No	No	No	No	No	No	No	,,	Yes	No	Yes	No	,,
1361	,, James Ross	No	No	Yes	No	No	No	Yes	,,	Yes	No	Yes	No	,,
2451	Serjeant James Ross	Yes	Yes	No	Yes	No	No	Yes	,,	Yes	No	Yes	No	,,
995	Private Robert Ross	No	No	No	No	No	No	No	,,	Yes	No	Yes	No	,,
2497	,, James Rourke	No	No	Yes	No	No	No	Yes	,,	Yes	No	No	No	Depot.
1266	,, David Rowan	No	No	Yes	No	No	No	Yes	,,	Yes	No	Yes	No	Regiment.
145	,, Robert Rowe	No	No	Yes	No	No	No	Yes	,,	Yes	No	No	No	,,
1971	,, Alexr. Rowes	No	No	No	No	No	No	No	,,	Yes	No	No	No	,,
220	,, Fredk. Rowley	No	No	Yes	No	No	No	Yes	,,	Yes	No	No	No	,, See 68/42/495.
2397	,, Allan Russell	Yes	Yes	No	Yes	Yes	No	No	,,	Yes	No	No	No	Regiment.
275	,, James Russell	No	No	No	No	No	No	No	,,	Yes	No	No	No	,,
761	,, John Russell	Yes	Yes	No	Yes	No	No	Yes	,,	Yes	No	Yes	No	,,
219	,, John Ryan	Yes	Yes	No	Yes	No	No	Yes	,,	Yes	No	No	No	,, See /620.
800	Serjeant Benj. Sadler	Yes	Yes	No	Yes	No	No	Yes	,,	Yes	No	Yes	No	,,
1105	Private William Schofield	Yes	Yes	No	Yes	No	No	Yes	,,	Yes	No	No	No	,,
773	,, Joseph Scothern	No	No	Yes	No	Yes	No	No	,,	Yes	No	Yes	No	,,
1280	,, Alexr. Scott	No	No	Yes	No	Yes	No	No	,,	Yes	No	No	No	,, Captain Stewart's Collection
2448	,, James Scott	No	No	No	No	No	No	No	,,	Yes	No	Yes	No	Regiment.
20	,, John Scott	Yes	Yes	No	Yes	Yes	No	No	/503 ,,	Yes	No	Yes	No	,,
691	,, Thomas Scott	Yes	Yes	No	Yes	Yes	No	No	,,	Yes	No	Yes	No	,,
1707	,, William Scrimgeour	No	No	Yes	No	No	No	Yes	,,	Yes	No	Yes	No	,,
870	,, John Sharp	Yes	Yes	No	Yes	No	No	Yes	,,	Yes	No	No	No	,,
966	,, Thomas Sharp	No	No	No	No	No	No	No	,,	Yes	No	Yes	No	2nd Battalion /588.
1110	,, Fredk. Shaw	Yes	Yes	No	Yes	No	No	Yes	,,	Yes	No	No	No	Depot.
289	,, Samuel Shaw	Yes	Yes	No	Yes	No	No	Yes	,,	Yes	No	Yes	No	,,
2318	,, Walter Shaw	No	No	No	No	No	No	No	,,	Yes	No	Yes	No	Regiment.
2620	,, Charles Shearer	Yes	Yes	No	Yes	No	No	No	,,	Yes	No	Yes	No	,,
2336	,, John Shepherd	No	No	Yes	No	No	No	Yes	,,	Yes	No	No	No	,,
1949	,, Peter Sheridan	No	No	Yes	No	No	No	Yes	/503 ,,	Yes	No	Yes	No	,,
223	,, Henry Shires	No	No	No	No	No	No	No	,,	Yes	No	No	No	,, See D.C.M. Roll.
2183	,, George Shirran	No	No	No	No	No	No	No	,,	Yes	No	Yes	No	Regiment.
2265	Lce.-Corpl. Francis de Sausmarez Shortt	No	No	No	No	No	No	No	,,	Yes	No	Yes	No	,, /588.
1443	Lce.-Corpl. Alex. Simpson	No	No	Yes	No	No	No	Yes	,,	Yes	No	No	No	Depot.
730	Private Charles Simpson	No	No	No	No	No	No	No	,,	Yes	No	Yes	No	Regiment.
1292	Corporal George Simpson	No	No	Yes	No	No	No	Yes	,,	Yes	No	Yes	No	,,
2377	Lce.-Corpl. James Simpson	No	No	No	No	No	No	No	,,	Yes	No	Yes	No	,,
86	Corporal Thomas Simpson	Yes	Yes	No	Yes	No	No	Yes	,,	Yes	No	No	No	,,
2115	Private William Simpson	No	No	Yes	No	No	No	Yes	,,	Yes	No	Yes	No	,,
706	Lce.-Corpl. Donald Sinclair	Yes	Yes	No	Yes	No	No	Yes	,,	Yes	No	Yes	No	,,
2101	,, Alexr. Singer	No	No	Yes	No	No	No	Yes	,,	Yes	No	Yes	No	,,
1222	Private William Skeet	No	No	Yes	No	Yes	No	No	,,	Yes	No	No	No	,,

Regtl. No.	Rank and Name at the time the Decoration was earned.	Whether in possession of Medal and Clasp for							Whether at Suakin between 26th March 1884 and 28th Feby. 1885.	Whether entitled to Clasps inscribed				Whether serving with Regt. or Depot, dead, discharged, deserted, etc.
		Egypt, 1882.	Tel-el-Kebir.	Medal Suakin, 1884.	Clasp Suakin, 1884.	El-Teb.	Tamaai.	El-Teb—Tamaai.		Nile, 1884-85.	Abu Klea.	Kirbekan.	Suakin, 1885.	
847	Private George W. Skillings	No	No	Yes	No	Yes	No	No	No	Yes	No	Yes	No	Regiment.
2349	„ Henry Skinner	No	No	No	No	No	No	No	„	Yes	No	Yes	No	„
93	„ David Slattie	Yes	Yes	No	Yes	No	No	Yes	„	Yes	No	No	No	„
2467	Drummer John Slattie	Yes	Yes	No	Yes	Yes	No	No	„	Yes	No	Yes	No	„
2002	Private Robert Sloggie	No	No	No	No	No	No	No	„	Yes	No	No	No	Depot.
2382	„ Alexr. Small	No	No	Yes	No	Yes	No	No	„	Yes	No	No	No	Regiment.
2087	„ Alexr. Smith	No	No	No	No	No	No	No	„	Yes	No	Yes	No	„
2387	„ Alexr. Smith	Yes	Yes	No	No	No	No	No	„	Yes	No	Yes	No	„
94	Corporal Charles Smith	Yes	Yes	No	Yes	Yes	No	No	„	Yes	No	Yes	No	„
237	Private Charles Smith	Yes	Yes	No	No	No	No	No	„	Yes	No	Yes	No	„
1144	„ Fredk. Smith	No	No	Yes	No	No	No	Yes	„	Yes	No	No	No	„
2664	Serjeant James Smith	Yes	Yes	No	Yes	Yes	No	No	„	Yes	No	Yes	No	„
1230	Lce.-Corpl. James Smith	No	No	No	No	No	No	No	„	Yes	No	Yes	No	„
53	Private James Smith	Yes	Yes	No	Yes	Yes	No	No	„	Yes	No	Yes	No	„
1004	„ James Smith	No	No	No	No	No	No	No	„	Yes	No	Yes	No	„ Forfeited /568.
1997	„ James Smith	No	No	Yes	No	No	No	Yes	„	Yes	No	No	No	Regiment.
2076	„ John Smith	No	No	No	No	No	No	No	„	Yes	No	No	No	„
2390	„ Robert Smith	Yes	Yes	No	Yes	No	No	Yes	„	Yes	No	No	No	„
1132	„ Stewart Smith	No	No	No	No	No	No	No	„	Yes	No	Yes	No	„
1187	„ William H. Smith	No	No	Yes	No	No	No	Yes	„	Yes	No	No	No	„
836	„ William Smith	No	No	Yes	No	No	No	Yes	„	Yes	No	No	No	„
2072	„ William A. Smith	No	No	No	No	No	No	No	„	Yes	No	Yes	No	„
2516	„ William Smith	No	No	Yes	No	No	No	Yes	„	Yes	No	No	No	„
2662	„ William Souter	No	No	Yes	No	Yes	No	No	„	Yes	No	Yes	No	„
1122	„ Robert Southgate	No	No	Yes	No	Yes	No	No	„	Yes	No	Yes	No	„
837	„ Joseph Spackman	No	No	Yes	No	No	No	Yes	„	Yes	No	Yes	No	„
775	„ Edward Speaks	No	No	Yes	No	No	No	Yes	„	Yes	No	No	No	Depot.
285	„ Archd. Speid	Yes	Yes	No	Yes	No	No	Yes	„	Yes	No	Yes	No	Regiment.
18	„ George Spence	Yes	Yes	No	Yes	No	No	Yes	„	Yes	No	No	No	„ Captain Stewart's Collection
2435	„ Andrew Spence	No	No	Yes	No	Yes	No	No	„	Yes	Yes	No	No	Regiment.
1010	„ Thomas Sprunt	No	No	Yes	No	Yes	No	No	„	Yes	No	No	No	„
596	Corporal Wm. Statham	Yes	Yes	No	Yes	Yes	No	No	„	Yes	No	No	No	„
801	Private Francis Stanley	No	No	Yes	No	No	No	Yes	„	Yes	No	Yes	No	„
1965	„ Keillock Steel	No	No	No	No	No	No	No	„	Yes	No	Yes	No	„
765	„ James Stenson	No	No	Yes	No	No	No	Yes	„	Yes	No	Yes	No	„
1174	„ William Stephenson	No	No	Yes	No	Yes	No	No	„	Yes	No	Yes	No	„
1256	„ James Stevenson	No	No	No	No	No	No	No	„	Yes	No	No	No	„
2649	„ Alexr. Stewart	No	No	Yes	No	No	No	Yes	„	Yes	No	Yes	No	„
13	„ Alexr. Stewart	Yes	Yes	No	Yes	No	No	Yes	„	Yes	No	Yes	No	„
1023	„ David Stewart	No	No	No	No	No	No	No	„	Yes	No	Yes	No	„
908	„ Donald Stewart	Yes	Yes	No	Yes	No	No	Yes	„	Yes	No	Yes	No	„
947	„ Donald Stewart	Yes	Yes	No	Yes	No	No	Yes	„	Yes	No	Yes	No	„
2471	„ George Stewart	Yes	Yes	No	Yes	No	No	Yes	„	Yes	No	No	No	„
1299	„ James Stewart	No	No	Yes	No	No	No	Yes	„	Yes	No	No	No	Depot.
96	„ Norman Stewart	Yes	Yes	No	Yes	No	No	Yes	„	Yes	No	Yes	No	Regiment.
1935	Serjeant Peter Stewart	No	No	Yes	No	No	No	Yes	„	Yes	No	Yes	No	„
906	Private William Stewart	Yes	Yes	No	Yes	No	No	Yes	„	Yes	No	Yes	No	„
1226	„ William Stewart	No	No	Yes	No	Yes	No	No	„	Yes	No	Yes	No	„

Regtl. No.	Rank and Name at the time the Decoration was earned.	Whether in possession of Medal and Clasp for							Whether at Suakin between 26th March 1884 and 28th Feby. 1885.	Whether entitled to Clasps inscribed				Whether serving with Regt. or Depot, dead, discharged, deserted, etc.
		Egypt, 1882.	Tel-el-Kebir.	Medal Suakin, 1884.	Clasp Suakin, 1884.	El-Teb.	Tamaai.	El-Teb—Tamaai.		Nile, 1884-85.	Abu Klea.	Kirbekan.	Suakin, 1885.	
1125	Private William Stewart	No	No	Yes	No	No	No	Yes	No	Yes	No	No	No	Regiment.
2646	Lce.-Corpl. Charles Stobbie	Yes	Yes	No	Yes	No	No	Yes	,,	Yes	No	No	No	,,
1016	Private David Stoddart	Yes	Yes	No	Yes	No	No	Yes	,,	Yes	No	Yes	No	,,
726	,, George Stokes	No	No	Yes	No	No	No	Yes	,,	Yes	No	No	No	,,
951	,, William Stokes	No	No	Yes	No	No	No	Yes	,,	Yes	No	No	No	,,
2492	Drummer Alexr. Stuart	Yes	Yes	No	Yes	No	No	Yes	,,	Yes	No	Yes	No	,,
47	Serjeant Harry Studley	Yes	Yes	No	Yes	No	No	Yes	,,	Yes	No	Yes	No	,,
2611	Private William Sullivan	No	No	No	No	No	No	No	,,	Yes	No	Yes	No	,,
97	,, Alexr. Sutherland	Yes	Yes	No	Yes	No	No	Yes	,,	Yes	No	Yes	No	,,
2204	,, James Sutherland	No	No	No	No	No	No	No	,,	Yes	No	Yes	No	,,
2374	Serjeant John Sutherland	Yes	Yes	No	Yes	No	No	Yes	,,	Yes	Yes	No	No	,, See D.C.M. Roll.
273	Private William Swan	Yes	Yes	No	Yes	No	No	Yes	,,	Yes	No	Yes	No	Regiment.
2275	,, William Tack	No	No	No	No	No	No	No	,,	Yes	No	Yes	No	,,
886	,, Thomas Tatton	No	No	No	No	No	No	No	,,	Yes	No	Yes	No	,,
2148	,, Alexr. Taylor	No	No	No	No	No	No	No	,,	Yes	No	No	No	,,
2558	,, David Taylor	No	No	Yes	No	No	No	Yes	,,	Yes	No	Yes	No	,,
1391	,, George Taylor	Yes	Yes	No	Yes	No	No	Yes	,,	Yes	No	Yes	No	,,
1727	,, John Taylor	No	No	Yes	No	No	No	Yes	,,	Yes	No	No	No	,,
2276	,, Richard Taylor	No	No	No	No	No	No	No	,,	Yes	No	Yes	No	,,
2118	,, Alexr. Terras	No	No	Yes	No	No	No	Yes	,,	Yes	No	Yes	No	,,
2633	,, William Terras	No	No	No	No	No	No	No	,,	Yes	No	Yes	No	,,
2153	,, John Thomas	No	No	No	No	No	No	No	,,	Yes	No	Yes	No	,,
1566	,, Charles Thompson	No	No	Yes	No	No	No	Yes	,,	Yes	No	Yes	No	,,
2160	,, Charles Thompson	No	No	No	No	No	No	No	,,	Yes	No	Yes	No	,,
98	,, David B. Thompson	Yes	Yes	No	Yes	No	No	Yes	,,	Yes	No	Yes	No	Depot.
2709	,, James Thompson	Yes	Yes	No	Yes	No	No	Yes	,,	Yes	No	No	No	Regiment.
139	,, James Thompson	Yes	Yes	No	Yes	No	No	Yes	,,	Yes	No	Yes	No	,,
790	,, John Thompson	Yes	Yes	No	Yes	No	No	Yes	,,	Yes	No	Yes	No	,,
297	,, William Thompson	No	No	No	No	No	No	No	,,	Yes	No	Yes	No	,,
105	,, William Thompson	Yes	Yes	No	Yes	No	No	Yes	,,	Yes	No	No	No	,,
1019	,, William Thompson	No	No	Yes	No	Yes	No	No	,,	Yes	No	Yes	No	,,
758	,, James Thorburn	Yes	Yes	No	No	No	No	No	,,	Yes	No	Yes	No	,,
1171	,, James Todd	No	No	No	No	No	No	No	,,	Yes	No	Yes	No	,, Restored 570.
839	,, Alfred C. Tombs	No	No	Yes	No	No	No	Yes	,,	Yes	No	No	No	Deceased. A.G. List 188.
2474	,, David Tosh	Yes	Yes	No	Yes	Yes	No	No	,,	Yes	No	Yes	No	Regiment.
1034	,, Thomas Totton	Yes	Yes	No	Yes	No	No	Yes	,,	Yes	No	Yes	No	,, 1032 correct No. Captain Stewart's Collection
1705	,, William Tough	No	No	Yes	No	No	No	Yes	,,	Yes	No	Yes	No	Regiment.
745	,, Henry Town	No	No	Yes	No	No	No	Yes	,,	Yes	No	Yes	No	,,
2548	,, Peter Toy	Yes	Yes	No	Yes	Yes	No	No	,,	Yes	No	No	No	,,
2498	,, Thomas Toy	No	No	Yes	No	No	No	Yes	,,	Yes	No	No	No	,,
1242	,, Matthew Tully	No	No	No	No	No	No	No	,,	Yes	No	No	No	,, Forfeited /511.
268	,, Alexr. Turner	Yes	Yes	No	Yes	No	No	Yes	,,	Yes	No	Yes	No	Regiment.
2321	Drummer James M. Turner	Yes	No	No	Yes	No	No	Yes	,,	Yes	No	Yes	No	,,
2665	Private John Turner	No	No	Yes	No	No	No	Yes	,,	Yes	No	Yes	No	,,

Regtl. No.	Rank and Name at the time the Decoration was earned.	Whether in possession of Medal and Clasp for							Whether at Suakin between 26th March 1884 and 28th Feby. 1885.	Whether entitled to Clasps inscribed				Whether serving with Regt. or Depot, dead, discharged, deserted, etc.
		Egypt, 1882.	Tel-el-Kebir.	Medal Suakin, 1884.	Clasp Suakin, 1884.	El-Teb.	Tamaai.	El-Teb—Tamaai.		Nile, 1884-85.	Abu Klea.	Kirbekan.	Suakin, 1885.	
2112	Private Thomas Turner	No	No	No	No	No	No	No	No	Yes	No	No	No	Regiment.
991	,, John Turnbull	No	No	No	No	No	No	No	,,	Yes	No	Yes	No	,,
1180	,, Charles Tuson	No	No	Yes	No	No	No	Yes	,,	Yes	Yes	No	No	Depot.
1234	,, William Trussler	No	No	No	No	No	No	No	,,	Yes	No	No	No	Regiment.
2198	Cr.-Serjt. James Tweedie	Yes	Yes	No	Yes	No	No	Yes	,,	Yes	No	Yes	No	,, See D.C.M. Roll.
258	Private William Vallance	Yes	Yes	No	Yes	No	No	Yes	,,	Yes	No	No	No	A. Reserve.
2509	Corporal John Vair	Yes	Yes	No	Yes	No	No	Yes	,,	Yes	No	Yes	No	Regiment.
49	,, Robert Vair	Yes	Yes	No	Yes	No	No	Yes	,,	Yes	No	Yes	No	,,
746	Private James Vickers	No	No	Yes	No	No	No	Yes	,,	Yes	No	No	No	,,
980	,, Frank Wade	No	No	Yes	No	No	No	Yes/503	,,	Yes	Yes	No	No	,,
737	,, Mark Wadmore	Yes	Yes	No	Yes	Yes	No	No	,,	Yes	No	Yes	No	Depot.
2437	Lce.-Corpl. Christr. Walker	Yes	Yes	No	Yes	No	No	Yes	,,	Yes	No	Yes	No	Regiment.
688	Private William Walker	Yes	Yes	No	Yes	No	No	Yes	,,	Yes	No	Yes	No	,,
890	,, James Wallace	No	No	No	No	No	No	No	,,	Yes	No	No	No	,,
1950	,, William Wallace	No	No	Yes	No	No	No	Yes	,,	Yes	No	Yes	No	,,
1700	,, Robert Wallace	No	No	Yes	No	No	No	Yes	,,	Yes	No	No	No	,,
2562	,, Henry Ward	Yes	Yes	No	Yes	Yes	No	No	,,	Yes	No	Yes	No	,,
953	,, James Washington	No	No	No	No	No	No	No	,,	Yes	No	No	No	,,
288	,, James Waters	No	No	No	No	No	No	No	,,	Yes	No	No	No	,,
538	Qr.-Mr.-Sjt. Alexr. B. Watson	Yes	No	No	No	No	No	No	,,	Yes	No	No	No	,,
2318	Private Robert Watson	No	No	Yes	No	Yes	No	No	,,	Yes	No	Yes	No	,,
1012	,, Thomas Watson	No	No	Yes	No	No	No	Yes	,,	Yes	No	Yes	No	,,
183	,, George G. Watt	Yes	Yes	No	Yes	No	No	Yes	,,	Yes	No	Yes	No	Depot.
2058	Lce.-Corpl. David Watt	No	No	Yes	No	No	No	Yes	,,	Yes	No	No	No	Regiment.
2666	Private John Watt	Yes	Yes	No	Yes	Yes	No	No	,,	Yes	No	Yes	No	,, Captain Stewart's Collection
1379	Serjeant Thomas Watt	Yes	Yes	No	Yes	Yes	No	No	,,	Yes	No	Yes	No	Regiment. See D.C.M. Roll.
123	Private David Webster	Yes	Yes	No	Yes	No	No	Yes	,,	Yes	No	Yes	No	Regiment.
2461	,, Herbert Webster	No	No	Yes	No	No	No	Yes	,,	Yes	No	Yes	No	,,
1224	,, John Webster	No	No	No	No	No	No	No	,,	Yes	No	Yes	No	,,
2320	,, Michael Welsh	No	No	Yes	No	No	No	Yes	,,	Yes	No	No	No	,,
2099	,, Fergus West	No	No	Yes	No	No	No	Yes	,,	Yes	No	Yes	No	,, 68/42/498.
152	,, George West	Yes	Yes	No	Yes	No	No	Yes	,,	Yes	No	No	No	,,
904	,, Alfred Wharton	No	No	Yes	No	No	No	Yes	,,	Yes	No	Yes	No	,,
2273	,, Alfred Wheatley	No	No	No	No	No	No	No	,,	Yes	No	No	No	,,
987	,, Benjn. Whitaker	No	No	No	No	No	No	No	,,	Yes	No	Yes	No	,,
786	,, Thomas White	Yes	Yes	No	Yes	No	No	Yes	,,	Yes	No	Yes	No	,,
2491	,, James Whitelaw	No	No	Yes	No	No	No	Yes	,,	Yes	No	Yes	No	,,
1967	Lce.-Corpl. Daniel Whyte	No	No	Yes	No	No	No	No	,,	Yes	Yes	No	No	,,
930	Private John Whytock	No	No	No	No	No	No	No	,,	Yes	No	Yes	No	,,
742	,, George Wilkes	Yes	Yes	No	No	No	No	No	,,	Yes	No	No	No	,,
2537	Corporal William Wilkie	Yes	Yes	No	Yes	No	No	Yes	,,	Yes	No	Yes	No	,,
2669	Serjeant Francis Wilkin	Yes	Yes	No	Yes	No	No	Yes	,,	Yes	No	Yes	No	,,
2379	Private John Williamson	Yes	Yes	No	Yes	Yes	No	No	,,	Yes	No	Yes	No	,,
199	,, William Willocks	Yes	Yes	No	No	No	No	No	,,	Yes	No	Yes	No	,,
2671	,, William Willox	Yes	Yes	No	Yes	No	No	Yes	,,	Yes	No	Yes	No	,,
48	,, Charles Wilson	Yes	Yes	No	Yes	No	No	Yes	,,	Yes	No	Yes	No	Deceased. A.G. List 198.

Regtl. No.	RANK AND NAME at the time the Decoration was earned.	Whether in possession of Medal and Clasp for							Whether at Suakin between 26th March 1884 and 28th Feby. 1885.	Whether entitled to Clasps inscribed				Whether serving with Regt. or Depot, dead, discharged, deserted, etc.
		Egypt, 1882.	Tel-el-Kebir.	Medal Suakin, 1884.	Clasp Suakin, 1884.	El-Teb.	Tamaai.	El-Teb—Tamaai.		Nile, 1884-85.	Abu Klea.	Kirbekan.	Suakin, 1885.	
1959	Private James Wilson . . .	No	No	Yes	No	No	No	Yes	No	Yes	No	No	No	Regiment.
185	Lce.-Serjt. John Wilson .	No	No	Yes	No	No	No	Yes	,,	Yes	No	Yes	No	Depot.
2640	Private Thomas Wilson .	No	No	Yes	No	No	No	Yes	,,	Yes	No	No	No	Regiment.
1028	,, Thomas Wilson .	Yes	Yes	No	Yes	Yes	No	No	,,	Yes	No	Yes	No	,,
101	,, William Wilson .	Yes	Yes	No	Yes	Yes	No	No	,,	Yes	No	Yes	No	,,
54	,, James H. Winter .	Yes	Yes	No	Yes	No	No	Yes	,,	Yes	No	No	No	,,
1713	,, Alexr. Wishart .	No	No	Yes	No	No	No	Yes	,,	Yes	No	No	No	,,
1049	,, Henry Wood .	Yes	Yes	No	Yes	No	No	Yes	,,	No	No	No	No	,,
1182	Corporal Sidney Wood .	No	No	Yes	No	No	No	Yes	,,	Yes	No	No	No	Discharged. A.G. List 250.
1852	Serjeant William Woodage .	Yes	Yes	No	Yes	No	No	Yes	,,	Yes	No	Yes	No	Regiment.
215	Private David Wooley .	Yes	Yes	No	No	No	No	No	,,	Yes	No	No	No	,,
1069	,, Alfred Wright . .	No	No	Yes	No	No	No	Yes	,,	Yes	No	Yes	No	,,
2019	,, James Wright . .	No	No	No	No	No	No	No	,,	Yes	No	Yes	No	,,
2162	,, Alexr. Young . .	No	No	No	No	No	No	No	,,	Yes	No	Yes	No	,,
1756	Serjt.-Major Isaac Young .	Yes	Yes	No	Yes	No	No	Yes	,,	Yes	No	Yes	No	Lieut. King's Liverpool Regt., O.C. 1st Battn.
14	Private William Young .	Yes	Yes	No	Yes	No	No	Yes	,,	Yes	No	Yes	No	Regiment.
103	Piper Robert Younger .	Yes	Yes	No	Yes	No	No	Yes	,,	Yes	No	Yes	No	,,
804	Private James P. Yule . .	No	No	Yes	No	No	No	Yes	,,	Yes	No	No	No	With 2nd Royal Highlanders, Curragh Camp.
1311	,, Robinson William .	..	..	..	..	..	..	..	,,	Yes	No	No	No	
	Lieut. J. G. Maxwell . . (Commandant Hd. Qr. Camp, N.E.F.)	Yes	Clasp	..	..	..	..	..	..	Yes	No	No	No	A.D.C. to M.-Genl. Grenfell, Comdg. F.F. Force.

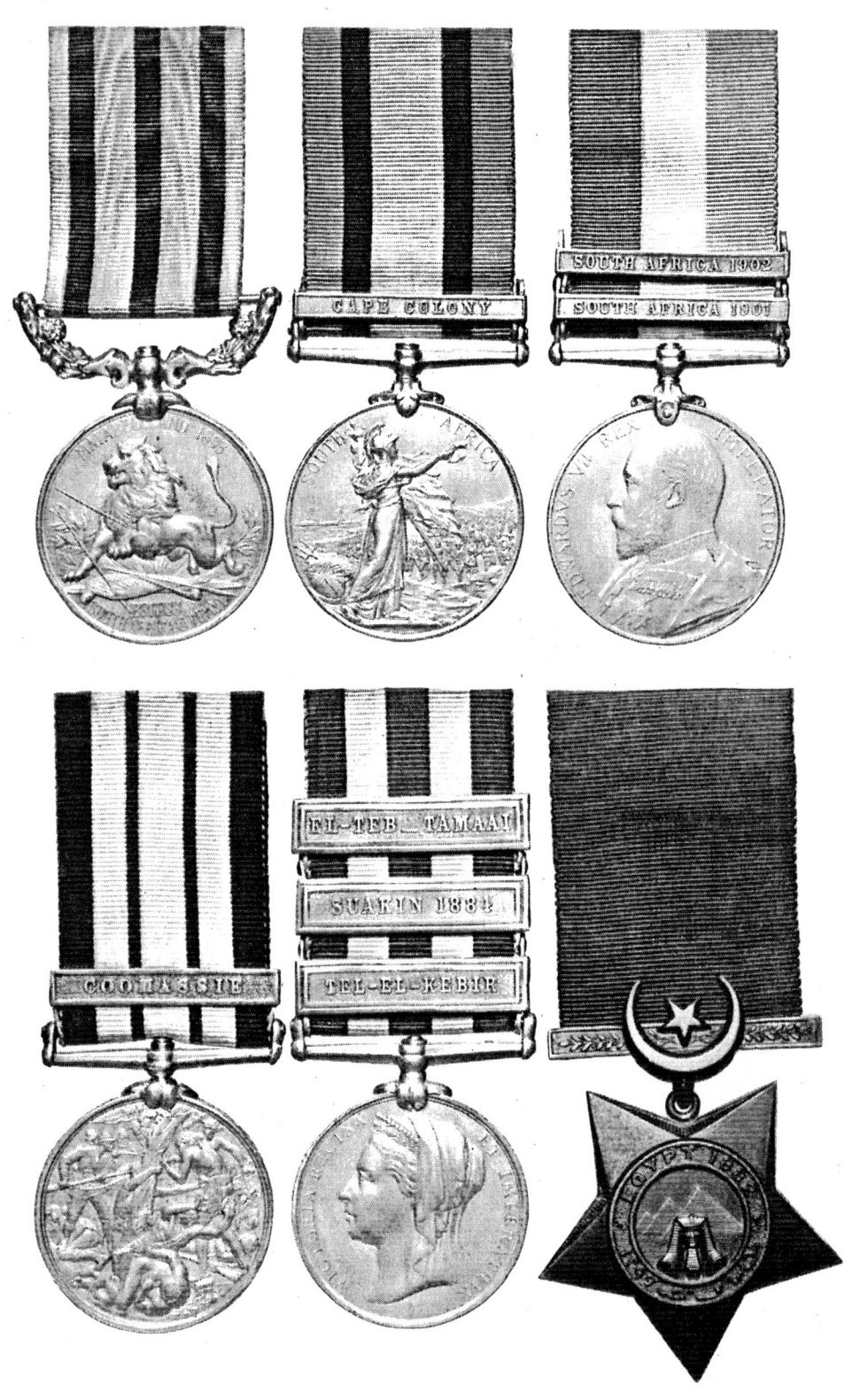

For Description of these Medals see List of Illustrations.

42ND

1ST BATTN. THE BLACK WATCH (ROYAL HIGHLANDERS)

ROLL OF OFFICERS,

WARRANT OFFICERS, N.C.O.'S AND MEN

ENTITLED TO THE

MEDAL FOR OPERATIONS IN

MATABELELAND

ROYAL HIGHLANDERS

ROLL OF OFFICERS, WARRANT OFFICERS, NON-COMMISSIONED OFFICERS AND MEN entitled to the MEDAL for Operations in MATABELELAND.

No.	Rank.	NAME.	Corps in which the Medal was earned.	Whether entitled to Medal.	Address.	REMARKS.
	Capt.	Wolridge-Gordon, Walter	1st Bn. R. Highrs.	Yes.	1st Bn. Royal Highlanders.	
3583	Pte.	Armstrong, John	do.	Yes.	c/o Pay-Master 42nd R. Dist.	
3781	,,	Diack, George .	do.	Yes.	do. do.	
3242	,,	Ferguson, William	do.	Yes.	1st Bn. Royal Highlanders.	
3213	,,	Forrester, William	do.	Yes.	c/o Pay-Master 42nd R. Dist.	
3804	,,	Gallacher, Peter .	do.	Yes.	Railway Dept., Cape Town.	
3261	,,	Galloway, Andrew	do.	Yes.	Police, Robben Island, Cape Town.	
3899	,,	Lucas, Archibald	do.	Yes.	1st Bn. Royal Highlanders.	
2962	,,	M'Callum, James	do.	Yes.	c/o Pay-Master 42nd R. Dist.	
4136	,,	M'Kinlay, John .	do.	Yes.	1st Bn. Royal Highlanders.	
4208	Corpl.	M'Lean, George [1]	do.	Yes.	do. do.	Capt. Stewart's Collection.
3709	Pte.	M'Lean, William	do.	Yes.	Railway Dept., Cape Town.	
3766	Sjt.	Morrison, David	do.	Yes.	do. do.	
4198	Pte.	Robinson, Herbert	do.	Yes.	1st Bn. Royal Highlanders.	Capt. Stewart's Collection.
4615	,,	Scott, Robert .	do.	Yes.	do. do.	Capt. Stewart's Collection.
3409	,,	Warnock, James .	do.	Yes.	c/o Pay-Master 42nd R. Dist.	
3874	,,	Watson, Andrew	do.	Yes.	Police Force, Cape Town.	
4145	,,	Wright, William .	do.	Yes.	1st Bn. Royal Highlanders.	

[1] This medal is stamped *Private* G. M'Lean, NOT Corporal. He was called up from the Reserve and served with the Bn. in S. Africa, receiving the Queen's Medal with Clasp, Cape Colony, and the King's with Clasps, 1901 and 1902.—J. S.

2ND BATTN. THE BLACK WATCH (ROYAL HIGHLANDERS)

ROLL OF INDIVIDUALS

ENTITLED TO THE

SOUTH AFRICAN MEDALS AND CLASPS

UNDER THE ARMY ORDERS GRANTING THE MEDALS

Issued on 1st April 1901 and 1st October 1902

2ND BATTALION THE BLACK WATCH

ROLL OF INDIVIDUALS entitled to the SOUTH AFRICAN MEDALS AND CLASPS under the Army Orders granting the MEDALS issued on 1st April 1901 and 1st October 1902.

Rank.	Name.	Paardeberg.	Driefontein.	Johannesburg.	Diamond Hill.	Belfast.	Wittebergen.	Cape Colony.	Orange Free State.	Transvaal.	Blandslaagte.	Defence of Ladysmith.	S. Africa, 1901.	S. Africa, 1902.	On what Roll name submitted for Queen's S. A. Medal.	If entitled to King's S. A. Medal.	Remarks.
Lieut.-Col.	Coode, J. H. C.						1										Killed in action.
Lieut.-Col.	Carthew Yorstoun, A. M., C.B.	1					1	1		1			1	1		Yes	
Major	Duff, A. G.						1						1	1		Yes	Killed in action.
,,	Willshire, E. M.					1	1									Yes	
,,	Maxwell, Hon. H. E.[1]	1					1	1		1			1	1		Yes	
,,	Berkeley, T. M. M.	1					1	1		1			1	1		Yes	Retired, Reserve of Officers.
,,	Livingston, P. J. C. (Bt.-Lt.-Col.).						1	1					1	1		Yes	
Captain	Wilson Farquharson, D. L.						1	1					1	1		Yes	1st Bn.
,,	Cumming Bruce, Hon. J. F. T.						1										Killed in action.
,,	Rennie, J. G., D.S.O.	1	1				1	1		1			1	1		Yes	
Cpt. and Ajt.	MacFarlan, W.						1										Killed in action.
Captain	Elton, E. G.						1										Killed in action.
,,	Stewart, C. E.	1	1				1	1					1	1		Yes	
,,	Eykyn, C.						1										Died of wounds.
Cpt. and Ajt.	Cameron, A. R. (Bt.-Major).						1	1		1			1	1		Yes	
Captain	MacRae, C. W.		1	1	1	1	1						1	1		Yes	
,,	Hamilton, J. G. H., D.S.O., Adjt.	1	1				1	1		1			1	1		Yes	
Maj. and Hon. Lt.-Col.	Bald, A. C., D.S.O.						1	1		1			1	1		Yes	Reserve of Officers
Captain	Moubray, W. H. H. C.						1	1		1			1	1		Yes	ditto.
,,	Scott, W. A.[2]							1	1				1	1		No	ditto.
,,	Pollok Morris, J. B.							1	1	1			1	1		Yes	On 6 Bn. I.Y.
Lieut.	Harvey, J.	1	1				1									Yes	1st Bn.
,,	Harvey, W. J. St. J.	1	1				1						1	1		Yes	1st Bn.
,,	MacLean, C.							1	1				1	1			3rd Bn. This officer served with 2nd Contingent Queensland M.I.
Captain	Stewart Richardson, Sir E. A., Bart.						1	1									
,,	Millar, R. H.						1	1					1		1st Vol. S. Coy.		
,,	Christie, R. M.							1	1	1			1	1	2nd Vol. S. Coy.	No	Killed in action.
Lieut.	Tait, F. G.						1										Died of wounds.
,,	Berthon, H. C. W.						1										Killed in action.
,,	Edmonds, N. G.						1										Killed in action.
,,	Stewart Murray, Lord G. (Capt.).							1	1	1	1	1	1	1	Adjt. 1st Regt. Scottish Horse.	Yes	1st Bn. Served with 2nd Gordon Highlanders in Natal.

[1] C.B., D.S.O.
[2] Chief Press Censor, 30/1/01 to 2/10/01. Assistant Press Censor from 12/7/00 to 30/1/01. Medal received at the hand of His Majesty the King.

Rank.	Name.	Paardeberg.	Driefontein.	Johannesburg.	Diamond Hill.	Belfast.	Wittebergen.	Cape Colony.	Orange Free State.	Transvaal.	Tugela Heights.	Relief of Ladysmith.	Laing's Nek.	Natal.	S. Africa, 1901.	S. Africa, 1902.	On what Roll name submitted for Queen's S. A. Medal.	If entitled to King's S. A. Medal.	Remarks.
Lieut.	Wauchope, A. G., D.S.O.						1												
,,	Ramsay, N. N.						1												Killed in action.
,,	Laverton, H. C.	1					1	1		1					1	1		Yes	
,,	Nunneley, W. P.						1	1		1					1				Resgnd. Commission.
,,	Innes, S. A.							1	1	1									
,,	Ferguson Davie, F. A. (Capt.).						1	1		1					1	1		Yes	Reserve of Officers.
,,	Mackay, J. A.						1	1		1					1	1	Resigned Commission.	Yes	Civilian commissioned during the war.
,,	Smith, H. K.						1	1							1		1st Vol. S. Coy.		
,,	Valentine, A.						1	1							1		1st Vol. S. Coy.		
,,	Tosh, E.							1	1	1					1		1st Vol. S. Coy.		
,,	Moubray, P. L.							1	1	1					1	1		Yes[1]	3rd Bn.
,,	Grant, A. S., D.S.O.							1	1	1					1	1		Yes	
,,	Drummond, Hon. M. C. A.							1	1	1					1	1		Yes	
,,	Hore Ruthven, Hon. C. M., D.S.O.						1	1		1					1	1		Yes	
,,	Bulloch, R. A.	1					1	1		1					1	1		Yes	
,,	West, C. C.	1	1				1	1		1					1	1		Yes	
,,	Gordon, C. W. E.	1	1					1	1	1					1	1		Yes	
,,	Buchanan White, F. H.							1	1	1					1	1		No	Vol. S.S. Coy.
,,	Corrie, A. B.							1	1	1					1	1		No	Vol. S.S. Coy.
,,	Evans, L. P.	1	1	1	1		1								1	1		Yes	
,,	Baillie Hamilton, N. A. B.							1	1	1					1	1	22nd Bn. Mtd. Inf.	Yes	
,,	Lamb, C. C.						1	1		1					1	1		Yes	
2nd Lieut.	Mackenzie, J.							1	1	1					1				Resgnd. Commission.
,,	Webber, R. G.							1	1										Resgnd. Commission.
,,	Comyn, D. C. E. ff.					1		1	1						1	1		Yes	
,,	Murray, H. F. F.							1	1						1	1		Yes	
,,	Campbell, D.						1	1											1st Bn.
,,	Parker, A. E.						1	1		1					1	1		Yes	
,,	Blair, J. M.							1	1	1									Served as Vol. Officer 2nd Hampshire Rgt.
,,	Forrester, R. E.							1	1	1					1	1		Yes	Served as No.8442 Sgt. R. E. Forrester in 19th Coy. 6th Bn. I.Y.
Qr.-Mr. and Hon. Lt.	Studley, H.	1	1				1	1		1					1	1		Yes	
ATTACHED.																			
Lieut. Permanent Land Forces.	Grieve, J. G. Staff, N. S. Wales	1						1											Killed in action.
R.A.M.C. Lt.	Goddard, G. H.	1					1	1											
,,	Douglas, H.E.M.							1	1										This officer left the Bn. Dec. 1899, wounded.
Scripture Reader	Revd. Lennox Fraser						1	1											

[1] In Supplementary 2nd Bn. King's Medal and Colony Clasp Roll, entry as follows: 'Attd. to 2nd Bn. The Black Watch from 7th March 1900 to 16th Aug. 1901, and from 17th Aug. 1901 to 18th July 1902 to the Remount Department at Newcastle, Natal.'

Regtl. No.	Rank.	Name.	Paardeberg.	Driefontein.	Johannesburg.	Diamond Hill.	Belfast.	Wittebergen.	Cape Colony.	Orange Free State.	Transvaal.	Tugela Heights.	Relief of Ladysmith.	Laing's Nek.	Natal.	S. Africa, 1901.	S. Africa, 1902.	On what Roll name submitted for Queen's S. A. Medal.	If entitled to King's S. A. Medal.	Remarks.
2752	Sgt.-Maj.	Anderson, J.	1	1					1		1					1	1		Yes	
6282	Piper	Ackroyd, G. (Private)	1	1				1	1							1				Home on demobilisation.
4216	Pte.	Ackroyd, T.							1	1								1			do. do.
2682	,,	Adams, T.			1	1			1	1							1	1		Yes	Home, time expired.
3890	,,	Adams, J. (Cpl).	1	1				1	1							1	1		Yes	
7582	,,	Adams, W.						1	1							1		1st Vol. S. Coy.		
4948	,,	Adams, J.							1											
4877	Sgt.	Adamson, J.	1	1					1											
4832	,,	Adamson, James	1	1					1											
3652	Pte.	Adamson, W.	1	1					1											
6723	,,	Adamson, A. J.	1	1				1	1		1					1	1		Yes	
2206	,,	Adamson, R.							1	1						1				Home, time exp.
3201	,,	Addison, D.						1	1		1					1	1		Yes	Home on demobn.
5651	,,	Agnew, W.							1	1	1					1	1		Yes	do. do.
4464	,,	Ailsworth, R.							1											
3093	,,	Airth, G.							1	1	1									B/785/S.A.C.
5504	,,	Aitken, K.	1	1	1	1	1		1							1	1		Yes	
6677	,,	Aitken, H.							1	1						1	1		Yes	Home, invalided.
6739	,,	Allison, A. J.	1	1					1	1	1					1	1		Yes	
3118	,,	Allison, S.							1	1										
7609	,,	Allison, H.							1	1						1		1st Vol. S. Coy.		
5593	,,	Allison, J.	1	1					1		1					1	1		Yes	Home on demobn.
5994	,,	Allan, A.	1	1					1										Yes	To 1st Blk. Watch.
7197	,,	Allan, J.						1	1		1					1	1			Home, invalided.
3464	Sgt.	Allan, A.							1	1	1					1				Home on demobn.
854	Pte.	Allan, W. A. (Lc.-Corpl.).						1	1											
4362	,,	Allan, T. B.	1						1											
2612	,,	Allan, A.						1	1		1					1	1		Yes	Home, time exp.
5368	,,	Allen, J.	1	1				1	1		1					1	1		Yes	To Army Reserve in S. A.
3648	,,	Allerdice, C.							1	1	1									
7420	,,	Alexander, H.							1	1	1					1	1		Yes	Home, invalided.
5607	,,	Alwell, J.							1	1	1					1	1	To 1st Blk. Watch	Yes	Home on demobn.
6548	Corpl.	Ambler, H. (Sgt.)	1	1					1		1					1	1		Yes	
7210	Pte.	Ames, J.							1											Killed in action.
5133	,,	Amey, C.	1						1	1	1					1	1		Yes	Home on demobn.
5916	Corpl.	Anderson, J. (Sgt.)							1	1							1		Yes	To 1st Blk. Watch.
6697	Pte.	Anderson, J.	1	1					1		1					1	1		Yes	
6431	,,	Anderson, D.	1	1				1	1		1					1	1		Yes	To 1st Blk. Watch.
5183	,,	Anderson, T.	1	1				1	1		1					1	1		Yes	Home on demobn.
7376	,,	Anderson, J.							1	1	1					1	1		Yes	
7064	,,	Anderson, J.						1	1		1					1	1		Yes	
3325	,,	Anderson, J.							1	1	1					1	1		Yes	Home on demobn.
3605	,,	Anderson, J.							1											Killed in action.
4170	,,	Anderson, J.							1	1	1					1	1		Yes	Home on demobn.

Regtl. No.	Rank.	Name.	Paardeberg.	Driefontein.	Johannesburg.	Diamond Hill.	Belfast.	Wittebergen.	Cape Colony.	Orange Free State.	Transvaal.	Tugela Heights.	Relief of Ladysmith.	Laing's Nek.	Natal.	S. Africa, 1901.	S. Africa, 1902.	On what Roll name submitted for Queen's S. A. Medal.	If entitled to King's S. A. Medal.	Remarks.
5574	Pte.	Anderson, R.			1	1	1		1	1						1	1		Yes	Home on demobn.
5892	Corpl.	Anderson, A. B.	1	1					1											
3947	Pte.	Anderson, M.	1	1				1	1		1					1	1	Home on demobn.	Yes	Discharged in S. A.
64	,,	Anderson, W.							1	1						1				Home on demobn.
3980	,,	Anderson, D.	1	1				1	1		1					1	1		Yes	Home on demobn.
6668	,,	Anderson, J.							1	1	1					1	1		Yes	
6802	,,	Anderson, J.	1	1				1	1		1					1	1		Yes	
6958	,,	Anderson, W.							1											
6948	,,	Anderson, C.						1	1		1					1	1		Yes	
6016	,,	Anderson, W.							1	1	1					1	1	To 1st Blk. Watch.	Yes	Home invalided.
6886	,,	Andrews, J.							1	1	1					1	1		Yes	
4553	Sgt.	Angus, J.							1											
8938	Pte.	Angus, G. C.							1	1	1					1		1st Vol. S. Coy.		No. 1484 J.M.R.
4246	,,	Archer, G.							1											Died of wounds.
6811	,,	Armit, G.							1											Killed in action.
6984	,,	Armit, J.	1					1	1		1					1	1		Yes	Home on demobn.
6318	Corpl.	Armstrong, J.							1											Killed in action.
3583	Pte.	Armstrong, J.							1											Killed in action.
6455	Corpl.	Arnold, G. (Sgt.)	1	1				1	1		1					1	1		Yes	
7298	Pte.	Bailey, R. H.						1	1		1					1	1		Yes	
8965	,,	Baillie, R. S.							1	1	1					1	1	2nd Vol. S. Coy.	No	
7635	,,	Bain, W.						1	1							1	1	1st Vol. S. Coy.		
4399	,,	Baker, J.	1	1				1	1		1					1	1		Yes	Home on demobn.
2189	Corpl.	Baldwin, F.						1	1		1									Home, time exp.
6238	,,	Balfour, G.							1											Died of wounds.
6744	Pte.	Ball, T.	1	1				1	1		1					1	1		Yes	Home, invalided.
9017	Sergt.	Band, D.							1	1	1					1	1	2nd Vol. S. Coy.	No	Dischd. at Harrismith, O.R.C.
3755	Pte.	Banks, J.	1	1				1	1							1				Home on demobn.
4368	,,	Banks, J.	1	1					1											
6717	Corpl.	Bannerman, T.[1]	1	1					1		1					1	1		Yes	
6778	Pte.	Balmain, C.							1											Died of disease.
3117	,,	Barclay, J.			1	1	1		1	1						1				Home on demobn.
6707	,,	Barr, A.							1											Died of wounds.
4867	,,	Barr, S.						1	1		1					1	1		Yes	Home on demobn.
3881	Sergt.	Barton, H. E.	1	1				1	1							1				do. do.
7069	Pte.	Barrett, W.						1	1		1					1	1		Yes	
4374	,,	Barrett, H.	1						1		1					1	1		No	To A. Reserve in S. Africa.
6995	,,	Barrie, S.	1						1											
3679	,,	Barnett, B.	1	1				1	1											
6622	,,	Barty, A.	1	1				1	1		1					1	1	To 1st Blk. Watch.	Yes	Home, invalided.
7021	,,	Barwick, A.							1	1	1					1	1		Yes	
3827	,,	Batchelor, D.	1						1							1			Yes	Home on demobn.
7124	,,	Batchelor, W.						1	1		1					1	1		Yes	No MEDAL. Deserted.
2410 6	,,	Bates, W.						1	1							1				Home on demobn.
7186 8	,,	Bates, J.						1	1		1					1	1		Yes	
6386	,,	Baxter, R.	1	1				1	1		1					1	1		Yes	To 1st Blk. Watch.

[1] Sergeant in 2nd Bn. Supplementary Roll.

Regtl. No.	Rank.	Name.	Paardeberg.	Driefontein.	Johannesburg.	Diamond Hill.	Belfast.	Wittebergen.	Cape Colony.	Orange Free State.	Transvaal.	Tugela Heights.	Relief of Ladysmith.	Laing's Nek.	Natal.	S. Africa, 1901.	S. Africa, 1902.	On what Roll name submitted for Queen's S. A. Medal	If entitled to King's S. A. Medal.	Remarks.
7542	Pte.	Baxter, M. R.						1	1							1		1st Vol. S. Coy.		
4872	Sergt.	Baxter, J.						1	1	1						1	1		Yes	Home, time exp. See D.C.M. Roll.
4529	L.-Cpl.	Baxter, T. (Cpl.)						1	1	1						1	1		Yes	
6349	Pte.	Bayne, J.	1	1				1	1		1					1	1		Yes	To 1st Blk. Watch.
7636	,,	Bayne, J. C.						1	1									1st Vol. S. Coy.		Died of disease. Died of enteric near Bloemfontein 27/4/00.
9012	L.-Sgt.	Bayne, T. M. (Corpl.)						1	1	1						1	1	2nd Vol. S. Coy.	No?	42014, 1st Scottish Horse,1/5/02 /03/5/02 St.
9056	L.-Cpl.	Beaton, J.						1	1	1						1	1	2nd Vol. S. Coy.	No	
3223	Pte.	Beattie, F.						1	1	1						1	1		Yes	Home on demobn.
6713	Corpl.	Beattie, J. (Sgt.)	1	1				1	1	1						1	1		Yes	
4336	Pte.	Beattie, M.						1	1							1				Home on demobn.
2597	,,	Beattie, J.						1	1											
3815	,,	Beattie, J.	1	1				1	1							1				Home on demobn.
9010	,,	Bethune, R.						1	1	1						1	1	2nd Vol. S. Coy.	No	
3654	,,	Belford, J.	1	1				1	1		1									Home on demobn.
3700	,,	Bell, D.	1	1				1	1							1				
3887	,,	Bell, J.	1						1											
3599	,,	Bell, N.	1	1				1	1											
7633	Sergt.	Bell, C.						1	1							1		1st Vol. S. Coy.		
3743	Pte.	Bell, A.							1											
3529	,,	Bennett, G.						1	1											
2394	,,	Bennett, T.						1	1											
4192	,,	Benson, W.	1					1	1							1	1		Yes	Home on demobn.
4540	,,	Bergin, S.						1	1	1						1	1		Yes	do. do.
4276	,,	Bergin, F.						1	1							1	1		Yes	do. do.
7008	,,	Bern, A.						1	1		1					1	1		Yes	
7557	,,	Bertie, F. J.						1	1							1		1st Vol. S. Coy.		
3689	,,	Bertie, D.	1	1				1	1											
5468	,,	Berwick, S.						1	1		1									Home, time exp.
6395	Corpl.	Beveridge, J.						1										1st Vol. S. Coy.		
7637	Pte.	Beveridge, J.						1	1							1		1st Vol. S. Coy.		
8948	,,	Beverley, N. G.						1	1	1						1	1	2nd Vol. S. Coy.	No	
3016	L.-Cpl.	Bews, G. (Bewes)						1	1		1					1	1	Home, time exp.	Yes	Home on demobn.
3842	Pte.	Bett, A.						1												Killed in action.
6839	,,	Binnie, D.	1	1				1	1		1					1	1		Yes	Home, invalided.
2600	,,	Binnie, C.						1	1	1						1	1		Yes	Home on demobn.
6304	,,	Biggs, S.	1	1				1	1		1					1	1		Yes	To 1st Blk. Watch.
6841	,,	Bird, W.[1]	1					1	1		1					1	1		No	
9062	,,	Birks, J.						1	1	1						1	1	2nd Vol. S. Coy.	No	
7385	,,	Birnie, C.						1	1	1						1	1		Yes	
9007	,,	Birrell, W.						1	1	1						1	1	2nd Vol. S. Coy.	No	
7561	,,	Bissett, L.					1	1								1		1st Vol. S. Coy.		
6376	Sergt.	Bissett, D.						1								1				Home, invalided.
3623	Pte.	Black, A.						1												Killed in action.

[1] In 1st Bn. King's Roll this man's name appears as entitled to that Medal and Clasps, 1901 and 1902, but the following remark appears: 'Expunge, Not entitled, Entered in error, A.G./2/M/13818. Returned to Woolwich, Clasps retained.'

Regtl. No.	Rank.	Name.	Paardeberg.	Driefontein.	Johannesburg.	Diamond Hill.	Belfast.	Wittebergen.	Cape Colony.	Orange Free State.	Transvaal.	Tugela Heights.	Relief of Ladysmith.	Laing's Nek.	Natal.	S. Africa, 1901.	S. Africa, 1902.	On what Roll name submitted for Queen's S. A. Medal.	If entitled to King's S. A. Medal.	Remarks.
7036	Pte.	Black, P.							1	1										
3760	,,	Black, R.							1	Yes										Died of disease.
7241	,,	Black, J.							1											
5338	,,	Black, H.	1	1					1	1	1					1				Home, time exp.
6819	,,	Black, J.	1	1					1	1	1					1				
3820	,,	Blackhall, R.							1	1						1				Died of disease.
6662	,,	Blackley, R.			1	1	1		1	1						1				
4302	L.-Cpl.	Blaney, J.	1	1					1	1	1					1	1		Yes	Home on demobn.
5950	Corpl.	Blyth, J. (Sgt.)	1	1					1	1	1					1	1		Yes	do. do.
6448	L.-Cpl.	Bogie, D. (Corpl.)							1	1						1	1		Yes	To 1st Blk. Watch.
3544	Pte.	Bolton, W.							1											Died of disease.
4294	,,	Bond, F.							1											Killed in action.
4871	,,	Bonnette, J.							1	1	1					1	1		Yes	Home on demobn.
5673	,,	Bowes, J. A. G.	1	1					1	1	1					1	1		Yes	Home, time exp.
8934	,,	Bowman, T.							1	1	1					1	1	2nd Vol. S. Coy.	No	
4500	,,	Boyd, J.	1	1					1							1	1		Yes	Home on demobn.
7243	,,	Boyd, W.							1											
3105	,,	Boyes, C.							1	1	1					1	1		Yes	Home on demobn.
6942	,,	Boyes, J.							1											Died of disease.
2662	,,	Boyle, J.						1	1		1					1	1	Home on demobn.	Yes	Home, time exp.
5875	L.-Cpl.	Boucher, J. F. (Corpl.)	1	1					1	1	1					1	1		Yes	To 1st Blk. Watch.
6519	Pte.	Brady, J.						1	1							1				Home, invalided.
4965	,,	Bradley, M.	1	1					1											
2913	,,	Braid, D.			1	1	1		1	1						1	1		Yes	Home on demobn.
7215	,,	Braid, G.							1	1	1					1	1		Yes	
3864	,,	Braid, A.	1	1					1	1	1					1	1	Home on demobn.	Yes	Home, time exp.
7581	,,	Brand, W.						1	1							1		1st Vol. S. Coy.		
9060	,,	Brand, R.[1]							1	1	1					1	1	2nd Vol. S. Coy.	No	
7560	L.-Cpl.	Brander, G. (Private)						1	1							1		1st Vol. S. Coy.		
6859	Pte.	Brannan, J.	1						1	1	1					1	1		Yes	
2474	,,	Brennan, M.			1	1			1	1						1				Home on demobn.
6873	,,	Brash, G.						1	1		1					1	1		Yes	Home, invalided.
7260	,,	Brearton, F.							1	1	1					1	1		Yes	
4525	,,	Bremner, J.	1						1											Killed in action.
4098	L.-Cpl.	Britt, E. (Brett)	1	1					1	1	1					1	1		Yes	Home on demobn.
7370	Pte.	Broadley, J.							1	1										
3956	,,	Brodie, J.	1						1											
3336	,,	Brogan, C.							1	1	1					1	1		Yes	Home on demobn.
7053	,,	Bromberg, J.	1	1					1	1							1			Home, time exp.
4039	Piper	Brown, D.							1	1	1					1	1		Yes	Home on demobn.
7190	Pte.	Brown, T. (Lc.-Corpl.)							1	1	1					1	1		No	Home, invalided.
6908	,,	Brown, R.							1											Died of wounds.
4467	,,	Brown, J.	1						1											
2803	,,	Brown, J.						1	1							1				Home, invalided.
2765	,,	Brown, A.							1	1	1					1				Home on demobn.
7356	,,	Brown, D.							1	1	1					1	1		Yes	
7055	,,	Brown, G.	1	1				1	1	1						1	1		Yes	
4566	,,	Brown, W.							1	1	1					1	1		Yes	Home on demobn.

[1] Served in both 2nd and 1st Vol. S. Coys.

Regtl. No.	Rank.	Name.	Paardeberg.	Driefontein.	Johannesburg.	Diamond Hill.	Belfast.	Wittebergen.	Cape Colony.	Orange Free State.	Transvaal.	Tugela Heights.	Relief of Ladysmith.	Laing's Nek.	Natal.	S. Africa, 1901.	S. Africa, 1902.	On what Roll name submitted for Queen's S. A. Medal.	If entitled to King's S. A. Medal.	Remarks.
4336	Pte.	Brown, J.	1	1	1	1	1		1							1	1		Yes	Home on demobn.
5476	Drmr.	Brown, J. (Private)							1	1	1					1	1		Yes	Discharged in S. Africa.
3758	L.-Cpl.	Brown, E.							1											
6720	Drmr.	Brown, G.	1	1					1											Died of disease.
4447	Pte.	Brown, S.	1					1	1	1						1	1		Yes	Home on demobn.
3637	,,	Brown, T.							1											
4345	,,	Brown, W.							1											
2777	,,	Brown, J.						1	1	1						1	1		Yes	Home, invalided.
6952	,,	Brown, G.	1	1					1											
7638	,,	Brown, J.						1	1							1		1st Vol. S. Coy.		
8987	,,	Brown, A.							1	1	1					1	1	2nd Vol. S. Coy.	No	
8995	,,	Brown, D.							1	1	1					1	1	2nd Vol. S. Coy.	No	
2175	,,	Browning, A.						1	1							1				Home, time exp.
4477	L.-Cpl.	Browning, J.							1											Killed in action.
7264	Pte.	Bruce, R.							1	1	1					1	1		Yes	
2366	Sergt.	Bruce, C.						1	1							1				Home, time exp.
3540	Pte.	Bruce, J.							1											
7613	,,	Bruce, G.						1	1							1		1st Vol. S. Coy.		
8966	L.-Cpl.	Bruce, W. B. (Pte.)							1	1	1					1	1	2nd Vol. S. Coy.	No	
9051	Pte.	Bryson, J. F.							1	1	1					1	1	2nd Vol. S. Coy.	No	
6812	L.-Cpl.	Buchan, D.(Pte.)	1	1				1	1	1						1	1	To 1st Blk. Watch	Yes	Home, invalided.
4773	Pte.	Buchan, A.	1	1					1											
8951	,,	Buchan, Q. Mungo							1	1	1					1		1st Vol. S. Coy.		
9064	L.-Cpl.	Buchan, A.							1	1	1					1	1	2nd Vol. S. Coy.	No	
2524	Pte.	Buchanan, G.							1	1										Died of disease at home.
8961	,,	Buchanan, J.							1	1	1					1	1	2nd Vol. S. Coy.	No	
2244	,,	Buchanan, J.							1	1	1					1	1		Yes	Home on demobn.
7128	,,	Buist, G.							1	1	1					1	1		Yes	
6899	,,	Bunch, A.						1	1		1					1	1		Yes	
5818	,,	Bunce, J.						1	1		1					1	1		Yes	Home on demobn.
3771	,,	Bunce, T.							1											
4716	,,	Burke, G.			1	1			1											
2327	,,	Burley, J.						1	1							Yes				
7010	L.-Cpl.	Burnett, W.	1						1		1					1	1		Yes	Discharged in S. Africa.
97																				
4795	Pte.	Burns, W.						1	1							1				Home on demobn.
7289	,,	Burns, W.						1	1		1					1	1		Yes	
2849	,,	Burns, E.							1	1										
3870	,,	Burns, E.						1	1		1					1	1		Yes	Home on demobn.
7162	,,	Burns, A.							1	1	1					1	1		Yes	To 1st Blk. Watch.
4987	Piper	Burns, D. (Private)	1	1				1	1		1					1	1		Yes	To A. Reserve in S. Africa.
7562	Pte.	Burt, J.							1	1						1	1	1st Vol. S. Coy.	No	No. 9127, 3rd V. S. C. Corpl.
3357	,,	Butler, J. (Butters)						1	1		1					1	1		Yes	Home on demobn.
3500	,,	Button, G. E.							1											

Regtl. No.	Rank.	Name.	Paardeberg.	Driefontein.	Johannesburg.	Diamond Hill.	Belfast.	Wittebergen.	Cape Colony.	Orange Free State.	Transvaal.	Tugela Heights.	Relief of Ladysmith.	Laing's Nek.	Natal.	S. Africa, 1901.	S. Africa, 1902.	On what Roll name submitted for Queen's S. A. Medal.	If entitled to King's S. A. Medal.	Remarks.
3515	Pte.	Cairns, P.							1	1						1				Home, time exp.
4436	,,	Cairns, J.	1	1				1	1	1	1					1	1		Yes	Home on demobn.
2171	,,	Cairns, J.			1	1	1		1	1						1				Home, time exp.
5243	Acting Band-Sgt.	Cain, H.	1	1				1	1		1					1	1		Yes	
7343	Pte.	Cairney, M.							1	1	1					1	1		Yes	
4060	,,	Calderwood, M.	1	1						1										
5902	,,	Caldwell, K.								1										Killed in action.
2741	,,	Callander, J. (Callendar)							1	1	1					1	1		Yes	
5200	,,	Callighan, J. (Calligan)						1	1		1					1	1		Yes	Home on demobn.
4504	,,	Calnan, F.	1	1					1	1	1					1	1		Yes	To 1st Blk. Watch.
6575	,,	Cameron, J.								1										Killed in action.
6142	Corpl.	Cameron, F. G.	1							1										Killed in action.
3660	,,	Cameron, D.								1										
6962	Pte.	Cameron, J.							1	1	1					1	1		Yes	To A. Reserve in S. Africa.
7607	,,	Cameron, A.						1	1							1		1st Vol. S. Coy.		
7564	,,	Cameron, J.						1	1							1		1st Vol. S. Coy.		
9074	,,	Cameron, W.							1	1	1					1	1	2nd Vol. S. Coy.	No	
6269	Piper	Cameron, D.	1	1					1	1	1					1	1		Yes	Discharged in S. Africa. See D.C.M. Roll.
7203	Pte.	Cameron, W.	1	1				1	1											Died of wounds.
3972	,,	Cameron, A.	1	1	1	1	1		1							1	1		Yes	Home on demobn.
6884	,,	Cameron, J.							1	1	1					1	1		Yes	
5585	,,	Caddle, J.							1	1	1									
2526	,,	Campbell, J.						1	1							1				Home on demobn.
4344	,,	Campbell, W.	1	1					1							1				do. do.
7099	,,	Campbell, T.	1	1				1	1	1	1					1*	1*		No	*Issd. 15/8/02. Trial dispensed with for offence of Fraudulent Enlistment. Medal re-earned. A.G.2/N/6684.
6807	,,	Campbell, W.							1	1										
6890	Corpl.	Campbell, A. (Lc.-Sgt.)	1	1					1		1					1	1		Yes	
5473	Drmr.	Campbell, H. (Pte.)							1	1						1	1		Yes	To 1st Blk. Watch.
7606	L.-Cpl.	Campbell, D. (Pte.)						1	1							1		1st Vol. S. Coy.		
7543	Pte.	Campbell, P. R.						1	1							1		1st Vol. S. Coy.		
9057	,,	Campbell, W.							1	1	1					1	1	2nd Vol. S. Coy.	No	
6927	,,	Campbell, J.	1	1					1	1	1					1	1	To 1st Blk. Watch.	Yes	Home, invalided.
6865	,,	Campbell, G.						1	1											
3480	,,	Campbell, J.						1	1	1						1	1		Yes	
2998	,,	Campbell, J.							1	1	1					1	1		Yes	Home on demobn.
7579	,,	Campsie, W.						1	1									1st Vol. S. Coy.		
4725	,,	Candy, W.							1	1	1					1	1		Yes	

Regtl. No.	Rank.	Name.	Paardeberg.	Driefontein.	Johannesburg.	Diamond Hill.	Belfast.	Wittebergen.	Cape Colony.	Orange Free State.	Transvaal.	Tugela Heights.	Relief of Ladysmith.	Laing's Nek.	Natal.	S. Africa, 1901.	S. Africa, 1902.	On what Roll name submitted for Queen's S. A. Medal.	If entitled to King's S. A. Medal.	REMARKS.
3629	Pte.	Candy, J.	1					1												Killed in action.
4354	,,	Cargill, J.	1	1					1	1							1	1		Yes	Home on demobn.
7657	,,	Cargill, J.							1	1	1						1	1		Yes	
4435	,,	Cannen, T. (Lc.-Corpl.)	1	1					1	1							1	1		Yes	Home on demobn.
6671	,,	Carling, W.	1	1				1	1		1						1	1	1st Vol. S. Coy.	Yes	
7576	,,	Carmichael, N.J.						1	1								1		1st Vol. S. Coy.		
3742	,,	Carnegie, L.							1										1st Vol. S. Coy.		
7563	,	Carnegie, W.							1	1							1				
2519	,,	Carr, M. J.						1	1		1						1	1	Home, time exp.	Yes	Home on demobn.
3233	,,	Carr, J.							1		1						1	1		Yes	do. do.
5143	,,	Carroll, G.	1	1				1	1		1						1	1		Yes	do. do.
6404	,,	Carroll, F.						1	1		1						1	1		Yes	do. do.
5954	,,	Carroll, C.						1	1		1						1	1		Yes	do. do.
3398	,,	Carrigan, J.							1	1	1						1	1		Yes	do. do.
4367	,,	Carter, C.							1												
6692	Corpl.	Casey, J. (Pte.)	1	1					1		1						1	1		Yes	
5776	Pte.	Cassidy, J.						1	1		1						1	1	2nd Vol. S. Coy.	Yes	Home on demobn.
9030	,,	Cassidy, W.							1	1	1						1	1		No	
5949	,,	Chalmers, A.							1	1	1						1	1		Yes	Home on demobn.
4257	,,	Chalmers, R.	1	1				1	1		1						1	1		Yes	do. do.
4457	,,	Chalmers, D.							1												
4460	,,	Chalmers, R.							1												
6845	,,	Chalmers, R.							1												Killed in action.
4791	,,	Chalmers, J.							1	1	1						1	1	1st Vol. S. Coy.	Yes	Home on demobn.
7559	Drmr.	Chalmers, A. (Bugler)						1	1								1		1st Vol. S. Coy.		
7614	Pte.	Chalmers, J.						1	1								1		1st Vol. S. Coy.		
8971	Sergt.	Chalmers, R.							1	1	1						1				
3610	Pte.	Chambers, R.	1	1				1	1												
6898	,,	Chaplin, T.						1	1		1						1	1		Yes	
6211	Corpl.	Chatfield, C.							1												
2763	Sgt.	Cattanach, J.			1	1			1	1							1	1	2nd Vol. S. Coy.	Yes	To 1st Blk. Watch.
9053	Pte.	Christie, P.							1	1	1						1	1		No	
2312	,,	Christie, W.							1	1											Died of disease.
5419	,,	Christie, J.	1	1					1												Died of disease.
4190	,,	Christie, D.	1	1	1	1	1		1								1	1		Yes	Home on demobn.
5057	,,	Christie, R.							1	1											
6879	,,	Clark, J.							1												
3729	,,	Clark, P.							1	1	1										
6930	,,	Clark, R.							1	1	1						1	1		Yes	
7154	L.-Cpl.	Clark, R. (Corpl.)						1	1		1						1	1		Yes	
4178	Pte.	Clark, W. T.	1						1		1						1	1		Yes	Home on demobn.
4395	Sergt.	Clark, E.	1	1				1	1		1						1	1		Yes	
7261	Pte.	Clark, J.							1	1	1						1	1		Yes	Home, invalided.
5560	,,	Clark, A.	1	1				1	1		1						1	1		Yes	Home on demobn.
4717	,,	Clark, J.	1	1					1											Yes	Home on demobn.
3589	,,	Clark, T.						1	1		1						1	1		Yes	To 1st Blk. Watch.
6870	,,	Clark, H. (L.-Cpl.)	1	1					1								1				Home on demobn.
3710	,,	Clark, W.	1						1								1				

Regtl. No.	Rank.	Name.	Paardeberg.	Driefontein.	Johannesburg.	Diamond Hill.	Belfast.	Wittebergen.	Cape Colony.	Orange Free State.	Transvaal.	Tugela Heights.	Relief of Ladysmith.	Laing's Nek.	Natal.	S. Africa, 1901.	S. Africa, 1902.	On what Roll name submitted for Queen's S. A. Medal.	If entitled to King's S. A. Medal.	Remarks.
7280	Pte.	Clark, P.							1	1	1					1	1		Yes	To 1st Blk. Watch.
5353	,,	Clark, C.							1	1	1					1				Home on demobn.
3917	,,	Cockburn, R.	1	1				1	1		1					1	1		Yes	Home on demobn.
3173	,,	Coen, M.						1	1		1					1	1		Yes	Home on demobn.
5470	,,	Clements, D.	1	1				1	1		1					1	1		Yes	
6649	Corpl.	Collier, R.	1		1	1	1		1							1	1		Yes	Discharged in S. A.
5636	L.-Cpl.	Collins, D. (Pte.)	1					1	1		1					1	1	Home, time exp.	Yes	Home on demobn.
2114	Pte.	Connolley, P.							1	1	1					1	1		Yes	do.　　do.
6868	,,	Connolley, P. (Connelly)							1	1	1					1				
6936	Drmr.	Connolly, T.	1	1					1	1 (Yes)						1	1		Yes	
3416	Pte.	Connolly, J.							1	1	1					1	1		Yes	Home on demobn.
4509	,,	Connolley, H.							1											Killed in action.
9065	,,	Connelly, P.							1	1	1					1	1	2nd Vol. S. Coy.	No	
6098	,,	Coleman, J.							1											
6625	,,	Coghill, J.	1	1				1	1	1	1					1	1		No	Medal issd. 29/12/02. Convicted of disgraceful conduct (theft) by F.G.C.M. Medal re-earned A.G.2/N/6684.
5024	,,	Coley, H.							1	1	1									
3958	,,	Connor, J.							1	1	1					1	1		Yes	Home on demobn.
3927	,,	Connor, J.	1						1		1					1				do.　　do.
3734	,,	Connor, T.						1	1							1				do.　　do.
5998	,,	Conway, J.[1]	1	1				1	1		1					1	1		Yes	Home on demobn.
3408	,,	Conway, T.			1	1	1		1	1						1	1		Yes	do.　　do.
4149	,,	Cook, N.	1	1				Yes	1		1					1	1		Yes	Discharged.
7262	,,	Cook, F.							1	1	Yes					1	1		Yes	
2391	,,	Cook, W.							1	1	1					1				Home on demobn.
5382	,,	Cooper, G.	1					1	1							1	1		Yes	Home to A. Reserve.
9005	,,	Cooper, J.							1	1	1					1	1	2nd Vol. S. Coy.	No	
4277	,,	Cooper, D.							1	1	1					1			Yes	Home on demobn.
6945	,,	Coull, T.	1	1				1	1											
5630	,,	Cousins, J.						1	1		1					1			Yes	
2683	,,	Couper, J.							1	1										Died of disease.
6973	,,	Cowper, J.	1						1											
5827	,,	Cowley, D.	1	1					1		1					1	1		Yes	Deceased.
4442	,,	Cowley, C. J.	1	1	1	1	1		1							1	1		Yes	Home, invalided.
5697	,,	Cowan, G.							1											Killed in action.
4146	,,	Coppard, W.							1											
7565	,,	Cosgrove, W.							1	1						1		1st Vol. S. Coy.		
3532	,,	Cowan, A.						1	1							1	1		Yes	Home on demobn.
2171	,,	Cowie, H.							1	1										No Medal. Sentenced by F.G.C.M. to penal servitude for manslaughter.
3879	,,	Cowie, W.	1	1				1	1							1				Home, invalided.
2837	,,	Cowie, D.						1	1	1						1	1		Yes	Deceased.
9066	L.-Cpl.	Cowie, J. M.						1	1	1	1					1	1	2nd Vol. S. Coy.	No	

[1] No. 6998 in King's Medal Roll.

Regtl. No.	Rank.	Name.	Paardeberg.	Driefontein.	Johannesburg.	Diamond Hill.	Belfast.	Wittebergen.	Cape Colony.	Orange Free State.	Transvaal.	Tugela Heights.	Relief of Ladysmith.	Laing's Nek.	Natal.	S. Africa, 1901.	S. Africa, 1902.	On what Roll name submitted for Queen's S. A. Medal.	If entitled to King's S. A. Medal.	Remarks.
2802	Pte.	Cox, J.						1	1							1				Home, invalided.
2799	,,	Craig, J.							1	1	1					1	1		Yes	Home on demobn.
3588	,,	Craig, D.							1											
4408	,,	Craig, J.						1	1		1					1	1		Yes	Home on demobn.
8932	,,	Craig, C.							1	1	1					1	1	2nd Vol. S. Coy.	No	
2141	,,	Craig, R.						1	1							1				Home, time exp.
7167	,,	Craigie, R.						1	1		1					1	1		Yes	
7013	L.-Cpl.	Craven, W. B. R.							1	1	1					1	1		Yes	Discharged in S. Africa.
4481	,,	Crawford, A. (Pte.)	1	1				1	1							1	1		Yes	Home for discharge.
3064	Pte.	Crawford, R.							1	1										
7342	L.-Cpl.	Crawford, J.							1	1	1					1	1		Yes	Home, invalided.
7578	Pte.	Crearer, J. M.						1	1							1		1st Vol. S. Coy.		
2221	,,	Critcher, C.						1	1							1				Home, time exp.
4130	,,	Cresswell, R. H.	1	1				1	1		1					1	1		Yes	Home on demobn.
2964	,,	Crichton, J.						1	1		1					1	1		Yes	do. do.
8204	,,	Cripps, J.	1	1					1											
7463	,,	Crombie, W.							1	1	1					1	1		Yes	No Medal. Deserted.
4596	,,	Crombie, R.	1	1	1	1	1		1							1	1		Yes	B/783 S.A.C.
3777	,,	Crombie, J.	1	1				1	1							1				Home, time exp.
2370	,,	Crook, H.							1	1										
6811	,,	Crosby, T. (Crosbie)							1	1	1					1	1	Home, time exp.	Yes	Home on demobn.
4085	,,	Cross, A.	1	1				1	1		1							Discharged in S. Africa.		E/137 S.A.C.
2228	,,	Crowe, A.						1	1							1				Home, time exp.
4013	,,	Cruickshanks, R.	1	1				1	1		1					1	1		Yes	Home on demobn.
7639	,,	Cruickshanks, M.						1	1							1		1st Vol. S. Coy.		
8937	Sgt.	Cruickshanks, D							1	1	1					1	1	2nd Vol. S. Coy.	No	
6800	Pte.	Cummings, G.							1											Killed in action.
4589	,,	Cummings, A.						1	1											
2605	,,	Cunning, R.							1	1										
6533	Corpl.	Cunningham, T. D. (Sgt.)							1	1	1					1	1		Yes	
4024	Pte.	Cusick, O.	1	1	1	1	1		1							1	1		Yes	Home on demobn.
5912	,,	Cushley, J.							1	1	1					1	1		Yes	do. do.
6852	,,	Cuthbert, J.							1											Killed in action.
4089	,,	Dalrymple, W.	1	1				1	1											
3866	,,	Dalziel, J.	1					1	1	1	1					1	1		Yes	Home on demobn.
7047	,,	Dalziel, D.						1	1		1					1	1		Yes	
3586	,,	Dargie, W.							1	1	1									
4824	,,	Davidson, A.	1	1				1	1		1					1	1		Yes	Home on demobn.
7615	L.-Cpl.	Davidson, A.						1	1							1		1st Vol. S. Coy.		
9001	Pte.	Davidson, W.							1	1	1					1	1	2nd Vol. S. Coy.	No	Discharged Cape Town, May /02.
7103	,,	Davidson, J.							1							1	1		Yes	Home on demobn.
3685	,,	Davidson, J.	1	1				1	1		1					1	1		Yes	To 1st Blk. Watch.
7139	,,	Davidson, J.							1	1	1					1	1			

Regtl. No.	Rank.	Name.	Paardeberg.	Driefontein.	Johannesburg.	Diamond Hill.	Belfast.	Wittebergen.	Cape Colony.	Orange Free State.	Transvaal.	Tugela Heights.	Relief of Ladysmith.	Laing's Nek.	Natal.	S. Africa, 1901.	S. Africa, 1902.	On what Roll name submitted for Queen's S. A. Medal	If entitled to King's S. A. Medal.	Remarks.
4259	Pte.	Davidson, A.	1	1	1				1											
6911	,,	Davidson, D.							1	1	1					1	1		Yes	
8947	,,	Davidson, J. L.							1	1	1					1		1st Vol. S. Coy.		
6417	L.-Cpl.	Davidson, C.	1	1					1											Died of disease.
6887	Pte.	Davie, R.							1											
3035	,,	Davis, W. (Davies)							1	1	1					1	1	Home, time exp.	Yes	Home on demobn.
2966	,,	Day, R.							1	1	1					1	1		Yes	do. do.
6979	,,	Dean, J.	1	1				1	1		1					1				Home, invalided.
5942	Corpl.	Deans, R.							1											
4528	Drmr.	Dellow, F.	1	1	1	1	1		1							1	1		Yes	To 1st Blk. Watch.
4015	Pte.	Devaney, J.							1	1						1	1		Yes	Home on demobn.
6637	,,	Devlin, R.	1	1				1	1		1					1	1		Yes	
6672	Corpl.	Dewar, J. (Pte.)	1	1					1		1					1	1		Yes	
6971	Pte.	Dewar, J. G.	1	1					1								1			
3781	,,	Diack, J.							1											
9046	,,	Dick, T.							1	1	1					1	1	2nd Vol. S. Coy.	No	
4122	,,	Dick, R.	1	1					1		1					1	1		No	Home on demobn.
7702	,,	Dick, G.							1	1	1					1	1		Yes	Home, invalided.
4483	,,	Dickson, J.	1						1		1					1	1		Yes	Home on demobn.
8354	,,	Dickson, T.														1	1		Yes	No. 1973 1/K.R.R.C. 3/K.R.R.C.
2082	,,	Dickson, J.	1						1											Died of wounds.
4121	L.-Cpl.	Dickson, A. (Private)	1	1				1	1		1					1	1		Yes	Home on demobn.
3979	Pte.	Dilly, S.	1						1											
9008	,,	Dingwall, A.							1	1						1		1st Vol. S. Coy.		
3976	L.-Cpl.	Dobie, A. (Pte.)	1	1					1		1					1	1		Yes	Home on demobn.
5578	Pte.	Dobie, R.	1	1	1	1	1		1							1	1		Yes	do. do.
4317	Drmr.	Dobson, J. H. (Corpl.)	1	1				1	1		1					1	1		Yes	Home, Permanent Staff.
3579	Pte.	Dobson, T.	1					1	1											
6640	,,	Doble, H.						1	1											Died of wounds.
4091	Corpl.	Docherty, W.	1						1											
3000	Pte.	Docherty, J.							1	1	1					1	1		Yes	Home on demobn.
3368	.,	Docherty, F.							1	1	1					1	1		Yes	do. do.
7044	,,	Docherty, W.						1	1											Died of disease.
2519	,,	Doctor, J.						1	1							1				Home, time exp.
8939	Drmr.	Doig, D.							1	1	1					1	1	2nd Vol. S. Coy.	No	
4983	Pte.	Doolan, W.							1											
5063	,,	Dolan, M. (Bandsman)	1	1				1	1		1					1	1		Yes	Home on demobn.
4673	,,	Dolan, M.	1	1				1	1		1					1				Home, time exp.
7003	,,	Dolan, L.	1	1				1	1		1					1	1		Yes	
6797	,,	Donald, J.						1	1		1					1	1		Yes	Home, invalided.
7566	,,	Donaldson, Wm.						1	1							1	1	1st Vol. S. Coy.		No. 9146, Sgt. 3rd V. S. C.
8950	,,	Donaldson, R.							1	1	1					1	1	2nd Vol. S. Coy.	No	
7271	,,	Donaldson, G.							1	1						1	1		Yes	To 1st Blk. Watch.
7384	L.-Cpl.	Donaldson, J.							1	1						1	1		Yes	

Regtl. No.	Rank.	Name.	Paardeberg.	Driefontein.	Johannesburg.	Diamond Hill.	Belfast.	Wittebergen.	Cape Colony.	Orange Free State.	Transvaal.	Tugela Heights.	Relief of Ladysmith.	Laing's Nek.	Natal.	S. Africa, 1901.	S. Africa, 1902.	On what Roll name submitted for Queen's S. A. Medal.	If entitled to King's S. A. Medal.	Remarks.
4090	Pte.	Donnelly, J.						1	1		1					1	1		Yes	Home on demobn.
6092	Sgt.	Dooley, M. H.							1	1	1					1	1		Yes	To 1st Blk. Watch.
5546	Pte.	Dorans, N.[1]	1	1				1	1		1					1	1		Yes	Home, time exp.
6838	,,	Dorward, S.						1	1	1	1					1	1			
9058	,,	Dorward, W.						1	1	1	1					1	1	2nd Vol. S. Coy.	No	
7616	,,	Dorward, D.						1										1st Vol. S. Coy.		Died of disease. Died of epilepsy, Cape Town, 1/4/00.
4280	,,	Douglas, R.							1											Killed in action.
7232	,,	Douglas, R.						1	1		1					1	1		Yes	
4112	,,	Douglas, D.	1						1		1					1				Home on demobn.
7075	,,	Douglas, D.						1	1		1					1	1		Yes	Home, time exp.
6490	,,	Douglas, W.							1	1										
7148	L.-Cpl.	Douglas, J.						1	1		1					1	1		Yes	Discharged in S. Africa.
3159	Pte.	Dowling, W.						1	1							1	1		Yes	E/134 S.A.C.
7216	,,	Dowell, J. (Dowall)	1	1				1	1		1					1	1		Yes	Discharged in S. Africa.
4320	,,	Dow, A.	1	1					1											
3925	,,	Dow, A.							1	1	1					1	1		Yes	Home on demobn.
5567	,,	Dowling, N.D.J.	1	1				1	1		1					1	1	Home on demobn.	Yes	Home, invalided.
5469	,,	Downie, J.	1	1				1	1		1					1				Home, time exp.
7129	L.-Cpl.	Drummond, J. (Corpl.)						1	1		1					1	1		Yes	
4077	Pte.	Drummond, P.	1	1				1	1							1				Home, invalided.
4764	,,	Drylie, T.	1	1				1	1							1	1		Yes	Home on demobn.
7640	,,	Drysdale, J.							1	1						1		1st Vol. S. Coy.		
6751	,,	Drysdale, W.							1											Killed in action.
6760	,,	Dryburgh, G.	1						1											Killed in action.
3917	,,	Dudley, J.	1	1				1	1		1					1	1		Yes	Home on demobn.
8955	Corpl.	Duff, D.							1	1	1					1	1	2nd Vol. S. Coy.	No	
8999	Sgt.	Duff, J.							1	1	1					1	1	2nd Vol. S. Coy.	No	
7121	Pte.	Duff, A.	1	1				1	1		1					1	1		Yes	
3885	,,	Duff, T.							1											
6638	,,	Duffus, A.							1	1	1					1	1	Home, time exp.	Yes	Home on demobn.
3948	,,	Duncan, H.	1	1				1	1		1					1	1		Yes	do. do.
2858	,,	Duncan, J.						1	1							1	1		Yes	do. do.
7545	Corpl.	Duncan, J. M.						1	1							1		1st Vol. S. Coy.		
7567	Pte.	Duncan, J.						1	1							1		1st Vol. S. Coy.		
7544	,,	Duncan, J.						1	1							1		1st Vol. S. Coy.		
8935	,,	Duncan, J.(Sgt.)							1	1	1					1	1	2nd Vol. S. Coy.	No	
3595	,,	Duncan, A.							1	1	1					1	1	Home on demobn.	Yes	Home, invalided.
6976	L.-Cpl.	Duncan, R. (Corpl.)			1	1	1		1	1						1			Yes	do. do.
3512	Pte.	Dunlop, W.							1	1	1					1	1	Home on demobn.	Yes	do. do.
6662	,,	Dunlop, J.							1											
5191	Corpl.	Dunn, R.	1	1				1	1											B/784 S.A.C.
3569	Pte.	Dunnigan, J.							1	1										
251	Sgt.	Durward, J.	1	1	1	1			1											
7265	Pte.	Durie, J.							1	1	1					1	1		Yes	Home, invalided.

[1] No. 5346 in King's Medal Roll.

Regtl. No.	Rank.	Name.	Paardeberg.	Driefontein.	Johannesburg.	Diamond Hill.	Belfast.	Wittebergen.	Cape Colony.	Orange Free State.	Transvaal.	Tugela Heights.	Relief of Ladysmith.	Laing's Nek.	Natal.	S. Africa, 1901.	S. Africa, 1902.	On what Roll name submitted for Queen's S. A. Medal.	If entitled to King's S. A. Medal.	Remarks.
2759	Pte.	Dye, C.							1	1	1					1	1		Yes	Home on demobn.
4468	,,	Dye, J.							1	1	1					1	1		Yes	
8960	,,	Easson, J. F.							1	1	1					1	1	2nd Vol. S. Coy.	No	
4373	,,	East, J.							1											
7468	,,	Edwards, D.							1	1	1					1	1		Yes	
8928	,,	Edwards, A.							1	1	1					1		1st Vol. S. Coy.		
7617	,,	Edwards, D.						1	1							1		1st Vol. S. Coy.		
7618	L.-Cpl.	Edwards, R. W. (Pte.)						1	1							1		1st Vol. S. Coy.		Dischd. in consequence of obtaining employment in S. A. 26/4/01.
3728	Pte.	Edwards, J.							1	1	1					1				Home, time exp.
4776	,,	Egan, H.							1											
7206	,,	Elder, J. (Lc.-Corpl.)							1	1	1					1	1		Yes	
2568	,,	Elder, W.							1	1						1	1		Yes	Home, time exp.
6540	,,	Elliot, J.	1	1				1	1											
4184	,,	Elliot, J.	1	1				1	1		1					1	1		Yes	Home on demobn.
7106	,,	Ellis, G.						1	1		1					1	1	Not entitled.	Yes	Tried by F.G.C.M. 29/12/01. Sentenced two years penal servitude.
4298	,,	Ellis, T.	1	1				1	1		1					1	1		Yes	Home on demobn.
3658	,,	Ellis, A.							1	1										
2215	Drum-Major	England, A. W.	1	1				1	1		1					1	1		Yes	To P.S. 3rd Black Watch.
4682	Pte.	English, E.	1	1					1		1					1	1	Home on demobn.	Yes	Home, invalided.
463	,,	Erroll, W.	1	1					1											
6473	,,	Erskine, A.							1	1	1									
7514	,,	Erskine, R.						1	1		1					1	1		Yes	Home on demobn.
7597	,,	Erskine, W.						1	1							1		1st Vol. S. Coy.		
7598	,,	Emslie, J. W.						1	1							1		1st Vol. S. Coy.		
4078	,,	Evans, S.	1	1				1	1		1					1	1		Yes	Home on demobn.
6698	,,	Evans, J.	1	1				1	1											
4279	,,	Evens, H.[1]						1	1		1					1	1		Yes	Home on demobn.
6737	,,	Evens, D.							1											
5197	,,	Ewan, A.	1	1				1	1		1					1	1		Yes	Home on demobn.
4136	,,	Fagan, J.							1	1										
3619	L.-Cpl.	Faichney, J.	1						1											
4699	Pte.	Fairbairn, T. G.	1						1		1					1	1		Yes	Home on demobn.
5169	,,	Fairley, F.							1											
4685	,,	Fairley, J.							1	1	1					1	1		Yes	Home on demobn.
7006	,,	Fairley, G.						1	1		1					1	1		Yes	
5429	,,	Fairley, R. (Fairlie)	1	1				1	1		1					1	1	Home, time exp.	Yes	To 1st Blk. Watch.
6291	,,	Fairweather, A.	1		1	1	1		1		1					1	1		Yes	To 1st Blk. Watch.
7619	,,	Falconer, J.						1	1							1		1st Vol. S. Coy.		
7301	,,	Falconer, W.							1	1	1					1	1		Yes	Home, invalided.
4231	,,	Fanning, P.	1	1					1	1	1					1	1		Yes	Home on demobn.
6715	,,	Farmer, G.	1	1				1	1		1					1	1	No Medal.	Yes	Deserted.
7188	,,	Farrell, T.						1	1		1					1	1		Yes	To 1st Blk. Watch.

[1] 'Evans' in Supplementary Roll.

Regtl. No.	Rank.	Name.	Paardeberg.	Driefontein.	Johannesburg.	Diamond Hill.	Belfast.	Wittebergen.	Cape Colony.	Orange Free State.	Transvaal.	Tugela Heights.	Relief of Ladysmith.	Laing's Nek.	Natal.	S. Africa, 1901.	S. Africa, 1902.	On what Roll name submitted for Queen's S. A. Medal.	If entitled to King's S. A. Medal.	Remarks.
6601	Pte.	Farquhar, W.	1	1				1	1		1					1				Died of disease.
7198	,,	Farrell, J.	1	1				1												
5548	,,	Farrell, J.			1	1	1		1	1						1	1		Yes	Home on demobn.
1526	,,	Farrell, T.						1	1							1				Invalided.
2626	,,	Farrell, W.							1	1									Yes	Home on demobn.
5016	,,	Fenwick, W.	1	1					1		1					1	1		Yes	do. do.
4179	,,	Fenwick, A.	1	1				1	1		1					1	1			
7587	,,	Ferguson, D.							1	1						1		1st Vol. S. Coy.		
8968	,,	Ferguson, J. (Corpl.)							1	1	1					1		1st Vol. S. Coy.		
7546	,,	Ferguson, T.							1	1						1		1st Vol. S. Coy.		
8974	,,	Ferguson, D.							1	1	1					1	1	2nd Vol. S. Coy.	No	
5620	,,	Ferguson, J.	1	1					1	1	1					1	1	Home on demobn.	Yes	Home, time exp.
7529	,,	Ferguson, T.							1	1	1					1	1		Yes	Home, invalided.
6596	L.-Cpl.	Ferguson, M. (Private)	1	1					1	1	1					1	1		Yes	do. do.
983	Pte.	Ferguson, A.	1	1					1	1	1					1	1		Yes	Home on demobn.
3273	,,	Ferguson, G.[1]							1	1	1					1	1		Yes	do. do.
3767	,,	Ferguson, D.							1											
5224	,,	Ferguson, W.							1	1						1				Home, time exp.
1812	,,	Ferguson, W.							1	1						1				Home on demobn.
2606	,,	Fergus, A.						1	1		1					1	1	Home on demobn.	Yes	Home, time exp.
7334	,,	Fernie, D.							1	1						1				Home on demobn.
6755	,,	Ferris, W.							1	1										
3711	,,	Ferry, A.							1											
4404	,,	Ferry, F.							1	1	1					1	1		Yes	Home on demobn.
5983	,,	Finch, E.	1						1	1	1					1	1		Yes	Home, invalided.
4293	L.-Sgt.	Finch, F. (Sergt.)	1	1	1	1	1		1							1	1		Yes	
7435	Pte.	Findlay, N. J.							1	1	1					1	1		Yes	
5795	Piper	Finnie, W. (Pte.)	1	1					1	1						1	1		Yes	To A. Reserve in S. Africa.
3802	Pte.	Fisher, A.	1	1					1	1	1					1				Home on demobn.
7179	,,	Fisher, A.							1	1	1						1		Yes	To 1st Blk. Watch.
5271	,,	Fitzpatrick, T.							1	1	1					1	1		Yes	Home on demobn.
7324	,,	Fitzsimmons, N.							1	1	1					1	1		Yes	Home, invalided.
2467	,,	Flannigan, J.						1	1							1				Home on demobn.
4531	Sgt.	Fleming, G.							1							1	1		Yes	
8931	Pte.	Fleming, N. W.							1	1	1					1	1	2nd Vol. S. Coy.	No	
3041	,,	Fletcher, J.							1	1	1						1			Home on demobn.
6197	,,	Flett, W.	1	1					1											
7568	,,	Florence, D.						1	1							1		1st Vol. S. Coy.		
5730	,,	Flynn, P.							1	1										
7177	,,	Forbes, W.							1											
5083	L.-Cpl.	Forbes, J. A.	1						1	1	1					1	1		Yes	Home on demobn.
4058	Pte.	Forbes, J.	1	Yes					1		1					1	1		Yes	do. do.
7620	,,	Forbes, G.							1							1		1st Vol. S. Coy.		
7621	,,	Forbes, W.							1	1								1st Vol. S. Coy.		
3033	,,	Folan, C.							1	1	1					1	1		Yes	Home on demobn.
6746	L.-Cpl.	Folan, J. (Corpl.)	1	1				1	1	1						1	1		Yes	B/782 S.A.C.
4379	Pte.	Foley, J.	1	1	1	1	1	1	1							1	1			Home on demobn.

1 No. 5273 in King's Medal Roll.

Regtl. No.	Rank.	Name.	Paardeberg.	Driefontein.	Johannesburg.	Diamond Hill.	Belfast.	Wittebergen.	Cape Colony.	Orange Free State.	Transvaal.	Tugela Heights.	Relief of Ladysmith.	Laing's Nek.	Natal.	S. Africa, 1901.	S. Africa, 1902.	On what Roll name submitted for Queen's S. A. Medal.	If entitled to King's S. A. Medal.	Remarks.
6550	L.-Cpl.	Foote, G. (Pte.)	1	1	1	1	1		1							1	1		Yes	To Regtl. Depot.
6219	Sgt.	Ford, T.	1	1				1	1		1					1	1		Yes	
4138	Pte.	Ford, M.						1	1		1					1	1		Yes	Home on demobn.
5428	,,	Forrester, J.							1	1	1					1	1		Yes	Home on demobn.
556	,,	Forrester, T.	1	1					1		1					1	1		Yes	do. do.
7087	,,	Forrester, J.	Yes	Yes					1											
6745	L.-Cpl.	Forret, W. (Cpl.)	1						1							1	1		Yes	
7209	Pte.	Fowler, R.	1	1				1	1		1					1	1		Yes	
7656	,,	Fox, J.							1	1	1					1	1		No	Home, invalided.
2873	,,	Fox, J.							1	1						1				do. do.
4377	,,	Fox, C.							1											Killed in action.
6888	,,	Fox, J.							1											Died of wounds.
4546	,,	Frampton, C.	1	1				1	1		1					1	1		Yes	
7596	,,	Fraser, D.						1	1									1st Vol. S. Coy.		Invalided 1900.
7547	,,	Fraser, D.						1	1							1		1st Vol. S. Coy.		
7590	,,	Fraser, W.						1	1							1		1st Vol. S. Coy.		
4087	Corpl.	Fraser, A. (Pte.)	1	1				1	1		1					1	1	Home, invalided.	Yes	To Regtl. Depot.
7650	Pte.	Fraser, A.							1	1	1[1]						1[1]	1[1]			Changed name to Patterson. See A. G. N/M/10854, additional Clasp Roll.
6471	,,	Fraser, J. (O.R. Sgt.)							1	1	1					1	1		Yes	
7047	,,	Fraser, H.	1	1					1		1					1	1		Yes	Home on demobn.
4470	,,	Fraser, R.	1	1				1	1		1					1	1		Yes	do. do.
6457	,,	Fraser, J.	1	1					1		1					1	1		Yes	Home, invalided.
4042	Sgt.	Fraser, W.	1	1	1	1	1		1							1	1		Yes	Home on demobn.
7242	L.-Cpl.	Fraser, D. (Cpl.)					1		1	1						1	1		Yes	
6628	,,	Fraser, A.							1											Killed in action.
6863	Pte.	Fraser, C.	1	1				1	1							1				Home, invalided.
4437	,,	Freckleton, J.							1	1	1					1	1		Yes	To A. Reserve in S. Africa.
4100	,,	French, W.							1											
3795	L.-Cpl.	Fulcher, C.	1	1					1											
4718	Corpl.	Furlong, J. (Private; Sergt.)	1	1					1		1					1	1	Home on demobn.	Yes	Home, invalided.
3443	Pte.	Fyfe, W.			1	1	1		1	1						1	1		Yes	Home on demobn.
3984	,,	Fyfe, J.							1	1										
2916	,,	Gallacher, P.							1	1	1					1	1		Yes	Home on demobn.
2914	,,	Gallacher, T. (Gallagher)						1	1		1					1	1	Home on demobn.	Yes	Home, invalided.
7034	,,	Gallacher, H. (Gallagher), (Lc.-Corpl.)						1	1		1					1	1		Yes	do. do.
4668	,,	Galloway, T.							1	1	1					1	1		Yes	Home on demobn.
4474	,,	Galloway, J.	1						1	1						1	1	Home on demobn.	Yes	Home, invalided.
4209	,,	Gardiner, W.							1											Killed in action.
4038	,,	Gagan, P.							1	1										Died of disease.
7145	,,	Garland, J.						1	1		1					1	1	No Medal. Re-issued 7/2/07.	Yes	Deserted.
5102	,,	Garland, J.						1	1		1					1	1		Yes	Home on demobn.

[1] These entries are under the name of No. 7650, Patterson, A., in both 2nd Bn. King's and Supplementary Medal Rolls.

Regtl. No.	Rank.	Name.	Paardeberg.	Driefontein.	Johannesburg.	Diamond Hill.	Belfast.	Wittebergen.	Cape Colony.	Orange Free State.	Transvaal.	Tugela Heights.	Relief of Ladysmith.	Laing's Nek.	Natal.	S. Africa, 1901.	S. Africa, 1902.	On what Roll name submitted for Queen's S. A. Medal.	If entitled to King's S. A. Medal.	Remarks.
6926	L.-Cpl.	Garvie, W.	1	1				1	1		1					1	1		Yes	Home, invalided.
7176	Pte.	Garvie, J.	1						1		1					1	1		Yes	
4662	„	Gavigan, H.							1							1				Home, invalided.
3825	„	Gavin, P.							1	1	1					1				Home, time exp.
2031	L.-Sgt.	Gaynor, G.	1						1									Presentation.		See D. C. M. Roll.
3894	Pte.	Geekie, J.							1	1										
8 7558	Sgt.	Gegan, J.						1	1							1		1st Vol. S. Coy.		
4267	Pte.	Gibbs, G.							1											Killed in action.
6816	„	Gibson, J.							1											Killed in action.
9067	„	Gibson, A.							1	1	1					1	1	2nd Vol. S. Coy.	No	
9003	„	Gibson, D.							1	1	1					1	1	2nd Vol. S. Coy.	No	
3790	L.-Cpl.	Gill, W.	1	1				1	1											
4059	Pte.	Gill, W.	1	1					1											
7132	„	Gillan, T.							1	1	1					1	1		Yes	
6421	L.-Cpl.	Gillies, W. A. (Corpl.)	1	1				1	1							1	1		Yes	Discharged in S. Africa.[1]
7739	Pte.	Gillies, P.							1	1	1					1	1		Yes	Home on demobn.
7459	„	Gillies, J.							1	1										
2705	„	Gilkinson, S.						1	1											
2251	„	Gillespie, A.							1	1	1					1	1	Home, time exp.	Yes	Home on demobn.
2648	„	Gilroy, A.						1	1		1					1	1		Yes	
7166	„	Glass, A.						1	1		1					1	1		Yes	Discharged in S. Africa.
8963	Corpl.	Glass, D.							1	1	1					1	1	2nd Vol. S. Coy.	No	
4548	Pte.	Glasgow, G.	1	1					1		1					1	1		Yes	Home on demobn.
7433	„	Glen, R.							1	1	1					1	1		Yes	
4148	„	Goddard, S.	1						1											
5749	„	Godfrey, D. (Corpl.)							1	1	1					1	1		Yes	Home on demobn.
4365	Sgt.	Godfrey, T.							1											Killed in action.
2325	Pte.	Golbie, J.						1	1		1									Home, time exp.
2 4053	„	Golden, J.	1	1					1	1						1	1		Yes	Home on demobn.
7223	„	Goldie, T.[2]							1	1	1					1	1		Yes	Home, invalided.
3113	Sgt.-Cook	Goldie, R. L.							1											
6791	Pte.	Gordon, F. N. (Drumr.)	1	1					1	1	1					1	1		Yes	
5357	„	Gordon, A.	1	1					1	1	1					1	1		No	Home on demobn.
7150	„	Gordon, J.	1	1					1	1							1			
4351	„	Gorman, W.			1	1	1		1	1						1	1		Yes	Home on demobn.
7531	„	Gorman, P.							1	1	1					1	1		Yes	To 1st Blk. Watch.
2353	„	Goodwin, D.						1	1											
7340	„	Gossling, E. E.						1	1		1					1	1		Yes	Discharged in S. Africa.
6552	„	Goulding, W.							1											
2497	„	Gourlay, J.							1	1	1					1	1	Home, time exp.	Yes	Home on demobn.
7536	„	Gourley, W.							1	1	1					1	1		Yes	Discharged in S. Africa.
2764	„	Gow, D.							1	1						1	1		Yes	Deceased.

[1] In 2nd Bn. Supplementary Roll: 'Dischd. in S. A. by purchase.'—J. S.
[2] No. 7123 in Supplementary Roll.

Regtl. No.	Rank.	Name.	Paardeberg.	Driefontein.	Johannesburg.	Diamond Hill.	Belfast.	Wittebergen.	Cape Colony.	Orange Free State.	Transvaal.	Tugela Heights.	Relief of Ladysmith.	Laing's Nek.	Natal.	S. Africa, 1901.	S. Africa, 1902.	On what Roll name submitted for Queen's S. A. Medal.	If entitled to King's S. A. Medal.	Remarks.
7361	Pte.	Gow, W. *Issue authd. 18/4/06. Restored under para. 2041 K. R. A. G. 2/M/15878.*							1	1						1	1	Q. M. C. O. and T. K. M. '01 and '02. Issd. 26/4/06. A.G. 2/M/15878.	Yes	Forfeited C.M. Sect. 18 A.A. 68/42/770.
7028 3531	L.-Cpl.	Gow. A.	1	1				1	1		1					1	1		Yes	Home, invalided.
3135	Pte.	Gow, F.			1				1	1						1	1		Yes	Home on demobn.
6877	,,	Gow, J.			1	1	1		1	1						1				Home, invalided.
3604	,,	Gowrie, T.							1											Killed in action.
3600	,,	Graham, W.							1											
3363	,,	Graham, A.						1	1		1					1	1		Yes	Home on demobn.
4898	,,	Graham, F.	1					1	1		1					1	1		Yes	do. do.
2618	,,	Graham, W.			1	1	1	1	1	1						1	1		Yes	Home, time exp.
4382	,,	Granger, J. (Grainger)	1	1				1	1		1					1	1		Yes	Dischd. on termn. of engagement.
6498	Corpl.	Grant, D. (Sgt.)	1	1				1	1		1					1	1		Yes	
4057 5	Pte.	Grant, J.	1	1					1		1					1	1	Home, time exp.	Yes	Home on demobn.
6372 2	,,	Grant, D.							1	1	1					1	1		Yes	To 1st Blk. Watch.
2123	,,	Grant, J.							1	1										Died of disease.
4081	,,	Grant, J.							1											Killed in action.
7266	,,	Grant, J.							1	1	1					1	1		Yes	
6529	,,	Grant, J. (L.-Cpl.)	1	1					1		1					1	1		Yes	To 1st Blk. Watch.
6889	,,	Grant, W.	1	1				1	1		1					1	1			
7071	,,	Grant, J.							1	1	1					1	1		Yes	To 1st Blk. Watch.
4465	,,	Grant, J.	1	1	1	1	1		1							1				Home on demobn.
6776	,,	Gray, W. (L.-Cpl.)	1	1				1	1		1					1	1		Yes	
2105	,,	Gray, J.							1	1										
7569	,,	Gray, J.						1	1							1		1st Vol. S. Coy.		
2748	,,	Gray, J.							1	1	1					1	1		Yes	Home, time exp.
3483	C.-Sgt.	Gray, A. J.							1	1	1					1	1		Yes	
7017	Pte.	Gray, J.							1	1	1					1	1		Yes	
3557	,,	Gray, R.							1											Killed in action. E/278 S.A.C.
6477	,,	Grey, H.	1	1					1		1									
2969	,,	Green, D.						1	1		1					1	1		Yes	Home on demobn.
5325	,,	Green, W. J.	1	1				1	1		1					1	1		Yes	do. do.
6951	,,	Greig, A.							1	1	1					1				Died of wounds received accidentally.
7570	,,	Greig, A.						1	1							1		1st Vol. S. Coy.		
3618	,,	Greive, A.	1						1											
4535	,,	Greive, T.	1	1					1											
3020	,,	Grelicke, E. (Grelick)						1	1		1					1	1	Home, time exp.	Yes	Home on demobn.
7117	,,	Grannon, J.	1	1				1	1		1					1	1		Yes	
3941	,,	Grewar, A.							1	1						1				Home, invalided.
4422	Sgt.	Grinstead, E.	1						1							1	1		Yes	Discharged in S. Africa.
7658	Pte.	Grubb, P. F.						1	1							1		1st Vol. S. Coy.		
4159	,,	Grundy, L.							1							1	1			
4904	L.-Sgt.	Gurney, A.							1	1	1					1	1		Yes	Home on demobn.

Regtl. No.	Rank.	Name.	Paardeberg.	Driefontein.	Johannesburg.	Diamond Hill.	Belfast.	Wittebergen.	Cape Colony.	Orange Free State.	Transvaal.	Tugela Heights.	Relief of Ladysmith.	Laing's Nek.	Natal.	S. Africa, 1901.	S. Africa, 1902.	On what Roll name submitted for Queen's S. A. Medal.	If entitled to King's S. A. Medal.	Remarks.
2845	Pte.	Guthrie, W.						1	1		1					1	1		Yes	Home on demobn.
6200	,,	Guthrie, R.						1	1		1					1	1		Yes	To 1st Blk. Watch.
6910	,,	Guthrie, P.							1	1										
7673 0	,,	Guthrie, A.						1	1	1						1	1		Yes	Home, invalided.
3479	,,	Hacker, W. (Bandsman)	1	1				1	1		1					1	1		Yes	do. do.
3564	,,	Hackney, J.	1	1				1	1											
4035	,,	Haddow, W.	1	1					1											
4686	,,	Hain, A.							1	1	1					1	1		Yes	Home on demobn.
2644	L.-Cpl.	Halkett, R.							1	1										Killed in action.
4748	Sgt. O.R.C.	Hall, A. (C.-Sgt.)	1	1				1	1		1					1	1		Yes	
5110	Sgt.	Hall, E. (C.-Sgt.)	1	1					1		1					1	1		Yes	
7105	Pte.	Hall, J.							1	1	1					1				Deceased.
3723 32	Sgt.	Hamilton, A. (Private ?)							1							1	1	22nd M.I.		
2417	Corpl.	Hamilton, R.						1	1							1				Home, time exp.
3054	Pte.	Hamilton, H.							1	1										
5026	,,	Hamilton, A.	1	1	1	1	1		1							1	1		Yes	Home on demobn.
5761	,,	Hamilton, D.							1	1	1					1	1		Yes	do. do.
4155	,,	Hammond, W.	1	1					1											
7585	,,	Hampton, J.						1	1							1		1st Vol. S. Coy.		
2646	,,	Hannah, J.							1	1	1					1	1		Yes	Home, time exp.
6673	,,	Hannan, A. (Lc.-Corpl.)	1	1					1	1	1					1	1		Yes	
7659	,,	Harcus, J.						1	1							1		1st Vol. S. Coy.		
4454	,,	Hardy, H. (Bandsman)	1	1					1	1	1					1	1		Yes	Discharged in S. Africa.
4462 4 2	,,	Hardie, J.	1	1					1	1	1					1	1		Yes	Home on demobn.
3969	,,	Hardie, J.							1											Killed in action.
2305	L.-Cpl.	Hardie, E.						1	1											
6665	Drmr.	Harding, W.	1	1					1											
6033	Pte.	Harding, J.							1	1	Yes									
6977	,,	Harkins, J.	1	1					1											
4295	,,	Harling, C.	1	1	1	1	1		1							1	1		Yes	Home on demobn.
8989	,,	Harrier, J.							1	1	1					1	1	2nd Vol. S. Coy.	No	
3638	,,	Harris, A.							1	1										
7571	,,	Harris, H.						1	1							1		1st Vol. S. Coy.		
6921	,,	Harris, H.						1	1		1					1	1		Yes	
6928	,,	Harris, J.							1											Killed in action.
6949	,,	Harris, R. R. J.	1	1				1	1		1					1	1		Yes	
4245	,,	Harris, W. G.	1	1					1											
3746	Sgt.	Harrison, H.	1	1				1	1		1					1	1		Yes	Deceased. See D.C.M. Roll.
7174	Pte.	Harrison, F.							1	1	1					1	1		Yes	Home, invalided.
3857	,,	Harrow, G.							1											
2915	,,	Hart, R. J.	1	1				1	1		1					1	1		Yes	Home, time exp.

Regtl. No.	Rank.	Name.	Paardeberg.	Driefontein.	Johannesburg.	Diamond Hill.	Belfast.	Wittebergen.	Cape Colony.	Orange Free State.	Transvaal.	Tugela Heights.	Relief of Ladysmith.	Laing's Nek.	Natal.	S. Africa, 1901.	S. Africa, 1902.	On what Roll name submitted for Queen's S. A. Medal.	If entitled to King's S. A. Medal.	Remarks.
6981	Pte.	Harvey, R.	1	1				1	1		1					1	1		Yes	Home, time exp.
7310	,,	Hassell, F.							1	1	1									
117	Actg. Armr.-Sergt.	Hastie, J. (Private)	1	1				1	1		1					1	1	Home, time exp. Home on demobn.	Yes	Promd. Actg. Armr.-Sgt., June 1900, and carried out duties till January 1901, when he reverted to Private. See D.C.M. Roll.
5373	Drmr.	Hastie, J.	1	1				1											
3978	Pte.	Hay, J.						1											
2738	,,	Hay, D.						1	1		1					1	1	Home on demobn.	Yes	Home, time exp.
3210	,,	Hay, G.							1	1	1					1	1		Yes	Home on demobn.
7389	L.-Cpl.	Hay, W.							1	1	Yes					1	1		Yes	Now No. 5022 in 16th Lancers.
4521	Pte.	Hay, R.	1	1				1	1		1					1	1		Yes	Home on demobn.
7112	,,	Hay, G.	1	1				1	1		1					1	1		Yes	
2586	,,	Hayden, M.						1	1		1					1	1		Yes	Home on demobn.
3285	,,	Hetherington, A. (Heatherington)							1	1	1					1	1		Yes	do. do.
6750	,,	Heathers, B.	1	1				1	1		1					1	1		Yes	
4325	,,	Hedley, A.	1					1												Yes	
3957	,,	Heenan, J.	1	1				1	1		1					1	1		Yes	Home on demobn.
7127	,,	Henderson, J.W.						1	1		1					1	1		Yes	
6774	,,	Henderson, D.						1													Died of disease.
3786	Sgt.	Henderson, S.	1	1				1	1		1					1				Home, time exp.
9068	Pte.	Henderson, W.L.							1	1	1					1	1	2nd Vol. S. Coy.	No	
4934	,,	Henderson, J.						1	1		1					1	1		Yes	Home on demobn.
5867	,,	Henderson, J.[1]							1	1	1									
7039	,,	Henderson, J.	1	1				1												Died of disease.
6486	,,	Henry, D. (Hendry)						1	1		1					1	1		Yes	To 1st Blk. Watch.
6860	,,	Hendry, J.						Yes	1		1					1	1		Yes	
4409	,,	Herbert, C.							1	1	1					1	1		Yes	Home on demobn.
7317	,,	Henley, G.							1		1					1	1		Yes	To 1st Blk. Watch.
7348	,,	Herschell, A.							1	1	1					1	1		Yes	Home, invalided.
7425	,,	Herschell, D.						1	1		1					1	1		Yes	Discharged in S. Africa.
3955	,,	Herschell, W.						1													
2591	,,	Herd, G.[2]	1	1				1	1							1				Home on demobn.
4693	,,	Herd, T. H.	1	1				1	1		1					1	1	Home on demobn.	Yes	Home, invalided.
7612	Sgt.	Hewison, G. W.							1	1	1*							1st Vol. S. Coy.		*Issd. authd. on A.G. 2/M/2746 6th Bn. I.Y.
3953	Pte.	Heylands, H.	1					1												
7224	,,	Hickie, J.	1					1												Killed in action.
7084	,,	High, D.						1												Killed in action.
9024	,,	High, E. S.							1	1	1				1			1st Vol. S. Coy.		
5277	,,	Hill, D.						1												Killed in action,
5537	,,	Hill, J.	1	1				1			1					1	1		Yes	Home on demobn.
3594	,,	Hill, D.	1	1	1	1	1	1												

[1] In 2nd Bn. King's Medal Roll is an entry of 5867, Piper J. Hogg, as being entitled to that medal and clasps for 1901-02 with the same number as Henderson. There is no man of the name of Hogg in the 2nd. Bn. Queen's Medal Roll. Hogg is shown as transferred to 1st Black Watch in King's Medal Roll.
[2] No. 5291 in King's Medal Roll.

Regtl. No.	Rank.	Name.	Paardeberg.	Driefontein.	Johannesburg.	Diamond Hill.	Belfast.	Wittebergen.	Cape Colony.	Orange Free State.	Transvaal.	Tugela Heights.	Relief of Ladysmith.	Laing's Nek.	Natal.	S. Africa, 1901.	S. Africa, 1902.	On what Roll name submitted for Queen's S. A. Medal.	If entitled to King's S. A. Medal.	Remarks.
3024	Pte.	Hill, M.							1	1	1					1	1		Yes	Home on demobn.
7119	,,	Hilson, A.							1	1	1					1	1		Yes	
4616	,,	Higgins, W.						1	1		1					1	1		Yes	Home on demobn.
2761	,,	Hindle, H.						1	1		1					1	1		Yes	do. do.
7083	L.-Cpl.	Hobbs, E. (Cpl.)							1	1	1					1	1		Yes	
4287	Pte.	Hobson, J.	1						1										Yes	Home, invalided.
7104	,,	Hogan, J.	1	1					1								1			Killed in action.
6652	,,	Holden, H.							1										Yes	Home on demobn.
4144	,,	Holland, H.	1	1				1	1		1					1	1		Yes	Home on demobn.
8976	,,	Hood, D.							1	1	1					1	1	2nd Vol. S. Coy.	No	
7138	,,	Hopkins, W.							1	1	1					1			Yes	Home, invalided.
4441	Sgt.	Hopkinson, W.							1											
4307	Pte.	Horner, F. J.	1	1				1	1		1					1	1		Yes	Home on demobn.
7583	L.-Sgt.	Hounan, J.						1	1							1		1st Vol. S. Coy.		
7052	Pte.	Houston, D.							1	1	1					1	1		Yes	Home, time exp.
1313	Pionr.-Sgt.	Howden, T.	1	1				1	1		1					1	1		Yes	To 1st Blk. Watch. See D.C.M. Roll.
3208	Pte.	Howden, A.	1	1				1	1		1					1	1		Yes	Home on demobn.
4135	,,	Howe, J.	1	1					1		1					1	1		Yes	do. do.
7278	,,	Howie, R.							1	1	1					1	1		Yes	Deceased.
4333	,,	Hoxley, W. (Sgt.)							1	1						1	1		Yes	To 1st Blk. Watch.
4217	,,	Huggett, T. A.	1						1										Yes	Home, time exp.
7076	,,	Hughes, F.							1	1	1					1	1		Yes	
6872	,,	Hughes, J.	1	1					1		1					1	1		Yes	
2791	,,	Hume, D.						1	1		1					1	1		Yes	Home on demobn.
4417	L.-Sgt.	Humphries, J. (Sgt.)	1	1				1	1		1					1	1	Home, time exp.	Yes	do. do.
7328	Pte.	Humphries, F.							1	1	1					1	1		Yes	Deceased.
3757	,,	Hunter, J.	1	1				1	1							1				Home, time exp.
6560	,,	Hunter, R. (Corpl.)	1	1				1	1		1					1	1		Yes	Discharged in S. Africa.
6868	,,	Hunter, R.	1	1				1	1		1					1	1		Yes	
1157	,,	Huntingdon, G.							1							1				Killed in action.
2213	,,	Hutchison, J.						1	1							1				Home, time exp.
7615	,,	Hutchison, J.	1	1				1	1		Yes					1	1		Yes	Home on demobn.
2465	,,	Hutchison, D.			1	1	1		1	1	1					1				Home, time exp.
7056	,,	Hutchesson, C. le M.							1	1	1					1	1		Yes	Discharged in S. Africa.
2367	,,	Hussey, P.			1	1	1		1	1						1				Home, time exp.
7191	,,	Husband, D.							1	1	1					1	1		Yes	To 1st Blk. Watch.
6762	,,	Hutchison, J.	1	1				1	1							1	1		Yes	
4637	,,	Hutton, J.							1	1	1					1	1		Yes	Home on demobn.
3666	,,	Hutton, G.	1	1				1	1										Yes	
7189	Corpl.	Hutton, T. (Sgt.-Drummer)	1	1				1	1		1					1	1		Yes	
7497	L.-Cpl.	Honeyman, T. (Corpl.)							1	1	1					1	1		Yes	
6643	Pte.	Hynd, A.	1						1							1	1		Yes	Home on demobn.
4213	,,	Hyslop, D.	1	1				1	1							1	1		Yes	do. do.
6395	,,	Imrie, J.							1	1	1					1	1		Yes	

Regtl. No.	Rank.	Name.	Paardeberg.	Driefontein.	Johannesburg.	Diamond Hill.	Belfast.	Wittebergen.	Cape Colony.	Orange Free State.	Transvaal.	Tugela Heights.	Relief of Ladysmith.	Laing's Nek.	Natal.	S. Africa, 1901.	S. Africa, 1902.	On what Roll name submitted for Queen's S. A. Medal.	If entitled to King's S. A. Medal.	Remarks.
4543	Pte.	Imrie, D.						1	1		1					1	1		Yes	Home on demobn.
6581	,,	Inches, A.							1											
6934	,,	Ingham, J.	1	1				1	1		1					1	1		Yes	Discharged in S. Africa.
7660	,,	Inglis, J.							1	1						1		1st Vol. S. Coy.		Home, invalided.
7336	,,	Inglis, A.							1	1	1					1	1	Forfeited. Deleted A.G. 2/M/13865.	Yes	do. do.
4169	,,	Inglis, W.							1							1	1			
3316	,,	Inglis, W.							1	1	1					1	1		Yes	Home on demobn.
6961	,,	Irvine, W.	1	1							1					1	1		Yes	
4599	,,	Irvine, J.	1	1				1	1		1					1	1		Yes	Home on demobn.
3412	,,	Irons, P.	1						1											
7240	,,	Izatt, J.							1	1	1					1	1		Yes	
7572	,,	Jack, J.						1	1							1		1st Vol. S. Coy.		
3202 97	,,	Jack, J.							1	1										Died of disease.
6796 79	,,	Jackson, W.						1	1		1					1	1		Yes	Home on demobn.
4269	,,	Jackson, E.	1		1	1	1		1							1	1		Yes	do. do.
2159	,,	Jackson, R.							1	1	1					1	1	Home on demobn.	Yes	Home, time exp.
4972	,,	Jackson, S.	1						1								Yes			
4043	,,	James, C.							1											Killed in action.
4133	Sgt.	Jenkins, W.							1							1				Home, invalided.
3573	,,	Jennings, J.							1											
6521	Pte.	Jepson, C.	1	1					1		1									
6116	Corpl.	Jess, A.							1											Killed in action.
3914	Pte.	Johnstone, J.	1	1				1	1											
7331	,,	Johnstone, M.							1	1	1					1	1		Yes	
6694	,,	Johnston, D.						1	1		1					1	1		Yes	Home on demobn.
7622	,,	Johnston, A.						1	1							1		1st Vol. S. Coy.		
6418	Corpl.	Johnston, R. J. R. J. (Sgt.)							1	1	1					1			Yes	To 1st Blk. Watch.
5704	Pte.	Johnston, J.	1					1	1		1					1	1	Home, time exp.	Yes	Home on demobn.
3960 74	,,	Johnston, T.	1	1				1	1		1					1	1	do. do.	Yes	do. do.
7196	,,	Jolly, J.							1	1	1					1	1		Yes	
3736	,,	Jolly, D.	1	1					1											
6917	,,	Jones, G.							1	1	1					1	1			
6892	Corpl.	Jones, T. (L.-Sgt.)	1	1				1	1		1					1	1		Yes	
3160	Pte.	Joyce, W.						1	1		1					1	1		Yes	Home on demobn.
4195	,,	Judd, G. (L.-Cpl.)	1	1				1	1		1					1	1	Home, time exp.	Yes	do. do.
6793	,,	Keddie, W.							1											Killed in action.
6725	,,	Keith, J. L.	1	1				1	1		1					1	1		Yes	Discharged in S. Africa.
6830	,,	Keith, J. (Piper)	1	1					1		1						1			
4256	,,	Keith, J.	1	1	1				1							1				Home, invalided.
7219	,,	Keith, R.							1	1						1				
6792	L.-Cpl.	Keith, A.							1											
6782	Pte.	Keir, A.							1	1	1									
6974	,,	Kelly, J.	1	1				1	1		1					1	1		Yes	Home, invalided.

Regtl. No.	Rank.	Name.	Paardeberg.	Driefontein.	Johannesburg.	Diamond Hill.	Belfast.	Wittebergen.	Cape Colony.	Orange Free State.	Transvaal.	Tugela Heights.	Relief of Ladysmith.	Laing's Nek.	Natal.	S. Africa, 1901.	S. Africa, 1902.	On what Roll name submitted for Queen's S. A. Medal.	If entitled to King's S. A. Medal.	Remarks.
3774	Pte.	Kelly, H.							1											
3614	,,	Kelly, T.							1	1										
2075	,,	Kelly, C.							1	1						1				Home, invalided.
7573	,,	Kelly, J.						1	1							1		1st Vol. S. Coy.		
3318	,,	Kelly, J.							1	1	1					1	1		Yes	Home on demobn.
3580	,,	Kelly, A.							1								1			do. do.
6931	,,	Kelman, G.	1						1											Killed in action.
5913	Corpl.	Kenny, J.							1											
4431	Pte.	Kelsall, J.	1	1					1	1						1	1		Yes	Home on demobn.
3568	,,	Kelt, T.							1										Yes	
6576	,	Kennedy, J.	1	1				1	1	1						1	1			
9047	,,	Kennedy, F. T.							1	1	1					1	1	2nd Vol. S. Coy.	No	
7532	,,	Kergan, J.							1	1	1					1	1		Yes	
4751	,,	Kerr, W.							1	1	1					1	1		Yes	Home on demobn.
6998	,,	Kerr, D.	1	Yes					1	1						1	1		Yes	
7510	,,	Kerr, R.							1	1						1	1		Yes	To 1st Blk. Watch.
6411	,,	Kidd, D.	1	1					1	1						1	1			Died of disease.[1]
7548	,,	Kidd, A.							1	1								1st Vol. S. Coy.		
4049	,,	Kidney, J.						1	1		1					1	1		Yes	Discharged in S. Africa.
4370	,,	Kilbourne, E. G.							1	1	1					1	1		Yes	Home on demobn.
2488	,,	King, W. B.							1	1										Died of disease. Died of enteric near Bloemfontein, 3/5/00.
3906	L.-Cpl.	King, W.							1	1	1					1	1		Yes	Home, time exp.
3678	,,	King, J.	1	1					1	1	1									do. do.
4802	Pte.	King, X. F.[2]							1	1	1					1	1		Yes	To 1st Blk. Watch.
3598	,,	King, J. W.	1	1					1											
5776	,,	King, A.							1	1	1					1	1	To 1st Blk. Watch.	Yes	Home on demobn.
5652	,,	King, D.	1						1											Killed in action.
5589	,,	Kingshorn, D.	1	1				1	1		1					1	1	Home, time exp.	Yes	Home on demobn.
3242	,,	Kinloch, W. P.	1					1	1		1					1			Yes	do. do.
3741	,,	Kinnear, T.	1	1	1	1	1		1							1				do. do.
9011	,,	Kinnell, G.							1	1	1					1	1	2nd Vol. S. Coy.	No	
2733	L.-Cpl.	Kirkcaldy, C.							1	1						1				Home on demobn.
6028	Pte.	Kirkwood, J.	1	1				1	1		1					1	1		Yes	To 1st Blk. Watch.
3981	,,	Kirkwood, J.							1											Killed in action.
2916	,,	Knight, D.							1	1									Yes	
6455	,,	Kyles, J.							1	1	1					1	1		Yes	Home on demobn.
2611	Sgt.	Laburn, D.						1	1	1	1					1	1		Yes	
6353	Pte.	Lackie, R.							1	1	1					1	1	Home, time exp.	Yes	Home on demobn.
6156	,,	Lafferty, F. R. F.						1	1		1					1	1	do. do.	Yes	do. do.
6476	,,	Laing, J.	1	1				1	1		1					1	1		Yes	Discharged in S. Africa.
7526	L.-Cpl.	Laing, D.							1	1	1					1	1	To 1st Blk. Watch.	Yes	Home for dischge.
7067	Pte.	Laing, J.							1	1	1					1	1		Yes	
2756	,,	Laing, A.							1	1	1					1	1		Yes	Home on demobn.
3891	,,	Laird, J.							1											Killed in action.
4351	,,	Lamb, J.	1	1					1	1	1					1	1		Yes	Home on demobn.
6373	,,	Lamond, J. (Lamont)							1	1	1					1	1		Yes	do. do.

[1] Died of enteric at Bloemfontein 3/5/00.
[2] Entry in 1st Bn. King's Roll as follows: 'Included in Roll of 1st Bn. A.G. 2/M/7311.'

Regtl. No.	Rank.	Name.	Paardeberg.	Driefontein.	Johannesburg.	Diamond Hill.	Belfast.	Wittebergen.	Cape Colony.	Orange Free State.	Transvaal.	Tugela Heights.	Relief of Ladysmith.	Laing's Nek.	Natal.	S. Africa, 1901.	S. Africa, 1902.	On what Roll name submitted for Queen's S. A. Medal.	If entitled to King's S. A. Medal.	Remarks.
7423	Pte.	Lamont, H.							1	1	1					1	1		Yes	To 1st Blk. Watch.
9033	L.-Sgt.	Lamont, P. (Cpl.)							1	1	1					1	1	2nd Vol. S. Coy.	No	
4459	Sgt. Mr.-Tailor	Land, O. O.							1	1	1					1	1		Yes	
5077	Pte.	Lauder, C.	1																	Killed in action.
7146	,,	Lavelle, J.[1]						1	1		1					1	1	Discharged in S. Africa.	Yes	Transvaal Clasp retd. A.D.O.S. 8/5/08. Queen's Medal not traced.
6582	,,	Law, R.							1											
4278	,,	Law, A.							1											
6849	,,	Law, W. M. J.						1	1		1					1	1		Yes	Home, invalided.
6377	L.-Sgt.	Law, A. D.	1	1					1		1					1	1			Promoted to Commission in Gloucester Rgt., serving in 1st Bn.
6992	Pte.	Lawrence, E.	1	1					1		1					1	1	Home on demobn.	Yes	Home, time exp.
3903	,,	Lawrie, W.	1	1				1	1		1					1	1	Home, time exp.	Yes	Home on demobn.
8929 3	,,	Lawrie, T.							1	1	1					1	1	2nd Vol. S. Coy.	No	
4520	,,	Lawrie, A.							1	1	1					1				
3855	,,	Lawrie, J.	1						1										Yes	Home on demobn.
6483	Corpl.	Lawson, J. M.	1	1				1	1		1					1	1		Yes	To 1st Blk. Watch.
4342	Pte.	Lawson, L.	1	1				1	1		1					1	1		Yes	Home on demobn.
6488	,,	Lawson, W. (Lc.-Corpl.)						1	1		1					1	1		Yes	To 1st Blk. Watch.
6653	,,	Lawson, G.							1	1	1					1	1			Home, invalided.
6613	,,	Lawson, W.	1	1				1	1		1					1	1		Yes	Discharged in S. Africa.
7252	,,	Leckie, J.	1	1				1	1		1					1	1		Yes	
6687	Corpl.	Leicester, O. H. (Sgt.)							1	1	1					1	1		Yes	
3806	Pte.	Leitch, G.							1							1				Home on demobn.
4766	,,	Leonard, F.							1											
3982	,,	Leroy, L.	1	1				1	1		1					1	1		Yes	Home on demobn.
2384	,,	Leroy, H.						1	1		1									Home, time exp.
9035	,,	Leslie, D. R.							1	1	1					1	1	2nd Vol. S. Coy.	No	
4771	,,	Lester, R.	1	1				1	1		1					1	1		Yes	Home on demobn. B/513 S.A.C.
7338	,,	Lewthwaite, A.							1	1	1					1	1		Yes	
4028	,,	Lindsay, J.	1						1		1					1	1		Yes	Home on demobn.
3822	Corpl.	Lindsay, D.							1											
6430 23	,,	Lindsay, R. (Sgt.)	1	1				1	1		Yes					1	1		Yes	To 1st Blk. Watch.
2932	Pte.	Lindsay, J.							1	1	1					1	1		Yes	Home on demobn.
6734	,,	Lindsay, D. (Cpl.)						1	1		1					1	1		Yes	
8986	,,	Lindsay, J.							1	1	1					1		1st Vol. S. Coy.		
2153	,,	Linnie, J. (Lennie)							1	1	1					1	1		Yes	Home, time exp.
3536	,,	Lister, A.	1	1				1	1											
5125	,,	Livingstone, T.							1	1	1					1	1		Yes	Home on demobn.

[1] Disposal of Queen's Medal not traced.

Regtl. No.	Rank	Name	Paardeberg	Driefontein	Johannesburg	Diamond Hill	Belfast	Wittebergen	Cape Colony	Orange Free State	Transvaal	Tugela Heights	Relief of Ladysmith	Laing's Nek	Natal	S. Africa, 1901	S. Africa, 1902	On what Roll name submitted for Queen's S. A. Medal	If entitled to King's S. A. Medal	Remarks
6693	Pte.	Livingstone, J.	1					1	1	1						1	1		No	Medal iss'd 29/12/02. Forfeits medal, conviction under Sect. 8 AA. Medal re-earned, A.G. 2/N 6/6684.
6836	L.-Cpl.	Livingstone, D. (Pte.)	1	1				1	1		1					1	1		Yes	
5263	Pte.	Livingstone, A.						1	1	1						1	1		Yes	
7491	,,	Livingstone, J.						1	1	1						1	1		Yes	Home, invalided.
3719	,,	Lochrie, J.					1	1								1				Home on demobn.
2343	,,	Loftus, J.						1	1	1						1	1		Yes	Home on demobn.
4215	L.-Cpl.	Lolly, A. W. (Private)						1	1	1						1	1		Yes	do. do.
6941	Pte.	Louie, J. (Louey) (Louie)						1	1		1					1	1		Yes	
7198	,,	Lord, W.						1	1	1						1	1		Yes	
7135	,,	Loudfoot, W.	1	1				1	1		1					1	1		Yes	
7624	,,	Loudon, W.						1	1							1		1st Vol. S. Coy.		
6862	,,	Love, W.						1										1st Vol. S. Coy.		
7574	,,	Low, H.						1	1									1st Vol. S. Coy.		E/284 S.A.C.
9032	L.-Cpl.	Low, J.						1	1	1						1	1	2nd Vol. S. Coy.	No	No
9036	Pte.	Low, R.						1	1	No						1	No	2nd Vol. S. Coy.	No	No
6631	,,	Low, D.	1	1				1												
7246	,,	Low, C.						1	1		1					1	1		Yes	
3708	,,	Low, D.	1	1				1												
4598	,,	Low, F.	1					1								1	1	2nd Vol. S. Coy.	No	
8940	Corpl.	Lowe, G. B. (Pte.)						1	1	1						1		1st Vol. S. Coy.		
7623	Pte.	Lowdon, T.						1	1							1		1st Vol. S. Coy.		
4297	,,	Lutman, R.	1	1				1	1		1					1	1	Home, time exp.	Yes	Home on demobn.
6900	,,	Lyall, W.						1	Yes											Changed name to Morrison, see additional Clasp Roll, A.G. 2/M/10854.
6656	L.-Cpl.	Lynch, J.						1											Yes	Home on demobn.
4468	Pte.	Lynch, T.						1	1	1						1	1			
4363	,,	Lyons, W.						1												
6540	,,	M'Adams, E.						1	1											
5897	,,	M'Ainsh, A. W. J.						1	1	1						1	1		Yes	Home on demobn.
4594	,,	M'Aleese, T.						1	1								1			To A. Reserve in S. Africa.
3007	,,	M'Allister, W.	1					1			1					1	1		Yes	Home on demobn.
7326	,,	M'Anarney, J.						1												Died of disease.
7518	,,	M'Andrew, P.						1	1	1						1	1		Yes	
7050	,,	M'Ara, J. (Lc.-Corpl.)	1	1				1	1		1					1	1		Yes	Home on demobn.
2391	,,	M'Arthur, P.						1	1	1						1	1		Yes	do. do.
5547	,,	M'Bain, A.				1		1	1	1						1	1		Yes	To 1st Blk. Watch.
5882	,,	M'Bride, T.	1	1				1	1		1					1	1		Yes	
7233	,,	M'Cabe, A.	1	1				1			1					1	1		Yes	
3469	,,	M'Cabe, B.						1	1		1					1	1			Home on demobn.

2 F

Regtl. No.	Rank.	Name.	Paardeberg.	Driefontein.	Johannesburg.	Diamond Hill.	Belfast.	Wittebergen.	Cape Colony.	Orange Free State.	Transvaal.	Tugela Heights.	Relief of Ladysmith.	Laing's Nek.	Natal.	S. Africa, 1901.	S. Africa, 1902.	On what Roll name submitted for Queen's S. A. Medal	If entitled to King's S. A. Medal	Remarks.
6915	Pte.	M'Cabe, J.	1		1	1	1		1							1	1		Yes	
6609	,,	M'Cabe, B.							1	1	1					1	1		Yes	Home on demobn.
3255	,,	M'Cafferty, M.	1	1				1	1		1					1	1		Yes	do. do.
5969	,,	M'Cann, P.							1	1	1					1	1		Yes	do. do.
6604	,,	M'Cann, P.	1	1				1	1		1					1	1		Yes	
5719	,,	M'Cann, P.							1							1				Home, invalided.
5943	,,	M'Carrol, T.	1	1				1	1		1					1	1		Yes	To 1st Blk. Watch.
6685	,,	M'Caskill, J.	1						1								1			
6647	Corpl.	M'Clellan, F. E.							1											Promoted to commission in Somerset L.I., serving in 2nd Battalion. Killed in action.
4415 3	Pte.	M'Coll, J.							1											
3457	,,	M'Coll, J.							1	1	1					1	1		Yes	Home on demobn.
7275	,,	M'Coll, A. (M'Call, J.)	1	1				1	1		1					1	1		Yes	To 1st Blk. Watch.
3267	Drmr.	M'Cormack, T.							1	1	1					1	1		Yes	Home on demobn.
4583	Sgt.	M'Crone, J.	1						1											Killed in action.
5579	Pte.	M'Dade, F. T.							1	1	1					1	1		Yes	Home on demobn.
4071	,,	M'Dade, H.	1	1					1	1	1					1	1		Yes	do. do.
3254	,,	M'Donald, J.							1	1	1					1	1		Yes	do. do.
4986	L.-Cpl.	M'Donald, J. (Pte.)	1	1					1	1	1					1	1		Yes	Home on demobn.
2513	Pte.	M'Donald, J.							1	1	1					1	1		Yes	do. do.
4221	,,	M'Donald, J.							1											Killed in action.
6097	,,	M'Donald, W.							1											Killed in action.
7608	,,	M'Culloch, D.						1	1							1		1st Vol. S. Coy.		
6458	,,	M'Donald, W.						1	1		1					1	1		Yes	To 1st Blk. Watch.
2441	L.-Cpl.	M'Donald, N.							1											
4430	,,	M'Donald, W.							1	1	1					1	1		Yes	
2824	,,	M'Donald, E.							1	1										Home, invalided.
6269	Pte.	M'Donald, M.			1	1	1		1							1	1		Yes	Home on demobn.
5207	Piper	M'Donald, W.	1	1				1	1		1					1	1		Yes	do. do.
4288	Pte.	M'Donald, C.	1	1				1	1		1					1	1		Yes	do. do.
9037	,,	M'Diarmid, P.							1	1	1					1	1	2nd Vol. S. Coy.	No	Deceased, Wynberg Hospl., May /02.
2707	,,	M'Bride, J.			1	1	1		1	1						1	1		Yes	Home on demobn.
5184	,,	M'Cormac, J.	1						1											
6718	,,	M'Donagh, P.	1	1				1	1		1					1	1		Yes	
3066	C.-Sgt.	M'Dougall, D.	1	1				1	1		1					1	1		Yes	
7258	Pipe-Major	M'Dougall, J.	1	1				1	1							1	1		Yes	
3512	C.-Sgt.	M'Dougal, R.	1	1				1	1		1					1	1		Yes	To Permanent Staff.
6847 1	L.-Cpl.	M'Dougall, P. (Pte.)	1					1	1		1					1	1		Yes[1]	Home, invalided.
2535	Pte.	M'Dowall, A.							1	1	1					1				Home, time exp.
3736	,,	M'Ewen, E.							1	1	1					1	1		Yes	Home on demobn.
3574	,,	M'Farlan, D.	1	1					1											
3353	,,	M'Farlan, W. W.							1	1	1					1	1		Yes	Home on demobn.

[1] No. 6847, M'Dougall, P., does not appear on the 2nd Bn. King's S. A. Roll. This entry 'Yes, Home, Invalided,' is taken from the Supplementary *Clasp* Roll 2nd Bn., and in it no mention is made of M'Dougall being entitled to the 1901 and 1902 Clasps, but they appear on the 1st Bn. King's Medal Roll.—J. S.

Regtl. No.	Rank.	Name.	Paardeberg.	Driefontein.	Johannesburg.	Diamond Hill.	Belfast.	Wittebergen.	Cape Colony.	Orange Free State.	Transvaal.	Tugela Heights.	Relief of Ladysmith.	Laing's Nek.	Natal.	S. Africa, 1901.	S. Africa, 1902.	On what Roll name submitted for Queen's S. A. Medal.	If entitled to King's S. A. Medal.	Remarks.
6290	Pte.	M'Farlan, S.							1	1							1			Home, invalided.
8972	,,	M'Farlane, G. F. T.							1	1	1					1	1	2nd Vol. S. Coy.	No	
7345	,,	M'Farlane, G.							1	1	1					1	1		Yes	
3872	,,	M'Farlane, J.	1	1					1										Yes	Died of disease.
7157	,,	M'Garry, J. W. (M'Garrie)							1	1	1					1	1		Yes	
7169	,,	M'Garry, J.							1							1	1		Yes	Home on demobn.
3438	,,	M'Garry, J.							1	1	1					1	1		Yes	do. do.
3962	,,	M'Geary, A.		1				1	1							1				Home, invalided.
3217	,,	M'Gee, S.							1	1	1					1	1		Yes	Home on demobn.
7286	,,	M'Gee, F.						1	1		1					1	1		Yes	
6940	,,	M'Gee, W.							1											
6939	,,	M'Gee, J.							1	1	1					1	1		Yes	
4126	,,	M'Gillivray, W.	1						1	1						1			Yes	Home on demobn.
7588	,,	M'Gillivray, R.							1	1						1		1st Vol. S. Coy.		
1110	,,	M'Ging, J.							1	1	1					1	1		Yes	Deceased.
5270	,,	M'Gouchan, F.	1	1				1	1		1					1	1		Yes	Home on demobn.
6014	,,	M'Govan, T. (M'Govern)						1	1		1					1	1		Yes	do. do.
4219	Sgt.	M'Gowan, J. L.	1	1					1											E/115 S.A.C.
5734	Pte.	M'Grath, J.							1	1										
7601	,,	M'Gregor, W. J.						1	1							1		1st Vol. S. Coy.		
7496	,,	M'Gregor, G. J. G.							1	1	1					1	1		Yes	
4114	,,	M'Gregor, J.							1											Killed in action.
5657	,,	M'Gregor, R.	1	1				1	1		1					1	1	To 1st Blk. Watch.	Yes	Home on demobn. See D.C.M. Roll.
5047	,,	M'Gregor, G.	1						1											
6439	,,	M'Guigan, J.							1	1	1					1	1		Yes	
6966	,,	M'Gurk, J.	1	1					1	1	1					1	1		Yes	
2653	,,	M'Gurty, F.			1	1			1	1	1					1				Time expired.
3737	,,	M'Hardy, J.							1											Killed in action.
2256	,,	M'Ilman, P.							1	1	1					1	1	Home on demobn.	No	Medal issd. 29/12/02. Convicted by F.G.C.M. of disgraceful conduct—theft. Medal re-earned, A.G.2/M/5684.
4329	,,	M'Ilroy, J.							1											
6874	,,	M'Inally, B.	1						1											
3648	,,	M'Innes, J.	1	1					1											
3596	,,	M'Innes, D.	1	1				1	1											
6202	,,	M'Inroy, J.							1											
7026	,,	M'Intosh, A.	1	1				1	1							1	1		Yes	
6301	L.-Cpl.	M'Intosh, J.	1						1											
4551	Pte.	M'Intosh, F.							1	1	1					1	1		Yes	Home on demobn.
7595	L.-Cpl.	M'Intosh, D.						1	1							1		1st Vol. S. Coy.		
8927	Pte.	M'Intosh, J.							1	1	1					1		1st Vol. S. Coy.		
8959	,,	M'Intosh, L. A.							1	1	1					1		1st Vol. S. Coy.		
8957	,,	M'Intosh, J.							1	1	1					1	1	2nd Vol. S. Coy.	No	
7038	,,	M'Intyre, J.							1	1						1	1		Yes	Home, invalided.

Regtl. No.	Rank.	Name.	Paardeberg.	Driefontein.	Johannesburg.	Diamond Hill.	Belfast.	Wittebergen.	Cape Colony.	Orange Free State.	Transvaal.	Tugela Heights.	Relief of Ladysmith.	Laing's Nek.	Natal.	S. Africa, 1901.	S. Africa, 1902.	On what Roll name submitted for Queen's S. A. Medal.	If entitled to King's S. A. Medal.	Remarks.
2272	Pte.	M'Intyre, J.						1	1							1				Home, time exp.
8953	,,	M'Intyre, J. F.							1	1	1					1		1st Vol. S. Coy.		
74849	,,	M'Intyre, J.							1	1	1					1	1		Yes	
6915	,,	M'Kay, J.						1	1		1					1	1		Yes	Home on demobn.
7231	,,	M'Kay, C. D.							1	1						1	1		Yes	Home for dischge.
3796	,,	M'Kay, A. E.							1											
3371	,,	M'Kay, A.						1	1		1					1	1		Yes	Home on demobn.
8994	,,	M'Kay, J. W.							1	1	1					1	1	1st Vol. S. Coy.	No	37492/S. Horse.
7029	,,	M'Kay, A.							1											
7447	,,	M'Kay, R.							1	1	1					1	1		Yes	
7024	,,	M'Kay, J.							1	1										
6887	,,	M'Kay, D.			1	1	1		1	1						1	1		Yes	Home on demobn.
5860	,,	M'Kay, J.							1	1						1	1		Yes	Home, invalided.
6288	,,	M'Kay, R.							1	1										
6482	,,	M'Kay, A.	1	1				1	1		1					1	1	To 1st Blk. Watch.	Yes	Medal issd. 29/12/02. Convicted by F.G. C.M. of disgraceful conduct—theft. Medal re-earned, A.G./M2/6684.
5304	,,	M'Kelvie, G.						1	1							1				
3865	,,	M'Kelvie, W.							1											Home, time exp.
4569	,,	M'Kenzie, J.	1	1				1	1		1					1	1		Yes	Home on demobn.
4180	,,	M'Kenzie, D.						1	1		1					1	1		Yes	do. do.
3871	,,	M'Kenzie, H.						1	1		1					1	1	Home, time exp.	Yes	do. do.
4492	,,	M'Kenzie, J.	1	1				1	1		1					1	1	do. do.	Yes	do. do.
2479	,,	M'Kenzie, J.						1	1							1				Home, time exp.
7594	,,	M'Kenzie, D. R. C. H.						1	1							1		1st Vol. S. Coy.		
90557	,,	M'Kenzie, D.							1	1	1					1	1	2nd Vol. S. Coy.	No	
2918	,,	M'Kenna, J.							1	1	1					1	1		Yes	Home on demobn.
2644	,,	M'Kernan, J.							1	1	1					1				Home, time exp.
3570	,,	M'Kerroll, D.							1											
7600	,,	M'Killop, D.						1	1		1							1st Vol. S. Coy.		
4136	,,	M'Kinley, J.	1	1				1	1		1					1	1		Yes	Home on demobn.
2464	,,	M'Kinnon, D.						1	1											
4564	,,	M'Knight, I.	1						1											Killed in action.
7591	,,	M'Laggan, J. I.						1	1									1st Vol. S. Coy.		E/131 S.A.C.
4337	,,	M'Laine, W.							1											Killed in action.
7677	,,	M'Laren, J.							1	1	1					1	1		Yes	
7593	,,	M'Laren, J.						1	1							1		1st Vol. S. Coy.		
5994	L.-Cpl.	M'Lauchlan, D.	1	1				1	1		1					1	1		Yes	To 1st Blk. Watch.
6918	Pte.	M'Lauchlan, J.						1	1											
6768	,,	M'Lauchlan, M.	1	1					1		1					1	1		Yes	
6585	L.-Cpl.	M'Lay, G. (Pte.)	1	1	1	1	1		1							1	1		Yes	
4000	Pte.	M'Lean, H.							1											
7201	L.-Cpl.	M'Lean, R. R. (Private)		1				1	1		1					1	1		Yes	
4208	Pte.	M'Lean, J. N. J.							1		1					1	1		Yes	Home on demobn.
3798	,,	M'Leish, A.	1	1				1	1							1				Home, invalided.

Regtl. No.	Rank	Name	Paardeberg	Driefontein	Johannesburg	Diamond Hill	Belfast	Wittebergen	Cape Colony	Orange Free State	Transvaal	Tugela Heights	Relief of Ladysmith	Laing's Nek	Natal	S. Africa, 1901	S. Africa, 1902	On what Roll name submitted for Queen's S. A. Medal	If entitled to King's S. A. Medal	Remarks
3154	Pte.	M'Leod, A.						1	1		1					1	1		Yes	Home on demobn.
2663	Sgt.	M'Leod, A.						1	1											
2268	Pte.	M'Leod, D.						1	1										Yes	Home, invalided.
4498	,,	M'Leish, C.	1	1					1							1	1		Yes	
8980	,,	M'Laren, L.							1	1	1					1	1	2nd Vol. S. Coy.	No	
9069	,,	M'Laren, P.							1	1	1					1	1	2nd Vol. S. Coy.	No	
2376	,,	M'Luckie, L.							1	1	1					1	1	To 1st Blk. Watch.	Yes	
6122	L.-Sgt.	M'Mahon, D. (Sgt.)	1	1					1							1	1		Yes	To 1st Blk. Watch.
8926	Pte.	M'Mahon, J.							1	1	1					1	1	2nd Vol. S. Coy.	No	
3683	,,	M'Manus, J.	1	1					1											E/130 S.A.C.
3331	Sgt.	M'Manus, A.							1	1	1					1	1		Yes	To 1st Blk. Watch.
3682	Pte.	M'Master, W.						1	1											
7184	L.-Cpl.	M'Master, D. (Pte.)	1	1					1								1			
2718	C.-Sgt.	M'Millan, J.							1											Killed in action.
4096	Pte.	M'Millan, J.							1											Killed in action.
7107	,,	M'Millan, J.							1	1	1					1	1		Yes	Home, invalided.
6418	,,	M'Millan, W.							1	1	1					1	1		Yes	Home on demobn.
5374	Sgt.	M'Millan, D.	1	1			1		1		1					1	1		Yes	
3491	,,	M'Murchy, N.							1	1	1					1	1	2nd Vol. S. Coy.	No	
9038	Pte.	M'Nab, P.							1	1	1					1	1		Yes	
7419	L.-Cpl.	M'Nab, W.							1	1	1					1	1		Yes	Discharged in S. Africa.
7399	Pte.	M'Namara, T.							1	1	1					1	1		Yes	
9002	,,	M'Naughton, J.							1	1	1					1	1	2nd Vol. S. Coy.	No	
3770	L.-Cpl.	M'Neil, T.	1	1				1	1											
7662	Pte.	M'Neil, K. H.						1	1									1st Vol. S. Coy.		
3952	,,	M'Neil, J.							1											No Medal. Sentenced by F.G.C.M. to penal servitude.
9020	,,	M'Nicoll, R.							1	1	1					1	1	2nd Vol. S. Coy.	No	
5565	Sgt.	M'Owan, D.							1	1	1					1	1		Yes	Home on demobn.
3532	Pte.	M'Quillan, J. O.			1				1											Home, time exp.
7063	,,	M'Quillan, J.			1				1											
5903	,,	M'Phee, A.							1	1	1					1	1		Yes	Home on demobn.
2345	,,	M'Phee, D.							1	1	1					1	1		Yes	do. do.
9049	,,	M'Pherson, J.							1	1	1					1	1	2nd Vol. S. Coy.	No	
8982	,,	M'Pherson, J. W.							1	1	1					1	1	2nd Vol. S. Coy.	No	
3668	,,	M'Pherson, D.	1						1											
3543	,,	M'Pherson, J.	1	1				1	1										Yes	
2943	,,	M'Pherson, A.							1	1	1					1	1		Yes	Home on demobn.
7438	,,	M'Robbie, G.A.G.						1	1	1	1					1	1		Yes	
6607	,,	M'Tavish, G. (Bandsman)	1	1				1	1		1					1	1		Yes	
6824	,,	M'Tavish, D.	1						1									2nd Vol. S. Coy.	No	
9018	,.	M'Walter, J.							1	1	1					1	1		Yes	To 1st Blk. Watch.
7249	,,	M'Williams, T.F.	1	1	1			1	1							1	1	Home on demobn.	Yes	Home, invalided.
5864	,,	M'Vey, J.	1	1				1	1		1					1	1		Yes	Home, invalided.
4572	Sgt.	Machray, A.	1	1				1	1		1					1	1		Yes	do. do.

Regtl. No.	Rank.	Name.	Paardeberg.	Driefontein.	Johannesburg.	Diamond Hill.	Belfast.	Wittebergen.	Cape Colony.	Orange Free State.	Transvaal.	Tugela Heights.	Relief of Ladysmith.	Laing's Nek.	Natal.	S. Africa, 1901.	S. Africa, 1902.	On what Roll name submitted for Queen's S. A. Medal.	If entitled to King's S. A. Medal.	Remarks.
6766	Pte.	Mackie, W.	1	1					1		1					1	1		Yes	
3571	„	Mackie, J.	1						1											
6916	„	Mackie, A.							1	1							1		Yes[1]	To 1st Blk. Watch.
834	„	Madden, P.							1	1										
3358	C.-Sgt.	Main, J.	1	1				1	1		1					1	1		Yes	To Auxiliary Forces.
6808	Pte.	Maison, A. (Lc.-Corpl.)							1							1	1		Yes	To 1st Blk. Watch.
6341	„	Malcolm, D.							1	1						1	1		Yes	To 1st Blk. Watch.
7180	L.-Cpl.	Malcolm, W. (Corpl.)						1	1		1					1	1		Yes	Home, invalided.
4945	Sgt.	Malcolm, W.							1											
2834	Pte.	Malcolm, J.							1	1						1	1		Yes	Home on demobn.
7575 6	„	Malcolm, W.						1	1							1		1st Vol. S. Coy.		
6996 9	„	Mackie, J.	1						1							1	1		Yes	
6917	„	Malone, J.							1	1	1					1	1		Yes	Home on demobn.
9045	„	Manson, N.							1	1	1					1	1	2nd Vol. S. Coy.	No	
6278	L.-Cpl.	Manson, G. (Cpl.)	1	1				1	1		1					1	1		Yes	To 1st Blk. Watch.
7230	Pte.	Mansfield, J.							1	1										
2910	„	Mann, A.						1	1							1	1		Yes	Home on demobn.
6925	„	Mann, J.							1											Killed in action.
3596	„	Markie, J.							1	1	1					1	1		Yes	Home on demobn.
2641	„	Marley, E.							1	1	1					1	1		Yes	Home on demobn.
9013	„	Marr, J.							1	1	1					1	1	2nd Vol. S. Coy.	No	
4032	Corpl.	Marrett, T. (Marret)							1	1	1					1	1	Home on demobn.	Yes	Home, invalided.
3725	Pte.	Marshall, D.	1	1				1	1		1									Home, time exp.
4449	„	Marshall, J.	1	1	1	1	1		1							1	1		Yes	Home on demobn.
6732	„	Martin, J. (Piper)							1		1					1	1		Yes	
4588	„	Martin, G.	1	1					1											
9000	„	Martin, E.							1	1	1					1	1	2nd Vol. S. Coy.	No	
5843	„	Martin, J.							1	1	1					1	1		Yes	To A. Reserve in S. Africa.
3828	„	Martin, J.	1	1	1	1	1		1											
1068	„	Martin, J.	1	1					1		1					1	1	Home, time exp.	Yes	Discharged in S. Africa.
3198 and 3197	„	Martin, John, *alias* Henry FitzGerald							1	1	1					1	1		Yes[2]	Attached to Black Watch. Served as 3197 A. & S. Highrs. and 1156 Fitzgerald, P.W.O. Yorkshire Regt. Forfeited medals for F.E.
4137	„	Masterton, A.							1											Died of wounds.
6783	„	Massie, J.							1											Killed in action.
3626	„	Markins, P.							1											
7464	„	Mathers, J.							1	1	1					1	1		Yes	
5136	„	Matthew, T. (Matthews)	1	1				1	1		1					1	1		Yes	Discharged in S. Africa.
9019	„	Mathew, A.							1	1	1					1	1	2nd Vol. S. Coy.	No	

[1] Note on 2nd Bn. King's Medal Roll: 'Through wounds in action invalided from S. Africa 1901, returned April 1902; granted sick furlough from 17/4/00 to 18/7/00, subsequently three months in convalescent home.' Entitled under para. 5 A.O. 1902.

[2] Attached to Black Watch only. Served as 3197 3rd A. & S. Highrs. and 1156 Henry FitzGerald, P.W.O. Yorkshire Regt. Forfeited medal for fraudulent enlistment; trial dispensed with 27/11/02. A. G. 2/C/17905, 6/11/03. Medal and Clasps lost. Home on demobilisation.

Regtl. No.	Rank.	Name.	Paardeberg.	Driefontein.	Johannesburg.	Diamond Hill.	Belfast.	Wittebergen.	Cape Colony.	Orange Free State.	Transvaal.	Tugela Heights.	Relief of Ladysmith.	Laing's Nek.	Natal.	S. Africa, 1901.	S. Africa, 1902.	On what Roll name submitted for Queen's S. A. Medal	If entitled to King's S. A. Medal.	Remarks.
6835	Pte.	Mathew, W. (Mathews)							1	1	1					1	1	To have medal.[1]	Yes	Medal issd. 29/12/02. Convicted by C.M. of disgraceful conduct. Medal re-earned A.G. 2/M /6684.
2990	,,	Mathewson, A. (Mathieson)							1	1	1					1	1		Yes	Home on demobn.
7549	,,	Mathewson, A.							1	1						1		1st Vol. S. Coy.		Died of disease. Died of enteric at Bloemfontein 28/4/01.
6705	,,	Maxwell, N. H.							1	1	1					1	1		Yes	Discharged in S. Africa.
4429	,,	Maxwell, R. .							1	1	1					1	1		Yes	Home, invalided.
2849	,,	Maxwell, J. .							1	1						1				Home on demobn.
4810	,,	Maxwell, H. .							1											Killed in action.
4584	,,	Mearns, P. .	1	1					1	1	1					1	1		Yes	Home on demobn.
3995	,,	Meek, D. .	1	1					1	1										
4291	,,	Meekison, J. .							1											
9004	,,	Meldrum, A. .							1	1	1					1	1	2nd Vol. S. Coy.	No	
5787	,,	Meldrum, S. .	1	1					1	1	1					1	1	To have medal.[2] Home on demobn.	Yes	Medal issd. 29/12/02. Convicted by C.M. of disgraceful conduct. Medal re-earned A.G. 2/M /6684.
7225	,,	Mellon, H. .	1	1					1		1					1	1		Yes	To 1st Blk. Watch.
2255	,,	Melvin, J. . .							1		1					1	1		Yes	Home on demobn.
7393	,,	Mellis, A. . .							1	1	1					1	1		Yes	Home for discharge.
2299	,,	Melville, J. .							1	1	1									Home, time exp.
9059	,,	Melville, W. .							1	1	1					1	1	2nd Vol. S. Coy.	No	
7192	,,	Menzies, J. .							1	1	1					1	1		Yes	To 1st Blk. Watch.
5162	,,	Menzies, D. .	1	1					1	1	1					1	1		Yes	Home on demobn.
9071	,,	Menzies, D. .							1	1	1					1	1	2nd Vol. S. Coy.	No	
9014	,,	Menzies, J. .							1	1	1					1	1	2nd Vol. S. Coy.	No	
6875	,,	Menzies, R. .	1						1		1					1	1	22nd Bn. M.I.	Yes	Discharged in S. Africa.
7144	,,	Mercer, A. .	1						1	1	1					1	1		Yes	
4281	,,	Mew, W. . .							1											
2214	Sgt.	Michie, W. .							1	1										
4659	Pte.	Middleton, A. .	1	1					1											
4800	,,	Middleton, A. .	1	1				1												
4308	,,	Millar, A. . .	1	1					1	1	1					1	1		Yes	Home on demobn.
4194	,,	Millar, A. . .	1	1					1	1	1					1	1		Yes	do. do.
6855	,,	Millar, A. . .	1	1					1	1	1					1	1		Yes	
4897	Sgt.	Millar, A. . .							1											
5722	,,	Miller, J. . .							1	1	1					1	1	Home, time exp.	Yes	Home on demobn.
4471	Pte.	Millar, C. . .	1	1					1											
6834	,,	Millar, J. . .	1	1					1										Yes	
4007	C.-Sgt.	Millar, A. . .	1						1	1	1					1	1			
7634	Corpl.	Millar, D. . .							1	1						1		1st Vol. S. Coy.		

[1] Notes on 2nd Bn. King's Medal Roll: 'Tried by F.G.C.M. for theft, 84 days I.H.L., 16/6/00. To duty, 8/9/00.'
[2] Tried by D.C.M. 14/4/00 for leaving guard without permission and stealing public goods, 15 months I.H.L., commuted to 3 months.

Regtl. No.	Rank.	Name.	Paardeberg.	Driefontein.	Johannesburg.	Diamond Hill.	Belfast.	Wittebergen.	Cape Colony.	Orange Free State.	Transvaal.	Tugela Heights.	Relief of Ladysmith.	Laing's Nek.	Natal.	S. Africa, 1901.	S. Africa, 1902.	On what Roll name submitted for Queen's S. A. Medal.	If entitled to King's S. A. Medal.	Remarks.
7550	Pte.	Millar, W. P.						1	1							1		1st Vol. S. Coy.		
4857	,,	Millington, F.							1	1										
2641	,,	Mills, T.						1	1		1					1	1		Yes	
3968	,,	Mills, J.							1											
4361	,,	Mills, E.	1	1	1	1	1		1							1	1		Yes	Home on demobn.
8925	L.-Cpl.	Milne, J. (Pte.)							1	1	1					1	1	2nd Vol. S. Coy.	No	
2694	Pte.	Milne, J.						1	1		1					1	1	Home on demobn.	Yes	Home, time exp.
4499	,,	Milne, J.							1	1	1					1	1		Yes	Home on demobn.
7367	,,	Milne, J.							1	1	1					1	1		Yes	Home, invalided.
6924	,,	Milne, J.						1	1		1					1	1		Yes	Home, invalided.
2423	,,	Milton, J. (Milne)						1	1							1				Home on demobn.
7507	,,	Mitchell, J.							1	1	1					1	1		Yes	To 1st Blk. Watch.
5380	,,	Mitchell, R.							1							1	1		Yes	To A. Reserve in S. Africa.
2134	,,	Mitchell, J.	1	1					1											
2677	,,	Mitchell, G.							1											
6040	Sgt.	Mitchell, W.	1	1	1	1	1		1							1	1		Yes	
8941	Pte.	Mitchell, D.							1	1	1					1	1	2nd Vol. S. Coy.	No	
6171	,,	Mitchell, D.							1	1										
3932	,,	Mitchell, A.	1	1				1	1		1					1	1		Yes	Home on demobn.
2610	,,	Mitchell, G.						Yes	1		1					1	1	Home on demobn.	Yes	Home, time exp.
4795	,,	Mitchell, T. (Lc.-Corpl.)		1					1		1					1	1		Yes	Home on demobn.
3452	,,	Mitchell, W.						1	1		1					1	1		Yes	Home, invalided.
6503	Drmr.	Mitchell, H.	1	1					1											
2300	C.-Sgt.	Mitchell, W.	1						1											Killed in action.
3714	Pte.	Mitchell, J.							1	1										
6796	,,	Mitchell, J.	1	1					1		1					Yes				
7344	,,	Mitchell, W.							1	1	1					1	1		Yes	
3330	Sgt.	Mitchell, W.						1	1		1					1	1		Yes	
3316	Corpl.	Mitchell, H. (Lc.-Sgt.)						1	1		1					1	1		Yes	
7058	Pte.	Mitchell, J.	1	1					1		1					1	1		Yes	
1849	,,	Mochan, D.							1	1						1	1		Yes	Home, invalided.
3833	,,	Moir, J.	1						1											
9048	,,	Moir, E.							1	1	1					1	1	2nd Vol. S. Coy.	No	
7217	,,	Money, A.	1						1		1					1	1		Yes	Home, invalided.
7366	,,	Montgomery, J.							1	1						1	1			Medal issd. 29/12/02. Sentenced by F.G.C.M. to penal servitude. Medal re-earned A.G. 2/M /6684.
6003	L.-Cpl.	Moodie, D. (Pte.) (Mooney)	1	1				1	1		1					1	1		Yes	To 1st Blk. Watch.
7661	Pte.	Moodie, D.							1	1						1		1st Vol. S. Coy.		
4001	,,	Moon, G.						1	1							1	1		Yes	Home, invalided.
7337	,,	Mooney, J.							1	1	1					1	1		Yes	
3582	,,	Mooney, D.	1	1					1		1					1	1		Yes	Home, time exp.
3672	,,	Moonlight, T.						1	1*	1*						1	1			*Issue authorised on 6th Bn. I. Y. /1193.

Regtl. No.	Rank	Name	Paardeberg	Driefontein	Johannesburg	Diamond Hill	Belfast	Wittebergen	Cape Colony	Orange Free State	Transvaal	Tugela Heights	Relief of Ladysmith	Laing's Nek	Natal	S. Africa, 1901	S. Africa, 1902	On what Roll name submitted for Queen's S. A. Medal	If entitled to King's S. A. Medal	Remarks
4560	Pte.	Moore, F.	1	1					1											Home on demobn.
2491	,,	Moore, W.			1	1	1		1	1						1				Died of wounds.
3926	,,	Moore, T.	1						1										Yes	
6608	,,	Moran, M.	1	1				1	1		1					1	1			
6516	Drmr.	Moran, C.							1										Yes	Home, invalided.
5098	Corpl.	Moran, G.	1	1				1	1							1	1		Yes	Home on demobn.
4188	Sgt.	Morgan, T.	1						1		1					1	1		Yes	
4928	Pte.	Morris, S.							1											Died of wounds.
7080	,,	Morris, J.							1											
4666	,,	Morrison, W.[1]							1	1	1					1	1		Yes	Home on demobn.
3625	,,	Morrison, A.	1	1					1											
3997	,,	Morrison, W.							1	1	1					1	1		Yes	Home on demobn.
3702	,,	Morrison, J.							1							1				Home, time exp.
5245	,,	Morrison, P. (Lc.-Corpl.)	1	1					1	1						1	1		Yes	Home on demobn.
5541	,,	Morrison, W.							1	1						1	1		Yes	do. do.
3602	,,	Morrow, W.	1	1					1											
5154	,,	Moyes, F. F. T.	1				1		1		1					1	1		Yes	
6895	,,	Moyes, H. (Lc.-Corpl.)	1	1			1		1		1					1	1		Yes	Home on demobn.
4153	,,	Morgan, J.	1	1			1		1							1	1		Yes	Home, time exp.
2674	,,	Mudie, D.							1	1	1					1	1		Yes	Deceased.
4919	,,	Mudie, J.	1	1					1	1	1					1	1			Died of disease.
7238	,,	Mudie, J.							1	1									Yes	Home on demobn.
6253	,,	Muir, T.	1	1	1	1	1		1							1	1		Yes	Home on demobn.
3398	,,	Muir, G. J.							1	1	1					1	1		Yes	do. do.
6675	,,	Muir, R.							1	1	1					1	1		Yes	do. do.
3157	,,	Muirhead, W.							1	1	1					1	1	Home, invalided.	Yes	do. do.
3317	,,	Mulheron, D. (Mulhearn)							1	1	1					1	1	Home, time exp.	Yes	do. do.
6970	,,	Mulgrew, T.							1	1	1					1	1	Home, invalided.	Yes	do. do.
6083	,,	Mulholland, J.	1						1											Killed in action.
2403	,,	Mumford, J.			1		1		1	1						1				Home on demobn.
3991	,,	Munro, R.	1	1					1							1	1		Yes	Home on demobn.
5865	,,	Murdoch, A.							1										Yes	
2420	,,	Murdoch, R. J.					1	1								1	1		Yes	
8942	,,	Murray, A. W.							1	1	1					1	1	2nd Vol. S. Coy.	No	
8958	,,	Murray, G.[2]							1	1	1					1	1	2nd Vol. S. Coy.	No	
4541	,,	Murray, J.							1	1	1									
6946	,,	Murray, J.	1	1			1		1		1					1	1		Yes	
7172	,,	Murray, G.							1											
1863	,,	Murray, J.							1	1	1					1	1		Yes	Home on demobn.
9070	,,	Murrie, J. W.							1	1	1					1	1	2nd Vol. S. Coy.	No	
3659	,,	Murrie, R.	1	1					1										Yes	
1660	,,	Murry, D. (Murray)							1	1						1	1			
6767	,,	Mustard, R.	1	1			1		1	1						1	1		No	Medal issd. 29/12/02. Convicted by F.G. C.M. of disgraceful conduct—theft. Medal re-earned A.G.2/NC/6684.

[1] Morrison. In 2nd Bn. King's Medal Roll there is a No. 6900, Morrison, W., entitled to King's Medal and 1901 and '02 Clasps. This number does not appear in Queen's Roll (nothing in King's Roll 'Remarks' column).—J. S.

[2] Lc.-Corpl. in 2nd Vol. S. Coy. Roll.

Regtl. No.	Rank.	Name.	Paardeberg.	Driefontein.	Johannesburg.	Diamond Hill.	Belfast.	Wittebergen.	Cape Colony.	Orange Free State.	Transvaal.	Tugela Heights.	Relief of Ladysmith.	Laing's Nek.	Natal.	S. Africa, 1901.	S. Africa, 1902.	On what Roll name submitted for Queen's S. A. Medal.	If entitled to King's S. A. Medal.	Remarks.
6564	Corpl.	Myers, G. (Lc.-Sgt.)			1	1	1		1	1						1	1		Yes	
6842	Pte.	Myers, W.	Yes	Yes					1		1					1	1		Yes	Discharged in S. Africa.
7037	,,	Myles, A.							1	1										Forfeited. Dischd. incorrigible and worthless. Medal and Clasps retd. to Woolwich 27/5/10, *vide* 68/42/981.
4031	,,	Myles, D.	1	1					1	1	1					1	1		Yes	Home on demobn.
4166	,,	Mylie, J.	1	1					1											
7062	,,	Neave, C.							1	1							1			
5171	,,	Neish, D.	1							1										Home, invalided.
2579	,,	Neish, J.							1	1	1					1	1		Yes	Home on demobn.
6087	,,	Neish, G.							1	1	1					1	1		Yes	do. do.
4420	,,	Newburg, G. J. (Newbury), J.G.	1	1					1	1	1					1	1		Yes	do. do.
5710	,,	Nicoll, J.	1	1					1	1	1					1	1		Yes	do. do.
6919	,,	Nicoll, W.	1	1					1		1					1	1		Yes	
2443	,,	Nicol, J.							1	1	1					1	1		Yes	Home on demobn.
7205	,,	Nicoll, J.							1	1	1					1	1		Yes	
7625	,,	Nicoll, J.							1	1	1					1	1	1st Vol. S. Coy.	No	No. 9176, Pte. 3/V.S.C.
7626	,,	Nicoll, T.							1	1								1st Vol. S. Coy.		
7237	,,	Nicoll, A. (Nicol)						1	1	1						1	1		Yes	
3693	,,	Nicol, J.	1	1					1	1						1				Home on demobn.
3308	,,	Nicol, J.	1	1					1		1					1	1		Yes	Home on demobn.
7164	,,	Nicolson, A.							1	1	1					1	1		Yes	Home, invalided.
3744	L.-Cpl.	Nisbet, W.	1	1					1	1	Yes					1				Home, invalided.
6935	Pte.	Niven, A.							1	1	1					1	1	Dischd. with ignominy. No medal, 68/42/815.	Yes	No MEDAL. Discharged with ignominy, 68/42/815.
2760	C.-Sgt.	Niven, D.	1	1					1	1	1					1	1		Yes	3rd Bn. Black Watch.
6994	L.-Cpl.	Niven, J. E. (Corpl.)	1	1					1		1					1	1	22nd Bn. M. I.	Yes	
5577	Pte.	Nivinson, G.	1	1					1		1					1	1		Yes	Home on demobn.
3720	,,	Nixon, J.	1	1					1	1	1									do. do.
6932	,,	Nixon, W.	1	1					1	1										
6215	L.-Cpl.	Noble, A. & J. J.G.	1	1					1	1	1					1	1		Yes	To 1st Blk. Watch.
4137	Pte.	Noble, A.							1	1	1					1	1		Yes	Home on demobn.
7551	,,	Norwell, J. P.							1	1						1		1st Vol. S. Coy.		
7627	,,	Oakley, D.							1	1						1		1st Vol. S. Coy.		
4383	,,	O'Brien, R.	1	1					1	1						1				Home on demobn.
7663	,,	O'Brien, F.							1	1						1		1st Vol. S. Coy.		
7422	,,	O'Brien, M.	1							1										
6729	,,	O'Connell, W.							1	1	1					1	1		Yes	
3581	,,	Ocral, J.								1										Died of disease.

Regtl. No.	Rank.	Name.	Paardeberg.	Driefontein.	Johannesburg.	Diamond Hill.	Belfast.	Wittebergen.	Cape Colony.	Orange Free State.	Transvaal.	Tugela Heights.	Relief of Ladysmith.	Laing's Nek.	Natal.	S. Africa, 1901.	S. Africa, 1902.	On what Roll name submitted for Queen's S. A. Medal.	If entitled to King's S. A. Medal.	Remarks.
5068	Pte.	Ogg, A.						1	1											
7664	,,	Ogg, A.					1	1								1		1st Vol. S. Coy.		
7552	,,	Ogg, J.					1	1								1		1st Vol. S. Coy.		
4662	,,	Ogg, J.						1												Killed in action.
6771	,,	Ogilvie, C.	1	1				1	1		1					1	1		Yes	Home, invalided.
6770	,,	Ogilvie, J.							1	1	1					1	1		Yes	Home on demobn.
3331	,,	O'Hara, J.							1	1	1					1	1		Yes	
3799	,,	Oliphant, W.	1	1				1												
6214	Corpl.	Oliver, W. (Sgt.)							1	1	1					1	1	Not entitled.[1]	Yes	
6721	Pte.	Oliver, J.							1	1	1					1	1		Yes	Medal issd. 29/12/02. Convicted by C.M. of disgraceful conduct. Medal re-earned A.G. 2/NC /6684.
7432	,,	Oram, W.							1	1	1					1	1		Yes	Discharged in S. Africa. See D.C.M. Roll.
4813	,,	Ormonde, R.	1					1												
6007	,,	Orr, H.			1			1	1			1	1	1		1	1		Yes	To 1st Blk. Watch.
6986	,,	Ormonde, A.					1	1		1						1	1		Yes	Home on demobn.
2744	,,	Osborne, W.					1	1		1						1	1		Yes	
7086	,,	Osborne, R.	1	1				1	1		Yes					1	1	Home on demobn.	Yes	Issue authd. 68/42 /905, 3/7105. Issued 10/7/05.
2219	,,	Oswald, J.						1	1											
6759	,,	Palmer, A.						1	1	1										
7182	,,	Palmer, J.					1	1			1					1	1		Yes	To 1st Blk. Watch.
4189	,,	Palmer, T.	1	1				1												
8943	,,	Parker, A.							1[2]	1[2]	1[2]					1		1st Vol. S. Coy.		Died of disease, 13/2/01. Died of enteric at Springfontein.
5226	Sgt.	Parker, E.	1	1				1			1					1	1	22nd Bn. M.I., Coy. Sgt.-Major	Yes	
4929	Pte.	Parsons, C.	1	1				1									1			Home on demobn.
3577	,,	Patterson, H.						1												
5587	,,	Patterson, J.	1	1			1	1	1							1	1		Yes	Home on demobn.
2240	C.-Sgt.	Paterson, J.						1												Died of wounds.
7116	Pte.	Paterson, J.						1												Killed in action.
3859	,,	Patterson, D. T.	1	1				1			1					1	1		Yes	Home, time exp.
32 6036	L.-Cpl.	Paterson, J. (Private)	1					1	1		1					1	1		Yes	To 1st Blk. Watch.
3824	Pte.	Paterson, N. W. M.							1	1	1					1	1		Yes	Home on demobn.
9075	,,	Paton, S.							1	1	1					1	1	2nd Vol. S. Coy.	No	
2625	.,	Paton, S.							1	1	1					1	1		Yes	Home on demobn.
6499	,,	Paton, P.						1	1	1						1	1		Yes	do. do.
2546	,,	Patton, N.							1	1	1					1				do. do.
5444	,,	Patton, J. (Paton)						1	1	1						1				do. do.
2147	Corpl.	Paul, H.						1	1							1				Home, time exp.

[1] Note from 2nd Bn. King's S. A. Medal Roll:—Entry as follows: 'Tried by F.G.C.M. 5/10/00 receiving stolen goods. Sentenced to 84 days I.H.L. To duty 28/12/00.'

[2] These entries are from the 1st V.S. Coy. Roll; they do not appear in 2nd Bn. Roll.

Regtl. No.	Rank.	Name.	Paardeberg.	Driefontein.	Johannesburg.	Diamond Hill.	Belfast.	Wittebergen.	Cape Colony.	Orange Free State.	Transvaal.	Tugela Heights.	Relief of Ladysmith.	Laing's Nek.	Natal.	S. Africa, 1901.	S. Africa, 1902.	On what Roll name submitted for Queen's S. A. Medal.	If entitled to King's S. A. Medal.	Remarks.
2640	Pte.	Payne, M.						1	1		1					1	1	Home on demobn.	Yes	Home, time exp.
2304	,,	Peck, J.						1	1							1				Home on demobn.
7665	,,	Peggie, J.						1	1							1		1st Vol. S. Coy.		
2831	,,	Penman, J.	1						1											
2665	,,	Penman, J.						1	1		1					1	1		Yes	Home, time exp.
7199	,,	Pert, J.							1											Killed in action.
3784	,,	Peters, J.							1											
9039	,,	Petrie, A.							1	1	1					1	1	2nd Vol. S. Coy.	No	Deceased Standerton, February/02.
3712	,,	Petrie, C.	1	1	1	1	1		1							1				Home on demobn.
969	,,	Petrie, W.							1	1	1					1	1		Yes	Home on demobn.
7628	,,	Phillip, D.						1	1							1		1st Vol. S. Coy.		Died of enteric at Netley, 9/6/01.
3377	L.-Cpl.	Philp, J. (Pte.)						1	1		1					1	1		Yes	Home on demobn.
5012	C.-Sgt.	Philip, J. (Philp)						1	1		1					1	1		Yes	
4202	,,	Philips, H. R.	1	1				1	1											
5911	Pte.	Phillips, H.	1						1		1					1	1		Yes	Home on demobn.
4608	,,	Pickett, F.							1											
7319	,,	Piggot, P.							1	1						1	1		Yes	
9009	,,	Porter, A.							1	1	1					1		1st Vol. S. Coy.		
4602	,,	Potter, G.							1											
2984	,,	Potts, S.							1	1						1	1		Yes	Home on demobn.
6773	Corpl.	Powell, A. (Sgt.)	1	1				1	1		1					1	1		Yes	
4222	Pte.	Powell, F.	1	1				1	1		1					1	1		Yes	Home on demobn.
6442	,,	Powrie, J.							1											Killed in action.
4300	,,	Price, W.	1						1		1					1	1		Yes	Home on demobn.
4723	Corpl.	Pritchatt, H.	1																	
7599	L.-Cpl.	Proudfoot, A.							1	1	1					1		1st Vol. S. Coy.		
7415	Pte.	Proudfoot, A.							1	1	1					1	1		Yes	
6586	Drmr.	Purdie, L. G. (Lc.-Corpl.)	1	1				1	1		1					1	1		Yes	
4255	Pte.	Purdie, R.	1						1											
3922	,,	Purvis, G.							1											
3808	,,	Pyott, C.							1											
7611	Drmr.	Quinn, J. (Bglr.)						1	1							1		1st Vol. S. Coy.		
6893	Pte.	Quinn, P.	1						1											
3722	,,	Quinn, G.							1	1	1					1				Home on demobn.
6570	,,	Quirk, A.	1	1					1		1					1	1		Yes	
7088	,,	Rae, J.							1	1	1					1	1		Yes	
2416	,,	Rae, E.							1	1	1					1	1		Yes	Home on demobn.
6866	,,	Rafferty, J.							1	1	1					1	1		Yes	do. do.
3023	Q.M.S.	Raisbeck, J.	1	1				1	1							1	1		Yes	
9050	Pte.	Ramsay, P.							1	1	1					1	1	2nd Vol. S. Coy.	No	
4119	,,	Ramsay, M.	1	1					1											
2698	,,	Ramsay, J.						1	1									No MEDAL.		Sentenced by F.G. C.M. to penal servitude.
6605	,,	Ramsay, E.						1	1	1						1	1		Yes	
6724	L.-Cpl.	Ramsay, H.							1											
4346	Pte.	Rattray, T.	1	1	1	1			1							1	1		Yes	Home on demobn.
7652	,,	Raynor, C.							1	1	1					1	1		Yes	

Regtl. No.	Rank.	Name.	Paardeberg.	Driefontein.	Johannesburg.	Diamond Hill.	Belfast.	Wittebergen.	Cape Colony.	Orange Free State.	Transvaal.	Tugela Heights.	Relief of Ladysmith.	Laing's Nek.	Natal.	S. Africa, 1901.	S. Africa, 1902.	On what Roll name submitted for Queen's S. A. Medal.	If entitled to King's S. A. Medal.	REMARKS.
4055	Pte.	Redfern, E.	1	1					1							1	1		Yes	Died of disease.
6806	Drmr.	Reeves, A. (Pte.)	1	1					1	1	1					1	1		Yes	
5721	Pte.	Reeve, W. (Lc.-Cpl.) (Reeves)							1	1	1					1	1	To 1st Blk. Watch	Yes	Home, invalided.
4700	,,	Regan, H.							1	1	1					1	1	Home on demobn.	Yes	Home, invalided.
5846	,,	Reid, J.	1	1				1	1		1					1	1			
6621	,,	Reid, A.	1					1	1							1		1st Vol. S. Coy.		68/T.F./198 KM.
7553	L.-Cpl.	Reid, J. M. (Private)						1	1											37213 L/Corpl. 1st Sc. Horse.
3904	Corpl.	Reid, J. N.	1	1					1	1	Yes *					1	1	Home, time exp.	Yes	*Issued 23/2/05.
4475	Pte.	Reid, T.	1	1					1	1	1					1	1		Yes	To 1st Blk. Watch.
6350	,,	Reid, J.							1	1	1					1	1		Yes	Home on demobn.
3941	,,	Reid, J.	1	1					1							1	1		Yes	Home, invalided.
3936	,,	Reid, A.	1	1					1	1	1					1	1		Yes	
7402	,,	Rennie, J.							1	1	1					1	1		Yes	
6678	L.-Cpl.	Rennie, J. (Cpl.)	1	1					1	1	1					1	1		Yes	Home on demobn.
2997	Pte.	Reilly, J.							1	1	1					1	1			
5354	,,	Reilly, P.							1	1	1									
2720	,,	Reilly, J.	1	1					1	1	1					1	1		Yes	Home on demobn.
4760	,,	Rest, M.							1										Yes	Home on demobn.
6908	,,	Reynolds, P.	1	1					1	1	1					1	1		Yes	To 1st Blk. Watch.
6451	,,	Reynolds, A.	1	1					1	1	1					1	1		Yes	Home on demobn.
4393	,,	Reynolds, A.	1	1					1	1	1					1	1	2nd Vol. S. Coy.	No	
9061	,,	Retigan, E.							1	1	1					1	1			Home, time exp.
2333	L.-Cpl.	Riddle, J.							1	1						1			Yes	
6747	Corpl.	Riddle, D.							1	1	1					1	1		Yes	Home on demobn.
2544	Pte.	Rice, P.							1	1	1					1	1		Yes	do. do.
2829	,,	Richings, H.							1	1	1					1	1		Yes	
7451	,,	Rintoul, J.							1	1	1					1	1		Yes	
7140	,,	Rintoul, A.	1	1					1											
7142	,,	Ritchie, L.							1	1	1					1	1		Yes	Home, invalided.
3556	,,	Ritchie, T.							1										Yes	Deserted.
7141	,,	Rivers, H.							1	1						1	1	No Medal.	Yes	To 1st Blk. Watch.
5844	L.-Cpl.	Robb, F. (Pte.)							1	1	1					1	1		Yes	
4301	Pte.	Roberts, C.							1											
3817	,,	Roberts, W.							1											
3719	,,	Robertson, J.							1											
6376	,,	Robertson, J.	1	1					1	1	1					1	1		Yes	To 1st Blk. Watch.
4476	,,	Robertson, H.	1						1	1	1					1	1		No	Home on demobn.
4381	Drmr.	Robertson, W.	1	1					1	1	1					1	1		Yes	To 1st Blk. Watch.
6398	Pte.	Robertson, W.							1	1						1	1	1st Vol. S. Coy.		
7584	,,	Robertson, J. L.							1	1						1		1st Vol. S. Coy.		
7629	,,	Robertson, J.							1	1						1		1st Vol. S. Coy.		
8981[1]	,,	Robertson, J.							1	1	1					1		1st Vol. S. C.		
8983	,,	Robertson, M. J.							1	1	1					1		1st Vol. S. C.		
7605	Sgt.	Robertson, T.							1	1						1		1st Vol. S. C.		
8992	Pte.	Robertson, T.							1	1	1					1	1	2nd Vol. S. Coy.	No	
2680	,,	Robertson, D.			1	1	1		1	1						1	1		Yes	Home, time exp.

1 No. 8973 in 1st V. S. C. Roll.

Regtl. No.	Rank.	Name.	Paardeberg.	Driefontein.	Johannesburg.	Diamond Hill.	Belfast.	Wittebergen.	Cape Colony.	Orange Free State.	Transvaal.	Tugela Heights.	Relief of Ladysmith.	Laing's Nek.	Natal.	S. Africa, 1901.	S. Africa, 1902.	On what Roll name submitted for Queen's S. A. Medal.	If entitled to King's S. A. Medal.	Remarks.
1752	Pte.	Robertson, J.	1	1	1	1	1		1							1	1		Yes	Home on demobn.
7000	,,	Robertson, G.							1											Died of wounds.
3014	C.-Sgt.	Robertson, J.	1						1											Killed in action.
3939	Pte.	Robertson, D.	1	1				1	1		1					1	1		Yes	Home on demobn.
3959	,,	Robertson, J.	1	1				1	1		1					1	1		Yes	do. do.
4625	,,	Robertson, J.						1	1		1					1	1		Yes	do. do.
2280	,,	Robertson, T.						1	1							1				Home, time exp.
2729	,,	Robertson, A. (Lc.-Corpl.)						1	1		1					1	1		Yes	Home, time exp.
7259	,,	Robertson, ℟. A.							1	1	1									Deceased.
4850	L.-Cpl.	Robertson, W.							1	1	1									
2428	Pte.	Robertson, A.						1	1							1		Home on demobn.		Medal, and Clasp Wittebergen, returned to A.D.O.S. 68 Garr. Regt. E4. Deserted from R.G. Regt. 22/8/02. No. 4229.
3671	,,	Robertson, ℟. J.	1	1				1	1							1				Home, time exp.
6568	,,	Robertson, P.	1					1	1		1					1	1		Yes	
5312	,,	Robertson, P.	1	1				1	1		1					1	1		Yes	Home on demobn.
4508	,,	Robins, E.							1											Killed in action.
4198	,,	Robinson, H.	1	1				1	1		1					1	1		Yes	Home on demobn.
4124	,,	Robinson, J.	1	1	1	1	1		1							1	1		Yes	Home on demobn.
5639	,,	Rodger, L. M.[1]	1	1				1	1		1					1	1		Yes	do. do.
7004	,,	Rodger, F.	1	1					1		1					1	1	No Clasps. No Medal.	Yes	Deserted.
6810	L.-Cpl.	Rodger, W. S. (Corpl.)							1	1	1					1	1		Yes	
6490	Pte.	Rodgers, A.							1	1	1					1	1		Yes	Home on demobn.
7014	L.-Cpl.	Rodger, A. (Cpl.)							1	1	1					1	1		Yes	
4331	Sgt.	Rose, H.							1											
3123	Pte.	Ross, G.							1	1						1	1		Yes	Home on demobn.
5887	,,	Ross, D.							1	1						1	1		Yes	do. do.
5886	,,	Ross, A. M.							1											Killed in action.
9063	,,	Ross, J.[2]							1	1	1					1	1	2nd Vol. S. Coy.	No	
3559	,,	Ross, R.	1						1	1										
6903	,,	Ross, W.							1	1										
3489	,,	Ross, W.							1	1	1					1	1		Yes	Home on demobn.
2714	,,	Ross, W.						1	1		1					1	1		Yes	do. do.
7111	L.-Cpl.	Ross, D. (Corpl.)							1	1	1					1	1		Yes	
3129	Pte.	Ross, D.							1	1	1					1	1		Yes	To A. Reserve in S. Africa.
6854	L.-Cpl.	Roote, C. P.							1											Killed in action.
4052	Pte.	Rothery, B.	1	1				1	1		1					1	1	Home, time exp.	Yes	Home on demobn.
5334	,,	Rougvie, ℟. D.	1	1				1	1							1				Home, invalided.
4185	L.-Cpl.	Rourk, W. (Cpl.)	1	1				1	1							1	1		Yes	Home on demobn.
4105	Pte.	Rowatt, D.	1					1	1		Yes*					1	1	Home, invalided.	Yes	*Authd. 68/42/905, 3/2/05. Issd.10/7/05.
4385	,,	Roy, Jas.	1	1				1	1		1					1	1		Yes	To A. Reserve in S. Africa.
6302	,,	Roy, D.						1	1	1						1	1		Yes	Home on demobn.

[1] Corporal in King's Medal Roll.
[2] Served also as No. 9063 3rd Vol. S. Coy.

Regtl. No.	Rank.	Name.	Paardeberg.	Driefontein.	Johannesburg.	Diamond Hill.	Belfast.	Wittebergen.	Cape Colony.	Orange Free State.	Transvaal.	Tugela Heights.	Relief of Ladysmith.	Laing's Nek.	Natal.	S. Africa, 1901.	S. Africa, 1902.	On what Roll name submitted for Queen's S. A. Medal.	If entitled to King's S. A. Medal.	Remarks.
3340	Pte.	Roy, J.							1	1	1					1	1		Yes	Home on demobn.
7163	,,	Ruddick, J.							1											
7114	,,	Rutherford, A. (Corpl.)							1	1	1					1	1		Yes	Home on demobn.
5049	,,	Russell, J.							1	1	1					1	1		Yes	
3892	,,	Russell, J.						1	1	1	1[1]					1	1	To 1st Blk. Watch	Yes	Forfeited. Incorrigible and worthless. Medal and Clasps returned Woolwich 27/5/10, vide 68/S.A./981.
6684	,,	Russell, R.	1	1					1											Died of disease.
2621	L.-Sgt.	Ruxton, F.							1											
4369	Sgt.	Sackett, F. E.	1	1					1	1	1					1	1		Yes	Home on demobn.
6965	Pte.	Sampson, A.							1											Died of disease.
4482	,,	Sandilands, J.	1	1					1	1	1					1	1		Yes	To A. Reserve in S. Africa.
5811	,,	Sandeman, C.							1	1										
2931	Corpl.	Sandison, J.	1						1	1	1									
6668	Pte.	Saxty, E.							1											
3981	,,	Scott, A.	1	1					1	1						1	1		Yes	Home on demobn.
3691	,,	Scott, J.							1	1	1									
4848	,,	Scott, A.	1	1					1											
2852	C.-Sgt.	Scott, J.							1											Home, invalided.
5881	Pte.	Scott, R. E.	1						1	1						1	1	Home on demobn.	Yes	Home, invalided.
2340	,,	Scott, A.	1	1					1	1	1									Home on demobn.
4519	,,	Scott, W. A.							1											Killed in action.
5836	,,	Scott, A.							1	1	1					1	1		Yes	Home on demobn.
5871	Sgt.	Scott, C.							1	1										
6798	Pte.	Scott, J.							1		1					1	1		Yes	To 1st Blk. Watch.
2332	,,	Scott, J.						1	1							1			Yes	Home, invalided.
5549	,,	Scott, J.	1	1					1	1	1					1	1		Yes	Home, invalided.
7411	,,	Scott, J.							1	1	1					1	1		Yes	To 1st Blk. Watch.
7027	,,	Scott, R.							1	1	1					1	1			Died of disease.
7666	,,	Scott, J.							1	1						1		1st Vol. S. Coy.		Died at De Aar 4/4/01.
7577	L.-Cpl.	Scott, J. B.							1	1	1					1		1st Vol. S. Coy.		
7630	Pte.	Scott, W.						1	1							1		1st Vol. S. Coy.		
9040	,,	Scott, M.							1	1	1					1	1	2nd Vol. S. Coy.	No	
7005	L.-Cpl.	Scott, D.	1	1	1	1	1		1							1				Home, invalided.
4990	Pte.	Scullin, T.							1											Killed in action.
3764	,,	Scullin, A.							1											
7554	,,	Scrimgeour, J.						1	1							1		1st Vol. S. Coy.		
9022	,,	Scroggie, T.							1	1	1					1	1	2nd Vol. S. Coy.	No	
4689	,,	Shanahan, J.							1											
6769	,,	Shand, A.							1											
2241	,,	Shankland, R.						1	1		1									Home on demobn.
7072	,,	Sharp, D.	1	1	1	1	1		1							1	1		Yes	
5437	L.-Sgt.	Sharp, C.							1											Killed in action.
6735	Pte.	Sharp, J.							1											Died of wounds.
4088	,,	Sharp, R.	1	1					1	1	1					1	1		Yes	Home on demobn.

1 In Supplementary Clasp Roll 2nd Bn. the entry is as follows: 'Clasp, Transvaal, returned to Woolwich 4/6/10. Forfeited, Desertion, 68/8a/99/88/10.'

Regtl. No.	Rank.	Name.	Paardeberg.	Driefontein.	Johannesburg.	Diamond Hill.	Belfast.	Wittebergen.	Cape Colony.	Orange Free State.	Transvaal.	Tugela Heights.	Relief of Ladysmith.	Laing's Nek.	Natal.	S. Africa, 1901.	S. Africa, 1902.	On what Roll name submitted for Queen's S. A. Medal.	If entitled to King's S. A. Medal.	Remarks.
4494	Pte.	Sharp, J.	1	1				1	1		1					1	1		Yes	Home on demobn.
4167	,,	Shaw, W.	1	1	1	1	1		1							1	1		Yes	do.　do.
2835	,,	Shaw, J.			1				1	1						1				do.　do.
6947	,,	Shaw, W.	1	1				1*	1		1					1	1		Yes	*Clasp returned. Claimed in error, 20/5/03.
3551	,,	Shaw, P.	1					1	1											
6433	Drmr.	Shaw, D. (Pte.)	1					1	1		1					1	1		Yes	To 1st Blk. Watch.
4319	Pte.	Shaw, J.							1	1	1					1	1		Yes	Home on demobn.
4341	,,	Shaw, H.							1											
3875	,,	Shaw, H.	1						1											
4132	,,	Shearby, G.	1						1								1			Home on demobn.
6619	,,	Shedden, J.	1	1				1	1		1					1	1		Yes	
2269	,,	Shepherd, J.							1	1						1	1		Yes	Home on demobn.
7096	,,	Shepherd, D.						1	1		1					1	1		Yes	
9025	,,	Sherrard, J.							1	1	1					1	1	2nd Vol. S. Coy.	No	
6357	,,	Sheret, D.							1		1					1	1		No	To 1st Blk. Watch.
4969	,,	Shirlaw, T.							1	1										Died of disease.
8988	L.-Cpl.	Short, J. (Pte.)							1	1	1					1	1	2nd Vol. S. Coy.	No	
2984	Pte.	Short, J.	1						1											
7341	,,	Sibbald, J.							1	1	1					1	1		Yes	Home, invalided.
8977	,,	Sidey, T.							1	1	1					1	1	2nd Vol. S. Coy.	No	
4645	,,	Sim, J.	1	1					1											
6876	Corpl.	Sim, R.						1	1		1					1	1		Yes	
7540	Sgt.	Sime, D. S.							1	1						1		1st Vol. S. Coy.		
6699	Pte.	Simons, J. (Simmons)	1					1*	1		Yes*					1	1		Yes	*Issued 28/12/03, 68/42/780.
2368	,,	Simpkins, F.							1	1						1				Home, time exp.
7369	,,	Simpson, T.							1	1	1					1	1		Yes	Home, invalided.
2601	L.-Cpl.	Simpson, J.							1	1										
2609	Pte.	Simpson, J.							1	1	1					1	1		Yes	Home, invalided.
7153	,,	Simpson, T.	1						1											Died of wounds.
5474	,,	Simpson, J.							1											
7066	,,	Simpson, A. J.							1	1	1					1	1		Yes	
5744	Sgt.	Simpson, W.	1	1	1	1	1		1							1	1		Yes	
4597	Pte.	Sinclair, J.							1											
9072	,,	Sinclair, J.							1	1	1					1	1	2nd Vol. S. Coy.	No	
4661	Sgt.	Sinclair, D.							1	1						1				Home, invalided.
6708	L.-Cpl.	Sinclair, J.							1											Killed in action.
3663	Pte.	Sinclair, J.							1	1	1							No Medal.		Sentenced by F.G. C.M. to penal servitude.
6795	,,	Sinclair, F.	1	1				1		1						1	1		Yes	Home on demobn.
4292	,,	Skates, A.	1	1				1	1	1						1	1		Yes	do.　do.
3405	,,	Skelly, J.			1			1	1							1	1		Yes	do.　do.
2355	,,	Skidmore, W.						1	1							1				Home, time exp.
4793	,,	Skirving, W.	1	1	1	1	1		1							1	1		Yes	Home on demobn.
7604	,,	Skinner, J.[1]						1	1							1		1st Vol. S. Coy.		Discharged in consequence of obtaining civil employment in S. A. 6/4/01.

[1] In 1st V. S. C. '1901' Clasp Roll entry: 'Promd. 2/Lt. 68/T.F./09.'

Regtl. No.	Rank.	Name.	Paardeberg.	Driefontein.	Johannesburg.	Diamond Hill.	Belfast.	Wittebergen.	Cape Colony.	Orange Free State.	Transvaal.	Tugela Heights.	Relief of Ladysmith.	Laing's Nek.	Natal.	S. Africa, 1901.	S. Africa, 1902.	On what Roll name submitted for Queen's S. A. Medal.	If entitled to King's S. A. Medal.	REMARKS.
7541	Corpl.	Skinner, R. C.						1	1	1						1		1st Vol. S. Coy.		1st Scottish Horse.
4262	L.-Cpl.	Sloan, W. (Cpl.)	1	1				1	1		1					1	1		Yes	Home on demobn.
6731	Pte.	Sloggie, J. . .							1	1	1					1	1		Yes	To 1st Blk. Watch.
7603	,,	Small, R. . .							1	1								1st Vol. S. Coy.		Died of disease. Died of dysentery, Bloemfontein, 10/4/00.
6879	,,	Smart, R. . .						1	1		1					1	1		Yes	Home on demobn.
6761	Corpl.	Smart, A. J. .	1	1				1	1		1					1	1		Yes	Home, invalided.
3918	Pte.	Smart, T. . .							1	1										
5296	,,	Smail, J. . .							1	1	1									Home, invalided.
2223	Q.M.S. O.R.S.	Smeaton, R. S.	1	1					1		1					1	1		Yes	To 1st Blk. Watch.
2373	Pte.	Smellie, J. . .							1	1	1					1	1		Yes	Home on demobn.
2431	,,	Smith, A. . .					1		1											
7340	,,	Smith, A. . .							1	1	1					1	1		Yes	Home on demobn.
7012	,,	Smith, A. . .					1		1											
7487	,,	Smith, M. . .							1	1						1	1		No	To 1st Blk. Watch.
6997	,,	Smith, J. . .	1	1				1	1		1					1	1		Yes	To 1st Blk. Watch.
4403	,,	Smith, J. W. .	1	1					1		1					1	1		Yes	Home on demobn.
3163	,,	Smith, J. . .							1	1	1					1	1		Yes	do. do.
7041	,,	Smith, G. . .							1											
2652	,,	Smith, J. . .							1	1	1					1	1	Home on demobn.	Yes	Home, time exp.
2946	,,	Smith, J. . .				1			1		1					1	1		Yes	Home on demobn.
7082	,,	Smith, A. . .	1	1				1	1		1					1	1		Yes	do. do.
6894	,,	Smith, J. . .							1											
2712	,,	Smith, J. . .	1	1				1	1		1					1	1		Yes	Home on demobn.
4695	,,	Smith, J. . .							1	1	1					1	1		Yes	do. do.
3913	,,	Smith, J. . .	1						1											Killed in action.
3909	,,	Smith, T. . .							1											Killed in action.
1789	,,	Smith, E. . .	1						1											Killed in action.
6772	Drmr.	Smith, J. . .							1											
5225	Sgt.	Smith, J. . .	1	1				1	1		1					1	1		Yes	Home on demobn.
5205	Pte.	Smith, W. . .							1	1	1					1	1		Yes	do. do.
4083	,,	Smith, J. . .	1	1				1	1		1					1	1		Yes	do. do.
4582	,,	Smith, L. . .	1	1				1	1		1					1	1		Yes	do. do.
2982	Corpl.	Smith, W. J. .							1	1	1					1	1		Yes	
9044	Pte.	Smith, Albert .							1	1	1					1	1	2nd Vol. S. Coy.	No	
8975	,,	Smith, Allan .							1	1	1					1	1	2nd Vol. S. Coy.	No	
8944	,,	Smith, G. . .							1	1	1					1	1	2nd Vol. S. Coy.	No	
9054	,,	Smith, J. N. R.							1	1	1					1	1	2nd Vol. S. Coy.	No	
8997	,,	Smith, T. . .							1	1	1					1	1	2nd Vol. S. Coy.	No	
8945	,,	Smith, W. . .							1	1	1					1	1	2nd Vol. S. Coy.	No	
7218	L.-Cpl.	Smith, J. (Cpl.)						1	1		1					1	1		Yes	
4641	Pte.	Smith, J. . .	1	1				1	1		1					1	1		Yes	Home on demobn.
3538	,,	Smith, H. . .	1	1					1											
7045	,,	Smith, W. . .							1	1	1					1	1		Yes	
7019	,,	Smith, A. J. H.							1	1										
7323	,,	Smith, J. . .							1	1						1	1		Yes	
7396	,,	Sinclair, D. .							1	1						1	1		Yes	
97 7679	,,	Sinclair, J. .							1	1						1	1		Yes	

Regtl. No.	Rank.	Name.	Paardeberg.	Driefontein.	Johannesburg.	Diamond Hill.	Belfast.	Wittebergen.	Cape Colony.	Orange Free State.	Transvaal.	Tugela Heights.	Relief of Ladysmith.	Laing's Nek.	Natal.	S. Africa, 1901.	S. Africa, 1902.	On what Roll name submitted for Queen's S. A. Medal.	If entitled to King's S. A. Medal.	Remarks.
7234	Pte.	Sinclair, R.							1	1						1	1		Yes	
7269	L.-Cpl.	Smart, J. (Cpl.)			1				1	1						1	1		Yes	To 1st Blk. Watch.
3826	Pte.	Sneddon, D.							1	1	1					1				Home on demobn.
6878	L.-Cpl.	Soper, G.							1											Killed in action.
652	Sgt.	Soper, W.	1	1					1	1	1					1				Discharged in S. Africa.
3114	Pte.	Soutar, W.							1	1	1					1	1		Yes	Home on demobn.
7631	,,	Spalding, P.							1	1						1		1st Vol. S. Coy.		
6728	,,	Spankie, A.	1	1					1	1	1					1	1		Yes	
4490	,,	Spareham, J.							1	1	1					1				Deceased.
7514	,,	Sparling, T.							1	1						1				do.
3940	,,	Speir, C.	1	1							1					1	1		No	Home on demobn.
3098	L.-Cpl.	Speirs, C. S.							1	1	1					1	1		Yes	Home on demobn.
2902	Pte.	Spence, H.			1	1	1		1	1						1	1		Yes	do. do.
4139	,,	Spicer, E.							1	1										Died of wounds.
7032	,,	Spink, J.							1	1							1			
9023	,,	Sprunt, T.							1	1	1					1		1st Vol. S. Coy.		
7134	,,	Stables, T.					1		1	1	1					1	1		Yes	
4030	,,	Stark, F.	1																	Killed in action.
7165	,,	Stephen, R.							1	1	1					1	1		Yes	
5630	,,	Steven, J. (Stevens)			1	1	1		1	1						1	1		Yes	Home on demobn.
4522	,,	Stevens, A.	1	1					1	1	1					1	1		Yes	do. do.
7002	,,	Stevens, W.							1	1										
4283	,,	Stevens, B.							1	1	1					1			Yes	Home on demobn.
4822	,,	Stanley, J.							1	1										
2767	,,	Stanley, R.			1	1	1		1	1						1	1		Yes	Home on demobn.
7040	,,	Steel, W.							1	1	1					1	1		Yes	
3889	,,	Stevenson, R.							1											Killed in action.
3695	L.-Cpl.	Stevenson, J.	1	1					1	1						1				Home, time exp.
7183	Pte.	Stevenson, J.							1	1	1					1	1		Yes	Home, invalided.
3878	,,	Stewart, D.							1											Killed in action.
8990	,,	Stewart, W. J.							1	1	1					1	1	2nd Vol. S. Coy.	No	
8954	,,	Stewart, J. C.							1	1	1					1	1	2nd Vol. S. Coy.	No	
9041	,,	Stewart, J.							1	1	1					1	1	2nd Vol. S. Coy.	No	
2749	,,	Stewart, T. J.					1		1		1					1	1		Yes	Home, time exp.
5296	,,	Stewart, C.	1	1					1											
4177	,,	Stewart, J.	1	1					1	1						1	1		Yes	Home on demobn.
2706	,,	Stewart, R.							1	1						1	1		Yes	Home, time exp.
5554	,,	Stewart, R.	1	1					1	1	1					1	1		Yes	To A. Reserve in S. Africa.
6827	,,	Stuart, G. (Stewart)	1						1		1					1	1		Yes	Home, invalided.
5259	,,	Stewart, H.	1	1					1		1					1	1		Yes	Home on demobn.
3621	,,	Stewart, W.							1	1	1									
4407	,,	Stewart, J.	1	1			1		1		1					1	1		Yes	Home on demobn.
5998	Corpl.	Stewart, G.	1	1					1		1					1	1		Yes	Home, invalided.
7149	Pte.	Stirling, A.					1		1		1					1	1		Yes	
6993	,,	Storrar, D.				1			1	1										
9015	,,	Strachan, J.							1	1	1					1	1	2nd Vol. S. Coy.	No	

Regtl. No.	Rank.	Name.	Paardeberg.	Driefontein.	Johannesburg.	Diamond Hill.	Belfast.	Wittebergen.	Cape Colony.	Orange Free State.	Transvaal.	Tugela Heights.	Relief of Ladysmith.	Laing's Nek.	Natal.	S. Africa, 1901.	S. Africa, 1902.	On what Roll name submitted for Queen's S. A. Medal.	If entitled to King's S. A. Medal.	Remarks.
7267	Pte.	Strachan, W.							1	1									Yes	
6730	,,	Strachan, H.	1	1					1	1	1					1	1		Yes	
6972	,,	Strachan, J.							1	1	1					1	1			Home on demobn.
918	,,	Strachan, J.	1	1					1							1				do. do.
3559	,,	Strachan, J.	1	1				1	1							1				
2513	,,	Strachan, W.						1	1							Yes			Yes	
7187	L.-Cpl.	Strang, J. (Pte.)						1	1		1					1	1			Discharged in S. Africa.
973	C.-Sgt.	Strathearn, G.							1	1						1		1st Vol. S. Coy., Sgt. Instr.		
4703	Sgt.	Strong, H.	1	1	1	1	1		1							1	1		Yes	Home on demobn.
4120	Pte.	Struther, D.							1	1	1					1	1		Yes	do. do.
7244	,,	Stuart, C.						1	1		1					1	1		Yes	Home, invalided.
7061	,,	Sturrock, J.	1	1				1	1		1					1	1	Home, time exp.	Yes	Home on demobn.
7592	,,	Sturrock, J.						1	1							1		1st Vol. S. Coy.		Home, invalided.
4366	,,	Suckling, C.	1	1				1	1		1					1			Yes	
6683	,,	Summers, A.							1	1						1	1			To 1st Blk. Watch.
2204	,,	Sutherland, J.						1	1											
7632	,,	Sutherland, A.						1	1							1		1st Vol. S. Coy.		
6846	L.-Cpl.	Sutherland, J. (Corpl.)	1	1					1							1	1		Yes	
3122	Sgt.	Suttie, D.							1	1	1					1				To A. Reserve in S. Africa.
7667	Pte.	Suttie, J.							1	1						1		1st Vol. S. Coy.		
9006	,,	Suttie, C.							1	1	1					1	1	2nd Vol. S. Coy.	No	
4749	,,	Swan, G.							1	1	1					1	1		Yes	Home on demobn.
6764	,,	Swan, A.							1	1	1					1	1	No Clasps. No Medal.	Yes	Deserted.
9027	,,	Sweeney, J.							1	1	1					1		1st Vol. S. Coy.		
3156	,,	Syme, J.							1	1						1	1		Yes	Home on demobn.
2275	,,	Tack, W.							1	1						1				do. do.
6780	,,	Tainsh, J.	1	1					1		1									Killed in action.
5741	,,	Tait, M.							1											
4040	L.-Cpl.	Tait, J.							1											Home on demobn.
2434	Pte.	Taylor, G.							1	1						1			Yes	Home on demobn.
4173	,,	Taylor, P.							1	1	1					1	1			Home on demobn.
8969	,,	Taylor, W.							1	1	1					1	1	2nd Vol. S. Coy.	No	
2148	C.-Sgt.	Taylor, A.	1	1					1	1						1	1		Yes	To 1st Blk. Watch.
7327	Pte.	Taylor, W.							1	1	1					1	1		Yes	Home for dischge.
6700	,,	Taylor, R.							1											Killed in action.
4485	,,	Taylor, W.	1	1					1		1					1	1		Yes	Home on demobn.
4178	L.-Cpl.	Taylor, A. (Cpl.)	1	1					1		1					1	1		Yes	
6151	Pte.	Taylor, D.							1										Yes	
5908	,,	Taylor, D.							1	1	1					1	1		Yes	
6920	,,	Taylor, W. J.	1	1					1	1	1					1	1		Yes	Home, invalided.
4322	Sgt.	Tedder, C.	1	1					1	1	1					1	1		Yes	
6906	Corpl.	Tedder, H.	1	1					1	1	1					1	1		Yes	Home, invalided.
2825	Pte.	Tuke, J.							1	1						1	1		Yes	
2768	,,	Thom, D.							1	1	1									
7068	,,	Thom, G.								1						1	1		Yes	To 1st Blk. Watch.

Regtl. No.	Rank.	Name.	Paardeberg.	Driefontein.	Johannesburg.	Diamond Hill.	Belfast.	Wittebergen.	Cape Colony.	Orange Free State.	Transvaal.	Tugela Heights.	Relief of Ladysmith.	Laing's Nek.	Natal.	S. Africa, 1901.	S. Africa, 1902.	On what Roll name submitted for Queen's S. A. Medal.	If entitled to King's S. A. Medal.	Remarks.
3675 0	Pte.	Thom, H.							1											
6642	,,	Thoms, J. (Thomas)						1	1		1					1	1		Yes	To 1st Blk. Watch.
2396	,,	Third, J.							1	1										
4076	,,	Thompson, J.							1											Killed in action.
7728	,,	Thompson, R.						1	1							1	1	Not entitled. *Vide* 68/42/976.	Yes	Home, invalided.
5894	,,	Thompson, E.						1	1		1					1	1		Yes	
4008	,,	Thompson, H.	1	1				1	1											
7173	L.-Cpl.	Thompson, J. (Thomson) (Pte.)	1	1				1	1		1					1	1		Yes	Home on demobn.
6479	Pte.	Thompson, J.	1	1					1		1					1	1		Yes	Dischd. in S. Africa.
1470	,,	Thompson, W.							1	1										
8949	L.-Cpl.	Thompson, D.							1	1	1					1	1	2nd Vol. S. Coy.	No	
9073	Pte.	Thompson, T.							1	1	1					1	1	2nd Vol. S. Coy.	No	
5434	Corpl.	Thompson, J.							1	1										Died of disease.
5498	Pte.	Thompson, W.	1	1					1							1	1		Yes	Home on demobn.
5273	,,	Thompson, T.	1	1				1	1		1					1	1		Yes	do. do.
3662	,,	Thomspon, J.							1											
3245	,,	Thompson, J.						1	1		1					1	1		Yes	Home on demobn.
5695	,,	Thompson, J.							1	1						1				do. do.
7668	L.-Cpl.	Thom, A. (Pte.)							1	1						1		1st Vol. S. Coy.		
7586	Pte.	Thomson, A.							1	1						1		1st Vol. S. Coy.		
9034	Corpl.	Thomson, D.							1	1	1					1	1	1st Vol. S. Coy.	No	No. 9129 Corpl. 3/V. S. C.
7589	Pte.	Thomson, J. (Cpl.)							1	1	1					1		1st Vol. S. Coy.		
7669	,,	Thomson, J.							1	1						1		1st Vol. S. Coy.		
7602	,,	Thomson, G.							1	1						1		1st Vol. S. Coy.		
9042	,,	Thomson, G.							1	1	1					1	1	2nd Vol. S. Coy.	No	
9076	,,	Thomson, J.							1	1	1					1	1	2nd Vol. S. Coy.	No	
5568	L.-Cpl.	Thomson, A.	1	1					1	1	1					1	1		Yes	Home on demobn.
7049	Pte.	Thomson, G.	1	1				1	1		1					1	1	Home, invalided.	Yes	do. do.
4530	,,	Thomson, J.	1	1				1	1							1				do. do.
4605	,,	Thomson, M.							1	1	1					1	1		Yes	Home on demobn.
6606	,,	Thomson, R.	1	1					1		1					1	1		Yes	
6969	,,	Thomson, S.	1	1				1	1		1					1	1		Yes	Home on demobn.
6902	L.-Cpl.	Teviotdale, J.	1						1											
4512	,,	Thomas, S.	1	1				1	1		1					1	1		Yes	To 1st Blk. Watch.
4428	Pte.	Thorburn, R.	1	1				1	1		1					1	1		Yes	Home on demobn.
6149	,,	Timmins, J.							1	1	1					1	1		Yes	do. do.
4480	,,	Trotter, R.							1	1	1					1	1		Yes	do. do.
3338	,,	Tolland, P.							1	1	1					1	1		Yes	do. do.
7015	,,	Tolmie, E.							1	1	1					1	1		Yes	
6383	,,	Torode, W.						1	1	1	1					1	1		Yes	To 1st Blk. Watch.
6292	Sgt.	Tough, J.							1	1	1					1	1		Yes	do. do.
6817	Pte.	Trueland, J.	1	1				1	1		1					1	1		Yes	
7035	,,	Trueland, R.							1	1										Died of disease.
4326	,,	Triggs, G.	1	1				1	1		1					1	1		Yes	Home on demobn.

Regtl. No.	Rank.	Name.	Paardeberg.	Driefontein.	Johannesburg.	Diamond Hill.	Belfast.	Wittebergen.	Cape Colony.	Orange Free State.	Transvaal.	Tugela Heights.	Relief of Ladysmith.	Laing's Nek.	Natal.	S. Africa, 1901.	S. Africa, 1902.	On what Roll name submitted for Queen's S. A. Medal.	If entitled to King's S. A. Medal.	Remarks.
6018	Pte.	Tucker, T.						1												
5544	,,	Tulloch, W. (Lc.-Corpl.)						1	1	1						1	1		Yes	Home on demobn.
3523	,,	Tulloch, W.						1	1											
6632	,,	Tulloch, T.						1	1	1						1	1		Yes	To 1st Blk. Watch.
3513	,,	Tully, M.						1	1	1						1	1		Yes	Home on demobn.
5417	,,	Turbett, W. (Lc.-Corpl.)					1	1			1					1	1	To 1st Blk. Watch.	Yes	Home, invalided.
6046	,,	Turkington, T.						1												
3064	Corpl.	Turner, G.						1												
4254	Pte.	Turner, C.	1	1				1								1	1		Yes	Discharged in S. Africa.
6752	,,	Urquhart, D.						1	1	1						1	1		Yes	
4916	Drmr.	Vance, C. (Lc.-Corpl.)						1	1		1					1	1		Yes	
5381	Sgt.	Veitch, W.						1								1	1		Yes	To A. Reserve in S. Africa.
7065	Pte.	Veitch, N.						1	1		1					1	1	Home, time exp.	Yes	Home on demobn.
7294	,,	Veitch, J. (Lc.-Corpl.)						1	1		1					1	1	do. do.	Yes	do. do.
6960	L.-Cpl.	Veitch, D. (Pte.)						1	1		1					1	1		No	Discharged.
7555	Pte.	Walker, W.						1	1									1st Vol. S. Coy.		E/132 S.A.C.
6109	,,	Walker, T.						1	1	1						1	1		Yes	To 1st Blk. Watch.
6967	,,	Walker, W.	1					1												Died of disease.
4304	,,	Walker, A.	1	1				1	1		1					1	1		Yes	Home on demobn.
7033	L.-Cpl.	Walker, G. (Cpl.)						1	1		1					1	1		Yes	Home, invalided.
2258	Pte.	Walker, T.						1	1							1				Home, time exp.
3187	,,	Walker, D.	1	1				1												
6345	Corpl.	Wale, P.						1												
4111	L.-Cpl.	Wall, W.	1		1	1	1	1												
3829	Sgt.	Wallace, W.						1												
6869	Pte.	Wallace, W.	1	1				1	1											
7093	,,	Wallace, J.	1	1				1	1		1					1	1	Home, time exp.	Yes	Home on demobn.
7059	,,	Wallace, A.						1	1		1					1	1		Yes	
6748	,,	Walters, C.	1	1				1	1		1					1	1		Yes	
4680	,,	Walton, J.	1	1				1												Died of disease.
6736	,,	Wannan, S.	1	1				1	1		1					1	1		Yes	To 1st Blk. Watch.
5888	Sgt.	Ward, R.						1	1	1	1					1	1		Yes	Home, invalided.
2365	Pte.	Ward, G.						1	1	1						1		Home on demobn.	Yes	Home, invalided.
3029	,,	Ward, R.							1	1										Home, time exp.
4676	L.-Cpl.	Ward, T. (Pte.)	1	1				1								1		Deceased.		Killed in action.
6983	Pte.	Watt, A.	1	1				1								1	1	Home, invalided.	Yes	To Regtl. Depot.
2157	,,	Watt, J. (L.-Cpl.)						1	1		1					1	1			Killed in action.
5949	,,	Watt, D.	1					1											Yes	Home on demobn.
5764	,,	Watts, R.								1	1			1	1	1	1		Yes	do. do.
5480	,,	Waterson, J.	1	1				1	1		1					1	1		Yes	do. do.
5294	Sgt.	Watson, A. (Pte.)						1	1	1						1	1	Home, invalided.	Yes	do. do.
6964	Pte.	Watson, T.						1												
7407	L.-Cpl.	Watson, W. B. (Corpl.)						1	1	1						1	1		Yes	Home, invalided.

Regtl. No.	Rank.	Name.	Paardeberg.	Driefontein.	Johannesburg.	Diamond Hill.	Belfast.	Wittebergen.	Cape Colony.	Orange Free State.	Transvaal.	Tugela Heights.	Relief of Ladysmith.	Laing's Nek.	Natal.	S. Africa, 1901.	S. Africa, 1902.	On what Roll name submitted for Queen's S. A. Medal.	If entitled to King's S. A. Medal.	Remarks.
7001	Pte.	Watson, F.							1	1	1					1	1		Yes	
4730	,,	Watson, G.							1											
9052	,,	Watson, R.							1	1	1					1	1	2nd Vol. S. Coy.	No	
5747	,,	Webb, G.						1	1		1					1	1		Yes	
2254	Band-Sgt.	Webb, W.							1	1										
4170	Pte.	Waterman, J.							1											
7299	,,	Waugh, H.							1	1	1					1	1		Yes	Killed in action.
3990	,,	Wedderspoon, S.	1	1				1	1							1	1		Yes	Discharged in S. Africa.
7284	L.-Cpl.	Weedon, W. (Pte.)							1	1						1				Home, invalided.
7556	Pte.	Welsh, N. M.						1	1							1		1st Vol. S. Coy.		
6402	,,	Welsh, D.							1											
7248	,,	Welsh, A.						1	1		1					1	1		Yes	
4265	Sgt.	Weir, G. M. G.							1	1	1					1	1	22nd Bn. M.I.	Yes	
6786	Pte.	Weir, A. W.						1	1		1					1	1		Yes	
2571	,,	Weir, G.			1	1	1	1	1							1	1		Yes	Home, time exp.
4282	,,	Welstead, C. C.	1	1				1	1	1						1	1		Yes	Home on demobn. E/135 S.A.C.
4433	,,	Whittaker, W.							1	1										
987	C.-Sgt.	Whittaker, B.							1	1	1					1	1	2nd Vol. S. Coy.	No	
9043	Pte.	West, D.							1	1	1					1	1	2nd Vol. S. Coy.	No	
6837	,,	Whitton, D.	1	1				1	1	1						1	1		Yes	
4488	,,	Whitehead, A.							1											Killed in action.
7133	,,	Whyte, W. (White)							1	1	1					1	1		Yes	
7185	,,	White, W.							1	1										
4843	,,	Whitworth, G.							1											
6714	,,	Whyte, G.							1											
3699	,,	Whyte, J.	1	1					1		1					1				Home on demobn.
3856	,,	Whyte, G.							1											
8979	,,	Whyte, D.							1	1	1					1	1	2nd Vol. S. Coy.	No	
8998	,,	Whyte, W.							1	1	1					1	1	2nd Vol. S. Coy.	No	
2336	Sgt.	White, D.							1	1	Yes*									*Issue authd. 68/42/905, 3/7/05. Issd. 10/7/05. Transvaal Clasp issd. off E.C. Roll /10854.
6880	Corpl.	Wicks, W. (Sgt.)							1	1	1					1	1		Yes	
6985	Pte.	Wightman, A.							1	1										
6929	,,	Wilkie, J.							1	1	1					1	1		Yes	To A. Reserve in S. Africa.
2349	,,	Williamson, D.						1	1											
3843	,,	Williamson, J.							1											
4099	,,	Williamson, G.	1	1				1	1		1					1	1		Yes	Home on demobn.
6626	,,	Williamson, D. J.	1	1					1		1					1	1		Yes	
2212	,,	Williamson, J.						1	1							1				Home on demobn.
6749	Corpl.	Williams, J.							1											
7100	Pte.	Wilkins, F. (Cpl.)	1	1				1	1		Yes*					1	1		Yes	*Issue authd. 68/42/905, 3/7/05. Issd. 10/7/05.

Regtl. No.	Rank.	Name.	Paardeberg.	Driefontein.	Johannesburg.	Diamond Hill.	Belfast.	Wittebergen.	Cape Colony.	Orange Free State.	Transvaal.	Tugela Heights.	Relief of Ladysmith.	Laing's Nek.	Natal.	S. Africa, 1901.	S. Africa, 1902.	On what Roll name submitted for Queen's S. A. Medal.	If entitled to King's S. A. Medal.	Remarks.
4398	Pte.	Wilkinson, J.	1	1				1	1		1					1	1		Yes	Home on demobn.
7048	L.-Cpl.	Willis, J. (Cpl.)	1	1					1		1					1	1		Yes	
3753	L.-Sgt.	Willson, J. E.							1	1						1				Home, time exp.
201	Pte.	Wilson, G.							1	1	1					1	1	Forfeited, felony. A.G.2C/18198.	Yes	Home, time exp.
5768	,,	Wilson, P.							1	1	1					1	1		Yes	Home on demobn.
4173	Sgt.	Wilson, T. H. (Cr.-Sgt.)	1	1					1		1					1	1		Yes	
3509	,,	Wilson, A.	1					1	1		1					1	1		Yes	Home on demobn.
4961	Pte.	Wilson, R.			1	1	1		1	1						1	1		Yes	Home on demobn.
2169	,,	Wilson, J.							1	1	1					1	1	Home on demobn.	Yes	Mila. Reserve 3rd A. and S. Highrs.
5323	,,	Wilson, R.							1											Killed in action.
7089	,,	Wilson, J.							1											Died of wounds.
4129	,,	Wilson, J.	1					1	1		1					1	1		Yes	Discharged in S. Africa.
6831	,,	Wilson, J.	1	1					1		1					1	1		Yes	
4713	,,	Wilson, W.							1	1	1					1	1	Home, invalided.	Yes	Home on demobn.
7095	,,	Wilson, W.							1	1	1					1	1		Yes	
4204	Sgt.	Wilson, A.	1						1	1	1					1	1	Home, time exp.	Yes	Home on demobn.
7318 6	Pte.	Wilson, R. (Lc.-Corpl.)							1	1	1					1	1		Yes	
3571	,,	Wilson, C.						1	1							1				Home on demobn.
3205	,,	Wilson, H.							1	1	1					1	1		Yes	Home on demobn.
7282	,,	Wilson, W.	1						1		1					1	1		Yes	
5002	,,	Winsor, W.							1	1						1	1		Yes	Home on demobn.
7610	,,	Winton, W.						1	1	1						1		1st Vol. S. Coy.		
2447	,,	Wishart, J.						1	1							1				Discharged in S. Africa.
3967	L.-Cpl.	Wishart, D. (Corpl.)	1	1				1	1		Yes*					1	1		Yes	Home on demobn. *Issd. 31/7/06.
3553	Pte.	Wishart, J.							1											
4004	,,	Wood, J.	1	1					1											
5204	,,	Wood, J.	1	1					1											Trial dispensed with for offence of Fraudulent Enlistment.
7495	,,	Woodcock, D.							1	1	1					1	1		Yes	Discharged in S. Africa.
5209	L.-Cpl.	Woolf, E. (Pte.)							1	1	1					1	1		Yes	Home, invalided.
4038	Pte.	Wright, W.	1	1					1		1					1	1		Yes	do. do.
6686	,,	Wright, J.							1											Died of disease.
7256	,,	Wright, J.							1	Yes*										* Issue authorised 68/42/905, 3/7/05. Issd. 10/7/05.
4145	L.-Cpl.	Wright, W. (Pte.)							1	1	1					1	1		Yes	Home on demobn.
2397	Pte.	Valentine, A.						1	1							1				Home, time exp.
4156	,,	Wyllie, W.	1	1				1	1		1					1	1		Yes	Home on demobn.
6891	,,	Wyseman, P.	1	1	1	1			1							1				Home, invalided.
4070	,,	Wynn, O.	1	1				1	1		Yes*					1	1	Home on demobn.	Yes	* Issue authorised 68/42/905, d/3/7/05. Issd. 10/7/05.

Regtl. No.	Rank.	Name.	Paardeberg.	Driefontein.	Johannesburg.	Diamond Hill.	Belfast.	Wittebergen.	Cape Colony.	Orange Free State.	Transvaal.	Tugela Heights.	Relief of Ladysmith.	Laing's Nek.	Natal.	S. Africa, 1901.	S. Africa, 1902.	On what Roll name submitted for Queen's S. A. Medal.	If entitled to King's S. A. Medal.	Remarks.
4401	Pte.	Yates, J. . .	1	1				1	1		1					1	1		Yes	Home on demobn.
6763	,,	Young, J. . .							1											Killed in action.
2162	,,	Young, A. . .						1	1											
4220	,,	Young, J. . .	1	1				1	1		1					1	1		Yes	Home on demobn.
7170	,,	Young, G. . .							1	1	1					1	1		Yes	Home, invalided.
8922	,,	Young, S. E. .							1	1	1					1	1	2nd Vol. S. Coy.	No	Discharged Cape Town, May /02.
6864	,,	Young, D. . .	1	1				1	1		1					1	1		Yes	
?2422 [1]	,,	Young, J. . .						1	1							1				Home on demobn.
7143	,,	Yale, S. (Yule)							1	1	1					1	1		Yes	
4484	,,	Henderson, R.							1											Killed in action.
5723	,,	Williams, C. .							1											Killed in action.
4975	,,	Culross, W. .							1											
5527	,,	Quinn, J. . .							1									No Medal.		Deserted 5 Decr. /99.

[1] Roll torn heie.—J.S.

SUPPLEMENTARY SOUTH AFRICAN MEDAL ROLL
2ND BATTALION THE BLACK WATCH

RANK.	NAME.	Cape Colony.	Orange Free State.	Transvaal.	S. Africa, 1901.	S. Africa, 1902.	On what Roll name submitted for Queen's S. A. Medal.	If entitled to King's S. A. Medal.	REMARKS.
Captain	Dawes, E. S.		1			1		No	
,,	Collins, J. G.		1	1	1	1		No	
,,	Murray, J. T. C.	1	1	1	1	1		No	
,,	Buyers, J.	1	1			1		No	3rd Vol. S. Coy.
Lieut.	Ferguson, T.	1	1			1		No	3rd Vol. S. Coy.
,,	Walker, C. E. C.	1	1			1		No	3rd Vol. S. Coy.
2nd Lieut.	Henderson, C. R. B.		1	1	1	1	22nd Bn. M.I.	No	
,,	Wavell, A. P.		1	1	1	1	22nd Bn. M.I.	No	
,,	Robertson, R. M.		1	1	1	1	22nd Bn. M.I.	No	
,,	Henderson, N. G. B.	Yes	1			1	22nd Bn. M.I.	No	

Regtl. No.	Rank.	NAME.								
7797	Pte.	Adams, J.								
7840	,,	Adamson, H.								
8										
8256	,,	Adamson, N.		1			1			On 1st B. W. Supplemetary Roll.
9128	Corpl.	Abbott, A.	1	1			1			3rd Vol. S. Coy.
7721	Pte.	Aineworth, W.								
7862	L.-Cpl.	Aikman, A.								
8179	Pte.	Aitken, J.								
8081	,,	Akers, D.								
7297	,,	Alexander, J.								
8254	,,	Allan, J.		1			1		No	On 1st B. W. Supplementary Roll.
7360	,,	Allen, W.								
7836	,,	Allerdyce, A.								
9144	,,	Anderson, D.	1	1			1			3rd Vol. S. Coy.
7281	,,	Anderson, W.								
8014	,,	Anderson, R.								
8134	,,	Armit, A.		1		1	1		No	On 1st B. W. Supplementary Roll.
8030	,,	Armstrong, J.		1		1	1		No	On 1st B. W. Supplementary Roll.
7725	,,	Ashworth, J.								
7687	,,	Bathgate, J.								
7306	,,	Bange, A.								
8387	,,	Barclay, W.		1			1		No	On 1st B. W. Supplementary Roll.
8270	,,	Bain, A.								
7889	,,	Band, W.								
8010	,,	Barr, H.								
3882	C.-Sgt.	Bain, W.	1	1		1	1			3rd Vol. S. Coy. Transfd. to ' D ' Coy. 2/B. W.
7440	Pte.	Bennett, R.								
7893	,,	Beveridge, R.								
8031	,,	Bell, R.		1			1		No	On 1st B. W. Supplementary Roll.
7941	,,	Berry, J.		1			1		No	On 1st B. W. Supplementary Roll.
7449	,,	Berry, J.								

Regtl. No.	Rank.	Name.	Cape Colony.	Orange Free State.	Transvaal.	S. Africa, 1901.	S. Africa, 1902.	On what Roll name submitted for Queen's S. A. Medal.	If entitled to King's S. A. Medal.	Remarks.
8263	Pte.	Beech, J.		1			1		No	On 1st B. W. Supplementary Roll.
9143	,,	Bell, A.	1	1			1			3rd Vol. S. Coy.
8181	,,	Bloy, A.								
8307	,,	Black, A.								
8048	,,	Black, R.								
7450	,,	Black, W.								
9094	,,	Blyth, A.	1	1			1			3rd Vol. S. Coy.
9159	,,	Blair, R. A.	1	1			1			3rd Vol. S. Coy.
7719	L.-Cpl.	Brown, T.								
7937	Pte.	Brown, W.								
7390	,,	Brodie, J.								
8043	,,	Breen, J.								
7654	,,	Burwood, W.								
8004	,,	Buchan, T. H.								
9139	,,	Buist, W.	1	1			1			3rd Vol. S. Coy.
9085	,,	Buntung, J. (Bunting)	1	1			1			3rd Vol. S. Coy.
9141	,,	Burgess, D.	1	1			1			3rd Vol. S. Coy.
8243	,,	Bonella, J.								
7993	,,	Bowman, C.								
9136	,,	Bowman, A.	1	1			1			3rd Vol. S. Coy.
9169	,,	Bowman, A.	1	1			1			3rd Vol. S. Coy.
9096	,,	Binny, W. (Binnie)	1	1			1			3rd Vol. S. Coy.
6160	,,	Carroll, J.								
7642	,,	Carr, W.		1		1	1		No	On 1st B. W. Supplementary Roll.
7969	,,	Carberry, S.								
9130	Corpl.	Carr, C.	1	1			1			3rd Vol. S. Coy.
9171	Pte.	Carr, R.	1	1			1			3rd Vol. S. Coy.
8360	,,	Cameron, R.								
8122	,,	Caird, D.		1			1		No	On 1st B. W. Supplementary Roll.
7970	,,	Campbell, D.								
8184	,,	Cairns, A.		1			1		No	On 1st B. W. Supplementary Roll.
7932	,,	Crinean, W.								
7792	,,	Chapman, J.								
8032	,,	Cooper, R. (Drumr.)		1			1		No	On 1st B. W. Supplementary Roll.
8187	,,	Cormack, G.								
8066	,,	Cook, J.		1			1		No	On 1st B. W. Supplementary Roll.
8021	,,	Cranie, D.								Changed name to P. Doyle. *Vide* A.G. 2/M/10854 additional Clasp Roll.
7474	,,	Cooper, J.								
4778	Drmr.	Cooper, J.								
7489	Pte.	Clarkson, E.		1			1		No	On 1st B. W. Supplementary Roll.
7829	,,	Chapman, W. A.		1			1		No	On 1st B. W. Supplementary Roll.
7717	,,	Cook, G.								
7443	,,	Crichton, P.								
9119	,,	Connell, T. D.	1	1			1			3rd Vol. S. Coy.
9090	,,	Coullie, J.	1	1			1			3rd Vol. S. Coy.
9098	,,	Couper, R.	1	1			1			3rd Vol. S. Coy.
9120	,,	Christie, A.	1	1			1			3rd Vol. S. Coy.
9140	,,	Cosgrove, F.	1	1			1			3rd Vol. S. Coy.
9121	,,	Connley, D.	1	1			1			3rd Vol. S. Coy.

Regtl. No.	Rank.	Name.	Cape Colony.	Orange Free State.	Transvaal.	S. Africa, 1901.	S. Africa, 1902.	On what Roll name submitted for Queen's S. A. Medal.	If entitled to King's S. A. Medal.	Remarks.
9101	Pte.	Cuthbert, F. J.	1	1			1			3rd Vol. S. Coy.
6518	,,	Dalling, J.		1			1		No	On 1st B. W. Supplementary Roll.
8053	,,	Dalloway, G.								
7295	,,	Crombie, D.								
7961	,,	Davidson, W.								
7799	,,	Davies, J.		1			1		No	On 1st B. W. Supplementary Roll.
5726	,,	Dailly, J.								
9151	L.-Cpl.	Davidson, F.	1	1			1			3rd Vol. S. Coy.
7843	Pte.	Dewar, R.								
8194	,,	Dewar, R.		1			1		No	On 1st B. W. Supplementary Roll.
9091	,,	Dewar, P.	1	1			1			3rd Vol. S. Coy.
8065	,,	Dearden, J.								
7902	L.-Cpl.	Dickson, A.								
8051	Pte.	Dickie, W.								
8130	,,	Dick, H. W.								
7530	,,	Dilly, T.								
7917	,,	Dick, W.		1			1		No	On 1st B. W. Supplementary Roll.
8220	,,	Doig, D.								
7999	,,	Downie, J.							No	On 1st B. W. Supplementary Roll.
8129	,,	Donaldson, A.		1			1		No	On 1st B. W. Supplementary Roll.
8275	,,	Doig, M.		1			1		No	On 1st B. W. Supplementary Roll.
7739	,,	Doyle, A.								
9118	,,	Doyle, J.	1	1			1			3rd Vol. S. Coy.
7387	,,	Duff, G.								
7957	,,	Duncanson, J.								
7765	,,	Douglas, J.								
7801	,,	Donoghue, P.		1			1	Forfeited. Incorrigible and worthless. Medal and Clasps returned to Woolwich 27/5/10. Vide 68/42/981.	No	On 1st B. W. Supplementary Roll.
7709	,,	Duff, J.								
9086	,,	Duncan, J.	1	1			1			3rd Vol. S. Coy.
9117	,,	Duncan, W.	1	1			1			3rd Vol. S. Coy.
9126	Sergt.	Donaldson, W.[1]	1	1		1	1	1st Vol. S. Coy.		3rd Vol. S. Coy.
7770	Pte.	Easson, W.								
9089	,,	Edminton, J.	1	1			1			3rd Vol. S. Coy.
9123	,,	Ellis, A.	1	1			1			3rd Vol. S. Coy.
9106	,,	Ettle, A. M'L.	1	1			1			3rd Vol. S. Coy.
9157	,,	Evans, J.	1	1			1			3rd Vol. S. Coy.
8098	,,	Fleming, A.		1			1		No	On 1st B. W. Supplementary Roll.
7671	,,	Forbes, A.								
8142	,,	Fairbairn, J.								
7906	,,	Foggo, J.								
8015	,,	Feeney, P.								
8095	L.-Cpl.	Feeney, M.								
7727	Pte.	Findlay, A.		1		1	1		No	On 1st B. W. Supplementary Roll.
9135	Drmr.	Forbes, A.	1	1			1			3rd Vol. S. Coy.
7963	Pte.	Forsyth, J.		1		1	1		No	On 1st B. W. Supplementary Roll.
8057	,,	Ferguson, P.								
8395	,,	Fleming, J.								

[1] No. 7566 in 1st Vol. S. Coy.

Regtl. No.	Rank.	Name.	Cape Colony.	Orange Free State.	Transvaal.	S. Africa, 1901.	S. Africa, 1902.	On what Roll name submitted for Queen's S. A. Medal.	If entitled to King's S. A. Medal.	Remarks.
7871	Pte.	Farrington, D.								
7901	,,	Flannagan, J.		1		1	1		No	On 1st B. W. Supplementary Roll.
7976	,,	Forrester, W.								
9095	,,	Forbes, D.	1	1			1			3rd Vol. S. Coy.
9083	,,	Fraser, A.	1	1			1			3rd Vol. S. Coy.
6145	,,	Garvie, W. J.		1			1		No	On 1st B. W. Supplementary Roll.
7313	,,	Gatherer, J.								
4316	,,	Green, G.								
8206	,,	Goldie, D.								
8207	,,	Gray, J.		1			1		No	On 1st B. W. Supplementary Roll.
7890	,,	Galloway, J.								
7442	,,	Grant, J.								
8224	,,	Gray, D.								
7226	,,	Gethins, J.								
7466	,,	Gibb, A.		1			1		No	On 1st B. W. Supplementary Roll.
8120	,,	Goar, F.								
4101	Drmr.	Goulden, J.								
8292	Pte.	Green, W. H.								
7842	,,	Greig, W.								
7391	,,	Grey, J.								
8146	,,	Gourlay, N. W.		1			1		No	On 1st B. W. Supplementary Roll.
8150	,,	Gordon, D.								
8160	,,	Gray, J.		1			1			
8036	,,	George, W.		1			1		No	On 1st B. W. Supplementary Roll.
9147	,,	Gibb, D. F.	1	1			1			3rd Vol. S. Coy.
9131	L.-Cpl.	Gregory, W.	1	1			1			3rd Vol. S. Coy.
9087	Pte.	Grant, R. G.	1	1			1			3rd Vol. S. Coy.
9174	,,	Gray, J.	1	1			1			3rd Vol. S. Coy.
7711	,,	Hall, C.								
8420	,,	Hastie, J.								
8009	,,	Harley, J.								
7508	,,	Harrison, H.		1		1	1		No	On 1st B. W. Supplementary Roll.
7380	,,	Harris, C.								
7865	,,	Hastie, W.								
8247	,,	Hastie, J.								
8133	,,	Hardie, D.								
7751	,,	Henderson, A.		1		1	1		No	On 1st B. W. Supplementary Roll.
8061	,,	Henderson, A.								
7819	,,	Hessell, T.								
7830	,,	Heap, S.								
9145	,,	Heron, W.	1	1			1			3rd Vol. S. Coy.
8041	,,	Howie, A.		1			1		No	On 1st B. W. Supplementary Roll.
7853	,,	Horsburgh, W.								
7848	,,	Hill, F.								
9125	Sergt.	Horne, J. T.	1	1			1			3rd Vol. S. Coy.
8096	Pte.	Hynd, J.								
9172	,,	Ireland, J.	1	1			1			3rd Vol. S. Coy.
7409	,,	Inglis, R.								
7994	,,	Irvine, J.		1			1		No	On 1st B. W. Supplementary Roll.
8058	,,	Inglis, J.								
8143	,,	Inglis, O.								

Regtl. No.	Rank.	Name.	Cape Colony.	Orange Free State.	Transvaal.	S. Africa, 1901.	S. Africa, 1902.	On what Roll name submitted for Queen's S. A. Medal.	If entitled to King's S. A. Medal.	Remarks.
5525	L.-Sgt.	Johnstone, J.								
7990	L.-Cpl.	Johnstone, T.							No	On 1st B. W. Supplementary Roll.
7958	Pte.	Johnstone, D. . .		1			1			3rd Vol. S. Coy.
9093	,,	Joiner, D. . . .	1	1			1			3rd Vol. S. Coy.
9170	,,	Johnstone, J. (L.-Cpl.)	1	1			1			3rd Vol. S. Coy.
9109	,,	Joiner, G. . . .	1	1			1			3rd Vol. S. Coy.
9115	,,	Keillor, T. T. . .	1	1			1			
7876	,,	Kerr, J.		1		1	1		No	On 1st B. W. Supplementary Roll.
8190	,,	Kelly, F.								
7803	,,	Kinloch, W.								
8103	,,	Kirk, J.								
8074	,,	Kirk, A.								
8132	,,	Kirk, D.		1			1		No	On 1st B. W. Supplementary Roll.
7740	,,	Kennedy, J.								
7919	,,	Louden, J.							No	On 1st B. W. Supplementary Roll.
8075	,,	Lorimer, J.[1] . . .		1			1		No	On 1st B. W. Supplementary Roll.
7430	L.-Cpl.	Laurie, T. . . .		1			1			
7486	,,	Love, H.								
8020	Pte.	Lawler, H.								Died 28/1/02.
7696	,,	Lamond, P. . . .								
7880	,,	Logie, J.								
8175	,,	Lugton, J.								
9102	,,	Lane, J. . . .	1	1			1			3rd Vol. S. Coy.
9175	Corpl.	Lannen, J. . . .	1	1			1			3rd Vol. S. Coy.
9152	Pte.	Lafferty, J. . . .	1	1			1			3rd Vol. S. Coy.
9116	,,	Mitchell, R. . . .	1	1			1			3rd Vol. S. Coy.
9150	,,	Milne, J. . . .	1	1			1			3rd Vol. S. Coy.
9155	,,	Morrison, J. . .	1	1			1			3rd Vol. S. Coy.
9122	,,	Matthews, J. . .	1	1			1			3rd Vol. S. Coy.
9146	,,	Miller, C. . . .	1	1			1			3rd Vol. S. Coy.
9134	,,	Morgan, C. . . .	1	1			1			3rd Vol. S. Coy.
9173	,,	Middleton, A. . .	1	1			1			3rd Vol. S. Coy.
7678	,,	Mann, R. . . .		1			1		No	On 1st B. W. Supplementary Roll.
5973	,,	Manson, W. . . .								
7161	,,	Miller, W.								
8035	,,	Millar, W. M. . .		1			1		No	On 1st B. W. Supplementary Roll.
7874	,,	Millar, J.								
7835	,,	Motion, G. . . .		1		1	1		No	On 1st B. W. Supplementary Roll.
8204	,,	Murdoch, A.								
7922	,,	Muchan, J.								
7991	,,	Mullen, G.								
7482	,,	Murray, R. M. . .		1		1	1		No	On 1st B. W. Supplementary Roll.
8157	,,	Melville, E.								
8259	,,	Mackie, J.								
8193	,,	Melville, T.								
7675	,,	Mitchell, W.								Died of disease.
7363	,,	Moir, D. . . .		1		1	1		No	On 1st B. W. Supplementary Roll.
8029	,,	Morrison, N.								
5310	Corpl.	Martin, A.								
7978	Pte.	Martin, M.								
2900	Corpl.	Melville, R.								

[1] Shown on two lists, on one the Clasp is 1902 and on the other 'Orange Free State.'—J. S.

Regtl. No.	Rank.	Name.	Cape Colony.	Orange Free State.	Transvaal.	S. Africa, 1901.	S. Africa, 1902.	On what Roll name submitted for Queen's S. A. Medal.	If entitled to King's S. A. Medal.	Remarks.
7911	L.-Cpl.	Muir, A.								
7954	Pte.	Milne, G.								
7884	,,	Malone, W.								
7997	,,	Marshall, W.		1			1		No	On 1st B. W. Supplementary Roll.
7986	,,	Milligan, W.								
7698	,,	Moore, R.								Died at Hielbron, 5/3/02.
7855	,,	Morrison, A.								
7869	,,	Morrison, F. W.								
8166	,,	Morrison, S.								
8073	,,	Murphy, T.								
8024	,,	Madden, P.								
7786	,,	Mathie, T.		1		1	1		No	On 1st B. W. Supplementary Roll.
8054	,,	Murdoch, R.								
7752	,,	Munro, H.								
6090	,,	Morrison, J.		1			1		No	On 1st B. W. Supplementary Roll.
8161	,,	M'Alpine, J.								
8141	,,	M'Kenzie, M.								
8198	,,	M'Kenzie, G.		1			1		No	On 1st B. W. Supplementary Roll.
3274	,,	M'Kenzie, G.								
7804	,,	M'Arthur, P.								
8127	,,	M'Aulay, M.								
8158	,,	M'Kay, W.								
7977	,,	M'Auley, W. M.		1		1	1		No	On 1st B. W. Supplementary Roll.
7924	,,	M'Gregor, J.								
7894	,,	M'Garry, J.								
6918	,,	M'Gregor, H.								
8056	,,	M'Leod, A.								
4825	,,	M'Queen, A.		1			1		No	On 1st B. W. Supplementary Roll.
8037	,,	M'Queen, J.								
7725	,,	M'Donald, A.								
8223	,,	M'Gill, A.		1			1		No	On 1st B. W. Supplementary Roll.
8046	,,	M'Leod, J.								
8001	,,	M'Neil, J.		1			1		No	On 1st B. W. Supplementary Roll.
7022	,,	M'Dougall, J.								
8107	,,	M'Intyre, J.								
8170	,,	M'Kenzie, J. (No Medal)		1			1	[1] Forfeited for Desertion. Medal and Clasps returned to Woolwich 27/5/10. Vide 68/42/981.	No	Tried and sentenced on 31/7/02 by D.C.M. to 49 days I.H.L. for stealing goods, the property of a comrade. On 1st B. W. Supplementary Roll.
4594	,,	M'Aleese, T.								See 2nd Bn. *original* Roll for clasps.
8077	,,	M'Kay, A. G.		1			1		No	On 1st B. W. Supplementary Roll.
8121	,,	M'Kenzie, A.								
7458 7	,,	M'Cullum, J.								
7926	,,	M'Farlane, W.		1		1	1		No	On 1st B. W. Supplementary Roll.
7766	,,	M'Intosh, J.		1		1	1		No	On 1st B. W. Supplementary Roll.
8039	,,	M'Ilroy, J.								
7364	,,	M'Kinnon, A.		1			1		No	On 1st B. W. Supplementary Roll.
5847	Sergt.	M'Lellan, H.								

[1] *This* entry is from the 1st B. W. Supplementary Roll.—J. S.

Regtl. No.	Rank.	NAME.	Cape Colony.	Orange Free State.	Transvaal.	S. Africa, 1901.	S. Africa, 1902.	On what Roll name submitted for Queen's S. A. Medal.	If entitled to King's S. A. Medal.	REMARKS.
8155	Pte.	M'Walters, A.								
9137	,,	M'Burney, B.	1	1			1			3rd Vol. S. Coy.
9160	,,	M'Innes, J.	1	1			1			3rd Vol. S. Coy.
9164	,,	M'Kenzie, M.	1	1			1			3rd Vol. S. Coy.
9148	,,	M'Nair, A.	1	1			1			3rd Vol. S. Coy.
9158	,,	M'Vicar, W.	1	1			1			3rd Vol. S. Coy.
9166	Sergt.	M'Pherson, J.	1	1			1			3rd Vol. S. Coy.
9084	Pte.	M'Callum, A.	1	1			1			3rd Vol. S. Coy.
9104	,,	M'Kinley, J.	1	1			1			3rd Vol. S. Coy.
9088	,,	M'Intosh, A.	1	1			1			3rd Vol. S. Coy.
9132	,,	M'Laren, R.	1	1			1			3rd Vol. S. Coy.
9138	,,	M'Queen, G.	1	1			1			3rd Vol. S. Coy.
7793	L.-Cpl.	Neeley, R.								
7757	Pte.	Neilson, G.								
7708	,,	Nicholson, W.								
8104	,,	Niven, W.								
6696	,,	Neave, A.								
7962	,,	Nicol, A. W.		1		1	1		No	On 1st B. W. Supplementary Roll.
7485	,,	Nicolson, D.								
7483	,,	Nuttal, F.								
7769	,,	Napier, M.		1		1	1		No	On 1st B. W. Supplementary Roll.
7851	,,	Nivison, W.								
8226	,,	Newberry, W.								
8063	,,	Neill, J.								
7939	,,	Neilson, W.								Died 28/8/02.
8295	,,	Ogilvie, C.								
8045	,,	O'Connor, P.								
7704	,,	Orr, T.								
7726	,,	Omerod, A.								
7947	,,	O'Brien, W.								
7805	,,	Paterson, W. J.		1			1		No	On 1st B. W. Supplementary Roll.
8092	,,	Paterson, A.		1			1		No	On 1st B. W. Supplementary Roll.
8116	,,	Parnell, H.								
7746	,,	Paterson, D.								
8090	,,	Pryce, J.								
7754	,,	Page, R.								
7912	,,	Proudfoot, R.								
8070	,,	Plimmer, W.								
7790	L.-Cpl.	Polson, W. (Private)		1			1		No	On 1st B. W. Supplementary Roll.
9113	Pte.	Petrie, A.	1	1			1			3rd Vol. S. Coy.
9100	,,	Pringle, J. D. H.								
9099	,,	Pringle, R. T.	1	1			1			3rd Vol. S. Coy.
8347	,,	Ritchie, F.								
7452	,,	Rushford, R.		1		1	1		No	On 1st B. W. Supplementary Roll.
7913	,,	Reid, W.								
8177	,,	Robertson, A.		1			1		No	On 1st B. W. Supplementary Roll.
7643	L.-Cpl.	Robson, J.								Died 18/4/02.
7987	Pte.	Reilly, J.								
7477	,,	Robertson, J.								
7964	,,	Rosenberg, H.								
7763	,,	Ross, A.								

Regtl. No.	Rank.	Name.	Cape Colony.	Orange Free State.	Transvaal.	S. Africa, 1901.	S. Africa, 1902.	On what Roll name submitted for Queen's S. A. Medal.	If entitled to King's S. A. Medal.	Remarks.
8287	Pte.	Russell, T.		1			1		No	On 1st B. W. Supplementary Roll.
7500	,,	Rodgers, W.		1	1		1	Medal and Clasps issued 16/7/04. E/27868/10. Next of kin (father) now deceased. Medal and Clasps sent O.C. 42nd Rgt. for custody 17/8/04.	No	Died 5/2/02.
7975	,,	Reynolds, W.								
8325	,,	Robertson, J.								
7796	,,	Reid, J.								
7670	,,	Robertson, J.								
8019	,,	Robertson, R.		1			1		No	On 1st B. W. Supplementary Roll.
8169	,,	Rooke, H.		1			1		No	On 1st B. W. Supplementary Roll.
7727	,,	Russell, A.								
8144 9	,,	Reekie, C.								
7957	,,	Reoch, T.		1			1		No	On 1st B. W. Supplementary Roll.
8203	,,	Robertson, A.								
8011	,,	Rencassell, D.								
7739	,,	Ritchie, S.								
8246	,,	Ross, T.		1			1		No	On 1st B. W. Supplementary Roll.
9149	,,	Ramsay, J. L.	1	1			1			3rd Vol. S. Coy.
9112	,,	Robertson, W.	1	1			1			3rd Vol. S. Coy.
9165	,,	Rae, J.	1	1			1			3rd Vol. S. Coy.
9107	,,	Robertson, A.	1	1			1			3rd Vol. S. Coy.
6320	,,	Scott, J.								
8050	,,	Sharp, J.		1			1		No	On 1st B. W. Supplementary Roll.
8139	,,	Sutherland, C.								
8078	,,	Scally, J.								
7732	,,	Stuttard, J.								
7513	,,	Sutherland, T.								
7898	,,	Seraphine, J.		1		1	1		No	On 1st B. W. Supplementary Roll.
7972	,,	Small, J.								
7439	,,	Smith, W.								
8119	,,	Stephen, J.								
7778	,,	Stowell, D.		1			1		No	On 1st B. W. Supplementary Roll.
5102	,,	Summersgill, T.								
8183	,,	Scott, T.								
7753	,,	Simpson, G.								
7965	,,	Skae, W.								
8040	,,	Smith, J.		1			1		No	On 1st B. W. Supplementary Roll.
7821	,,	Smith, D.		1		1	1		No	On 1st B. W. Supplementary Roll.
8038	,,	Swan, T.								
7822	,,	Scott, W.								
7382	,,	Simpson, M.								
7909	,,	Small, J.								
7405	,,	Smitton, D.								
3271	,,	Stewart, W.								
7956	,,	Smith, D.								
8136	,,	Stanley, J.								

Regtl. No.	Rank.	NAME.	Cape Colony.	Orange Free State.	Transvaal.	S. Africa, 1901.	S. Africa, 1902.	On what Roll name submitted for Queen's S. A. Medal.	If entitled to King's S. A. Medal.	REMARKS.
7808	Pte.	Sylvester, G. J. W. . .		1			1		No	On 1st B. W. Supplementary Roll.
8148	,,	Smith, J. . . .		1			1		No	On 1st B. W. Supplementary Roll.
8332	,,	Storrar, T. . . .		1			1		No	On 1st B. W. Supplementary Roll.
7329	,,	Sword, E. A.								
8159	,,	Scott, J. H.								
8101	,,	Scott, J.								
7883	,,	Scott, R.								
7781	,,	Simpson, J.								
5197	Corpl.	Sutherland, A.								
9124	L.-Cpl.	Simpson, D. . . .	1	1			1			3rd Vol. S. Coy.
9111	Pte.	Scott, D. . . .	1	1			1			3rd Vol. S. Coy.
9092	,,	Singleton, E. . .	1	1			1			3rd Vol. S. Coy.
9168	,,	Struth, W. . . .	1	1			1			3rd Vol. S. Coy.
9097	Sgt.	Swaddel, R. . . .	1	1			1			3rd Vol. S. Coy.
9108	Pte.	Scott, D. . . .	1	1			1			3rd Vol. S. Coy.
9161	,,	Scrimgeour, G. . .	1	1			1			3rd Vol. S. Coy.
9110	,,	Smith, D. . . .	1	1			1			3rd Vol. S. Coy.
9154	,,	Sutherland, G. C. .	1	1			1			3rd Vol. S. Coy.
8003	,,	Tulloch, D. . . .		1					Yes	On 1st B. W. Supplementary Roll.
7728	,,	Thomson, R.								
7720	,,	Thomson, T. H.								
8097	,,	Tagg, A.								
8154	,,	Tod, J.								
7877	,,	Timmins, F.								
8114	,,	Tod, D. G.								
8064	,,	Tait, J.								
8258	,,	Taylor, J.								
9103	,,	Thomson, R. . .	1	1			1			3rd Vol. S. Coy.
9156	,,	Thomson, J. . .	1	1			1			3rd Vol. S. Coy.
9153	,,	Thomson, J. . .	1	1			1			3rd Vol. S. Coy.
9162	,,	Thomson, P. . .	1	1			1			3rd Vol. S. Coy.
7815	,,	Wilkinson, A.								
7904	,,	Wilson, R.								
7953	,,	Wilson, T. . . .		1			1	Forfeited. P. Assault. Medal and Clasps returned to Woolwich 27/5/10. *Vide* 68/42/981.	No	On 1st B. W. Supplementary Roll.
8060	,,	Waterson, D.								
8240	,,	Whitcombe, H. W. .		1			1		No	On 1st B. W. Supplementary Roll.
8128	,,	Whitelaw, J.								
8202	,,	Wright, J.								
8052	,,	Warden, G.								
7499	,,	Wilson, T.								
7290	,,	Weir, G.								
8188	,,	Wallace, J.								
8115	,,	Welsh, J.								
7448	,,	Wilson, J.								
7850	,,	Wilson, G.								
7784	,,	Wright, T.								
7905	,,	Watson, D.								

Regtl. No.	Rank.	Name.	Cape Colony.	Orange Free State.	Transvaal.	S. Africa, 1901.	S. Africa, 1902.	On what Roll name submitted for Queen's S. A. Medal.	If entitled to King's S. A. Medal.	Remarks.
7903	Pte.	Williamson, A.								
7408	,,	Wilson, G.								
7539	,,	Wilson, W.								
7272	,,	Wishart, E.								
7776	,,	Wasson, R.								
8083	,,	Watson, A.					1		No	On 1st B. W. Supplementary Roll.
8140	,,	Watson, T.								
7839	::	Ward, A.								
7501	,,	Wilkie, J.								
9133	,,	Watson, R.	1	1			1			3rd Vol. S. Coy.
9167	,,	Whittet, T.	1	1			1			3rd Vol. S. Coy.
9142	,,	Wilkie, A.	1	1			1			3rd Vol. S. Coy.
9105	,,	Whyte, J. D.	1	1			1			3rd Vol. S. Coy.
9163	,,	Wighton, F.	1	1			1			3rd Vol. S. Coy.
8137	,,	Young, E.		1			1		No	On 1st B. W. Supplementary Roll.
7736	,,	Young, R.								
6007	,,	Orr, H.[1]								
5764	,,	Watts, R.[2]								
9114	,,	Oakley, A.[3]	1	1			1			3rd Vol. S. Coy.
9176	,,	Nicol, J.[4]		1		1	1	1st Vol. S. Coy.		3rd Vol. S. Coy.
9129	Corpl.	Thomson, D.[5]				1	1	1st Vol. S. Coy.		3rd Vol. S. Coy.
9127	,,	Burt, J.[6]				1	1	1st Vol. S. Coy.		3rd Vol. S. Coy.

[1] See 2nd Battalion Original Roll. Entitled to clasps for Belfast, Cape Colony, Orange Free State, Tugela Heights, Relief of Ladysmith, and Laing's Nek.

[2] See 2nd Battalion Original Roll. Entitled to clasps for Orange Free State, Transvaal, and Natal.

[3] This man is the only member of the 3rd Vol. S. Coy. whose name does not appear on the 2nd Bn. Supplementary Roll (for what reason I do not know). I have therefore added his name above, thus completing the three Volunteer Service Companies, the 1st and 2nd having already appeared in the original 2nd Bn. Roll.—J. S.

[4] No. 9176 Pte. J. Nicol, see 2nd Bn. Original Roll, No. 7625 1st Vol. S. Coy.

[5] No. 9129 Corpl. D. Thomson, see 2nd Bn. Original Roll, No. 9034 1st Vol. S. Coy.

[6] No. 9127 Corpl. J. Burt, see 2nd Bn. Original Roll, No. 7562 1st Vol. S. Coy.

1st BATTN. THE BLACK WATCH (ROYAL HIGHLANDERS)

ROLL OF INDIVIDUALS

ENTITLED TO THE

SOUTH AFRICAN MEDALS AND CLASPS

UNDER THE ARMY ORDERS GRANTING THE MEDALS

Issued on 1st April 1901 and 1st October 1902

ROLL of Individuals entitled to the South African Medals and Clasps under the Army Orders granting the Medals issued on 1st April 1901 and 1st October 1902.

Note.—In this Roll all those with ' * ' in the Cape Colony clasp column formed the M.I. section.

Rank.	Name.	Whether application already made for Queen's S.A. Medal.	On what Roll name submitted for Queen's S.A. Medal.	Cape Colony.	Orange Free State.	Transvaal.	S. Africa, 1901.	S. Africa, 1902.	If entitled to King's S.A. Medal.	Remarks.
Colonel	E. G. Grogan . . .				1	1	1	1		
Lt.-Colonel	A. G. Duff ¹ . . .	Yes	2nd Black Watch, 8/9/01.		1	1	1	1	Yes	1st Battalion.
Major	St. G. E. W. Burton .			1	1	1	1	1		
"	W. G. Wolrige-Gordon			*1	1	1	1	1		
"	H. Rose				1	1	1	1		
"	D. L. Wilson Farquharson ¹	Yes	2nd Black Watch, 8/9/01.			1	1	1	Yes	
Captain	T. O. Lloyd				1	1	1	1		
"	A. Grant-Duff . . .			1	*1			1		
"	J. G. Collins . . .				1	1	1	1		
"	A. H. Marindin ² . .	Yes	From Staff College.	1	1			1		
"	Sir W. Dick-Cunningham, Bart.									
"	W. J. St. J. Harvey ¹ .	Yes	1st Black Watch, 1/7/01.			1	1	1	Yes	
"	C. M'Lean ¹	Yes	2nd Black Watch, 8/9/01.			1	1	1	Yes	
"	E. F. M. Urquhart .			1	1	1	1			
Lieutenant	S. H. Eden			1	1	1	1			
"	O. H. D'A. Steward .			1	1	1	1			
"	G. D. Grant-Suttie .			1	1	1	1			
"	W. Stewart			1	1	1		1*		* The original Medal Roll is torn here, but these clasps were issued to those two officers.—J.S.
"	W. Green			1	1		1*	1*		
"	B. C. A. Steuart . .	Yes	1st Black Watch, 1/7/01.				1	1	Yes	Lumsden's Horse.
2nd Lieut.	D. Campbell . . .	Yes	2nd Black Watch, 8/9/01.			1	1	1		1st Battalion.
"	C. A. de G. Dalglish .			1	1	1	1			
"	K. J. Campbell .			1	1	1	1			
"	W. T. Kedie . .			1	1	1	1			
"	R. W. Hadow . .			1	1	1	1			
"	A. D. C. Krook .			1	1	1	1		Yes	
"	G. M. Richmond .			1				1		
"	C. E. Strahan . .			1				1		
"	W. D. Allan . .			1				1		
Lt. and Qr.-Mr.	W. B. F. Davidson .			1	1	1	1			

¹ See 2nd Bn. Roll.

² On a list marked 'Black Watch (Special Service)' Capt. Marindin's name appears alone, with the following in the column of Remarks: 'Employed on Special Service March 13th to May 7th in Cape Colony at Base, and on Transport'; 'May 7th to Nov. 13th in Orange River Colony as S. O. to O. C. Rest Camp Btn. and S. O. to O. C. Troops Btn. and S. L. of C.; L. of C. Orders, 16/3/00, 1; Orders O. C. Btn., 30/5/00, 2; A. O. S. Africa, 4/10/00, 6.'—J. S.

Regtl. No.	Rank.	Name.	Whether application already made for Queen's S. A. Medal.	On what Roll name submitted for Queen's S. A. Medal.	Cape Colony.	Orange Free State.	Transvaal.	S. Africa, 1901.	S. Africa, 1902.	If entitled to King's S. A. Medal.	Remarks.
2440	S.-Maj.	William Fowler				1	1	1	1		
1361	Bandmaster	Wm. J. Scott				1		1	1		
6232	Pte.	Alexander Able				1	1	1	1		
5246	,,	William Adam						1	1		
6500	,,	Charles Adamson				1	1	1	1		
6412	,,	John Adamson				1	1	1	1		
5278	Pr.-Sgt.	Wm. Adamson				1	1	1	1		
6670	Pte.	Archibald Addie				1	1	1	1		
6546	,,	William Addison				1	1	1	1		
5299	,,	Hugh Aitken				1	1	1	1		
6163	,,	Andrew Aitken				1	1	1	1		
5251	,,	Thomas Allan				1	1	1	1		
5210	,,	William Allan				1	1	1	1		
6511	,,	Robert Allan				1	1	1	1		Forfeited. Conviction C.M.—theft. Medal and Clasps returned to Woolwich 27/5/10. *Vide* 68/42/981.
5322	,,	William Alexander				1	1	1	1		
5391	,,	William Alexander				1	1	1	1		
4789	,,	James Alexander				1	1	1	1		
5502	,,	John Anderson				1	1	1	1		
6658	,,	Peter Anderson				1	1	1	1		
5932	,,	James Anderson				1	1	1	1		
3763	Sgt.	Robert Anderson				1	1	1	1		
8023	Pte.	Edward Anderson				1	1	1	1		
6452	,,	Robert Anderson				1	1	1	1		
5924	,,	Archibald Anderson				1	1	1	1		
5695	,,	Thomas Anderson				1	1	1	1		
5769	,,	George Anderson				1	1	1	1		
2711	Q.-Mr.-Sgt.	James Anderson				1	1	1	1		
4812	Pte.	Arthur Appleyard				1	1	1	1		
6313	,,	James Armour				1	1	1	1		
6010	,,	Joseph Arthur				1	1	1	1		
7395	,,	William Arthur				1	1	1	1		
5689	,,	David Arthur				1	1	1	1		
5541	Sgt.	Samuel Arthur				1	1	1	1		
4860	Pte.	Alfred Baildon				1	1	1	1		
5775	,,	Peter Bain				1	1	1	1		
5765	,,	John Bain				1	1	1	1		
4720	,,	John Bain				1	1	1	1		
6343	,,	James Baird				1	1	1	1		
7359	,,	Peter Balfour				1	1	1	1		
5280	,,	Charles Banfield				1	1	1	1		
6080	,,	Wm. Bannerman				1	1	1	1		
6339	,,	David Barclay				1	1	1	1		
6161	,,	Mark Barker						1	1		
4926	,,	Thomas Barty				1	1	1	1		
6284	,,	Thomas Barty				1	1	1	1		

Regtl. No.	Rank.	NAME.	Whether application already made for Queen's S. A. Medal.	On what Roll name submitted for Queen's S. A. Medal.	Cape Colony.	Orange Free State.	Transvaal.	S. Africa, 1901.	S. Africa, 1902.	If entitled to King's S. A. Medal.	REMARKS.
5686	Pte.	Archibald Barr . .				1	1	1	1		
5694	,,	Charles Barr . . .				1	1	1	1		
6506	,,	Henry Barr . . .				1	1	1	1		
4182	Sgt.	Walter Barlow . . .				1	1	1	1		
6466	Pte.	William Barrett . .				1	1	1	1		
5508	,,	Neil Baxter . . .				1	1	1	1		
5309	,,	William Beaton . .				1	1	1	1		
2597	,,	James Beattie . . .	Yes	1st Black Watch, 1/7/01.		1	1	1	1		
4837	,,	Alexander Beattie . .				1	1	1	1		
6434	,,	David Bell				1	1	1	1		
4788	,,	Henry Bell				1	1	1	1		
4982	,,	James Bell				1	1	1	1		
6691	,,	William G. Beeby . .				1	1	1	1		
5611	,,	Joseph Bentley . .				1	1	1	1		
4650	,,	William Bertram . .				1	1	1	1		
2813	Cr.-Sgt.	James Birch . . .				1	1	1	1		
6841	Pte.	William Bird [1] . . .	Yes	1st Black Watch, 1/7/01.			1	1	1	Yes	Expunge. Not entitled. Entered in error. A.C./2 /M/13818. Retd. Woolwich. Clasps 1901-2 retained.
6361	,,	Andrew Black . . .				1	1	1	1		
6580	Lc.-Cpl.	William H. Black . .				1	1	1	1		
6115	Pte.	Alexander Black . .				1	1	1	1		
6382	,,	Robert Blair . . .				1	1	1	1		
5490	,,	Roderick Blyth . .				1	1	1	1		
5718	,,	Charles Bogue . . .				1	1	1	1		
5321	,,	Owen Bogue . . .				1	1	1	1		
6326	,,	John Bokie				1	1	1	1		
5106	,,	George Bonnar . .				1	1	1	1		
5180	,,	Joseph Bonnette . .				1	1	1	1		
6287	,,	William Bonnette . .				1	1	1	1		
5460	Sgt.	Robert Bowden . .				1	1	1	1		
6562	Pte.	George Bowler . . .				1	1	1	1		
5529	,,	William Boyd . . .				1	1	1	1		
5597	,,	John Boyd				1	1	1	1		
5003	,,	George Boyes . . .				1	1	1	1		
5539	,,	Stewart Boyle . . .				1	1	1	1		
5576	,,	Peter Breckenridge . .				1	1	1	1		
4765	,,	William Brady . . .				1	1	1	1		
5481	,,	Henry Brand . . .				1	1	1	1		
2078	Sgt.	David Brodie . . .				1	1	1	1		
5689	Pte.	John Brogan . . .				1	1	1	1		
6174	Lc.-Sgt.	David Brook . . .				1	1	1	1		
4628	Pte.	Albert Brown . . .				1	1	1	1		
6414	,,	James Brown . . .				1	1	1	1		
6271	,,	Peter Brown . . .				1	1	1	1		
6414	,,	James Brown . . .				1	1	1	1		
5336	,,	David Brown . . .				1	1	1	1		
5966	,,	David Brown . . .				1	1	1	1		

[1] See 2nd Bn. Roll.

Regtl. No.	Rank.	Name.	Whether application already made for Queen's S. A. Medal.	On what Roll name submitted for Queen's S. A. Medal.	Cape Colony.	Orange Free State.	Transvaal.	S. Africa, 1901.	S. Africa, 1902.	If entitled to King's S. A. Medal.	Remarks.
6615	Lc.-Cpl.	John Brown				1	1	1	1		
5483	Pte.	James Brown				1	1	1	1		
6332	,,	David Brown				1	1	1	1		
4849	,,	John Brown				1	1	1	1		
5025	,,	Robert Brown				1	1	1	1		
5713	,,	Thomas Brown				1	1	1	1		
4762	Sgt.	George Bruce				1	1	1	1		
5410	Pte.	James Bruce				1	1	1	1		
4846	,,	Alexr. Bryson				1	1	1	1		
5456	Sgt.	James Buchan				1	1	1	1		
6556	Pte.	Allan Buchanan				1	1	1	1		
5820	,,	Archibald Buchanan				1	1	1	1		
7856	,,	Thomas Bunting				1	1	1	1		
7505	Corpl.	Robert Burnett				1	1	1	1		
7861	Pte.	David Burt						1	1		
6037	,,	Leonard Burn				1	1	1	1		
2532	Sgt.	Alexander Burnett				1	1	1	1		
5677	Lc.-Cpl.	James Burns				1	1	1	1		
6162	Pte.	John Burns				1	1	1	1		
6286	Corpl.	Andrew Burns				1	1	1	1		
6689	Pte.	John Burns				1	1	1	1		
6327	,,	James Burns				1	1	1	1		
5050	,,	William Burns				1	1	1	1		
5550	,,	David Burns			*1	1	1	1	1		
4140	,,	Arthur Bush				1	1	1	1		
5707	,,	James Byrne				1	1	1	1		
5984	,,	Allan Caldwell				1	1	1	1		
5042	Corpl.	James Callery				1	1	1	1		
5219	Pte.	Kenneth Cameron				1	1	1	1		
5835	,,	Edward Cameron				1	1	1	1		
5032	,,	Finlay Campbell				1	1	1	1		
5574	,,	James Campbell				1	1	1	1		
5075	,,	Robert Campbell				1	1	1	1		
3877	Colour-Sgt.	David Campbell				1	1	1	1		
5433	Pte.	Peter Campbell				1	1	1	1		
5625[1]	,,	Robert Campbell				1	1	1	1		
7273	,,	Robert Campbell				1	1	1	1		
5283	,,	John Campbell				1	1	1	1		
6569	,,	John Campbell				1	1	1	1		
5292	,,	John Cardie				1	1	1	1		
6082	,,	Andrew Carnegie				1	1	1	1		
6088	,,	William Carr				1	1	1	1		
5938	,,	William Carrie				1	1	1	1		
5745	,,	James Carse				1	1	1	1		
5884	,,	John Cassidy				1	1	1	1		
5088	,,	John Cassidy			*1	1	1	1	1		
5418	,,	Peter Cation				1	1	1	1		
5039	,,	Joseph Cavanagh				1	1	1	1		
6074	,,	Thomas Chalmers				1	1	1	1		
4693	,,	James Chalmers				1	1	1	1		

[1] This number belongs to Private Wm. Rutherford. My authority is Private R. Campbell himself, who told me this at Hamilton 19th January 1911. He said he mentioned the matter to his Colour-Sergeant, who told him that 'it did not matter' ! ! ! !—J. S.

Regtl. No.	Rank.	Name.	Whether application already made for Queen's S. A. Medal.	On what Roll name submitted for Queen's S. A. Medal.	Cape Colony.	Orange Free State.	Transvaal.	S. Africa, 1901.	S. Africa, 1902.	If entitled to King's S. A. Medal.	Remarks.
7297	Pte.	John Chalmers . .				1	1	1	1		
6497	,,	William Chalmers . .				1	1	1	1		
4782	Corpl.	Charles Checkley . .				1	1	1	1		
5111	Pte.	William Cheyne . .				1	1	1	1		
4072	Lc.-Cpl.	Alexr. Chisholm . .				1	1	1	1		
6370	,,	John Chivas . . .				1	1	1	1		
6358	Pte.	William Clark . . .				1	1	1	1		
4044	Sgt.	William Clark . . .				1	1	1	1		
6870	Pte.	Hugh Clark [1] . . .	Yes	1st Black Watch, 1/7/01.			1	1	1	Yes	
4621	Sgt.	Thomas Clark . . .				1	1	1	1		
6484	Pte.	Duncan Clark . . .				1	1	1	1		
5506	,,	Ernest Clements . .				1	1	1	1		
6231	,,	Peter Cockrane . .				1	1	1	1		
5357	,,	Thomas Colgrave . .				1	1	1	1		
6342	,,	John Colville . . .				1	1	1	1		
6032	,,	Francis Colyer . . .				1	1	1	1		
5515	,,	Francis Connor . .				1	1	1	1		
5208	,,	Peter Connor . . .				1	1	1	1		
5827	,,	Daniel Conway . .				1	1	1	1		
5972	,,	William Cooper . .				1	1	1	1		
6610	Corpl.	John Cooper . . .				1	1	1	1		
4979	Pte.	John Cooper . . .				1	1	1	1		
5087	,,	Alexander Cormack .				1	1	1	1		
6325	,,	Adam Coupar . . .				1	1	1	1		
6013	,,	John Cowen . . .				1	1	1	1		
8163	,,	Wilfred Cowgill . .				1	1	1	1		
6650	,,	Edwin Cowie . . .				1	1	1	1		
4786	,,	William Cox . . .				1	1	1	1		
8028	,,	William Craig . . .						1	1		
5823	Lc.-Cpl.	James Craig . . .				1		1	1		
5964	Pte.	Thomas Craig . . .				1	1	1	1		
5804	Sgt.	George Craik . . .				1	1	1	1		
5390	Pte.	James Crawford . .				1	1	1	1		
5642	,,	Charles Crawford . .				1	1	1	1		
5200	Lc.-Cpl.	Robert Crawford . .				1	1	1	1		
7775	Pte.	William Crookston .				1	1	1	1		
5188	,,	George Crosson . .				1	1	1	1		
7364	,,	Thomas Crowe . . .				1	1	1	1		
5105	,,	James Culley . . .				1	1	1	1		
5060	,,	James Cumming . .				1	1	1	1		
7783	Lc.-Cpl.	Alexr. Cumming . .				1	1	1	1		
6446	Pte.	William Cummison .				1	1	1	1		
5031	Corpl.	Charles Wm. Curtis .				1	1	1	1		
7042	Pte.	James Curtis . . .				1	1	1	1		
5351	,,	William Cuthbert . .				1	1	1	1		
4651	,,	G. Charles Dalziel . .				1		1	1		*Alias* John M‘Intyre.
6351	,,	Joseph Dair . . .				1	1	1	1		
6056	,,	Alexander Davidson .				1	1	1	1		
5284	,,	Andrew Davidson . .				1	1	1	1		
6578	,,	Daniel Davidson . .				1	1	1	1		

[1] See 2nd Bn. Roll.

Regtl. No.	Rank.	Name.	Whether application already made for Queen's S. A. Medal.	On what Roll name submitted for Queen's S. A. Medal.	Cape Colony.	Orange Free State.	Transvaal.	S. Africa, 1901.	S. Africa, 1902.	If entitled to King's S. A. Medal.	Remarks.
7255	Pte.	David Davis				1	1	1	1		
5326	,,	George Day				1	1	1	1		
6031	,,	John Day				1	1	1	1		
5952	,,	William Day				1	1	1	1		
6583	,,	David Deas				1	1	1	1		
4958	,,	Ernest Dellow				1	1	1	1		
7945	Boy	George Dempster				1	1	1	1		
3276	Pte.	Robert Dempster				1	1	1	1		
4687	,,	John Devine				1	1	1	1		
5699	,,	George Devlin				1	1	1	1		Deserted.
5397	,,	George Devlin		Not entitled. This Medal and Clasps retd. to K.C.O. O. 19/5/03, A.G. 2/M/8458 Roll of 2/N/Fusrs.		1	1	1	1		Transferred to 2nd Northumberland Fusiliers 25/2/02. No. 8540.
5365	,,	John Devlin				1	1	1	1		
5789	,,	Andrew Dewar				1	1	1	1		
6630	,,	Peter Dewar				1	1	1	1		
5272	Sgt.	William Dewar				1	1	1	1		
6189	Pte.	James Dick				1	1	1	1		
4999	,,	James Dickson				1	1	1	1		
5516	,,	Robert Dickson				1	1	1	1		
5441	,,	James Dickson				1	1	1	1		
6566	,,	James Dingwall				1	1	1	1		
5354	,,	William Dobie				1	1	1	1		
5955	,,	David Doig				1	1	1	1		
5189	,,	John Dolenn						1	1		
5762	Corpl.	John Donald				1	1	1	1		
4696	Pte.	William Donald				1	1	1	1		
4874	,,	Arthur Donaldson				1	1	1	1		
7271	,,	George Donaldson [1]	Yes	1st Black Watch, 1/7/01.			1	1	1	Yes	
5671	,,	Henry Dorans				1	1	1	1		
5856	,,	Archibald Douglas				1	1	1	1		
6467	,,	Henry Douglas				1	1	1	1		
4616	,,	John Douglas				1	1	1	1		
6192	,,	James Dow				1	1	1	1		
5500	,,	William Dow				1	1	1	1		
4785	,,	Daniel Downie				1	1	1	1		
7750	,,	John Doyle				1	1	1	1		
4793	,,	Alexr. Drummond				1	1	1	1		
4761	Drumr.	William Drury				1	1	1	1		
6251	Pte.	George Dryden				1	1	1	1		
8102	Drumr.	John Duff				1	1	1	1		
5079	Lc.-Cpl.	David Duncan				1	1	1	1		
5846	Pte.	David Duncan			*1	1	1	1	1		
5399	,,	James Duncan				1	1	1	1		
5033	,,	John Duncan				1	1	1	1		
4878	,,	Thomas Duncan				1	1	1	1		
7312	Corpl.	Thomas Duncan				1	1	1	1		Deceased.
5706	Sgt.	Walter Duncan				1	1	1	1		
6321	Pte.	William Duncan				1	1	1	1		

[1] See 2nd Bn. Roll.

Regtl. No.	Rank.	Name.	Whether application already made for Queen's S. A. Medal.	On what Roll name submitted for Queen's S. A. Medal.	Cape Colony.	Orange Free State.	Transvaal.	S. Africa, 1901.	S. Africa, 1902.	If entitled to King's S. A. Medal.	Remarks.
6462	Pte.	William Duncan				1	1	1	1		
6169	,,	George Duncanson [1]	Yes	Clasp, Defence of Ladysmith. 1st Blk. Watch 1/7/01.		1	1	1	1	Yes	Attd. to 2nd Bn. K.R.R. Corps as mule-driver.
5675	,,	James Dunbar				1	1	1	1		
6987	,,	Cornelius Dunnegan				1	1	1	1		
5027	,,	John Dunnegan				1	1	1	1		
5065	,,	Alexr. Durham				1	1	1	1		
6212	,,	George Durie				1	1	1	1		
6445	,,	Crombie Duthie				1	1	1	1		
4851	Corpl.	Henry P. Eden				1	1	1	1		
5432	Lc.-Cpl.	William Elder				1	1	1	1		
7816	Pte.	Arthur Ellam				1	1	1	1		
6465	,,	Samuel Ewen				1	1	1	1		
4383	,,	James Fairley				1	1	1	1		
7410	,,	James Fairweather				1	1	1	1		Forfeited. Dischd. incorrigible and worthless. Medal and Clasps retd. to Woolwich 27/5/10. Vide 68/42/981.
5455	,,	James Fairweather				1	1	1	1		
6740	Drumr.	James Falconer				1	1	1	1		
6592	Pte.	James Fenton				1	1	1	1		
6252	Corpl.	Andrew Ferguson				1	1	1	1		
4769	Pte.	Robert Findlay				1	1	1	1		
5592	,,	William Finlay			*1	1	1	1	1		
6356	,,	Thomas Finnigan				1	1	1	1		
6095	,,	James Fisher			*1	1	1	1	1		
4732	,,	Robert Flatters				1	1	1	1		
6054	,,	George Fleming				1	1	1	1		
7427	,,	Thomas Fleming				1	1	1	1		
6528	,,	James Flood				1	1	1	1		
5910	,,	Henry Flood				1	1	1	1		
6170	,,	William Forbes				1	1	1	1		
5376	,,	Alexr. Forbes				1	1	1	1		
6409	,,	David Ford				1	1	1	1		
4968	,,	Alexr. Forrest				1	1	1	1		
6559	,,	Andrew Foreman				1	1	1	1		
5375	,,	Peter Forrester				1	1	1	1		
6427	,,	Alexr. Forsyth				1	1	1	1		
7230	,,	Alexander Fraser				1	1	1	1		
6401	,,	James Fraser				1	1	1	1		
6415	,,	John Fraser				1	1	1	1		
7900	,,	Mathew Fraser				1	1	1	1		
5494	,,	Thomas Fraser				1	1	1	1		
6148	,,	John Fraser				1	1	1	1		
3031	Sgt.	James St. G. French				1	1	1	1		
5138	Corpl.	John Fullarton				1	1	1	1		
5514	Pte.	Arthur Funnie				1	1	1	1		
5211	,,	Thomas Fyffe				1	1	1	1		

[1] See 2nd Bn. Roll.

Regtl. No.	Rank.	Name.	Whether application already made for Queen's S. A. Medal.	On what Roll name submitted for Queen's S. A. Medal.	Cape Colony.	Orange Free State.	Transvaal.	S. Africa, 1901.	S. Africa, 1902.	If entitled to King's S. A. Medal.	Remarks.
4747	Pte.	Robert Gailey						1	1		
5674	,,	Donald Galbraith				1	1	1	1		
5766	Corpl.	John Galloway				1	1	1	1		
5895	Pte.	James Gardiner				1	1	1	1		
5019	,,	William Gardiner				1	1	1	1		
5819	,,	Alexander Garvie				1	1	1	1		
5807	,,	James Gardyne				1	1	1	1		
5468	,,	George Geddis				1	1	1	1		
6660	,,	James Geekie				1	1	1	1		
4142	,,	William George				1	1	1	1		
5617	,,	John Gibson				1	1	1	1		
7858	,,	Henry Gatens				1	1	1	1		
7881	,,	George Gibson				1	1	1	1		
7429	Lc.-Cpl.	James Gilbert				1	1	1	1		
6574	Pte.	James Glennie				1	1	1	1		Deceased.
7755	,,	John Gloag				1	1	1	1		
7852	Lc.-Cpl.	William Gray				1	1	1	1		
5619	Sgt.	Albert Green				1	1	1	1		
6106	Pte.	David Greig			*1	1	1	1	1		
5976	,,	John Greig				1	1	1	1		
5242	,,	James Guthrie				1	1	1	1		
4807	,,	Walter Grimshaw				1	1	1	1		
6408	,,	James Grubb				1	1	1	1		
7992	,,	James Gillespie				1	1	1	1		
5890	,,	John Glancy						1	1		
5735	,,	George Glasgow[1]	Not entitled. Did not land. E/28006.					1			Deceased.
5815	,,	James Glendinning				1	1	1	1		
5158	,,	James Goodwin				1	1	1	1		
7774	,,	David Gordon			1	1	1	1	1		
5186	,,	John Gordon				1	1	1	1		
8345	,,	Alexr. Gordon				1	1	1	1		
3440	Sgt.	James Grant				1	1	1	1		
6404	Pte.	Adam Graham			*1	1	1	1	1		
4273	,,	Harry Graham				1	1	1	1		
7838	,,	John Graham				1	1	1	1		
7102	,,	John Graham				1	1	1	1		
4090	,,	Alexander Gray				1	1	1	1		
5646	,,	Andrew Gray				1	1	1	1		
4966	,,	Charles Gray				1	1	1	1		
4955	,,	John Gray				1	1	1	1		
6353	,,	John Gray				1	1	1	1		
6335	,,	Peter Gray				1	1	1	1		
6294	,,	Thomas Gray				1	1	1	1		
4710	,,	Samuel Grice						1	1		
5580	,,	John Grieve				1	1	1	1		
4873	,,	James Gruar				1	1	1	1		
5080	,,	David Guillan				1	1	1	1		
4127	Sgt.	Thomas Gunn				1	1	1	1		
7535	Pte.	George Hadow				1	1	1	1		
4894	,,	William Haggerty				1	1	1	1		

[1] This man fell overboard and was drowned at Durban.

Regtl. No.	Rank.	NAME.	Whether application already made for Queen's S. A. Medal.	On what Roll name submitted for Queen's S. A. Medal.	Cape Colony.	Orange Free State.	Transvaal.	S. Africa, 1901.	S. Africa, 1902.	If entitled to King's S. A. Medal.	REMARKS.
7030	Pte.	David Halley . . .				1	1	1	1		
3242	,,	Joseph Hall . . .				1	1	1	1		
7112	,,	Ernest Hamilton . .				1	1	1	1		
5837	,,	William Hamilton . .				1	1	1	1		
6765	,,	William Hamilton . .				1	1	1	1		
6324	,,	David Hamilton . .						1	1		
3074	Cr.-Sgt.	Thomas Hampton . .				1	1	1	1		
6369	Corpl.	James Hannan . .				1	1	1	1		
7915	Pte.	John Hardy . . .				1	1	1	1		
6977	Lc.-Cpl.	John Harkins [1] . .	Yes	1st Black Watch, 1/7/01.			1	1	1	Yes	
7791	Pte.	John Harley . . .				1	1	1	1		
5603	,,	William Harman . .				1	1	1	1		
4892	,,	William G. Harper .				1	1	1	1		
6240	,,	John Harrison . .				1	1	1	1		
3933	,,	Alexander Harvey .				1	1	1	1		
5792	,,	Philip Haswell . . .				1	1	1	1		
4831	,,	Joseph Hatton . . .				1	1	1	1		
6629	,,	Andrew Haxton . .				1	1	1	1		
6149	,,	Peter Hay				1	1	1	1		
4372	Lc.-Cpl.	Reuben Heales . .				1	1	1	1		
5609	Pte.	Thomas Healey . .			*1	1	1	1	1		
5388	,,	Alexr. Henderson . .				1	1	1	1		
5078	Corpl.	Alonza Henderson . .				1	1	1	1		
5363	Pte.	William Henderson .				1	1	1	1		
7759	,,	William Henderson .				1	1	1	1		
6532	,,	Charles Hendry . .				1	1	1	1		
4941	,,	William Hendry . .				1	1	1	1		
6675	,,	John Herd				1	1	1	1		
2997	Corpl.	Henry Hewetson . .				1	1	1	1		
4407	Pte.	James Higgenbottom .				1	1	1	1		
3848	,,	Edward Higgs . . .				1	1	1	1		
4953	,,	William Hindle . .				1	1	1	1		Killed in action.
3330	,,	David Hogg . . .				1	1	1	1		
5093	Sgt.	Henry Holford . . .				1	1	1	1		
6283	Pte.	Archibald Hood . .				1	1	1	1		
6624	,,	James Hood . . .				1	1	1	1		
4707	,,	Thomas Hood . . .				1	1	1	1		
5851	,,	William Horsburgh .				1	1	1	1		
4756	,,	William Howarth . .				1	1	1	1		
5838	,,	James Hughes . . .				1	1	1	1		
778	Armr.-Sgt.	Fred Howell . . .				1	1	1	1		Army Ordnance Corps.
3584	Corpl.	John Hunter . . .				1	1	1	1		
5634	Pte.	William Hunter . .				1	1	1	1		
6193	,,	William Hunton . .				1	1	1	1		
4787	,,	Alexr. Hutchison . .				1	1	1	1		
4469	,,	William Hutchison .						1	1		
7827	,,	James Hutton . . .				1	1	1	1		
6419	,,	James Hutton . . .				1	1	1	1		
5020	,,	Robert Hutton . . .				1	1	1	1		

[1] Shown as No. 5971 Lc.-Cpl. J. Harkins in King's Medal Roll.

Regtl. No.	Rank.	Name.	Whether application already made for Queen's S. A. Medal.	On what Roll name submitted for Queen's S. A. Medal.	Cape Colony.	Orange Free State.	Transvaal.	S. Africa, 1901.	S. Africa, 1902.	If entitled to King's S. A. Medal.	Remarks.
6199	Pte.	William Hutton				1	1	1	1		
3676	Sgt.	Francis Illingworth				1	1	1	1		
5045	Pte.	David Imrie				1	1	1	1		
5466	,,	Andrew Inglis				1	1	1	1		
6463	,,	George Innes				1	1	1	1		
7943	Drumr.	Arthur Irvine						1	1		
5488	Pte.	George Irvine				1	1	1	1		
5449	,,	William Irvine				1	1	1	1		
5810	Drumr.	William Irving				1	1	1	1		
6866	Pte.	William Ives				1	1	1	1		
5857	,,	Archibald Izzatt				1	1	1	1		
5873	,,	John Izzett				1	1	1	1		
3167	Sgt.	Adam Jack				1	1	1	1		
2870	,,	David Jack				1	1	1	1		
4623	Pte.	George Jack				1	1	1	1		
6260	,,	Alexander Jamie			*1	1	1	1	1		
5931	,,	David Jamieson				1	1	1	1		
5430	,,	James Jamieson				1	1	1	1		
5237	,	James Johnston				1	1	1	1		
7762	,,	John Johnston				1	1	1	1		
4865	Corpl.	Robert Johnston				1	1	1	1		
3951	Sgt.	William Johnston				1	1	1	1		
5275	Pte.	Angus Johnstone				1	1	1	1		
7818	,,	David Johnstone				1	1	1	1		
7043	,,	John Johnstone				1	1	1	1		
4721	,,	John Jolly				1	1	1	1		
5402	,,	William Jones				1	1	1	1		
4890	,,	James Kavanagh				1	1	1	1		
5616	,,	John Kay				1	1	1	1		
5489	,,	Thomas Kay				1	1	1	1		
7392	,,	Walter Kay				1	1	1	1		
4162	Lc.-Cpl.	William Kedge				1	1	1	1		
5557	Pte.	Samuel Kelly				1	1	1	1		
5872	Sgt.	Arthur Kenewell				1	1	1	1		
6062	Pte.	Hugh Kennedy				1	1	1	1		
5344	,,	Joseph Kennedy				1	1	1	1		
6519	,,	Robert Kennedy				1	1	1	1		
5427	,,	Andrew Kerr						1	1		
5822	,,	James Kerr			1	1	1	1			
6125	,,	Charles Kidd			1	1	1	1			
4646	,,	James Kilgour			1	1	1	1			
4866	,,	Robert Kilgour			1	1	1	1			
5446	,,	John King			1	1	1	1			
5126	,,	Robert King			1	1	1	1			
5053	,,	William King			1	1	1	1			
6191	Lc.-Sgt.	William King			1	1	1	1			
5553	Sgt.	John Kinghorn			1	1	1	1			
8482	Pte.	James Kinnear			1			1	1		
7375	,.	Andrew Kirk			1	1	1	1			
3716	,,	James Kirk			1	1	1	1			
5451	,,	Michael Kirk			1	1	1	1			

Regtl. No.	Rank.	NAME.	Whether application already made for Queen's S. A. Medal.	On what Roll name submitted for Queen's S. A. Medal.	Cape Colony.	Orange Free State.	Transvaal.	S. Africa, 1901.	S. Africa, 1902.	If entitled to King's S. A. Medal.	REMARKS.
4740	Pte.	John Knight				1	1	1	1		
5727	,,	Thomas Knight				1	1	1	1		
5123	,,	Thomas Kyd				1	1	1	1		
5701	Lc.-Cpl.	John G. Kyle				1	1	1	1		
5431	Pte.	John Laffy				1	1	1	1		
5689	,,	Charles Laing				1	1	1	1		
4901	,,	Herbert Laing				1	1	1	1		
5990	Corpl.	William Laing				1	1	1	1		
4772	Lc.-Sgt.	Andrew Lambert				1	1	1	1		
5963	Pte.	Peter Lamont				1	1	1	1		
4816	,,	James Lawrence				1	1	1	1		
6428	,,	Robert Lawrence				1	1	1	1		
6328	,,	Robert Lawrie				1		1	1	1		
6264	,,	John Lawless				1	1	1	1		
5848	,,	Alexander Lawson				1	1	1	1		
5509	,,	Joseph Lawson				1	1	1	1		
6611	,,	Thomas Lawson				1	1	1	1		
5635	,,	Edward Leavie				1	1	1	1		
4340	,,	William Lee				1	1	1	1		
6190	,,	Thomas Lee				1	1	1	1		
7686	,,	John Lees				1	1	1	1		
4694	,,	Andrew Leitch				1	1	1	1		
5290	,,	William Leitch				1	1	1	1		
6107	,,	Alexr. Leonard				1	1	1	1		
7473	,,	James Leslie				1	1	1	1		
5531	,,	George Levey				1	1	1	1		
4750	,,	John Lewis				1	1	1	1		
6255	,,	Graham Lindsay				1	1	1	1		
6391	,,	Robert Linton				1	1	1	1		
4985	,,	Henry Lisle				1	1	1	1		
4794	,,	Samuel Lloyd				1	1	1	1		
5452	,,	Alexander Logan				1	1	1	1		
5959	Corpl.	David Longwell				1	1	1	1		
6226	Pte.	James Lonie				1	1	1	1		
4726	,,	James Lord				1	1	1	1		
5040	,,	Andrew Love				1	1	1	1		
5440	,,	George B. Low				1	1	1	1		
6071	Lc.-Cpl.	Alexr. Lownie				1	1	1	1		
6360	Pte.	Alexr. Lumsden				1	1	1	1		
5279	Sgt.	William Lumsden				1	1	1	1		
5396	Lc.-Cpl.	Thomas Lunn				1	1	1	1		
5891	Pte.	Alexr. Lyall				1	1	1	1		
6126	,,	David Lyall				1	1	1	1		
6403	,,	James Lynch				1	1	1	1		
5687	,,	Michael Lynch				1	1	1	1		
2617	,,	Malcolm Macara				1	1	1	1		
5828	,,	Robertson Maccready				1	1	1	1		
7748	,,	Alexr. Mackay				1	1	1	1		
4665	,,	Henry Mackel				1	1	1	1		
6243	,,	James E. Magin				1	1	1	1		
6808	Lc.-Cpl.	Arthur Maison [1]	Yes	1st Black Watch, 1/7/01.		1	1	1	1	Yes	

[1] See 2nd Bn. Roll.

Regtl. No.	Rank.	Name.	Whether application already made for Queen's S. A. Medal.	On what Roll name submitted for Queen's S. A. Medal.	Cape Colony.	Orange Free State.	Transvaal.	S. Africa, 1901.	S. Africa, 1902.	If entitled to King's S. A. Medal.	Remarks.
7323	Pte.	Samuel Manuel				1	1	1	1		
5119	,,	Archd. Malcolm				1	1	1	1		
5316	,,	William Maltman				1	1	1	1		
4642	Lc.-Cpl.	John Marnie				1	1	1	1		
7456	Pte.	Christopher Marshall				1	1	1	1		
6620	,,	David Marshall				1	1	1	1		
5526	Sgt.	John Marshall				1	1	1	1		
5285	Pte.	William Marshall				1	1	1	1		
4773	,,	James Martin				1	1	1	1		
4909	,,	Patrick Martin				1	1	1	1		
4187	Sgt.	Joseph Masters				1	1	1	1		
5532	Pte.	Wm. Masterton				1	1	1	1		
5497	Lc.-Cpl.	Richard Matchett				1	1	1	1		
6584	Pte.	James Mathew				1	1	1	1		
5155	,,	William Mathew				1	1	1	1		
5645	,,	William Mathie				1	1	1	1		
6181	Corpl.	Alfred Mathieson				1	1	1	1		
5206	Pte.	Lindsay Mathieson				1	1	1	1		
6549	,,	Alexr. Maxwell				1	1	1	1		
6166	Corpl.	Alister M'Andrew				1	1	1	1		
5230	Pte.	Thomas M'Andrew				1	1	1	1		
5250	,,	Alexr. M'Aulay				1	1	1	1		
5178	,,	Hugh M'Aulay				1	1	1	1		
4944	,,	Joseph M'Beth				1	1	1	1		
3993	,,	James M'Bride				1	1	1	1		
5089	,,	James M'Cafferty				1	1	1	1		
4886	,,	Philip M'Cairns				1	1	1	1		
6222	Corpl.	Fred M'Cann				1	1	1	1		
5765	Drumr.	John M'Cann				1	1	1	1		
5408	Pte.	William M'Carl				1	1	1	1		
5510	,,	Anthony M'Caskill				1	1	1	1		
5958	Corpl.	Martin M'Cheyne				1	1	1	1		
6137	Cr.-Sgt.	Creighton M'Clellan				1	1	1	1		
6535	Pte.	Thomas M'Cluskey				1	1	1	1		
6141	,,	John M'Coombs				1	1	1	1		
6344	,,	William M'Culloch				1	1	1	1		
6194	,,	James M'Dade [1]	Yes	1st Black Watch, 1/7/01.		1	1	1	1	Yes	
7946	Boy	John M'Dade			1			1	1		
5629	Pte.	James M'Diarmid			1		1	1			
6005	,,	Alexr. M'Donald			1	1	1	1			
5648	,,	Alexr. M'Donald			1	1	1	1			
6265	,,	Alexr. M'Donald			1	1	1	1			
6272	,,	James M'Donald						1	1		
5523	,,	John M'Donald									
6011	Corpl.	Neil M'Donald			1	1	1	1			
5305	Pte.	Peter M'Donald			1	1	1	1			
6273	,,	Thomas M'Donald			1	1	1	1			
6524	,,	Peter M'Donald			1	1	1	1			
7782	,,	John M'Donald			1	1	1	1			
5712	,,	Robert M'Donald			1	1	1	1			

[1] See 2nd Bn. Roll.

Regtl. No.	Rank.	NAME.	Whether application already made for Queen's S. A. Medal.	On what Roll name submitted for Queen's S. A. Medal.	Cape Colony.	Orange Free State.	Transvaal.	S. Africa, 1901.	S. Africa, 1902.	If entitled to King's S. A. Medal.	REMARKS.
5947	Pte.	Frederick M'Ewan	.			1	1	1	1		
5643	,,	John M'Ewan . .	.			1	1	1	1		
6617	,,	Peter M'Ewan .	.		*1	1	1	1	1		
4862	Corpl.	William M'Ewan	.			1	1	1	1		
6089	Pte.	Charles M'Fadden .				1		1	1		
5558	,,	James M'Farlane .	.			1	1	1	1		
5448	Pioneer	Edward M'Farlane	.			1	1	1	1		
5267	Pte.	William M'Farlane	.			1	1	1	1		
5349	,,	Francis M'Glenn .	.			1	1	1	1		
6136	,,	Blayne M'Gilvray .	.		*1	1	1	1	1		
4834	,,	George M'Inally .	.			1	1	1	1		
6794	,,	Thomas M'Intosh .	.			1	1	1	1		
6502	,,	William M'Intosh .	.			1	1	1	1		
6128	,,	Peter M'Intyre .	.			1	1	1	1		
5420	,,	John M'Intyre . .	.			1	1	1	1		
5901	,,	Thomas M'Intyre .	.			1	1	1	1		
5682	,,	Norman M'Ivor .	.			1	1	1	1		
4947	,,	Alexr. M'Kay . .	.			1	1	1	1		
5748	Corpl.	George E. M'Kay .	.		*1	1	1	1	1		
5258	Pte.	James M'Kay . .	.			1	1	1	1		
5112	,,	John M'Kay . .	.			1	1	1	1		
6706	,,	William M'Kay .	.			1	1	1	1		
5666	,,	William M'Kell .	.			1	1	1	1		
4714	,,	Neil M'Kellar . .	.			1	1	1	1		
8088	Boy	John M'Kenna . .	.			1	1	1	1		
5214	Pte.	James M'Kenzie .	.			1		1	1		
5693	,,	John M'Kenzie .	.			1	1	1	1		
4819	,,	Robert M'Kenzie .	.					1	1		
5790	,,	Donald M'Kercher .				1	1	1	1		
4940	,,	Malcolm M'Kie .	.			1	1	1	1		
4439	Sgt.	Robert M'Kie . .	.			1	1	1	1		
5331	Pte.	Archd. M'Killop .	.			1	1	1	1		
4895	Corpl.	William M'Kinlay .	.			1	1	1	1		
6100	Pte.	Donald M'Laren .	.			1	1	1	1		
5496	,,	Peter M'Laren . .	.			1	1	1	1		
5918	,,	William M'Laren .	.			1	1	1	1		
5621	,,	John M'Latchie .	.			1	1	1	1		
7346	,,	James M'Lean . .	.			1	1	1	1		
5409	,,	James M'Lean . .	.			1	1	1	1		
6508	,,	John M'Lean . .	.			1	1	1	1		
6310	,,	Neil M'Lean . .	.			1	1	1	1		
6103	,,	Peter M'Lean . .	.			1	1	1	1		
5436	,,	Peter M'Lean . .	.			1	1	1	1		
6014	,,	Gregor M'Leod .	.			1	1	1	1		
7401	,,	John M'Leod . .	.			1	1	1	1		
4635	,,	Samuel M'Mullen .	.			1	1	1	1		
5085	Sgt.	Alexr. M'Nab . .	.			1	1	1	1		
6337	Corpl.	John M'Naughton .	.			1	1	1	1		
5676	Pte.	Thomas M'Neil .	.			1	1	1	1		
4884	,,	Donald M'Phee .	.			1	1	1	1		
7718	,,	Johnstone M'Pherson .				1	1	1	1		

Regtl. No.	Rank.	Name.	Whether application already made for Queen's S. A. Medal.	On what Roll name submitted for Queen's S. A. Medal.	Cape Colony.	Orange Free State.	Transvaal.	S. Africa, 1901.	S. Africa, 1902.	If entitled to King's S. A. Medal.	Remarks.
6069	Pte.	Thomas M'Pherson				1	1	1	1		
7655	Corpl.	Alexr. M'Quire				1	1	1	1		
5224	Pte.	John M'Shane				1	1	1	1		
5961	,,	John M'Williams				1	1	1	1		
5968	Corpl.	John Melville				1	1	1	1		
5231	Pte.	James Mill				1	1	1	1		
3081	Corpl.	Robert Mill				1	1	1	1		
5153	Pte.	Alexr. Millar				1	1	1	1		
4885	,,	Charles Millar				1	1	1	1		
4632	,,	Charles Millar				1	1	1	1		
5829	Sgt.	David Millar				1		1	1		
8085	Pte.	Douglas Millar				1	1	1	1		
7847	,,	James Millar				1	1	1	1		
6573	Lc.-Cpl.	John Millar				1	1	1	1		
5177	Corpl.	William Millar				1	1	1	1		
3059	Cr.-Sgt.	Randolph Miller				1	1	1	1		
5254	Pte.	Samuel Millikin				1	1	1	1		
5334	,,	Alexander Milne				1	1	1	1		
5814	,,	Alexr. Mitchell				1	1	1	1		
5338	Sgt.	Alexr. Mitchell				1	1	1	1		
5575	,,	David Mitchell				1	1	1	1		
5445	Pte.	David Mitchell				1	1	1	1		
6298	Sgt.-Drumr.	Duncan Mitchell				1	1	1	1		
4502	Pte.	James Mitchell				1	1	1	1		
6066	,,	James Mitchell				1	1	1	1		
6472	,,	Robert Mitchell				1	1	1	1		
6443	,,	William Mitchell				1	1	1	1		
7841	,,	William Mitchell				1	1	1	1		
3035	,,	William Mitchell				1	1	1	1		
6127	,,	Thomas Mochan				1	1	1	1		
4818	,,	Joseph Moore				1	1	1	1		
5148	,,	Robert Moore				1	1	1	1		
7875	,,	William Moore				1	1	1	1		
6795	,,	Henry Moran				1	1	1	1		
6004	,,	John More				1	1	1	1		
6108	,,	Peter More				1	1	1	1		
5618	,,	John Morgan				1	1	1	1		
4863	,,	William Morgan				1	1	1	1		
4804	,,	John Morley				1	1	1	1		
6478	,,	Alexr. Morris				1	1	1	1		
7810	,,	Charles Morris				1	1	1	1		
5054	,,	David Morris				1	1	1	1		
5797	,,	William Morrice			*1	1	1	1	1		
4905	,,	Alexr. Morrison				1	1	1	1		
6305	,,	Joseph Morrison				1	1	1	1		
6248	,,	David Mowbray				1	1	1	1		
5979	,,	Allan Muir				1	1	1	1		
5067	,,	David Muir				1	1	1	1		
5157	,,	Charles Mulholland				1	1	1	1		
4626	,,	Andrew Munro				1	1	1	1		

Regtl. No.	Rank.	NAME.	Whether application already made for Queen's S. A. Medal.	On what Roll name submitted for Queen's S. A. Medal.	Cape Colony.	Orange Free State.	Transvaal.	S. Africa, 1901.	S. Africa, 1902.	If entitled to King's S. A. Medal.	REMARKS.
5863	Pte.	George Munro				1	1	1	1		
7722	,,	Hugh Munro						1	1		
7701	,,	John Murdoch				1	1	1	1		
5306	Sgt.	William Murdoch				1	1	1	1		
5752	Pte.	John Murphy				1	1	1	1		
6157	,,	David Murray				1	1	1	1		
6374	,,	John Murray				1	1	1	1		
5046	,,	George Murray				1	1	1	1		
5064	,,	William Murray				1	1	1	1		
4411	Sgt.	Joseph Myers				1	1	1	1		
5401	Pte.	Robert Myles				1	1	1	1		
6833	,,	Alexr. Neil				1	1	1	1		
5905	,,	John Newland				1	1	1	1		
5660	,,	David Newlands				1	1	1	1		
7444	,,	Alexr. Nicoll				1	1	1	1		
7724	,,	Alexr. Nicoll				1	1	1	1		
5716	,,	William Nicoll				1	1	1	1		Forfeited. Dischd. incorrigible and worthless. Medal and Clasps returned to Woolwich 27/5/10. *Vide* 68/42/981.
4967	,,	William Nicoll				1	1	1	1		
6410	Lc.-Cpl.	James Nisbett				1	1	1	1		
6322	Pte.	Charles Noble				1	1	1	1		
6196	,,	William Ogg				1	1	1	1		
5227	,,	John E. O'Keefe				1	1	1	1		
5904	,,	Adam Oldham				1	1	1	1		
5816	,,	George Oldham				1	1	1	1		
7653	,,	Robert Oliphant				1	1	1	1		
2871	Corpl.	John Openshaw				1	1	1	1		
6280	Pte.	Alexr. Orcheson				1	1	1	1		
5954	,,	David B. Orr				1	1	1	1		
4961	,,	William Orr				1	1	1	1		
6633	,,	Robert Oswald				1	1	1	1		
5487	,,	Henry Owens				1	1	1	1		
4743	,,	David Patterson				1	1	1	1		
6112	,,	Archibald Phillip				1	1	1	1		
6610	,,	John Player				1	1	1	1		
4924	Corpl.	Duncan Palmer				1	1	1	1		
5057	,,	John Palmer				1	1	1	1		
5047	Drumr.	Ralph Palmer				1	1	1	1		
4104	Lc.-Cpl.	Malcolm Parker				1	1	1	1		
5946	Pte.	Robert Parmenter				1	1	1	1		
5015	,,	Robert Partington				1	1	1	1		
5683	,,	William Paton				1	1	1	1		
5414	,,	Alexr. Patterson				1	1	1	1		
5334	,,	Andrew Patterson				1	1	1	1		
4347	Cr.-Sgt.	Peter Patton				1	1	1	1		
6225	Pte.	Peter Patton				1	1	1	1		
4728	,,	Alexr. Patullo				1	1	1	1		

Regtl. No.	Rank.	NAME.	Whether application already made for Queen's S. A. Medal.	On what Roll name submitted for Queen's S. A. Medal.	Cape Colony.	Orange Free State.	Transvaal.	S. Africa, 1901.	S. Africa, 1902.	If entitled to King's S. A. Medal.	REMARKS.
6227	Pte.	James Peden . . .				1	1	1	1		
6444	,,	David Pert . . .				1	1	1	1		
6336	,,	James Pert . . .				1	1	1	1		
5248	,,	David Peters . . .				1	1	1	1		
7247	,,	Robert Peters . . .				1	1	1	1		
6365	Corpl.	Robert Philp . . .				1	1*	1	1		*From a 1st Battn. Supplementary Roll.
5157	,,	Joseph Philips . . .				1	1	1	1		
6262	Pte.	James Pirie . . .				1	1	1	1		
5579	Lc.-Cpl.	Andrew Plowman . .				1	1	1	1		
6180	Corpl.	James Porteous . .						1	1		
5249	Pte.	James Porteous . .				1	1	1	1		
4840	,,	Charles Potts . .				1	1	1	1		
5034	,,	Thomas Powell . .				1	1	1	1		
5146	,,	John Pryde . .				1	1	1	1		
6006	,,	Charles Pyott . . .						1	1		
5536	,,	Joseph Player . . .				1	1	1	1		
6397	,,	John Potts . . .				1	1	1	1		
5887	,,	Robert Quade . . .				1	1	1	1		
4913	,,	James Quinn . . .				1	1	1	1		
5730	,,	Robert Rae . . .				1	1	1	1		
5120	,,	Alexr. Rankine . .				1	1	1	1		
4757	,,	Henry Rattray . .				1	1	1	1		
8374	,,	Joseph Rae . . .				1	1	1	1		
6676	Lc.-Cpl.	William Reekie . .				1	1	1	1		
5903	Pte.	Frank Reid . . .				1	1	1	1		
6118	,,	George Reid . . .				1	1	1	1		
7350	,,	William Reid . . .				1	1	1	1		
5709	,,	James Reynolds . .				1	1	1	1		
6073	,,	Hugh Reilly . . .				1	1	1	1		
6387	,,	James Rennie . . .				1	1	1	1		
7355	,,	Alexr. Richardson . .				1	1	1	1		
7031	Lc.-Cpl.	Cecil Richardson . .				1	1	1	1		
4413	Pte.	Peter Richardson . .				1	1	1	1		
7967	,,	William Richmond .				1	1	1	1		
4961	,,	James Ritchie . . .				1	1	1	1		
5528	,,	James Ritchie . .				1	1	1	1		
1153	,,	William Riley . .				1	1	1	1		
5353	,,	William Riley . . .				1	1	1	1		
6423	,,	William Robb . . .				1	1	1	1		
4389	Sgt.	Alexr. Robertson . .				1	1	1	1		
6553	Pte.	Charles Robertson . .				1	1	1	1		
5922	,,	David Robertson . .				1	1	1	1		
5411	,,	David Robertson . .				1	1	1	1		
5914	,,	Henry Robertson . .				1	1	1	1		
5426	Sgt.	James Robertson . .				1	1	1	1		
5264	Pte.	James Robertson . .				1	1	1	1		
5586	,,	James Robertson . .				1	1	1	1		
7460	,,	John Robertson . .				1	1	1	1		
5703	,,	Robert Robertson . .				1	1	1	1		

Regtl. No.	Rank.	Name.	Whether application already made for Queen's S. A. Medal.	On what Roll name submitted for Queen's S. A. Medal.	Cape Colony.	Orange Free State.	Transvaal.	S. Africa, 1901.	S. Africa, 1902.	If entitled to King's S. A. Medal.	Remarks.
5492	Pte.	Thomas Robertson				1	1	1	1		
5551	,,	William Robertson				1	1	1	1		
5665	Sgt.	Colin C. Robinson				1	1	1	1		
5142	Pte.	Thomas Robinson				1	1	1	1		
4754	,,	Alexr. Rodgers						1	1		
5438	,,	Charles Rodgers				1	1	1	1		
6091	,,	Gordon Rodgers				1	1	1	1		
5919	,,	Hugh Roden				1	1	1	1		
5811	,,	Patrick Roden				1	1	1	1		
5915	,,	George Ronald				1	1	1	1		
5160	,,	Alexander Rose				1	1	1	1		
6152	,,	George Ross				1	1	1	1		
4647	,,	George Ross			*1	1	1	1	1		
8162	,,	James Ross				1	1	1	1		
5223	,,	James Ross				1	1	1	1		
6198	,,	John G. Ross				1	1	1	1		
6263	,,	John Ross				1	1	1	1		
7649	,,	John Ross				1	1	1	1		
4574	,,	William Roy				1	1	1	1		
5097	,,	John Runcy				1	1	1	1		
5556	,,	Alexander Russell				1	1	1	1		
6438	Drumr.	Archibald Russell				1	1	1	1		
6492	Pte.	John Russell				1	1	1	1		
6867	,,	Peter Rutherford				1	1	1	1		
6753	,,	Robert Rutherford				1	1	1	1		
5493	,,	Michael Ryan				1	1	1	1		
6259	,,	Peter Ryan				1	1	1	1		
4523	Lc.-Sgt.	George Sage				1	1	1	1		
6657	Pte.	Hugh Samson				1	1	1	1		
6134	,,	William Sandeman			*1	1	1	1	1		
7814	,,	John Sandeman				1	1	1	1		
5252	,,	William Sawers				1	1	1	1		
4576	,,	John Sawyers				1	1	1	1		
7195	,,	John Scanlon				1	1	1	1		
4784	,,	Alexander Scotland				1	1	1	1		
5216	,,	Andrew Scott				1	1	1	1		
6348	Corpl.	Andrew Scott				1	1	1	1		
6267	Pte.	David Scott				1	1	1	1		
5831	,,	David Scott				1	1	1	1		
6485	,,	David Scott				1	1	1	1		
6315	,,	George Scott				1	1	1	1		
5641	,,	Henry Scott				1	1	1	1		
4774	,,	James Scott				1	1	1	1		
5291	,,	Joseph Scott				1	1	1	1		
6501	,,	Robert Scott				1	1	1	1		
5841	,,	Robert Scott				1	1	1	1		
4615	,,	Robert Scott				1	1	1	1		
5599	Lc.-Cpl.	Walter Scott				1	1	1	1		Killed in action, 27/3/02.[1]
5244	Pte.	William Scott				1	1	1	1		
5893	,,	William Scott				1	1	1	1		

[1] The son of Bandmaster Scott. Killed on the blockhouse line between Harrismith and Bethlehem.—J. S.

Regtl. No.	Rank.	Name.	Whether application already made for Queen's S. A. Medal.	On what Roll name submitted for Queen's S. A. Medal.	Cape Colony.	Orange Free State.	Transvaal.	S. Africa, 1901.	S. Africa, 1902.	If entitled to King's S. A. Medal.	Remarks.
6378	Pte.	William Scott . . .				1	1	1	1		
6526	,,	William Scott . . .				1	1	1	1		
6185	,,	George Scrimgeour .				1	1	1	1		
6600	,,	John Scully . . .				1	1	1	1		Forfeited. Dischd. incorrigible and worthless. Medal and Clasps returned to Woolwich 27/5/10. *Vide* 68/42/981.
6775	,,	Charles Sexton . . .				1	1	1	1		
5977	,,	Charles Sharkey . .				1	1	1	1		
6276	,,	John Sharkey . . .				1	1	1	1		
5626	,,	John Sharp . . .				1	1	1	1		
5581	,,	William Sharp . . .				1	1	1	1		
5668	,,	William Shaw . . .				1	1	1	1		
5779	,,	Joseph Shepherd . .				1	1	1	1		
2183	Cr.-Sgt.	George Shirran . .				1	1	1	1		
2165	Pte.	Alexr. Short . . .				1	1	1	1		
5522	,,	Bernard Short . . .				1	1	1	1		
6268	,,	Alexander Sibbald .			1	1	1	1	1		
5337	,,	Peter Sim . . .				1	1	1	1		
5159	,,	James Sime . . .				1	1	1	1		
5612	,,	Alexander Simpson .				1	1	1	1		
4997	,,	George Simpson . .				1	1	1	1		
4554	,,	George Simpson . .				1	1	1	1		
6354	,,	David Simpson . . .				1	1	1	1		
5667	,,	James Simpson . . .				1	1	1	1		
7892	,,	James Simpson . . .				1	1	1	1		
6020	,,	Joseph Simpson . .				1	1	1	1		
5194	,,	Joseph Simpson . .				1	1	1	1		
6024	,,	William Simpson . .				1	1	1	1		
5858	,,	William Simpson . .				1	1	1	1		
5777	,,	Mark Sinclair . . .				1	1	1	1		
5845	,,	Robert Sinclair . .				1	1	1	1		Deceased.
5235	,,	Hugh Slavin . . .				1	1	1	1		
4763	Lc.-Sgt.	John Slattie . . .				1	1	1	1		
6000	Pte.	Andrew Smart . . .				1	1	1	1		
6493	,,	James Smart . . .				1	1	1	1		
6499	,,	John Smart . . .				1	1	1	1		
6538	,,	Benjamin Smith . .				1	1	1	1		
6012	,,	Charles Smith . . .				1	1	1	1		
4444	,,	Charles Smith . . .				1	1	1	1		
7891	,,	George Smith . . .				1	1	1	1		
6156	,,	James Smith . . .				1	1	1	1		
6389	,,	James Smith . . .				1	1	1	1		
5301	,,	James Smith . . .				1	1	1	1		
4739	,,	John Smith . . .				1	1	1	1		
4962	,,	John Smith . . .				1	1	1	1		
5944	,,	Peter Smith . . .				1	1	1	1		
6595	,,	Joseph Smith . . .				1	1	1	1		
6464	,,	William Smith . . .				1	1	1	1		

Regtl. No.	Rank.	Name.	Whether application already made for Queen's S. A. Medal.	On what Roll name submitted for Queen's S. A. Medal.	Cape Colony.	Orange Free State.	Transvaal.	S. Africa, 1901.	S. Africa, 1902.	If entitled to King's S. A. Medal.	Remarks.
7680	Pte.	William Smith				1	1	1	1		
4911	,,	Clement Standing				1	1	1	1		
3057	Sgt.	William Statham				1	1	1	1		
6086	Pte.	Henry Stephen				1	1	1	1		
3905	Q.-Mr.-Sgt.	John Stephen				1	1	1	1		
4827	Pte.	George Stevens				1	1	1	1		
5070	,,	Alexander Stewart				1	1	1	1		
13	,,	Alexander Stewart				1	1	1	1		
6087	,,	Charles Stewart				1	1	1	1		
6381	,,	David Stewart				1	1	1	1		
5511	,,	Donald Stewart				1	1	1	1		
6249	,,	Hugh Stewart				1	1	1	1		
5424	,,	Isaac Stewart			*1	1	1	1	1		
6038	,,	James Stewart				1	1	1	1		
3207	Sgt.	John Stewart				1	1	1	1		
5786	Pte.	John D. Stuart				1	1	1	1		Deceased.
6247	,,	John Stewart				1	1	1	1		
6228	,,	John Stewart				1	1	1	1		
6102	,,	John Stewart			*1	1	1	1	1		
5644	,,	Robert Stewart				1	1	1	1		
5491	,,	Thomas Stewart				1	1	1	1		
4199	,,	William Stewart				1	1	1	1		
5130	,,	George Still				1	1	1	1		
6019	,,	Donald Storey				1	1	1	1		
5056	,,	Alexander Strachan				1	1	1	1		
4722	,,	George Strachan				1	1	1	1		.
6029	,,	Peter Strachan				1	1	1	1		
5512	,,	William Strachan				1	1	1	1		
6236	,,	John Sullivan				1	1	1	1		
6683	,,	Archibald Summers[1]	Yes	1st Black Watch, 1/7/01.			1	1	1	Yes	
5999	,,	Alexander Sutherland				1	1	1	1		
5513	,,	William Sutherland				1	1	1	1		
6008	,,	William Swan				1	1	1	1		
8093	Boy	John Sowersby						1	1		
6140	Pte.	James Storrance				1	1	1	1		
6086	,,	Thomas Smith				1	1	1	1		
5824	,,	Robert Tait				1	1	1	1		
5889	Lc.-Sgt.	Charles Taylor				1	1	1	1		
6663	Pte.	James H. Taylor				1	1	1	1		
6338	,,	James Taylor			1	1	1	1	1		
5542	,,	Hugh Taylor				1	1	1	1		
5193	,,	Alexr. Teviotdale				1	1	1	1		
4654	,,	Andrew Thom				1	1	1	1		
7068	,,	George Thom[1]	Yes	1st Black Watch, 1/7/01.	*1	1	1	1		Yes	
6319	,,	James Thompson				1	1	1	1		
5260	,,	James Thompson				1	1	1	1		
5422	,,	Peter Thompson				1	1	1	1		
5520	Piper	Robert Thompson				1	1	1	1		

[1] See 2nd Bn. Roll.

Regtl. No.	Rank.	Name.	Whether application already made for Queen's S. A. Medal.	On what Roll name submitted for Queen's S. A. Medal.	Cape Colony.	Orange Free State.	Transvaal.	S. Africa, 1901.	S. Africa, 1902.	If entitled to King's S. A. Medal.	Remarks.
6470	Pte.	David Thomson				1	1	1	1		
6143	,,	James Thomson				1	1	1	1		
5479	,,	John Thomson				1	1	1	1		
5715	,,	Robert Thomson				1	1	1	1		
5967	,,	Thomas Thomson			*1	1	1	1	1		
6980	,,	Thomas Thomson				1	1	1	1		
6239	,,	James Timothy				1	1	1	1		
5467	,,	Edward Tolmie				1	1	1	1		Deceased.
5760	,,	John Toner				1	1	1	1		
6183	,,	Joseph Topping				1	1	1	1		
5874	,,	George Tresadern				1	1	1	1		
4918	Lc.-Cpl.	James Trobe				1	1	1	1		
5654	Pte.	Robert Tunnah				1	1	1	1		
4995	,,	John Turnbull				1	1	1	1		
6435	,,	Archibald Turner				1	1	1	1		
6184	,,	William Turner				1	1	1	1		
5866	Drumr.	James Tyrell				1	1	1			
5515	Pte.	David Urquhart			1		1	1	1		
49	Q.-Mr.-Sgt.	Robert Vair			1	1	1	1			
4242	Pte.	George Varndall				1	1	1	1		
5733	,,	Albert Viney				1	1	1	1		
6133	,,	Albert Walker				1	1	1	1		
6256	,,	Charles Walker				1	1	1	1		
6436	,,	John Walker [1]	Yes	Clasp Defence of Ladysmith. 1st Black Watch, 1/7/01.		1	1	1	1	Yes	2nd Bn. K. R. Rifles, attd. from 1st B. W. as mule-driver.
6742	,,	David Wallace				1	1	1	1		
5185	,,	David Wallace				1	1	1	1		
6017	,,	John Wallace				1	1	1	1		
6206	,,	William Wallace				1	1	1	1		
4915	,,	Alexander Watson				1	1	1	1		
6065	,,	James Watson				1	1	1	1		
7794	,,	John Watson				1	1	1	1		
6355	,,	William Watt				1	1	1	1		
5746	,,	Sigmund Wehrle			*1	1	1	1	1		
5692	,,	John Weir				1	1	1	1		
6359	,,	James Welsh				1	1	1	1		
6205	,,	William Welsh				1	1	1	1		
6096	,,	Charles West				1	1	1	1		
5335	,,	George White				1	1	1	1		
4808	,,	James White				1	1	1	1		
5980	,,	Thomas White			*1	1	1	1	1		
4627	,,	James Whiteley				1	1	1	1		
7406	,,	Charles Whyte				1	1	1	1		
1967	Corpl.	Daniel Whyte				1	1	1	1		
6094	Pte.	David Whyte				1	1	1	1		
5817	,,	Frederick Whyte				1	1	1	1		
6201	,,	William Whyte				1	1	1	1		Deceased.
6105	Lc.-Cpl.	Charles Wilkie				1	1	1	1		

[1] See 2nd Bn. Roll.

Regtl. No.	Rank.	Name.	Whether application already made for Queen's S. A. Medal.	On what Roll name submitted for Queen's S. A. Medal.	Cape Colony.	Orange Free State.	Transvaal.	S. Africa, 1901.	S. Africa, 1902.	If entitled to King's S. A. Medal.	Remarks.
2715	Sgt.	John Wilkie				1	1	1	1		
6144	Pte.	William Wilkie				1	1	1	1		
5883	,,	George Wilkins				1	1	1	1		
6475	,,	John Williams				1	1	1	1		
4814	,,	John Williams				1	1	1	1		
4465	Cr.-Sgt.	Thomas Willis				1	1	1	1		
5172	Pte.	David Willocks				1	1	1	1		
6330	,,	David Wilson				1	1	1	1		
5927	,,	David Wilson				1	1	1	1		
9353	,,	David Wilson				1			1		
5559	,,	David Wilson				1	1	1	1		
6690	,,	George Wilson				1	1	1	1		
5796	,,	George Wilson				1	1	1	1		
5048	Drumr.	James Wilson				1	1	1	1		
5415	Corpl.	James Wilson				1	1	1	1		
6111	Pte.	James Wilson				1	1	1	1		
5638	Sgt.	John Wilson				1	1	1	1		
6537	Pte.	Charles Witherwick				1	1	1	1		
7397	,,	George Wishart				1	1	1	1		
3900	Cr.-Sgt.	David Wright			*1	1	1	1	1		
6531	Pte.	Fred. L. H. Wright				1	1	1	1		
5459	,,	George Wright				1	1	1	1		
5017	,,	James Wright				1	1	1	1		
6651	,,	James Wright				1	1	1	1		
2019	Sgt.	James Wright				1	1	1	1		
6104	Pte.	William Wright				1	1	1	1		
5907	,,	John Wynn				1	1	1	1		
5877	,,	John Yorkston				1	1	1	1		
6030	,,	Frederick Young				1	1	1	1		
6352	,,	Hastie Young				1	1	1	1		
6554	,,	James Young				1	1	1	1		
6523	,,	John Young				1	1	1	1		
5464	,,	Robert Young				1	1	1	1		
804	,,	James P. Yule				1	1	1	1		

SUPPLEMENTARY LIST 1st BATTALION THE BLACK WATCH.

Regtl. No.	Rank.	Name.	Whether application already made for Queen's S. A. Medal.	On what Roll name submitted for Queen's S. A. Medal.	Cape Colony.	Orange Free State.	Transvaal.	S. Africa, 1901.	S. Africa, 1902.	If entitled to King's S. A. Medal.	Remarks.
8461	Pte.	J. Gallacher.									
7743	Le.-Cpl.	D. Anderson				1	1	1			See 22nd Bn. M. I. Roll.
7764	Pte.	A. Henderson			1	1	1	1	1		See 22nd Bn. M. I. Roll.
6220	,,	J. Ballantyne.									
6561	,,	M'Connell, T.		Clasp Defence of Ladysmith							Attached to K.R. R. Corps as mule-driver.
Civil Transport Conductor		Morris, Thomas.									

22ND BATTALION MOUNTED INFANTRY, DETACHMENT 2ND ROYAL HIGHLANDERS.

Regtl. No.	Rank.	Name.	Whether application already made for Queen's S. A. Medal.	On what Roll name submitted for Queen's S. A. Medal.	Cape Colony.	Orange Free State.	Transvaal.	S. Africa, 1901.	S. Africa, 1902.	If entitled to King's S. A. Medal.	Remarks.
	Lieut.	Duff, P. A.			1	1	1	1	1		
	,,	Baillie Hamilton, N. A. B.[1]		Served with Regt. in S. Africa.	1	1	1				See 2nd Bn. Roll.
5226	Coy. Sgt.-Mj.	Parker, E. . . .		Served with Regt. in S. Africa.	1		1				See 2nd Bn. Roll.
4265	Sgt.	Weir, G.		Served with Regt. in S. Africa.	*1	1	1				See 2nd Bn. Roll.
6994	Corpl.	Niven, J.		Served with Regt. in S. Africa.	*1		1				See 2nd Bn. Roll.
7194	,,	Malloch, J.			1	1	1				
7538	Lc.-Cpl.	Johnstone, W. . . .			1	1	1				
7309	,,	Eden, B.			1	1	1				
7743	Pte.	Anderson, D. . . .			1	1	1				See 1st Bn. Supplementary List.
7503	,,	Beattie, J.			1	1	1				
7512	,,	Blair, W.			1	1	1				
7455	,,	Blake, M.			1						
7798	,,	Cairns, A.			1	1	1				
7834	,,	Campbell, J. . . .			1	1	1				E/26058/6 'S. A. 1901.'
7807	,,	Carroll, M.			1	1	1				
7263	,,	Cross, A.			1	1	1				
7689	,,	Drummond, T. . . .			1	1	1				
7426	,,	Duncan, J.			1	1	1				
7311	,,	Dunn, J.			1	1	1				
7453	,,	Ferguson, P. . . .			1	1	1				
6514	Sgt.	Tyrie, J.			1	1	1				
7788	Pte.	Fitzpatrick, J. . . .			1	1	1				
7308	,,	Fraser, D.			1	1	1				
7480	,,	Gardiner, A. . . .			1	1	1				
7332	,,	Hamilton, A. . . .			1	1	1				
7428	,,	Hardie, P.			1	1	1				
7823	,,	Harkins, J.			1	1	1				
7764	,,	Henderson, A. . . .			1	1	1	1	1		See 1st Bn. Supplementary Roll.
7780	,,	Kelly, J.			1	1	1				
7208	,,	Kennedy, J. . . .			1	1	1				
7767	,,	Lindsay, J. C. . . .			1	1	1				
7695	,,	Leonard, J.			1	1	1				
7314	,,	M'Farlane, J. . . .			1	1	1				
7214	,,	M'Hardy, J. . . .			1	1	1				
7679	,,	M'Intyre, N. . . .			1	1	1				
7494	,,	M'Kay, W.			1	1	1				

[1] Transvaal Clasp earned with 23rd Bn. M. I. ; for others see 2nd Bn. Roll.—J. S.

Regtl. No.	Rank.	Name.	Whether application already made for Queen's S. A. Medal.	On what Roll name submitted for Queen's S. A. Medal.	Cape Colony.	Orange Free State.	Transvaal.	S. Africa, 1901.	S. Africa, 1902.	If entitled to King's S. A. Medal.	Remarks.
7417	Pte.	M'Laren, J.			1	1	1				
7431	,,	Mascott, E.			1	1	1				
6875	Lc.-Cpl.	Menzies, R.		Served with Regt. in S. Africa.	*1		1				See 2nd Bn. Roll.
7741	Pte.	Mitchell, G.			1	1	1				
7688	,,	Moir, C.			1	1	1				
7221	,,	Murray, L.			1	1	1				
7222	,,	Murray, R.			1	1	1				
7706	,,	Ogilvie, D.			1	1	1				
7773	,,	Omerod, J.			1	1	1				
7672	,,	Paton, J.			1	1	1				
7710	,,	Pool, J.			1	1	1				
7330	,,	Rowell, P.			1	1	1				
7386	,,	Russell, P.			1	1	1	1			
7756	,,	Sheret, W.			1	1	1				
7524	,,	Small, F.			1	1	1				
7771	,,	Stewart, W.			1	1	1				
7758	,,	Taylor, W.			1	1	1				Discharged.
7772	,,	Thompson, W.			1	1	1				
7516	,,	Walker, J.			1	1	1				
7365	,,	Walker, T.			1	1	1				
7820	,,	Watson, A.			1	1	1				
7712	,,	Waugh, J.			1	1	1				
7809	,,	White, J.			1	1					
7648	,,	Woodcock, J.			1	1	1				
7742	,,	Young, P.			1	1	1				
7394	,,	Yule, S.		Name expunged from Roll. A.G. 2/m/734 1/B. Watch.	1	1	1				Authority A.G. 2/M/11127.

NOTE.—The men of this Company were nearly all recruits from Perth, who, after being trained at Tidworth, were sent direct to the 22nd Bn. M. I. in S. Africa.—J. S.

The following NAMES appear mostly on single MEDAL ROLL forms, but the last three are from Rolls on which all the other Names are traceable to either the 1st or 2nd Battn. Original Rolls, but these particular three cannot be traced in any other BLACK WATCH ROLL.

Regtl. No.	Rank.	NAME.	Whether application already made for Queen's S. A. Medal.	On what Roll name submitted for Queen's S. A. Medal.	Cape Colony.	Orange Free State.	Transvaal.	S. Africa, 1901.	S. Africa, 1902.	If entitled to King's S. A. Medal.	REMARKS.
5458	Lieut.	R. E. Scott Erskine .	Yes		*1	1	1	1	1	No	3rd Battalion.
	Corpl.	Mackenzie, H. . . .	No			1	1	1	1	No	To Army Reserve.
	Hon. Lt.-Col.	Scott, Angel. William [1]		Not known, but Medal received at the hand of His Majesty the King.	1	1		1			Employed as Chief Censor, Cape Town, from 30/1/01 to 2/10/01. Assistant Press Censor from 12/7/00 to 30/1/01.
	Major	N. W. Cuthbertson .	Yes	Special application on return home as Equerry to H.R.H. Princess Louise. Clasps for Paardeberg and Driefontein also.	1		1	1		No	Served in Transvaal with Hickman's column, also as D.A.A.G. Intelligence Hd.-Qr. Staff. Regimental application has been requested to be cancelled.
	Lieut. Capt. and Bt.-Major and Local Lt.-Col.	Watson, E. C. . . . H. Scott Turner . .		Clasp for Defence of Kimberley.	1	1	1				32nd Bn. M.I. Killed in action, 28/11/1899.
	Bt.-Major	Murray, F. D. . . .		Clasps for Belfast, Cape Colony, Orange Free State, Talana, Tugela Heights, Relief of Ladysmith, Laing's Nek.							Killed in action.
	Lieut.	Pearth, H. A. . . .			1	1	1				3rd Bn. R. Highrs. 12th M.I.
	Capt.	W. M. Campbell . .			1		1		1		Scottish Horse.
	Capt.	J. D. G. Walker, D.S.O.[2]						1	1	Yes	

UNTRACEABLE IN OTHER ROLLS.

| 5867 | Pte. | J. Hogg [3] . . . . | | | | | | 1 | 1 | Yes | |
| 9489 | ,, | Alex. Smith . . . | | | | | | 1 | 1 | Yes | |

[1] See Capt. Scott, W. A., 2nd Bn. Original Roll. I think this is the same officer.—J. S.
[2] From 1st Bn. King's Medal Roll.
[3] Pte. Hogg changed his name from Henderson to Hogg at Standerton. See No. 5867 Jn. Henderson in 2nd Bn. Roll; his Queen's Medal has the name Henderson erased and Hogg inserted unofficially.—J. S.

68/Genl. No./1976.

THE BLACK WATCH (ROYAL HIGHLANDERS).

LIST OF MEDALS AND CLASPS returned to the Assistant-Director of Ordnance Stores, Woolwich, by the Officer in Charge of Records, No. 1 District, Perth.

Regtl. No.	RANK AND NAME.	Description of Medals Returned.				REMARKS.
		King's		Queen's		
		Medals.	Clasps.	Medals.	Clasps.	
6744	Pte. Ball, T.	1	2			Discharged.
2524	,, Buchanan, G.			1	2	Deceased.
7010	Corpl. Burnett, W.	1	2			Discharged.
7834	Pte. Campbell, J.			1	3	Deceased.
2312	,, Christie, W.			1	2	Deceased.
4509	,, Connolly, H.			1	1	Deceased.
4149	,, Cook, N.	1	2			Discharged.
5827	,, Cowley, D.	1	2		1	Deceased.
5735	,, Glasgow, G.¹			1	1	Drowned.
2764	,, Gow, D.	1	2			Deceased.
3557	,, Gray, R.			1	1	Killed in action.
2646	,, Hannah, J.			1	3	Discharged.
2305	,, Hardie, E.	1	2	1	2	Discharged.
4454	,, Hardy, H.	1	2	1	4	Discharged.
7583	,, Honnan, J.			1	2	Discharged.
7278	,, Howie, R.	1	2		1	Deceased.
7328	,, Humphries, F.	1	2		1	Deceased.
6725	,, Keith, J.	1	2		1	Discharged.
5344	,, Kennedy, J.			1	4	Deceased.
8161	,, M'Alpine, J.			1	2	Discharged.
6561	,, M'Connel, J. T.²			1	1	Deceased.
2441	,, M'Donald, N.			1	1	Discharged.
6097	,, M'Donald, W.			1	1	Deceased.
1110	,, M'Ging, J.	1	2		1	Deceased.
3683	,, M'Manus, J.			1	3	Discharged.
7419	,, M'Nab, W.	1	2		1	Discharged.
4137	,, Masterton, A.			1	1	Deceased.
3859	,, Patterson, D.	1	2		1	Deceased.
2640	,, Payne, H.			1	3	Discharged.
7599	Lc.-Corpl. Proudfoot, A.			1	3	Discharged.
7142	Pte. Ritchie, L.	1	2		1	Discharged.
2621	,, Ruxton, F.			1	1	Discharged.
4139	,, Spicer, E. A.			1	1	Deceased.
7772	,, Thompson, W.			1	3	Discharged.
6436	,, Walker, J.			1	2	Discharged.
7287	,, Welsh, J.	1	2		1	Deceased.
9163	,, Wighton, F.			1	3	Discharged.
3911	,, Williamson, D.			1	1	Discharged.
201	,, Wilson, G.	1	2		1	Discharged.

¹ See note on page 268.—J. S.   ² Attached to 2nd Bn. K. R. R. Corps as mule-driver.

Victoria Cross

RECIPIENTS OF THE VICTORIA CROSS, with Accounts of the Acts of Bravery for which they were awarded.

Regtl. No.	RANK.	NAME.	Campaign.	'London Gazette.'	REMARKS.
	Private	Walter Cook	India, 1857-9.	18 June 1859.	
	Private	James Davis	India, 1857-9.	27 May 1859.	
	Lieut.	F. E. H. Farquharson . .	India, 1857-9.	18 June 1859.	
	Cr.-Sgt.	W. Gardner	India, 1857-9.	23 Augt. 1858.	
	Private	Duncan Millar	India, 1857-9.	18 June 1859.	
	Qr.-Mr.-Sgt.	John Simpson	India, 1857-9.	27 May 1859.	
	Lc.-Corpl.	A. Thompson	India, 1857-9.	27 May 1859.	
	Lc.-Sgt.	Samuel M'Gaw	Ashanti, 1873-4.	28 March 1874.	
	Private	Thomas Edwards . . .	Soudan, 1884.	21 May 1884.	
	Private	E. Spence [1]	India, 1858.	15 Jan. 1907.	

[1] Private EDWARD SPENCE, 42nd Foot, would have been recommended for V.C. for India, 1858, had he survived.

PRIVATE WALTER COOK AND PRIVATE DUNCAN MILLAR.
Date of act of bravery, Jany. 15th, 1859.

In the action at MAYLAH GHAUT, on the 15th Jany. 1859, Brigadier General Walpole reports that the conduct of Privates Cook and Millar deserves to be particularly pointed out. At the time the fight was the severest, and the few men of the 42nd Regiment were skirmishing so close to the enemy (who were in great numbers) that some of the men were wounded by sword cuts, and the only officer of the 42nd was carried to the rear, severely wounded, and the Colour-Sergeant was killed, these soldiers went to the front, took a prominent part in directing the Company, and displayed a courage, coolness, and discipline which was the admiration of all who witnessed it.

PRIVATE JAMES DAVIS.
Date of act of bravery, April 15th, 1858.

For conspicuous gallantry at the attack on the fort of RUHYA, when, with an advanced party to point out the gate of the fort to the Engineer officer, Private Davis offered to carry the body of Lieutenant Bramley, who was killed at the point, to the regiment. He performed this duty of danger and affection under the very walls of the fort.

2 o

Lieutenant FRANCIS EDWARD HENRY FARQUHARSON.
Date of act of bravery, March 9th, 1858.

For conspicuous bravery, when engaged before Lucknow, on the 9th March 1858, in having led a portion of his company, stormed a bastion mounting two guns, and spiked the guns, by which the advanced position held during the night of the 9th March was rendered secure from the fire of artillery. Lieutenant Farquharson was severely wounded, while holding an advanced position, on the morning of the 10th of March.

Captain Farquharson served at the Siege of Sebastopol from 14th July 1855 (medal and clasp and Turkish medal). Served the campaign of 1857-8 against the mutineers in India, including the actions at Cawnpore, 6th December 1857, Seriaghat, Kudygunge, and Shumsabad, Siege and Fall of Lucknow, and assault of the Martiniere and Banks Bungalow (medal and clasp).

Colour-Sergeant WILLIAM GARDNER.
Date of act of bravery, May 5th, 1858.

For his conspicuous and gallant conduct on the morning of the 5th May, in having saved the life of Lieutenant-Colonel Cameron, his commanding officer, who, during the action of Bareilly, on that day had been knocked from his horse, when three fanatics rushed upon him. Colour-Sergeant Gardner ran out, and in a moment bayoneted two of them, and was in the act of attacking the third, when he was shot down by another soldier of the regiment.

Letter from Captain Macpherson, 42nd Regiment, to Lt.-Colonel Cameron commanding that Regiment.

Quarter-Master-Sergeant JOHN SIMPSON.
Date of act of bravery, April 15th, 1858.

For conspicuous bravery at the attack on the fort of Ruhya on the 15th April 1858, in having volunteered to go to an exposed point within forty yards of the parapet of the fort under a heavy fire, and brought in, first Lieutenant Douglas, and afterwards a private soldier, both of whom were dangerously wounded.

Lance-Corporal ALEXANDER THOMPSON.
Date of act of bravery, April 15th, 1858.

For daring gallantry on the 15th April 1858, when at the attack of the fort of Ruhya, in having volunteered to assist Captain Cafe, commanding the 4th Punjaub Rifles, in bringing the body of Lieutenant Willoughby, of that corps, from the top of the glacis, in a most exposed situation, under a heavy fire.

Lance-Sergeant SAMUEL M'GAW.
Ashanti, January 31st, 1874.

At Amoaful, on the 31st January 1874, skilfully leading his section through the bush for a whole day, although badly wounded early in the battle.

Private THOMAS EDWARDS.
Soudan (Red Sea), March 13th, 1884.

At Tamaai, on the 13th March 1884, defending a gun, and though wounded, remaining by it throughout.

Private EDWARD SPENCE.[1]
Date of act of bravery, April 15th, 1858.

Private Edward Spence would have been recommended to Her Majesty for the decoration of 'The Victoria Cross' had he survived. He and Lance-Corporal Thompson volunteered, at the attack of the fort of Ruhya on the 15th of April 1858, to assist Captain Cafe, commanding the 4th Punjaub Rifles, in bringing in the body of Lieutenant Willoughby from the top of the glacis. Private Spence dauntlessly placed himself in an exposed position, so as to cover the party bearing away the body. He died on the 17th of the same month from the effects of wounds which he received on the occasion.

[1] The decoration earned by Private Spence was awarded to his relatives by His Majesty King Edward, the notification appearing in the *Gazette* dated 15th January 1907.—J. S.

42ND AND 73RD

1ST AND 2ND BNS. ROYAL HIGHLANDERS, THE BLACK WATCH

I.

DISTINGUISHED SERVICE ORDER

II.

MERITORIOUS SERVICE MEDAL

III.

DISTINGUISHED CONDUCT IN THE FIELD

DISTINGUISHED SERVICE ORDER

ROLL of Officers to whom the D.S.O. has been granted whilst serving in the ROYAL HIGHLANDERS, THE BLACK WATCH.

NAME.	RANK.	Date of Appointment.	REMARKS.
Maxwell, John Grenfell	Lieutenant.	26/11/86.	
Rennie, John George	Captain.	29/11/00.	
Walker, John Douglas Glen	Lieutenant.	29/11/00.	
Wauchope, Arthur Grenfell	Lieutenant.	29/11/00.	
Maxwell, Hon. Henry Edward	Major.	29/11/00.	
Hamilton, John George Harry	Captain.	29/11/00.	
Bald, A. C.	Captain.	26/6/02.	
Wilson-Farquharson, David Lorraine . . .	Major.	22/8/02.	
Grant, Archibald Seafield	Lieutenant.	22/8/02.	
Hore-Ruthven, Hon. Christian Malise . . .	Lieutenant.	22/8/02.	

MERITORIOUS SERVICE MEDAL

LIST OF WARRANT AND NON-COMMISSIONED OFFICERS OF THE 42ND AND 73RD FOOT who were awarded the 'MERITORIOUS SERVICE MEDAL' with Annuity, since the institution of the Decoration in the year 1845.

Regiment.	RANK.	Regtl. No.	NAME.	Annuity.	Date.	REMARKS.
42nd Foot	Qr.-Mr.-Sgt.		Robert Robertson .	£15	23/5/1847	
73rd ,,	Cr.-Sgt.		John Riley . . .	£15	24/8/1847	
42nd ,,	Sgt.-Major		Alexander Geddes .	£15	15/12/1849	
73rd ,,	Sgt.-Major		Francis Rennie . .	£15	21/6/1851	
73rd ,,	Hospl.-Sgt.		Hope Duff	£10	2/6/1853	
73rd ,,	Drum-Major		John Young . . .	£10	2/6/1853	
42nd ,,	Pay-Mr.-Sgt.		John Grant . . .	£10	13/4/1854	
42nd ,,	Qr.-Mr.-Sgt.		Alexr. M'Gregor . .	£20	5/1/1855	
42nd ,,	Sgt.-Major		John Granger . . .	£20	20/7/1855	
42nd ,,	Cr.-Sgt.		William Gardner . .	£20	26/9/1855	
73rd ,,	Garrn. Sgt.-Maj.		Edward Robins . .	£10	5/6/1872	
42nd ,,	Sgt.-Major		John Barclay . . .	£10	7/5/1874	
73rd ,,	Sgt.-Piper		William Stark . . .	£10	6/11/1892	
73rd ,,	Band-Mr.		Walter Greeson Buck	£10	29/8/1894	
42nd ,,	Sgt.-Major		Joseph Knight . .	£10	25/10/1897	
42nd ,,	Sgt.-Major		Andrew Graham . .	£10	18/8/1899	
42nd ,,	Sgt.-Major		Henry Barton . . .	£10	20/7/1900	
73rd ,,	Cr.-Sgt.		Patrick Lewin . . .	£10	13/5/1910	Late Staff R. Military College.
Late R. Highrs.	Sgt.-Maj.		J. Knight } See above.			
Late 2nd Bn. R. H.	Band-Mr.		W. G. Buck }			
73rd Foot	Sgt.		B. Kilkeary . . .		Sept. 1905	Late Royal Artillery, formerly 73rd.
1st V. B. Black Watch	Actg. S.-Maj.		J. Tait		June 1910	Formerly 4th Rifle Bde., late P.S. 1st V. Bn.

DISTINGUISHED CONDUCT IN THE FIELD

NOMINAL ROLL of WARRANT OFFICERS, NON-COMMISSIONED OFFICERS AND MEN OF THE BLACK WATCH, awarded the MEDAL for 'DISTINGUISHED CONDUCT IN THE FIELD.'

Regtl. No.	RANK.	NAME.	Campaign for which awarded.	REMARKS.
2217	Private	Bowie, A.	Crimea.	
888	,,	Christison, C.	,,	
2129	,,	Grant, J.	,,	
1075	,,	Haddow, D.	,,	
1986	,,	Hartley, J.	,,	
1336	,,	Hislop, D.	,,	
1156	,,	Holmes, R.	,,	
1025	,,	Kerr, W.	,,	
918	,,	Logg, D.	,,	
1209	Corporal	M'Clelland, J.	,,	
785	Qr.-Mr.-Sgt.	M'Gregor, A.	,,	With an annuity of £20.
	Private	Miller, J.	,,	
3209	Corporal	Mumford, J.	,,	
1619	,,	Patterson, J.	,,	
1204	,,	Petrie, W.	,,	
2230	Cr.-Sergt.	White, P.	,,	
1800	Private	Adams, T.	Ashanti, 1873-4.	
2854	Sgt.-Major	Barclay J.	Ashanti, 1873-4.	With an annuity of £10.
921	Sergt.	Barton, H.	,, ,,	
154	Private	Bell, W.	,, ,,	
209	,,	Cameron, G.	,, ,,	and 79th Foot.
120	,,	Jones, H.	,, ,,	and 79th Foot.
1882	Sergt.	Nicol, W.	,, ,,	
1561	Private	Ritchie, G.	,, ,,	Private in Ashanti Roll.
269	Sergeant	Street, W.	,, ,,	Sgt.-Instr. of Musketry in Ashanti Roll.
1187	Piper	Weatherspoon, J.	,, ,,	
1534	Private	White, J.	,, ,,	
2189	,,	Baldwin, F.	Sudan, 1884.	
2223	Cr.-Sergt.	Connan, J.	,, ,,	
21	Hospl.-Sergt.	Davidson, W.	,, 1883.	
1797	Private	Henderson, J.	,, 1884.	
1017	Cr.-Sergt.	Morrison, D.	,, 1883.	
2655	Drummer	Mumford, H.	,, ,,	Lc.-Corpl. in Egypt Roll.
223	Private	Shires, H.	,, ,,	
2374	Sergeant	Sutherland, J.	,, ,,	
2198	Cr.-Sergt.	Tweedie, J.	,, 1884.	
1379	Sergeant	Watt, T.	,, ,,	
2099	Private	West, F.	,, 1884-5.	Subsequently granted a bar to his medal for service in West Africa (Rank, Colour-Sergeant). Clasp awarded Jany. 1903.
2752	Sgt.-Major	Anderson, J. A.	S. Africa, 1899-1902	

Regtl. No.	RANK.	NAME.	Campaign for which awarded.	REMARKS.
4872	Sergeant	Baxter, J.	S. Africa, 1899-1902	
6269	Piper	Cameron, D. . . .	,, ,,	
6745	Lce.-Corpl.	Forrett, W.	,, ,,	
2031	Lce.-Sergt.	Gaynor, G.	,, ,,	
3746	Sergeant	Harrison, H. . . .	,, ,,	
	Pioneer	Hastie, J.	,, ,,	
1313	Pioneer-Sgt.	Howden, T.	,, ,,	
5657	Private	M'Gregor, R. . . .	,, ,,	
4007	Cr.-Sgt.	Millar, A.	,, ,,	
4813	Private	Ormond, R.	,, ,,	
	,,	Smith, J.	,, ,,	
3509	Sergeant	Wilson, A.	,, ,,	
	Qr.-Mr.-Sgt.	J. Mackenzie . . .		Late 3rd Bn. R. Highrs. and 79th Foot. Granted Oct. 1895.
	Cr.-Sergt.	King, W.		Awarded when serving in 1st Bn. S. Nigeria Regt. W.A.F.F.

MISCELLANEOUS
INCLUDING PENINSULAR GOLD MEDAL AND CROSS

MISCELLANEOUS

SERINGAPATAM MEDAL.

1799.

Struck by the Honourable East India Company, and issued to all who took part in the siege and capture of Seringapatam. It was issued in silver-gilt to field officers, silver for captains and subalterns, copper for non-commissioned officers, and tin for privates. None of these medals were impressed with the name of the recipient.

All ranks of the 73rd who were present received the medal, but unfortunately no roll of the names is in existence.

CEYLON MEDAL.

73RD FOOT.

In the year 1818 the 73rd were engaged in suppressing a rebellion of the Kandyans in Ceylon. A small party of the regiment, in charge of Lance-Corporal R. M'Laughlin, while on a march, was attacked by a numerous body of the enemy, and two men were killed. As the Kandyans generally mutilated the remains of British soldiers, the little party of the 73rd divided, part remaining to guard the bodies, and the other part, at an equal risk, forcing their way to Badulla, a few miles distant. From this place they returned with a reinforcement, drove back the enemy, and carried off the bodies of their slain comrades. To reward this gallant conduct a medal was struck by the Ceylon Government for presentation to Corporal M'Laughlin and three privates, but they all died of fever before it was issued.

The following would have received the medal :—

Lance-Corporal M'Laughlin.   Private Christopher Sheppard.
Private John Wilson.   ,,   William Connor.

PENINSULAR WAR.

GOLD MEDAL AND CROSS.

The following officers of the 42nd received the Medal or Cross for services in Egypt and the Peninsula, 1801-1814 :—

Lieut.-Colonel Alexr. Anderson.—Served with 11th Portuguese Regt.
    Badajoz, Salamanca, Vittoria, Pyrenees, Nivelle, Orthes, and Toulouse.   Cross and 3 Clasps.

Lieut.-Colonel Lord Blantyre, 2nd Bn. 42nd.
    Fuentes d'Onor.   Medal.

Lieut.-Colonel Robert Henry Dick.
    Fuentes d'Onor, Salamanca, Busaco.   Medal and 2 Clasps.

Lieut.-Colonel Robert Macara.
    Pyrenees, Nive, Nivelle, Orthes, Toulouse.   Cross and 1 Clasp.

Colonel George Murray—Qr.-Mr. General.   Hon. Colonel 42nd.
> Corunna, Talavera, Busaco, Fuentes d'Onor, Vittoria, Pyrenees, Nive, Nivelle, Orthes, and Toulouse.   Cross and 6 Clasps.

Lieut.-Colonel Maxwell Grant.—Served with 6th Portuguese Regt.
> Vittoria, Pyrenees, Nive, Nivelle, and Orthes.   Cross and 1 Clasp.

Major William Cowell.—Commanded a Light Battalion.
> Nivelle and Orthes.   Medal and 1 Clasp.

Captain John Campbell.—Succeeded to command of Light Companies.
> Orthes and Toulouse.   Medal and 1 Clasp.

Lieut.-Colonel James Stirling.
> Corunna, Salamanca, Pyrenees.   Medal and 2 Clasps.

Captain George Stewart.—Commanded Light Company.
> Nive.   Medal.

CHINA, 1902.

The following N.C.O.'S received the Medal and Clasp 'Relief of Pekin.'
> 2930 Cr.-Sgt. C. Young.   4334 Cr.-Sgt. E. Dunn.
> Both served with the Chinese Regiment.

The following received the Medal without the Clasp:—
> 5990 Lc.-Cpl. W. B. Laing.—Attached Indian Medical Service.
> 5280 Private C. J. Banfield.—Attached Telegraph Coy. R.E.

INDIAN FRONTIER MEDAL.

> Lieut. H. H. Sutherland.—Medal and Clasp, 'Punjab Frontier, 1897-98.'
> Lieut. J. M. Blair.—Medal and Clasp 'North-West Frontier, 1908.'
3522 Private J. Hannan.—Medal and Clasp 'Punjab Frontier, 1897-98.'
> Corporal E. J. Cheesman.   ,,   ,,   ,,
4547 Sgt. T. Munro.—Medal and Clasps 'Punjab Frontier 1897-98,' 'Samana 1897,' and 'Tirah 1897-98.'
> Capt. J. B. Pollok Morris.—Medal for Tibet and Clasp 'Gyantse.'
> Capt. J. T. C. Murray.—Medal and Clasp 'North-West Frontier, 1908.'
> Capt. P. A. Duff.—Medal and Clasp 'North-West Frontier, 1908.'

WEST AFRICA.

> Capt. D. Campbell.—Medal and Clasp 'N. Nigeria, 1906.'

INDIAN VOLUNTEER LONG SERVICE AND GOOD CONDUCT MEDAL.

Private James Robertson.—Served in the 42nd Foot, 1864-71, and G.I.P. Railway Volunteers, 1878-1904.

VOLUNTEER LONG SERVICE AND GOOD CONDUCT MEDAL.

182 Sgt. R. Sime, 1st Bn. The Black Watch, earned the Medal in 7th V.B. Royal Scots.
> See also First Egyptian Roll.
2124 Pte. David Cairns, 42nd Foot, earned the Medal in 4th V.B. Royal Scots.
> See also Gold Coast Medal Roll.

MEDALS AND DECORATIONS

OF

FOREIGN NATIONS

CONFERRED ON OFFICERS, N.C. OFFICERS AND MEN

OF

THE 42ND AND 73RD REGIMENTS OF FOOT

NOW

THE 1ST AND 2ND BNS. THE BLACK WATCH
(ROYAL HIGHLANDERS)

MEDALS AND DECORATIONS OF FOREIGN NATIONS CONFERRED ON OFFICERS, N.C. OFFICERS AND MEN OF THE 42ND AND 73RD REGIMENTS OF FOOT, NOW THE 1ST AND 2ND BNS. THE BLACK WATCH (ROYAL HIGHLANDERS).

1854–55.

TURKISH MEDAL FOR THE CRIMEA.

This Medal—the gift of H.M. the Sultan of Turkey—was issued to all soldiers and sailors engaged in the war.

1882–86.

KHEDIVE'S STAR.

This Decoration—presented by the Khedive of Egypt—was given to all who took part in the operations in Egypt from 1882 to 1886.

1854–55.

FRENCH ORDER

'VALEUR ET DISCIPLINE.'

Presented by H.I.M. the Emperor of France to certain non-commissioned officers and men of the British forces in the Crimea for distinguished gallantry. The following are those of the 42nd to whom it was given:—

Colour-Sergeant Thomas Ridley.
Sergeant George Fox.
,,   William Strathearn.
Lance-Corporal William Bennett.

Lance-Corporal Robert M'Nair.
Private Neil Carmichael.
,,   Andrew Cromtie.
,,   Donald M'Kenzie.

SARDINIAN ORDER

'AL VALORE MILITARE.'

Given to selected officers, non-commissioned officers and men by the King of Sardinia for services rendered during the Crimean campaign. The following are those of the 42nd who received it:—

Colonel D. A. Cameron, C.B.
Lieut.-Colonel A. Cameron.
Major A. Pitcairn.
Captain H. Montgomery.

Captain Sir P. A. Halkett, Bt.
Colour-Sgt. D. Dalgleish.
Private E. M'Millan.

TURKISH ORDER OF THE MEDJIDIEH.

Colonel D. A. Cameron, C.B.—For services in the Crimea, 1854-55.
Lieut. J. C. M'Leod.   ,,   ,,   ,,
   ,,   J. C. Ross Grove.   ,,   ,,   ,,
Lt. and Qr.-Mr. W. Wood.   ,,   ,,   ,,
Capt. A. G. Wauchope.—For services in Egypt, 1882-86.
Capt. H. F. S. Amery.—For services in Egypt.

TURKISH ORDER OF THE OSMANIEH.

Colonel D. Macpherson, C.B.—For services in Egypt, 1882-86.
Lt.-Colonel W. Green.   ,,   ,,
Major R. K. Bayly.   ,,   ,,
   ,,   A. F. Kidston.   ,,   ,,
   ,,   W. J. St. J. Harvey.—For services in Egypt.
Capt. H. F. S. Amery.   ,,   ,,

FRENCH LEGION OF HONOUR.

Lieut.-General Sir J. C. M'Leod.

42ND AND 73RD

REGISTER OF N.C.O.'S AND MEN

RECOMMENDED FOR

THE GOOD CONDUCT MEDAL

UNDER THE PROVISIONS OF

ROYAL WARRANTS OF 1829, 1845, and 1847

ALSO

LONG SERVICE AND GOOD CONDUCT MEDAL

THE ROYAL HIGHLAND REGIMENT

From 1881

42ND REGIMENT OF ROYAL HIGHLANDERS

REGISTER OF MEN recommended for the GRATUITY AND GOOD CONDUCT MEDAL, in addition to PENSION, under the Provisions of Royal Warrants of 1829, 1845, and 1847.

Year.	RANK AND NAME.	Regtl. No.	Description and Amount of Gratuity.		Date of Issue of Medal.	To whom sent.	REMARKS.
1850-1	Serjt. John Henderson .	502	S.	£15	7/9/50	S.O.P., Glasgow.	
	C.-Sjt. John Rawson . .	346	S.	£10	7/9/50	,, Edinburgh.	
	Pte. Alexr. Mitchell . .	547	P.	£5	7/9/50	,, Stirling.	
1851-2	Actg.-S.-Maj. Alexr. Vigrow	553	Serjt.	£15	19/2/52	O.C.D. 42nd Regt.	Vigrow, not Vigors.
	Pt. Quintin Chalmers .	..	Pt.	£5	22/5/52	ditto.	
	,, James Potter . .	..	Pt.	£5	,,	ditto.	
	Corpl. Peter M'Cowan .	..	Pt.	£5	,,	ditto.	
1852-3	Qr.-Mr.-Sjt. John Shields	606	Sergt.	£15	22/5/52	O.C. 42nd Regt.	
	Pte. James Baxter . .	604	P.	£5	9/7/52	do. Stirling.	
	,, James Cramb . .	607	P.	£5	9/7/52	do. ,,	
	,, Alexr. M'Kay . .	678	P.	£5	9/7/52	do. ,,	
1853-4	Sjt.-Major James Rankin	690	Sergt.	£15	23/9/53	O.C. 42nd Regt.	
	Pte. Robt. Lang . . .	764	Pt.	£5	23/9/53	do.	
	C.-Sjt. George Dick . .	769	Corp.	£10	13/12/53	S.O.P., Perth.	No Corporal eligible.
1854-5	Pte. Meek Wright . . .	782	Pt.	£5	11/5/54	O.C. 42nd, Portsth.	
	,, David Pithie . .	798	Pt.	£5	11/5/54	do. do.	
	,, John M'Lean . .	833	Pt.	£5	11/5/54	do. do.	
	,, David M'Nab . .	846	Pt.	£5	11/5/54	do. do.	
	Sergt. John Morrison .	875	Corpl.	£10	18/7/54	O.C.D.B., Winchester	
	Pte. John Donald . . .	734	Pt.	£5	22/8/54	O.C. 42nd, Turkey.	
	Col.-Sgt. Peter White .	2230	Sergt.	£15	26/3/55	Adjt.-Genl. in Crimea	Under Royal Warrant 4 Decr. 1854. 'For Distinguished Conduct in the Field.'
	Corpl. Josh. Mumford .	3209	Corpl.	£10	,,	,, ,,	do. do.
	,, Jas. M'Clelland .	1209	,,	£10	,,	,, ,,	do. do.
	,, Wm. Petrie . .	1204	,,	£10	,,	,, ,,	do. do.
	,, Jno. Patterson .	1619	,,	£10	,,	,, ,,	do. do.
	Pte. Jas. Miller . .	1748	Private	£5	,,	,, ,,	do. do.
	,, Jas. Grant . .	2129	,,	£5	,,	,, ,,	do. do.
	,, Robert Holmes .	1156	,,	£5	,,	,, ,,	do. do.
	,, Angus Bowie . .	2217	,,	£5	,,	,, ,,	do. do.
	,, Josh. Hartley .	1986	,,	£5	,,	,, ,,	do. do.
	,, Chas. Christison .	888	,,	£5	,,	,, ,,	do. do.
	,, Wm. Kerr . .	1025	,,	£5	,,	,, ,,	do. do.
	,, David Haddow .	1075	,,	£5	,,	,, ,,	do. do.
	,, Daniel Logg . .	918	,,	£5	,,	,, ,,	do. do.
	,, David Hislop .	1336	,,	£5	,,	,, ,,	do. do.
1855-6	Cr.-Sergt. Jas. Veitch .	1085	Sergt.	£15	25/1/56	O.C.D. 42nd, Stirling.	
	Sergt. John Stonar .	810	Pte.	£5	,,	,,	
	,, Archd. M'Callum .	1046	Sergt.	£15	6/3/56	O.C.D. 42nd.	
	Pte. Edward Conolly . .	820	Pte.	£5	,,	A.G., Crimea.	

Year.	Rank and Name.	Regtl. No.	Description and Amount of Gratuity.		Date of Issue of Medal.	To whom sent.	Remarks.
1856-7	Sergt. Wm. Simpson . .	1184	Pte.	£5	21/8/60	S.O.P., Carlisle.	
	Pte. Wm. M'Math . . .	978	Pte.	£5	,,	S.O.P., Glasgow.	
	Pte. Daniel Logg . . .	918	Pte.	£5	,,	S.O.P., Glasgow.	
	Pte. Donald Bain . . .	959	Pte.	£5	,,	S.O.P., Stirling.	
	Pte. David Haddow . .	1075	Pte.	£5	{E 31/8/60 E}	S.O.P., {York. Glasgow.	{Medal returned from York and sent to Glasgow.
1857-8	Pte. William Gibson . .	1076	Pte.	£5	7/5/57	O.C. Regt., Dover.	
	Sergt. John Duff . . .	873	Pte.	£5	,,	O.C. Depot, Stirling.	
	Pte. Andrew Shedden .	1045	Pte.	£5	,,	,, ,,	
	Sergt. Wilson Brown .	1153	Corpl.	£10	,,	O.C. Regt., Dover.	d£5 ; 117/4757.
	Pte. Neil Carmichael .	1170	Pte.	£5	,,	,,	
	Pte. John Mutrie . . .	1730	Pte.	£5	21/8/60	O.C. 22nd D. Bn., Stirling.	
	Pte. John M'Kay . . .	1231	Pte.	£5	,,	,, ,,	
1858-9	Pte. William Simpson .	1352	Pte.	£5	6/12/58	O.C. Regt., E. Indies.	
	,, James O'Neill . .	1252	Pte.	£5	6/12/58	,, ,,	
	,, John Cronan . . .	81	Pte.	£5	6/12/58	O.C. Regt., E. Indies.	Deceased previous to grant. *Vide* O.C.'s letter dated 8/4/59 in Ld. Clyde's letter 24/4/59. Medal to be given to another man. Notified to W.O.
	,, Alexr. Stephen . .	1412	Pte.	£5	,,	,, ,,	
	,, Chas. Sanderson .	1712	Pte.	£5	,,	,, ,,	
	,, Jas. Montgomery .	1297	Pte.	£5	,,	,, ,,	
	,, Joseph Bogle . .	1234	Pte.	£5	,,	,, ,,	
	Corpl. George Grant . .	826	Pte.	£5	,,	O.C.D. Bn., Stirling.	Returned from India, and sent to Stirling. Receipt ackd. 25/8/59.
	Pte. Jas. Douglass . .	1382	Pte.	£5	21/8/60	,, ,,	
1859-60	Pr.-Sergt. James Brown .	1327	Corpl.	£10	10/9/59	O.C. Regt., Bengal.	
	Pte. Fredk. M'Kenzie .	1389	Pte.	£5	,,	,, ,,	
	,, Geo. Ritchie . .	1413	Pte.	£5	,,	,, ,,	
	,, John Graham .	1751	Pte.	£5	,,	,, ,,	
	Cr.-Sergt. Alex. Reid . .	1406	Sergt.	£10	,,	O.C. 22 D.B., Stirling.	
	Sergt. Geo. Donald . .	822	Pte.	£5	,,	,, ,,	
1860-1	Pte. James Lockhart . .	1626	Pte.	£5	19/7/60	O.C. Regt., Bengal.	
	Pte. Alex. Chisholm . .	1351	Pte.	£5	,,	,, ,,	M.G.
	Pte. Chas. Brothwell .	3251	Pte.	£5	,,	,, ,,	
	Pte. Robt. M'Moran . .	1780	Pte.	£5	,,	,, ,,	
	Corpl. Wm. Bain . . .	1835	Pte.	£5	,,	,, ,,	
	Pte. Wm. Brown . . .	1981	Pte.	£5	,,	,, ,,	
	Sergt. Chas. Robertson .	1580	Pte.	£5	,,	,, ,,	
	Sergt. David Peebles . .	1869	Pte.	£5	,,	,, ,,	
1861-2	Sergt. Thomas Stiven .	2120	Corpl.	£10	5/7/61	Regt., Bengal.	M.G. in P.M.
	Pte. Wm. Healey . . .	1456	Pte.	£5	,,	,, ,,	
	Pte. John Buchanan . .	1809	Pte.	£5	,,	,, ,,	
	Pte. John M'Kinnon . .	1908	Pte.	£5	,,	,, ,,	

Year.	RANK AND NAME.	Regtl. No.	Description and Amount of Gratuity.		Date of Issue of Medal.	To whom sent.	REMARKS.
1861-2	Pte. Archd. M'Farlane .	1915	Pte.	£5	5/7/61	Regt., Bengal.	
	Pte. John M'Alpine . .	2000	Pte.	£5	,,	,, ,, ,,	
	Pte. Wm. Sideserf . .	2061	Pte.	£5	,,	,, ,, ,,	
1862-3	Cr.-Serjt. Wm. Strathearn	2156	Pte.	£5	3/7/62	Regt., Bengal.	
	Pte. Jas. Bell	2099	Pte.	£5	,,	,, ,, ,,	
	Pte. Wm. Dewar . . .	2081	Pte.	£5	,,	,, ,, ,,	
	Pte. John Dorthwaite .	86	Pte.	£5	,,	,, ,, ,,	
	Pte. John Arneil . .	2140	Pte.	£5	,,	,, ,, ,,	
	Pte. Alexr. Herron . .	2103	Pte.	£5	,,	,, ,, ,,	
	Pte. George Glen . .	2134	Pte.	£5	,,	,, ,, ,,	
	Pte. John Orr	1796	Pte.	£5	,,	,, ,, ,,	
1863-4	Pte. Alexr. Lindsay .	2446	Pte.	£5	21/7/63	Regt., Bengal.	
	,, Jno. Wilson . .	1901	Pte.	£5	,,	Commt., Netley.	
	,, Geo. Howard . .	96	Pte.	£5	,,	Regt., Bengal.	
	Corpl. Rodk. Ross .	4317	Pte.	£5	,,	,, ,,	
	Pte. Chas. Richardson .	114	Pte.	£5	,,	,, ,,	Claim £10; 117/2747.
	Sergt. Andw. Johnstone .	1999	Pte.	£5	,,	Commt., Netley.	
	Pte. Wm. M'Luskey .	2014	Pte.	£5	,,	Regt., Bengal.	
	Corpl. James M'Gregor .	1388	Pte.	£5	18/9/63	,, ,,	
1864-5	Pte. Thomas Delaney .	85	Pte.	£5	14/7/64	Regt., Bengal.	
	,, Wm. Barclay .	2117	Pte.	£5	2/9/64	S.O.P., Stirling.	
	,, Alexr. Robbin .	2058	Pte.	£5	,,	Comdt., Netley.	
	,, Jas. Cumpsty . .	2290	Pte.	£5	,,	Dep., Edinburgh.	
1865-6	Hospl. - Sergeant David M'Farlane	25	Sergt.	£15	29/9/65	Regt., Bengal.	M.G. in P.M. I. H. Tidy, Adjt.
	Pte. Ambrose Ledger . .	1071	Pte.	£5	,,	,, ,, ,,	M.G. in P.M. I. H. Tidy, Adjt.
	Armr.-Sgt. James Pattison	1196	Sergt.	£15	,,	Depot, Aberdeen.	M.G. in P.M. I. H. Tidy, Adjt.
	Pte. Alexr. M'Kenzie . .	2313	Pte.	£5	20/10/65	,, ,,	M.G. in P.M. Robt. C. Stewart, D.A.A.G.
1866-7	Sergt.-Maj. Charles Christie	1480	Sergt.	£15	25/8/66	15 D.B., Aberdeen.	
	Sergt. Alexr. Moir . .	2084	Sergt.	£15	,,	,, ,, ,,	
1867-8	Pte. Alexr. M'Pherson .	967	Pte.	£5	22/6/67	Appt.	
	Qr.-Mr.-Sgt. Thos. Torrance	2647	Sergt.	£15	24/7/67	Appt.	
	Qr.-Mr.-Sergt. John Stephen	2255	Corpl.	£10	20/8/67	O.C. 15 Dep. Bn.	
1868-9	Sergt. Wm. Brown . .	2582	Pte.	£5	30/6/68	Regiment.	
	Corpl. James Menzies .	2505	Pte.	£5	,,	,, ,,	
	Pte. George M'Lean . .	2607	Pte.	£5	,,	,,	
	,, Neil M'Kechnie . .	2609	Pte.	£5	,,	,,	
1869-70	Cr.-Sgt. Wm. H. French .	64	Corpl.	£10	7/7/69	Regiment.	
	Pte. Thomas Brown . .	2703	Pte.	£5	,,	,,	
	,, Michael Mahoney .	3305	Pte.	£5	,,	,,	
1870-1	Pte. Malcolm M'Phee .	3012	Pte.	£5	4/7/70	Regiment.	
	Cr.-Sergt. David Moodie .	2820	Corpl.	£10	16/12/70	,,	
	Sergt. Andw. Brown . .	2816	Pte.	£5	,,		

Year.	RANK AND NAME.	Regtl. No.	Description and Amount of Gratuity.	Date of Issue of Medal.	To whom sent.	REMARKS.
1871-2	Q. M. Sgt. John Barclay .	2854	Corpl. £10	5/10/71	O.C. Regt.	C. 10439 see fm. 4/ Tronbridge /36. Relinqd. on being granted Medal with Annuity.
	Sgt. Major John Forbes .	2825	Corpl. £10	6/2/72	,,	Relinqd. on promotion to Qr.-Master /43.
	Corporal George Christie .	2753	Pte. £5			Already in possession of medal without gratuity.
	Pte. John Angus . . .	3154	Pte. £5	..	.. ..	
	,, Wm. Cox . . .	3254	Pte. £5			
1872-3	Sergt. John Barr . . .	3609	Corpl. £10	29/3/73	Regiment.	
	Pte. Guilford Dudley . .	3375	Pte. £5	,,	,,	
	Armr.-Sergt. Richd. Warry	1849	Pte. £5	2/8/73	,,	
	Pte. Michael Leonard .	3464	Pte. £5	,,	,,	
	,, John Neilson . .	3688	Pte. £5	,,	,,	
1873-4	Sergt. James Butters . .	3454	Pte. £5	21/3/74	Regiment.	
	Cr.-Sergt. Quibel Cooper .	4086	Corpl. £10	,,	,,	
	Cr.-Sergt. Thos. M'Laren .	3995	Pte. £5	,,	,,	
	Cr.-Sergt. James Paterson	3685	Corpl. £10	,,	,,	
1874-5	Sergt. Robert Leishman .	4295	Pte. £5			
	Sergt. Wm. Matheson .	3409	Corpl. £10			
	Sergt. Daniel Kelly . .	797	Corpl. £10			
	Pte. Thomas Panton . .	4314	Pte. £5			
				Date of Recommendation.		
1876-7	Pay-Mr.-Sergeant Charles Bateman	1551	.. £5	30/6/75		
	Corpl. Andrew Howie .	231	.. £5	1/1/76		
	Pte. James Campbell . .	134	.. £5	4/11/75		
	Sgt. I. of My. William Street	269	.. £5	15/1/76		
	Sgt. John Todhunter . .	172	.. £5	1/10/75		
	Sgt. Samuel Wilson . .	198	.. £5	18/10/75		
	Pte. James Walker . .	200	.. £5	20/10/75		
	Pte. Patrick Docharty .	1672	.. £5	18/10/75		
	Corpl. Hugh M'Kerney .	264	.. £5	21/1/76		
	Corpl. John Stewart . .	195	.. £5	1/4/76		
	Cr.-Sgt. Wm. Farquharson	333	.. £5	1/4/76		
	Pte. Alexr. Finlayson .	305	.. £5	1/4/76		
	Sgt.-Mr.-Tailor John Whyte	1604	.. £5	1/4/76		
	Pte. Wm. Rennie . . .	1641	.. £5	1/4/76		
	Cr.-Sgt. John White . .	355	.. £5	1/7/76		
	Pte. Martin Dunn . .	422	.. £5	1/7/76		
	Pte. Wm. M'Callum . .	1314	.. £5	1/7/76		
	Sgt.-Maj. Andw. Graham	386	.. £5	1/7/76		
	Cr.-Sgt. Wm. Mitchell .	1386	.. £5	1/7/76		
	Pte. James M'Kay . .	434	.. £5	1/7/76		
	Pte. Wm. Munro . . .	1630	.. £5	1/7/76		
	Corpl. Thomas Milne . .	476	.. £5	1/10/76		
	Pte. Michael Rogers . .	416	.. £5	1/10/76		
	Pte. James Walker . .	425	.. £5	1/10/76		

Year.	Rank and Name.	Regtl. No.	Description and Amount of Gratuity.		Date of Recommendation.	To whom sent.	Remarks.
1877-8	Cr.-Sgt. Wm. Cockburn .	506	..	£5	1/1/77		
	Sergt. Peter Gairns . .	526	..	£5	1/1/77		
	Pte. John M'Tavish . .	1759	..	£5	1/1/77		
	Sergt. John Bisset Wilson	4323	..	£5	1/1/77		
	Corpl. James Gunn . .	548	..	..	1/4/77		
	Corpl. Alexr. Robertson .	488	..	..	,,		
	Pte. Geo. Aitken . .	38	..	..	,,		
	Pte. Thos. Hindon . .	579	..	..	,,		
	Pte. John Sim . . .	639	..	..	,,		
	Pte. Robert Buswell .	1076	..	..	1/7/77	O.C. Regiment.	
	Sergt. James Cornfoot .	653	..	..	,,	,,	
	Pte. James Dewar . .	591	..	..	,,	,,	
	Pte. Peter Lafferty .	646	..	..	,,	,,	
	Pte. John Mitchell . .	206	..	..	,,	,,	
	Cr.-Sgt. John Simpson .	624	..	..	,,	,,	
	Pte. Luke Todd . . .	692	..	..	,,	,,	
	Pte. David Todd . . .	645	..	..	,,	O.C. Depot.	
	Pte. John Howie . . .	1559	..	..	1/10/77	O.C. Regiment.	
	Sergt. Archd. M'Lachlan .	753	..	..	,,	,,	
1878	Pte. George Aitken . .	38	..	..	1/4/78	O.C. 57 Bde. Depot.	
	Sergt. James M'Lean . .	4321	..	..	,,	O.C. Perth Militia, Perth.	
	Pte. Patrick M'Elroy . .	754	..	..	1/7/78	O.C. 57th Bde. Depot.	
	Sergt. Joseph Tyson . .	889	..	..	,,	O.C. 57th Bde. Depot.	
	Pte. David Beattie . .	1707	..	..	,,	O.C. Regiment.	
	Cr.-Sgt. James Chapman	888	..	..	,,	,,	
	Pte. Joseph Bertie . .	338	..	..	1/1/79	,,	
1879	~~Pte. David Beattie . .~~	~~1707~~	~~..~~	~~..~~	~~1/4/79~~	~~O.C.R.~~	Awarded A.G. List 38.
	Pte. John Slattie . . .	786	..	..	1/10/79	O.C.R.	

42ND REGIMENT OF HIGHLANDERS

REGISTER OF MEN recommended for a GOOD CONDUCT MEDAL *without* GRATUITY, under the Provisions of the Royal Warrant of 16th January 1860.

Year.	RANK AND NAME.	Regtl. No.	Date of Recommendation, and by whom.	Date of Issue of Medal.	Officer to whom the Medal was sent.	REMARKS.
1859-60	.. ..	..	..	..	.. ..	
1860-1	.. ..	..	..	..	.. ..	
1861-2	Qr.-Mr.-Sgt. William Gardner	1469	O.C.D.	16/4/66	16/6/66	S.O.P., Glasgow.	Claims £15 ; 117/1629.
	~~Armr.-Sgt. Jas. Pattison~~	~~1196~~	~~O.C.D.~~	~~8/6/62~~	~~29/7/62~~	~~Dep., Stirling.~~	
	Sergt. Alexr. M'Kay .	1563	Do.	Do.	,,	,,	
	Pte. Joshua Holland .	95	Do.	Do.	,,	S.O.P., Newcastle-under-Lyme.	
1862-3	Pte. Wm. Gray . .	1877	O.C.R.	14/4/62	3/7/62	O.C. Regt., Bengal.	
1863-4	.. ..	..	..	..	.. ..	
1864-5	.. ..	..	..	..	.. ..	
1865-6	.. ..	..	..	..	.. ..	
1866-7	.. ..	..	..	..	.. ..	
1870-1	Pte. Robert Smith .	2826	O.C.R.	7/9/70	19/12/70	O.C. Regt.	
	Pte. John Brown . .	2889	O.C.R.	1/4/71	19/8/71	,,	
	Army School-Mr. Wm. M'Ewan	..	O.C.R.	4/9/71	6/2/72	,,	
1871-2	~~Corpl. George Christie~~	~~2759~~	~~O.C.R.~~	~~4/9/71~~	~~6/2/72~~	~~Regt.~~	} Subsequently awarded Gratuity. See /43. Subsequently awarded Gratuity.
	~~Pte. John Angers .~~	~~3154~~	~~O.C.R.~~	~~4/9/71~~	~~,,~~	~~Regt.~~	
	~~Pte. William Cox .~~	~~3254~~	~~O.C.R.~~	~~20/1/72~~	~~11/6/72~~	~~Regt.~~	
1872-3	Pte. Daniel Hill . .	1166	O.C.R.	12/3/73	2/8/73	Regt.	
	Hospl.-Sgt. John Hynd	3363	O.C.R.	25/4/73	,,	,,	
1873-4	Pte. Alexr. Symington	3863	O.C.R.	2/10/73	21/3/74	Regt.	
	Band-Mr. James Wilson	2815	O.C.R.	2/10/73	,,	,,	
	Corpl. James M'Laren	1585	O.C.R.	4/4/74	19/12/74	,,	
1874-5	Pte. John Calderwood	4111	O.C.R.	23/3/75	..		
	~~Corpl. Methven Clarke~~	~~4311~~	~~O.C.R.~~	~~23/3/75~~	forfeited, see /79.		
	Pte. Wm. Clark . .	3536	O.C.D.	30/3/75			

73RD REGIMENT OF FOOT

REGISTER OF MEN recommended for the GRATUITY and GOOD CONDUCT MEDAL, in addition to PENSION, under the Provisions of the Royal Warrants of 1829, 1845, and 1847.

Year.	RANK AND NAME.	Regtl. No.	Description and Amount of Gratuity.	Date of Issue of Medal.	To whom sent.	REMARKS.
1850-1	No man eligible,	*vide*	O.C.'s letter 31/5/53.			
1851-2	Private George Merchant	760	Pte. £5	10/9/52	P. at Chatham.	
	„ John Snow . .	729	Pte. £5	do.	do.	
1852-3	Private Wm. Small . .	1183	Pte. £5	15/6/53	S.O.P., Cardiff.	
	„ Saml. Casson .	1060	„ £5	27/8/53	O.C. 73, Cape.	
1853-4	Private Saml. Candler .	838	Pte. £5	27/8/53	O.C. at Chatham.	
	Qr.-Mr.-Sgt. James Carroll	1924	Serjt. £15	1/8/54	O.C. 73, Cape.	
	Corpl. Michl. Eagan . .	..	Pte. £5	18/8/54	S.O.P., Dublin.	
UNDER ROYAL WARRANT, 13 APRIL 1854.						
1854-5	Private John Early . .	982	Pte. £5	9/12/54	O.C.D. 73, Jersey.	
	„ Bernard King .	987	Pte. £5	20/1/55	do.	
1855-6	Corpl. And. Halliey . .	1067	Pte. £5	16/6/56	O.C. Cape.	
	Pte. John Dunan . .	1103	Pte. £5	„	„	
1856-7	.. ..	..	..	..	..	..
1857-8	Sergt. James Holihan .	1252	Sergt. £15	23/8/58	O.C., Colchester.	
	Private James White .	1192	Pte. £5	29/6/60	S.O.P., Tralee.	
	„ Meredith Roberts	1161	Pte. £5	29/6/60	„ Cardiff.	
1858-9	Private Patk. Halloran .	1393	Pte. £5	29/1/59	O.C. Regt., E. Indies.	Duplicate Medal, see below.
	„ Patk. Maloney .	1384	„ £5	12/3/59	„ „	
	~~„ Patk. Halloran .~~	~~1393~~	~~„ £5~~	~~„~~	~~„ „~~	Cancelled, see above.
	„ Samuel Moffatt	1310	„ £5	19/11/59	O.C. Regt., Bengal.	To receive Medal sent in duplicate for Halloran.
	„ James Hopper .	1336	„ £5		„ „	
	„ Wm. Bonnyman	2	„ £5	23/4/59	„ „	
	„ John Finch . .	1402	„ £5	„	„ „	
	„ Alexr. Ferguson	3	„ £5	„	„ „	
	Sergt. John Daly . .	1450	„ £5	„	„ „	
1859-60	Private Edward Rock .	1008	Pte. £5	9/5/59	O.C.D.Bn., Plymouth	
	Sgt.-Major Jas. FitzGerald	1383	Serjt. £15	„	„ Colchester	
	Private Patrick Cassidy	1349	Pte. £5	1/3/60	O.C. Regt., Bengal.	This gratuity is granted for 1859-60, there being no vacancies for 1858-9, the year for which you recommend Cassidy.
	Qr.-Mr.-Sjt. Wm. Darling	1631	Serjt. £15	24/3/60	„ Calcutta.	*P.S.*—No vacancies for Haughey or Fell.

Year.	RANK AND NAME.	Regtl. No.	Description and Amount of Gratuity.		Date of Issue of Medal.	To whom sent.	REMARKS.
1860-1	Private Mattw. M'Dermott	1618	Pte.	£5	29/6/60	G.O.C., Chatham.	
	,, James O'Brien .	1622	,,	£5	,,	,,	
	,, Willm. Bond .	1554	,,	£5	19/7/60	O.C. Regt., Calcutta.	
	,, Thos. Hartrope	1769	,,	£5	21/8/60	,, ,,	
	,, Wm. Britton .	1429	,,	£5	,,	,, ,,	
	C.-Sergt. Jas. S. Barson .	1794	Sergt.	£15	,,	G.O.C., Chatham.	
1861-2	Sergt. Swain Atkinson .	1890	Corpl.	£10	9/5/62	Regt., Devonport.	
	Corpl. Joshua Fell . .	1711	Pte.	£5	,,	,, ,,	
	Sergt. Thos. Drinkwater	1825	Pte.	£5	,,	,, ,,	
	Drummer John W. Best	1020	Pte.	£5	,,	,, ,,	
	Private Jas. Kedwell	1814	Pte.	£5	,,	,, ,,	
	Private Patk. Conlon .	1865	Pte.	£5	,,	,, ,,	
	Private John Tilley . .	1974	Pte.	£5	,,	,, ,,	
1862-3	Dr.-Major Thos. Bosanquet	648	Pte.	£5	9/5/62	Regt., Devonport.	
	Sergt. Richd. Lewis . .	2055	Pte.	£5	,,	,, ,,	
	Corpl. John Rich .	2042	Pte.	£5	,,	,, ,,	
	Private John Watt . .	1229	Pte.	£5	,,	,, ,,	
	Private Richd. Proudley	1898	Pte.	£5	,,	,, ,,	
	Private John Fisher .	1966	Pte.	£5	,,	,, ,,	
	Private John Lough .	1977	Pte.	£5	,,	,, ,,	
	Private Jas. Illsley . .	2022	Pte.	£5	,,	,, ,,	
1863-4	Private Willm. Bingham	2030	Pte.	£5	2/5/63	Regt., Aldershot.	
	Private John Trendell .	2124	Pte.	£5	,,	,, ,,	
	Cr.-Sergt. Wm. Conway .	1140	Pte.	£5	11/6/63	4 D.Bn., Colchester.	Cl. £5 ; 117/3581.
	Sergt. Wm. Ashfield .	1704	Pte.	£5	,,	,, ,,	Cl. £10 ; 117/3580.
	Private Josh. Henry .	1859	Pte.	£5	,,	,, ,,	
	Private Jno. Crawforth .	1906	Pte.	£5	,,	Comdt. Kneller Hall, Whilton.	
1864-5	Sergt. Jno. Williams .	2061	Pte.	£5	21/5/64	Regt., Aldershot.	
	Sergt. Jno. Murtaugh .	2091	Pte.	£15	16/7/64	I.F.O., Glasgow.	
	Sergt. Eli Sumners . .	6	Pte.	£5	,,	Dep., Colchester.	
	Private David Viney	1955	Pte.	£5	,,	,, ,,	
1865-6	Cr.-Sergt. George Shuter	2178	Sergt.	£15	8/7/65	Regt., Shorncliff.	
	Corpl. Nicholas Connolly	2067	Pte.	£5	,,	,, ,,	
	Private Manus Day . .	2167	Pte.	£5	,,	,, ,,	
	Private Patrick Fennaghty	2504	Pte.	£5	,,	,, ,,	
1866-7	Cr.-Sgt. Robert Whitby .	2316	Sergt.	£15	16/6/66	Regt., Limerick.	
	Private John O'Grady .	2347	Pte.	£5	,,	,, ,,	
1867-8	Sergt. John Lewin . .	2647	Corpl.	£10	20/8/67	O.C., W. Suffolk Mila.	
	Corpl. John Ibett . .	2384	Pte.	£5	,,	Depot.	
	Private John Donoghoe .	2511	Pte.	£5	,,	,,	
	Private William Higgins	2528	Pte.	£5	,,	,,	
	Private David Riley .	11	Pte.	£5	,,	,,	
1868-9	Sgt.-Maj. Joseph L. Murray	2766	Sergt.	£15	22/7/68	O.C. Regt.	
	Private John Hopkins .	2627	Pte.	£5	,,	Depot.	
	Private Patrick Jordan .	2475	Pte.	£5	,,	S.O.P., Ennis.	
	Private Patrick Hayes .	2484	Pte.	£5	,,	Depot.	

Year.	RANK AND NAME.	Regtl. No.	Description and Amount of Gratuity.		Date of Issue of Medal.	To whom sent.	REMARKS.
1869-70	Private James Fitzpatrick	2839	Pte.	£5	26/7/69	Regt.	
	Private Patrick Moran .	2639	Pte.	£5	,,	S.O.P., Limerick.	
	Private Michael Bird .	2743	Pte.	£5	,,	S.O.P., Cork.	
	Private James Ritchie .	2911	Pte.	£5	,,	Depot.	
	Private John Buckley .	2444	Pte.	£5	,,		
	Private Michael Howley	2637	Pte.	£5	,,	S.O.P., Galway.	
1870-1	Private Patrick Murphy	2853	Private	£5	25/7/70	S.O.P., Plymouth.	
	Qr.-Mr.-Sgt. James Rowland	2800	Sergt.	£15	23/8/70	Regt.	Appd. Qr.-Mr. Gave up gratuity.
	Cr.-Sgt. Thomas J. Berry	2934	Sergt.	£15			
	Private Timothy Alrom	2653	Pte.	£5	12/10/71	S.O.P., Cork.	
	Sergt. William Mitchell .	2909	Pte.	£5	..	P.A.Ml. without grat.	
1871-2	Private John May . .	2846	Pte.	£5	5/10/71	O.C. Regt.	
	Private George Geffries .	2991	Pte.	£5	,,	,,	
	Private Andrew Hickey	3098	Pte.	£5	,,	,,	
	Cr.-Sergt. William Rowe	3129	Sergt.	£15	18/11/71	Depot.	
	Private Timothy Sullivan	2983	Pte.	£5	10/8/72	Regiment.	
	Private John Fisher .	3001	Pte.	£5	11/1/73	,,	
1872-3	Private William Flint .	3135	Pte.	£5	11/1/73	Regt.	
	Sergt. George Henry Noble	3187	Sergt.	£15	,,	,,	
	Corpl. Philip Sage . .	3112	Pte.	£5	,,	Depot.	
	Private Michael Burk .	3145	Pte.	£5	,,	,,	
	Private James Logan .	3429	Pte.	£5	16/2/74	Regt.	
	Private James Kilkenny	3469	Pte.	£5	,,	,,	
1873-4	Sgt.-Major Robert Haw .	1501	Sergt.	£15	16/2/74	Regt.	
	Cr.-Sgt. Samuel Bland .	3441	Sergt.	£15	,,	,,	
	Cr.-Sgt. James Cummins	3729	Corpl.	£10	Date of Recommendation.		
1874-5	Sergt. Joseph Ferris .	775	Corpl.	£10	1/4/74		
	Corpl. John Geary . .	745	Pte.	£5	,,		
	Private Israel Hobbs .	3635	Pte.	£5	,,		
	Private James Farrell .	3722	Pte.	£5	,,		
	Private George Warding	3680	Pte.	£5	,,		
	Qr.-Mr.-Sgt. Jos. Parkins	3521	Pte.	£10	24/6/75		
1876-7	Private John M'Grath .	1127	..	..	17/4/75		
	Private James Segrave .	3358	..	..	,,		
	~~Qr.-Mr.-Sgt. Jos. Parkins~~	~~3521~~	..	..	,,		Awarded 1874-5.
	Band-Master Walter G. Buck	1531	..	..	,,		
	Private Richd. Richardson	51	..	..	1/4/76		
	Cr.-Sgt. Joseph Brown .	3357	..	..	,,		
	Sergt. Henry Trydell .	3426	..	..	,,		
	Private John Garvey .	892	..	..	,,		
	Private Frederick Harding	72	..	..	,,		
	Private Joseph Horne .	24	..	..	,,		
	Private William Lowe .	60B. /662	..	..	,,		
	Private John Pollock .	60B. /665	..	..	,,		

Year.	RANK AND NAME.	Regtl. No.	Description and Amount of Gratuity.		Date of Recommendation of Medal.	To whom sent.	REMARKS.
1876-7	Private James Tipple .	55	..	..	1/4/76		
	Private William Truscott	3770	..	..	,,		
1877-8	Private Charles Bean .	229	..	..	1/1/77		
	Private Thomas Selvester	83	..	..	,,		
	Private Isaac Bell . .	139	..	..	,,		
	Private Henry Goodfellow	256	..	..	,,		
	Cr.-Sgt. Amos Jenkins .	150	..	..	,,		
	Private Mark Brooks .	60B. /868	..	..	,,		
	Private Solomon Harris	336	..	..	,,		
	Sgt. I. of M. Walter Gow	340	..	..	1/4/77		
	Cr.-Sgt. Edwin Sidwell .	401	..	..	,,		
	Sergt. John Briggs . .	407	..	..	,,		
	Private Robert Aird .	60B. /658	..	..	,,		
	Private John Laughlam	834	..	..	,,		
	Private James Mapston	889	..	..	,,		
1878	Private Thomas Clarke .	60B. /656	..	..	1/4/78	O.C. Regt.	
	Private Thomas Burns .	1258	..	..	1/7/78	S.O.P., Galway.	
	Private Mark Dempsey .	793	..	..	,,	O.C. Regt.	
	Private George Good .	836	..	..	,,	,,	
	Private Patrick M'Garron	644	..	..	1/10/78	S.O.P., Limerick.	
	Qr.-Mr.-Sgt. Robert Cartledge	685	..	..	,,	O.C. Regt.	
	Cr.-Sgt. Jacob Frampton	823	..	..	,,	,,	
	Cr.-Sgt. Charles Masters	798	..	..	,,	,,	
	Private George Deasey .	690	..	..	,,	,,	
	Sergt. Charles Wilkin .	659	..	..	4/11/78	S.O.P., Ipswich.	
1879	Private James Donald .	60B. /690	..	..	1/7/79	O.C. Depot.	
	Army School-Mr. George Green	..	..	..	,,	O.C. Regt.	
	Corporal George Ingman	615	..	..	1/8/79	S.O.P., Derby.	
	Sergt. John Bull . . .	109	..	..	1/10/79	O.C.R.	
1880	Drum-Majr. William Boyd	1185	..	..	1/1/80	O.C.R.	
1880-1	Sergt. Charles Smith .	484	..	..	1/1/81	O.C.R.	
	Sergt. Daniel Cornell .	997	..	..	1/1/81	O.C.D.	
	Cr.-Sgt. James Fitzgerald	929	..	..	1/10/80	O.C.R.	
1881-2	Cr.-Sgt. James H. I. Beach	948	..	..	1/4/81	,,	
	Armr.-Sergeant Thomas Higginson	423	..	..	,,	,,	
	Lce.-Corpl. George Gurney	934	..	..	,,	,,	

73RD REGIMENT OF FOOT

REGISTER OF MEN recommended for a GOOD CONDUCT MEDAL *without* GRATUITY, under the Provisions of the Royal Warrant of 16th January 1860.

Year.	RANK AND NAME.	Regtl. No.	Date of Recommendation, and by whom.		Date of Issue of Medal.	Officer to whom the Medal was sent.	REMARKS.
1859-60	Sergt. George Knott	2230	O.C.R.	18/3/63	2/5/63	Regt., Plymouth.	
	Private Haughey .	1388	,,	,,	,,	P.M., ,,	
1860-1	Sergt. Fredk. Perry .	2794	O.C.D.	7/5/64	20/7/64	Adjt., Renfrew Vols., Gourock.	
1861-2							
1862-3	Sergt. Jno. Popple .	1992	O.C.D.	7/5/64	20/7/64	Dep., Colchester.	£5; 117/1084.
	Private Patk. Byrne	2159	,,	,,	,,	,, ,,	£5; 117/395.
	Private Jno. Cox .	2126	,,	,,	,,	,, ,,	
1863-4	Corpl. Josh. Campbell	1347	O.C.R.	25/4/64	1/6/64	Rt., Aldershot.	£5; 117/885.
	Private Jas. Doran .	2157	O.C.D.	26/5/64	20/7/64	Dep., Colchester.	£5; 117/60.
	Private Michl. Kerr .	2148	,,	,,	,,	,, ,,	£5; 117/1655.
1864-5	Sergt. Saml. Woolcott	2217	O.C.D.	26/5/64	20/7/64	Dep., Colchester, 31/8/65.	Claim £15; 117/53.
	Sergt. George Lucas	2044	O.C.R.	18/4/65	22/8/65	Regt., Curragh, 31/8/65	Claim £15; 117/1736.
	Private James Pead	2920	O.C.R.	15/4/65	,,	,, ,, ,,	£5; 117/2402.
1866-7	Sergt. Michl. Weir .	682	O.C.R.	23/3/68	22/7/68	Regt., 16/11/68.	
	Private Patrick White	2445	O.C.D.	18/5/68	,,	S.O.P., Ennis.	£5; 117/1735.
	Private James Cody	2658	,,	,,	,,	Depot.	£5; 117/1300.
1867-8	.. ..	..	..	..	..	.. ..	Claims £15; 117/1856.
	Sergt. John Flinn .	2322	O.C.D.	14/5/69	29/7/69	Depot.	
	Private Thos. Nolan	2651	,,	,,	,,	,,	
1868-9	Private Daniel Darcy	2857	O.C.R.	1/4/69	29/7/69	Regt.	£5; 117/521.
	Private Chas. Woods	760	,,	22/4/70	21/6/70	Regt.	£5; 117/203.
1869-70	Cr.-Sgt. Thos. J. Berry	2934	O.C.D.	23/5/70	21/7/70	Depot.	
1870-1	~~Sergt. Wm. Mitchell .~~	~~2009~~	~~O.C.R.~~	~~6/8/70~~	~~10/12/70~~	O.C. Regt.	Subsequently awarded a gratuity.

LONG SERVICE AND GOOD CONDUCT MEDAL
THE ROYAL HIGHLAND REGIMENT
1881

Year.	Regtl. No.	RANK.	NAME.	Battn.	Date of Recommendation, and by whom Recommended.		REMARKS.
1881-2	924	Lce. Corpl.	George Gurney	2nd	1/7/81	O.C.R.	/1 see /3.
,,	440	Private	John Crawford	,,	1/1/82	,,	/2 N. S.
,,	457	,,	James Durney	,,	,,	,,	,, N. S.
,,	2367	Qr.-Mr.-Sgt.	James Hay	R.D.	,,	O.C.D.	/1.
,,	1038	Sergeant	Henry Jones	2nd	,,	O.C.R.	/2.
1882-3	654	Cr.-Sergt.	Patrick M'Cormac	R.D.	1/10/82	O.C.D.	42/2.
,,	536	Private	Rodk. Mathieson	2nd	,,	O.C.R.	/4 N. S.
,,	331	Sergt.	William Day	,,	1/1/83	,,	/5.
1883-4	1375	Sgt.-Ins.-Musy	John George	1st	,,	,,	/6.
,,	1373	Sgt.-Piper	John M'Donald	,,	,,	,,	,,
,,	2027	,,	William Stark (see below)	2nd	1/7/83	,,	/7 N. S.
,,	1379	Sergt.	Thomas Watt	1st	,,	,,	/8.
,,	1340	Sgt.-Instr.	William Cameron	,,	,,	O.C.D.	Miscel. /82.
,,	442	Private	Thomas Cooney	2nd	1/10/83	O.C.R.	/9 N. S.
,,	317	Cr. Sgt.	Richd. M'Cutcheon	,,	,,	,,	,, N. S.
,,	328	Sergt.	John Slonn (see below)	,,	,,	,,	,, N. S.
,,	404	Private	Samuel Bailey	,,	1/1/84	,,	2/42/11.
,,	1320	Sergt.	Simpson Henderson	1st	,,	O.C. 1st R.D.	1/42/15.
,,	2109	Sgt.-Drumr.	George W. Large	,,	,,	O.C.D.	42/4.
,,	332	Sergt.	John Roach	,,	,,	,,	,,
1884-5	1448	Corporal	Alexr. Simpson	,,	1/4/84	,,	1/42/17 N. S.
1885-6	392	Drummer	Thomas Maloney	2nd	1/4/85	O.C.R.	/17 N. S.
,,	328	Cr.-Sergt.	John Slonn	,,	,,	,,	,,
,,	2027	Sgt.-Piper	William Stark	,,	,,	,,	,,
,,	2494	Qr.-Mr.-Sgt.	John M'Kenzie	3rd	,,	,,	42/8.
,,	419	Private	Innes Bryan	2nd	1/10/85	,,	/22.
,,	663	,,	James Martin	,,	,,	,,	,,
,,	541	,,	John Menzies	,,	,,	,,	,, N. S.
,,	590	,,	Frederick Shipp	,,	,,	,,	,,
,,	521	,,	Patrick M'Carthy	,,	1/1/86	,,	/24.
1886-7	322	Cr.-Sergt.	Herbert Button	,,	1/4/86	,,	42/11 W. G.
,,	666	Private	Thomas Carter	,,	,,	,,	/22 N. S.
,,	1654	Sergt.	Alexr. Henderson (see below)	1st	,,	,,	/22 N. S.
,,	562	Private	Alfred Pink	2nd	,,	,,	/46.
,,	2473	Sergt.	Robert Stewart	,,	1/7/86	O.C.D.	42/14 W. G.
,,	436	Private	James Carr	2nd	1/10/86	O.C.R.	/30 N. S.
,,	1188	,,	Ronald M'Donald	,,	,,	O.C.D.	42/18
,,	1101	Cr.-Sergt.	William Murray	,,	,,	,,	,, N. S.

Year.	Regtl. No.	Rank.	Name.	Battn.	Date of Recommendation, and by whom Recommended.		Remarks.
1887-8	1683	Cr.-Sergt.	Henry Milne . .	2nd	1/1/87	O.C.D.	42/10 W. G.
,,	340	,,	Joseph Walker .	,,	,,	,,	,, N. S.
,,	1654	Sergt.	Alexr. Henderson	1st	,,	O.C.R.	/28 W. G.
,,	1653	,,	James Donaldson	,,	,,	,,	,, N. S.
,,	1724	Sergt.-Drumr.	William Clark .	,,	,,	,,	,, W. G.
,,	491	Private	William Hooton .	2nd	,,	,,	/32.
,,	—	Private	Mark Farley . .	late 73rd Foot.	7/4/87	See R.H. Chelsea.	42/36 N. S.
,,	305	Q.-M.-Sgt.	Wallis Atkinson .	2nd	1/4/87	O.C.R.	2/42/34 N. S.
,,	333	Cr.-Sgt.	Robert Binning .	,,	,,	,,	2/42/34 N. S.
,,	339	Sgt.-Cook	William I. Church	,,	,,	,,	,, W. G.
,,	360	Cr.-Sgt.	Watson Senior .	,,	,,	,,	,, N. S.
,,	358	Corpl.	John Pearce . .	Depot.	1/7/87	O.C.D.	42/22.
,,	—	School-Master	John Tough . .	1st	,,	O.C.R.	1/42/22 W. G.
,,	597	Private	Charles Stinton .	2nd	,,	,,	242/38 N. S.
,,	1818	Cr.-Sgt.	Alexr. M'Swain .	Depot.	1/10/87	O.C.D.	42/24 W. G.
,,	319	Sergt.	George Collyer .	,,	1/1/88	,,	42/27 W. G.
1888-9	1794	Private	James Miller . .	1st	1/7/88	O.C.	1/42/36.
,,	327	Cr.-Sergt.	Thos. Quinn . .	Depot.	1/10/88	O.C.D.	/31 W. G.
,,	2040	,,	L. Jagoe . . .	,,	1/1/89	,,	/35 W. G.
,,	436	Private	J. Carr . . .	2nd	,,	O.C. }	2/42/43.
,,	543	Bandsman	W. Mitchell . .	,,	,,	,,	
1889-90	326	Cr.-Sergt.	G. Orwin . . .	4 Vol.Bn.	1/4/89	,,	/37 W. G.
,,	1982	Qr.-Mr.-Sgt.	R. Burnett . .	1st	,,	,,	1/42/39 W. G.
,,	323	Sergt.	Chas. Clarke . .	2nd	1/10/89	,,	2/42/46 W. G.
,,	468	Private	T. Ford . . .	,,	1/1/90	,,	2/42/48 N. S.
1890-1	2414	Sergt.	Wm. M'Lachlan .	Depot.	1/7/90	,,	1/42/40 W. G.
,,	330	Cr.-Sgt.	Albert Sylvester .	,,	,,	,,	42/40 N. S.
,,	392	Drummer	Thomas Maloney	2nd	1/10/90	..	2/42/49 N. S.
,,	333	Cr.-Sgt.	Robert Binning .	3/Shrop. L.I.	1/1/91	..	See Shropshire Lt. Infy.
1891-2	2028	,,	Wm. Johnson .	2nd	1/4/91	..	2/42/50 N. S.
,,	348	,,	Jas. Connolly .	,,	1/7/91	..	/53 W. G.
,,	606	Private	Hy. Tattersall .	,,	,,	..	/42 W. G.
,,	545	Sergt.	Wm. Morton . .	Depot.	1/10/91	..	/42 W. G.
1892-3	2793	Bandsman	J. Kemp . . .	1st	1/1/92	..	1/42/41 N. S.
,,	2794	Corporal	T. E. Simpson .	,,	,,	..	,, N. S.
,,	341	Qr.-Mr.-Sgt.	F. Oliver . . .	2nd	1/4/92	..	2/42/54 W. G.
,,	347	Cr.-Sgt.	T. W. Clark . .	Depot.	,,	..	42/44 W. G.
,,	2028	,,	W. Johnson . .	2nd	1/7/92	..	2/42/55 N. S.
,,	2197	Qr.-Mr.-Sgt.	J. Lockhart . .	Depot.	1/10/92	..	42/45 W. G.
,,	2801	,,	R. Logan . . .	,,	,,	..	42/45 W. G.
,,	3009	,,	A. B. Watson .	,,	,,	..	,, W. G.
1893-4	3754	Bandsman	T. Wilson . . .	1st	1/4/93	..	1/42/43.
,,	2794	Corpl.	T. E. Simpson .	,,	,,	..	/42 N. S.
1894-5	377	Cr.-Sgt.	P. Byrne . . .	Depot.	1/1/94	..	/47 W. G.
,,	2028	,,	W. Johnson . .	2nd	,,	..	2/42/57 W. G.

Year.	Regtl. No.	RANK.	NAME.	Battn.	Date of Recommendation, and by whom Recommended.		REMARKS.
1894-5	4690	Cr.-Sgt.	J. Downey	Depot.	1/7/94	..	42/49 W. G.
,,	2794	Corpl.	E. Simpson	2nd	,,	..	2/42/60.
1895-6	1444	Cr.-Sgt.	Geo. Luscombe	Depot.	1/4/95	..	/50 W. G. *Without* gratuity.
,,	4677	,,	Alexr. White	,,	,,	..	,, W. G. do. do.
,,	5900	,,	Robt. Robertson	5/V.B.	1/7/95	..	/51 W. G. do. do.
,,	4841	,,	David Ross	6/V.B.	,,	..	,, W. G. do. do.
,,	1957	Mila. Sgt.-Maj.	Geo. Childs	3rd	1/10/95	..	/53 W. G. do. do.
,,	169	Private	Jas. Wilson	,,	personal	..	/57 N. S.
,,	300	,,	John Anderson	2nd	1/1/96	..	2/42/64 N. S.
,,	1101	Cr.-Sgt.	Wm. Murray	Depot.	,,	..	/55 W. G. *Without* gratuity.
,,	5956	Sergt.	Wm. Brown	2/V.B.	1/4/96	..	/58 N. S.
1896-7	2584	Pioneer Sgt.	W. Limeburn	2nd	1/1/97	..	
,,	2462	Sergt.	C. Johnstone	Depot.	,,	..	/60 N. S.
1897-8	3905	Qr.-Mr.-Sgt.	John Stephen	..	1/4/97	..	/62 W. G. *Without* gratuity.
,,	3164	Private	G. W. Skillings	..	,,	..	/61. With gratuity.
,,	4515	Bandsman	Alfred Wheatley	..	1/7/97	..	/63 N. S.
,,	2057	Band-Sgt.	Wm. Statham	..	1/1/98	..	128 of '98 N. S.
,,	5014	Cr.-Sgt.	David Osler	..	1/1/98	..	128a of '98 W. G. Without gratuity.
,,	5956	Sergt.	Wm. Brown	..	,,	..	,, ,, W. G. do. do.
1898-9	371	Cr.-Sgt.	Wm. Black	..	1/4/98	..	334 ,, W. G. do. do.
,,	426	Private	Samuel Beresford	..	,,	..	335 ,, With gratuity.
,,	4513	,,	Alfred Wheatley	..	1/7/98	..	530 ,, do. do.
,,	4774	,,	James Scott	..	1/10/98	..	753 ,, do. do.
,,	4763	Corpl.	John Slattie	..	,,	..	,, ,, N. S.
1899--1900	5060	Cr.-Sgt.	John Paterson	..	1/1/99	..	174 of '99 N. S.
,,	370	,,	T. J. Wiltshire	..	,,	..	,, ,, N. S.
,,	5023	Private	Edwd. Ledran	..	1/1/99	..	,, ,, With gratuity.
,,	370	Cr.-Sergt.	T. J. Wiltshire	..	1/4/99	..	397 ,, W. G. Without gratuity.
,,	2462	Sergt.	Chas. Johnston	..	,,	..	,, ,, N. S.
,,	4459	Sgt.-Mr.-Tailor	Oscar Land	..	1/7/99	..	484 ,, W. G. Without gratuity.
,,	5133	Private	C. G. Amey	..	,,	..	,, ,, With gratuity.
,,	1068	,,	Jonas Martin	..	,,	..	,, ,, do. do.
,,	4763	Corpl.	John Slattie	..	,,	..	612 ,, N. S.
,,	13	Bandsman	Alexr. Stewart	..	,,	..	,, ,, With gratuity.
,,	249	Cr.-Sgt.	Gilbert Berry	..	1/10/99	..	611 ,, W. G. Without gratuity.
,,	5217	,,	John Falconer	..	,,	..	,, ,, W. G. do. do.
,,	22	,,	James Hutchison	..	,,	..	,, ,, W. G. do. do.
,,	800	,,	Benjamin Sadler	..	1/1/1900	..	66 of 1900 W. G. do. do.
,,	3882	Sgt.-Piper	William Bain	..	,,	..	65 ,, W. G. do. do.
1900-01	943	Cr.-Sgt.	David Swan	..	1/4/00	..	118 ,, W. G. do. do.
,,	1003	,,	A. D. Neal	..	1/10/00	..	372 ,, N. S.
1901-2	820	Private	John Cripps	..	1/4/01	..	233 of 1901. With gratuity.
,,	1313	Sergt.	Thomas Howden	..	,,	..	,, ,, With gratuity.
,,	2462	Cr.-Sgt.	Chas. Johnstone	..	,,	..	,, ,, N. S.
,,	652	Sergt.	W. C. Soper	..	,,	..	,, ,, With gratuity.
,,	682	Cr.-Sgt.	Alexr. Fraser	..	,,	..	,, ,, do. do.
,,	1247	,,	George Bedson	..	1/10/01	..	586 ,, do. do.
,,	973	,,	George Strathearn	..	,,	..	,, ,, do. do.

Year.	Regtl. No.	RANK.	NAME.	Battn.	Date of Recommendation, and by whom Recommended.		No. of Paper.	REMARKS.
1902	4674	Sergt.-Major	John Vair	..	1/10/02	..	..	Without gratuity.
,,	2462	Cr.-Sgt.	Charles Johnstone	..	,,	..	780 of '02 W. G.	With gratuity.
1903	2440	Sgt.-Major	William Fowler	..	1/1/03	..	,, ,,	Without gratuity.
,,	1361	Bandmaster	W. J. Scott	..	,,	..	109 ,, W. G.	do. do.
,,	2569	Q.-M.-S. (O.R. Sgt.)	Alexr. Kelman	..	1/7/03	..	240 of '03.	With gratuity.
,,	2630	Cr.-Sgt.	David Graham	..	,,	..	,, ,,	do. do.
1904	2755	,,	George Miller	..	1/1/04	..	3 of '04.	do. do.
,,	2828	,,	William Carnegie	..	,,	..	,, ,,	do. do.
,,	2760	,,	David Niven	..	,,	..	,, ,,	do. do.
,,	2514	Lce.-Sgt.	Alexander Reid	..	,,	..	45 ,,	do. do.
,,	2752	Sgt.-Major	James Anderson	..	,,	..	14 ,,	Without gratuity.
,,	2597	Private	James Beattie	..	1/7/04	..	60 ,,	With gratuity.
,,	2851	Cr.-Sgt.	George Sellars	..	,,	..	,, ,,	do. do.
,,	2183	,,	George Shirran	..	,,	..	,, ,,	do. do.
,,	2852	,,	Joseph Scott	..	,,	..	,, ,,	do. do.
,,	1081	,,	William Curtis	..	,,	..	,, ,,	do. do.
1905	3031	,,	J. St. George French	..	1/1/05	..	12 of '05.	do. do.
,,	3113	,,	R. L. Goldie	..	,,	..	,, ,,	do. do.
,,	3055	Private	John Mackie	..	,,	..	,, ,,	do. do.
,,	3065	Cr.-Sgt.	George Turner	..	1/1/05	..	,, ,,	do. do.
,,	2534	Private	Archibald Ness	..	,,	..	,, ,,	do. do.
,,	3023	Qr.-Mr.-Sgt.	James Raisbeck	..	,,	..	32 ,,	do. do.
,,	2997	Corpl.	H. C. Hewetson	..	1/7/05	..	59 of '05.	do. do.
,,	3250	Cr.-Sgt.	Patrick C. Goady	..	,,	..	,, ,,	do. do.
,,	3358	,,	James Main	..	,,	..	,, ,,	do. do.
,,	2148	,,	Alexr. Taylor	..	,,	..	,, ,,	do. do.
,,	49	Qr.-Mr.-Sgt.	Robert Vair	..	,,	..	,, ,,	do. do.
,,	2711	,,	James Anderson	..	,,	..	,, ,,	do. do.
1906	3547	Sergt.	Thomas Clark	..	1/1/06	..	6 of '06.	do. do.
,,	3081	Lce.-Sgt.	Robert Mill	..	,,	..	,, ,,	do. do.
,,	3575	Drummer	William Dolan	..	1/7/06	..	52 ,,	do. do.
,,	3676	Sergt.	F. W. Illingworth	..	,,	..	79 ,,	do. do.
1907	3500	Private	G. E. Button	..	1/1/07	..	8 of '07.	do. do.
,,	3848	Bandsman	E. J. H. Higgs	..	1/7/07	..	53 ,,	do. do.
,,	1323	Sgt.-Major	James M'Lachlan	..	,,	..	54 ,,	Without gratuity.
,,	198	Cr.-Sgt.	John Johnston	..	,,	..	,, ,,	With gratuity.
,,	1186	,,	G. S. Fulton	..	,,	..	,, ,,	do. do.
,,	3059	,,	Randolph Miller	..	,,	..	,, ,,	do. do.
,,	3426	,,	David Fairweather	..	,,	..	,, ,,	do. do.
,,	3852	Lce.-Corpl.	Thomas Graham	..	,,	..	,, ,,	do. do.
,,	3877	Cr.-Sgt.	David Campbell	..	,,	..	,, ,,	do. do.
,,	5028	,,	William M'Laren	..	,,	..	,, ,,	do. do.
,,	3838	Drummer	Alexr. Hardie	..	,,	..	,, ,,	do. do.
1908	3140	Sgt.-Major	J. Y. Fenwick	..	1/1/08	..	12 of '08.	Without gratuity.
,,	2344	Cr.-Sgt.	Henry Sinnett	..	,,	..	,, ,,	With gratuity.
,,	2930	,,	C. M. C. Young	..	,,	..	,, ,,	do. do.
,,	3074	,,	Thomas Hampton	..	,,	..	,, ,,	do. do.

Year.	Regtl. No.	RANK.	NAME.	Battn.	Date of Recommendation, and by whom Recommended.		No. of Paper.	REMARKS.	
1908	3681	Cr.-Sgt.	David Birse . .	..	1/1/08	..	12 of '08.	With gratuity.	
,,	4673	,,	John King . .	..	,,	..	,, ,,	do.	do.
,,	3064	Sergt.	Grantley Turner .	..	,,	..	,, ,,	do.	do.
,,	2870	,,	David Jack . .	..	1/7/08	..	48 ,,	do.	do.
,,	4032	,,	Thomas Marett .	..	,,	..	57 ,,	do.	do.
,,	4007	Cr.-Sgt.	Alexr. Millar . .	..	,,	..	70 ,,	do.	do.
1909	4400	Sergt.	William Donaldson	..	1/1/09	..	26 of '09.	do.	do.
,,	4322	,,	Charles Tedder .	..	,,	..	,, ,,	do.	do.
,,	4317	Drummer	John Dobson . .	..	,,	..	27 ,,	do.	do.
,,	4439	Sergt.	Robert M'Kie .	..	,,	..	,, ,,	do.	do.
,,	4187	Cr.-Sgt.	Joseph Masters .	..	,,	..	,, ,,	do.	do.
,,	3744	Private	William Nisbet .	..	,,	..	,, ,,	do.	do.
,,	2813	Cr.-Sgt.	J. W. Birch . .	..	,,	..	,, ,,	do.	do.
,,	4173	,,	T. H. Wilson . .	..	,,	..	,, ,,	do.	do.
,,	4411	,,	J. R. W. Myers .	..	,,	..	,, ,,	do.	do.
1910	5110	Qr.-Mr.-Sgt.	Edgar Hall . .	..	1/1/10	..	10 of '10.	do.	do.
,,	4578	Cr.-Sgt.	John Lindsay .	..	,,	..	,, ,,	do.	do.
,,	4646	Private	James Kilgour .	..	,,	..	,, ,,	do.	do.
,,	4529	Sergt.	Thomas Baxter .	..	,,	..	25 ,,	do.	do.
,,	9507	Cr.-Sgt.	William Charles .	..	,,	..	,, ,,	do.	do.
,,	4389	,,	Alexr. Robertson	..	,,	..	29 ,,	do.	do.
,,	4748	,,	Allan Hall . .	..	1/7/10	..	61 ,,	do.	do.
,,	4202	,,	H. R. Phillips .	..	,,	..	,, ,,	do.	do.
,,	2254	,,	W. G. Webb .	..	,,	..	,, ,,	do.	do.
,,	4661	,,	David Sinclair .	..	,,	..	,, ,,	do.	do.
,,	5012	,,	John Philp . .	..	,,	..	,, ,,	do.	do.

THE MILITIA (SPECIAL RESERVE) LONG SERVICE MEDAL

LIST OF N.C. OFFICERS AND MEN OF THE 3RD SPECIAL RESERVE BN. (LATE MILITIA) ROYAL HIGHLANDERS, who have been awarded THE MILITIA (OR SPECIAL RESERVE) MEDAL FOR LONG SERVICE.

	Regtl. No.	RANK.	NAME.	REMARKS.
Per. Staff	59	Drummer	M. Flynn.	1st Feby. 1905.
'H' Coy.	918	Private	J. Strachan.	do. do.
'B' ,,	1752	,,	J. Robertson.	
'B' ,,	8898	,,	P. Clark.	
'C' ,,	3028	,,	A. Hughes.	
'G' ,,	8842	,,	W. M'Allister.	
'G' ,,	2948	,,	J. Short.	
'B' ,,	521	,,	A. Ferguson.	
'E' ,,	371	,,	J. Reilly.	
'D' ,,	890	,,	G. Hood.	Awarded while serving in the S.E. of Scotland R. G. A. Militia.

VOLUNTEER OFFICERS' DECORATION

AND

TERRITORIAL OFFICERS' DECORATION

VOLUNTEER OFFICERS' DECORATION

LIST OF OFFICERS of the 1st, 2nd, 3rd, 4th, 5th, and 6th VOLUNTEER BATTALIONS, THE BLACK WATCH, who have been awarded 'THE VOLUNTEER OFFICERS' DECORATION.' 6/9/93 *et seq.*

Date.	Corps.	RANK.	NAME.	REMARKS.
	1st Vol. Bn. City of Dundee.	Lt.-Col. and Hony. Col.	James Rankin.	
	,, ,,	Major and Hon. Lt.-Col.	William W. Turnbull.	
	,, ,,	Capt. and Hon. Major	David A. Watson.	
	,, ,,	,, ,,	John Nelson.	
	,, ,,	Lt.-Col. and Hony. Col.	George Mitchell.	Retired.
	,, ,,	Capt. and Hon. Major	Henry Plenderleath . . .	Retired.
	2nd V. B. (Angus)	Hony. Colonel	John Grant Kinloch.	
	,, ,,	Lt.-Col. Commdt. and Hony. Col.	William A. Gordon.	
	,, ,,	Lieut.-Colonel	Alexr. M'Hardy.	
	,, ,,	Maj. and Hon. Lt.-Col.	John Duke.	
	,, ,,	Bde. Surgn. Lt. Col.	John Mackie, jr., M.D.	
	,, ,,	Surgn. Lt.-Col.	William F. Murray, M.D.	
	,, ,,		James K. Anderson, M.D.	
	,, ,,		George P. Alexander, M.D.	
	,, ,,	,, ,,	The Revd. T. Alexr. Cameron.	
	,, ,,	Actg. Chaplain	James A. Dickson.	
	,, ,,	Lt.-Col. and Hony. Col.	William Scott	Retired.
	,, ,,	,, ,,	James P. Dowall	Retired.
	,, ,,	Major and Hon. Lt.-Col.	Samuel Laurence, M.D. . .	Retired.
	3rd V. B. (Dundee)	Surgn. Lt.-Col.	William Smith.	
	,, ,,	Lt.-Col. and Hony. Col.	John Crerar Macdonald.	
	,, ,,	Qr.-Mr. and Hon. Capt.	The Revd. Peter Grant, D.D.	
	,, ,,	Hony. Chaplain	John Jessiman	Retired.
	4th V. B. (Perthshire)	Maj. and Hony. Lt.-Col.	John Hally.	
	,, ,,	Maj. and Hony. Lt.-Col.	Archibald Gibson.	
	,, ,,	Capt. and Hony. Maj.	George Mailer.	
	,, ,,		Duncan Kippen.	
	,, ,,	Lieutenant	James Clark	Retired.
	5th V. B. (Perthshire) Highland.	Capt. and Hony. Maj.	William M. Macdonald.	
	,, ,,	Hony. Colonel	Sir Robt. Menzies, Bt.	
	,, ,,	Lieut.-Col.	David Buttar.	
	,, ,,	Maj. and Hony. Lt.-Col.	Charles Munro.	
	,, ,,	Capt. and Hony. Maj.	David M. Robertson.	
	,, ,,		John Baxter.	
	,, ,,	Captain	Charles Stewart	Retired.
	,, ,,	Maj. and Hony. Lt.-Col.	William Japp	Retired.
	,, ,,	Capt. and Hony. Maj.	David Chalmers	Retired.
	,, ,,	,, ,,	Donald Fisher	Retired.
	,, ,,	,, ,,	John Borrie	Retired.

Date.	Corps.	Rank.	Name.	Remarks.
	5th V. B. (Perthshire) Highland.	Lt. and Hony. Capt.	Robert M'Laren	Retired.
	,, ,,	,, ,,	Peter Davidson	Retired.
	,, ,,	,, ,,	James B. Ritchie	Retired.
	6th V. B. (Fifeshire)	Capt. and Hony. Maj.	James Cusin, junr.	
	,, ,,	,, ,,	Charles G. Dawson.	
	,, ,,	,, ,,	Andrew R. Shearer.	
	,, ,,	,, ,,	Peter Herd.	
	,, ,,	,, ,,	John M'Quillan.	
	,, ,,	Qr.-Mr. and Hony. Maj.	Thomas Brown.	
	,, ,,	Lt.-Col. and Hony. Col.	James M'Farlane	Retired.
	,, ,,	Capt. and Hony. Maj.	John Tait	Retired.
13/12/92	,, ,,	,, ,,	William Roger	Retired.
,,	5th Vol. Bn.	Captain	Charles Boyd	Retired.
20/1/93	6th ,,	Lt. and Hony. Capt.	William Boak	Retired.
,,	1st Vol. Bn.	Major	Howard Hill.	
,,	3rd ,,	Capt. and Hony. Maj.	James Arinett	Retired.
2/5/93	4th ,,	Hony. Chaplain	The Revd. John Cunningham .	Retired.
,,	4th Vol. Bn.	Actg. Chaplain	The Revd. Wm. Blair, D.D.	
6/6/93	6th ,,	Hony. Chaplain	The Rev. Andw. K. H. Boyd, D.D.	
	,, ,,		The Revd. Robert Edgar, D.D.	
6/6/93	4th Vol. Bn.	Surgn. Lt.-Col.	James MacFee.	
12/12/93	2nd Vol. Bn.	Maj. and Hony. Lt.-Col.	James Davidson.	
13/2/94	3rd Vol. Bn.	Qr.-Mr. and Hon. Capt.	William Anderson.	
,,	6th ,,	Hony. Colonel	Peter G. Walker.	
3/7/94	3rd Vol. Bn.	Hony. Colonel	Sir J. T. Stewart Richardson, Bt.	
25/9/94	1st Vol. Bn.	Capt. and Hony. Maj.	Alfred G. Primrose.	
14/5/95	6th Vol. Bn.	Capt. and Hony. Maj.	John Jamieson.	
21/1/96	3rd Vol. Bn.	Major	Robert W. Laburn.	
12/5/96	2nd Vol. Bn.	Capt. and Hony. Maj.	James Buyers.	
,,	,, ,,	,, ,,	John Smart Roy.	
14/8/96	2nd Vol. Bn.	Capt. and Hony. Maj.	John P. Anderson.	
,,	,, ,,	Actg. Chaplain	The Revd. John Boyd.	
29/7/97	2nd Vol. Bn.	Qr.-Mr. and Hony. Capt.	Robert Ross Balfour.	
,,	,, ,,	Surgn. Lieut.	Robert Grant.	
,,	,, ,,	Actg. Chaplain	The Revd. John Stephenson.	
,,	3rd Vol. Bn.	Major	Charles Batchelor.	
9/4/97	5th Vol. Bn.	Lieutenant	David S. Johnston.	
,,	6th Vol. Bn.	Capt. and Hony. Maj.	James Gillespie.	
,,	,, ,,	Captain	Charles Anderson	Retired.
,,	,, ,,	Lieutenant	James D. Connel.	
18/1/98	1st Vol. Bn.	Major	David Scroggie.	
21/2/98	5th Vol. Bn.	Surgn. Lt.-Col.	John Mackay, M.B.	
15/8/98	2nd Vol. Bn.	Capt. and Hony. Maj.	David Duke.	
,,	,, ,,	Actg. Chaplain	The Revd. William Duke.	
12/11/98	2nd Vol. Bn.	Capt. and Hony. Maj.	John A. MacLean.	
,,	4th Vol. Bn.	Maj. and Hony. Lt.-Col.	David T. Reid	Retired.
,,	5th Vol. Bn.	Captain	Hugh M'Kerracher.	
7/6/99	1st Vol. Bn.	Qr.-Mr. and Hony. Capt.	George Malcolm.	
,,	,, ,,	Actg. Chaplain	The Revd. Colin Campbell, D.D.	
5/8/99	2nd Vol. Bn.	Capt. and Hony. Maj.	Archibald Whyte.	
,,	,, ,,	,, ,,	David Corsar.	
7/11/99	4th Vol. Bn.	Hony. Colonel	David R. Williamson.	
5/6/00	2nd Vol. Bn.	Capt. and Hony. Maj.	Robert H. Millar.	
4/12/00	4th Vol. Bn.	Major	Duncan M'Ewen.	

Date.	Corps.	Rank.	Name.	Remarks.
4/12/00	4th Vol. Bn.	Capt. and Hony. Maj.	Robert M'Naughtan.	
,,	6th Vol. Bn.	Lieut.-Col.	James Dewar.	
5/3/01	4th Vol. Bn.	Capt. and Hony. Maj.	David C. Campbell.	
7/5/01	6th Vol. Bn.	Capt. and Hony. Maj.	Andrew Burt.	
,,	2nd ,,	,, ,,	William F. M'Intosh.	
19/11/01	4th Vol. Bn.	Qr.-Mr. and Hony. Capt.	Thomas Sanderson.	
,,	5th ,,	Captain	Thomas Buttar.	
,,	6th ,,	,,	Thomas Clark.	
1/7/02	5th Vol. Bn.	Maj. and Hony. Lt.-Col.	William S. Ferguson . . .	Retired.
6/2/03	3rd Vol. Bn.	Capt. and Hony. Maj.	David Milne.	
,,	6th ,,	,, ,,	Wm. Prattie Wilson . . .	Retired.
,,	,, ,,	Surgn. Major	Charles E. Douglas, M.D.	
3/6/03	6th Vol. Bn.	Capt. and Hony. Maj.	Harry D. Henderson.	
23/9/04	4th Vol. Bn.	Lt.-Col. and Hony. Col.	Sir R. D. Moncreiff, Bt.	
10/11/04	6th Vol. Bn.	Capt. and Hony. Maj.	George Fergusson.	
30/3/05	2nd Vol. Bn.	Capt. and Hony. Maj.	John F. Dickson.	
1/8/05	6th Vol. Bn.	Lieutenant	John A. Romanes.	
,,	,, ,,	Capt. and Hony. Major	John W. Robertson.	
27/4/06	4th Vol. Bn.	Capt. and Hony. Major	Charles E. Colville	Instructor of Musketry.
,,	6th ,,	Hony. Colonel	Sir ff. W. Erskine, Bt.	
19/6/06	3rd Vol. Bn.	Major	Sinclair G. M'Donald.	
,,	,, ,,	,,	David M. Small.	
6/11/06	6th Vol. Bn.	Maj. and Hony. Lt.-Col.	James S. Davidson.	
,,	2nd ,,	Capt. and Hony. Major	David W. Fairweather.	
15/3/07	4th Vol. Bn.	Major and Hon. Lt.-Col.	Andrew T. Reid.	
,,	6th ,,	Capt. and Hony. Major	David Williamson.	
30/8/07	2nd Vol. Bn.	,, ,,	David A. Spence.	
19/11/07	6th Vol. Bn.	Actg. Chaplain	Revd. David Imrie.	
,,	,, ,,	,, ,,	Revd. John R. Soutar.	
3/3/08	6th Vol. Bn.	Surgeon Major	Charles N. Lee, M.B.	
,,	,, ,,	Actg. Chaplain	Revd. Alexander Legge.	
1/1/09	3rd Vol. Bn.	Surgeon Major	William Kinnear, M.D.	
11/1/10	6th Vol. Bn.	Capt. and Hony. Major	George J. Lumsden . . .	Retired.
,,	5th ,,	,, ,,	John Moffat	Retired.

TERRITORIAL OFFICERS' DECORATION

Date.	Corps.	Rank.	Name.	Remarks.
14/5/09	5th Bn.	Capt. and Hony. Major	Peter S. Nicoll.	
4/1/10	Attached to 4th Bn.	Lt.-Col. and Hon. Surgn. Col.	David Lennox, M.D.	
3/5/10	5th Bn.	Captain	John Sim.	
,,	Attached to 6th Bn.	Major	Robert Stirling, R.A.M.C.	
14/10/10	7th Bn.	Lt.-Col. and Hony. Col.	Sir R. W. Anstruther, Bt.	
,,	,,	Capt. and Hony. Major	John L. Macpherson.	
4/1/10	,,	,, ,,	Peter MacDuff.	

VOLUNTEER LONG SERVICE MEDAL

AND

TERRITORIAL EFFICIENCY MEDAL

VOLUNTEER LONG SERVICE MEDAL

LIST of Officers, Non-Commissioned Officers and Men of the 1st, 2nd, 3rd, 4th, 5th, and 6th Volunteer Battalions, The Black Watch, who have been awarded 'The Volunteer Long Service Medal.'

Date.	Corps.	Regtl. No.	Rank.	Name.
Jan./95	1st V.B.	2966	Colour-Sgt.	W. Cochrane.
,,	,,	3217	,,	W. Crighton.
,,	,,	3879	Private	W. Gloag.
,,	,,	2949	,,	A. Gray.
,,	,,	3491	Colour-Sgt.	S. Lumsden.
,,	,,	619	Lce.-Sergt.	J. Mitchell.
,,	,,		Qr.-Mr.	G. Malcolm.
,,	,,	1205	Qr.-Mr.-Sgt.	P. Scott.
,,	,,	3222	Private	A. Smith.
,,	,,	2709	Corporal	J. Stewart.
,,	,,	2599	Private	J. Watson.
,,	2nd V.B.		Capt. and Qr.-Mr.	R. R. Balfour.
,,	,,	3537	Private	J. Brown.
,,	,,	49	Colour-Sgt.	J. Cunningham.
,,	,,	199	Private	W. Dall.
,,	,,	846	Sergeant	J. D. Duncan.
,,	,,	642	,,	J. Dures.
,,	,,	446	Colour-Sgt.	W. Findlay.
,,	,,	929	Qr.-Mr.-Sgt.	G. Forbes.
,,	,,	932	Sergeant	W. Forbes.
,,	,,	459	,,	J. Ford.
,,	,,	189	Colour-Sgt.	W. Fox.
,,	,,	956	Private	A. Gibb.
,,	,,	773	Colour-Sgt.	A. Greenhill.
,,	,,	444	,,	J. Hardie.
,,	,,	737	,,	W. Hardie.
,,	,,	738	Private	J. Hill.
,,	,,	781	Sergeant	W. Hogg.
,,	,,	452	,,	A. Jack.
,,	,,	979	,,	J. Johnson.
,,	,,	930	Colour-Sgt.	T. Kyd.
,,	,,	483	Private	A. B. Kydd.
,,	,,	15	Qr.-Mr.-Sgt.	J. M'Beth.
,,	,,	641	Colour-Sgt.	J. M'Gregor.
,,	,,	805	Corporal	F. M'Nicoll.
,,	,,	839	Colour-Sgt.	J. M. Marnie.
,,	,,	490	Private	J. Masson.
,,	,,	202	,,	D. Mathew.
,,	,,	37	Sergeant	J. Ogilvie.
,,	,,	442	Qr.-Mr.-Sgt.	J. Oliphant.
,,	,,	211	Sergeant	A. Rennig.

Date.	Corps.	Regtl. No.	Rank.	Name.
Jan./95	2nd V.B.	181	Colour-Sgt.	D. Renny.
,,	,,	565	Private	J. Richmond.
,,	,,	936	,,	J. Ritchie.
,,	,,	3539	,,	A. Ross.
,,	,,	187	Colour-Sgt.	T. Ross.
,,	,,	191	Private	G. Smith.
,,	,,	257	Sgt.-Bugler	J. Stirling.
,,	,,	460	Sergeant	J. L. Strachan.
,,	,,	585	Colour-Sgt.	G. Taylor.
,,	,,	774	Sergeant	C. Thomson.
,,	,,	184	Colour-Sgt.	D. Tosh.
,,	,,	22	,,	D. Tyrie.
,,	,,	644	Sergeant	T. Whyte.
,,	,,	207	,,	M. Wilkie.
,,	,,	514	Private	D. Wyllie.
,,	3rd V.B.	9	Sergeant	J. Alexander.
,,	,,		Capt. and Hony. Maj.	C. Batchelor.
,,	,,	15	Colour-Sgt.	D. Davidson.
,,	,,	102	,,	W. Drysdale.
,,	,,	56	Qr.-Mr.-Sgt.	J. Stewart.
,,	,,	671	Sergeant	W. Stewart.
,,	4th V.B.	11	Private	A. Allen.
,,	,,	120	Sergeant	J. Anderson.
,,	,,	25	Colour-Sgt.	P. Arnott.
,,	,,	224	Lance-Sgt.	P. Brown.
,,	,,	16	Corporal	P. Brown.
,,	,,	134	Sergeant	J. Calder.
,,	,,	393	Colour-Sgt.	J. Cameron.
,,	,,	228	Sergeant	J. Campbell.
,,	,,	124	,,	P. Campbell.
,,	,,	100	Colour-Sgt.	J. Cruickshank.
,,	,,	260	Sergeant	D. Ferguson.
,,	,,	246	Private	A. Fraser.
,,	,,	116	,,	J. Kinnaird.
,,	,,	185	Sergeant	M. M'Cabe.
,,	,,	183	Colour-Sgt.	D. M'Farlane.
,,	,,	278	Corporal	J. M'Farlane.
,,	,,	75	,,	D. M'Gillivray.
,,	,,	63	,,	A. M'Niven.
,,	,,	7	Private	D. Moir.
,,	,,	29	,,	A. Patton.

Date.	Corps.	Regtl. No.	Rank.	Name.	Date.	Corps.	Regtl. No.	Rank.	Name.
Jan./95	4th V.B.	165	Private	R. Patton.	Jan./95	6th V.B.	70	Sergeant	J. Henderson.
,,	,,	151	,,	J. Rutherford.	,,	,,	71	Lce.-Corpl.	J. Herd.
,,	,,	797	Colour-Sgt.	T. Scoble.	,,	,,	131	Private	A. Howie.
,,	,,	230	,,	J. Sinclair.	,,	,,	146	Colour-Sgt.	A. B. Keddie.
,,	,,	419	Private	J. Smith.	,,	,,	425	Sergeant	T. Kenny.
,,	,,	133	,,	A. Smitton.	,,	,,		Captain	J. Lawson.
,,	,,	127	,,	P. Thomson.	,,	,,	45	Colour-Sgt.	J. M'Laren.
,,	,,	140	Qr.-Mr.-Sgt.	J. Whitton.	,,	,,	83	Corporal	J. Mackie.
,,	5th V.B.	43	Sergeant	D. Anderson.	,,	,,	133	,,	M. Miller.
,,	,,	114	Corporal	J. Brow.	,,	,,	64	Colour-Sgt.	W. Ness.
,,	,,	110	Sergeant	J. Bryson.	,,	,,	3984	Private	G. Oake.
,,	,,	58	Colour-Sgt.	A. Carr.	,,	,,	126	Colour-Sgt.	T. Philp.
,,	,,	27	,,	W. Davidson.	,,	,,	187	Sergeant	H. Robertson.
,,	,,	97	,,	J. C. Dewar.	,,	,,	195	,,	A. Scott.
,,	,,	5	,,	R. Forbes.	,,	,,	212	Corporal	D. Scott.
,,	,,	55	Sergeant	W. Gellately.	,,	,,	35	Sergeant	J. Smith.
,,	,,	22	,,	P. Grant.	,,	,,	109	Colour-Sgt.	T. Sutherland.
,,	,,	2199	Corporal	W. Hebenton.	,,	,,	52	Sergeant	A. Thom.
,,	,,	68	Colour-Sgt.	A. Hill.	,,	,,	68	,,	A. Thomson.
,,	,,		Lieutenant	D. S. Johnson.	,,	,,	57	Corporal	J. Thomson.
,,	,,	108	Colour-Sgt.	D. Lamont.	,,	,,	3668	,,	A. Wildridge.
,,	,,	92	Lce.-Sgt.	A. Lindsay.	,,	,,	111	Sergeant	T. Williamson.
,,	,,	73	Colour-Sgt.	P. M'Andrew.	,,	,,	2	Corporal	A. Young.
,,	,,	48	Sergeant	R. M'Diarmid.	,,	,,	165	,,	J. Young.
,,	,,		Lieutenant	D. M'Farlane.	April/95	4th V.B.	34	Private	D. Farquharson.
,,	,,	40	Corporal	J. M'Laren.	,,	5th V.B.	975	,,	D. M'Dougall.
,,	,,	135	,,	H. M'Martin.	,,	,,	116	,,	J. Stewart.
,,	,,	118	Sergeant	W. Macpherson.	Oct./95	1st V.B.	794	Colour-Sgt.	W. Crockatt.
,,	,,	115	,,	J. Martin.	,,	,,	4104	Sergeant	J. Crowlie.
,,	,,	61	,,	D. Paterson.	,,	,,	407	Private	A. Donaldson.
,,	,,		Lieutenant	A. Robertson.	,,	,,	4108	Armr.-Sgt.	G. Fender.
,,	,,	86	Sergeant	A. Robertson.	,,	,,	2443	Private	J. Henderson.
,,	,,	122	Corporal	H. Robertson.	,,	,,	3887	Sergeant	G. MacFarlane.
,,	,,	120	Sergeant	J. Scott.	,,	,,	739	Private	W. M'Nab.
,,	,,	28	,,	P. Shepherd.	,,	,,	6240	,,	R. M'Rostie.
,,	,,	51	,,	W. Sidey.	,,	,,	317	,,	A. Macpherson.
,,	,,	80	Sergeant	P. Stewart.	,,	,,	503	Sergeant	J. Monro.
,,	,,	16	Colour-Sgt.	J. Tod.	,,	,,	5131	,,	P. Morris.
,,	,,	83	,,	J. Walker.	,,	,,	2799	Colour-Sgt.	W. Patrick.
,,	6th V.B.	54	Colour-Sgt.	J. Adam.	,,	,,		Capt. and Hony. Maj.	D. Scroggie.
,,	,,	143	,,	T. Aitken.					
,,	,,	92	Private	F. W. Archibald.	,,	,,	8040	Private	A. Smith.
,,	,,	50	Corporal	J. Berwick.	,,	,,	5771	,,	D. Walker.
,,	,,	169	Colour-Sgt.	P. Bissett.	,,	2nd V.B.	748	Sergeant	G. Anderson.
,,	,,	114	Sergeant	D. Bruce.	,,	,,	2376	Private	G. Beedie.
,,	,,	104	,,	A. Buchanan.	,,	,,	196	Sergeant	W. Carnegie.
,,	,,	48	,,	G. Clelland.	,,	,,	584	Qr.-Master-Sergeant	D. Dakers.
,,	,,		Lieutenant	J. D. Connell.					
,,	,,	105	Colour-Sgt.	W. Couper.	,,	,,	845	Sergeant	G. Duncan.
,,	,,	631	Lce.-Corpl.	W. A. Dick.	,,	,,		Lieutenant	J. Jack.
,,	,,	633	Sergeant	A. Downie.	,,	,,	1453	Sergeant	J. Kennedy.
,,	,,	72	,,	W. Drummond.	,,	,,	4030	Private	W. M'Farlane.
,,	,,	115	Private	J. Finlay.	,,	,,	643	Sergeant	J. M'Kay.
,,	,,	31	Colour-Sgt.	A. Foster.	,,	,,	185	Private	D. Muckart.
,,	,,	59	Sergeant	C. Grieve.	,,	,,	711	Colour-Sgt.	J. Ogilvie.

Date.	Corps.	Regtl. No.	Rank.	Name.	Date.	Corps.	Regtl. No.	Rank.	Name.
Oct./95	2nd V.B.	589	Private	J. Strachan.	Oct./95	5th V.B.	39	Sergeant	D. Ross.
,,	3rd V.B.	3548	,,	J. Carnegie.	,,	,,	13	Colour-Sgt.	J. Simpson.
,,	,,	1	,,	J. Coutts.	,,	6th V.B.	834	Corporal	W. Aitchison.
,,	,,	1528	,,	A. Findlay.	,,	,,	36	Colour-Sgt.	G. Anderson.
,,	,,	8	,,	D. Kidd.	,,	,,	32	,,	T. Archibald.
,,	,,	2370	Sergeant	W. Knipes.	,,	,,	52	Colour-Sgt.	W. Ayton.
,,	,,		Major	R. Laburn.	,,	,,	73	Qr.-Mr.-Sgt.	A. Balsillie.
,,	,,		Captain	D. Milne.	,,	,,	21	Corporal	G. Booth.
,,	,,	3511	Private	H. Officer.	,,	,,	160	Sergeant	J. Brown.
,,	,,	2100	,,	G. Reid.	,,	,,	85	Corporal	S. Campbell.
,,	,,	3004	,,	J. Ritchie.	,,	,,	30	Sergeant	J. Clunie.
,,	,,	3563	Sergeant	W. G. Taylor.	,,	,,	32	,,	R. Craigie.
,,	,,	917	Colour-Sgt.	J. Walls.	,,	,,	20	Colour-Sgt.	R. Davidson.
,,	4th V.B.	12	,,	J. Brown.	,,	,,	234	Corporal	J. Dewar.
,,	,,	137	Sergeant	D. Cameron.	,,	,,	11	Sergeant	J. Douglas.
,,	,,	47	Colour-Sgt.	J. Campsie.	,,	,,		Lieutenant	J. Foster.
,,	,,	189	Sergeant	W. Deuchars.	,,	,,	153	Sergeant	J. Graham.
,,	,,	30	Private	D. Don.	,,	,,	28	Colour-Sgt.	W. Greig.
,,	,,	141	Sergeant	O. Duncan.	,,	,,	340	Sergeant	J. Harcus.
,,	,,	368	Private	W. Elliott.	,,	,,		Captain	H. D. Henderson.
,,	,,	40	Sergeant	D. Ferguson.	,,	,,	4076	Private	W. Henderson.
,,	,,	45	,,	J. Gibson.	,,	,,	249	,,	D. Johnston.
,,	,,	32	Private	J. Grant.	,,	,,	253	Corporal	T. Johnston.
,,	,,	325	Corporal	D. Henderson.	,,	,,	90	Sergeant	J. M'Quire.
,,	,,	163	Colour-Sgt.	J. Innes.	,,	,,		Lieutenant	G. Macpherson.
,,	,,	411	Private	J. Kennedy.	,,	,,		,,	A. Martin.
,,	,,	79	,,	J. M'Gregor.	,,	,,	17	Sergeant	J. Morris.
,,	,,	202	Lce.-Sergt.	M. M'Naughton.	,,	,,	2013	Private	J. Paterson.
,,	,,	102	Sergeant	A. MacDonald.	,,	,,	237	Sergeant	T. Pearson.
,,	,,	89	Corporal	J. Munro.	,,	,,	3733	Private	T. Peebles.
,,	,,	1355	Sergeant	W. Munro.	,,	,,	233	Sergeant	J. Ritchie.
,,	,,	47	Private	W. Neilson.	,,	,,	10	Colour-Sgt.	D. Robertson.
,,	,,	5	Colour-Sgt.	J. Petty.	,,	,,		2nd Lieut.	J. A. Romanes.
,,	,,	336	Sergeant	A. Reid.	,,	,,	8	Qr.-Mr.-Sgt.	J. Russell.
,,	,,	502	,,	J. Rigg.	,,	,,	1955	Private	G. Swan.
,,	,,	78	Private	J. Robertson.	,,	,,	27	Colour-Sgt.	A. Waddel.
,,	,,	416	Sergeant	P. Rutherford.	,,	,,	60	Private	A. Wallace.
,,	,,	66	Colour-Sgt.	J. Stewart.	,,	,,	26	Sergeant	R. Wilson.
,,	,,	30	,,	P. Stewart.	,,	,,	164	Colour-Sgt.	W. Williamson.
,,	,,	13	Sergeant	R. Whyte.	,,	,,	98	,,	D. Young.
,,	,,	175	Private	A. Wotherspoon.	Feb./05[1]	2nd V.B.	3783	Sergeant	W. M'Lean.
,,	5th V.B.	228	Sergeant	A. Ambrose.	,,	4th V.B.	58	Colour-Sgt.	J. M'Kenzie.
,,	,,	18	Colour-Sgt.	D. Bruce.	,,	5th V.B.	1023	Sergeant	W. Davidson.
,,	,,	21	Sergeant	J. Buttar.	,,	6th V.B.	2781	Corporal	W. Fowlis.
,,	,,	229	Corporal	J. Gellately.	July/05	1st V.B.	6068	Armr.-Sgt.	G. MacFarlane.
,,	,,	24	Colour-Sgt.	D. Harris.	,,	,,	6076	Colour-Sgt.	D. Pyott.
,,	,,	44	Corporal	S. How.	,,	3rd V.B.	2481	Private	W. Dargie.
,,	,,	20	Sergeant	J. Imrie.	,,	,,	2470	Sergeant	W. Scott.
,,	,,	19	,,	J. Kay.	,,	4th V.B.	66	Bugler	J. S. Rylance.
,,	,,	26	Private	D. Kennedy.	,,	5th V.B.	1207	Private	J. Smith.
,,	,,	203	,,	D. Leslie.	,,	6th V.B.	4379	,,	J. Cuthbert.
,,	,,	3	Colour-Sgt.	R. M'Lean.	,,	,,	3312	Corporal	R. Gair.
,,	,,	38	Corporal	A. Mitchell.	,,	,,	4812	Private	J. M'Kinlay.
,,	,,	15	Lce.-Sergt.	C. Murray.	,,	,,	2041	Sergeant	S. Melville.
,,	,,	136	Sergeant	A. Robertson.	,,	,,	2085	,,	R. Peebles.

[1] NOTE.—The Rolls jump from October 1895 to February 1905, but on page 338 the list is continued from January 1896 up to December 1904.

Date.	Corps.	Regtl. No.	Rank.	Name.	Date.	Corps.	Regtl. No.	Rank.	Name.
July/05	6th V.B.	1956	Corporal	A. Russell.	Aug./06	3rd V.B.	2819	Qr.-Mr.-Sgt.	D. Low.
,,	,,	4550	,,	J. C. Thomson.	,,	,,	2818	Lce.-Sergt.	J. Bain.
,,	,,	2126	Sergeant	J. Wilson.	,,	4th V.B.	605	Private	G. S. Gibb.
Aug./05	1st V.B.	9564	Private	J. Craig.	,,	,,	368	Lce.-Sergt.	C. Moir.
,,	,,	6130	Colour-Sgt.	J. Galloway.	,,	5th V.B.	1196	Private	W. Davidson.
,,	,,	6136	Corporal	J. Lumgair.	,,	,,	1469	,,	P. Duff.
,,	,,	7383	,,	J. Robb.	,,	,,	1439	,,	T. Ferguson.
,,	2nd V.B.	2083	Private	J. Burnett.	,,	,,	528	,,	R. Robertson.
,,	,,	3267	,,	W. Forrest.	,,	6th V.B.	3568	Sergeant	A. Wallace.
,,	,,	2189	Lce.-Corpl.	G. Mann.	Nov./06	4th V.B.	362	Private	A. Ferguson.
,,	,,	1936	Corporal	D. Watson.	,,	6th V.B.	4545	Lce.-Corpl.	G. M'Kinlay.
,,	3rd V.B.		Surgn.-Maj.	W. Kinnear.	Feb./07	3rd V.B.	4048	Sergeant	G. Fisher.
,,	4th V.B.	647	Colour-Sgt.	J. Connon.	,,	,,	4623	Private	J. S. Lyall.
,,	,,	677	Drummer	A. Drummond.	,,	4th V.B.	657	Corporal	J. Drummond.
,,	,,	709	Private	J. M'Laren.	May/07	1st V.B.	8976	Colour-Sgt.	C. Anderson.
,,	,,	234	Corporal	J. M'Naughton.	,,	,,	9878	Private	A. Graham.
,,	,,	92	Sergeant	D. M'Dougall.	,,	,,	7624	,,	J. Patullo.
,,	,,	145	Lce.-Corpl.	J. Paton.	,,	,,	6480	Sergeant	P. Pullen.
,,	,,		Major	A. T. Reid.	,,	,,	4660	,,	J. Sedgewick.
,,	,,	348	Colour-Sgt.	D. Strang.	,,	,,	643	Private	D. Smith.
,,	,,	738	Private	J. Watson.	,,	4th V.B.	500	,,	J. Connelly.
,,	5th V.B.	2174	Lce.-Sergt.	T. Gellatly.	,,	,,	524	Lce.-Corpl.	H. Elliott.
,,	6th V.B.	2092	Sergeant	J. Morris.	,,	,,	6	Qr.-Mr.-Sgt.	W. M'Cowan.
,,	,,	2091	Lce.-Corpl.	S. Normand.	,,	,,	653	Sergeant	J. M'Gregor.
Nov./05	3rd V.B.	5403	,,	A. Kay.	,,	5th V.B.	729	Sgt.-Piper	D. Campbell.
,,	,,	4446	Private	D. Lamont.	,,	6th V.B.	3946	Lce.-Corpl.	R. Johnstone.
,,	4th V.B.	157	Lce.-Sergt.	R. Cairns.	Aug./07	4th V.B.	495	Private	J. Manning.
,,	,,	649	,,	T. Turnbull.	,,	,,	838	Sergeant	D. Scott.
Feb./06	1st V.B.	7662	Sergeant	W. Lennox.	,,	5th V.B.	1827	,,	J. Campbell.
,,	,,	6175	Private	J. Wilson.	,,	6th V.B.	4972	,,	A. Gray.
,,	2nd V.B.	2321	Colour-Sgt.	A. Peffers.	,,	,,	2489	Private	A. Michie.
,,	,,	5750	Lce.-Corpl.	J. Ritchie.	Nov./07	1st V.B.	6568	Sergeant	J. Brown.
,,	3rd V.B.	6162	Bandsman	J. Robertson.	,,	,,	8083	Private	J. Constable.
,,	4th V.B.	503	Sergeant	B. Reid.	,,	,,	8402	Sergeant	J. Hall.
,,	,,	637	Private	J. Younger.	,,	,,	8084	Lce.-Corpl.	J. Knowles.
,,	5th V.B.	3058	,,	A. Menzies.	,,	5th V.B.	2728	Sergeant	D. Scotland.
,,	,,	1279	,,	J. M'Donald.	,,	,,	1687	Private	D. Fraser.
,,	,,	1304	,,	A. M'Kinlay.	Feb./08	1st V.B.	313	Sergeant	W. Marquis.
,,	,,	1326	Corporal	A. MacNaughton.	,,	5th V.B.	2196	Colour-Sgt.	R. S. Ferrier.
,,	,,	1185	Private	W. L. Mac-Naughton.	,,	6th V.B.	2653	Sergeant	J. Gow.
,,	,,	1181	,,	J. Robertson.	May/08	4th V.B.	52	Lce.-Corpl.	W. Young.
,,	,,	1187	Lce.-Sergt.	W. Stewart.	,,	5th V.B.	1720	Colour-Sgt.	S. Robertson.
,,	,,		Major	G. J. Haynes.	,,	6th V.B.	4268	Corporal	J. Nicol.
,,	6th V.B.	3167	Private	W. Clark.	,,	,,		Lieutenant	T. J. Robertson.
May/06	2nd V.B.	3664	Sergeant	W. Davidson.	,,	,,		Lieutenant	J. Shirlaw.
,,	,,	5787	,,	W. Forsyth.		B.W.Bde Bearer Coy.R.A. M.C.Vols	5	Staff-Sgt.	J. Cleland.
,,	,,	2915	,,	C. Hastings.					
,,	3rd V.B.	2758	Bandsman	A. Rutherford.	Jan./09	1st V.B.	7653	Colour-Sgt.	R. Annan.
,,	6th V.B.	2402	Sergeant	D. Annan.	,,	,,	6892	Sergeant	E. Arkile.
,,	,,	2312	Colour-Sgt.	T. Batchelor.	,,	,,	7362	Private	C. Clayton.
,,	,,	2328	Corporal	D. Swan.	,,	,,	7422	Sergeant	P. Cochrane.
,,	,,	2245	Sergeant	J. Taylor.	,,	,,	7553	,,	W. Davidson.
,,	,,	2257	,,	A. Westwood.	,,	,,	7277	Private	A. Dewar.
Aug./06	3rd V.B.		Capt. and Hony. Maj.	P. S. Nicoll.					

Date.	Corps.	Regtl. No.	RANK.	NAME.	Date.	Corps.	Regtl. No.	RANK.	NAME.
Jan./09	1st V.B.	8232	Sergeant	T. Dewar.	Jan./09	2nd V.B.	5853	Private	A. Young.
,,	,,	7640	Private	G. Easson.	,,	3rd V.B.	2722	,,	J. Forbes.
,,	,,	8157	,,	G. Fender.	,,	,,	4940	Colour-Sgt.	W. Fraser.
,,	,,	6950	,,	D. Gove.	,,	,,	4026	,,	J. Gegan.
,,	,,	8277	Corporal	R. Heggie.	,,	,,	4967	Sergeant	W. Lancett.
,,	,,	6964	Lce.-Corpl.	W. Ireland.	,,	,,	6341	Private	G. Liddle.
,,	,,	849	Corporal	G. Keillor.	,,	,,	7029	Sergeant	R. Phillips.
,,	,,	6929	Private	A. M'Dougall.	,,	4th V.B.	354	,,	T. Callanan.
,,	,,	6877	Colour-Sgt.	G. M'Laren.	,,	,,	236	,,	R. Comrie.
,,	,,	7449	Private	D. M'Pherson.	,,	,,	501	Private	J. Connolly.
,,	,,	7145	,,	G. M'Pherson.	,,	,,	672	Corporal	W. Connon.
,,	,,	7442	Sergeant	J. Ogg.	,,	,,	2223	Private	P. Crerar.
,,	,,	6076	,,	R. Pyott.	,,	,,	248	Lce.-Corpl.	W. Dron.
,,	,,	9690	,,	J. Ross.	,,	,,	678	Private	A. Drummond.
,,	,,	6903	Corporal	A. Scott.	,,	,,	2103	Sergeant	J. S. Hood.
,,	,,	7123	Private	D. Simpson.	,,	,,	88	Lce.-Sergt.	P. Jack.
,,	,,	8505	,,	G. Webster.	,,	,,	825	Sgt.-Piper	D. Kennedy.
,,	,,	6848	Sergeant	J. Wilkie.	,,	,,	240	Corporal	P. M'Farlane.
,,	2nd V.B.	2967	Private	G. Allan.	,,	,,	375	,,	J. M'Intyre.
,,	,,	3451	Lce.-Corpl.	W. Bennett.	,,	,,	705	Private	A. M'Kee.
,,	,,	6847	Sergeant	M. G. Beverley.	,,	,,	707	Piper	M. M'Kenzie.
,,	,,	4807	Colour-Sgt.	J. Bruce.	,,	,,	619	Colour-Sgt.	W. M'Kenzie.
,,	,,	4044	Sergeant	A. Christie.	,,	,,	241	Corporal	W. M'Phail.
,,	,,	3249	Corporal	D. Christie.	,,	,,	147	Sergeant	A. Paton.
,,	,,	3712	Private	A. Clark.	,,	,,	42	Private	J. Peebles.
,,	,,	4809	Corporal	A. Craik.	,,	,,	528	Corporal	T. Sim.
,,	,,	3749	Sergeant	D. Croall.	,,	,,	729	Sergeant	G. Smart.
,,	,,	4991	Corporal	A. Donaldson.	,,	,,	529	,,	W. Smitton.
,,	,,	3837	,,	J. S. Dow.	,,	,,	740	Private	R. Wingate.
,,	,,	3272	,,	A. Duncan.	,,	,,	635	Sergeant	J. L. Wood.
,,	,,	6344	Colour-Sgt.	W. Hampton.	,,	,,	243	Private	H. Wylie.
,,	,,	3693	,,	T. J. Ivison.	,,	,,	162	,,	J. Wylie.
,,	,,	3593	Corporal	G. Japp.	,,	5th V.B.	1881	Colour-Sgt.	D. Adam.
,,	,,	3667	Sergeant	A. Kydd.	,,	,,	2027	Private	J. Alcorn.
,,	,,	3070	Corporal	G. M'Kenzie.	,,	,,	2231	,,	J. Campbell.
,,	,,	2825	Lce.-Corpl.	W. M'Pherson.	,,	,,	2230	Sergeant	H. S. Duff.
,,	,,	4873	Private	J. Mamby.	,,	,,	2206	Private	W. Erskine.
,,	,,	4040	,,	W. Marshall.	,,	,,	4574	,,	D. Gellatly.
,,	,,	3172	Lce.-Corpl.	W. Matthew.	,,	,,	2207	,,	W. Forbes.
,,	,,	3594	Private	A. Millar.	,,	,,	3658	Corporal	J. P. M'Alpine.
,,	,,	5502	Sergeant	J. Milne.	,,	,,	2314	Private	D. M'Culloch.
,,	,,	5124	Private	J. Milne.	,,	,,	2805	Pioneer-Sgt.	C. B. M'Farlane.
,,	,,	3569	Sergeant	J. Morris.	,,	,,	1957	Private	R. M'Glashan.
,,	,,	3656	,,	W. Morton.	,,	,,	3004	Sergeant	J. M'Lean.
,,	,,	3214	Colour-Sgt.	J. Napier.	,,	,,	1870	Colour-Sgt.	J. Moon.
,,	,,	3499	Sergeant	W. Nicol.	,,	,,	2528	Corporal	P. Murray.
,,	,,	3933	,,	W. Prain.	,,	,,	2171	Sergeant	J. Pennycook.
,,	,,	4832	Lce.-Corpl.	J. Scott.	,,	,,	3245	Private	T. A. Richardson.
,,	,,	2868	Piper	J. Shepherd.	,,	,,	2065	Sergeant	W. Robertson.
,,	,,	2792	Sergeant	R. L. Sinclair.	,,	,,	2248	Qr.-Mr.-Sgt.	W. Scott.
,,	,,	4775	Private	D. Spence.	,,	,,	1843	Corporal	J. Stewart.
,,	,,	3069	Corporal	D. Stewart.	,,	,,	2536	Drummer	W. Stewart.
,,	,,	3948	Private	G. Thompson.	,,	,,	2834	Sergeant	A. Wighton.
,,	,,	3665	Lce.-Corpl.	S. Winter.	,,	6th V.B.	3029	Colour-Sgt.	A. Aitken.
,,	,,	3329	Corporal	D. Wylie.	,,	,,	2789	,,	J. Band.

Date.	Corps.	Regtl. No.	Rank.	Name.	Date.	Corps.	Regtl. No.	Rank.	Name.
Jan./09	6th V.B.	6773	Lce.-Corpl.	W. Bease.	Aug./09	4th V.B.		Captain	C. Stewart Murray.
,,	,,	3350	Sergeant	C. Bell.	,,	,,	78	Private	T. Moncrieff.
,,	,,	3423	,,	G. Bissett.	,,	5th V.B.		Capt. and Hony. Maj.	T. Buchanan.
,,	,,	3955	Colour-Sgt.	R. Borthwick.	,,	6th V.B.		Lt.-Col. and Hony. Col.	Sir R. W. Anstruther, Bt.
,,	,,	6249	Lce.-Corpl.	M. Brown.	,,	,,		Surgn. Capt.	R. T. Ferguson.
,,	,,	4652	Sergeant	R. Brown.	,,	,,		Capt. and Hony. Maj.	P. Macduff.
,,	,,	4073	,,	D. C. Clark.	,,	,,		Surgn. Capt.	J. S. Mackay.
,,	,,	6170	Lce.-Corpl.	T. Crombie.	Oct./09	1st V.B.	9506	Private	J. Robertson.
,,	,,	6616	Private	H. Dexter.	,,	2nd V.B.	206	Sergeant	W. Scott.
,,	,,	4291	Sergeant	G. Dobie.	,,	4th V.B.		Actg. Chaplain	Revd. D. R. Henderson.
,,	,,	3106	Colour-Sgt.	W. Greig.	Dec./09	6th V.B.		Lieutenant	W. B. Brown.
,,	,,	4465	,,	W. Hunter.	Jan./96[1]	1st V.B.	2065	Colour-Sgt.	T. Adamson.
,,	,,	3460	Lce.-Corpl.	J. Jackson.	,,	,,	5114	Private	J. Belford.
,,	,,	3444	Lce.-Sergt.	D. Leslie.	,,	,,		Actg. Chaplain	Revd. C. Campbell, D.D.
,,	,,	4571	Corporal	G. M'Kinlay.	,,	,,		Captain	J. Fleming.
,,	,,	3271	,,	J. M'Laren.	,,	,,	4061	Colour-Sgt.	D. Fyffe.
,,	,,	3618	,,	W. M'Murray.	,,	,,	4076	Private	D. Ness.
,,	,,	4170	,,	H. J. Manson.	,,	2nd V.B.	11	,,	A. Brown.
,,	,,	3483	Private	T. Melville.	,,	,,	2332	,,	J. Chalmers.
,,	,,	2868	,,	D. Paterson.	,,	,,	2585	,,	W. Collie.
,,	,,	7511	Lce.-Corpl.	J. Pool.	,,	,,	14	Colour-Sgt.	J. Findlay.
,,	,,	5401	Private	D. Ramage.	,,	,,		Lieutenant	W. Findlay.
,,	,,	7094	,,	C. Rankin.	,,	,,	38	Sergeant	W. Piggot.
,,	,,	4502	Corporal	A. Reddie.	,,	3rd V.B.	23	Colour-Sgt.	D. M'Leod.
,,	,,	4337	Sergeant	J. Ripley.	,,	,,	915	,,	A. Reid.
,,	,,	7154	,,	A. Robertson.	,,	5th V.B.	168	Corporal	W. Cattanach.
,,	,,	2856	,,	J. Stewart.	,,	,,	9	Sergeant	G. Christie.
,,	,,	3528	Corporal	R. A. Taylor.	,,	,,	8	,,	P. Ferguson.
,,	,,	2881	Private	J. Thomson.	,,	,,	169	Private	D. Livingstone.
,,	,,	2918	Sergeant	P. Walker.	,,	,,	143	Sergeant	D. M'Gibbon.
,,	,,	2911	,,	A. Wilkie.	,,	,,	670	Private	W. M'Gregor.
,,	,,	3306	Colour-Sgt.	D. Williamson.	,,	,,	10	,,	J. M'Intyre.
,,	,,	7817	Corporal	A. Wilson.	,,	,,	454	Corporal	D. M'Laren.
April/09	1st V.B.	8250	Private	J. Carden.	,,	,,	167	Colour-Sgt.	J. M'Leish.
,,	,,	6745	,,	R. Simpson.	,,	,,	7	,,	P. M'Naughton.
,,	5th V.B.	2109	Qr.-Mr.-Sgt.	J. E. Adamson.	,,	6th V.B.	3417	Private	B. Bain.
,,	,,	1779	Colour-Sgt.	R. Chalmers.	,,	,,	147	Corporal	C. Batchelor.
,,	,,	2169	Private	J. Hall.	,,	,,	1691	Private	J. Birrell.
,,	,,	1788	Corporal	J. M'Glashan.	,,	,,	22	Colour-Sgt.	A. Craighead.
,,	,,	1825	Colour-Sgt.	J. A. M'Gregor.	,,	,,	667	Private	D. Foster.
Aug./09	B.W. Bearer Coy. R.A.M.C.	230	Private	W. Edwards.	,,	,,	283	,,	G. Hogg.
,,	,,	244	,,	D. Todd.	,,	,,	66	,,	J. M'Kinlay.
,,	1st V.B.		Lieutenant	C. B. Anderson.	,,	,,	58	Corporal	H. Norman.
,,	,,		Major	D. Pirie.	,,	,,	24	,,	G. Simpson.
,,	2nd V.B.	2907	Private	W. F. Kydd.	,,	,,	324	Sergeant	T. Wallace.
,,	,,	3529	Corporal	J. M'Caffery.	July/96	1st V.B.	6624	Private	C. P. Robertson.
,,	,,	2999	Sergeant	J. M'Intosh.	,,	,,	6362	,,	G. Thomson.
,,	3rd V.B.	6767	,,	W. Crockart.	,,	,,	5466	,,	W. Will.
,,	,,	3533	,,	R. Duncan.	,,	2nd V.B.	853	Corporal	A. Bey.
,,	,,	5093	,,	G. Ogilvie.	,,	,,	935	,,	A. Milne.
,,	,,	3229	Private	H. Petrie.					
,,	,,	6352	Sergeant	C. S. Reid.					
,,	,,	2758	Private	A. Rutherford.					

[1] See page 335.—J. S.

Date.	Corps.	Regtl. No.	Rank.	Name.
July /96	2nd V.B.	4353	Private	R. Milne.
„	„	193	Sergeant	C. Sim.
„	3rd V.B.	2261	Colour-Sgt.	J. Bell.
„	„	899	Sergeant	J. Grubb.
„	„	2844	Private	J. M'Inroy.
„	„	4275	„	F. Matthew.
„	4th V.B.	19	Private	J. Crow.
„	„	363	„	G. Honeyman.
„	„	29	„	W. Lawrie.
„	„	234	Sergeant	A. M'Ewan.
„	„	335	Private	J. M'Geogh.
„	„	290	Sergeant	D. Munro.
„	„	452	„	A. Robertson.
„	„	34	Private	D. Shaw.
„	„	263	Sergeant	W. Sinclair.
„	„	236	Private	P. Smitton.
„	6th V.B.	37	Sergeant	W. Barnett.
„	„	3327	Private	T. Black.
„	„	307	Corporal	R. Brodie.
„	„	34	Private	D. Brown.
„	„	319	„	J. Brown.
„	„	320	Sergeant	J. Duncan.
„	„	315	„	D. Elder.
„	„		Capt. and Hony. Maj.	J. Gillespie.
„	„	314	Corporal	J. Gordon.
„	„	329	Sergeant	J. M'Donald.
„	„	322	Corporal	D. Robertson.
„	„	333	„	J. Scott.
„	„	331	Colour-Sgt.	J. Spence.
Jan./97	1st V.B.	7986	Private	D. Anderson.
„	3rd V.B.	1130	Sergeant	J. Thomson.
July/97	2nd V.B.	2579	Private	D. Shephard.
„	4th V.B.	271	Sergeant	P. Cramb.
„	„	17	Corporal	D. Dewar.
„	„	34	„	D. Dewar.
„	„	22	Private	D. M'Culloch.
„	„		Captain	R. M'Naughton.
„	„	1389	Private	A. M'Neill.
„	„	269	Sergeant	T. Patterson.
„	5th V.B.	207	„	J. Leslie.
„	„	201	Corporal	R. Menzies.
„	„	164	Private	J. Paterson.
„	„	163	Sergeant	E. Robertson.
„	„	120	Lce.-Sergt.	A. Scott.
„	„	206	Corporal	D. Waters.
„	6th V.B.	1931	Private	A. Herd.
„	„	1935	„	R. Kinnaird.
„	„	43	Sergeant	J. Patton.
Oct./97	1st V.B.	7621	Private	A. J. Robertson.
„	„	4415	Sergeant	J. Roy.
Jan./98	1st V.B	6563	Lance-Sergt.	J. T. Dewar
„	2nd V.B.	468	„	J. Beattie.
„	„	855	Sergeant	J. Corstorphine.
„	„	802	Corporal	R. Johnston.
„	„	944	Sergeant	R. Kirkland.
Jan./98	2nd V.B.	550	Corporal	R. Matthew.
„	„	886	Private	W. Morrison.
„	„	1826	Corporal	A. Pettie.
„	„	1812	Lance-Sergt.	J. Ripley.
„	„	3988	„	C. Shepherd.
„	3rd V.B.	2851	Corporal	G. Chalmers.
„	„	4605	Private	W. Hunter.
„	„	1205	„	J. Lindsay.
„	4th V.B.	72	„	P. Comrie.
„	„	289	Lance-Sergt.	J. Hally.
„	„	410	Sergeant	J. M'Farlane.
„	„	269	Lance-Sergt.	J. Tran.
„	6th V.B.	354	Private	A. Bell.
„	„	3289	Lance-Corpl.	R. Black.
„	„		Captain	J. S. Davidson.
„	„		„	H. M. Hewison.
„	„	362	Sergeant	W. Liddell.
April/98	2nd V.B.	1618	Corporal	J. Mitchell.
„	„	687	Sergeant	W. Sandeman.
„	3rd V.B.	2113	„	D. Ferguson.
„	4th V.B.	80	Private	George Hally.
„	„	581	Sergeant	J. Morrison.
„	„	24	Lce.-Corpl.	W. Murphy.
„	„	655	„	A. Robertson.
July /98	5th V.B.	462	Sergeant	W. Davidson.
„	„	1658	Private	G. Low.
„	„	954	Corporal	B. Paterson.
„	„	25	Private	D. Scott.
„	6th V.B.	2019	„	P. Beveridge.
„	„	4479	„	D. Brooks.
„	„	1785	„	R. W. Brown.
„	„	374	„	J. Campbell.
„	„	467	Colour-Sgt.	J. Deuchars.
„	„	1416	Sergeant	W. Elliot.
„	„	439	„	W. Irvine.
„	„	449	Private	D. Leslie.
„	„	4497	„	D. M'Farlane.
„	„	2617	Sergeant	C. Thomson.
„	„	472	Private	W. White.
Oct./98	1st V.B.		Surgn.-Maj.	A. Campbell.
„	„	4620	Corporal	A. Glass.
„	„	5592	„	S. M'Gregor.
„	„	7105	„	J. Smith.
„	„	4448	O.R. Sergt.	G. Telfer.
„	„	4495	Sergeant	D. Walker.
„	2nd V.B.	296	„	H. Bryan.
„	4th V.B.		„	J. Thom.
„	6th V.B.	3050	„	A. Benzie.
„	„		Lieutenant	T. Clark.
„	„		Captain	G. Fergusson.
„	„	1429	Private	J. Young.
Jan./99	1st V.B.	4709	„	J. Smart.
„	4th V.B.	103	Corporal	J. Marshall.
„	6th V.B.	537	Colour-Sgt.	G. Dingwall.
April/99	2nd V.B.	838	„	J. Davidson.
„	„	664	Sergeant	W. Drummie.

Date.	Corps.	Regtl. No.	Rank.	Name.	Date.	Corps.	Regtl. No.	Rank.	Name.
April/99	2nd V.B.	2553	Corporal	J. Gordon.	Oct./00	2nd V.B.	1173	Private	W. Black.
,,	4th V.B.	57	Sergeant	S. Emslie.	,,	,,	117	Sergeant	W. Duncan.
,,	,,		Major	D. M'Ewen.	,,	,,	913	,,	G. L. Stewart.
July/99	1st V.B.	4783	Sergeant	J. Carey.	,,	4th V.B.	4	Private	D. Banks.
,,	,,	6377	Private	J. Simpson.	,,	6th V.B.	2082	Sergeant	J. Beattie.
,,	3rd V.B.	1997	Colour-Sgt.	W. Clarke.	,,	,,	1879	Private	J. Swan.
,,	,,	2270	Private	A. Jackson.	,,	,,	350	,,	W. White.
,,	,,	1777	,,	J. M'Nab.	Jan./01	1st V.B.	5267	,,	T. Coults.
,,	5th V.B.	453	,,	J. C. Beaton.	,,	,,	5831	,,	J. Craig.
,,	,,	629	Sergeant	R. Boyd.	,,	,,	5209	,,	J. M'Gonigal.
,,	,,	290	,,	J. Craig.	,,	4th V.B.	519	Sergeant	A. Martin.
,,	,,	346	,,	D. Robertson.	,,	6th V.B.	4095	Private	G. Adamson.
,,	6th V.B.	608	Corporal	J. Kellie.	,,	,,	2526	,,	J. Smart.
Oct./99	1st V.B.	6835	Private	J. Elliott.	April/01	2nd V.B.	2576	Corporal	G. Kennison.
,,	,,	4773	,,	J. Millar.	,,	,,	5018	Sergeant	J. Robertson.
,,	,,	4885	Corporal	A. Simpson.	,,	,,	765	Lce.-Corpl.	D. Thompson.
,,	,,	4920	Private	A. Thoms.	,,	,,	3538	Private	J. Wrighton.
,,	2nd V.B.	1829	,,	J. Black.	,,	5th V.B.	2275	Sergeant	F. T. Garden.
,,	,,	86	Sergeant	G. Hutcheon.	,,	,,	1772	Private	H. Grant.
,,	,,	1316	,,	C. M'Donald.	,,	,,	2529	,,	J. Gray.
,,	,,	3544	Private	J. Milne.	,,	,,	3016	,,	D. M'Naughton.
,,	4th V.B.	513	Corporal	J. Anderson.	,,	,,	504	Sergeant	W. Miller.
,,	,,	686	Private	D. K. Gray.	,,	,,	2258	,,	J. Robertson.
,,	,,		Qr.-Mr. and Capt.	T. Sanderson.	,,	,,	433	,,	W. Robertson.
,,	6th V.B.	627	Private	D. Mollison.	,,	6th V.B.		Captain	W. P. Wilson.
Jan./00	2nd V.B.	2523	Sergeant	W. Britcher.	July /01	1st V.B.	5275	Sergeant	J. Begbie.
,,	,,	3314	Private	D. Eggo.	,,	,,	6241	Private	A. Gardner.
,,	,,	1361	Sergeant	G. Gordon.	,,	,,	5292	,,	G. Thomson.
,,	,,	3540	Private	G. Webster.	,,	2nd V.B.	3715	,,	J. Baird.
,,	4th V.B.	13	,,	D. Barker.	,,	,,	3443	,,	A. Glen.
,,	,,	618	,,	J. M'Leish.	,,	,,	439	,,	D. Milne.
,,	5th V.B.	417	Colour-Sgt.	J. Robertson.	,,	,,	370	,,	G. Smith.
,,	,,	415	Sergeant	D. Stewart.	,,	,,	989	,,	J. Spark.
,,	6th V.B.	895	Colour-Sgt.	W. Oswald.	,,	4th V.B.	64	,,	J. Smith.
,,	,,	3654	Private	T. Scott.	,,	6th V.B.	937	,,	J. Beveridge.
July/00	2nd V.B.	1971	Sergeant	J. Cameron.	,,	,,	2888	Lce.-Corpl.	R. Smith.
,,	,,	3831	Private	C. Coleman.	Oct./01	1st V.B.	5407	Colour-Sgt.	W. Cathro.
,,	,,	114	Sergeant	P. Craig.	,,	2nd V.B.	1248	Private	J. Wilkie.
,,	,,	526	Colour-Sgt.	J. Donnar.	,,	,,	1043	Corporal	D. Wilson.
,,	,,	1659	Private	R. Mitchell.	,,	6th V.B.	1120	Colour-Sgt.	R. Bett.
,,	,,	1792	Sergeant	G. M'Kay.	,,	,,	3524	Private	J. Fairbairn.
,,	,,	5621	Private	J. Robertson.	,,	,,	1092	Corporal	J. Herd.
,,	3rd V.B.	4537	,,	J. Innis.	,,	,,	3421	Sergeant	W. Peggie.
,,	,,	1573	,,	W. Miller.	Jan./02	2nd V.B.	1302	Colour-Sgt.	A. Mitchell.
,,	,,	1636	Sergeant	T. Taylor.	,,	3rd V.B.	1907	,,	T. Carstairs.
,,	4th V.B.	889	,,	J. Smith.	,,	4th V.B.	645	Corporal	R. Allan.
,,	,,	588	Corporal	W. Wilson.	,,	,,	664	Private	J. Bell.
,,	6th V.B.	790	Private	G. Crichton.	,,	,,	138	Sergeant	H. R. Hume.
,,	,,	726	Colour-Sgt.	G. Howie.	,,	,,	139	,,	J. Kerr.
,,	,,	720	Sergeant	J. M'Kinney.	,,	,,	149	Corporal	J. Scott.
Oct./00	1st V.B.	5838	Private	J. Carson.	,,	,,	137	Lce.-Corpl.	J. Strong.
,,	,,	5050	Colour-Sgt.	J. Crigton.	,,	,,	741	Private	D. Wright.
,,	,,	4993	Private	J. Edward.	,,	5th V.B.	399	Corporal	J. Carr.
,,	,,	5075	Sgt.-Bugler	G. Johnston.	,,	,,	2129	Private	J. Fender.
,,	,,	3749	Private	W. Lamb.	,,	,,	1943	,,	D. M'Leish.
					,,	,,	542	Drummer	J. M'Pherson.

Date.	Corps.	Regtl. No.	Rank.	Name.
Jan./02	6th V.B.		Surgn.-Capt.	C. E. Douglas.
,,	,,	2562	Sergeant	J. Bain.
April/02	1st V.B.		Capt. and Hony. Maj.	T. Cappon.
,,	2nd V.B.	2766	Qr.-Mr.-Sgt.	J. Cameron.
,,	3rd V.B.		Capt. and Hony. Maj.	D. Small.
,,	,,	4455	Sergeant	G. Aird.
,,	,,	1952	Private	A. M'Donald.
,,	,,	1975	Sgt.-Piper	J. Stewart.
,,	5th V.B.	1152	Private	E. Devine.
,,	,,	1732	,,	J. Spottiswood.
,,	6th V.B.	3226	,,	A. Bain.
July /02	2nd V.B.	4089	,,	D. Ramsay.
,,	3rd V.B.	2014	Sergeant	J. Balharrie.
,,	,,	2054	Colour-Sgt.	W. Christie.
,,	4th V.B.		Capt. and Hony. Maj.	C. E. Colville.
,,	,,		Captain	G. Ferguson.
,,	,,	244	Corporal	D. Halley.
,,	,,	5	Sergeant	H. Wilkie.
,,	6th V.B.	1236	Private	J. Beveridge.
,,	,,	3523	Lce.-Corpl.	G. Thomson.
,,	,,	1285	Sergeant	A. Turpie.
Oct./02	2nd V.B.		Lieutenant	D. P. Booth.
,,	,,	5743	Band-Sgt.	H. R. Campbell.
,,	,,	1383	Corporal	D. Corstorphine.
,,	,,	1459	,,	W. Rae.
,,	,,	2764	Private	J. Strachan.
,,	3rd V.B.	2080	Lce.-Sergt.	D. Bain.
,,	4th V.B.	18	Sergeant	J. Millar.
,,	,,	516	,,	R. Maltman.
,,	,,	517	Private	E. Sinclair.
,,	,,	912	,,	J. Tait.
,,	5th V.B.	699	,,	J. Irvine.
,,	,,	1914	Sergeant	J. Kidd.
,,	,,	3404	Private	J. M. Menzies.
,,	,,	1499	Corporal	J. Patterson.
,,	,,	735	,,	J. Small.
,,	6th V.B.	1430	,,	R. Pratt.
Jan./03	4th V.B.	890	Private	A. Fenwick.
,,	,,	141	Sergeant	A. C. Guthrie.
,,	1st V.B.	5267	Bandsman	T. Coutts.
April/03	,,	7409	Private	D. Kiddie.
,,	,,	5601	,,	A. Manzie.
July /03	,,	6921	Colour-Sgt.	W. Mackay.
,,	,,	9048	Private	W. Hall.
,,	2nd V.B.	2995	Corporal	W. Simpson.
,,	4th V.B.	521	,,	J. Allen.
,,	,,	226	Sergeant	J. F. Don.
,,	,,	520	Lce.-Corpl.	J. Martin.
,,	,,	761	Sgt.-Bugler	J. M. Miller.
,,	,,	343	Sergeant	W. M'Anish.
,,	,,	233	,,	J. Roy.
,,	,,	47	Private	D. Wallace.

Date.	Corps.	Regtl. No.	Rank.	Name.
July /03	6th V.B.	1458	Sergeant	G. Gould.
,,	,,	2303	Private	A. Kinnaird.
,,	,,	1234	Sergeant	G. Meiklejohn.
Oct./03	2nd V.B.	1810	Bandsman	J. Campbell.
,,	,,	2116	Sergeant	J. Millar.
,,	,,	1785	,,	W. Whyte.
,,	4th V.B.	645	Colour-Sgt.	P. Buchanan.
,,	,,	834	,,	J. M'Cracken.
,,	,,	345	Sergeant	J. Pegott.
,,	,,	56	,,	A. K. Robertson.
,,	5th V.B.	1519	Private	J. Menzies.
,,	6th V.B.		Captain	D. D. Blair.
Jan./04	5th V.B.	2861	Corporal	J. Campbell.
,,	,,	3038	Private	W. M'Intosh.
,,	,,	1006	Corporal	J. M'Leish.
,,	,,	2567	Sergeant	R. Mitchell.
,,	6th V.B.		Lieutenant	J. A. Porteous.
,,	,,	2380	Sergeant	T. Wishart.
July /04	4th V.B.	522	Corporal	G. Duff.
,,	,,	569	Private	D. Steel.
,,	5th V.B.	938	,,	C. Ayling.
,,	,,	1661	Sergeant	D. S. Grant.
,,	,,	2624	Private	P. Kilgour.
,,	,,	874	Lce.-Sergt.	A. Low.
,,	,,	1378	Sergeant	M. Reid.
,,	6th V.B.	1698	Private	J. Addison.
,,	,,	1703	Piper	P. Bardner.
,,	,,	2495	Bugler	D. Baxter.
,,	,,	1727	Private	E. Danks.
,,	,,	4274	,,	J. Haig.
,,	,,	2962	,,	W. Hutton.
,,	,,	1728	Drummer	G. Spence.
,,	,,	1702	Sergeant	T. Strachan.
,,	,,		,,	J. Brown.
Sept./04	1st V.B.	6859	Private	A. Lawrie.
,,	2nd V.B.	2100	Corporal	A. Craig.
,,	,,	1944	,,	G. Davie.
,,	,,	1590	Sergeant	P. Ogilvie.
,,	3rd V.B.	6699	Corporal	J. Bennie.
,,	5th V.B.		Hony. Major	J. Scott.
,,	,,	1057	Private	D. Grewer.
,,	,,	1059	,,	J. Jack.
,,	,,	1179	Sergeant	D. Keir.
,,	,,	1060	Private	J. M'Diarmid.
,,	6th V.B.	1511	Sergeant	R. Batchelor.
,,	,,	1915	Colour-Sgt.	W. Brown.
,,	,,	1911	,,	D. Foster.
,,	,,	1838	Sergeant	A. Nicol.
,,	,,	2422	Corporal	J. Spence.
Dec. /04	,,	2615	,,	W. Edie.
,,	,,	1861	,,	J. Peggie.
Sept. 1910	Colonel the Rt. Honble. the Marquis of Bredalbane, K.G., A.D.C., formerly 5th V. Bn. R. H.			
Oct./10	1st V.B.	8013	Private	J. Elder.

TERRITORIAL FORCE EFFICIENCY MEDAL

Date.	Corps.	Regtl. No.	Rank.	Name.	Date.	Corps.	Regtl. No.	Rank.	Name.
July /09	4th Bn.	377	Corporal	H. Brock.	July /09	7th Bn.	504	Corporal	J. Funkie.
,,	,,	430	Private	J. Brown.	,,	,,	453	Private	D. Gordon.
,,	,,	482	,,	J. Carrie.	,,	,,	132	,,	C. Grant.
,,	,,	209	Sergeant	D. Cruikshank.	,,	,,	558	,,	A. Handyside.
,,	,,	393	Corporal	D. Grieve.	,,	,,	301	Lce.-Sergt.	C. Hutchison.
,,	,,	395	Private	J. M'Mahon.	,,	,,	147	Sergeant	A. Louden.
,,	,,	101	Corporal	J. Martin.	,,	,,	191	,,	D. Millar.
,,	,,	261	Sergeant	F. Matthew.	,,	,,	419	,,	P. Muir.
,,	,,	49	Private	J. Moonie.	,,	,,	72	Lce.-Corpl.	J. M'Kinlay.
,,	,,	471	Corporal	W. Morris.	,,	,,	644	Corporal	T. M'Kinlay.
,,	,,	442	Private	J. Porter.	,,	,,	485	Lce.-Sergt.	A. Macnab.
,,	,,	223	,,	A. Stewart.	,,	,,	154	Qr.-Mr.-Sgt.	W. Ness.
,,	,,	30	,,	D. Thomson.	,,	,,	64	Lce.-Corpl.	J. D. Thomson.
,,	,,	20	Corporal	G. Towns.	,,	,,	519	Colour-Sgt.	J. B. Walker.
,,	,,	445	Private	W. Watson.	,,	,,	62	Corporal	A. Westwater.
,,	,,	517	,,	W. Watson.	,,	,,	126	Sergeant	A. R. Wilson.
,,	5th Bn.	265	,,	A. Birse.	,,	,,	605	Private	J. Young.
,,	,,	237	Sergeant	W. Burgess.	Jan./10	6th Bn.	296	,,	J. Callanin.
,,	,,	32	Private	A. Glen.	,,	,,	141	Colour-Sgt.	J. M. Crerar.
,,	,,	470	Sergeant	T. W. Guild.	,,	,,	161	Corporal	D. M'Neil.
,,	,,	587	,,	R. Innes.	,,	,,	206	,,	J. B. Paton.
,,	,,	35	Private	J. Ironsides.	,,	7th Bn.	142	Qr.-Mr.-Sgt.	D. Todd.
,,	,,	893	Sergeant	J. Kane.	April/10	4th Bn.	220	Sergeant	T. Bowman.
,,	,,	471	,,	G. Kyd.	,,	,,	516	Private	C. Craig.
,,	,,	353	Colour-Sgt.	J. Law.	,,	,,	226	Colour-Sgt.	J. Dryden.
,,	,,	11	Corporal	A. Littlejohn.	,,	,,	36	Lce.-Corpl.	G. Hood.
,,	,,	41	Private	J. Liveson.	,,	,,	144	Sergeant	J. Lundie.
,,	,,	12	Lce.-Sergt.	G. B. Lowe.	,,	,,	66	Private	J. Mason.
,,	,,	48	Lce.-Corpl.	W. M'Kay.	,,	,,	32	Colour-Sgt.	G. Simmie.
,,	,,	589	Lce.-Sergt.	D. K. Mitchell.	,,	5th Bn.	405	Piper	J. Cowieson.
,,	,,	760	Drummer	J. Pennycook.	,,	,,	406	,,	F. Reid.
,,	,,	813	Colour-Sgt.	J. Pont.	,,	7th Bn.	645	,,	J. Chisholm.
,,	,,	74	Lce.-Sergt.	J. Ross.	,,	,,	455	Corporal	G. Thomson.
,,	,,	286	Corporal	A. Shepherd.	July /10	5th Bn.	22	Lce.-Corpl.	W. Ballingall.
,,	,,	143	Sergeant	D. Simpson.	,,	,,	276	Private	J. Beedie.
,,	,,	654	Lce.-Sergt.	J. Whyte.	,,	,,	6	Sergeant	J. Christie.
,,	6th Bn.	136	Sergeant	A. W. Allison.	,,	,,	236	Drummer	C. Fairweather.
,,	,,	92	,,	P. C. Arnott.	,,	,,	613	Sgt.-Cook	J. Fraser.
,,	,,	669	Lce.-Sergt.	W. Campsie.	,,	,,	786	Corporal	J. Marr.
,,	,,	53	Private	A. Dow.	,,	,,	9	Sergeant	J. Mathewson.
,,	,,	85	Colour-Sgt.	A. Innes.	,,	,,	900	Lce.-Sergt.	J. Nairn.
,,	,,	1164	Private	J. Martin.	,,	,,	55	Lce.-Corpl.	A. Petrie.
,,	,,	274	Corporal	G. Mailer.	,,	,,	119	Sergeant	W. Smith.
,,	,,	48	Private	G. Millar.	,,	,,	588	,,	A. Whyte.
,,	,,	254	Corporal	R. M'Donald.	,,	6th Bn.	268	Private	A. Park.
,,	,,	209	Private	C. M'Lauchlan.	,,	,,	102	Corporal	J. Soutar.
,,	,,	722	Lce.-Corpl.	W. J. Reid.	,,	7th Bn.	370	Lce.-Corpl.	H. Craigie.
,,	,,	117	Private	R. Spiers.	,,	,,	221	Sergeant	R. Bethune.
,,	,,	375	,,	W. Stokes.	,,	,,	596	Corporal	J. Dutch.
,,	,,	737	,,	D. Watson.	,,	,,	304	Sergeant	G. M'Cathie.
,,	7th Bn.	300	Lce.-Sergt.	A. Alexander.	,,	,,	254	,,	D. Rodger.
,,	,,	266	Corporal	H. R. Annan.	Oct./10	4th Bn.	515	Private	A. Middleton.
,,	,,	1	,,	W. Bissett.	,,	,,	534	Sergeant	J. Milne.
,,	,,	265	,,	J. W. Clunie.	,,	7th Bn.	434	Lce.-Corpl.	A. B. Robertson.
,,	,,	473	Sergeant	A. Farmer.					

5TH REGIMENT

THE ROYAL HIGHLANDERS OF CANADA
THE BLACK WATCH

MEMBERS OF THE REGIMENT who were transferred for Service to the
1st, 2nd, and 3rd CANADIAN CONTINGENT, SOUTH AFRICA, 1900-02

5TH REGIMENT

THE ROYAL HIGHLANDERS OF CANADA, THE BLACK WATCH.

MEMBERS OF THE REGIMENT who were transferred for Service to the 1st, 2nd, and 3rd CANADIAN CONTINGENT, SOUTH AFRICA, 1900-02.

Major G. W. Cameron.	Private J. G. Gardiner.	Private Jno. Walters.
Lieut. C. J. Armstrong.	„ F. G. Corner.	„ J. Currie.
„ G. B. Mackay.	„ C. R. Molynaux.	„ F. Wasdell.
„ J. W. Allan.	„ M. Gunn.	„ J. S. Lawson.
„ A. H. Gault.	„ R. G. D. M'Lean.	„ F. Coons.
Col.-Sergt. A. Pope.	„ J. Malin.	„ J. A. M'Donald.
„ P. Evans.	„ R. C. Goodfellow.	„ A. Hannaford.
Pipe-Sgt. D. Ferguson.	„ A. A. Burke.	„ F. Erskine.
Sergt. W. Jeffrey.	„ W. J. Hale.	„ H. A. M'Dougall.
Corpl. A. Sword.	„ W. M'Iver.	„ H. W. Coates.
„ J. Cockburn.	„ J. S. Youngson.	„ G. Hampson.
„ C. Allan.	„ A. W. Wilkins.	„ T. H. Doyle.
„ J. Yelland.	„ R. O'Toole.	„ F. J. Daly.
Private J. Phillips.	„ W. Stenning.	„ F. G. W. Thomas.
„ C. Black.	„ L. Stanton.	„ S. W. Hateley.
„ F. B. Irwin.	„ A. J. Tullock.	„ W. Wilkin.
„ G. W. Foster.	„ A. Mackellar.	„ R. J. Ryan.
„ J. Gamble.	„ J. Lampton.	„ J. C. Macpherson.
„ A. F. Cameron.	„ P. Hynes.	„ H. Dougall.
„ J. M'Goldrick.	„ F. M. Jones.	„ T. Byrnes.

NOTE.—The above are given the ranks held by the various members in The Highlanders at the time they joined the Contingents.

SERVICE MEDALS EARNED IN REGIMENT.

FENIAN RAID.

Musketry Instructor T. A. Gardiner.

LONG SERVICE MEDALS EARNED IN REGIMENT.

OFFICERS.

Lt.-Colonel G. S. Cantlie.	Major C. E. Gault.	Lt.-Colonel J. G. Ross.

Private R. P. Niven.	Private A. Sword.	Staff Sergt. B. Howard.
„ J. Currie.	„ E. Morgan.	Sergt.-Major A. Pope.
„ J. Kamberry.	Sergt. P. Ford.	Regt. Sergt.-Major D. A. Bethune.
„ J. B. Logan.	Staff Sergt. John Munn.	Musketry Instructor T. A. Gardiner.

2 x

1ST BATTN. N.S.W. SCOTTISH RIFLE REGIMENT

(AFFILIATED TO THE BLACK WATCH)

NAMES OF OFFICERS, N.C.O.'S AND MEN

who served in SOUTH AFRICA

1st BATTN. N.S.W. SCOTTISH RIFLE REGIMENT
(Affiliated to THE BLACK WATCH).

NAMES OF OFFICERS, N.C.O.'S AND MEN who served in SOUTH AFRICA.

RANK.		NAME.	In what Contingent, and for how long.		REMARKS.
Major		Dibbs, T. B.	Special Service Officer.	12 mos.	Queen's Medal.
„		Dove, F. A.	Infantry Contingent.	18 „	D.S.O., Queen's Medal. Mentioned in Despatches.
Lieut.		Grieve, G. J.	Special Service Officer. Served 2nd Battn. Royal Highlanders.	..	Killed in action.
„		MacKellar, K.	Australian Light Horse. Subsequently in 7th Dragoon Guards.	..	Killed in action.
„		MacLean, A. L.	N.S.W. Bushmen.	12 mos.	Queen's Medal.
„		Dickson, B. B.	5th Commonwealth Light Horse.	5 „	Nil.
Regtl. No.					
37	Sergt.	Fraser, J. E.	Infantry Contingent.	14 „	Queen's Medal.
124	„	Coxhead, A. D.	„ „	14 „	„ „
231	„	M'Donald, W. T.	„ „	14 „	„ „ Mentioned in Despatches.
208	„	Stevenson, W. O.	2nd Mounted Rifles.	18 „	Queen's Medal.
281	Corpl.	M'Lennan, S.	Infantry Contingent.	..	Killed in action.
1230	„	Apps, J.	1st Mounted Rifles.	12 mos.	Queen's Medal.
25	Piper	Bell, W. J.	4th Commonwealth Light Horse.	6 „	„ „
216	Bugler	M'Leod, W.	1st Mounted Rifles.	12 „	„ „
1243	„	Parkes, V.	2nd „ „	12 „	„ „
797	„	Hardwick, C.	5th Commonwealth Light Horse.	5 „	Nil.
22	Pte.	Andrews, A.	Infantry Contingent.	14 „	Queen's Medal.
572	„	Southey, C. M.	„ „	14 „	„ „
41	„	Goodsal, S. J.	„ „	14 „	„ „
772	„	Wilson, J.	„ „	14 „	„ „
182	„	Spilsbury, G. H.	„ „	14 „	„ „
300	„	Hebblewhite, D. H.	„ „	11 „	„ „
587	„	Russell, H. H.	„ „	11 „	„ „
385	„	Fraser, D.	„ „	..	Killed in action.
753	„	Atchison, S.	„ „	..	Killed in action.
115	„	Brown, H.	Imperial Bushmen.	12 mos.	Queen's Medal.
545	„	Ritchie, A. M.	2nd Mounted Rifles.	11 „	„ „
489	„	Blackett, R. G.	Imperial Bushmen.	11 „	„ „
516	„	Gammidge, T. A.	„ „	11 „	„ „
404	„	Bratten, T.	3rd Mounted Rifles.	8 „	„ „
597	„	Mitchell, T. D.	Imperial Bushmen.	15 „	„ „
	„	Smith, G. A.	2nd Mounted Rifles.	18 „	„ „
908	„	Blair, R. J.	„ „	12 „	„ „
877	„	M'Donald, J.	„ „	12 „	„ „
475	„	M'Ilveen, T. J.	„ „	12 „	„ „
1132	„	Tourle, E. A.	„ „	12 „	„ „

Regtl. No.	Rank.	Name.	In what Contingent, and for how long.		Remarks.
1096	Pte.	Apthorpe, A. V.	3rd Mounted Rifles.	..	D.D.
856	,,	Christansen, D.	,, ,,	12 mos.	Queen's Medal.
758	,,	White, E. C.	,, ,,	12 ,,	,, ,,
873	,,	Nossiter, R. A.	,, ,,	10 ,,	,, ,,
1187	,,	Spedding, R.	,, ,,	12 ,,	,, ,,
412	,,	Fulton, J.	,, ,,	18 ,,	,, ,,
454	,,	Holt, D. L.	,, ,,	18 ,,	,, ,,
710	,,	Hattersley, A.	,, ,,	18 ,,	,, ,,
843	,,	Kenny, F. C.	2nd Mounted Rifles.	8 ,,	,, ,,
898	,,	Yarrow, S.	,, ,,	18 ,,	,, ,,
1030	,,	Kibble, A.	,, ,,	12 ,,	,, ,,
503	,,	Pettigrew.	N.S.W. Lancers.	18 ,,	,, ,,
615	,,	Golledge, H. W.	A.A.M. Corps.	12 ,,	,, ,,
639	,,	Bell, R.	Imperial Bushmen.	12 ,,	,, ,,
506	,,	Adams, A.	,, ,,	12 ,,	,, ,,
900	,,	Meecham, J. W.	1st Mounted Rifles.	12 ,,	,, ,,
818	,,	Meecham, M. R.	,, ,,	12 ,,	,, ,,
840	,,	Charlton, J.	,, ,,	12 ,,	,, ,,
804	,,	Davis, S.	,, ,,	12 ,,	,, ,,
959	,,	Garrard, R. M.	1st N.S.W. Draft.	6 ,,	,, ,,
815	,,	M'Kell, H. K.	,, ,,	8 ,,	,, ,,
947	,,	Clarke, F.	,, ,,	8 ,,	,, ,,
885	,,	Chambers, T.	4th Commonwealth Light Horse.	6 ,,	,, ,,
1194	,,	Markham, C.	5th ,, ,,	5 ,,	Nil.
600	,,	Chalmers, A.	,, ,, ,,	5 ,,	Nil.
1249	,,	See, E.	,, ,, ,,	5 ,,	Nil.
787	,,	May, D.	,, ,, ,,	5 ,,	Nil.
1269	,,	Davis, G.	,, ,, ,,	5 ,,	Nil.
1529	,,	Anderson, J.	,, ,, ,,	5 ,,	Nil.
451	,,	Ford, A. T.	2nd Mounted Rifles.	18 ,,	Queen's Medal.
1313	,,	M'Ilveen, J.	1st ,, ,,	12 ,,	,, ,,
983	,,	Matheson, J. K.	Queensland Mounted Rifles.	..	D.D.
1001	,,	Saville, G.	,, ,, ,,	12 mos.	Queen's Medal.
1110	,,	Saville, F.	,, ,, ,,	12 ,,	,, ,,

Printed in the United Kingdom
by Lightning Source UK Ltd.
112658UKS00002B/116